KU-271-873

Major Problems
in the History
of the American West

DOCUMENTS AND ESSAYS

EDITED BY
CLYDE A. MILNER II
UTAH STATE UNIVERSITY

D. C. HEATH AND COMPANY
Lexington, Massachusetts   Toronto

Cover: *New Mexican Village,* by Andrew Dasburg. (The Museum of New Mexico, negative #32274)

Copyright © 1989 by D. C. Heath and Company.

All rights reserved. No part of this publication may be reproduced or transmitted in any form or by any means, electronic or mechanical, including photocopy, recording, or any information storage or retrieval system, without permission in writing from the publisher.

Published simultaneously in Canada.

Printed in the United States of America.

International Standard Book Number: 0-669-15134-3

Library of Congress Catalog Card Number: 88-80718

10 9 8 7 6 5 4 3

To my mentors in western history
Howard R. Lamar
and
Charles S. Peterson

Preface

The chance to prepare this collection of essays and documents has been a delightful opportunity, and it came at a most appropriate time. Since the autumn of 1984, I have helped edit the *Western Historical Quarterly,* a scholarly journal published by the Western History Association. In this capacity, I have become aware of not only the national, but also the international, interest of scholars and students in the history of the American West. An impressive range of research that considers topics in both western and frontier history has developed. The editing of this volume gave me a chance to learn even more about this field.

The important contributions of the past three decades have been the primary focus of my research for this volume. The task was to create a balanced collection for the undergraduate student. The first and final chapters consider how to interpret the history of the West and where the concept of the frontier may fit. Along with this central "problem," many of the other thirteen chapters share important themes. For example, several chapters attempt to illuminate the lives of real "westerners." Popular misconceptions abound about Indians, mountain men, cowboys, and outlaws. Recent writings have presented more realistic pictures of them, as well as of other members of the West's diverse population, including blacks, Hispanics, and Asians. Understanding the history of women in the West is another major thread that connects several essays. Finally, several selections highlight federal actions and economic realities that have shaped western life.

The selection of essays followed certain pedagogic goals. Quality of writing and breadth of presentation were the primary concerns. I chose some essays because of their provocative interpretations, which I hope will stimulate discussion and further reading. The documents illuminate aspects of each chapter's essays. Through them, students see firsthand the kind of evidence that might lead to different interpretations in the essays. Because not every document supports the conclusions presented in the subsequent essays, some points of debate may arise for student readers. Chapter introductions and section headnotes place the readings in historical context and pose questions for further consideration. A list of additional readings, encompassing recent scholarship as well as a few classics of interpretation, accompanies each chapter.

I owe thanks to many people who helped me prepare this collection. Thomas G. Paterson of the University of Connecticut, general editor for the Heath Major Problems in American History Series anthologies, invited me to compile this book as one volume of the series, and he has since assisted in many ways. Linda Halvorson, Sylvia Mallory, James Miller,

Margaret Roll, and Bryan Woodhouse, all editors at D. C. Heath, lent professional support and personal encouragement. In an early stage of planning, a request for course syllabuses and letters of advice brought generous responses from W. David Baird, Richard Maxwell Brown, Kathleen N. Conzen, the late Arrell Morgan Gibson, Robert A. Goldberg, Robert V. Hine, Norris Hundley, jr., Albert L. Hurtado, Roger W. Lotchin, Michael P. Malone, Michael L. Nicholls, Roger L. Nichols, Walter Nugent, Kenneth N. Owens, Paula E. Petrik, Donald J. Pisani, Carlos A. Schwantes, Duane A. Smith, David H. Stratton, William R. Swagerty, Michael L. Tate, Robert A. Trennert, Kathleen Underwood, and most especially, Carter Blue Clark. Advice and aid in acquiring documents came from Peter J. Blodgett, John Mack Faragher, Craig Fuller, Peter Nabokov, Carol A. O'Connor, Floyd A. O'Neil, F. Ross Peterson, Gregory Thompson, and Barbara Walker.

Six individuals were most generous in supplying copies of important documents for this book: my warm thanks to Bradford Cole, Jay Gitlin, David G. Gutierrez, Paul Andrew Hutton, William L. Lang, and Katherine G. Morrissey. I received a most helpful critique of the book's outline from Richard Etulain and Patricia Nelson Limerick. Two colleagues, Richard White and William Cronon, helped at all important stages of development with letters of advice and words of encourgement. Barbara L. Stewart and Carolyn Fullmer supplied invaluable aid with statistical charts and word processing. My graduate and undergraduate students have helped me learn how to teach western history. Three of them—Kim M. Gruenwald, Christiane A. Mitchell, and Thomas E. Staton—gave timely assistance to my editorial and research efforts. Finally, this volume is dedicated to my two mentors in western history, both excellent teachers, remarkable scholars and good friends, who have kept me intellectually out West.

C.A.M. II

Contents

C H A P T E R   7
Overland Migration and Family Structure
Page 261

C H A P T E R   8
Miners and Cowboys
Page 311

C H A P T E R 12
Cultural Complexities
Page 487

C H A P T E R 13
The Federal West
Page 546

C H A P T E R 14
The Changing West
Page 602

C H A P T E R 15
New Meanings of the West
Page 654

Maps

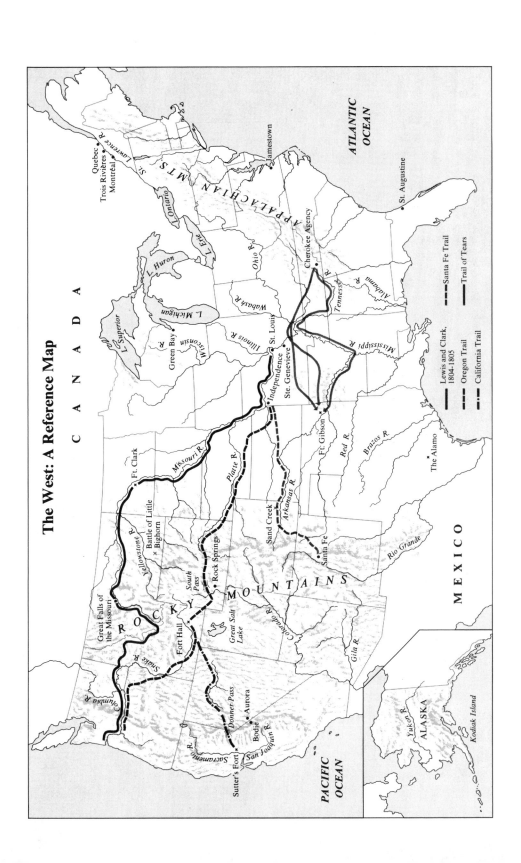

The West: A Reference Map

*Major Problems
in the History
of the American West*

Frontier and the Meaning

of the West

Υ

Frederick Jackson Turner's theory of the frontier seems indelibly linked to the study of the American West. In 1893, at age thirty-two, Turner presented his essay "The Significance of the Frontier in American History" to a meeting of the American Historical Association in Chicago. In his thesis this young assistant professor from the University of Wisconsin disputed the significance of the "germ theory," which insisted that American institutions and values had originated from distinctive elements, or "germs," in European history. Instead, he empha-sized the "germ" of the frontier experience as the critical influence on the shaping of the American character and commitment to democracy. Turner's ideas had a clear nationalistic tone that impressed many of his contemporaries. In 1910 he moved to Harvard University and became the scholarly mentor, di-rectly or indirectly, for several generations of American historians. Turner's frontier theory has been the subject of revision, rejection, and seemingly constant dispute. Turner himself refined, adjusted, and expanded his ideas in later essays and books. Today most historians do not consider the frontier to be the crucial, definitive element for all of American history. Nonetheless, the frontier experi-ence remains "significant" for many scholars who study the history of the West.

Υ E S S A Y S

Because Turner's famous essay may itself be considered a major problem in at-tempting to define and understand the history of the American West, it is worth-while to read the main text unabridged, so it appears as the first essay. Exactly how he defined the frontier, and whether the frontier is synonymous with the West, are worth careful consideration. Donald Worster, an environmental histo-rian and professor at Brandeis University, in the second essay advocates aban-doning Turner's frontier, with its emphasis on process, and accepting the con-cept of region, with its emphasis on place. Among others Worster points to the ideas of Walter Prescott Webb, a historian from Texas, whose monumental study, *The Great Plains,* appeared in 1931. After reading Worster's essay and again after reading the fourteen chapters that follow in this volume, it would be enlightening to review Turner's essay to consider whether his ideas stand up in the face of so many different approaches to western history.

The Significance of the Frontier in American History

FREDERICK JACKSON TURNER

In a recent bulletin of the superintendent of the census for 1890 appear these significant words: "Up to and including 1880 the country had a frontier of settlement, but at present the unsettled area has been so broken into by isolated bodies of settlement that there can hardly be said to be a frontier line. In the discussion of its extent, its westward movement, etc., it cannot, therefore, any longer have a place in the census reports." This brief official statement marks the closing of a great historic movement. Up to our own day American history has been in a large degree the history of the colonization of the Great West. The existence of an area of free land, its continuous recession, and the advance of American settlement westward, explain American development. Behind institutions, behind constitutional forms and modifications, lie the vital forces that call these organs into life, and shape them to meet changing conditions. Now, the peculiarity of American institutions is, the fact that they have been compelled to adapt themselves to the changes of an expanding people—to the changes involved in crossing a continent, in winning a wilderness, and in developing at each area of this progress out of the primitive economic and political conditions of the frontier into the complexity of city life. Said [John C.] Calhoun in 1817, "We are great, and rapidly—I was about to say fearfully—growing!" So saying, he touched the distinguishing feature of American life. All peoples show development: the germ theory of politics has been sufficiently emphasized. In the case of most nations, however, the development has occurred in a limited area; and if the nation has expanded, it has met other growing peoples whom it has conquered. But in the case of the United States we have a different phenomenon. Limiting our attention to the Atlantic coast, we have the familiar phenomenon of the evolution of institutions in a limited area, such as the rise of representative government; the differentiation of simple colonial governments into complex organs; the progress from primitive industrial society, without division of labor, up to manufacturing civilization. But we have in addition to this *a recurrence of the process of evolution in each western area reached in the process of expansion.* Thus American development has exhibited not merely advance along a single line, but a return to primitive conditions on a continually advancing frontier line, and a new development for that area. American social development has been

Frederick Jackson Turner, "The Significance of the Frontier in American History," *Proceedings of the Forty-First Annual Meeting of the State Historical Society of Wisconsin* (Madison, Wis., 1894), 79–112.

continually beginning over again on the frontier. This perennial rebirth, this fluidity of American life, this expansion westward with its new opportunities, its continuous touch with the simplicity of primitive society, furnish the forces dominating American character. The true point of view in the history of this nation is not the Atlantic coast, it is the Great West. Even the slavery struggle, which is made so exclusive an object of attention by writers like Professor [Hermann E.] von Holst, occupies its important place in American history because of its relation to westward expansion.

In this advance, the frontier is the outer edge of the wave—the meeting point between savagery and civilization. Much has been written about the frontier from the point of view of border warfare and the chase, but as a field for the serious study of the economist and the historian it has been neglected.

What is the frontier? It is not the European frontier—a fortified boundary line running through dense populations. The most significant thing about it is, that it lies at the hither edge of free land. In the census reports it is treated as the margin of that settlement which has a density of two or more to the square mile. The term is an elastic one, and for our purpose does not need sharp definition. We shall consider the whole frontier belt, including the Indian country and the outer margin of the "settled area" of the census reports. This paper will make no attempt to treat the subject exhaustively; its aim is simply to call attention to the frontier as a fertile field for investigation, and to suggest some of the problems which arise in connection with it.

In the settlement of America we have to observe how European life entered the continent, and how America modified and developed that life, and reacted on Europe. Our early history is the study of European germs developing in an American environment. Too exclusive attention has been paid by institutional students to the Germanic origins, too little to the American factors. Now, the frontier is the line of most rapid and effective Americanization. The wilderness masters the colonist. It finds him a European in dress, industries, tools, modes of travel, and thought. It takes him from the railroad car and puts him in the birch canoe. It strips off the garments of civilization, and arrays him in the hunting shirt and the moccasin. It puts him in the log cabin of the Cherokee and the Iroquois, and runs an Indian palisade around him. Before long he has gone to planting Indian corn and plowing with a sharp stick; he shouts the war cry and takes the scalp in orthodox Indian fashion. In short, at the frontier the environment is at first too strong for the man. He must accept the conditions which it furnishes, or perish, and so he fits himself into the Indian clearings and follows the Indian trails. Little by little he transforms the wilderness, but the outcome is not the old Europe, not simply the development of Germanic germs, any more than the first phenomenon was a case of reversion to the Germanic mark. The fact is, that here is a new product that is American. At first, the frontier was the Atlantic coast. It was the frontier of Europe in a very real sense. Moving westward, the frontier became more and more American. *As successive terminal moraines result from successive glaciations, so each frontier leaves its traces behind it, and when it becomes a settled area the region still partakes of the frontier characteristics.* Thus the advance of the frontier has meant a steady movement away from the influence of Europe, a steady growth of independence on American lines. And to study this advance, the men who grew up under these conditions, and the political, economic and social results of it, is to study the really American part of our history.

Stages of Frontier Advance

In the course of the seventeenth century the frontier was advanced up the Atlantic river courses, just beyond the "fall line," and the tidewater region became the settled area. In the first half of the eighteenth century another advance occurred. Traders followed the Delaware and Shawnese Indians to the Ohio as early as the end of the first quarter of the century. Gov. Spottswood, of Virginia, made an expedition in 1714 across the Blue Ridge. The end of the first quarter of the century saw the advance of the Scotch-Irish and the Palatine Germans up the Shenandoah Valley into the western part of Virginia, and along the Piedmont region of the Carolinas. The Germans in New York pushed the frontier of settlement up the Mohawk to German Flats. In Pennsylvania the town of Bedford indicates the line of settlement. Settlements had begun on New River, a branch of the Kanawha, and on the sources of the Yadkin and French Broad. The king [George III of England] attempted to arrest the advance by his proclamation of 1763, forbidding settlements beyond the sources of the rivers flowing into the Atlantic; but in vain. In the period of the Revolution the frontier crossed the Alleghanies into Kentucky and Tennessee, and the upper waters of the Ohio were settled. When the first census was taken in 1790, the continuous settled area was bounded by a line which ran near the coast of Maine, and included New England except a portion of Vermont and New Hampshire, New York along the Hudson and up the Mohawk about Schenectady, eastern and southern Pennsylvania, Virginia well across the Shenandoah Valley, and the Carolinas and eastern Georgia. Beyond this region of continuous settlement were the small settled areas of Kentucky and Tennessee and the Ohio, with the mountains intervening between them and the Atlantic area, thus giving a new and important character to the frontier. The isolation of the region increased its peculiarly American tendencies, and the need of transportation facilities to connect it with the East called out important schemes of internal improvement, which will be noted farther on. The "West," as a self-conscious section, began to evolve.

From decade to decade distinct advances of the frontier occurred. By the census of 1820 the settled area included Ohio, southern Indiana and Illinois, southeastern Missouri, and about one-half of Louisiana. This settled area had surrounded Indian areas, and the management of these tribes became an object of political concern. The frontier region of the time lay along the Great Lakes, where Astor's American Fur Company operated in the Indian trade, and beyond the Mississippi, where Indian traders extended their activity even to the Rocky Mountains; Florida also furnished frontier conditions. The Mississippi river region was the scene of typical frontier settlements.

The rising steam navigation on western waters, the opening of the Erie canal, and the westward extension of cotton culture added five frontier states to the Union in this period. [F.J.] Grund, writing in 1836, declares: "It appears then that the universal disposition of Americans to emigrate to the western wilderness, in order to enlarge their dominion over inanimate nature, is the actual result of an expansive power which is inherent in them, and which by continually agitating all classes of society is constantly throwing a large portion of the whole population on the extreme confines of the state, in order to gain space for its development. Hardly is a new state or territory formed before the same principle manifests itself again and gives rise to a further emigration; and so it is destined to go on until a physical barrier must finally obstruct its progress."

In the middle of this century the line indicated by the present eastern boundary of Indian Territory, Nebraska, and Kansas, marked the frontier of the Indian country. Minnesota and Wisconsin still exhibited frontier conditions, but the distinctive frontier of the period is found in California, where the gold discoveries had sent a sudden tide of adventurous miners, and in Oregon, and the settlements in Utah. As the frontier had leaped over the Alleghanies, so now it skipped the Great Plains and the Rocky Mountains; and in the same way that the advance of the frontiersmen beyond the Alleghanies had caused the rise of important questions of transportation and internal improvement, so now the settlers beyond the Rocky Mountains needed means of communication with the East, and in the furnishing of these, arose the settlement of the Great Plains, and the development of still another kind of frontier life. Railroads, fostered by land grants, sent an increasing tide of immigrants into the far West. The United States army fought a series of Indian wars in Minnesota, Dakota, and the Indian Territory.

By 1880, the settled area had been pushed into northern Michigan, Wisconsin, and Minnesota, along Dakota rivers, and in the Black Hills region, and was ascending the rivers of Kansas and Nebraska. The development of mines in Colorado had drawn isolated frontier settlements into that region, and Montana and Idaho were receiving settlers. The frontier was found in these mining camps and the ranches of the great plains. The superintendent of the census for 1890 reports, as previously stated, that the settlements of the West lie so scattered over the region that there can no longer be said to be a frontier line.

In these successive frontiers we find natural boundary lines which have served to mark and to affect the characteristics of the frontiers, namely: The "fall line"; the Alleghany Mountains; the Mississippi; the Missouri where its direction approximates north and south; the line of the arid lands, approximately the 99th meridian; and the Rocky Mountains. The fall line marked the frontier of the seventeenth century; the Alleghanies that of the eighteenth; the Mississippi that of the first quarter of the nineteenth; the

Missouri that of the middle of this century (omitting the California movement); and the belt of the Rocky Mountains and the arid tract, the present frontier. Each was won by a series of Indian wars.

The Frontier Furnishes a Field for Comparative Study of Social Development

At the Atlantic frontier one can study the germs of processes repeated at each successive frontier. We have the complex European life, sharply precipitated by the wilderness into the simplicity of primitive conditions. The first frontier had to meet its Indian question, its question of the disposition of the public domain, of the means of intercourse with the older settlements, of the extension of political organization, of religious and educational activity. And the settlement of these and similar questions for one frontier served as a guide for the next. The American student needs not to go to the "prim little townships of Sleswick" for illustrations of the law of continuity and development. For example, he may study the origin of our land policies in the colonial land policy; he may see how the system grew by adapting the statutes to the customs of the successive frontiers. He may see how the mining experience in the lead region of Wisconsin, Illinois, and Iowa was applied to the mining laws of the Rockies, and how our Indian policy has been a series of experimentations on successive frontiers. Each tier of new states has found, in the older ones, material for its constitutions. Each frontier has made similar contributions to American character, as will be discussed farther on.

But with all these similarities there are essential differences due to the place element and the time element. It is evident that the farming frontier of the Mississippi Valley presents different conditions from the mining frontier of the Rocky Mountains. The frontier reached by the Pacific railroad, surveyed into rectangles, guarded by the United States army, and recruited by the daily immigrant ship, moves forward at a swifter pace and in a different way than the frontier reached by the birch canoe or the pack horse. The geologist traces patiently the shores of ancient seas, maps their areas, and compares the older and the newer. It would be a work worth the historian's labors to mark these various frontiers and in detail compare one with another. Not only would there result a more adequate conception of American development and characteristics, but invaluable additions would be made to the history of society.

[Achille] Loria, the Italian economist, has urged the study of colonial life as an aid in understanding the stages of European development, affirming that colonial settlement is for economic science what the mountain is for geology, bringing to light primitive stratifications. "America," he says, "has the key to the historical enigma which Europe has sought for centuries in vain, and the land which has no history reveals luminously the course of universal history." He is right. The United States lies like a huge page in the history of society. Line by line as we read from west to east we find the record of social evolution. It begins with the Indian and the hunter; it goes on to tell of the disintegration of savagery by the entrance of the trader, the path-finder of civilization; we read the annals of the pastoral stage in ranch life; the exploitation of the soil by the raising of unrotated crops of corn and wheat in sparsely settled farming communities; the intensive culture of the denser farm settlement; and finally the manufacturing organization with city and factory system. This page is familiar to the student of census statistics, but how little of it has been used by our historians. Each of these areas has had an influence in our economic and political history; the evolution of each into a higher stage has worked political transformations. But what constitutional historian has made any adequate attempt to interpret political facts by the light of these social areas and changes?

The Atlantic frontier was compounded of fisherman, fur trader, miner, cattle raiser and farmer. Excepting the fisherman, each type of industry was on the march toward the West, impelled by an irresistible attraction. Each passed in successive waves across the continent. Stand at Cumberland Gap and watch the procession of civilization, marching single file—the buffalo, following the trail to the salt springs, the Indian, the fur trader and hunter, the cattle raiser, the pioneer farmer,—and the frontier has passed by. Stand at South Pass in the Rockies a century later, and see the same procession with wider intervals between. The unequal rate of advance compels us to distinguish the frontier into the trader's frontier, the rancher's frontier, or the miner's frontier, and the farmer's frontier. When the mines and the cowpens were still near the fall line the traders' pack trains were tinkling across the Alleghanies, and the French on the Great Lakes were fortifying their posts, alarmed by the British trader's birch canoe. When the trappers scaled the Rockies, the farmer was still near the mouth of the Missouri.

The Indian Trader's Frontier

Why was it that the Indian trader passed so rapidly across the continent? What effects followed from the trader's frontier? The trade was coeval with American discovery. The Norsemen, Vespuccius, Verrazano, Hudson, John Smith, all trafficked for furs. The Plymouth pilgrims settled in Indian cornfields, and their first return cargo was of beaver and lumber. The records of the various New England colonies show how steadily exploration was carried into the wilderness by this trade. What is true for New England is, as would be expected, even plainer for the rest of the colonies. All along the coast from Maine to Georgia the Indian trade opened up the river courses. Steadily the trader passed westward, utilizing the older lines of French trade. The Ohio, the Great Lakes, the Mississippi, the Missouri and the Platte, the lines of western advance, were ascended by traders. They found the passes in the Rocky Mountains and guided Lewis and Clark, Frémont, and [John] Bidwell. The explanation of the rapidity of this advance is bound up with the effects of the trader on the Indian. The trading post left the unarmed tribes at the mercy of those that had purchased fire-arms—a truth which the Iroquois Indians wrote in blood, and so the remote and unvisited tribes gave eager welcome to the trader. "The savages," wrote La Salle, "take better care of us French than of their own children; from us only can they get guns and goods." This accounts for the trader's power and the rapidity of his advance. Thus the disintegrating forces of civilization entered the wilderness. Every river valley and Indian trail became a fissure in Indian society, and so that society became honeycombed. Long before the pioneer farmer appeared on the scene, primitive Indian life had passed away. The farmers met Indians armed with guns. The trading frontier, while steadily undermining Indian power by making the tribes ultimately dependent on the whites, yet, through its sale of guns, gave to the Indians increased power of resistance to the farming frontier. French colonization was dominated by its trading frontier; English colonization by its farming frontier. There was an antagonism between the two frontiers as between the two nations. Said Duquesne to the Iroquois, "Are you ignorant of the difference between the king of England and the king of France? Go see the forts that our king has established and you will see that you can still hunt under their very walls. They have been placed for your advantage in places which you frequent. The English, on the contrary, are no sooner in possession of a place than the game is driven away. The forest falls before them as they advance, and the soil is laid bare so that you can scarce find the wherewithal to erect a shelter for the night."

And yet, in spite of this opposition of the interests of the trader and the farmer, the Indian trade pioneered the way for civilization. The buffalo trail became the Indian trail, and this became the trader's "trace"; the trails widened into roads, and the roads into turnpikes, and these in turn were transformed into railroads. The same origin can be shown for the railroads of the South, the far West, and the Dominion of Canada. The trading posts reached by these trails were on the sites of Indian villages which had been placed in positions suggested by nature; and these trading posts, situated so as to command the water systems of the country, have grown into such cities as Albany, Pittsburgh, Detroit, Chicago, St. Louis, Council Bluffs, and Kansas City. Thus civilization in America has followed the arteries made by geology, pouring an ever richer tide through them, until at last the slender paths of aboriginal intercourse have been broadened and interwoven into the complex mazes of modern commercial lines; the wilderness has been interpenetrated by lines of civilization, growing ever more numerous. It is like the steady growth of a complex nervous system for the originally simple, inert continent. If one would understand why we are to-day one nation, rather than a collection of isolated states, he must study this economic and social consolidation of the country. In this progress from savage conditions lie topics for the evolutionist.

The effect of the Indian frontier as a consolidating agent in our history is important. From the close of the seventeenth century various intercolonial congresses have been called to treat with Indians and establish common measures of defense. Particularism was strongest in colonies with no Indian frontier. This frontier stretched along the western border like a cord of union. The Indian was a common danger, demanding united action. Most celebrated of these conferences was the Albany congress of 1754, called to treat with the Six Nations, and to consider plans of union. Even a cursory reading of the plan proposed by the congress reveals the importance of the frontier. The powers of the general council and the officers were, chiefly, the determination of peace and war with the Indians, the regulation of Indian trade, the purchase of Indian lands, and the creation and government of new settlements as a security against the Indians. It is evident that the unifying tendencies of the Revolutionary period were facilitated by the previous co-operation in the regulation of the frontier. In this connection may be mentioned the importance of the frontier, from that day to this, as a military training school, keeping alive the power of resistance to aggression, and developing the stalwart and rugged qualities of the frontiersman.

The Rancher's Frontier

It would not be possible in the limits of this paper to trace the other frontiers across the continent. Travellers of the eighteenth century found the "cowpens" among the canebrakes and peavine pastures of the South, and the "cow drivers" took their droves to Charleston, Philadelphia, and New York. Travellers at the close of the War of 1812 met droves of more than a thousand cattle and swine from the interior of Ohio going to Pennsylvania to fatten for the Philadelphia market. The ranges of the Great Plains, with ranch and cowboy and nomadic life, are things of yesterday and of today. The experience of the Carolina cowpens guided the ranchers of Texas. One element favoring the rapid extension of the rancher's frontier is the fact that in a remote country lacking transportation facilities the product must be in small bulk, or must be able to transport itself, and the cattle raiser could easily drive his product to market. The effect of these great ranches on the subsequent agrarian history of the localities in which they existed should be studied.

The Farmer's Frontier

The maps of the census reports show an uneven advance of the farmer's frontier, with tongues of settlement pushed forward and with indentations of wilderness. In part this is due to Indian resistance, in part to the location of the river valleys and passes, in part to the unequal force of the centers of frontier attraction. Among the important centers of attraction may be mentioned the following: fertile and favorably situated soils, salt springs, mines and army posts.

Army Posts

The frontier army post, serving to protect the settlers from the Indians, has also acted as a wedge to open the Indian country, and has been a nucleus for settlement. In this connection mention should also be made of the government military and exploring expeditions in determining the lines of settlement. But all the more important expeditions were greatly indebted to the earliest pathmakers, the Indian guides, the traders and trappers, and the French voyageurs, who were inevitable parts of governmental expeditions from the days of Lewis and Clark. Each expedition was an epitome of the previous factors in western advance.

Salt Springs

In an interesting monograph, Victor Hehn has traced the effect of salt upon early European development, and has pointed out how it affected the lines of settlement and the form of administration. A similar study might be made for the salt springs of the United States. The early settlers were tied to the coast by the need of salt, without which they could not preserve their meats or live in comfort. Writing in 1752, Bishop Spangenburg says of a colony for which he was seeking lands in North Carolina, "They will require salt & other necessaries which they can neither manufacture nor raise. Either they must go to Charleston, which is 300 miles distant. . . . Or else they must go to Boling's Point in Virginia on a branch of the James & is also 300 miles from here. . . . Or else they must go down the Roanoke—I know not how many miles—where salt is brought up from the Cape Fear." This may serve as a typical illustration. An annual pilgrimage to the coast for salt thus became essential. Taking flocks or furs and ginseng root, the early settlers sent their pack trains after seeding time each year to the coast. This proved to be an important educational influence, since it was almost the only way in which the pioneer learned what was going on in the East. But when discovery was made of the salt springs of the Kanawha, and the Holston, and Kentucky, and central New York, the West began to be freed from dependence on the coast. It was in part the effect of finding these salt springs that enabled settlement to cross the mountains.

From the time the mountains rose between the pioneer and the seaboard, a new order of Americanism arose. The West and the East began to get out of touch of each other. The settlements from the sea to the mountains kept connection with the rear and had a certain solidarity. But the over-mountain men grew more and more independent. The East took a narrow view of American advance, and nearly lost these men. Kentucky and Tennessee history bears abundant witness to the truth of this statement. The East began to try to hedge and limit westward expansion. Though Webster could declare that there were no Alleghanies in his politics, yet in politics in general they were a very solid factor.

Land

Good soils have been the most continuous attraction to the farmer's frontier. The land hunger of the Virginians drew them down the rivers into Carolina, in early colonial days; the search for soils took the Massachusetts men to

Pennsylvania and to New York. The exploitation of the beasts took hunter and trader to the west, the exploitation of the grasses took the rancher west, and the exploitation of the virgin soil of the river valleys and prairies attracted the farmer. As the eastern lands were taken up migration flowed across them to the west. Daniel Boone, the great backwoodsman, who combined the occupations of hunter, trader, cattle raiser, farmer and surveyor,—learning, probably from the traders, of the fertility of the lands on the upper Yadkin, where the traders were wont to rest as they took their way to the Indians, left his Pennsylvania home with his father, and passed down the Great Valley road to that stream. Learning from a trader whose posts were on the Red River in Kentucky of its game and rich pastures, he pioneered the way for the farmers to that region. Thence he passed to the frontier of Missouri, where his settlement was long a landmark on the frontier. Here again he helped to open the way for civilization, finding salt licks, and trails, and land. His son was among the earliest trappers in the passes of the Rocky Mountains, and his party are said to have been the first to camp on the present site of Denver. His grandson, Col. A. J. Boone, of Colorado, was a power among the Indians of the Rocky Mountains, and was appointed an agent by the government. Kit Carson's mother was a Boone. Thus this family epitomizes the backwoodsman's advance across the continent.

The farmer's advance came in a distinct series of waves. In Peck's *New Guide to the West,* published in Cincinnati in 1848, occurs this suggestive passage:

"Generally, in all the western settlements, three classes, like the waves of the ocean, have rolled one after the other. First, comes the pioneer, who depends for the subsistence of his family chiefly upon the natural growth of vegetation, called the 'range,' and the proceeds of hunting. His implements of agriculture are rude, chiefly of his own make, and his efforts directed mainly to a crop of corn and a 'truck patch.' The last is a rude garden for growing cabbage, beans, corn for roasting ears, cucumbers and potatoes. A log cabin, and, occasionally, a stable and corn-crib, and a field of a dozen acres, the timber girdled or 'deadened,' and fenced, are enough for his occupancy. It is quite immaterial whether he ever becomes the owner of the soil. He is the occupant for the time being, pays no rent, and feels as independent as the 'lord of the manor.' With a horse, cow, and one or two breeders of swine, he strikes into the woods with his family, and becomes the founder of a new county, or perhaps state. He builds his cabin, gathers around him a few other families of similar tastes and habits, and occupies till the range is somewhat subdued, and hunting a little precarious, or, which is more frequently the case, till neighbors crowd around, roads, bridges, and fields annoy him, and he lacks elbow room. The pre-emption law enables him to dispose of his cabin and corn-field to the next class of emigrants; and, to employ his own figures, he 'breaks for the high timber,' 'clears out for the New Purchase,' or migrates to Arkansas or Texas, to work the same process over.

"The next class of emigrants purchase the lands, add field to field, clear out the roads, throw rough bridges over the streams, put up hewn log houses, with glass windows and brick or stone chimneys, occasionally plant orchards, build mills, school-houses, court-houses, etc., and exhibit the picture and forms of plain, frugal, civilized life.

"Another wave rolls on. The men of capital and enterprise come. The settler is ready to sell out, and take advantage of the rise in property— push farther into the interior and become, himself, a man of capital and enterprise in turn. The small village rises to a spacious town or city; substantial edifices of brick, extensive fields, orchards, gardens, colleges and churches are seen. Broadcloths, silks, leghorns, crapes, and all the refinements, luxuries, elegancies, frivolities and fashions are in vogue. Thus wave after wave is rolling westward:—the real *Eldorado* is still farther on.

"A portion of the two first classes remain stationary amidst the general movement, improve their habits and condition, and rise in the scale of society.

"The writer has traveled much amongst the first class—the real pioneers. He has lived many years in connection with the second grade; and now the third wave is sweeping over large districts of Indiana, Illinois and Missouri. Migration has become almost a habit in the West. Hundreds of men can be found, not over fifty years of age, who have settled for the fourth, fifth or sixth time on a new spot. To sell out and remove only a few hundred miles makes up a portion of the variety of backwoods life and manners."

Omitting the pioneer farmer who moves from the love of adventure, the advance of the more steady farmer is easy to understand. Obviously the immigrant was attracted by the cheap lands of the frontier, and even the native farmer felt their influence strongly. Year by year the farmers who lived on soil, whose returns were diminished by unrotated crops, were offered the virgin soil of the frontier at nominal prices. Their growing families demanded more lands, and these were dear. The competition of the unexhausted, cheap and easily tilled prairie lands compelled the farmer either to go west and continue the exhaustion of the soil on a new frontier, or to adopt intensive culture. Thus the census of 1890 shows, in the Northwest, many counties in which there is an absolute, or a relative, decrease of population. These states have been sending farmers to advance the frontier on the plains, and have themselves begun to turn to intensive farming and to manufacture. A decade before this, Ohio had shown the same transition stage. Thus the demand for land and the love of wilderness freedom drew the frontier ever onward.

Having now roughly outlined the various kinds of frontiers, and their modes of advance, chiefly from the point of view of the frontier itself, we may next inquire what were the influences on the East and on the Old World. A rapid enumeration of some of the more noteworthy effects is all that I have time for.

Composite Nationality

First, we note that the frontier promoted the formation of a composite nationality for the American people. The coast was preponderantly English, but the later tides of continental immigration flowed across to the free lands. This was the case from the early colonial days. The Scotch-Irish and the Palatine Germans, or "Pennsylvania Dutch," furnished the stock of the colonial frontier. With these people were also the free indentured servants, or redemptioners, who at the expiration of their time of service passed to the frontier. Governor Spottswood of Virginia writes in 1717, "The inhabitants of our frontiers are composed generally of such as have been transported hither as servants, and, being out of their time, settle themselves where land is to be taken up and that will produce the necessarys of life with little labour." Very generally these redemptioners were of non-English stock. In the crucible of the frontier the immigrants were Americanized, liberated and fused into a mixed race, English in neither nationality or characteristics. The process has gone on from the early days to our own. [Edmund] Burke and other writers in the middle of the eighteenth century believed that Pennsylvania was "threatened with the danger of being wholly foriegn in language, manners, and perhaps even inclinations." The German and Scotch-Irish elements in the frontier of the South were only less great. In the middle of the present century the German element in Wisconsin was already so considerable that leading publicists looked to the creation of a German state out of the commonwealth by concentrating their colonization. Such examples teach us to beware of misinterpreting the fact that there is a common English speech in America into a belief that the stock is also English.

Industrial Independence

In another way the advance of the frontier decreased our dependence on England. The coast, particularly of the South, lacked diversified industries, and was dependent on England for the bulk of its supplies. In the South there was even a dependence on the Northern colonies for articles of food. Governor [James] Glenn of South Carolina writes in the middle of the eighteenth century: "Our trade with New York and Philadelphia was of this sort, draining us of all the little money and bills we could gather from other places for their bread, flour, beer, hams, bacon, and other things of their produce, all which, except beer, our new townships begin to supply us with, which are settled with very industrious and thriving Germans. This no doubt diminishes the number of shipping and the appearance of our trade, but it is far from being a detriment to us." Before long the frontier created a demand for merchants. As it retreated from the coast it became less and less possible for England to bring her supplies directly to the consumer's wharfs, and carry away staple crops, and staple crops began to give way to diversified agriculture for a time. The effect of this phase of the frontier action upon the northern section is perceived when we realize how the advance of the frontier aroused seaboard cities like Boston, New York, and Baltimore, to engage in rivalry for what Washington called "the extensive and valuable trade of a rising empire."

Effects on National Legislation

The legislation which most developed the powers of the national government, and played the largest part in its activity, was conditioned on the frontier. Writers have discussed the subjects of tariff, land, and internal improvement, as pendants to the slavery question. But when American history comes to be rightly viewed it will be seen that the slavery question is an incident. In the period from the end of the first half of the present century to the close of the Civil War, slavery rose to primary but far from exclusive importance. But this does not justify Professor von Holst (to take an example) in treating our constitutional history in its formative period down to 1828 in a single volume, and giving six volumes to the history of slavery from 1828 to 1861, under the title of a *Constitutional History of the United States*. The growth of nationalism and the evolution of American political institutions were dependent on the advance of the frontier. Even so recent a writer as [James Ford] Rhodes, in his *History of the United States since the Compromise of 1850,* has treated the legislation called out by the western advance as incidental to the slavery struggle.

This is a wrong perspective. The pioneer needed the goods of the coast, and so the grand series of internal improvement and railroad legislation began, with potent nationalizing effects. But the West was not content with bringing the farm to the factory. Under the lead of [Henry] Clay—"Harry of the West"—protective tariffs were passed, with the cry of bringing the factory to the farm.

The Public Domain

The public domain has been a force of profound importance in the nationalization and development of the government. The effects of the struggle of the landed and the landless states, and of the Ordinance of 1787, need no discussion. Administratively the frontier called out some of the highest and most vitalizing activities of the general government. The purchase of Louisiana was perhaps the constitutional turning-point in the history of the republic, inasmuch as it afforded both a new area for national legislation, and the occasion of the downfall of the policy of strict construction. But the purchase of Louisiana was called out by frontier needs and demands. As frontier states accrued to the Union, the national power grew. In a speech on the dedication of the Calhoun monument, [Lucius Q. C.] Lamar explained: "In 1789 the states were the creators of the federal government; in 1861, the federal government was the creator of a large majority of the states."

When we consider the public domain from the point of view of the sale and disposal of the public lands, we are again brought face to face with the frontier. The policy of the United States in dealing with its lands is in sharp contrast with the European system of scientific administration. Efforts to make this domain a source of revenue, and to withhold it from emigrants in order that settlement might be compact, were in vain. The jealousy and the fears of the East were powerless in the face of the demands of the frontiersmen. John Quincy Adams was obliged to confess: "My own system of administration, which was to make the national domain the inexhaustible fund for progressive and unceasing internal improvement, has failed." The reason is obvious; systems of administration was not what the West demanded; it wanted land. Adams states the situation as follows: "The slave holders of the South have bought the co-operation of the western country by the bribe of the western lands, abandoning to the new western states their own proportion of the public property and aiding them in the design of grasping all the lands into their own hands. Thomas H. Benton was the author of this system, which he brought forward as a substitute for the American system of Mr. Clay and to supplant him as the leading statesman of the West. Mr. Clay, by his tariff compromise with Mr. Calhoun, abandoned his own American system. At the same time he brought forward a plan for distributing among all the states of the Union the proceeds of the sales of the public lands. His bill for that purpose passed both Houses of Congress, but was vetoed by President Jackson, who, in his annual message of December, 1832, formally recommended that all public lands should be gratuitously given away to individual adventurers and to the states in which the lands are situated."

"No subject," said Henry Clay, "which has presented itself to the present, or perhaps any preceding, congress, is of greater magnitude than that of the public lands." When we consider the far-reaching effects of the government's land policy upon political, economic, and social aspects of American life, we are disposed to agree with him. But this legislation was framed under frontier influences, and under the lead of Western statesmen like Benton and Jackson. Said Senator Scott of Indiana in 1841: "I consider the pre-emption law merely declaratory of the custom or common law of the settlers."

National Tendencies of the Frontier

It is safe to say that the legislation with regard to land, tariff, and internal improvements—the American system of the nationalizing Whig party—was conditioned on frontier ideas and needs. But it was not merely in legislative action that the frontier worked against the sectionalism of the coast. The economic and social characteristics of the frontier worked against sectionalism. The men of the frontier had closer resemblances to the Middle region than to either of the other sections. Pennsylvania had been the seed-plot of frontier emigration, and, although she passed on her settlers along the Great Valley into the west of Virginia and the Carolinas, yet the industrial society of these Southern frontiersmen was always more like that of the

Middle region than like that of the tide-water portion of the South, which later came to spread its industrial type throughout the South.

The Middle region, entered by New York harbor, was an open door to all Europe. The tide-water part of the South represented typical Englishmen, modified by a warm climate and servile labor, and living in baronial fashion on great plantations; New England stood for a special English movement— Puritanism. The Middle region was less English than the other sections. It had a wide mixture of nationalities, a varied society, the mixed town and county system of local government, a varied economic life, many religious sects. In short it was a region mediating between New England and the South, and the East and the West. It represented that composite nationality which the contemporary United States exhibits, that juxtaposition of non-English groups, occupying a valley or a little settlement, and presenting reflections of the map of Europe in their variety. It was democratic and non-sectional, if not national; "easy, tolerant and contented;" rooted strongly in material prosperity. It was typical of the modern United States. It was least sectional, not only because it lay between North and South, but also because with no barriers to shut out its frontiers from its settled region, and with a system of connecting waterways, the Middle region mediated between East and West as well as between North and South. Thus it became the typically American region. Even the New Englander, who was shut out from the frontier by the Middle region, tarrying in New York or Pennsylvania on his westward march, lost the acuteness of his sectionalism on the way.

Until the spread of cotton culture into the interior gave homogeneity to the South, the western part of it showed tendencies to fall away from the faith of the fathers into internal improvement legislation and nationalism. In the Virginia convention of 1829–30, called to revise the constitution, Mr. Leigh, of Chesterfield, one of the tide-water counties, declared:

"One of the main causes of discontent which led to this convention, that which had the strongest influence in overcoming our veneration for the work of our fathers, which taught us to contemn the sentiments of Henry and Mason and Pendleton, which weaned us from our reverence for the constituted authorities of the state, was an overweening passion for internal improvement. I say this with perfect knowledge; for it has been avowed to me by gentlemen from the West over and over again. And let me tell the gentleman from Albemarle (Mr. Gordon) that it has been another principal object of those who set this ball of revolution in motion, to overturn the doctrine of state rights, of which Virginia has been the very pillar, and to remove the barrier she has interposed to the interference of the federal government in that same work of internal improvement, by so reorganizing the legislature that Virginia, too, may be hitched to the federal car."

It was this nationalizing tendency of the West that transformed the democracy of Jefferson into the national republicanism of Monroe and the democracy of Andrew Jackson. The West of the War of 1812, the West of Clay, and Benton, and Harrison, and Andrew Jackson, shut off by the Middle states and the mountains from the coast sections, had a solidarity of its own with national tendencies. On the tide of the Father of Waters, North and South met and mingled into a nation. Interstate migration went steadily on—a process of cross-fertilization of ideas and institutions. The fierce struggle of the sections over slavery on the western frontier does not diminish the truth of this statement; it proves the truth of it. Slavery was a sectional trait that would not down, but in the West it could not remain sectional. It was the greatest of frontiersmen [Abraham Lincoln] who declared: "I believe this government cannot endure permanently half slave and half free. It will become all of one thing, or all of the other." Nothing works for nationalism like intercourse within the nation. Mobility of population is death to localism, and the western frontier worked irresistibly in unsettling population. The effects reached back from the frontier and affected profoundly the Atlantic coast, and even the Old World.

Growth of Democracy

But the most important effect of the frontier has been in the promotion of democracy here and in Europe. As has been pointed out, the frontier is productive of individualism. Complex society is precipitated by the wilderness into a kind of primitive organization based on the family. The tendency is anti-social. It produces antipathy to control, and particularly to any direct control. The tax-gatherer is viewed as a representative of oppression. Professor [Herbert L.] Osgood, in an able article, has pointed out that the frontier conditions prevalent in the colonies are important factors in the explanation of the American revolution, where individual liberty was sometimes confused with absence of all effective government. The same conditions aid in explaining the difficulty of instituting a strong government in the period of the confederacy. The frontier individualism has from the beginning promoted democracy.

The frontier states that came into the Union in the first quarter of a century of its existence came in with democratic suffrage provisions, and had reactive effects of the highest importance upon the older states whose people were being attracted there. It was *western* New York that forced an extension of suffrage in the constitutional convention of that state in 1820; and it was *western* Virginia that compelled the tide-water region to put a more liberal suffrage provision in the constitution framed in 1830, and to give to the frontier region a more nearly proportionate representation with the tide-water aristocracy. The rise of democracy as an effective force in the nation came in with western preponderance under Jackson and William Henry Harrison, and it meant the triumph of the frontier—with all of its good and with all of its evil elements. An interesting illustration of the tone of frontier democracy in 1830 comes from the same debates in the Virginia convention already referred to. A representative from western Virginia declared: "But, sir, it is not the increase of population in the West which this gentleman ought to fear. It is the energy which the mountain breeze and western habits impart to those emigrants. They are regenerated, politically I mean, sir. They soon become *working politicians*; and the difference, sir, between a *talking* and a *working* politician is immense. The Old Dominion has long been celebrated for producing great orators; the ablest metaphysicians in policy; men that can split hairs in all abstruse questions of political economy. But at home, or when they return from congress, they have negroes to fan them asleep. But a Pennsylvania, a New York, an Ohio, or a western Virginia statesman, though far inferior in logic, metaphysics and rhetoric to an old Virginia statesman, has this advantage, that when he returns home he takes off his coat and takes hold of the plough. This gives him bone and muscle, sir, and preserves his republican principles pure and uncontaminated.''

So long as free land exists, the opportunity for a conpetency exists, and economic power secures political power. But the democracy born of free land, strong in selfishness and individualism, intolerant of administrative experience and education, and pressing individual liberty beyond its proper bounds, has its dangers as well as its benefits. Individualism in America has allowed a laxity in regard to governmental affairs which has rendered possible the spoils system, and all the manifest evils that follow from the lack of a highly developed civic spirit. In this connection may be noted also the influence of frontier conditions in permitting lax business honor, inflated paper currency and wild-cat banking. The colonial and revolutionary frontier was the region whence emanated many of the worst forms of an evil currency. The West in the War of 1812 repeated the phenomenon on the frontier of that day, while the speculation and wild-cat banking of the period of the crisis of 1837 occurred on the new frontier belt of the next tier of states. Thus each one of the periods of lax financial integrity coincides with periods when a new set of frontier communities had arisen, and coincides in area with these successive frontiers for the most part. The recent Populist agitation is a case in point. Many a state that now declines any connection with the tenets of the Populists, itself adhered to such ideas in an earlier stage of the development of the state. A primitive society can hardly be expected to show the intelligent appreciation of the complexity of business interests in a developed society. The continual recurrence of these areas of paper-money agitation is another evidence that the frontier can be isolated and studied as a factor in American history of the highest importance.

Attempts to Check and Regulate the Frontier

The East has always feared the result of an unregulated advance of the frontier, and has tried to check and guide it. The English authorities would have checked settlement at the headwaters of the Atlantic tributaries and allowed the ''savages to enjoy their deserts in quiet lest the peltry trade should decrease.'' This called out Burke's splendid protest:

"If you stopped your grants, what would be the consequence? The people would occupy without grants. They have already so occupied in many places. You cannot station garrisons in every part of these deserts. If you drive the people from one place, they will carry on their annual tillage and remove with their flocks and herds to another. Many of the people in the back settlements are already little attached to particular situations. Already they have topped the Appalachian mountains. From thence they behold before them an immense plain, one vast, rich, level meadow; a square of five hundred miles. Over this they would wander without a possibility of restraint; they would change their manners with their habits of life; would soon forget a government by which they were disowned; would become hordes of English Tartars; and, pouring down upon your unfortified frontiers a fierce and irresistible cavalry, become masters of your governors and your counselors, your collectors and comptrollers, and of all the slaves that adhered to them. Such would, and in no long time must, be the effect of attempting to forbid as a crime, and to suppress as an evil, the command and blessing of Providence, 'Increase and multiply.' Such would be the happy result of an endeavor to keep as a lair of wild beasts that earth which God, by an express charter, has given to the children of men.''

But the English government was not alone in its desire to limit the advance of the frontier, and guide its destinies. Tide-water Virginia and South Carolina gerrymandered those colonies to ensure the dominance of the coast in their legislatures. Washington desired to settle a state at a time, in the Northwest; Jefferson would reserve from settlement the territory of his Louisiana purchase north of the 32d parallel, in order to offer it to the Indians in exchange for their settlements east of the Mississippi. ''When we shall be full on this side,'' he writes, ''we may lay off a range of states on the western bank from the head to the mouth, and so range after range, advancing compactly as we multiply.'' Madison went so far as to argue to the French minister that the United States had no interest in seeing population extend itself on the right bank of the Mississippi, but should rather fear it. When the Oregon question was under debate, in 1824, [Alexander] Smyth, of Virginia, would draw an unchangeable line for the limits of the United States at the outer limit of two tiers of states beyond the Mississippi, complaining that the seaboard states were being drained of the flower of their population by the bringing of too much land into market. Even Thomas Benton, the man of widest views of the destiny of the West, at this stage of his career declared that along the ridge of the Rocky Mountains ''the western limits of the republic should be drawn, and the statue of the fabled god Terminus should be raised upon its highest peak, never to be thrown down.'' But the attempts to limit our boundaries, to restrict land sales and settlement, and to deprive the West of its share of political power, were all in vain. Steadily that frontier of settlement advanced and carried with it individualism, democracy and nationalism, and powerfully affected the Old World.

Missionary Activity

The most effective efforts of the East to regulate the frontier came through its educational and religious activity, exerted by interstate migration and by organized societies. Speaking in 1835, Dr. Lyman Beecher declared:

"It is equally plain that the religious and political destiny of our nation is to be decided in the West," and he pointed out that the population of the West "is assembled from all the states of the Union, and from all the nations of Europe, and is rushing in like the waters of the flood, demanding for its moral preservation the immediate and universal action of those institutions which discipline the mind and arm the conscience and the heart. And so various are the opinions and habits, and so recent and imperfect is the acquaintance, and so sparse are the settlements of the West, that no homogeneous public sentiment can be formed to legislate immediately into being the requisite institutions. And yet they are all needed immediately in their utmost perfection and power. A nation is being 'born in a day.' . . . But what will become of the West if her prosperity rushes up to such a majesty of power, while those great institutions linger which are necessary to form the mind and the conscience, and the heart of that vast world. It must not be permitted. . . . Let no man at the East quiet himself and dream of liberty, whatever may become of the West. . . . Her destiny is our destiny."

With this appeal to the conscience of New England, he adds appeals to her fears lest other religious sects anticipate her own. The New England preacher and school teacher left their mark on the West. The dread of western emancipation from New England's political and economic control was paralleled by fears lest the West cut loose from her religion. Commenting in 1850 on reports that settlement was rapidly extending northward in Wisconsin, the editor of *The Home Missionary* writes: "We scarcely know whether to rejoice or to mourn over this extension of our settlements. While we sympathize in whatever tends to increase the physical resources and prosperity of our country, we cannot forget that with all these dispersions into remote and still remoter corners of the land, the supply of the means of grace is becoming relatively less and less." Acting in accordance with such ideas, home missions were established and western colleges were erected. As seaboard cities like Philadelphia, New York and Baltimore strove for the mastery of western trade, so the various denominations strove for the possession of the West. Thus an intellectual stream from New England sources fertilized the West. On the other hand, the contest for power and the expansive tendency furnished to the various sects by the existence of a moving frontier, must have had important results on the character of religious organizations in the United States. It is a chapter in our history which needs study.

Intellectual Traits

From the conditions of frontier life came intellectual traits of profound importance. The works of travellers along each frontier from colonial days onward describe for each certain traits, and these traits have, while softening down, still persisted as survivals in the place of their origin, even when a higher social organization succeeded. The result is that to the frontier the American intellect owes its striking characteristics. That coarseness and strength combined with acuteness and inquisitiveness, that practical, inventive turn of mind, quick to find expedients, that masterful grasp of material things, lacking in the artistic but powerful to effect great ends, that restless, nervous energy, that dominant individualism, working for good and for evil, and withal that buoyancy and exuberance which comes with freedom,—these are traits of the frontier, or traits called out elsewhere because of the existence of the frontier. Since the days when the fleet of Columbus sailed into the waters of the New World, America has been another name for opportunity, and the people of the United States have taken their tone from the incessant expansion which has not only been open but has even been forced upon them. He would be a rash prophet who should assert that the expansive character of American life has now entirely ceased. Movement has been its dominant fact, and, unless this training has no effect upon a people, the American intellect will continually demand a wider field for its exercise. But never again will such gifts of free land offer themselves. For a moment at the frontier the bonds of custom are broken, and unrestraint is triumphant. There is not *tabula rasa*. The stubborn American environment is there with its imperious summons to accept its conditions; the inherited ways of doing things are also there; and yet, in spite of environment, and in spite of custom, each frontier did indeed furnish a new field of opportunity, a gate of escape from the bondage of the past; and freshness, and confidence, and scorn of older society, impatience of its restraints and its ideas, and indifference to its lessons, have accompanied the frontier. What the Mediterranean Sea was to the Greeks, breaking the bond of custom, offering new experiences, calling out new institutions and activities, that, and more, the ever retreating frontier has been to the United States directly, and to the nations of Europe more remotely. And now, four centuries from the discovery of America, at the end of a hundred years of life under the Constitution, the frontier has gone, and with its going has closed the first period of American history.

New West, True West

DONALD WORSTER

I say to my colleague in Chinese studies that I teach western history. "Doesn't almost everyone in this department," he complains. "The history of England, Germany, France, Italy—it is all western history in our courses. Nobody here knows or cares anything about the East." I cut him short to explain that what I mean by the West is not Europe, not the whole of western civilization. My West is the *American* West: that fabled land where the restless pioneer moves ever forward, settling one frontier after another; where the American character becomes self-reliant, democratic, and endlessly

---

Copyright by Western History Association. Reprinted by permission. The article first appeared as "New West, True West: Interpreting the Region's History" by Donald Worster, *Western Historical Quarterly*, 18 (April 1987), 141–156.

eager for the new; where we strip off the garments of civilization and don a rude buckskin shirt; where millions of dejected immigrants gather from around the world to be rejuvenated as Americans, sounding together a manly, wild, barbaric yawp of freedom. That is my West: precisely that and nothing more. "Oh," my colleague ventures, more perplexed now than cantankerous, "you mean 'the West'—the frontier, Indians, Clint Eastwood?" I nod vaguely and sidle off. It is all so hard to convey over a single, polite glass of academic sherry.

For a field that has been around so long, western American history can be frustratingly difficult to pin down. Soon it will be a full century old. Often, with such advanced age comes a clarity of purpose as well as a record of achievement. Not so in this case. The record is impressive enough: the field now has several excellent journals, regularly holds good scholarly conferences, and boasts an immense bibliography that no one could read in a lifetime. But as for clarity of purpose, the field is still groping about in adolescence. It doesn't quite know who it is or what it wants to be when it grows up. What are its boundaries? Where is "West" and where is not? There is still no settled, mature answer.

There is, to be sure, an established body of writing about the history of the West, and usually it would be to such a body that we would turn for resolving what the field of study is or ought to be. In this case, however, the traditional literature is more a cause of confusion than a remedy. For it reveals that the West is just about anything that anyone has ever wanted it to be. That it has been located anywhere and everywhere.

My own private confusions of place may, in their ordinariness, illustrate that wonderful ambiguity we sense about the field. I was born in the Mohave Desert of southern California, an area the books say is indubitably part of the West. I grew up on the Great Plains, and again the books tell me that that is West too. But when I moved some years ago to Hawaii, was I still in the West or was I out of it? For an answer I might consult the *Western Historical Quarterly,* which reassures me in its index to recent articles in the field that the islands do indeed belong. The Hawaiian monarchs, resplendent in their feather capes and fed on taro, mullet, and the milk of coconuts, are to be understood (whatever their personal views of the matter) as having lived in the American West alongside Chief Sitting Bull and Geronimo; while Captain James Cook of Yorkshire was as much a western adventurer as Meriwether Lewis or John Charles Fremont. Now then, go to the other geographical extreme of the country. Move, as I have recently done, five thousand miles from Honolulu to the small Massachusetts town of Concord, founded in 1635 as the first inland settlement of the Bay colony. You will learn that it too, is, or has been, in the realm of the West! The authorities have it so. For example, that grand and indispensable reference work, *The Reader's Encyclopedia of the American West,* includes an entry on the settlement of Massachusetts, and it is a longer entry than the one on the Oregon Trail. Thus, you may go west or east, young man or woman, and you will always in fact be going west.

As defined by its historians, the West has been nothing less than all of America, or all that we have conquered. For further evidence of how the part has swallowed the whole, consider the last work of the Harvard historian Frederick Merk, *A History of the Westward Movement*, published in 1978, one year after his death. He might as well have called it the story of the nation. There are chapters on Indian culture, cotton growing in the South, the Dred Scott decision, the industrialization of the Great Lakes, the Tennessee Valley Authority, and farm policy in the Kennedy-Johnson years. After more than six hundred pages of tracking American development, Professor Merk, in his moving peroration, expands even further his notion of the West as an "open frontier" to sweep in all of science and technology, all human control over the environment, all "the relations of man to his fellow man." "This is the frontier," he concludes, "now challenging the national energies." If we follow his reasoning, the West is to be found wherever there is optimism, a love of freedom and democracy, an indomitable will to overcome all obstacles, a determination to make things better for the future. That is, I will grant you, the state of Oregon he is describing, but it also might be Australia or Hong Kong.

But hold: there is still more to the West than we have yet fathomed. Long before there was Merk's cotton gin, long before there was a colony planted on the cold Massachusetts shore in the seventeenth century, long before America was even discovered and named, the historians tell us of an even more ancient, shadowy West. On its existence we have, for example, the magisterial authority of the man who, until his death in 1981, was regarded by many as the dominant name in western history: Ray Allen Billington, senior research associate at the Huntington Library. His textbook, *Westward Expansion: A History of the American Frontier*, may be taken as one of the most authoritative delineations of the field. According to this book (4th ed., 1974), the American West was merely "the last stage in a mighty movement of peoples that began in the twelfth century when feudal Europe began pushing back the barbaric hordes" pressing in on Christendom. The Crusaders, off to do battle with the Moslems, were the first pioneers, and Jerusalem was their frontier. They did not prevail, but after them came the more triumphant Marco Polo, Christopher Columbus, and Ponce de Leon—came a whole multitude pushing the domain of the West out to the remote corners of the earth. In Billington's account the great saga rolls along for eight centuries, until it reaches the American Populists defending themselves against "ruthless exploitation of eastern interests." If I have the story right, there is an undeniable grandeur to it, stretching as it does from the armies of Richard the Lionhearted to those of old Sockless Jerry Simpson in droughty, dusty Kansas. My grandfather, himself a raggletaggle populist with tobacco juice streaming from his mouth, would have loved it. But then, just as we are ready to spring with Billington into the future, the grandeur abruptly fades away. With the defeat of the Populists in 1896, he declares in one of his last chapters, the West came to a sad death. It will have no more history to make in the twentieth century. Once the West was going everywhere, now it is gone.

To discover where the American West is supposed to be, I have been consulting major books published within the last ten or twelve years, books by scholars of stature from whom we have learned much. But having read them, I could not put my finger on the map and say, "There is the West." The books have attached too abstract a meaning to the word, so abstract in fact that it has become bewildering. The West is "movement," "expansion," the "frontier," they all say, and apparently any kind of movement, any expansion, any frontier will do.

The primal source of this abstractness, this elusiveness of subject, must be located in the mind of the scholar who has gotten so much praise for imagining the field in the first place: Frederick Jackson Turner. He started historians down a muddy, slippery road that ultimately leads to a swamp. That destination was not apparent for a long while. The route signs Turner put up had a deceptively concrete promise to them. In a letter written in the 1920s, he pointed out that "the 'West' with which I dealt, was a *process* rather than a fixed geographical region." Earlier, he had made the same distinction in the notes for his Harvard course on the West: it was described as "a study of selected topics in the history of the West considered as a process rather than an area." That process, he explained in an unpublished essay, included:

1. the spread of settlement steadily westward, and
2. all the economic, social, and political changes involved in the existence of a belt of free land at the edge of settlement;
3. the continual settling of successive belts of land;
4. the evolution of these successive areas of settlement through various stages of backwoods life, ranching, pioneer farming, scientific farming, and manufacturing life.

In short, Turner's "process" was really four of them, or rather, was a tangled web of many processes, all going on at once and including the whole development of American agriculture and industry, the history of population growth and movement, the creation of national institutions, and, somewhere in the tangle, the making of an American personality type. No wonder western history has ever after had trouble staying on track.

When you are lost, the most sensible strategy is to go back to the point of departure, back where Mr. Turner once stood pointing the way, and look for another road. Ignore the signs saying, "[t]his way to process," and look instead for the one reading, "[T]o a fixed geographical region." Or better yet, look for the specific processes that went on in the specific region. We may grope and argue a lot that way too, but we won't end up back in Massachusetts befuddled by Puritan theology or back with the Crusaders defeated and dead.

My strategy of diverging from Turner and his frontier theme is hardly original. It was implicitly recommended almost thirty years ago, in a 1957 article published in *Harper's Magazine,* by a man then described as "the West's leading historian," Walter Prescott Webb. The article was entitled "The American West: Perpetual Mirage." Had it been taken more fully to heart, it might have started the field off in a more promising direction. There was absolutely nothing in it of Turner's vaporous notion of the West as frontier advance. On the contrary, Webb gave the West a set of firm coordinates on the North American landscape. In his second paragraph he declared,

> Fortunately, the West is no longer a shifting frontier, but a region that can be marked off on a map, traveled to, and seen. Everybody knows when he gets there. It starts in the second tier of states west of the Big River.

The West, in other words, begins with the Dakotas, Nebraska, Kansas, Oklahoma, and Texas. So defined, the West would become, along with the North and South, one of the three great geographical regions of the co-terminous United States.

In Webb's view, what sets this western region off from the other two major regions is the lack of enough rainfall to sustain traditional, European-derived agriculture. In that second tier of states the average yearly precipitation falls below the twenty-inch minimum needed to grow crops in the accustomed way. From there to the California coast the region is mainly dry: in its extremes it is a desert, elsewhere it is a subhumid environment. Admittedly, within it are some anomalies and further diversities—the Pacific northwest coast outstanding among them—which, for the sake of analysis, Webb had to ignore. Every region is, after all, only a generalization and is subject to exceptions.

This more mappable West, as everyone in the field knows, was an idea Webb took from the nineteenth-century explorer John Wesley Powell, whose *Report on the Lands of the Arid Region of the United States,* published in 1878 as a House of Representatives document, identified the 100th meridian as the line roughly dividing a humid from a subhumid America. Webb nudged the line eastward a couple of degrees so it lay right outside Austin, Texas, where he lived. And he boldly declared that Powell's arid region was one and the same as the American West. For the post-World War Two generation, he sensed, the two regions had merged completely, and historians had better acknowledge the fact and stop harking back to Turner.

I know in my bones, if not always through my education, that Webb was right. His notion of the West as the arid region of the country fits completely my own experience and understanding. Born eighty years to the day after Frederick Jackson Turner—on the 14th of November, 1941 (Turner was born on the 14th of November, 1861)—I have never been able to think of the West as Turner did, as some process in motion. Instead, I think of it as a distinct place inhabited by distinct people: people like my parents, driven out of western Kansas by dust storms to an even hotter, drier life in Needles, California, working along the way in flyblown cafes, fruit orchards, and on railroad gangs, always feeling dwarfed by the bigness of the land and by the economic power accumulated there. In my West, there are no coonskin caps, nor many river boats, axes, or log cabins.

Those things all belong to another time, another place—to an eastern land where nature offered an abundance of survival resources near at hand. My West is, by contrast, the story of men and women trying to wrest a living from a condition of severe natural scarcity and, paradoxically, of trying to survive in the midst of entrenched wealth.

This picture of the West, I submit, is the closer to the one most western historians carry around in their heads today. When pushed hard to make a stand, we usually line up with Webb and Powell, not Turner. For instance, on the first page or so of the introduction to his book *Historians and the American West,* Michael Malone grants that he means by the West more or less what Webb meant: "the entire region lying west of the 98th meridian, the line of diminishing rainfall which runs from the eastern Dakotas on the north through central Texas on the south." But having admitted that much to ourselves, we often resist the logical implications in what we have done. We still feel obliged to keep feeding Turner's ghost at the table. We may accept the modern view that the West is a settled region distinct unto itself, but we are not always steadfast, clear-minded regionalists in writing its history.

The main questions I now want to raise are these: What is regional history and what is it not? And what strategies should we employ for analyzing this West as region, as opposed to the West as frontier? For the sake of intellectual and moral vitality, regional history should be as inclusive as possible, dealing with anything and everything that has happened to anyone in its territory; it should be total history. Clarifying its purpose should never mean imposing a rigid, doctrinaire formula, especially on so wonderfully diverse a place as the West. But some things are more significant than others in the making of a region. The region has its core influences, just as it has peripheral ones. What we must do is determine what is in that core and what is not.

Begin with what is not. Regional history is not, in the strictest sense, merely the history of the American nation replicating itself, politically, economically, or culturally. Any regional historian must proceed from the assumption that his region is, in some important way, a *unique* part of that greater whole. To find nothing but sameness in it would make his entire enterprise useless. Felix Frankfurter once wrote, "Regionalism is a recognition of the intractable diversities among men, diversities partly shaped by nature but no less derived from the different reactions of men to nature." I will come back to the complicated role of nature in a moment, but for now let us concentrate on that word diversity. The regional historian must be out looking earnestly for it, even when it's hard to find or define, even when it's hard to feel good about when located. But do we do this? Not systematically enough. In fact, one school of thought denies that there has been anything unique or innovative about the West to discover.

Such was the position taken by Earl Pomeroy in 1955, when, in another heroic effort to free us from the influence of Turner, he wrote that "the Westerner has been fundamentally imitator rather than innovator." By example after example, ranging from architecture to territorial government, Pomeroy showed how people in the West drew on the East for their ideas and institutions. To a point he was right, and the argument long overdue. But carry his argument too far and the objection must be raised, why then study the West at all? Why bother with uncovering more and more examples—with mere copies of the original? Better to examine the original itself. If we insist too strenuously that the West has been merely a borrower from the East, it becomes not a region but a province, a dull little backwater of conformists and copycats, all looking to some eastern capital for their inspiration. Nothing would be more tiresome to an active mind than to dwell year after year in such a place. The more ambitious would quickly go elsewhere. Pomeroy certainly did not want that to happen; indeed, he warned the field against slipping into intellectual mediocrity. Yet too much emphasis on the West as continuity would certainly lead us straight to mediocrity and boredom.

Pomeroy properly admonished us against the excesses of exceptionalism. It can lead to extravagant claims of originality, a bumptious chauvinism, a sagebrush rebellion against "outside interference." It can conceal the crucial formative role the federal government has played in the region, particularly through its evolving territorial system, as both Pomeroy and Lamar have shown. But, finally, regionalism is about telling differences or it has nothing to tell.

Nor should regional history be confused, as it sometimes is, with the history of ethnic groups migrating into a place and taking up residence. In fact, I will venture to say that ethnic history and regional history are often conflicting endeavors. In America, ethnic history commonly deals with those "intractable diversities" that have been introduced into this country from abroad and their struggle to survive in the face of pressures to assimilate. Whereas in Europe an ethnic group usually had a regional base—that is, was rooted in a specific geographical place—in the United States it became a moveable identity: a language, some music, holidays and foods, religion, all journeying through space, to a steel town, the prairie, suburbia, yet marvelously remaining intact. Many ethnic groups have come to live in the American West, of course, but the fact of their being in the West is not necessarily the same as their being *of* the West. The ethnic group becomes central to the region's history when and where and to the extent it becomes altered by that region, or develops an active voice in defining the region's "intractable diversity."

Quite different from ethnic history, and presenting an even more intricate problem of fit, is the history of the indigenous peoples who have been invaded and conquered, in this case the Indians and, more ambiguously, the Hispanics. To a greater extent than anyone else, by the fact of their much longer occupation and engagement with the environment, they belong. They are not immigrants, they are natives. But for all that, they are not to be readily or casually absorbed into the study of region. They are sovereign nations that have been unwillingly regionalized—made a part of the "West" (also of the "South" and "Northeast", but especially of the "West") as they have been made by force a part of America. The regionalist who does not begin with their story, their interaction with the place, continues the injustice of their expropriation. But inclusion alone will not do; it is not adequate now merely to make them regional Americans.

Finally, in a mood of rigorous clarification, we must caution that regional history is not quite the same thing as the history of the American or world economic system and their hierarchies of superior and subordinate parts. The western terrain has again and again come under the thumb of some eastern entrepreneur. As William Robbins has recently argued, we need to develop "a broad theoretical formulation that examines the West in the context of its national and international relations" in order to understand that outside exploitation. Quite so, and we ought to ask where all the region's coal, gold, uranium, and timber have gone, and who has profited from them, ask how they have helped build a system of industrial capitalism. But one must be careful not to simply substitute that investigation of outside exploitation for a more complex inquiry into regionalism and its tensions.

The region, the nation, the world: all three are terms in this historical equation, all interacting through time, continually shifting in weight and value, and the regional historian, though committed mainly to understanding the first of them, must not ignore the others. His special task is to understand how those outside economic and political forces, empire and capital, have entered the West and dealt with its regional peculiarities, either by trying to stamp them out or by becoming themselves transformed into new, more indigenous forms.

Those are some of the things, it seems to me, that lie on the periphery, or pose as potential traps, to regional history. What then lies in that core history of the West? What forces and events are to be found there? Recurring to Frankfurter's words, it is the story of the West as one of those intractable diversities which have been "partly shaped by nature but no less derived from the different reactions of men to nature." In other words, the history of the region is first and foremost one of an evolving human ecology. A region emerges as people try to make a living from a particular part of the earth, as they adapt themselves to its limits and possibilities. What the regional historian should first want to know is how a people or peoples acquired a place and, then, how they perceived and tried to make use of it. He will identify the survival techniques they adopted, their patterns of work and economy, and their social relationships.

Put more modishly, the region derives its identity primarily from its ecologically adapted modes of production—or more simply, from its ecological modes. If those modes are precisely the same as those existing elsewhere in the country or world, then we have not got much of a region to study. On the other hand, if the modes are too radically different, we may not have a region at all but rather a foreign civilization. Somewhere between those poles of conformity and differentiation lies the region.

So, leave aside as a related but separate kind of inquiry Merk's wide open frontier, and Turner's process of settlement, and Pomeroy's insistence on continuities. Forget for a while the broader tides of imperialism and

Christendom and urbanization and the marketplace. We want to concentrate our attention first on how people have tried to wrest their food, their energy, their income from the specific land in question and what influence that effort has had on the shaping of the West's society and culture.

In our oldest and most distinctive region, the American South, there has been only one dominant ecological mode over most of its history, the plantation system of agriculture in which tobacco and cotton were cultivated by African slave labor. That mode has given the south an enduring identity, a fate that, even now, it has not escaped. More than a hundred years after its defeat in the Civil War, the South can still read its past mode of living in the present condition of its soils, its long backward economic status, and its still troubled racial relations.

In the West, however, we have to deal with not one, but two, primary ecological modes under white occupation. The first of these modes is the life of the cowboy and sheepherder. The second is the life of the irrigator and water engineer. Call these the *pastoral West* and the *hydraulic West*. Neither is found anywhere else in the United States; they are unique to the lands lying beyond Webb and Powell's line of demarcation. What we must understand is how they have evolved side by side, what social impact each has had, where and how they have been in competition with each other, how they have coexisted into our own time, and what cultural values are embedded in each.

All the world knows that the American West is fundamentally a land of cowboys. It is not a myth, however much the fact may have been mythologized in fiction and movies. When the cowboy arrived and commenced punching cows, the West ceased to be a vague frontier of exploration and began, over broad reaches of its territory, in every state from the Great Plains to the Pacific, to take shape as an articulated region.

This West did not develop the way Turner had anticipated. For in his West as process, as social evolution, the pastoral life is supposed to be only a passing stage of settlement and soon must give way to the farmer and the manufacturer. Beyond the hundredth meridian such was not to be the case.

The fur trapper, the miner, and the dirt farmer came to the West, as they did elsewhere on the continent; so too did the missionary and the Indian fighter. All of them had important roles, but none was distinctive to the region, with the possible exception of the hardrock miner. The cowboy, on the other hand, came to stay and built a special way of life. By the early twentieth century that life was firmly rooted in place and being depicted in such works as Wister's *The Virginian* (1902) and Adams's *The Log of a Cowboy* (1903). Even now, in this last quarter of the twentieth century, the pastoral life thrives as well as it ever did. The techniques of range and herd management may have changed, but the basic ecological mode has remained intact. So also endures the cult of self-reliant individualism that has grown up around this mode. We are not in any danger of losing the way of life, nor of missing its historical significance. But even were it to disappear abruptly, it would leave as lasting a mark on the West as the cotton plantation has left on the South.

The hydraulic West, on the other hand, has been much less noticed by western historians. It has taken us by surprise, and we have still not fully comprehended its meaning. This is so for several reasons. The hydraulic West came of age only after World War Two, while western historians have, until late, been preoccupied with the nineteenth century. It is a more technically abstruse and more organizationally complex mode than ranching, therefore requires more effort to penetrate. And, although it has inspired a few songs, movies, and novels, there is too little romance about it to attract much popular attention. It is, in fact, too faceless, anonymous, impersonal, even at times too sinister, to be celebrated and loved. This West has been created by irrigation ditches, siphons, canals, and storage dams. In it daily existence depends on the intensive management of that scarce, elusive, and absolutely vital natural resource, water.

The hydraulic mode of living is much older than the grazier's, going back as it does hundreds of years to the Hohokam Indians of Arizona and other native societies. In the modern era of white dominion, the mode first appears in 1847 among the Mormons in their state of Deseret and, soon thereafter, in the Greeley vicinity of Colorado and in California's Central Valley. California would eventually become the principal center of hydraulic development, radiating an influence all the way to Montana and Texas. By 1978, the Census of Agriculture reported 43,668,834 irrigated acres in the seventeen western states: one-tenth of the world's total. California counted 8.6 million acres; Texas, 7 million; Nebraska, 5.7 million; and Idaho and Colorado, 3.5 million each. The market sales from those lands amounted to one-fourth of the nation's total, or $26 billion. Taken by counties, all but one of the top ten agricultural producers in the nation are in the hydraulic West, and eight of them are in California alone.

This water empire is a purely western invention. To be sure, a lot of capital and technology has been invested on farms all over the United States, in the form of machinery, pesticides, fertilizer, and the like; looked at as merely another form of technology, the hydraulic West may appear to be nothing more than an advanced version of modern agribusiness. However, the regional distinctiveness lies in the fact that the typical irrigator is not merely trying to enhance his production by buying a little water now and then. He is critically dependent on that single resource and, to survive, must have it delivered on a steady, reliable basis. There is no room for marketplace competition in his life, no freedom to buy or do without, no substitute available. The western farmer does not have any real choice in the matter; he lives or dies by the level of water in his ditches. This stark fact of utter dependence on an indispensable resource creates a special mode of production.

Given such dependency, the regional historian wants to know what social changes the hydraulic West has worked. How are people organized in this mode? What are their relationships with one another? What qualities of mind and thought appear or take on new emphasis? In what ways does the irrigation infrastructure make this West different from the East or, for that matter, from the pastoral West?

Oddly enough, though he did not think of the West as region, Frederick Jackson Turner was among the first to discern the peculiar characteristics of this hydraulic life. In an *Atlantic Monthly* article of 1903, he noted that in the preceding fifteen years western settlement had reached the Great Plains, where "new physical conditions have . . . accelerated the social tendency of Western democracy." The conquest of that country would be impossible, he went on, "by the old individual pioneer methods." The new region required "expensive irrigation works," "cooperative activity," and "capital beyond the reach of the small farmer." The condition of water scarcity, he wrote, "decreed that the destiny of this new frontier should be social rather than individual." He compared it to the changes in social structure going on elsewhere in America: this West would be from the outset an "industrial" order, giving rise to "captains of industry," home-grown or imported versions of men like Andrew Carnegie, who were taking charge of the country generally. The task of settling the arid West, like that of creating an industrial society, was too monumental for ordinary people using ordinary skills to carry out; they must therefore "combine under the leadership of the strongest." They would also be forced to rely on the federal government to build for them huge dams and canals as well as show them "what and when and how to plant." "The pioneer of the arid regions," Turner concluded, "must be both a capitalist and the protégé of the government." That these were fundamental differences from the requirements of raising food and fiber in the East, Turner clearly understood, yet strangely he assumed that his vaunted frontier democracy would be unaffected by them. To see matters otherwise would have shattered the hopeful, nationalistic pride he felt in the westward movement. We, on the other hand, can put realistic names to the social conditions emerging in this West: hierarchy, concentration of wealth and power, rule by expertise, dependency on government and bureaucracy. The American deserts could be made to grow some crops all right, but among them would be the crop of oligarchy.

The fact was already faintly discernible eighty-three years ago. By the late 1930s, John Steinbeck could confirm them in his novel, *The Grapes of Wrath*, which portrays the hydraulic West through the eyes of the Joads of Oklahoma. Forced to migrate west, the Joads become members of a permanent underclass of stoop-and-pick laborers, an underclass that had access neither to the land nor the water needed to make it flourish. Steinbeck sensed that there was no simple alternative to that undemocratic outcome, not so long as the West wanted or needed a hydraulic system and wanted it to grow more and more elaborate. Some form of power elite, whether possessing capital, or expertise, or both, would be required to carry out that ambition. It need not be a capitalistic elite that would rise to command. Government could intervene in the outcome, not only to develop more water but also to distribute it into more hands. But in doing so, the government would itself become a form of concentrated power, threatening to dominate people's lives to an often intolerable degree. Quite simply, the domination of nature in the water empire must lead to the domination of some people by others.

Another outcome of the hydraulic mode, likewise unanticipated at the beginning and even now not commonly realized, is an intensification and concentration of urban growth. Cities need water too; and in a region of scarcity, where water sources are few and far between, the city must reach out over great distances to fill that necessity. The bigger the city, the more power it has to wield over its rivals. In this competition, the small community is at a disadvantage, short as it is of both capital and technical virtuosity. Inevitably, it loses out or it becomes a dependent on the metropolis, as the Owens Valley of California has done in its struggle with Los Angeles. Webb noted the outcome of this unequal competition: "The West is today virtually an oasis civilization." Despite an abundance of space, people have found themselves being driven to a few isolated oases where they live packed closely together, while all around them the land stretches away like a great, wild void.

Finally, the hydraulic West has touched and shaped people's imaginations in ways we have hardly yet understood. Old ideas have been reborn there, or they have been applied in new ways. For example, the Americans who came into the region brought with them a deeply rooted drive for mastery over the natural world. They did not come to contemplate the land, nor would they easily tolerate any deprivations it imposed on them. We will make a stand here in this awesome canyon, westerners began to say, and hold back with our common force the full might of the Columbia, the Snake, the Missouri, the Platte, the Rio Grande, the Colorado. No individual or small knot of people among us can achieve that triumph. It will require all of us working as one, all of us united in the pursuit of power. In contrast to the pastoral West, with its glorification of rugged individualism, this hydraulic mode has promoted the cultish idea of the collective domination of nature.

There are many resemblances between this hydraulic West and the modern technological society, as found today in Moscow, New York, or Tokyo. But they are not quite the same thing—not yet anyway. The technological society believes it has escaped all environmental restraint, overcome all limits, and at last stands free of nature. But in today's West such a boast would be ludicrous. The region obviously has not yet learned how to manufacture a single molecule of water, let alone water in unlimited quantities, nor even to find a single substitute for it. Water remains a severely limited resource, yet it is irreplaceable. Until the West discovers how to produce this resource in unstinting abundance, it must continue to obey nature's demands. And in that obedience the West remains a region set apart from other regions.

Through this recapitulation of the two major western modes, I have been indicating a strategy of analysis that, if followed, would take us to the true West at last. Walter Prescott Webb told us where we might find it some time ago, but then he himself got discouraged and turned back. There was not enough intellectual substance along the way, he feared, to satisfy the historian. "Western history," he wrote in his 1957 essay, "is brief and it is bizarre. It is brief because the time is so short and its material deficient. Western history is bizarre because of the nature of what it has got." Having spent some time in England as a visiting professor, having travelled widely around the East and South, he had come home to the West in the fifties with a heightened sense of it as a place "full of negatives and short on positives." Above all, the region's lack of water seemed to him responsible somehow for its failure to achieve a larger cultural significance.

> What is the biographer going to do for a region that has so few men of distinction: What is the historian going to do with a country almost without chronology or important battles or great victories or places where armies have surrendered or dead soldiers were buried? How can he make a thick history out of such thin material?

We have heard such laments before. It is the old, piteous cry of the provincial who has lost confidence in himself and his ability to find complex meaning in his surroundings. Perhaps, to avoid such doubt, the western historian ought to stay away from places like Oxford. Or if he insists on visiting them, he ought to remind himself that, looked at up close, their old kings and warriors were not any better than the new ones; that, anyway, battles and armies are not the only stuff of history. He ought to read and reread as often as possible what Ortega y Gasset once wrote, that arid lands do not necessarily make arid minds. But Webb forgot all that. Late in his life he seems to have lost enthusiasm for the West as region and instead began denigrating it. Now it falls to a later generation—our generation—to push ahead toward a deeper, fuller, and more intellectually complex regionalism.

If Clifford Geertz can find large meanings in the cockfights of Bali and Emmanuel Le Roy Ladurie in the peasants of Languedoc, the western historian need not despair of the West. For those with imagination to find it, there is plenty of thick history to be written about this region. Within its spacious boundaries and across its spare, dry expanses, through what is now more than two hundred years of European settlement and many thousand of Indian life, this region offers for study all the greed, violence, beauty, ambition, and variety anyone could use. Given enough time and effort, it may someday also offer a story of careful, lasting adaptation of people to the land.

We are beginning to know where the true West is, what it has been, what it might have been, what it might still be. We are beginning to know the place for the first time.

ʏ *F U R T H E R   R E A D I N G*

Lee Benson, *Turner and Beard: American Historical Writing Reconsidered* (1960)
Ray A. Billington, *America's Frontier Heritage* (1966)
——, *The American Frontier Thesis: Attack and Defense* (1971)

——, *Frederick Jackson Turner* (1973)

——, ed., *Frontier and Section: Selected Essays of Frederick Jackson Turner* (1961)

——, ed., *The Frontier Thesis: Valid Interpretation of American History?* (1966)

Ronald H. Carpenter, *The Eloquence of Frederick Jackson Turner* (1983)

Stanley Elkins and Eric McKitrick, "A Meaning for Turner's Frontier," *Political Science Quarterly*, 69 (1954), 321–53, 562–602

Gene M. Gressley, "The Turner Thesis: A Problem in Historiography," *Agricultural History*, 32 (1958), 227–49

Richard Hofstadter, *The Progressive Historians: Turner, Beard, Parrington* (1968)

—— and Seymour Martin Lipset, eds., *Turner and the Sociology of the Frontier* (1968)

Wilbur R. Jacobs, *Frederick Jackson Turner's Legacy: Unpublished Writings in American History* (1965)

——, ed., *The Historical World of Frederick Jackson Turner* (1968)

Murray Kane, "Some Considerations on the Frontier Concept of Frederick Jackson Turner," *Mississippi Valley Historical Association, Proceedings*, 27 (1940), 379–400

George Wilson Pierson, "American Historians and the Frontier Hypothesis in 1941," *Wisconsin Magazine of History*, 26 (1942), 36–60, 170–85

——, "The Frontier and American Institutions: A Criticism of the Turner Theory," *New England Quarterly*, 15 (1942), 224–55

Jackson K. Putnam, "The Turner Thesis and the Westward Movement: A Reappraisal," *Western Historical Quarterly*, 7 (1976), 378–404

Martin Ridge, "Frederick Jackson Turner, Ray Allen Billington, and American Frontier History," *Western Historical Quarterly*, 19 (1988), 5–20

Jerome O. Steffen, "Some Observations on the Turner Thesis: A Polemic," *Papers in Anthropology*, 14 (1973), 16–30

George Rogers Taylor, ed., *The Turner Thesis Concerning the Role of the Frontier in American History* (rev. ed. 1956)

Frederick Jackson Turner, *The Early Writings of Frederick Jackson Turner* (1938)

Walter Rundell, Jr., "Concepts of the 'Frontier' and the 'West'," *Arizona and the West*, 1 (1959), 13–41

Norman J. Simler, "The Safety-Valve Doctrine Reevaluated," *Agricultural History*, 32 (1958), 250–57

Walter P. Webb, *Divided We Stand: The Crisis of a Frontierless Society* (1937)

——, *The Great Frontier* (1952)

——, *The Great Plains* (1931)

David J. Weber, "Turner, the Boltonians, and the Borderlands," *American Historical Review*, 91 (1986), 66–81

Benjamin F. Wright, Jr., "American Democracy and the Frontier," *Yale Review*, 20 (1930), 349–65

Native Lands

Y

*Scholars may disagree about whether to view the West historically as a frontier
or a region, but for the native peoples of North America, this continent has
been a homeland for thousands of years. Misnamed "Indians" by the European
newcomers, these native peoples had established an "old world" of their own
long before 1492. The interaction between native Americans and European newcomers is the first major story of both American and western history. Understanding the profound changes that occurred when Europeans swept into these
native homelands is a formidable challenge to the student of the American past.
Evidence from a wide range of disciplines, such as archaeology, anthropology,
folklore, linguistics, climatology, and epidemiology, has been used by historians
to recapture the early era of Indian-white contact. The full story may be impossible to reconstruct, but most recent scholarship is demonstrating that American
Indians are very much actors and survivors in this postcontact history, not passive victims of an overwhelming invasion.*

Y *D O C U M E N T S*

The oral traditions of many native American tribes contain clear memories of the
first contact with Europeans. These stories were written down by white visitors
who came later. The first two documents indicate how truly foreign these newcomers appeared to native people. The events described in the first document, a
Chippewa narrative first written down in 1855, occurred in the Great Lakes region. The second document, a Chinook story recorded in 1894, took place near
the mouth of the Columbia River in what today is Oregon.

The next two documents are accounts of the Pueblo revolt of 1680 in colonial New Mexico. The third document is a report to the king of Spain by the
recently arrived viceroy of New Spain, the count of Paredes, who learned of this
rebellion on the northern frontier before he reached Mexico City to take up his
post. The testimony before his Spanish inquisitors of Pedro Naranjo, an imprisoned Pueblo Indian, indicates how traditional religious beliefs and one native
leader helped launch the revolt. This event remains a vivid memory in the minds
of present-day Pueblo Indians—as significant to them as the American Revolu-

tion for Anglo-Americans. Although New Mexico would be reconquered after the revolt, Spanish domination would never be as intense as before 1680.

The final two documents, written over two hundred years apart, demonstrate the deadliest aspect of the European "invasion" of America—the introduction of epidemic diseases, especially smallpox. The first account, concerning an epidemic in 1633, was written by William Bradford, the governor of Plymouth Colony in Massachusetts. The second is from the 1837 journal of Francis Chardon, a trader at Fort Clark, located on the Missouri River some fifty-five miles above present-day Bismarck, North Dakota. In 1633 in many of the native villages of southern New England, up to 95 percent of the Indians died. Similar catastrophic rates of death occurred in 1837 in villages of the Arikaras, Mandans, Hidatsas, Assiniboins, and Blackfeet.

A Chippewa Narrative, Recorded in 1855

For a long time before this story began, my people had lived on a small promontory on Lake Superior. It is called the Point of the Old Village.

One night one of my grandfathers, a prophet of the tribe, had a dream which had a strange effect on him. For days he busied himself very earnestly, as a result of this dream. He fasted, he took sweat baths every day, he shut himself alone in his prophet lodge.

His penance was so thorough, so unusual, that the people of the village were curious. What was about to happen? Was there to be a great famine or an unusually successful hunting season? Was there to be a serious war with the Sioux? Or was something else of equal importance about to take place?

At last when the prophet had considered everything carefully, and after he had the whole story of his dream clear in his mind, he called together the other prophets and the chiefs of his people. He had astonishing news for them.

"Men of strange appearance have come across the great water," he told them. "They have landed on our island. Their skins are white like snow, and on their faces long hair grows. These people have come across the great water in wonderfully large canoes which have great white wings like those of a giant bird. The men have long and sharp knives, and they have long black tubes which they point at birds and animals. The tubes make a smoke that rises into the air just like the smoke from our pipes. From them come fire and such terrific noise that I was frightened, even in my dream."

Half a day it took the prophet to tell his dream. He described the sails and the masts of the ships, the iron corslets, the guns and cannon. The other prophets and the chiefs listened in amazement. When he finished speaking, all agreed at once that they should prepare a fleet of several canoes and send it eastward along the Great Lakes and the great river. There at the big water, their messengers should find out about these strange people and, on their return home, should make a report to the tribe.

Canoes were made ready for the long journey, and trusted men were selected. For many suns and several moons they travelled over the waters of the lakes and down the great river, through the lands of friendly tribes. These people knew nothing yet of the white strangers, for they had no gifted dreamer and prophet among them.

At last the travellers from the Point of the Old Village came to the lower part of the great river. One evening they found a clearing in the forest, where even the largest trees had been cut down quite smoothly. The Indians camped there and examined the stumps closely. Giant beavers with huge, sharp teeth had done the cutting, the men thought.

"No," said the prophet. "These trees were probably cut by the long knives I saw in my dream. The white strangers must have camped here."

His companions were filled with awe, and with terror also. Using their own stone-headed axes, they could not cut down such large trees or cut anything so smoothly. Then they found some long, rolled-up shavings that puzzled them, and also some pieces of bright-coloured cloth. The shavings they stuck in their hair and in their ears; the cloth they wound around their heads.

Wearing these decorations, the travellers went on. Soon they came to the camp of the strangers. The men had white faces and bushy beards, just as the prophet had said. They had long knives, thundering fire-tubes, and giant canoes with white wings, just as the prophet had said. Now we know that these first white men were Frenchmen.

When the travellers had finished their visit, they made the long journey back to their home on Lake Superior and reported what they had seen. They were excited, and their story excited all the village. Everyone crowded round, to see the things the men had brought back: the shavings, the pieces of wood cut with sharp tools, the gaily-coloured cloth. This cloth was torn into small pieces, so that each person might have one.

To impress other chiefs and other tribes, the Chippewas followed an old custom. In former days they had bound the scalps of their enemies on long poles and sent them from one tribe to another; now they fastened splinters of wood and strips of calico to poles and sent them with special messengers.

And so these strange articles were passed from hand to hand around the whole lake. In this way the people of Lake Superior gained their first knowledge of the white men from Europe.

A Chinook Story, Recorded in 1894

An old woman in a Clatsop village near the mouth of Big River mourned because of the death of her son. For a year she grieved. One day she ceased her wailing and took a walk along the beach where she had often gone in happier days.

As she returned to the village, she saw a strange something out in the water not far from shore. At first she thought it was a whale. When she came nearer, she saw two spruce trees standing upright on it.

"It is not a whale," she said to herself. "It is a monster."

When she came near the strange thing that lay at the edge of the water, she saw that its outside was covered with copper and that ropes were tied to the spruce trees. Then a bear came out of the strange thing and stood on it. He looked like a bear, but his face was the face of a human being.

"Oh, my son is dead," she wailed, "and now the thing we have heard about is on our shore."

The old woman returned to her village, weeping and wailing. People hearing her called to each other, "An old woman is crying. Someone must have struck her."

The men picked up their bows and arrows and rushed out to see what was the matter.

"Listen!" an old man said.

They heard the old woman wailing, "Oh, my son is dead, and the thing we have heard about is on our shore."

All the people ran to meet her. "What is it? Where is it?" they asked.

"Ah, the thing we have heard about in tales is lying over there." She pointed toward the south shore of the village. "There are two bears on it, or maybe they are people."

Then the Indians ran toward the thing that lay near the edge of the water. The two creatures on it held copper kettles in their hands. When the Clatsop arrived at the beach, the creatures put their hands to their mouths and asked for water.

Two of the Indians ran inland, hid behind a log awhile, and then ran back to the beach. One of them climbed up on the strange thing and entered it. He looked around inside it. He saw that it was full of boxes, and he found long strings of brass buttons.

When he went outside to call his relatives to see the inside of the thing, he found that they had already set fire to it. He jumped down and joined the two creatures and the Indians on shore.

The strange thing burned just like fat. Everything burned except the iron, the copper, and the brass. The Clatsop picked up all the pieces of metal. Then they took the two strange-looking men to their chief.

"I want to keep one of the men with me," said the chief.

Soon the people north of the river heard about the strange men and the strange thing, and they came to the Clatsop village. The Willapa came from across the river, the Chehalis and the Cowlitz from farther north, and even the Quinault from up the coast. And people from up the river came also—the Klickitat and others farther up.

The Clatsop sold the iron, brass, and copper. They traded one nail for a good deerskin. For a long necklace of shells they gave several nails. One man traded a piece of brass two fingers wide for a slave.

None of the Indians had ever seen iron and brass before. The Clatsop became rich selling the metals to the other tribes.

The two Clatsop chiefs kept the two men who came on the ship. One stayed at the village called Clatsop, and the other stayed at the village on the cape.

The Count of Paredes' Report
on the Pueblo Indians' Revolt, 1681

Before entering upon this government I received information (while on the road from Vera Cruz to the city of Mexico, and more fully as soon as I entered the latter city, from the letters and certified documents which the archbishop viceroy, my predecessor, delivered to me) of the general uprising of the Indians of the provinces of New Mexico. According to the *autos*, reports, and documents which were remitted to this government, on the thirteenth day of August of the past year 1680 the rebellious Indians, by prearranged conspiracy, fell upon all the pueblos and farms at the same time with such vigor and cruelty that they killed twenty-one missionary religious—nineteen priests and two lay brothers—and more than three hundred and eighty Spaniards, not sparing the defenselessness of the women and children. They set fire to the temples, seizing the images of the saints and profaning the holy vessels with such shocking desecrations and insolences that it is indecent to mention them. They left thirty-four pueblos totally desolated and destroyed, not counting many other farms and haciendas at a distance from them. . . .

The ferocity of these Indians met with no resistance except in the villa and capital of Santa Fe, where the governor resides, who was, and is, Don Antonio de Otermín. He defended himself in the casas reales [royal mansions] where he was besieged for nine days, having gathered therein all the people and cattle that he could. Realizing that they had cut off his water supply, that provisions were becoming scarce, and that the number of the enemy who were arriving from other pueblos and nations was increasing, and that such were their boldness and fury that they had set fire to the houses and the temples, attempting also to fire the casas reales, and considering that no help could reach him from any direction, alike because of the multitude of the barbarians who had taken all the passes, and because of the information that he had received from some of them whom our people captured and from others who fled from the enemy, that all the religious and the Spaniards from the surrounding pueblos had been killed, the governor resolved, in accordance with the opinion of a junta of the besieged, seeing the imminent danger of starvation or death at the hands of the Indians, to go out to attack them and retreat as well as he could. This he did, breaking through the chief division of the barbarians with the loss of one Spaniard [killed] and many wounded, the governor himself receiving two wounds in the face and a gunshot in the breast. This movement having put the barbarians to flight, our people turned quickly upon some houses where forty-seven Indians were fortified, whom they shot with harquebuses after they had declared that the uprising had been deliberated upon for a long time, at the instance of the Teguas Indians of the pueblo of Tesuque.

Notwithstanding that more than three hundred Indians had been killed in the affray, fearing that they would be joined by those from other pueblos and that all the heathen nations would be convoked, [the Spaniards] resolved to withdraw from the villa, taking all the provisions they could and the few cattle that remained to them.

Pedro Naranjo's Testimony, 1681

Declaration of Pedro Naranjo of the Queres Nation. [Place of the Río del Norte, December 19, 1681.]

In the said plaza de armas on the said day, month, and year, for the prosecution of the judicial proceedings of this case his lordship caused to appear before him an Indian prisoner named Pedro Naranjo, a native of the pueblo of San Felipe, of the Queres nation, who was captured in the advance and attack upon the pueblo of La Isleta. He makes himself understood very well in the Castilian language and speaks his mother tongue and the Tegua. He took the oath in due legal form in the name of God, our Lord, and a sign of the cross, under charge of which he promised to tell the truth concerning what he knows and as he might be questioned, and having understood the seriousness of the oath and so signified through the interpreters, he spoke.

Asked whether he knows the reason or motives which the Indians of this kingdom had for rebelling, forsaking the law of God and obedience to his Majesty, and committing such grave and atrocious crimes, and who were the leaders and principal movers, and by whom and how it was ordered; and why they burned the images, temples, crosses, rosaries, and things of divine worship, committing such atrocities as killing priests, Spaniards, women, and children, and the rest that he might know touching the question, he said that since the government of Señor General Hernando Ugarte y la Concha they have planned to rebel on various occasions through conspiracies of the Indian sorcerers, and that although in some pueblos the messages were accepted, in other parts they would not agree to it; and that it is true that during the government of the said señor general seven or eight Indians were hanged for this same cause, whereupon the unrest subsided. Some time thereafter they [the conspirators] sent from the pueblo of Los Taos through the pueblos of the custodia two deerskins with some pictures on them signifying conspiracy after their manner, in order to convoke the people to a new rebellion, and the said deerskins passed to the province of Moqui, where they refused to accept them. The pact which they had been forming ceased for the time being, but they always kept in their hearts the desire to carry it out, so as to live as they are living to-day. Finally, in the past years, at the summons of an Indian named Popé who is said to have communication with the devil, it happened that in an estufa* of the pueblo of Los Taos there appeared to the said Popé three figures of Indians who never came out of the estufa. They gave the said Popé to understand that they were going underground to the lake of Copala. He

---

* ceremonial chamber, often called a "kiva."

saw these figures emit fire from all the extremities of their bodies. . . . They told him to make a cord of maguey fiber and tie some knots in it which would signify the number of days that they must wait before the rebellion. He said that the cord was passed through all the pueblos of the kingdom so that the ones which agreed to it [the rebellion] might untie one knot in sign of obedience, and by the other knots they would know the days which were lacking; and this was to be done on pain of death to those who refused to agree to it. As a sign of agreement and notice of having concurred in the treason and perfidy they were to send up smoke signals to that effect in each one of the pueblos singly. The said cord was taken from pueblo to pueblo by the swiftest youths under the penalty of death if they revealed the secret. Everything being thus arranged, two days before the time set for its execution, because his lordship had learned of it and had imprisoned two Indian accomplices from the pueblo of Tesuque, it was carried out prematurely that night, because it seemed to them that they were now discovered; and they killed religious, Spaniards, women, and children. This being done, it was proclaimed in all the pueblos that everyone in common should obey the commands of their father whom they did not know, which would be given through El Caydi or El Popé. This was heard by Alonso Catití, who came to the pueblo of this declarant to say that everyone must unite to go to the villa to kill the governor and the Spaniards who had remained with him, and that he who did not obey would, on their return, be beheaded; and in fear of this they agreed to it. Finally the señor governor and those who were with him escaped from the siege, and later this declarant saw that as soon as the Spaniards had left the kingdom an order came from the said Indian, Popé, in which he commanded all the Indians to break the lands and enlarge their cultivated fields, saying that now they were as they had been in ancient times, free from the labor they had performed for the religious and the Spaniards, who could not now be alive. He said that this is the legitimate cause and the reason they had for rebelling, because they had always desired to live as they had when they came out of the lake of Copala. . . .

Asked for what reason they so blindly burned the images, temples, crosses, and other things of divine worship, he stated that the said Indian, Popé, came down in person, and with him El Saca and El Chato from the pueblo of Los Taos, and other captains and leaders and many people who were in his train, and he ordered in all the pueblos through which he passed that they instantly break up and burn the images of the holy Christ, the Virgin Mary and the other saints, the crosses, and everything pertaining to Christianity, and that they burn the temples, break up the bells, and separate from the wives whom God had given them in marriage and take those whom they desired. In order to take away their baptismal names, the water, and the holy oils, they were to plunge into the rivers and wash themselves with amole, which is a root native to the country, washing even their clothing, with the understanding that there would thus be taken from them the character of the holy sacraments. They did this, and also many other things which he does not recall, given to understand that this mandate had come from the Caydi and the other two who emitted fire from their extremities in the said estufa of Taos, and that they thereby returned to the state of their antiquity, as when they came from the lake of Copala; that this was the better life and the one they desired, because the God of the Spaniards was worth nothing and theirs was very strong, the Spaniards's God being rotten wood. These things were observed and obeyed by all except some who, moved by the zeal of Christians, opposed it, and such persons the said Popé caused to be killed immediately. He saw to it that they at once erected and rebuilt their houses of idolatry which they call estufas, and made very ugly masks in imitation of the devil in order to dance the dance of the cacina;* and he said likewise that the devil had given them to understand that living thus in accordance with the law of their ancestors, they would harvest a great deal of maize, many beans, a great abundance of cotton, calabashes, and very large watermelons and cantaloupes; and that they could erect their houses and enjoy abundant health and leisure. As he has said, the people were very much pleased, living at their ease in this life of their antiquity, which was the chief cause of their falling into such laxity. . . .

Asked what arrangements and plans they had made for the contingency of the Spaniards' return, he said that what he knows concerning the question is that they were always saying they would have to fight to the death, for they do not wish to live in any other way than they are living at present; and the demons in the estufa of Taos had given them to understand that as soon as the Spaniards began to move toward this kingdom they would warn them so that they might unite, and none of them would be caught. . . . He greatly fears in his heart that he may have offended God, and that now having been absolved and returned to the fold of the church, he has spoken the truth in everything he has been asked. His declaration being read to him, he affirmed and ratified all of it. He declared himself to be eighty years of age, and he signed it with his lordship and the interpreters and assisting witnesses.

William Bradford on the Great Sickness Among New England Indians, 1633

I am now to relate some strange and remarkable passages. There was a company of people lived in the country up above in the River of Connecticut a great way from their trading house there, and were enemies to those Indians which lived about them, and of whom they stood in some fear, being a stout people. About a thousand of them had enclosed themselves in a fort which they had strongly palisadoed about. Three or four Dutchmen went up in the beginning of winter to live with them, to get their trade and prevent them for bringing it to the English or to fall into amity with them;

---

* *Cacinas* (now most commonly spelled *kachinas*) are powerful spirits impersonated by the dancers.

but at spring to bring all down to their place. But their enterprise failed. For it pleased God to visit these Indians with a great sickness and such a mortality that of a thousand, above nine and a half hundred of them died, and many of them did rot above ground for want of burial. And the Dutchmen almost starved before they could get away, for ice and snow; but about February they got with much difficulty to their trading house; whom they kindly relieved, being almost spent with hunger and cold. Being thus refreshed by them divers days, they got to their own place and the Dutch were very thankful for this kindness.

This spring also, those Indians that lived about their trading house there, fell sick of the small pox and died most miserably; for a sorer disease cannot befall them, they fear it more than the plague. For usually they that have this disease have them in abundance, and for want of bedding and linen and other helps they fall into a lamentable condition as they lie on their hard mats, the pox breaking and mattering and running one into another, their skin cleaving by reason thereof to the mats they lie on. When they turn them, a whole side will flay off at once as it were, and they will be all of a gore blood, most fearful to behold. And then being very sore, what with cold and other distempers, they die like rotten sheep. The condition of this people was so lamentable and they fell down so generally of this disease as they were in the end not able to help one another, no not to make a fire nor to fetch a little water to drink, nor any to bury the dead. But would strive as long as they could, and when they could procure no other means to make fire, they would burn the wooden trays and dishes they ate their meat in, and their very bows and arrows. And some would crawl out on all fours to get a little water, and sometimes die by the way and not be able to get in again. But of those of the English house, though at first they were afraid of the infection, yet seeing their woeful and sad condition and hearing their pitiful cries and lamentations, they had compassion of them, and daily fetched them wood and water and made them fires, got them victuals whilst they lived; and buried them when they died. For very few of them escaped, notwithstanding they did what they could for them to the hazard of themselves. The chief sachem himself now died and almost all his friends and kindred. But by the marvelous goodness and providence of God, not one of the English was so much as sick or in the least measure tainted with this disease, though they daily did these offices for them for many weeks together. And this mercy which they showed them was kindly taken and thankfully acknowledged of all the Indians that knew or heard of the same. And their masters here did much commend and reward them for the same.

Francis Chardon on the Destruction of the Arikaras and Mandans by Smallpox, 1837

[*July*] *Wednesday 26,*   The Rees [Arikaras] And Mandans all arrived to Day Well loaded With Meat, Mitchel also arrived with 15 pieces, The 4 Bears (Mandan) has caught the small pox, and got crazy, and has disappeared from camp—he arrived here in the afternoon—The Indians of the Little Village all arrived in the evening Well loaded—With dried Meat—the small Pox has broke Out among them, several has died,

Thursday 27, Indians all Out after berries, No News from Any quarter, the small pox is Killing them of at the Village, four died to day—

Friday 28, Rain in the Morning—This day was very Near being my last—a young Mandan came to the Fort with his gun cocked, And secreted under his robe, With the intention of Killing Me, after hunting Me in 3 or 4 of the houses he at last found Me, the door being shut, he waited some time for Me to come Out, just as I Was in the Act of going Out, Mitchel caught him, and gave him in the hands of two Indians Who Conducted him to the Village, had Not Mitchel perceived him the instant he did, I would Not be at the trouble of Makeing this statement—I am upon my guard, the Rees are Out rageous against the Mandans, they say that the first Mandan that Kills a White, they Will exterminate the whole race, I have got 100 Guns ready And 1000 Powder, ready to hand Out to them when the fun Commences—The War Party of Rees that left here the 7th inst came back to day—With five horses, that they stole from the Sioux—a lodge that was encamped at the Little Miss^r they attacked it in the Night, after fireing several shots they departed takeing with them all the Horses they think to have Killed 3 or 4 in the lodge—The Mandans & Rees gave us two splendid dances, they say they dance, on account of their Not haveing a long time to live, as they expect to all die of the Small Pox— and as long as they Are alive, They Will take it Out in danceing.

Saturday 29, Several More Mandans died last night. Two GrosVentres arrived from their dried Meat camp, it appears that it has Not broke Out Among them as yet—

Sunday 30, An other report from the GrosVentres to day say, they are Arrived at their Village, and that 10 or 15 of them have died, two big fish Among them, they threaten Death And Distruction to us all at this Place, saying that I was the Cause of the small pox Makeing its appearance in this Country—One of Our best friends of the Village (The Four Bears) died today, regretted by all Who Knew him,

Monday 31, Mandans are getting worse Nothing Will do them except revenge. Three of the War party that left here the 26th of last Month Arrived to day. With each of them One horse, that they stole from the Yanctons on White River,

Killed 61 Rats this Month—total 1778

August 31 Days—1837

Tuesday 1st The three horses that the war party brought in yesterday they say that they belong to the Compy that they were stole on the Island below the Little Missr the Soldiers was takeing them from them, but I told them to Waite untill the Arrival of Lachapelle Who I expect to Arrive in 4 or 5 days—

The Mandans Are Makeing their Medicine for rain, As their Corn is all drying up—to day we had several light showers—

Wednesday 2nd   Yesterday an Indian that was Out after berris discovered a band of Cows, all hands Out to run them, they all Arrived in the Afternoon Well laden With fresh meat haveing ran three Bands—

Thursday 3rd   All quiet, No News from Any quarter the GrosVentres Not yet Arrived from their Dried Meat excursion—

Friday 4th   Same As Yesterday—Nothing New, Only two deaths today—sprinkled with rain in the Morning—

Saturday 5th   Portrá a half breed from the North started to day—alone, for Red River, Indians Out after berries, others Out After Meat—News from the GrosVentres, they say that they are encamped this side of Turtle Mountain, And that a great Many of them have died of the Small Pox—several chiefs Among them, they swear vengence Against all the Whites, As they say the small Pox Was brought here by the S. B. [Steamboat].

Sunday 6   One More Ree died last Night—To day we had a tremendous storm of rain, hale, And Wind, which Continued for ½ hour With great Violence, the Fort came very Near blowing down, 40 or 50 Loads of hay that I have Out is Much damaged

Monday 7   Six More died to day—several Rees left the Mandan Village and pitched their Lodges Out in the Prairies—rain all day—report from the GrosVentres say they will be at their Village tomorrow—

Tuesday 8   Four More died to day—the two thirds of the Village are sick, to day I gave six pounds of Epsom salts in doses to Men, Women, and children   the small Pox has broke Out at the Little Mandan Village. three died yesterday, two chiefs—

Wednesday 9   Seven More died to day—the Men came back from the hay at full speed haveing saw enemies, all hands out for the fight, False alarm,

Thursday 10   All the Rees that were encamped in the Mandan lodges, except a few that are sick, Moved down to the Island hoping to get rid of the small Pox—the Mandans talk of Moveing to the other side of the river, 12 or 15 died to day—

Friday 11,   Sent old Charboneau up to the GrosVentres with some tobacco; and a bag full of good talk, as yesterday they sent a very severe threat to Me, Mandans all crossed to the other Side of the river to encamp—leaveing all that were sick in the Village, I Keep No A/c of the dead, as they die so fast that it is impossible—

Saturday 12,   Cool And pleasant Weather, one of My best friends of the Little Village died to day—(Le Fort)—News of a War party of GrosVentres And Rees (70) being used up by the Saons [Sioux], quicker Work than the small Pox.

Sunday 13,   Several reports from the GrosVentres that they are bent on the distruction of us all, As yet I do Not place Much confidence in what report says, Charboneau Will bring us the strait News—The Mandan are dying 8 and 10 every day—an Old fellow who has lost the whole of his family to the Number of 14, harrangued to day, that it was time to begin to Kill the Whites, as it was them that brought the small Pox in the Country—

Tuesday 22,   Cool pleasant Weather, The disease still Keeps ahead 8 and 10 die off daily, thirty five Mandans (Men) have died, the Women and Children I keep No Account of—Several Mandans have come back to remain in the Village, One of My Soldiers a (Ree) died to day—Two Young Mandans shot themselves this Morning—News from the Little Village, that the disease is getting worse and worse every day. it is now two months that it broke Out—A Ree that has the small Pox, And thinking that he was going to die, approached Near his Wife, a Young Woman of 19—And struck her in the head With his tommahawk, With the intent to Kill her, that she Might go With him in the Other World—she is badly Wounded   a few Minutes after he cut his throat, a report is in Circulation, that they intend to fire the Fort, Stationed guards in the Bastion

Wednesday 23,   May and Charboneau arrived late last night from the GrosVentres   all appears to be quiet in that quarter. The little Sioux a *Mandan* died last night, We had three allerts to day—all hands under Arms, all false reports   Several Rees Arrived from their camp at the GrosVentres

Thursday 24,   Seven More died at the Village last Night, and Many More at the Ree camp at the point of Woolds below   The fellow that we Killed on the 17th all his band Came to day to smoke With us and Make Peace, how long it will last I Cannot tell, however We Must put up With it, good or bad—

Friday 25,   May And Charboneau started last Night for the GrosVentres sent a few pounds of powder & Ball to the GrosVentres And Rees—An other Mandan chief died to day—(The long fingers)   total Number of Men that has died—50, I have turned Out to be a first rate doctor St Grado, an Indian that has been bleeding at the Nose all day, I gave him a decoction of all sorts of ingredients Mixed together, enough to Kill a Buffaloe Bull of the largest size, and stopped the effusion of Blood, the decoction of Medicine, Was, a little Magnisia, peppermint, sugar lead, all Mixed together in a phial, filled With Indian grog—and the Patient snuffing up his nose three or four times—I done it out of experiment And Am Content to say, that it proved effectual, the Confidence that an Indian has in the Medicine of the whites, is half the Cure,

Saturday 26,   The Indians all started Out on the North side in quest of Buffaloe, As they have Nothing to eat A Young Ree, the Nephew of Garreau, died at the Village last Night, Much regretted by us all, As he was one of the foresmost in aideing to Kill the dog on the 17th inst & A Mandan of the Little Village Came to the Fort to day to Sing his Medicine Song, got paid for his trouble, and Went off—glad to get clear of him— A young Ree that has the Small Pox, told his Mother to go and dig his grave, she accordingly did so—after the grave Was dug, he walked With the help of his Father to the Grave, I Went Out With the Interpreter to try to pursuade him to return back to the village—but he would not, Saying for the reason that all his young friends Were gone, And that he wished to follow them, torwards evening he died—

Sunday 27,   Strong east Wind, rain in the Morning, The Indians Came back from the *Cerne* Well loaded With fresh Meat, report Cattle in abundance 20 Miles off—News from the GrosVentres of the disease breaking Out amongst them,

Monday 28,   Wind from the North, rain, disagreeable Weather, several More Indians Arrived With fresh Meat—from the North Side gave us a small quantity which we found very good—Three More fell sick in the Fort to day—My interpreter for one, if I loose him I shall be badly off, the bad Weather continued all day—and no Prospects of Clearing off—

Tuesday 29,   Last Night I Was taken Very Sick With the Fever, there is Six of us in the Fort that has the Fever, and One the Small Pox—An Indian Vacinated his child, by Cutting two small pieces of flesh Out of her Arms, and two on the belly—and then takeing a Scab from One, that Was getting Well of the disease, and rubbing it on the Wounded part, three days after, it took effect, and the child is perfectly Well—

Wednesday 30,   All those that I thought had the small Pox turned out to be true, the fever left them yesterday, and the disease showed itself, I Am perfectly Well, as last Night, I took a hot Whiskey Punch, Which Made Me sweat all last Night, this Morning I took My daily Bitters as usual, Indians Arrived with fresh Meat, report Cattle in abundance opposite the Little Lake below—

Thursday 31,   A Young Mandan that died 4 days ago, his Wife haveing the disease also Killed her two Children. one a fine Boy of eight years, and the other six, to complete the affair she hung herself.

Month of August I bid you farewell With all My heart, after running twenty hair breadth escapes, threatened every instant to be all Murdered, however it is the Wish of [your] humble Servant that the Month of September Will be More Favorable. the Number of Deaths up to the present is Very Near five hundred   The Mandans are all Cut off except 23 young and Old Men

Killed 89 Rats this Month   Total 1867—

September 30 Days—1837

Friday 1,   This Morning two dead bodies wrapped in a White skin, and laid on a raft passed by the Forks on their way to the regions below. May success attend them. The Rees that are encamped in the Point of Woods below, Are Moving up to encamp at the Mandans Corn fields No doubt with the intention of takeing all from them, as what few Mandans are left are Not able to Contend with the Rees—Mitchels squaw fell to day.

Saturday 2,   Being Out of wood, risqued the Men—to the point of Woods below   hauled eight loads. Several Indians Arrived With fresh Meat, out 2 days, but one death to day, although several are sick, those that catch the disease at Present, seldom die. One Fellow I saw on horseback to day— he looked More like a gohst than a [human] being—

Sunday 3,   A Young Mandan came to pay us a Visit from the Little Village, he informes us, that they are all Most all used up, and that it is his opinion that before the disease stops, that there will not One be left, except 8 or 10 that has Weathered Out the Sickness—. . . .

[*December*] *Sunday 31,*   Sent a Man down to the Ree camp to collect some News—Caught three foxes last Night—Charboneau Arrived from the GrosVentre camp. he was accompanied by 2 Mandan and one GrosVentre, he is encamped with only Ten Lodges, the rest of the Lodges are scattered, on the Little Misso he has had No News of them, for two Months, in all Probability they Are all Dead, the last News that he had from them was, that 117 had died, and the disease was still rageing—

Killed 85 Rats this Month—   total 2294

Speech of the 4 Bears a Mandan Warrior to the Arricarees and Mandan—30th July 1837

My Friends one And all, Listen to what I have to say—Ever since I Can remember, I have loved the Whites, I have lived With them ever since I was a Boy, and to the best of My Knoweledge, I have Never Wronged a White Man, on the Contrary, I have always Protected them from the insults of others, Which they Cannot deny, The 4 Bears Never saw a White Man hungry, but what he gave him to eat, Drink, and a Buffaloe skin to sleep on, in time of Need, I was always ready to die for them, Which they Cannot deny. I have done every thing that a red Skin could do for them, And how have they repaid it! With ingratitude! I have Never Called a White Man a Dog, but to day, I do Pronounce them to be a set of Black harted Dogs, they have deceived Me, them that I Always Considered as Brothers, has turned Out to be My Worst enemies, I have been in Many Battles, and often wounded, but the Wounds of My enemies, I exhalt in, but to day I am Wounded, And by Whom, by those same White Dogs that I have Always Considered, and Treated as Brothers, I do Not fear Death My friends, You Know it, but to *die* With My face rotton, that even the Wolves will shrink With horror at seeing Me, And say to themselves, that is the 4 Bears the Friend of the Whites—Listen well what I have to say, as it will be the last time you will hear Me. think of your Wives, children, Brothers, Sisters, Friends, and in fact all that you hold dear, are all Dead, or Dying, with their faces all rotton, caused by those dogs the whites, think of all that My friends, and rise all together and Not leave one of them Alive, The 4 Bears Will act his part. . . . [Four Bears died the same day.]

ϒ *E S S A Y S*

Elizabeth A. H. John, a historian who lives in Austin, Texas, has written extensively on the complex history of the Southwest. Her *Storms Brewed in Other Men's Worlds* (1975) considered the confrontations among the Indians, Spanish, and French in that region between 1540 and 1795. Her essay, published here for the first time, provides an overview of the interactions between the Spanish and the diverse native American tribes who lived, raided, and traded in the Southwest. It demonstrates that the Spanish were important, but not always dominant, actors who helped establish a wider peace in the region. Alfred W. Crosby is a member of the American studies faculty at the University of Texas at Austin and a noted historian of environmental transformations after the European invasion of America. Reprinted as the second selection here is his brief essay on why certain diseases devastated native populations. James Axtell, a professor of history at the College of William and Mary, is currently writing an impressive three-volume study of the cultural origins of North America. In the final essay, he challenges us to consider how the history of colonial America might have developed without the presence of native peoples. Such a counterfactual exercise is worth applying to John's and Crosby's essays. What if the Spanish in the Southwest had not confronted any native American tribes? What if European diseases had had little or no effect on the native population of North America? Whatever our answers to such speculations, the realities of the interaction between people of native American and European descent continue to the present day.

Indians in the Spanish Southwest

ELIZABETH A. H. JOHN

Consider first a question of perspective. To Indians and Spaniards, that grand sweep of deserts and mountains, plains and prairies, never was "the Southwest." That term reflects the stance of Anglo-Americans who grabbed it a mere century and a half ago and made it the southwestern quadrant of the United States. For three centuries before that, Spaniards made it the far nothern frontier of New Spain, and "El Norte" still looms enticing on the upper horizon of Hispanic America. But it was the center of the universe for Indian peoples whose homeland it had been for a much longer time, and for many of their descendants it remains so. The term *Southwest* serves as a handy contemporary usage, but only with the clear understanding that it is a misnomer in the context of Indian and Spanish experience.

Now consider the complex interplay of Indian and European cultures that molded the historic Southwest. What about the notion of "Indians in the Spanish Southwest"? Equally valid would be "Spaniards in the Indian Southwest." Great legends of conquistadors notwithstanding, New Spain's northern frontier provinces survived only by coming to terms with Indian realities. The conditions of Indian-Spanish coexistence evolved over decades, with countless clashes and grievous suffering on all sides. But there were also triumphs of humane intent, of law and justice, and of intelligent, purposeful adaptation to sweeping change. Our responsibility is to understand as fairly as possible the formative interactions among a diverse array of Indian and European peoples.

The catalyst was Spain's late-sixteenth-century thrust into the upper

Elizabeth A. H. John, "Indians in the History of the Spanish Southwest." Much of this analysis was initially presented at a Newberry Library Conference on "The Impact of Indian History on the Teaching of United States History" at the University of California at Los Angeles, 1986. Reprinted with the permission of the author.

Rio Grande basin, homeland of the culturally advanced, settled Indians whom Spaniards lumped together as "Pueblos" after seeing their compact towns. There were so many apparent similarities among the various Pueblos—their agricultural practices, their stone and adobe villages, their preoccupation with ceremonials—that their considerable differences were not immediately obvious to the Spaniards. In fact, they spoke four or five mutually incomprehensible languages, each with several dialects. Each of the more than seventy pueblos was autonomous, and wars among them were not unusual.

The common misfortune of those Indians was to look so admirable: skillful, industrious farmers, with impressive stores of food, especially corn; producers of good cotton and feather textiles; excellent potters; builders of substantial, well-ordered villages. What empire could not wish to gain such a valuable population? And what a grand harvest of Pueblo souls seemed to beckon the Faith! Who could doubt that such intelligent Indians needed only the opportunity to abandon their strange pagan rites for those of Roman Catholicism?

But Spanish assumptions erred on two vital points. The Pueblos' apparent prosperity was precarious, vulnerable to drought and to nomadic raiders. Conversely, their complex religion was virtually unassailable, so profoundly was it enmeshed with every aspect of Pueblo being. Missionaries thinking to extirpate native belief and ritual were dangerously deluded.

Could the Spaniards truly expect the Pueblos tamely to accept Spanish sovereignty and colonization in their homeland? Yes. In the wane of the sixteenth century, Spaniards saw themselves offering those Indians everything reasonable persons could desire: the blessings of Spanish civilization in this world and eternal salvation in the next. The king would extend his peace to the Pueblo world, giving them justice, the orderly rule of law, and protection from all enemies. In return, the Pueblos had only to accept the proud status of direct free vassals of the king of Spain, promising to obey his laws and receive the missionaries of his Faith.

So alien were such concepts and so great the language barrier that the Pueblos' understanding of those propositions could only have been vague and garbled at best. Promises of economic gain were more comprehensible. Perhaps it was not altogether clear that the invaders meant to instruct the crown's new vassals in Spanish arts and crafts, improve their existing skills in building and agriculture, and introduce valuable new crops. But the usefulness of the livestock brought by the Spaniards—horses, cattle, sheep, swine, chickens—was obvious enough, and so was the importance of their metal implements and weaponry, especially the deadly guns.

Pueblos already knew the force of the Spaniards' weapons and the advantage of their horses. Five limited encounters—the major expedition of Francisco Vásquez de Coronado in the 1540s and four minor incursions in the 1580s and 1590s—had taught the Pueblos how untrustworthy and dangerous even a few Spaniards could be. These newcomers violated the laws of hospitality and devoured precious stores, and resisting them invited destruction and death.

What, then, must the Pueblos have felt in the summer of 1598 when

Don Juan de Oñate arrived with more than five hundred persons apparently equipped for permanent residence? Licensed by the crown to colonize this New Mexico, entrepreneur Oñate brought not only men-at-arms but families (both Spanish and Mexican Indian), sixty-one wagons laden with Spanish goods and domestic gear, and great herds of livestock—truly a massive incursion into the austere Pueblo environment. With the caravan, but supported by royal benefaction and quite independent of Oñate's authority, came nine Franciscans to begin the missionary enterprise that was the official reason for the colonization of New Mexico.

Truly concerned for Indian souls and appalled by the destruction that earlier conquests had wrought among natives of the New World, Spain's King Philip II meant this enterprise of New Mexico to be "apostolic and Christian, and not a butchery"—indeed, not a conquest at all but a "pacification." Oñate's mandate was to obey and enforce the New Laws of 1573, which embodied the humane intent of the crown and would remain the governing principle to the end of Spanish empire. Indians were not to be enslaved or destroyed but instead incorporated into Spanish Christian civilization, with full rights of property, political liberty, and human dignity.

Unfortunately, the king's investment did not match his piety. Although it underwrote all the expenses of the missionaries, the royal treasury would not bear the costs of colonization. Against the urgent advice of his viceroy, who foresaw disaster, Philip II entrusted the colonization of New Mexico to a private contractor, who naturally would risk such an onerous, costly venture only in the expectation of enormous profit. Oñate, heir to one of the great silver mining fortunes of New Spain, gambled everything on the New Mexican enterprise, hoping to strike new mineral riches and counting on illegal requisition of Indian labor and property. From the moment Oñate entered the Pueblo world in the summer of 1598, he defied the law by commandeering food from the Indians.

Oñate nevertheless observed the formalities of pacification, explaining to Pueblo leaders that the greatest king in the world had sent him to save the Indians' souls and embrace them as subjects of the Two Majesties: God and the king of Spain. Describing the great advantages they would gain, he asked them to submit voluntarily, becoming the king's vassals and receiving the missionaries of his Faith.

Whatever they understood of the propositions of Don Juan de Oñate, assembled Pueblo leaders nodded their acquiescence, apparently thinking it wiser to accept possible gains from the Spanish connection than to resist and so risk the horrors of Spanish warfare. It was not unreasonable to entertain eight Franciscans in as many pueblos while their leader returned to headquarters to fetch more missionaries. The broad Pueblo pantheon could embrace more spirits, and it was obvious that the Spaniards' gods had given them great power and many wonderful things. Their rituals with the crossed sticks [Indians did not perceive a "cross"] might well bear learning. How could Pueblos have guessed that the missionaries would not wish merely to share their Christian god and ceremonies but also to eradicate those of the Pueblos?

For better or for worse, from 1598 to 1821, Pueblos held the status of vassals of the Spanish crown. Despite the just laws and the profound piety of the king, the first decade was a horrible ordeal at the mercy of a robber baron and his henchmen. Repudiating from the outset his commitments to build exemplary Spanish settlements and foster agriculture, Oñate focused all efforts upon a desperate search for exploitable resources, especially minerals. To house his colony, he dispossessed the residents of pueblos at the confluence of the Rio Grande and the Chama River. To feed his people, he instituted monthly requisitions of food from the Indians; for warmth, he exacted tributes of skins and blankets. His devastation of Pueblo resources was appalling, but the first Indian resistance, at Acoma in the winter of 1598, brought such swift, cruel punishment as to discourage any further revolt.

Within three years, Oñate destroyed the Pueblos' economy, meanwhile failing miserably in his wide search for riches. The piteous suffering of the Indians horrified the missionaries, who protested to Oñate vehemently, only to be ignored. Conscientious colonists also deplored the wrongful exploitation, and the Franciscans warned them that complicity in sins against the Pueblos jeopardized Spaniards' own immortal souls. In the fall of 1601, most of the colonists fled back to Mexico, where they denounced Oñate to the viceroy.

Assuming that Oñate's abuses had rendered the missionary effort hopeless, the crown nearly decided to withdraw from New Mexico. It would protect the four hundred baptized Pueblos through subsidized relocation in Mexico. But the Spanish intrusion had already triggered such far-reaching, unintended changes as to rule out disengagement. Suddenly the Spaniards found themselves morally trapped in New Mexico by a surge in 1608 of several thousand Pueblos to baptism. Relocating so many was impracticable: Spain would have to protect and minister to them in their homeland.

Why the startling change? All the abuses that Pueblos suffered from the Spaniards had begun to pale in comparison to the ravages of Apache raiders. In their despair, many Pueblos looked to the Spaniards for help, perhaps pinning their hopes on the missionaries' magic, perhaps only counting on the mounted, armored soldiers and their guns, perhaps both. Indeed, the desire for powerful allies against the Apaches had probably figured in the Pueblos' initial acceptance of the Spanish colony. Whatever the Pueblos' motives, baptism clinched the Spanish obligation to protect them.

Why the Apache onslaught? For a century or so, ever since those countless little groups of Athapaskan-speaking nomads had drifted southward into the Pueblo sphere, they had preyed on the villages there intermittently, particularly at harvest time. But there had also evolved some moderating interdependence of villagers and nomads, based upon mutually advantageous trade: dried meat, hides, and tallow taken by Apache hunters and processed by their women in exchange for the Pueblos' surplus produce and sometimes their textiles and pottery. Visiting Apaches often camped beside the sheltering walls of frontier pueblos, and friendships evolved between some Apache and Pueblo families.

But the Spaniards wrecked those constructive relationships. After three years of Oñate's exactions of corn and blankets, Pueblos had no surplus to trade to Apaches, who had therefore to seize what they needed. Weakened by starvation and by excessive Spanish demands on their labor, Pueblos lay nearly helpless against marauders. Worse, Apaches found irresistibly attractive the metal implements and livestock that Spaniards had brought into the pueblos. Metal was immediately adapted to Apache uses. At first, Apaches perceived livestock only as food and slaughtered horses, cattle, and sheep indiscriminately. But soon they began stealing horses and became superb riders. Spain had unwittingly sparked among Apaches an equestrian revolution that would spread among Indian peoples far into the interior, transforming native economies and upsetting balances of power for centuries to come.

The immediate impact was to lock Pueblos and Spaniards into a system of mutual defense. Understanding now that New Mexico's sparse resources could not support the costs of colonization, mmuch less yield a profit, the crown reconstituted the enterprise as a royal colony with an appointed governor and fifty married soldier-settlers, solely to sustain the missionary program into which the royal treasury would pour millions. Twelve Franciscans would continue teaching and ministering to the Pueblos. If they wished, the friars could peacefully and discreetly seek converts farther afield, but the crown would support no further exploration.

The first royal governor, Pedro de Peralta, took command of the province in 1609, shipping Oñate and his henchmen back to Mexico to be punished for their crimes in New Mexico. Strains on the Pueblos eased as Peralta stabilized the turbulent Spanish colony, which at last built homes and established fields and gardens instead of expropriating Pueblo dwellings and food. With Peralta's founding of Santa Fe as a proper Spanish villa in 1610, the colonists were now able to elect their local government and live under Spanish law rather than at an outlaw's whim.

Peralta also established the Pueblos' right to local self-governance, as enjoyed by other vassals of the king. Not comprehending the Pueblos' traditional leadership structure, Peralta decreed a system on the Spanish model: a governor and other officers to be elected in January of each year by majority vote in each pueblo, with no Spaniards allowed in any pueblo on election day lest they interfere in the process. In practice, the "Spanish" officials of the pueblos evolved into a convenient set of functionaries to manage the pueblo's temporal, external affairs, while the old theocratic system of caciques and their assistants carried on the essential functions of leadership in the ancient tradition.

External jurisdiction over the Indians belonged only to the royal governor, whose prime duty was to enforce their legal rights and protect them against hostile Indians. He could allot Indians in *encomienda*—grant fruits of their labor in compensation for services rendered them—but was required to account to the king for the qualifications and services of the *encomenderos* and to moderate both the amount and the manner of collecting tribute so as to prevent exploitation. Some thirty-five *encomenderos* bore primary responsibility for defending the Pueblos, although Pueblo warriors were expected to fight alongside the Spaniards. Based upon long experience on the Iberian peninsula, it was not an unreasonable system, *if* the crown could enforce its humane intentions in the remote vastness of New Mexico.

With better order in the Spanish community and more systematic defense, conditions among the Pueblos improved for the first time in a dozen years. The Franciscans poured their pent-up energies and the king's materials into the long-deferred missionary effort, which was as much economic as doctrinal in emphasis. For two decades the mission program flourished in many pueblos. Largely cooperating in indoctrination and worship, Pueblos realized tangible benefits: new skills and arts and goods, new crops, and herds of cattle and sheep.

But the new prosperity carried the seeds of destruction. The herds and newly accumulating possessions attracted more Apache raiders than ever. New skills and expanded productivity also made Pueblos more vulnerable to unlawful exploitation by Spaniards—not only by *encomenderos* collecting excessive tribute in goods and services but by a series of corrupt royal governors exploiting unmercifully the Indians they were sworn to protect. Even Franciscans, waxing overzealous to aggrandize their missions, demanded intolerable amounts of Pueblo time and labor. Worse still, the governor's jurisdiction over the Indians conflicted with the prerogatives of the missionaries. Bewildered Pueblos often found themselves caught up in vicious contests between the provincial leaders of church and state, with *encomenderos* sometimes joining in the squabbles.

Such constant discord horrified Pueblos. Believing strife to invite supernatural wrath, they valued above all else harmony within their communities and with the spirits of their universe. In the context of that belief, it was hardly surprising that pestilence had entered the Pueblo world with the contentious Spaniards. Smallpox, measles, assorted fevers—all endemic among Europeans but hitherto unknown in New Mexico—ravaged Pueblos again and again.

As their ordeal worsened, Pueblos turned increasingly to their traditional ceremonies to propitiate the spirits and mend their torn universe. Outraged missionaries, seeing the Pueblos' dances and ritual paraphernalia as witchcraft, set about eradicating them forcibly, often with the help of secular forces.

By 1680, some Pueblos would brook no more abuse, spiritual or economic. A concerted revolt, involving all Pueblos north of Isleta and west to the Hopis, rid the Pueblo world of Spanish presence for a dozen years. But during their respite from the Spaniards, devastating wars broke out among various Pueblo groups, and nomads seized the opportunity to plunder them relentlessly. So grim became the ordeal that some Pueblos judged the Spaniards a lesser evil and were prepared to welcome them back. Still, reconquest and recolonization of New Mexico cost the Spaniards and their Pueblo allies several grueling campaigns in the mid-1690s. By 1700, Spanish rule—and with it, relative order—was largely restored in the Pueblo world.

From the anguish of revolt, the Pueblos salvaged lasting victory on their two key issues: spiritual and economic. Never again would they be subject to the *encomienda*, which had been their principal economic grievance and the worst cause of friction wth Spaniards. Their only obligation would be the military service expected of all vassals of the Spanish crown: Pueblo warriors would campaign alongside Spanish New Mexicans when called upon. In return, they relied upon Spanish authorities to keep peace among pueblos and defend them against external enemies.

The Pueblos also established their right to practice their native religion. Although they had to submit to the forms of Catholicism and let the missionaries return as the price of peace and pardon, the Pueblos had taught the Spaniards the futility of force against profound belief. Much of the official blame for the revolt had fallen on the excesses of the missionaries, and the crown made it clear that it would not tolerate further attacks on Indian rituals. However reluctantly, the Franciscans would have to abide the coexistence of native and Christian practices, as evolved by the Pueblos.

In the Pueblo heartland, the sorely diminished population settled into patterns of existence that would prevail into this century. Preserving old Pueblo values, they observed traditional rituals in the kivas but dutifully attended mass as well. Friars baptized, married, and buried them. But native religious leaders maintained the key relationships with the spirit world and dealt with the heart of community concerns, while the elected "Spanish" officials of each pueblo managed secular and external affairs. Only the Hopis held aloof, deeming Catholicism so inimical to their traditional ways as to rule out any readmission of missionaries to their remote mesas. Their decision cost the Hopis dearly in terms of the trade, economic assistance, and protection from external enemies that they might have enjoyed as vassals of the crown, but they never wavered from their fierce resolve, and the Spaniards sadly acquiesced.

Other Pueblos would make the most of their legal standing as vassals of the king of Spain. Beyond their internal jurisdiction, Pueblos were entitled to the full protection of Spanish law; New Mexican officialdom included an appointed "protector of the Indians," whose duty was to ensure their rights. Secured on their communal lands by decrees of the Spanish crown and no longer forced to pay tribute, Pueblos now could rebuild their economy, making what they wished of new crops, livestock, tools, and skills that they had assimilated from the Spaniards. With horses and mules and two-wheeled carts revolutionizing transportation and Spanish serving as a useful common language throughout the province, trade expanded among New Mexican Pueblos and Spaniards and, intermittently, their roving neighbors as well.

The Pueblo experience warrants emphasis because it was the formative encounter; the lessons that the Pueblos so painfully taught the Spaniards bore fruit throughout the Southwest. *Encomienda* was a dead issue, and the only allowable methods of conversion were persuasion and kind example. No other people would suffer from the Spaniards such indignities as the Pueblos had borne.

The earliest beneficiaries of the Pueblos' impact on the Spaniards were the comparably advanced Caddo peoples, whose agricultural hamlets dotted the humid woodlands eastward from the branches of the upper Trinity to

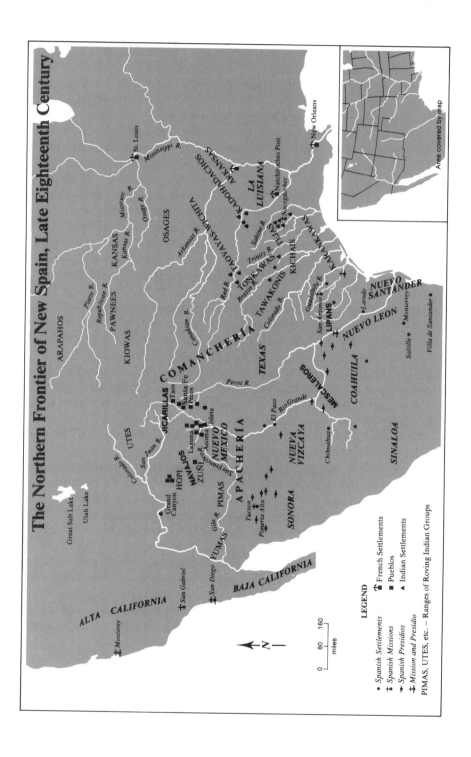

The Northern Frontier of New Spain, Late Eighteenth Century

New Orleans

St. Louis

Mississippi R.

Missouri R.

Osage R.

Kansas R.

Platte R.

Republican R.

Arkansas R.

Canadian R.

Red R.

Brazos R.

Trinity R.

Sabine R.

Pecos R.

Colorado R.

Guadalupe R.

San Antonio R.

Rio Grande

Gila R.

Colorado R.

San Juan R.

Sta. Francisca R.

ARAPAHOS

PAWNEES

KIOWAS

KANSAS

OSAGES

WICHITA

TAOVAYAS-WICHITA

KADOHADACHOS

ARKANSAS

LA LUISIANA

Natchitoches Post

Nacogdoches

TEJAS

KARANKAWAS

KICHAIS

TAWAKONIS

TONKAWAS

COMANCHERIA

TEXAS

LIPANS

NUEVO SANTANDER

Laredo

NUEVO LEON

Monterrey

Saltillo

Villa de Santander

COAHUILA

MESCALEROS

SINALOA

Chihuahua

NUEVA VIZCAYA

El Paso

APACHERIA

Santa Fe

Taos

Pecos

JICARILLAS

Isleta

NUEVO MEXICO

Acoma

Laguna

ZUNI

NAVAJOS

HOPI

Grand Canyon

Pimeria Alta

Tucson

SONORA

PIMAS

YUMAS

UTES

Great Salt Lake

Utah Lake

San Diego

San Gabriel

Monterey

ALTA CALIFORNIA

BAJA CALIFORNIA

Area covered by map

LEGEND

• *Spanish Settlements*
‡ *Spanish Missions*
⚔ *Spanish Presidios*
‡ *Mission and Presidio*
PIMAS, UTES, etc. — *Ranges of Roving Indian Groups*

⚓ French Settlements
■ Pueblos
▲ Indian Settlements

N

miles
0   80   160

the great bend of the Red River. Although famous warriors, the Caddos were essentially peaceful people: architects of handsome, functional grass houses; successful farmers and hunters; accomplished craftsmen and traders; heirs to rich ceremonial traditions and impressive civil order. In the late seventeenth century, the Caddos seemed to Spaniards as promising a mission field as had the Pueblos a century before. Just before the Reconquest of New Mexico in the 1690s, Franciscans won permission to open a new mission frontier among the western Caddos whom they knew as Tejas. So began the easternmost sector of the "Spanish Southwest," the province of Texas.

The Tejas received the few missionaries and supporting soldiery cordially enough in 1690 but angrily ordered them out after three years of mounting displeasure with their impact on village life. Not the least of the strains was the smallpox that ravaged the Caddo populace in the first winter of the Spaniards' residence among them, their first direct experience of the terrible cost to Indians of contact with Europeans, however peaceful or well intentioned.

Two decades passed before Spain resumed the effort on a larger scale, spurred more by rival French activity among eastern Caddo groups than by the Franciscans' ardent desire to win Tejas souls. In 1716 the western Caddos graciously welcomed families of settlers, as well as more missionaries and soldiers than before, and pledged themselves vassals of the Spanish crown, probably to bolster their defenses against aggressive Indian enemies then menacing the Caddo world from the north, east, and west. On that basis of mutual need evolved an important interdependence of Caddos and Spaniards that would also embrace the eastern Caddos after France yielded Louisiana to Spain in the 1760s. But it was an alliance only of comrades-at-arms and trading partners, not of coreligionists. Although the Caddos tolerated the six missions established among them, they largely rejected the Faith, which they found superfluous to their well-ordered lives. Thus the Caddos taught the Spaniards another essential lesson: that religious conversion was not a necessary condition of practical alliance with any nation. That paved the way for the network of Indian relationships necessary for the survival and development of New Spain's northern frontier provinces.

While missions in east Texas withered under Caddo indifference, Indian enthusiasm spawned others to the southwest. A motley array of roving hunters and gatherers, mostly Coahuiltecan speakers who were little organized above the level of family camps, had long begged for missions in their own territory. Why? Perhaps they were attracted to what they saw of Christianity at missions in northern Coahuila. Certainly they were in desperate need of the secure subsistence and protection from enemies that missions and their supporting soldiers offered, because far-riding Apache warriors now jeopardized the very existence of such little groups. In 1718 Franciscans found the headwaters of the San Antonio River the ideal spot to serve those importunate souls while also providing a vital way-station on the long supply route to the missions in east Texas. By mid-century, five missions flourished there, along with the supporting presidio [military fort and garrison] and the civil settlement that made San Antonio the capital of Spanish Texas and its principal hub on interaction with Indians.

The clear successes of those missions—in indoctrination, in acculturation, in material benefits to their neophytes—were overshadowed by the terrible toll of deaths from epidemic diseases that swept each generation of recruits. By the end of the eighteenth century, Indians of the missions communities were so few that some priests suspected that God had never meant those natives to be garnered to the Faith and that the costly, well-intended missionary effort had been tragically misguided. Descendants of the mission Indians, nevertheless, persist around San Antonio to this day, whereas there is little trace of those who took their chances in the open against the Apache onslaught.

The Pimas and Papagos of present Arizona gleaned more encouraging, durable results from the mission program that the Jesuits launched among them in the 1690s. That northern sector of Spanish Sonora was the homeland of perhaps thirty thousand Upper Piman Indians, who varied in life-style from simple hunters and gatherers to irrigation farmers. By the time the Franciscans replaced the Jesuits in 1768, two dozen mission stations served Piman settlements; the Franciscans persevered into the 1840s. Major Piman revolts in 1695 and 1751 attest to the frictions of early decades. But from the outset, hard-hitting Apache raiders made refuge in missions as desirable in the Pimería Alta as in New Mexico and Texas. Here, too, the supposed safety of missions cost countless Indian deaths from the Europeans' endemic diseases. But the spiritual impact of the missions endures to the present in Pima and Papago parishes, where the forms of Roman Catholicism blend with aboriginal beliefs and symbols in ways that the Indians have found right and useful for themselves.

There were important material gains. Among the usual array of crops and livestock introduced by the Jesuits, wheat and cattle particularly flourished in Piman territory, generating unprecedented prosperity. But the new riches drew more Apache raiders than ever, so presidios became necessary to protect the neophytes against predators. Piman warriors served regularly with the Spanish military against the common enemy. Presidios attracted civilian settlers, thus broadening Piman experience of Spaniards other than friars and soldiers. Mineral finds in the region brought rougher Spanish seekers of wealth, and wages lured some Indians, particularly from the roving Upper Piman groups, to work in the mines. Both mining and presidial communities were profitable outlets for Piman agricultural products. Through several decades, Pimas and Papagos participated in a burgeoning market economy that prepared them better than most other Indians to cope with the next wave of invaders. Piman prosperity developed within the framework of Spanish law, with its vital protections of Indian rights to life and property and its provisions for their local self-governance, which helped to preserve and even strengthen their communities.

What of the formidable, far-ranging Apaches, who forced the Spaniards to persevere in New Mexico in order to protect the Pueblos and also drove

Indians of southwestern Texas and northern Sonora to seek refuge in missions? From the 1720s on, the crown's policy was to conciliate and court alliance with Apaches, encouraging peaceful trade and hoping for, though never counting on, their eventual conversion to the Faith. In the early eighteenth century, when newly mounted Comanche and Ute warriors drove Apaches from the front ranges of the Rocky Mountains and neighboring buffalo plains, some Apaches found refuge on the frontiers of Spanish provinces. In northwestern New Mexico, the Jicarilla Apaches swore themselves vassals of the Spanish crown in 1723, settling into mountains near the pueblos of Taos and Pecos. Lipan Apaches, driven south into Texas by Comanches, contracted an alliance with the Spaniards at San Antonio in 1749. While those alliances held to the end of the Spanish era, other Apache groups ensconced themselves in the more southerly ranges of the Rockies, whence their raiders took grievous tolls of lives and property from both Indian and Spanish communities over many decades.

Hence, the roles of Apaches in the Spanish Southwest were contradictory: vengeful foes and rapacious raiders; allies, indispensable scouts, guides, and couriers; denizens, often erratic, of presidial settlements and mission communities; and peaceful traders and sometime poachers. The dilemma was that, however meritorious the peaceful Apaches, Spanish provinces could not thrive at the mercy of marauding Apaches. Late in the eighteenth century, Spanish authorities presented the predators this choice: to settle peacefully in the vicinity of designated presidios near their homelands, with subsidies from the crown to compensate them for giving up their livelihood as raiders, or to be the targets of systematic military campaigns searching them out for destruction on their own turf. The resulting settlements of peaceful Apaches in three frontier provinces were successful enough to suggest that the program might eventually have resolved the Apache dilemma if time had not run out for the Spanish sponsors in 1821 with Mexico's achievement of national independence.

What of the myriad Comanches, the Shoshone-speaking horde whose enmity drove so many Apaches to accommodation with the Spaniards? Descending in little groups from the northern Rockies at the dawn of the eighteenth century, Comanches built the most powerful yet of the new equestrian societies and, with the help of kindred Utes, quickly shattered the eastern Apachería.

New Mexico and Texas first knew Comanches as relentless raiders of horse herds and implacable foes of Apaches. Caught up in that vendetta by Spanish obligations to protect certain Apaches, mid-century New Mexicans and Texans found their provinces threatened with destruction by Comanches. How astonishing, then, seemed the crown's decision in the 1760s to seek alliance with the Comanches to save the northern provinces and its demand that frontier officials attain that objective. But it worked. Within two decades Comanche leaders concluded that a Spanish connection would serve their nation's interests better than continual wars, and they labored heroically to bring their far-flung people to a binding consensus for peace. In the resulting treaties, of eastern Comanches in Texas in 1785 and western Comanches in New Mexico in 1786, they pledged themselves vassals of the king of Spain, friends of his friends, and enemies of his enemies.

The Comanche alliance functioned remarkably well in New Mexico from the outset and evolved toward stability in Texas by 1803. Now channeling their New Mexican trade largely through Pecos rather than Taos, Comanches accelerated their migration southward, surging into the milder grasslands of the upper Brazos and Colorado river basins of Texas. On those lush buffalo ranges, the Comanches evolved a pastoral economy, developing vast herds of horses. San Antonio, as well as Santa Fe, became a hub of Comanche commerce and interaction with other Indian allies of the Spanish crown. Generous reciprocal hospitality in Comanche camps welcomed visitors from both Texas and New Mexico. Hispanic and Pueblo hunters and traders, as well as explorers and soldiers on official business, traveled regularly into the Comanchería in the early decades of the nineteenth century.

However greatly their profitable new alliance delighted Comanches and New Mexican Hispanos and Pueblos, it dismayed the Jicarilla Apaches and the Utes, whose friendship with the Spaniards was nearly as old as their tribal enmities with Comanches.* Now that they were all vassals of the king of Spain, they were obliged to forgo the customary hostilities and rely on Spanish authorities to reconcile any grievances arising between nations. Lapses did occur on all sides, but to a remarkable degree the old enemies strove to maintain the king's peace and to live within the new rule of law.

Navajos also felt repercussions of the Comanche rapprochement with New Mexico. The Spaniards had long courted the Navajos, a people of remarkable genius established on the northwestern periphery of New Mexico. Apparently the Navajos differed little from kindred Apaches when the Athapaska-speaking groups first drifted into the region a century or so before the Spaniards. But the Navajos had wrought the most elaborate of the cultural revolutions sparked by Spain's thrust northward, surpassing even the Comanches' transformation. In addition to materials introduced by the Spaniards, the Navajos had adapted Pueblo skills and ceremonials. Within the century they had become successful farmers and owners of sheep, goats, and horses, and their superb woolen textiles were the most prized in the northern provinces. The Navajos also possessed a worldview of great strength and coherence and stubbornly rejected missionary efforts. Greatly dismayed, the Spaniards could only assume that such intelligent Indians, who had voluntarily progressed so far in the arts and skills of civilization, would in time establish towns in which to live as vassals of God and king.

Through most of the eighteenth century, Navajos maintained relative

---

* The early eighteenth-century alliance of Utes and Comanches on the northern frontier of New Mexico had ended in the 1730s with a violent dispute said to have originated with a quarrel over a horse. The Utes and Comanches ceremonially reconciled their differences in the 1970s, resuming their active friendship.

peace with the Spaniards, the better to enjoy the fruits of their labor, their livestock, and their increasingly important trade with New Mexico. But occasional clashes resulted as Spanish settlers moved into lands claimed by Navajos and Navajos stole New Mexican livestock. There were also mounting, sometimes irresistible, pressures on Navajo warriors from western Apaches demanding help against the Spaniards. But in 1786, Navajos joined in New Mexico's burgeoning network of Indian alliances, making unprecedented commitments as vassals of the Spanish crown, with reciprocal obligations and guarantees very like those in the Comanche treaties. Not the least of their incentives was the knowledge that Comanche warriors would be campaigning for the Spaniards: Navajos had felt enough of Comanche prowess to prefer being on the same side.

The Navajo alliance with the Spaniards proved less stable than that of the Comanches, partly because the fragmentary nature of Navajo society militated against unified, sustained commitments. The principal difficulty, however, was mounting rivalry over mutually desired lands, which sparked intermittent hostilities in the last two decades of the Spanish era. Punitive invasions of Navajo territory by New Mexican forces caused great suffering and lasting bitterness, a sad reversal of the largely positive trend of Navajo-Spanish relations in the eighteenth century.

In the 1790s rumors of the advantages of Spanish connection reached obscure Indian peoples roving the upper Missouri basin. Some groups were feeling threatened, not only by westward-thrusting Sioux but by Anglo-Americans, who menaced Indians of the northern plains from the outset of their nationhood. Desiring counterweight and perhaps refuge, some of those northerly groups collaborated to seek a Spanish connection. Santa Fe assiduously encouraged those surprising overtures. BY 1807 the Kiowas, Kiowa Apaches, and Arapahos were among the allied nations maintaining peace and commerce with New Mexico on treaty terms like those celebrated two decades earlier with the Comanches and Navajos. That initially appalled the Comanches, for whom the new arrivals were old enemies. But their common interest in peaceful access to New Mexico soon led the Comanches and Kiowas to form their own lasting alliance, affirming the southward movement of both nations by making the Arkansas River a new boundary between them.

That alliance is a useful reminder of both the unpredictability and the complexity of the Indian experience in the Spanish Southwest. The quality of interaction between Spaniards and Indians varied enormously according to cultural differences among the Indians and also according to the time. Eighteenth-century Spaniards brought much more sophistication to Indian affairs than had their sixteenth-century counterparts; and Indian perceptions of the problems and the potentialities of the Spanish presence also changed over the decades. Greatly compounding the complexities were the manifold interactions among Indian groups that Spanish activity fortuitously triggered. The resulting web of historical accident involved so many Indian peoples of such wide diversity that this brief analysis has touched only upon pivotal examples.

Far from pivotal—indeed, so peripheral in time and space as to be nearly disjoint from the rest—was the California dimension of Indian experience in the Spanish Southwest. Spanish occupation of Alta California was a late, strategic initiative of the crown, designed to check trespassers from rival European powers. The authorities provided for a missionary effort as an obligatory component of any Spanish colonization, but in Alta California missions were not the initiating, predominant force that they had been in the older provinces.

It is impossible to know the extent of the native peoples' experience of Spaniards in California before establishment of the first presidio and mission at San Diego in 1769. From the 1530s onward, coastal Indians had fleeting encounters with seaborne Spaniards and occasionally other Europeans—official explorers, private adventurers, victims of accidents at sea. Some trade, plundering, and hostilities occurred, but there is no record of any lasting impact. In 1697, far to the south, the Jesuits established the first of seventeen missions that their order created among the Indians of Baja California before the crown expelled all Jesuits from the New World in 1767. The Franciscan successors had barely taken charge in Baja when the crown invited them to participate in its purposeful thrust into Alta California, beginning with Mission San Diego in 1769.

The California missions were on the whole successful. Extraordinarily vigorous, experienced Franciscan leadership made the most of California's rich agricultural potential, so that, after some early starving times, those missions produced an abundance of food. That was a crucial attraction, particularly to Indians whose traditional subsistence was comparatively sparse and sometimes precarious. But Indian relationships with Spaniards varied over the years from sustained congeniality at some missions to severe friction at others. Ultimately, twenty-one missions stretched from San Diego to Sonoma, exerting significant acculturative impact upon nearby Indian peoples but having little or no effect on the many peoples living in the interior valleys and mountains.

In California, as elsewhere, the mission program was as much economic and political as doctrinal. Indians participating in the mission program reaped obvious material benefits: new crops, livestock, and agricultural skills, arts, and crafts. Mission communities provided experience with self-governance on the Spanish pattern, and some intertribal feuds faded under Spanish pressures to keep the peace. Some Indians participated in the market economy developing around the presidial communities and the three secular pueblos of San Diego, Los Angeles, and San Jose. But inevitably the interaction with Europeans exacted a grim toll from Indian populations, who had no immunity against such alien diseases as smallpox and measles. Syphilis also is cited as a major killer of California Indians, as well as a sterilizing factor that deterred recovery of dwindling populations.

The comparatively late and remote California phase of the encounter of Indians and Spaniards differed significantly from the earlier, more formative encounters in New Mexico, Texas, and Sonora. But in each of those arenas, the confrontations were initially fraught with pain for the Indians: always from epidemic disease, often from exacerbation of conflict among Indian nations, sometimes from direct conflict with Spaniards. The longer trend, over two and a half centuries, was toward wider peace among all peoples than the region had known before, under principles of law dating back to the Roman empire. The crucial accommodations involved Indian, as well as Spanish, vision and enterprise.

Virgin Soil Epidemics

ALFRED W. CROSBY

During the last few decades historians have demonstrated increasing concern with the influence of disease in history, particularly the history of the New World. For example, the lastest generation of Americanists chiefly blames diseases imported from the Old World for the disparity between the number of American aborigines in 1492—new estimates of which soar as high as one hundred million or approximately one-sixth of the human race at that time—and the few million pure Indians and Eskimos alive at the end of the nineteenth century. There is no doubt that chronic disease was an important factor in the precipitous decline, and it is highly probable that the greatest killer was epidemic disease, especially as manifested in virgin soil epidemics.

Virgin soil epidemics are those in which the populations at risk have had no previous contact with the diseases that strike them and are therefore immunologically almost defenseless. The importance of virgin soil epidemics in American history is strongly indicated by evidence that a number of dangerous maladies—smallpox, measles, malaria, yellow fever, and undoubtedly several more—were unknown in the pre-Columbian New World. In theory, the initial appearance of these diseases is as certain to have set off deadly epidemics as dropping lighted matches into tinder is certain to cause fires.

The thesis that epidemics have been chiefly responsible for the awesome diminution in the number of native Americans is based on more than theory. The early chronicles of America are full of reports of horrendous epidemics and steep population declines, confirmed in many cases by recent quantitative analyses of Spanish tribute records and other sources. The evidence provided by the documents of British and French America is not as definitely supportive of the thesis because the conquerors of those areas did not establish permanent settlements and begin to keep continuous records until the seventeenth century, by which time at least some of the worst epidemics of imported diseases had probably already taken place. Furthermore, the British tended to drive the Indians away, rather than ensnaring them as slaves and peons, as the Spaniards did, with the result that many of the most important events

Alfred W. Crosby, "Virgin Soil Epidemics as a Factor in the Aboriginal Depopulation in America," *William and Mary Quarterly,* 3 ser. 33 (April 1976), 289–299.

of aboriginal history in British America occurred beyond the range of direct observation by literate witnesses.

Even so, the surviving records for North America do contain references—brief, vague, but plentiful—to deadly epidemics among the Indians, of which we shall cite a few of the allegedly worst. In 1616–1619 an epidemic, possibly of bubonic or pneumonic plague, swept coastal New England from Cape Cod to Maine, killing as many as nine out of every ten it touched. During the 1630s and into the next decade, smallpox, the most fatal of all the recurrent Indian killers, whipsawed back and forth through the St. Lawrence–Great Lakes region, eliminating half the people of the Huron and Iroquois confederations. In 1738 smallpox destroyed half the Cherokees, and in 1759 nearly half the Catawbas. During the American Revolution it attacked the Piegan tribe and killed half its members. It ravaged the plains tribes shortly before they were taken under United States jurisdiction by the Louisiana Purchase, killing two-thirds of the Omahas and perhaps half the population between the Missouri River and New Mexico. In the 1820s fever devastated the people of the Columbia River area, erasing perhaps four-fifths of them. In 1837 smallpox returned to the plains and destroyed about half of the aborigines there.

Unfortunately, the documentation of these epidemics, as of the many others of the period, is slight, usually hearsay, sometimes dated years after the events described, and often colored by emotion. Skepticism is eminently justified and is unlikely to be dispelled by the discovery of great quantities of first-hand reports on epidemics among the North American Indians. We must depend on analysis of what little we now know, and we must supplement that little by examination of recent epidemics among native Americans.

Let us begin by asking why the American aborigines offered so little resistance to imported epidemic diseases. Their susceptibility has long been attributed to special weakness on their part, an explanation that dates from the period of colonization, received the stamp of authority from such natural historians as the Comte de Buffon, and today acquires the color of authenticity from the science of genetics. In its latest version, the hypothesis of genetic weakness holds that during the pre-Columbian millennia the New World Indians had no occasion to build up immunities to such diseases as smallpox and measles. Those aborigines who were especially lacking in defenses against these maladies were not winnowed out before they passed on their vulnerabilities to their offspring. Although there is no way to test this hypothesis for pre-Columbian times, medical data on living American aborigines do not sustain it, and the scientific community inclines toward the view that native Americans have no special susceptibility to Old World diseases that cannot be attributed to environmental influences, and probably never did have.

The genetic weakness hypothesis may have some validity, but it is unproven and probably unprovable, and is therefore a weak reed to lean upon. What is more, we have no need of it. The death rate among white United States soldiers in the Civil War who contacted smallpox, a disease to which their ancestors had been exposed for many generations, was 38.5

percent, probably about the percentage of Aztecs who died of that disease in 1520. The difference between the Union troops and the Aztec population is, of course, that most of the former had been vaccinated or exposed to the disease as children, while the latter was a completely virgin soil population.

It should also be asked why the decline in numbers of the American aborigines went on as long as it did, 400 years or so, in contrast to the decline caused by Europe's most famous virgin soil epidemic, the Black Death, which lasted no more than 100 to 200 years. The answer is that the Indians and Eskimos did not experience the onslaught of Old World diseases all at the same time and that other factors were also responsible for depressing their population levels. As far as we can say now, Old World diseases were the chief determinants in the demographic histories of particular tribes for 100 to 150 years after each tribe's first full exposure to them. In addition, the newcomers, whose dire influence on native Americans must not be underestimated just because it has been overestimated, reduced the aboriginal populations by warfare, murder, dispossession, and interbreeding. Thereafter the Indians began a slow, at first nearly imperceptible, recovery. The greatest exceptions were the peoples of the tropical lowlands and islands who, under the extra heavy burden of insect-borne fevers, mostly of African provenance, held the downward course to oblivion.

The Indians of Mexico's central highlands perfectly fit this pattern of sharp decline for four to six generations followed by gradual recovery. Appalling depopulation began with the nearly simultaneous arrival of Cortés and smallpox; the nadir occurred sometime in the seventeenth century; and then Indian numbers slowly rose. The pattern of European population history was approximately the same in the two centuries following the Black Death. The recovery in numbers of the Indians of the United States in the twentieth century is probably part of a similar phenomenon.

But why did Europeans lose one-third or so to the Black Death, imported from Asia, while the American aborigines lost perhaps as much as 90 percent to the diseases imported from the Old World? The answers are probably related to the factors that have caused many fatalities in recent virgin soil epidemics among native Americans, not of such deadly diseases as smallpox and plague, which are tightly controlled in our era, but of such relatively mild maladies as measles and influenza. In 1952 the Indians and Eskimos of Ungava Bay, in Northern Quebec, had an epidemic of measles: 99 percent became sick and about 7 percent died, even though some had the benefit of modern medicine. In 1954 an epidemic of measles broke out among the aborigines of Brazil's remote Xingu National Park: the death rate was 9.6 percent for those of the afflicted who had modern medical treatment and 26.8 percent for those who did not. In 1968 when the Yanomamas of the Brazilian-Venezuelan borderlands were struck by measles, 8 or 9 percent died despite the availability of some modern medicines and treatment. The Kreen-Akorores of the Amazon Basin, recently contacted for the first time by outsiders, lost at least 15 percent of their people in a single brush with common influenza.

The reasons for the massive losses to epidemics in the last four hundred years and the considerable losses to the epidemics just cited can be grouped conveniently in two categories, the first relating to the nature of the disease or diseases, and the second having to do with how individuals and societies react to the threat of epidemic death.

First, we must recognize that the reputations of measles and influenza as mild diseases are not entirely justified. Contemporary native Americans who contract them are not cured by "miracle drugs," even when modern medical treatment is available, because there are no such drugs. Modern physicians do not *cure* measles, influenza, and such other viral maladies as smallpox, chicken pox, and mumps, but try, usually successfully, to keep off other infections until the normal functioning of undistracted immune systems kills off the invading viruses. If doctors fail in this task or are not available, the death rate will be "abnormally high." Measles killed more than 6 percent of all the white Union soldiers and almost 11 percent of all the black Union soldiers it infected during the Civil War, even though the waves of this disease that swept the army were not virgin soil epidemics.

Virgin soil epidemics are different from others in the age incidence of those they kill, as well as in the quantity of their victims. Evidence from around the world suggests that such epidemics of a number of diseases with reputations as Indian killers—smallpox, measles, influenza, tuberculosis, and others—carry off disproportionately large percentages of people aged about fifteen to forty—men and women of the prime years of life who are largely responsible for the vital functions of food procurement, defense, and procreation. Unfortunately little evidence exists to support or deny the hypothesis that native American virgin soil epidemics have been especially lethal to young adults. There is no doubt, however, that they have been extremely deadly for the very young. Infants are normally protected against infectious diseases common in the area of their births by antibodies passed on to them before birth by their immunologically experienced mothers, antibodies which remain strong enough to fend off disease during the first precarious months of life. This first line of defense does not exist in virgin soil epidemics. The threat to young children is more than just bacteriological: they are often neglected by ailing adults during such epidemics and often die when their ailing mother's milk fails. Infants in traditional aboriginal American societies are commonly two years of age or even older before weaning, so the failure of mothers' milk can boost the death rate during epidemics to a greater extent than modern urbanites would estimate on the basis of their own child-care practices.

Mortality rates rise sharply when several virgin soil epidemics strike simultaneously. When the advance of the Alaska Highway in 1943 exposed the Indians of Teslin Lake to fuller contact with the outside world than they had ever had before, they underwent in one year waves of measles, German measles, dysentery, catarrhal jaundice, whooping cough, mumps, tonsillitis, and miningococcic meningitis. This pulverizing experience must have been common among aborigines in the early post-Columbian generations, although the chroniclers, we may guess, often put the blame on only the most spectacular of the diseases, usually smallpox. A report from Española

Epidemics among the Dakota Indians, 1780–1851

1780–1781	Smallpox.
1801–1802	Smallpox ("all sick winter").
1810	Smallpox.
1813–1814	Whooping cough.
1818–1819	Measles ("little smallpox winter").
1837	Smallpox.
1845–1846	Disease or diseases not identified ("many sick winter").
1849–1850	Cholera ("many people had the cramps winter").
1850–1851	Smallpox ("all the time sick with the big smallpox winter").

in 1520 attributed the depopulation there to smallpox, measles, respiratory infection, and other diseases unnamed. Simultaneous epidemics of diseases, including smallpox and at least one other, possibly influenza, occurred in Meso-America in the early 1520s. The action of other diseases than the one most apparently in epidemic stage will often cause dangerous complications, even if they have been long in common circulation among the victims. In the Ungava Bay and Yanomama epidemics the final executioner was usually bronchopneumonia, which advanced when measles leveled the defenses of aborigines weakened by diseases already present—malaria and pneumonia among the South Americans, and tuberculosis and influenza among the North Americans.

Successive epidemics may take longer to dismantle societies than simultaneous attacks by several diseases, but they can be as thorough. The documentation of American Indians' experience of successive epidemics is slim and not expressed as statistics, but the records are nonetheless suggestive. The Dakotas kept annual chronicles on leather or cloth showing by a single picture the most important event of each year. These records indicate that all or part of this people suffered significantly in the epidemics listed above, at least one of which, cholera, and possibly several others were virgin soil. It should be noted that the considerable lapses of time between the smallpox epidemics meant that whole new generations of susceptibles were subject to infection upon the return of the disease and that the repeated ordeals must have had much of the deadliness of virgin soil epidemics.

Virgin soil epidemics tend to be especially deadly because no one is immune in the afflicted population and so nearly everyone gets sick at once. During a period of only a few days in the 1960s every member of the Tchikao tribe of Xingu Park fell ill with influenza, and only the presence of outside medical personnel prevented a general disaster. Witnesses to the Ungava Bay and Yanomama epidemics noted the murderous effect of nearly universal illness, however brief in duration. The scientists with the Yanomamas found that when both parents and children became sick, "there was a drastic breakdown of both the will and the means for necessary nursing." The observers saw several families in which grandparents, parents, and their children were simultaneously ill.

The fire goes out and the cold creeps in; the sick, whom a bit of food and a cup of water might save, die of hunger and the dehydration of fever; the seed remains above the ground as the best season for planting passes, or there is no one well enough to harvest the crop before the frost. In the 1630s smallpox swept through New England, and William Bradford wrote of a group of Indians who lived near a Plymouth colony trading post that "they fell down so generally of this disease as they were in the end not able to help one another, no not to make a fire nor to fetch a little water to drink, nor any to bury the dead. But would strive as long as they could, and when they could procure no other means to make fire, they would burn the wooden trays and dishes they ate their meat in, and their very bows and arrows. And some would crawl out on all fours to get a little water, and sometimes die by the way and not to be able to get in again."

The second category of factors—those which pertain to the ways native Americans reacted to epidemic diseases—often had as decisive an influence on the death rate as did the virulency of the disease. American aborigines were subjected to an immense barrage of disease, and their customs and religions provided little to help them through the ordeal. Traditional treatments, though perhaps effective against pre-Columbian diseases, were rarely so against acute infections from abroad, and they were often dangerous, as in the swift transfer of a patient from broiling sweathouse to frigid lake. Thus, to take a modern example, when smallpox broke out among the Moqui Indians in Arizona in 1898, 632 fell ill but only 412 accepted treatment from a physician trained in modern medical practice. Although he had no medicines to cure smallpox or even to prevent secondary bacterial infections, only 24 of his patients died. By contrast, 163 of the 220 who refused his help and, presumably, put their faith in traditional Indian therapy, died.

Native Americans had no conception of contagion and did not practice quarantine of the sick in pre-Columbian times, nor did they accept the new theory or practice until taught do so by successive disasters. The Relation of 1640 of the Jesuit missionaries in New France contains the complaint that during epidemics of the most contagious and deadly maladies the Hurons continued to live among the sick "in the same indifference, and community of all things, as if they were in perfect health." The result, of course, was that nearly everyone contracted the infections, "the evil spread from house to house, from village to village, and finally became scattered throughout the country."

Such ignorance of the danger of infection can be fatal, but so can knowledge when it creates terror, leading to fatalism or to frenzied, destructive behavior. A large proportion of those who fall acutely ill in an epidemic will die, even if the disease is a usually mild one, like influenza or whooping cough, unless they are provided with drink, food, shelter, and competent nursing. These will be provided if their kin and friends fulfill the obligations of kinship and friendship, but will they do so? Will the sense of these obligations be stronger thar fear, which can kill by paralyzing all action to help the sick or by galvanizing the healthy into flight?

If we may rely on negative evidence, we may say that aboriginal kin and tribal loyalties remained stronger than the fear of disease for a remarkably long time after the coming of the micro-organisms from the Old World. We will never be able to pinpoint chronologically any change as subtle as the failure of these ties, but whenever it happened for a given group in a given epidemic the death rate almost certainly rose. In most epidemics, contagious disease operating in crowded wigwams and long houses would spread so fast before terror took hold that panicky flight would serve more to spread the infection than to rob it of fresh victims, and any decline in the number of new cases, and consequently of deaths that might result from flight, would at the very least be cancelled by the rise in the number of sick who died of neglect. Observers of the Ungava Bay epidemic reported that a fatalistic attitude toward the disease caused the loss of several entire families, whose members would not help each other or themselves. Scientists with the Yanomamas during their battle with measles recorded that fatalism killed some and panic killed more: the healthy abandoned the sick and fled to other villages, carrying the disease with them.

When a killing epidemic strikes a society that accepts violence as a way of reacting to crises and believes in life after death—characteristics of many Christian and many Indian societies—the results can be truly hideous. Many fourteenth-century Europeans reacted to the Black Death by joining the Flagellants or by killing Jews. Some Indians similarly turned on the whites whom they blamed for the epidemics, but most were obliged by their circumstances to direct their fear and rage against themselves. During the epidemic of 1738 many Cherokees killed themselves in horror of permanent disfigurement, according to their contemporary, James Adair. Members of the Lewis and Clark expedition were told that in the 1802 smallpox epidemic the Omahas "carried their franzey to verry extrodinary length, not only burning their Village, but they put their *wives* and children to *Death* with a view of their all going to some better Countrey." In 1837 smallpox killed so many of the Blackfeet and so terrified those left alive after the first days of the epidemic that many committed suicide when they saw the initial signs of the disease in themselves. It is estimated that about 6,000, two-thirds of all the Blackfeet, died during the epidemic.

The story of that same epidemic among the Mandans, as George Catlin received it, cannot be exceeded in its horror:

> It seems that the Mandans were surrounded by several war-parties of their most powerful enemies the Sioux, at that unlucky time, and they could not therefore disperse upon the plains, by which many of them could have been saved; and they were necessarily inclosed within the piquets of their village, where the disease in a few days became so very malignant that death ensued in a few hours after its attacks; and so slight were their hopes when they were attacked, that nearly half of them destroyed themselves with their knives, with their guns, and by dashing their brains out by leaping head-foremost from a thirty foot ledge of rocks in front of their village. The first symptoms of the disease was a rapid swelling of the body, and so very virulent had it become, that very many died in two or three hours after their attack, and in many cases without the appearance of disease upon their skin. Utter dismay seemed to possess all classes and ages and

they gave themselves up in despair, as entirely lost. There was but one continual crying and howling and praying to the Great Spirit for his protection during the nights and days; and there being but few living, and those in too appalling despair, nobody thought of burying the dead, whose bodies, whole families together, were left in horrid and loathsome piles in their own wigwams, with a few buffalo robes, etc. thrown over them, there to decay, and be devoured by their own dogs.

During that epidemic the number of Mandans shrank from about 1,600 to between 125 and 145.

Whether the Europeans and Africans came to the native Americans in war or peace, they always brought death with them, and the final comment may be left to the Superior of the Jesuit Missions to the Indians of New France, who wrote in confusion and dejection in the 1640s, that "since the Faith has come to dwell among these people, all things that make men die have been found in these countries."

Colonial America Without the Indians

JAMES AXTELL

It is taking us painfully long to realize that throughout most of American history the Indians were "one of the principal *determinants* of historical events." A growing number of scholars understand that fact, but the great majority of us still regard the native Americans—if we regard them at all— as exotic or pathetic footnotes to the main course of American history.

This is patently clear from American history textbooks. As Virgil Vogel, Alvin Josephy, and most recently Frederick Hoxie have shown in embarrassing detail, "Indians in textbooks either do nothing or they resist." In their colonial and nineteenth-century manifestations, they are either "obstacles to white settlement" or "victims of oppression." "As victims or obstacles, Indians have no textbook existence apart from their resistance." In short, the texts reflect our "deep-seated tendency to see whites and Indians as possessing two distinct species of historical experience" rather than a mutual history of continuous interaction and influence.

Attempts to redress the balance have suffered from serious flaws. Some observers have exaggerated and oversimplified the Indian impact. We certainly ought to avoid the fatuity of the argument that "what is distinctive about America is Indian, through and through" or that Americans are simply Europeans with "Indian souls." Historians have been more drawn to other, less sweeping, approaches. Robert Berkhofer described four well-meaning but unproductive remedial approaches to "minority " history, especially the history of American Indians. They are the "great man" or "heroes" approach (the "devious side of treaty-making"), the "who-is-more-civilized"

Axtell, James, "Colonial America without the Indians: Counterfactual Reflections," *Journal of American History,* 73 (March 1987), 981–996. Copyright Organization of American Historians, 1987.

approach ("barbarities committed by whites against Indians" contrasted with the "civilized" contributions of Indians), the "crushed personality" and "cultural theft" approach ("change only destroys Indian cultures, never adds to them"), and—by far the most important—the "contributions" approach ("long lists of the contributions Native Americans made to the general American way of life"). The first two approaches offer variations on the theme of Indian heroism and resistance. The third presents Indians as victims. None of the three gives much help in analyzing processes in which both Indians and whites played varying and evolving roles. At best they alert us to the moral dimensions of Indian-white history.

The contributions approach, although flawed, is useful. We inevitably employ it when we seek to define the Indian role in American history, rather than the white role in Indian history. Since most scholars who refer to Indian history are primarily interested in the evolution of the dominant Anglo-American "core culture" and political nationhood they will write in terms of Indian contributions. It is therefore essential to understand the pitfalls in the approach and to devise ways of avoiding them.

A relative disregard for chronology weakens the contributions approach. By focusing on the modern legacy of Indian culture, it usually ignores the specific timing of the various white adaptations and borrowings. Generic "Indian" contributions seem to have been made any time after 1492, it hardly matters when. Such cavalier chronology ought to offend historians not only because it is imprecise but also because it prevents us from determining causation with any accuracy. If we do not know *which* Indian group lent the word, trait, or object and *when,* we will be unable to measure the impact of the adaptive changes in Anglo-American culture at the time they occurred and as they reverberated.

An even more serious flaw is an almost exclusive focus on native material culture (and names of native or American objects and places) that neglects how those items were used, perceived, and adapted by their white borrowers. That focus and the neglect of chronology restrict discussion to a narrow range of additions to contemporary American"life" (i.e., material culture) rather than opening it up to the cultural and social fullness of American *history*. What the approach sadly ignores are the changes wrought in Anglo-American culture, not by borrowing and adapting native cultural traits, words, and objects, but by reacting negatively and perhaps unconsciously to the native presence, threat, and challenge. Without consideration of these deeply formative *reactive* changes, we can have no true measure of the Indians' impact on American history.

In seventeenth- and eighteenth-century Anglo-America, the adaptive changes whites made in response to their contacts with Indians significantly shaped agriculture, transport, and economic life. The more elusive reactive changes significantly shaped the identity of a new people and the nation they founded.

One striking way to register the sheer *indispensability* of the Indians for understanding America's past is to imagine what early American history might have looked like in the utter *absence* of Indians in the New World. The emphasis should be on historical control, not the free flight of fancy. If we posited an Indian-less New World in 1492 and then tried to reconstruct the course of later history, we would end up in a speculative quagmire because each dependent variable could develop in many alternative ways, depending on the others. By the time we reached 1783 we might have a familiar historical product or, more likely, a virtually unrecognizable one. Whatever the outcome, its artificiality would make it heuristically useless. But by following the historical course of events in America and at selected points imaginatively removing the Indians from the picture, we reduce the artificiality of the exercise and the opportunity for conjectural mayhem. Such a controlled use of the counterfactual can invigorate the search for historical causation.

The following series of counterfactual reflections is offered as a heuristic exercise. . . . "Had the Europeans colonists found an utterly unpopulated continent," we ask, "would colonial American life have differed in any major respect from its actual pattern?"

To begin at the beginning, in the period of European discovery and exploration, we can say with confidence that if Christopher Columbus had not discovered the people whom he called *los Indios* (and they him), the history of Spanish America would have been extremely short and uneventful. Since Columbus was looking for the Far East, not America or its native inhabitants, it would not have surprised him to find no Indians in the Caribbean—the new continent was surprise enough. But he would have been disappointed, not only because the islands of the Orient were known to be inhabited but also because there would have been little reason to explore and settle an unpopulated New World instead of pursuing his larger goal. He would have regarded America as simply a huge impediment to his plan to mount an old-fashioned crusade to liberate Jerusalem with profits derived from his shortcut to Cathay.

If the Caribbean and Central and South America had been unpopulated, the placer mines of the islands and the deep mines of gold and silver on the mainland probably would not have been discovered; they certainly would not have been quickly exploited without Indian knowledge and labor. It is inconceivable that the Spanish would have stumbled on the silver deposits of Potosí or Zacatecas if the Incas and Aztecs had not set Spanish mouths to watering with their sumptuous gold jewelry and ornaments. Indeed, without the enormous wealth to be commandeered from the natives, it is likely that the Spanish would not have colonized New Spain at all except to establish a few supply bases from which to continue the search for the Southwest Passage.

It is equally possible that without the immediate booty of Indian gold and silver, the Spanish would have dismissed Columbus after one voyage as a crack-brained Italian and redirected their economic energies eastward in the wake of the Portuguese, toward the certifiable wealth of Africa, India, and the East Indies. Eventually, sugar cane might have induced the

Iberians to colonize their American discoveries, as it induced them to colonize the Cape Verde, Madeira, and Canary islands, but they would have had to import black laborers. Without Indian labor and discovery, however, saltwater pearls and the bright red dye made from the cochineal beetle—the second largest export of the Spanish American empire in the colonial period—would not have contributed to Spain's bulging balance sheets, and to the impact of that wealth on the political and economic history of Europe in the sixteenth and early seventeenth centuries.

Perhaps most important, without the millions of native Americans who inhabited New Spain, there would have been no Spanish conquest—no "Black Legend," no Cortés or Montezuma, no brown-robed friars baptizing thousands daily or ferreting out "idolatry" with whip and fagot, no legalized plunder under the encomienda system, no cruelty to those who extracted the mines' treasures and rebuilt Spanish cities on the rubble of their own, no mastiffs mangling runaways. And without the fabulous lure of Aztec gold and Inca silver carried to Seville in the annual bullion fleets, it is difficult to imagine Spain's European rivals racing to establish American colonies of their own as early as they did.

Take the French, for example. As they did early in the sixteenth century, the cod teeming on the Grand Banks off Newfoundland would have drawn and supported a small seasonal population of fishermen. But without the Indians, the French would have colonized no farther. Giovanni da Verrazzano's 1524 reconnaissance of the Atlantic seaboard would have been an even bigger bust than it was, and Jacques Cartier would probably have made two voyages instead of three, the second only to explore the St. Lawrence River far enough to learn that China did not lie at the western end of Montreal Island. He would have reported to Francis I that "the land God gave to Cain" had no redeeming features, such as the greasy furs of Indian fishermen and the promise of gold and diamonds in the fabled Kingdom of the Saguenay, of which the Indians spoke with such apparent conviction.

If by chance Samuel de Champlain had renewed the French search for the Northwest Passage in the seventeenth century, he would have lost his backers quickly without the lure of an established fur trade with the natives of Acadia and Canada, who hunted, processed, and transported the pelts in native canoes or on native showshoes and toboggans. And without the "pagan" souls of the Indians as a goad and challenge, the French religious orders, male and female, would not have cast their lot with Champlain and the trading companies that governed and settled New France before 1663. In short, without the Indian fur trade, no seigneuries would have been granted along the St. Lawrence, no *habitants, engagés* (indentured servants) or marriageable "King's girls" shipped out to Canada. Quebec and Montreal would not have been founded even as crude *comptoirs,* and no Jesuit missionaries would have craved martyrdom at an Iroquois stake. No "French and Indian" wars would mar our textbooks with their ethnocentric denomination. North America would have belonged solely to settlements of English farmers, for without the Indians and their fur trade, the Swedish and the Dutch would have imitated the French by staying home or turning to the Far East for economic inspiration.

Without the lure of American gold and the Elizabethan contest with Spain that it stimulated, the English, too, would probably have financed fewer ocean searches for the Northwest Passage. If no one thought that Indian chamber pots were made of gold, far fewer gentle-born investors and lowborn sailors would have risked their lives and fortunes on the coasts of America. Unless the Spanish had reaped fabulous riches from the natives and then subjected them to cruel and unnatural bondages, Sir Walter Raleigh would not have sponsored his voyages of liberation to Guiana and Virginia. If the Spanish bullion fleets had not sailed regularly through the Straits of Florida, English privateers would not have preyed on the West Indies nor captured the booty they used to launch permanent colonies in Ireland and North America. Arthur Barlowe's 1584 voyage to North Carolina would probably not have been followed up soon, if he had not discovered friendly natives able to secure a fledgling colony from Spanish incursions.

Sooner or later, the English would have established colonies in America as a safety valve for the felt pressures of population growth and economic reorganization and as a sanctuary for religious dissenters. Once English settlement was under way, the absence of native villages, tribes, and war parties would have drastically altered the chronology of American history. In general, events would have been accelerated because the Indian presence acted as a major check on colonial development. Without a native barrier (which in the colonial period was much more daunting than the Appalachians), the most significant drag on colonial enterprise would have been the lack of Indian labor in a few minor industries, such as the domestic economy of southern New England (supplied by Indians captured in the Pequot and King Philips wars) and the whale fisheries of Cape Cod, Long Island, and Nantucket. Indians were not crucial to wheat farming, lumbering, or rice and tobacco culture and would not have been missed by the English entrepreneurs engaged in them.

Without Indians to contest the land, English colonists would have encountered opposition to their choice of prime locations for settlement only from English competitors. They would not have had to challenge Indian farmers for the fertile river valleys and coastal plains the natives had cultivated for centuries. Without potential Indian or European enemies, sites could be located for economic rather than military considerations, thus removing Jamestown, Plymouth, and St. Mary's City from the litany of American place-names. Boston, New York, Philadelphia, and Charleston would probably be where they are, either because Indian opposition did not much affect their founding or because they were situated for optimal access to inland markets and Atlantic shipping lanes.

In an empty land, English leaders would also have had fewer strategic and ideological reasons for communal settlement of the classic New England type. Without the military and moral threat of Indian war parties, on the one hand, and the puzzling seduction of native life, on the other, English colonists would have had to be persuaded by other arguments to cast their lots together. One predictable result is that New England "Puritans" would have become unbridled "Yankees" even faster than they did. Other colonies would have spread quickly across the American map. By 1776, Anglo-American farmers in large numbers would have spilled over the Appalachians, headed toward their "Manifest Destiny" in the West. Without Indians, Frenchmen, or Spaniards in the Mississippi Valley and beyond to stop them, only the technology of transportation, the supply of investment capital, and the organization of markets en route would have regulated the speed of their advance.

Another consequence of an Indian-less America would be that we could not speak with any accuracy of "the American frontier" because there would be no people on the other side; only where two peoples and cultures intersect do we have a bona fide frontier. The movement of one people into uninhabited land is merely exploration or settlement; it does not constitute a frontier situation. In fact, without viable Indian societies, colonial America would have more nearly resembled Frederick Jackson Turner's famous frontier in which Indians are treated more as geographical features than as sociological teachers. In Turner's scenario, the European dandy fresh from his railroad car is "Americanized" less by contact with palpably attractive human societies than by the "wilderness" or Nature itself. Moreover, the distinctively American character traits that Turner attributed to life on the edge of westering "civilization" would have been exaggerated by the existence of truly limitless cheap land and much less control from the Old World and the Eastern Establishment.

Not only would Turner's mythopoeic frontier really have existed in a non-Indian America, but three other common misunderstandings of colonial history would have been realities. First, America would indeed have been a virgin land, a barren wilderness, not home to perhaps four million native people north of Mexico. If those people had not existed, we would not have to explain their catastrophic decline, by as much as 90 percent, through warfare, injustice, forced migrations, and epidemics of imported diseases— the "widowing" of the once-virgin land, as Francis Jennings has so aptly called it.

Second, colonial history would be confined roughly to the eastern and midwestern parts of the future United States (which themselves would be different). Without Indians, we could ignore French Canada and Louisiana, the Spanish Southwest, the Russian Northwest (whose existence depended on the Indian-staffed seal trade), and the borderless histories of Indian-white contact that determined so much of the shape and texture of colonial life.

And third, we would not have to step up from the largely black-and-white pageant of American history we are offered in our textbooks and courses to a richer polychromatic treatment, if the Indians had no role in the past. We would not even have to pay lip service to the roll call of exclusively male Indian leaders who have been squeezed into the corners of our histories by Indian militance during the last twenty years. Still less would we have to try to integrate into our texts an understanding of the various native peoples who were here first, remained against staggering odds, and are still here to mold our collective past and future.

To get a sharper perspective on an Indian-free scenario of colonial history, we should increase our focal magnification and analyze briefly four distinguishable yet obviously related aspects of colonial life—economics, religion, politics, and acculturation. The economy of Anglo-America without the Indians would have resembled in general outline the historical economy, with several significant exceptions. Farming would certainly have been the mainstay of colonial life, whether for family subsistence or for capitalist marketing and accumulation. But the initial task of establishing farms would have required far more grubbing and clearing without the meadows and park-like woods produced by seasonal Indian burning and especially without the cleared expanses of Indian corn fields and village sites. Many colonists found that they could acquire cleared Indian lands with a few fathoms of trading cloth, some unfenced cows, or a well-aimed barrel of buckshot.

There would have been no maize or Indian corn, the staple crop grown throughout the colonial period to feed people and sometimes to fatten livestock for export. If Indians had not adapted wild Mexican corn to the colder, moister climates of North America and developed the agricultural techniques of hilling, fertilizing by annual burning, and co-planting with nitrogen-fixing beans to reduce soil depletion, the colonists would have lacked a secure livelihood, particularly in the early years before traditional European cereal crops had been adapted to the American climate and soils. Even if traditional crops could have been transplanted with ease, colonial productivity would not have benefitted from the efficiency and labor savings of native techniques, which were often taught by Indian prisoners (as at Jamestown) or by allies like Squanto at Plymouth. So central was maize to the colonial economy that its absence might have acted as a severe brake on westward settlement, thereby somewhat counteracting the magnetic pull of free land.

The colonial economy would also have been affected by the lack of Indian trade, whose profits fueled the nascent economies of several colonies, including Massachusetts, Rhode Island, New York, Pennsylvania, Virginia, and South Carolina. Without fortunes made from furs, some of the "first families" of America—the Byrds, Penns, Logans, Winthrops, Schuylers—would not have begun to accumulate wealth so soon in the form of ships, slaves, rice, tobacco, or real estate. Nor would the mature economies of a few major colonies have rested on the fur trade well into the eighteenth century. New York's and Pennsylvania's balance of payments with the mother country would have been badly skewed if furs supplied by Indians had not accounted for 30 to 50 percent of their annual exports between 1700 and 1750. A substantial portion of English exports to the colonies would not have been sent to colonial traders for Indian customers, whose desire for English cloth and appetite for West Indian rum were appreciatd even though throughout the colonial period furs accounted for only .5 percent of England's colonial imports, far less than either tobacco or sugar.

The lack of Indians and Indian property rights in America would have narrowed another classic American road to wealth. If the new land had been so close to inexhaustible and "dirt cheap," the range of legal and extralegal means to acquire relatively scarce land for hoarding and speculation would have been markedly reduced. Within the unknown confines of the royal response to a huge, open continent, every man, great and small, would have been for himself. If the law condoned or fostered the selective aggrandisement of colonial elites, as it tended to do historically, unfavored farmers and entrepreneurs could simply move out of the government's effective jurisdiction or find leaders more willing to do their bidding. The proliferation of new colonies seeking economic and political independence from the felt tyranny of an Eastern Establishment would have been one certain result, as would a flattening of social hierarchy in all the mainland colonies.

Finally, in an America without Indians the history of black slavery would have been different. It is likely that, in the absence of Indians, the colonial demand for and use of African slaves would have begun earlier and accelerated faster. For although the historical natives were found to be poor workers and poorer slaves, the discovery took some time. Not only would the rapid westward spread of settlements have called for black labor, perhaps more of it indentured, but the rice and tobacco plantations of the Southeast probably would have been larger than they were historically, if scarce land and high prices had not restricted them. In a virgin-land economy, agricultural entrepreneurs who wanted to increase their acreage could easily buy out their smaller neighbors, who lacked no access to new lands in the west. Greater numbers of black laborers would have been needed because white indentured servants would have been extremely hard to get when so much land and opportunity beckoned. The slaves themselves would have been harder to keep to the task without surrounding tribes of Indians who could be taught to fear and hate the African strangers and to serve the English planters as slave catchers. The number of maroon enclaves in the interior would have increased considerably.

While most colonists came to the New World to better their own material condition, not a few came to ameliorate the spiritual condition of the "godless" natives. Without the challenge of native "paganism" in America, the charters of most English colonies would have been frankly materialistic documents with pride of motive going to the extension of His (or Her) Majesty's Eminent Domain. Thus American history would have lost much of its distinctively evangelical tone, though few of its millenarian, utopian strains. Without the long, frustrated history of Christian missions to the Indians, there would have been one less source of denominational competition in the eighteenth century. And we would lack a sensitive barometer of the cultural values that the European colonists sought to transplant in the New World.

Without Indian targets and foils, even the New England colonists might not have retained their "Chosen People" conceit so long or so obdurately. On the other hand, without the steady native reminder of their evangelical mission in America, their early descent into ecclesiastical tribalism and spiritual exclusiveness might have been swifter. The jeremiads of New England would certainly have been less shrill in the absence of the Pequot War and King Philip's War, when the hostile natives seemed to be "scourges" sent by God to punish a sinful people. Without the military and psychological threat of Indians within and without New England's borders, the colonial fear of limitless and unpredictable social behavior would have been reduced, thereby diminishing the harsh treatment of religious deviants such as Roger Williams, Anne Hutchinson, the Quakers, and the Salem witches. Finally, the French "Catholic menace" to the north would have been no threat to English Protestant sensibilities without hundreds of Indian converts, led by "deviously" effective Jesuit missionaries, ringing New England's borders. The French secular clergy who would have ministered to the handful of fishermen and farmers in Canada would have had no interest in converting Protestant "heretics" hundreds of miles away and no extra manpower to attempt it.

Colonial politics, too, would have had a different complexion in the absence of American natives. Even if the French had settled the St. Lawrence Valley without a sustaining Indian fur trade, the proliferating English population and European power politics would have made short work of the tiny Canadian population, now bereft of Indian allies and converts in the thousands. In all likelihood, we would write about only one short intercolonial war, beginning much earlier than 1689. Perhaps the English privateers, David and Jarvis Kirke, who captured New France in 1629, would not have given it back to the French in 1632. Without the Catholic Indian *reserves* (praying towns) of Lorette, Caughnawaga, and St. François to serve as military buffers around French settlements, Canada would quickly have become English, at least as far north as arable land and lumber-rich forests extended.

Without a formidable French and Indian threat, early Americans would not have developed—in conjunction with their conceit as God's "Chosen People"—such a pronounced garrison mentality, picturing themselves as innocent and holy victims threatened by heavily armed satanic forces. If the English had not been virtually surrounded by Indian nations allied with the French and an arc of French trading forts and villages from Louisiana to Maine, the Anglo-American tendencies toward persecuted isolationism would have been greatly reduced.

As the colonies matured, the absence of an Indian military threat would have lightened the taxpayers' burden for colonial defense, lessening the strains in the political relations between governors and representative assemblies. Indeed, the assemblies would not have risen to political parity with the royal administrators without the financial crises generated by war debts and defense needs. Intercolonial cooperation would have been even rarer than it was. Royal forces would not have arrived during the eighteenth century to bolster sagging colonial defenses and to pile up imperial debts that the colonies would be asked to help amortize. Consequently, the colonies would have had few grievances against the mother country serious enough to ignite an American Revolution, at least not in 1776. On the other hand, without the concentration of Indian allies on the British side, the colonists might have achieved independence sooner than they did.

Indeed, without the steady impress of Indian culture, the colonists would probably not have been ready for revolution in 1776, because they would not have been or felt sufficiently Americanized to stand before the world as an independent nation. The Indian presence precipitated the formation of an American identity.

Without Indian societies to form our colonial frontiers, Anglo-American culture would have been transformed only by internal developments, the evolving influence of the mother country, and the influence of the black and other ethnic groups who shared the New World with the English. Black culture probably would have done the most to change the shape and texture of colonial life, especially in the South. But English masters saw little reason to emulate their black slaves, to make *adaptive* changes in their own cultural practices or attitudes in order to accommodate perceived superiorities in black culture. English colonial culture changed in response to the imported Africans largely in *reaction* to their oppositional being, and pervasive and often virulent racism was the primary result. Other changes, of course, followed from the adoption of staple economies largely but not necessarily dependent on black labor.

English reactions to the Indians, on the other hand, were far more mixed; the "savages" were noble as well as ignoble, depending on English needs and circumstances. Particularly on the frontier, colonists were not afraid or loath to borrow and adapt pieces of native culture if they found them advantageous or necessary for beating the American environment or besting the Indians in the contest for the continent. Contrary to metropolitan colonial opinion, this cultural exchange did not turn the frontiersmen into Indians. Indian means were simply borrowed and adapted to English ends. The frontiersmen did not regard themselves as Indians nor did they appreciably alter their basic attitudes toward the native means they employed. But they also knew that their American encounters with the Indians made them very different from their English cousins at home.

While the colonists borrowed consciously and directly from Indian culture only on the frontier, English colonial culture as a whole received a substantial but indirect impress from the Indians by being forced to confront the novel otherness of native culture and to cope with its unpredictability, pride, and retaliatory violence. Having the Indians as adversaries sometimes and contraries at all times not only reinforced the continuity of vital English traits and institutions but also Americanized all levels of colonial society more fully than the material adaptations of the frontiersmen. The colonial experience of trying to solve a series of "Indian problems" did much to give the colonists an identity indissolubly linked to America and their apprenticeship in political and military cooperation. In large measure, it was the *reactive* changes that transformed colonial Englishmen into native

Americans in feeling, allegiance, and identity, a transformation without which, John Adams said, the American Revolution would have been impossible.

What identity-forming changes would *not* have taken place in colonial culture had the continent been devoid of Indians? The adaptive changes are the easiest to describe. Without native precedent, the names of twenty-eight states and myriad other place-names would carry a greater load of Anglophonic freight. The euphonious Shenandoah and Monongahela might well be known as the St. George and the Dudley rivers. We might still be searching for suitable names for the *moose, skunk,* and *raccoon,* the *muskellunge* and *quahog,* the *hickory* tree and marshy *muskeg.* It would be impossible, no doubt, to find *moccasins* in an L. L. Bean catalog or canned *succotash* in the supermarket. We would never refer to our children playfully as *papooses* or to political bigshots as *mugwumps.* Southerners could not start their day with *hominy* grits.

Without Indian guides to the New World, the newly arrived English colonists could not have housed themselves in bark-covered wigwams and longhouses. Not only would their diet have depended largely on imported foods, but even their techniques for hunting American game and fowl and coping in the woods would have been meager. Without native medicines, many colonists would have perished and the *U.S. Pharmacopeia* would lack most of the 170 entries attributable to Indian discovery and use. Without Indian snowshoes and toboggans, winter hunting and travel would have been sharply curtailed. Without the lightweight bark canoe, northern colonists would have penetrated the country on foot. English hunters probably would have careered around the woods in gaudy colors and torn English garments much longer, unaware that the unsmoked glint of their musket barrels frightened the game. And what would Virginia's patriotic rifle companies have worn in 1775 as an alternative to moccasins, leggings, fringed hunting shirts, scalping knives, and tomahawks?

Without native opponents and instructors in the art of guerilla warfare, the colonists would have fought their American wars—primarily with the British—in traditional military style. In fact, without the constant need to suppress hostile natives and aggressive Europeans, they might have lost most of their martial spirit and prowess, making their victory in the now-postponed Revolution less than certain. Beating the British regulars at their own game without stratagems and equipment gained from the Indians would have been nearly impossible, particularly after the British gained experience in counterinsurgent warfare in Scotland and on the continent.

The absence of such adaptive changes would have done much to maintain the Anglicized tone and texture of colonial life; the absence of Indians would have preserved more fundamental cultural values that were altered historically. The generalized European fear of barbarism that colonial planners and leaders manifested would have dissipated without the Indian embodiment of a ''heathenism'' that seemed contagious to English frontiersmen or the danger of Englishmen converting to an Indian way of life in captivity or, worse still, voluntarily as ''apostates'' and ''renegades.'' Without the seduction of an alternative lifestyle within easy reach, hundreds of colonists would not have become white Indians.

More generally, the Anglo-Americans' definition of themselves would have lacked a crucial point of reference because the Indians would no longer symbolize the "savage" baseness that would dominate human nature if man did not "reduce" it to "civility" through government, religion, and the capitalist work ethic. Only imported Africans, not American natives, would then have shown "civilized men [what] they were not and must not be." Because the settlers were "especially inclined to discover attributes in savages which they found first but could not speak of in themselves," they defined themselves "less by the vitality of their affirmations than by the violence of their abjurations." All peoples define themselves partly by contrast with other peoples, but the English colonists forged their particular American identity on an Indian anvil more than on a (non-English) European or African one.

The Indians were so crucial to the formation of the Anglo-American character because of the strong contrasts between their culture and that of the intruders, which the English interpreted largely as native deficiencies. While English technology had reached the Age of Iron, Indian technology was of the Stone Age, without wheels, clocks, compasses, cloth, iron, glass, paper, or gunpowder. While the English participated in a capitalist economy of currency and credit, the natives bartered in kind from hand to hand. While the English were governed by statutes, sheriffs, parliaments, and kings, the Indians' suasive polities of chiefs and councils seemed to be no government at all. While the English worshipped the "true God" in churches with prayer books and scripture, native shamans resembled "conjurers" who preyed on the "superstitious" natures of their dream-ridden, "devil-worshipping" supplicants. While the English enjoyed the benefits of printing and alphabetic literacy, the Indians were locked in an oral culture of impermanence and "hearsay." While the English sought to master nature as their religion taught them, the natives saw themselves as part of nature, whose other "spirits" deserved respect and thanks. While English men worked in the fields and women in the house, Indian women farmed and their menfolk "played" at hunting and fishing. While English time shot straight ahead into a progressive future, Indian time looped and circled upon itself, blurring the boundaries between a hazy past, a spacious present, and an attenuated future. While the English lived in permanent towns and cities, the Indians' annual subsistence cycle of movement seemed aimlessly "nomadic." While the English waged wars of state for land, crowns, wealth, or faith, Indian warriors struck personally for revenge, honor, and captives. While English society was divided into "divinely sanctioned" strata of wealth, power, and prestige, Indian society fostered an "unnatural" sense of democratic individualism in the people. And while English ethnocentrism was based on a new religion, technology, social evolution, and ultimately race, the Indians' own strong sense of superiority, color-blind and religiously tolerant, could not be undermined except by inexplicable European diseases.

For the whole spectrum of colonial society, urban and rural, the Indians as cultual contraries were not so frustrating, alarming, or influenttial as the Indian enemy. As masters of an unconventional warfare of terror, they seared the collective memories, imaginations, and even subconscious of the colonists, leaving a deep but blurred intaglio of fear and envy, hatred and respect. Having the American natives as frequent and deadly adversaries— and even as allies—did more to "Americanize" the English colonists than any other human factor and had two contradictory results. When native warfare frustrated and humbled the English military machine, its successes cast into serious doubt the colonists' sense of superiority, especially when the only recourse seemed to be the hiring of mercenaries from other tribes. At the same time, victorious Indians seemed so insufferably insolent—a projection of the Christians' original sin—that the colonists redoubled their efforts to claim divine grace and achieve spiritual and social regeneration through violence. One of the pathetic ironies of early America is that in attempting to exterminate the wounding pride of their Indian enemies, the colonists inflated their own pride to sinful proportions.

The Indians' brand of guerilla warfare, which involved the "indiscriminate slaughter of all ranks, ages and sexes," torture, and captivity for adoption, gave rise to several colonial reactions. The first reaction was a well-founded increase in fear and paranoia. The second reaction was the development of a defensive garrison mentality, which in turn reinforced the colonists' sense of being a chosen if momentarily abandoned people. And the colonists' third response was a sense of being torn from their own "civilized" moorings and swept into the kind of "savage" conduct they deplored in their enemies, motivated by cold-blooded vengeance. Without Indian enemies, it is doubtful if the colonists would have slaughtered and tortured military prisoners, including women and children, taken scalps from friends and enemies to collect government bounties, encouraged the Spanish-style use of dogs, or made boot tops and tobacco pouches from the skin of fallen foes. It is a certainty that non-Indian enemies would not have been the target of frequent if unrealized campaigns of genocide; it is difficult to imagine English settlers coining an aphorism to the effect that "the only good Dutchman is a dead one."

It is both fitting and ironic that the symbol chosen by Revolutionary cartoonists to represent the American colonies was the Indian, whose love of liberty and fierce independence had done so much to Americanize the shape and content of English colonial culture. It is fitting because the Indians by their long and determined opposition helped to meld thirteen disparate colonies into one (albeit fragile) nation, different from England largely by virtue of having shared that common history of conflict on and over Indian soil. It is ironic because after nearly two centuries of trying to take the Indians' lives and lands, the colonists appropriated not only the native identity but the very characteristics that thwarted the colonists' arrogations.

ϒ *F U R T H E R   R E A D I N G*

Gary C. Anderson, *Kinsmen of Another Kind: Dakota-White Relations in the Upper Mississippi Valley, 1500–1862* (1984)
James Axtell, *The European and the Indian* (1981)
———, *The Invasion Within: The Contest of Cultures in Colonial North America* (1985)
Robert F. Berkhofer, Jr., *Salvation and the Savage: An Analysis of Protestant Missions and American Indian Response, 1787–1862* (1965)
———, *The White Man's Indian: Images of the American from Columbus to the Present* (1977)
William Cronon, *Changes in the Land: Indians, Colonists, and the Ecology of New England* (1983)
Alfred Crosby, *The Columbian Exchange: Biological and Cultural Consequences of 1492* (1972)
R. David Edmunds, *The Potawatomis: Keepers of the Fire* (1978)
———, *The Shawnee Prophet* (1983)
———, *Tecumseh and the Quest for Indian Leadership* (1984)
John C. Ewers, "Intertribal Warfare as Precursor of Indian-White Warfare on the Northern Great Plains," *Western Historical Quarterly*, 6 (1975), 397–410
Brian M. Fagan, *The Great Journey: The Peopling of Ancient America* (1987)
Charles Gibson, "Conquest, Capitulation and Indian Treaties," *American Historical Review*, 83 (1978), 1–15
Gary C. Goodwin, *Cherokees in Transition: A Study of Changing Culture and Environment Prior to 1775* (1977)
Cornelius J. Jaenen, *Friend to Foe: Aspects of French-Amerindian Cultural Contact in the Sixteenth and Seventeenth Centuries* (1976)
Francis Jennings, *The Ambiguous Iroquois Empire* (1984)
———, *Empire of Fortune: Crowns, Colonies and Tribes in the Seven Years War in America* (1988)
———, *The Invasion of America: Indians, Colonialism, and the Cant of Conquest* (1975)
Elizabeth A. H. John, *Storms Brewed in Other Men's Worlds: The Confrontation of Indians, Spaniards, and the French in the Southwest, 1540–1795* (1975)
John L. Kessell, *Kiva, Cross and Crown: The Pecos Indians and New Mexico, 1540–1840* (1979)
Karen O. Kupperman, *Settling with the Indians: The Meeting of English and Indian Cultures in America, 1580–1640* (1980)
James H. Merrell, "The Indians' New World: The Catawba Experience," *William and Mary Quarterly*, 41 (1984), 537–65
Roxanne Dunbar Ortiz, *Roots of Resistance: Land Tenure in New Mexico, 1680–1980* (1980)
Neal Salisbury, *Manitou and Providence: Indians, Europeans, and the Making of New England, 1500–1643* (1982)
Karl H. Schlesier, "Epidemics and Indian Middlemen: Rethinking the Wars of the Iroquois, 1609–1653," *Ethnohistory*, 23 (1976), 129–45
Bernard W. Sheehan, *Savagism and Civility: Indians and Englishmen in Colonial Virginia* (1980)
William S. Simmons, *Spirit of the New England Tribes: Indian History and Folklore, 1620–1984* (1986)
Richard Slotkin and James K. Folsom, *So Dreadful a Judgement: Puritan Responses to King Philip's War, 1676–1677* (1978)
Edward H. Spicer, *Cycles of Conquest: The Impact of Spain, Mexico, and the United States on the Indians of the Southwest, 1533–1960* (1962)
Peter A. Thomas, "Contrastive Subsistence Strategies and Land Use as Factors

for Understanding Indian-White Relations in New England," *Ethnohistory*, 23 (1976), 1–18

Russell Thornton, *American Indian Holocaust and Survival: A Population History Since 1492* (1987)

Michael K. Trimble, *An Ethnohistorical Interpretation of the Spread of Smallpox in the Northern Plains Utilizing Concepts of Disease Ecology* (1979)

Richard White, "The Winning of the West: The Expansion of the Western Sioux in the 18th and 19th Centuries," *Journal of American History*, 65 (1978), 319–43

Colonial Frontier Societies

Υ

Within a three-year period between 1607 and 1610, three important frontier communities were established by three different European empires: Jamestown by the English in 1607, Quebec by the French in 1608, and Santa Fe by the Spanish in 1610. For England and France, these small communities represented their first permanent settlements in North America. Spain had established St. Augustine in Florida in 1565 as a northern outpost of its New World empire. Russia would not have a permanent post in North America, on Alaska's Kodiak Island, until 1784. Of these European powers, the Spanish and French had the earliest sustained presence in the interior region that later became the frontier, and eventually the West, of the United States. The French in the St. Lawrence and Mississippi river valleys, and the Spanish in Texas, New Mexico, and California, created frontier settlements that mirrored the values of each European society and also demonstrated the adaptations necessary in an American frontier setting. In this way, the Spanish and French provided the first examples of a distinctive western frontier style of settlement that was not native to the region. Whether each frontier society created new ''American'' patterns of life or modestly modified traditions carried over from Europe has been a major source of debate. The relative success of Spanish and French frontier settlement is also a contested issue.

Υ *DOCUMENTS*

The first two documents compare the personal property of two Spanish soldiers. Captain Don Luís de Velasco accompanied Don Juan de Oñate in his colonizing expedition to the area that became New Mexico. His manifest of 1597 shows that the captain was a wealthy man who, one may assume, anticipated acquiring even more wealth in New Mexico. In the second document, dated 1663, Nicolás de Aguilar appears less fortunate in two ways: First, he has been excommunicated from the Catholic church, arrested by the Inquisition, and taken to Mexico City because he accused New Mexican clerics of fathering children by Indian women under their care. Second, his worldly goods, as recorded by the religious court, are far more modest than those of Captain de Velasco. Like most of the other colonists of New Mexico, Nicolás de Aguilar had not become a wealthy man. Should the success of frontier societies be judged by the acquisition of wealth in European terms?

The third and fourth documents are accounts of visitors to New Mexico and rural Canada, respectively, in the mid-1700s. Dr. Pedro Tamarón y Romeral, the sixteenth bishop of Durango, had official ecclesiastical reasons for touring the New Mexican part of his vast diocese. His description of the communities of El Paso, Santa Fe, and Taos reveals a diverse population of Spanish, mixed-heritage, and Indian peoples who shared limited access to water and fear of Comanche raiders as two realities of their daily lives. Peter Kalm, a traveler from Sweden, paid close attention to the fields, farmhouses, villages, and peoples of rural French Canada during an excursion there in 1749. His account notes the "mixed blood" of some of the residents, as well as the preference of Indians to retain their culture and not take up European ways. Judging from these accounts, how well established do the French and Spanish frontier societies appear to have been?

In the final document, Henry Marie Brackenridge fondly recalls his experiences as a child in the French community of Sainte Genevieve in present-day Missouri, west of the Mississippi River. After his mother's death in 1788, Brackenridge was only seven in 1792 when his father, a prominent Pennsylvania lawyer, sent him under the care of a guardian to live with the Bauvais family. He enjoyed his three-year interlude among the French before returning to his father's home in Pittsburgh. Like Kalm, Brackenridge, *le petit Anglais*, shows little cultural prejudice in his depiction of French frontier life. Would he or Kalm have left such positive accounts if they had lived or toured in the Spanish Southwest?

Don Luís de Velasco's Manifest, 1597

Manifest made by Captain Don Luís de Velasco of the goods, arms, and horses which he is taking to serve his Majesty in the expedition to New Mexico, of which Don Juan de Oñate goes as governor and captain-general.

Being at the mines of Casco, where is encamped the army of his Majesty, which is going to the conquest and pacification of the provinces of New Mexico, on the nineteenth day of May, 1597, before Señor Don Juan de Oñate, governor and captain-general of the provinces of New Mexico and its kingdoms and the adjacent territories for the king, our Lord, and before me, Juan Pérez de Donis, clerk of his royal Majesty and secretary of the said expedition, appeared Captain Don Luís de Velasco, whom I swear that I know. He declared that in fulfillment of what some captains and officers of the royal army have petitioned before his lordship, he wished to make a manifest of the goods that he is taking; and, so doing, he exhibited and brought into the presence of the señor governor and myself, to which I swear, the following things:

First, he exhibited and brought before his lordship a standard of figured white Castilian silk, with fringes and trimmings of gold and crimson silk, which has stamped on one side the pictures of Our Lady and Saint John the Baptist. Encircling these two figures is painted the rosary of Our Lady with large gold beads, and at their feet the escutcheon and arms of the governor. On the other side it has the figure of the lord Saint James, with an inscription encircling it which says *Sic ut sanguino centa,* and at the feet of the horse of the lord Saint James the escutcheon and arms of the Velascos, with large tassels trimmed with gold and crimson silk.

Item: A silver lance, in its handle, for the exercise of his office as captain, with tassels of gold and yellow and purple silk.

Item: For the said purpose three complete suits of armor, to arm himself and two other soldiers in coat of mail, with thigh piece, beaver, and helmet, all complete, and with nothing lacking.

Item: Three calivers, with their large and small powder horns, firelocks, bullet screws, moulds, and all the rest that pertains to each one.

Item: Three sets of horse armor of buckskin, lined with undressed leather, for the flanks, foreheads, breasts, necks—all, without anything lacking.

Item: A halberd, garnished with yellow velvet and purple tassels, and all studded with nails, which he bought for his sergeant to carry.

Item: Thirty war-horses of different brands and marks, marked with his brand, which is in the margin.

Item: Two saddle mules to take on the said expedition and two pack mules.

Item: A sword and a gilded dagger with their waist belts stitched with purple, yellow, and white silk.

Item: One broadsword with shoulder belt, and two shields for defense against arrows.

Item: Two trooper saddles of Cordovan leather, with housings of blue flowered Spanish cloth bound with Cordovan leather, all complete and with loose stirrups.

Item: Two *estradiotas* [light cavalry] saddles of Cordovan leather, with the stirrups, bridles, girths, halters, and reins that go with them, one *estradiote* and two troopers' bridles.

Item: One bed with two mattresses, a coverlet, sheets, pillow-cases, pillows, and a canvas mattress-bag bound with sole leather.

Item: He is taking in his service two Spanish servants, from eighteen to twenty years old, to serve his Majesty on the expedition, to each of whom he has given four horses and complete equipment of armor for themselves and their horses.

Item: One suit of blue Italian velvet trimmed with wide gold passementerie, consisting of doublet, breeches, and green silk stockings with blue garters with points of gold lace.

Item: Another suit of rose-colored lustrous Castilian satin, consisting of a Walloon doublet, trimmed with narrow gold passementerie and a short cloak of gray cloth trimmed with wide gold and silver fringe, rose-colored silk stockings, and garters of striped rose-colored taffeta.

Item: Another suit of straw-colored Castilian satin, slashed with wide slashes and trimmed with interlinings of crimson Castilian taffeta, consisting of breeches, doublet, stockings of straw-colored silk and garters of purple taffeta with points.

Item: Another suit of purple Castilian cloth, consisting of Walloon breeches and doublet, trimmed with narrow gold passementerie, a cape with a wide gold fringe and ruffles of purple taffeta, purple silk stockings and garters of purple taffeta with points of gold lace.

Item: Another suit of chestnut-colored London cloth in the Walloon style, doublet and short cloak all trimmed with silver passementerie embroidery.

Item: Another suit of Chinese flowered silk, tan and green, trimmed with very narrow gold passementerie, consisting of breeches, doublet, and a jacket of ordinary cloth.

Item: Two doublets of kid dressed in Castile, one from the royal city being trimmed with gold and purple silk passementerie, and the other with wide silver passementerie.

Item: Another doublet of royal lion skin trimmed with gold and purple passementerie, with buttons of the same.

Item: One rain-cloak of gray cloth of the country.

Item: Two Rouen linen shirts with collars and cuffs of Holland cambric.

Item: Six handkerchiefs of Rouen linen and eight pairs of linen breeches with their socks.

Item: Six pairs of trimmed Rouen linen breeches.

Item: Eight pairs Cordovan leather boots, six white pairs and four black, and four pairs of laced gaiters.

Item: Fourteen pairs of Cordovan leather shoes, white and black, and four pairs of boots of sole leather and buckskin.

Item: Two hats, one black, trimmed around the crown with a silver cord, with black, purple, and white feathers, and the other gray, with yellow and purple feathers.

Item: Another hat of purple taffeta with blue, purple, and yellow feathers, and trimmed with a band of gold and silver passementerie.

Item: Four pairs of spurs for long stirrups, two for short stirrups, and some Moorish spurs with tassels and cords of silk.

Item: Fifty yards of striped canvas of Michoacan bindweed for a tent, with all the appurtenances necessary for setting it up with forked stakes, and everything else belonging to it.

The said goods having been thus declared, Captain Don Luís de Velasco begged his lordship to declare them manifested. Besides the aforesaid—as his lordship is aware, and, as is well known—some of his officers and soldiers are in debt to him for a large quantity of goods which they carried off when they absconded because of the delay in the expedition. With all this he came to serve his Majesty, and he will also give a report separately, presenting a petition that it be received. With this declaration he said that at present he has nothing more to manifest.

Nicolás de Aguilar's Worldly Goods, 1663

First Hearing and Deposition of Nicolás de Aguilar, April 12 and May 8, 1663

Nicolás de Aguilar, [a native of the pueblo of Yorerapudaro, Michoacán,] and a resident of Las Salinas in New Mexico, thirty-six years of age; his occupation, past and present, is that of a soldier in those provinces of New Mexico, having served the king, our lord, since he was ten years old. He has been sergeant and aide in the villa of Santa Fé, and *visitador* [wagonmaster] of the wagons of Andrés de Gracias, which went to the provinces of New Mexico; he has also twice been field captain of New Mexico and *alcalde mayor* [principal town clerk] of the jurisdiction of Las Salinas. One year and six days ago he was made prisoner in the pueblo of La Isleta in that kingdom by order of this Holy Office; he was brought here and entered the secret prisons, where he now is. . . .

He is a man of large body, coarse, and somewhat brown; . . . He wears a gabardine of buff and black wool, adorned with very small points of black wool [lace], a doublet of white cloth embroidered with blue wool, trousers of dark red flannel with small points of black wool lace, blue woolen stockings, a cotton neckcloth adorned with drawn work, and shoes of buckskin from New Mexico. Apparently he brought nothing else with him. In a [1] white wooden box, the [2] key of which he handed over, there were also found:

3. A doublet of buff and black wool, badly worn, with cotton sleeves embroidered with blue wool.

4. Another doublet of buff and black woolen cloth, with the same sort of sleeves.

5. Item. An old cotton shirt, adorned with drawn work.

6. Item. Another cloth shirt, worn out.

7. Item. A shirt of ordinary Rouen linen.

8. A cotton shirt, embroidered with dark red wool.

9. A short jacket of dark red flannel, decorated with black wool.

10. Two pairs of woollen stockings, one pair red and the other buff-colored.

11. One pair of white cotton stockings.

12. One pair of shoes of Córdovan leather, worn out.

13. A book, entitled, "Catechism in the Castilian and Timuquana languages." Inside of this was another very small book, entitled, "Instructions for examining the conscience."

14. A bar of soap and a little *alucema* [polishing brush] wrapped in an old black rag.

15. An antelope skin muffler lined with yellow linen.

16. A cloth containing, apparently, roots of dry grass, which he said they call bear grass in New Mexico, used for curing fevers.

17. Three small pieces of dried grass roots, which he said is called *manso* grass, and is good for healing wounds.

18. A fair-sized bag of relics, inside of which was another bag containing a paper telling of the restitution which must be made. It covers about half of a half-sheet of paper.

19. A little printed copy of the four Gospels.

20. A quantity of folded papers, which he said were relics.

21. A rosary strung on *coyole* wire, having large beads, and a little silver cross.

22. A small and very old book bound with small black boards, which had no title at the beginning, and seems to consist, in the middle, of exercises and reflections.

23. A very old cloak of olive-colored cloth.

24. A very old black hat.

25. A buckskin bag within which is a cotton pillow filled with sheep's wool.

26. A mattress of coarse black and white stuff, filled with sheep's wool.

27. Two black woollen blankets.

28. Two woollen sheets.

29. A large buckskin into which the leather bag goes. He has apparently brought nothing else.

Bishop Tamarón Visits New Mexico, 1760

The boundaries of New Mexico, if we seek them from Sonora and Janos, are the Santa María River on the west, and the line with Vizcaya is in that region. From there it is fifty leagues to El Paso, and I took this route when I made my episcopal visitation. The captain of Janos and his men left me there and returned to their presidio thirty leagues away. In the south the boundary is Carrizal, which is thirty-six leagues from El Paso. The eastern boundary is eighty leagues downstream from El Paso at the junction with the Conchos River. The northern limit is unknown. On the west flank there are Gila, Navaho, and Ute Indians; on the northeast, Apaches and Faraones, and other tribes.

El Paso

This town's population is made up of Spaniards, Europeanized mixtures, and Indians. Its patron saints are Our Lady of the Pillar [of Saragossa] and St. Joseph. There is a royal presidio with a captain and fifty soldiers in the pay of the King. . . .

El Paso has 354 families of Spanish and Europeanized citizens, with 2479 persons. There are 72 Indian families with 249 persons.

They gave me a solemn reception here, for not only did the captain of the presidio, Don Manuel de San Juan, who is also the chief magistrate, the Father Custos, and the vicar come out to the Río de Santa María, but when I entered El Paso, everyone came marching out in fine order and display. This cost me a night's sojourn in the country three leagues from El Paso, which I did not like at all, because it is a very dangerous region, even though I had been in the same situation for the six preceding nights from the time I left Janos since there are no settlements en route. But this last night was at their request so that they might make better preparations for my reception, for I was then near enough to have been able to enter El Paso that night. But I arrived on the following day, April 23, 1760. . . .

There is a large irrigation ditch with which they bleed the Río del Norte. It is large enough to receive half its waters. This ditch is subdivided into others which run through broad plains, irrigating them. By this means they maintain a large number of vineyards, from which they make *generoso* wines even better than those from Parras, and also brandy, but not as much. They grow wheat, maize, and other grains of the region, as well as fruit trees, apples, pears, peaches, figs. It is delightful country in summer.

That settlement suffers a great deal of trouble caused by the river. Every year the freshet carries away the conduit they make to drain off its waters. The flood season lasts three months, May, June, and July. They told me about this before I came, and I traveled with more speed, since I had to cross it before it was in flood. Three or four days after my arrival, I went to see the river, a trip which requires an armed escort. It was already rising. It is at its peak on May 3. It was necessary for me to wait while supplies for the journey to the interior of New Mexico were made ready.

The method of restoring the conduit every year is to make some large round baskets of rather thick rods. When the freshets are over, they put them in the current, filling them with stones, and they act as dams and force the water to seek the mouth of the ditch. This is not necessary when the river is in flood. Indeed, so much water flows that if the river is somewhat higher than usual, they are alarmed, fearing that they may be flooded and innundated with great damage. . . .

Santa Fe

This villa is the capital of New Mexico. It is four leagues east of the house of El Alamo, which I left the afternoon of the same day. And a half a league before we reached Santa Fe, the governor came forth with a numerous and brilliant retinue. He dismounted from his horse and joined me in the coach. This reception was very noteworthy. We proceeded to the villa among a crowd of people, and my entrance to Santa Fe was made with the same solemnity that the Roman ceremonial prescribes for cathedrals. After this function the governor himself lodged me in the very casa reales [royal mansions], and he moved to another house. And he provided food during my sojourn there. I accepted this, and the same from the captain at El Paso, because there was no other way of obtaining it; and they conformed, according to what I heard, to the practice of their predecessors with my predecessors, as likewise with regard to providing mules and horses.

On May 25, which was Whitsunday, the visitation was made with all possible solemnity in the principal church, which serves as the parish church. It is large, with a spacious nave and a transept adorned by altars and altarscreens, all of which, as well as the baptismal font and the other things mentioned in the Roman ritual, were inspected after the edict concerning public sins had been read and a sermon on the aims of the visitation given. . . .

This villa of Santa Fe has 379 families of citizens of Spanish and mixed blood, with 1285 persons. Since I have confirmed 1532 persons in the said villa, I am convinced that the census they gave me is very much on the low side, and I do not doubt that the number of persons must be at least twice that given in the census.

In this villa I visited another church dedicated to the Archangel St. Michael. It is fairly decent; at that time they were repairing the roof.

In the plaza, a very fine church dedicated to the Most Holy Mother of Light was being built. It is thirty varas long and nine wide, with a transept. Eight leagues from there a vein of very white stone had been discovered, and the amount necessary for an altar screen large enough to fill a third [of the wall] of the high altar was brought from this place. This was then almost carved. Later both it and the church were finished. The dedication of this church was also celebrated, and I was informed that it was all well adorned. The chief founder of this church was the governor himself, Don Francisco Marín del Valle, who simultaneously arranged for the founding of a confraternity which was established while I was there. I attended the first meeting and approved everything.

The buildings of this villa, both churches and houses, are all adobe. There is no fortress there, nor any formal presidio building. The garrison consists of 80 mounted soldiers in the pay of the King. In that villa, in Galisteo, and in Taos there was need of a stone fort in the vicinity of each. Santa Fe is a very open place; the houses are far apart; and therefore it does not have the least defence. If there had been a fort at the time of the uprising in the year 1680, the Indians would not have dared to do what they did.

This villa lies at the foot of a sierra, which is east of it and runs to the north. Water is scarce, because the river that traverses it dries up entirely in the months just before harvest, when only an inadequate small spring remains for drinking water, in addition to the wells. On May 25 it rained and hailed, and the sierra was covered with snow which soon melted. That people rejoiced, since they thought that such early precipitation augured a good winter. The villa of Santa Fe is located in latitude 37°28', longitude 262°40'.

Since the two pueblos of Pecos and Galisteo are off the beaten track, the decision to break off the visitation of Santa Fe and to proceed to make that of the said two pueblos was taken. . . .

From Galisteo I returned to Santa Fe. I also experienced another alarm about the Comanches, the news of whose coming was given by the peaceful heathen Apaches. The governor took precautions, and the Comanches went in another direction. And the force marched on the day of Corpus, on which I celebrated a pontifical high mass and organized the procession with His Divine Majesty. The street through which the procession passed was decorated with branches and splendid altars; there were salvos by the military squadrons, and a large crowd was present. I consecrated six altar stones at Santa Fe.

Here I received a petition which I shall relate because of its unusual nature. A woman fifteen years of age, who had already been married for five years, presented herself, asking for the annulment of her marriage because she had been married at the age of ten. Then the husband, who was a soldier of the presidio, appeared. The fact that the marriage had taken place when she was ten years old was verified, but there was also proof that she immediately conceived and bore a son, and then another, and that she was already pregnant with the first child at the age of eleven. For this reason her petition was not valid, and the couple was ordered to continue in the state of matrimony. . . .

Taos

The titular patron of this Indian pueblo is San Jerónimo. To reach it we traveled through pine forests and mountains until we descended to the spacious and beautiful valley they call the valley of Taos. In this valley we kept finding encampments of peaceful infidel Apache Indians, who have sought the protection of the Spaniards so that they may defend them from the Comanches. Then we came to a river called Trampas, which carries enough water. The midday halt was made at the large house of a wealthy Taos Indian, very civilized and well-to-do. The said house is well walled in, with arms and towers for defense. In the afternoon the journey through that valley continued. Three rivers of similar current and water were crossed. The first one in particular provided abundant ditches for irrigation. They are about a league and a half from one another. And, crossing the last one, we entered the pueblo of Taos, where a Franciscan missionary parish priest resides.

. . . It is the last and most distant pueblo. . . . It lies at the foot of a very high sierra. . . . This pueblo has 159 families of Indians, with 505 persons. There are 36 families of Europeanized citizens, with 160 persons. There is a very decent and capacious church.

I also put forth every effort there to induce those best acquainted with Spanish to perform the act of contrition and confess. I therefore left this group until last, confirming the children first. And in fact some did confess, and, encouraged to contrition, were confirmed. But since they do not know the catechism except in Spanish, I did not feel as pleased and easy in my mind as I should have liked. Therefore I reprimanded the mission father and duly reminded him of his duty, ordering him to continue receiving their confessions.

This pueblo is divided into three many-storied tenements. It would have been better, as I told them, if they had been kept together, for one is on the other side of the river about two hundred varas away. There is a wooden bridge to cross the river. It freezes every year, and they told me that when it is thus covered with ice, the Indian women come with their naked little ones, break the ice with a stone, and bathe them in those waters, dipping them in and out. And they say it is for the purpose of making them tough and strong.

When I was in the pueblo two encampments of Ute Indians, who were friendly but infidels, had just arrived with a captive woman who had fled from the Comanches. They reported that the latter were at the Río de las Animas preparing buffalo meat in order to come to trade. They come every year to the trading, or fairs. The governor comes to those fairs, which they call *rescates* [barter, trade], every year with the majority of his garrison and people from all over the kingdom. They bring captives to sell, pieces of chamois, many buffalo skins, and, out of the plunder they have obtained elsewhere, horses, muskets, shotguns, munitions, knives, meat, and various other things. Money is not current at these fairs, but exchange of one thing for another, and so those people get provisions. I left Taos on June 12, and a few days later seventeen tents of Comanches arrived. They make these of buffalo hide, and they say that they are good and well suited for defense; and a family occupies each one. And at the end of the said month of June seventy of these field tents arrived. This was the great fair.

The character of these Comanches is such that while they are peacefully trading in Taos, others of their nation make warlike attacks on some distant pueblo. And the ones who are at peace, engaged in trade, are accustomed to say to the governor, "Don't be too trusting. Remember, there are rogues among us, just as there are among you. Hang any of them you catch."

Peter Kalm Visits Rural Canada, 1749

August the 2nd [1749]

En Route for Quebec.   Early this morning we left Montreal and went in a bateau on our journey to Quebec in company with the second major of Montreal, M. de Sermonville. We went down the St. Lawrence River, which was here pretty broad on our left; on the northwest side was the isle of Montreal, and on the right a number of other isles, and the shore. The isle of Montreal was closely inhabited along the river; it was very flat and the rising land near the shore consisted of pure earth and was between three or four yards high. The woods were cut down along the riverside for the distance of an English mile. The dwelling houses were built of wood or stone indiscriminately, and whitewashed on the outside. The other buildings, such as barns, stables, etc. were all of wood. The ground next to the river was turned either into grain fields or meadows. Now and then we perceived churches on both sides of the river, the steeples of which were generally on that side of the church which looked towards the river, because they are not obliged here to put the steeples on the west end of the churches as in Sweden. Within six French miles of Montreal we saw several islands of different sizes in the river, and most of them were inhabited. Those without houses were sometimes turned into grain fields, but generally into grazing land. We saw no mountains, hills, rocks or stones to-day, the country being flat throughout, and consisting of pure earth.

All the *farms in Canada* stand separate from one another, so that each farmer has his possessions entirely separate from those of his neighbor. Each church, it is true, has a little village near it; but that consists chiefly of the parsonage, a school for the boys and girls of the place, and of the houses of tradesmen, but rarely of farmhouses; and if that was the case, their fields were still separated. The farmhouses hereabouts are generally all built along the rising banks of the river, either close to the water or at some distance from it, and about three or four arpens from each other. To some farms are annexed small orchards but they are in general without them; however, almost every farmer has a kitchen-garden.

Peach Trees. I have been told by all those who have made journeys to the southern parts of Canada and to the Mississippi River that the woods there abound with peach trees which bear excellent fruit, and that the Indians of those parts say that the trees have been there since time immemorial.

The *farmhouses* are generally built of stone, but sometimes of timber, and have three or four rooms. The windows, seldom of glass, are most frequently of paper. They have iron stoves in one of the rooms and fireplaces in the rest, always without dampers. The roofs are covered with boards, and the crevices and chinks are filled up with clay. Other farm buildings are covered with straw. The fences are like our common ones.

Road Shrines. There are several crosses put up by the roadside, which is parallel to the shores of the river. These crosses are very common in Canada, and are put up to excite devotion in the travellers. They are made of wood, five or six yards high, and proportionally broad. In that side which faces the road is a square hole, in which they place an image of our Savior, the Cross, or of the Holy Virgin with the Child in her arms, and before that they put a piece of glass, to prevent its being spoiled by the weather. Everyone who passes by crosses himself, raises his hat or does some other bit of reverence. Those crosses which are not far from churches, are very much adorned, and they put up about them all the instruments which they think the Jews employed in crucifying our Savior, such as a hammer, tongs, nails, a flask of vinegar, and perhaps many more than were really used. A figure of the cock, which crowed when St. Peter denied our Lord, is commonly put at the top of the cross.

The country on both sides was very delightful to-day, and the fine state of its cultivation added greatly to the beauty of the scene. It could really be called a village, beginning at Montreal and ending at Quebec, which is a distance of more than one hundred and eighty miles, for the farmhouses are never above five arpens and sometimes but three apart, a few places excepted. The prospect is exceedingly beautiful when the river flows on for several miles in a straight line, because it then shortens the distances between the houses, and makes them form one continued village.

Women's Dress. All the women in the country without exception, wear caps of some kind or other. Their jackets are short and so are their skirts, which scarcely reach down to the middle of their legs. Their shoes are often like those of the Finnish women, but are sometimes provided with heels. They have a silver cross hanging down on the breast. In general they are very industrious. However I saw some, who, like the English women in the colonies, did nothing but prattle all day. When they have anything to do within doors, they (especially the girls) commonly sing songs in which the words *amour* and *coeur* are very frequent. In the country it is usual that when the husband receives a visit from persons of rank and dines with them, his wife stands behind and serves him, but in the town the ladies are more distinguished, and would willingly assume an equal if not superior position to their husbands. When they go out of doors they wear long cloaks, which cover all their other clothes and are either grey, brown or blue. Men sometimes make use of them when they are obliged to walk in the rain. The women have the advantage of being in a *déshabillé* under these cloaks, without anybody's perceiving it.

We sometimes saw *windmills* near the farms. They were generally built of stone, with a roof of boards, which together with its wings could be turned to the wind. . . .

August the 3rd

Trois Rivières is a little market town which had the appearance of a large village. It is, however, numbered among the three great towns of Canada, which are Quebec, Montreal, and Trois Rivières. It is said to lie in the middle between the two first, and is thirty French miles distant from each. The town is built on the north side of the St. Lawrence River on a flat, elevated sandbar and its location is very pleasant. On one side the river passes by, and it is here an English mile and a half broad. On the other side are fine grain fields, though the soil is very sandy. In the town are two churches of stone, a nunnery, and a house for the friars of the order of St. Francis. This town is likewise the seat of the third governor in Canada, whose house is also of stone. Most of the other houses are of timber, a single story high, tolerably well built, and stand very much apart. The streets are crooked. The shore here consists of sand, and the rising grounds along it are pretty high. When the wind is very violent here, it raises the sand, and blows it about the streets, making it very troublesome to walk in them. The nuns, who are about twenty in number, are very ingenious in all kinds of needlework. This town formerly flourished more than any other in Canada, for the Indians brought their goods to it from all sides; but since that time they have gone to Montreal and Quebec, and to the English, on account of their wars with the Iroquois, or Five Nations, and for several other reasons, so that this town is at present very much reduced by it. Its present inhabitants live chiefly by agriculture, though the neighboring ironworks may serve in some measure to support them. About an English mile below the town a great river flows into the St. Lawrence River, but first divides into three branches, so that it appears as if three rivers emptied themselves there. This has given occasion to call the river and this town, Trois Rivières (the Three Rivers). . . .

August the 12th

Mixed Blood. This afternoon I and my servant went out of town, to stay in the country for a couple of days that I might have more leisure to examine the plants which grow in the woods here, and the nature of the country. In order to proceed the better, the governor-general had sent for an Indian from Lorette to show us the way and teach us what use they make of the wild plants hereabouts. This Indian was an Englishman by birth, taken by the Indians thirty years ago when he was a boy and adopted by them according to their custom in the place of a relation of theirs killed by the enemy. Since that time he had constantly stayed with them, become a Roman Catholic and married an Indian woman. He dressed like an Indian, spoke English and French and many of the Indian dialects. In the wars between the French and English in this country, the French Indians made many prisoners of both sexes in the English plantations, adopted them afterwards, and married them to people of the Indian nations. Hence the Indian blood in Canada is very much mixed with European blood, and a large number of the Indians now living owe their origin to Europe. It is also remarkable that a great number of the people they had taken during the war and incorporated with their nations, especially the young people, did not choose to return to their native country, though their parents and nearest relations came to them and endeavored to persuade them to, and though it was in their power to do so. The free life led by the Indians pleased them better than that of their European relations; they dressed like the Indians and regulated all their affairs in their way. It is therefore difficult to distinguish them, except by their color, which is somewhat whiter than that of the Indians. There are likewise examples of some Frenchmen going amongst the Indians and following their mode of life. There is on the contrary scarcely one instance of an Indian adopting the European customs; for those who were taken prisoners in the war always endeavored to return to their own people again, even after several years of captivity, though they enjoyed all the privileges that were ever possessed by the Europeans in America. . . .

Haymaking. Farmers were now busy making hay and getting it in and I was told they had begun about a week ago. The scythes are like our Swedish ones; the men mow and the women rake. The hay was prepared in much the same way as with us, but the tools are a little different. The head of the rake is smaller, has tines on both sides and is a little heavier. The hay is raked into rows; and they also use a kind of wooden fork for both pitching and raking. In so doing, however, a good deal of the hay is left on the field since this does not rake as clean as an ordinary rake. There were no hillocks on these meadows. The hay is taken away in four-wheeled carts drawn by either horses or oxen. The oxen are hitched in such a way as to pull with their horns instead of their shoulders. Some of the hay barns were out on the fields. They have haystacks near most of their meadows, and on the wet ones they make use of conic haystacks. Their grass lots are usually without fences, the cattle being in the pastures on the other side of the woods and cowherds take care of them where they are necessary.

The *grain fields* are pretty large. I saw no ditches anywhere, though they seemed to be needed in some places. They are divided into ridges, of the breadth of two or three yards broad, between the shallow furrows. The perpendicular height of the middle of the ridge, from the level to the ground is near one foot. All the grain is summer sown, for as the cold in winter destroys the grain which lies in the ground, it is never sown in autumn. I found white wheat most common in the fields. There are likewise large fields with peas, oats, in some places summer rye, and now and then barley. Near almost every farm I found cabbages, pumpkins, and melons. The fields are not always sown, but lie fallow every two years. The fallow fields not being plowed in summer the weeds grow without restraint in them and the cattle are allowed to roam over them all season.

There was a superabundance of fences around here, since every farm was isolated and the fields divided into small pastures. It will be difficult to obtain material for these fences when the woods are used up; in the future they will probably have to use hedges for their enclosures. It is a stroke of good fortune though, that there is a large amount of cockspur hawthorn growing in the neighborhood. Happy they who will think of it in time! . . .

The houses in the country are built of stone or wood. The stone houses are not of bricks, as there is not yet any considerable quantity of brick made here. People therefore take what stones they can find in the neighborhood, especially the black slate. This is quite compact when quarried, but shatters when exposed to the air; however, this is of little consequence as the stones stick fast in the wall, and do not fall apart. For want of it they sometimes make their buildings of limestone or sandstone, and sometimes of gray stone. The walls of such houses are commonly two feet thick and seldom thinner. The people here can have lime everywhere in this neighborhood. The greater part of the houses in the country are built of wood, and sometimes plastered over on the outside. The chinks in the walls are filled with clay instead of moss. The houses are seldom above one story high. The windows are always set in the inner part of the wall, never in the outer, unless double windows are used. The panes are set with putty and not lead. In the city glass is used for the windows for the most part, but further inland they use paper. In opening the windows they use hooks as with us. The floors are sometimes of wood and sometimes of clay. The ceiling consists generally of loose boards without any filling, so that much of the internal heat is wasted. In every room is either a chimney or a stove, or both. The stoves have the form of an oblong square; some are entirely of iron, about two feet and a half long, one foot and a half or two feet high, and near a foot and a half broad. These iron stoves are all cast at the ironworks at Trois Rivières. Some are made of bricks or stones, not much larger than the iron stoves, but covered at the top with an iron plate. The smoke from the stoves is conveyed up the chimney by an iron pipe in which there are no dampers, so that a good deal of their heat is lost. In summer the stoves are removed. The roofs are always very steep, either of the Italian type or with gables. They are made of long boards, laid horizontally, the upper overlapping the lower. Wooden shingles are not used since they are too liable to catch fire, for which reason they are forbidden in Quebec. Barns have thatched roofs, very high and steep. The dwelling houses generally have three rooms. The baking oven is built separately outside the house, either of brick or stone, and covered with clay. Brick ovens, however, are rare.

Henry Marie Brackenridge's Life with a French Family, 1792–1795

I was placed in a French or Spanish family [at New Madrid on the Mississippi River] for a couple of weeks, during which time I saw nothing of my guardian. Although it was an agreeable circumstance, to be once more on firm land, and have room to run about, yet I was among strangers, whose language I did not understand, and my fare was not as good as that I might have expected if I had been apprenticed to an anchorite. Coarse black bread, a kind of catfish soup, hot with pepper, and seasoned with garlick, was almost the only food they gave me. When I look back, the time spent at this dreary place seems to be a black speck on my past life. In the mean time, my guardian was probably making preparations for a journey through the wilderness, to the settlements of Upper Louisiana, on the Illinois, as they were called, and I was glad when he came to take me away.

He had procured horses for himself and his guide, and a small poney for me. A supply of provisions was provided, a part packed on each horse, with a coffee pot, tin cups, and a hatchet, the usual outfits of travellers through the wilderness. A blanket for each was all our bedding, and there being no houses on the way, we took our chance for the weather. Many years afterwards, I travelled over the same way, passed the same swamps, and swam the same streams, and a more disagreeable country to travel over cannot easily be found in the United States. Our path lay through an Indian village of Shawanese, who treated us well; but I trembled at the sight of them, having learned to look upon these people as demons. Being on Spanish ground, they would not have molested us, even if they had known that we were not Spaniards. After a week or ten days, we arrived, without any material accident, at the village of St Genevieve, situated on the Mississippi, although not immediately on its banks.

My guardian carried me directly to the house of M. Bauvais, a respectable, and comparatively wealthy inhabitant of the village, and then took his departure the same evening. Not a soul in the village, except the curate, understood a word of English, and I was possessed of but two French words, *oui* and *non*. I sallied into the street, or rather highway, for the houses were far apart, a large space being occupied for yards and gardens by each. I soon found a crowd of boys at play; curiosity drew them around me, and many questions were put by them, which I answered alternately, with the aid of the before mentioned monosyllables, "Where have you come from?" "Yes."—"what is your name?" "No." To the honour of these boys be it spoken, or rather to the honour of their parents who had taught them true politeness—instead of turning me into ridicule, as soon as they discovered I was a strange boy, they vied with each other in showing me every act of kindness.

M. Bauvais was a tall, dry, old French Canadian, dressed in the costume of the place: that is, with a blue cotton handkerchief on his head, one corner thereof descending behind and partly covering the eel skin which bound his hair; a check shirt; coarse linen pantaloons on his hips; and the Indian sandal, or moccasin, the only covering to the feet worn here by both sexes. He was a man of a grave and serious aspect, entirely unlike the gay Frenchmen we are accustomed to see; and this seriousness was not a little heightened, by the fixed rigidity of the maxillary muscles, occasioned by having his pipe continually in his mouth, except while in bed, or at mass, or during meals. Let it not be supposed that I mean to speak disrespectfully, or with levity, of a most estimable man; my object in describing him, is to give an idea of many other fathers of families of the village. Madame Bauvais was a large fat lady, with an open cheerful countenance, and an expression of kindness and affection to her numerous offspring, and to all others excepting her coloured domestics, towards whom she was rigid and severe. She was, notwithstanding, a most pious and excellent woman, and, as a French wife ought to be, completely mistress of the family. Her eldest daughter was an interesting young woman; two others were nearly grown, and all were handsome. I will trespass a little on the patience of the reader, to give some account of the place where I was domiciliated; that is, of the house in which I lived, and of the village in which it was situated.

The house of M. Bauvais was a long, low building, with a porch or shed in front, and another in the rear; the chimney occupied the centre, dividing the house into two parts, with each a fire place. One of these served for dining room, parlour and principal bed chamber; the other was the kitchen; and each had a small room taken off at the end for private chambers or cabinets. There was no loft or garret, a pair of stairs being a rare thing in the village. The furniture, excepting the beds and the looking glass, was of the most common kind, consisting of an armoire, a rough table or two, and some coarse chairs. The yard was enclosed with cedar pickets, eight or ten inches in diameter, and six feet high, placed upright, sharpened at the top, in the manner of a stockade fort. In front, the yard was narrow, but in the rear, quite spacious, and containing the barn and stables, the negro quarters, and all the necessary offices of a farm yard. Beyond this, there was a spacious garden enclosed with pickets, in the same manner with the yard. It was, indeed, a garden—in which the greatest variety, and the finest vegetables were cultivated, intermingled with flowers and shrubs: on one side of it, there was a small orchard containing a variety of the choicest fruits. The substantial and permanent character of these enclosures, is in singular contrast with the slight and temporary fences and palings of the Americans. The house was a ponderous wooden frame, which, instead of being weather-boarded, was filled in with clay, and then white-washed. As to the living, the table was provided in a very different manner from that of the generality of Americans. With the poorest French peasant, cookery is an art well understood. They make great use of vegetables, and prepared in a manner to be wholesome and palatable. Instead of roast and fried, they had soups and fricassees, and gumbos, (a dish supposed to be derived from the Africans) and a variety of other dishes. Tea was not used at meals, and coffee for breakfast, was the privilege of M. Bauvais only.

From the description of this house, some idea may be formed of the rest of the village. The pursuits of the inhabitants were chiefly agricultural, although all were more or less engaged in traffic for peltries with the Indians, or in working the lead mines in the interior. But few of them were mechanics, and there were but two or three small shops, which retailed a few groceries. Poultry and lead constituted almost the only circulating medium. All politics, or discussions of the affairs of government, were entirely unknown: the commandant took care of all that sort of thing. But instead of them, the processions and ceremonies of the church, and the public balls, furnished ample matter for occupation and amusement. Their agriculture was carried on in a field of several thousand acres, in the fertile river bottom of the Mississippi, enclosed at the common expense, and divided into lots, separated by some natural or permanent boundary. Horses or cattle, depastured, were tethered with long ropes, or the grass was cut and carried to them in their stalls. It was a pleasing sight, to mark the rural population going and returning morning and evening, to and from the field, with their working cattle, carts, old fashioned wheel ploughs, and other implements of husbandry. . . . About a quarter of a mile off, there was a village of Kickapoo Indians, who lived on the most friendly terms with the white people. The boys often intermingled with those of the white village, and practised shooting with the bow and arrow; an accomplishment which I acquired with the rest, together with a little smattering of the Indian language, which I forgot on leaving the place.

Such were the place, and the kind of people, where, and among whom, I was about to pass some of the most important years of my life, and which would naturally extend a lasting influence over me. A little difficulty occurred very soon after my arrival, which gave some uneasiness to Madame Bauvais. She felt some repugnance at putting a little heretic into the same bed with her own children. This was soon set right by the good curate, Pere St Pierre, who made a Christian of me, M. and Madame Bauvais becoming my sponsors, by which a relationship was established almost as strong as that formed by the ties of consanguinity. Ever after this, they permitted me to address them by the endearing names of father and mother; and more affectionate, careful, and anxious parents I could not have had. It was such as even to excite a kind of jealousy among some of their own children. They were strict and exemplary Catholics; so indeed, were most of the inhabitants of the village. Madame Bauvais caused me every night to kneel by her side, to say my *pater noster* and *credo*, and then whispered those gentle admonitions which sink deep into the heart. To the good seed thus early sown, I may ascribe any growth of virtue, in a soil that might otherwise have produced only noxious weeds.

But a few days elapsed after my arrival, before I was sent to the village school, where I began to spell and read French before I understood the language. My progress was such, that, in a few weeks, I learned to read and speak the language, and it is singular enough, that half a year had scarcely elapsed before I had entirely forgotten my native tongue, a consequence which had not, most certainly, been foreseen by my father, who expected that I should be possessed of two languages instead of one, and who could not have supposed that I should be sent home a French boy to learn English. So completely had every trace disappeared from my memory, with the exception of the words *yes*, and *no*, that when sent for occasionally to act as interpreter to some stray Anglo-American, the little English boy, *le petit Anglais*, as they called me, could not comprehend a single word beyond the two monosyllables.

Y ESSAYS

Ramón A. Gutiérrez, who teaches Latin American and Chicano history at the University of California, San Diego, has received a prestigious MacArthur grant for his intellectually challenging studies of the history of the Spanish borderlands of North America. In the first essay, he examines patterns of marriage in colonial New Mexico as a way to uncover other patterns of race, class, and gender. R. Cole Harris, a distinguished historical geographer at the University of British Columbia, looks closely in the second essay at French life on the land. Much of what he finds reflects ideas present in Turner's famous essay, but his emphasis on the role of the agricultural market is something that Turner neglected. Since Gutiérrez and Harris have different ways of examining each frontier society, it would be enlightening to consider how Gutiérrez might try to present rural Canada in terms of marriage, race, class, and gender; and to ponder what questions Harris might ask about land use and markets in colonial New Mexico. The categories employed in the study of each society may help explain where each essay falls in the debate over the impact of European traditions and frontier adaptations.

Honor and Marriage in New Mexico

RAMÓN A. GUTIÉRREZ

The ways in which societies organize marriage provide us an important window into how economic and political arrangements are construed. When people marry, they forge affinal alliances, change residence, establish rights to sexual service, and exchange property. Besides being about the reproduction of class and power, however, marriage is about gender. The marital exchange of women gives men rights over women that women never gain over men. This feature of marriage provides a key to the political economy of sex, by which cultures organize "maleness" and "femaleness," sexual desire, fantasy, and concepts of childhood and adulthood.

With these theoretical moorings in mind, I present here an essay on the history of marriage in a colonial setting, New Mexico between 1690 and 1846, an environment in which class domination was culturally articulated and justified through hierarchies of status based on race, ethnicity, religion, and gender. My major concern will be to examine the key role that control over marriage choice played in the maintenance of social inequality, focusing on changes in the mode of marriage formation during the period under study—a decline in the incidence of parentally arranged nuptials and an increase in those freely contracted by adolescents on the basis of love and personal attraction. Rather than discussing the roots of these changes abstractly, I will explore how parents and children negotiated their behavior, the disparities of power that constrained their actions, and the ambiguities, tensions, and contradictions within the ideological superstructure that gave historical agency meaning.

Historical Setting

Once the ancient temples of Mexico City had been leveled and cities of gold had failed to materialize, the business of colonizing Mexico's central plateau began. The 1548 discovery of silver at Zacatecas quickly moved the frontier north and set the pace for the establishment of a rapid succession of towns: Guanajuato, Queretaro, San Luis Potosí, Durango. The far north, the areas we know today as New Mexico, California, and Texas, was explored in the first half of the sixteenth century by such men as Álvar Núñez Cabeza de Vaca, Fray Marcos de Niza, and Francisco Vásquez de Coronado. Nonetheless, it remained a fantasy of future enrichment in the Spanish imagination until the end of the century. Then, in 1598, Don Juan de Oñate, the son of one of Zacatecas's wealthiest silver miners, mustered 129 soldiers and together with their dependents ventured into the land of the Chichimecas—the fierce nomadic Indian tribes that had effectively curtailed Spanish expansion north—to establish the Kingdom of New Mexico.

Arriving in August of 1598 armed with the cross of Christ and the sword to impose it, the soldier-settlers and friars quickly set about the task of "civilizing" the Indians through baptism, the introduction of European seeds and livestock, and the imposition of Spanish mores of comportment and dress. To ensure the presumed physical and spiritual well-being of New Mexico's Pueblo Indians, they were divided into 41 *encomiendas* awarded to notables of the conquest. For this "entrustment" to the protection and

Ramón A. Gutiérrez, "Honor Ideology, Marriage Negotiation, and Class-Gender Domination in New Mexico, 1690–1846," *Latin American Perspectives*, 12 (Winter 1985), 81–93, 98–101. Reprinted by permission of the author.

spiritual care of the Spanish, the natives paid dearly in tribute, labor, and, often, lives.

Though "savages" were all the Spaniards saw when they arrived in the Rio Grande Valley, the word is hardly adequate to describe the Indians living there. Since the thirteenth century, the river basin had been occupied by the compact agricultural villages of the Pueblo Indians. The 90 pueblos— so named by the Spanish because their multistoried dwellings resembled Aztec cities—were economically independent, politically autonomous, and best described as city-states. In 1598 the Pueblo population totaled approximately 60,000. Though several nomadic Indian tribes, notably the Apache and Navajo, hunted in the surrounding plains and mountains, their low level of material culture and social organization spared them the yoke of subjugation until the early 1700s.

The years 1598–1680 were brutal ones for the Pueblo peoples. Their food reserves were depleted by the colonists; their lives were disrupted by Spanish labor demands; their religious images were desecrated by the friars and their rituals suppressed. Many saw their kin driven to the point of death; women were raped and children enslaved. In 1680 they formed a confederation and routed the Spanish from the area, a feat that reverberated throughout New Spain and spurred other Indians to similar action. When the fury of the Pueblo Revolt was over, 21 out of 33 Franciscan friars were dead and 380 settlers had lost their lives. The 2,300 white survivors fled south to El Paso (Texas), where they regrouped and remained until 1693.

Don Diego de Vargas was charged with the reconquest of the territory and in 1693 led 100 soldiers, 70 families, and 18 friars to reestablish Spanish presence in Santa Fe. A second Spanish town, Santa Cruz de la Cañada, was founded in 1695, followed by Albuquerque in 1706. Colonists who did not live in one of these three towns resided in small dispersed ranches or hamlets situated along the banks of the Rio Grande. The white population in 1700 was perhaps no more than 3,000. The Pueblo population by that year had declined to 15,000.

The period following the reconquest saw a major readjustment in Indian-white relations. Faced with the realization that there was a limit to the exploitation the Pueblo would tolerate and that they would not be cowed into abandoning their native religious beliefs easily, the crown abolished the encomienda and replaced it with the *repartimiento*, a less onerous rotational labor levy. New Mexico's governors were ordered to observe Indian rights strictly, and the martyrdom of their brothers impressed on the friars that their evangelical zeal would have to be tempered.

But the problem of extracting labor and wealth from the native population in its various forms remained. The revolt had not altered the practice of using political office as a vehicle for personal enrichment. Someone still had to construct the imposing mission compounds that were to dot the landscape, and the aristocracy's sense of preeminence was still dependent on the labor of others. For these ends, then, a new enemy was necessary. The "Apaches"—as the Spanish called all the nomadic Indians whose hunting grounds bordered on the agricultural settlements of the river basin

(Jicarilla, Mescalero, Navajo, Ute, and Comanche)—were quickly defined as Satan's minions; this status made them eligible for "just war." Scores of men, women, and particularly children were brought into Spanish villages enslaved as prisoners of war. Some *genízaros*, as these detribalized Indians became known, were retained in local households for the performance of domestic tasks while others were traded for luxury goods in the mining centers of northern New Spain. The growth of this commerce in captives during the eighteenth century was directly responsible for the constant warfare the kingdom's colonists were to experience.

In this environment, the Spanish colonists of the post-reconquest period fashioned a society that they perceived as ordered hierarchically by honor, a prestige system based on principles of inherent personal worth. Honor was a complex gradient of status that encompassed several other measures of social standing such as descent, ethnicity, religion, profession, and authority over land. The summation and ordering of these statuses and the pragmatic outcome of evaluations of honor resulted in the organization of society into three broadly defined groups: the nobility, the landed peasantry, and the genízaros.

The status hierarchy did not completely encompass class standing as structured by relations of production. The Pueblo Indians on whose labor and tribute the colonists so heavily relied fell outside the groups to whom honor mattered and refused to accept, cherish, and validate the ideals by which Spanish society organized its interactions. From the colonists' point of view, the physical tasks the Pueblo Indians performed were intrinsically dishonorable and conquest by a superior power itself dishonoring. Obviously, the Pueblo did not consciously share this view. In colonial New Mexico, honor and class were nevertheless interdependent. Social power ultimately gained its effectiveness from the combination of the two.

The nobility consisted of 15–20 families that intermarried to ensure their continued dominance. Their sense of aristocracy was rooted in the legally defined honor granted to the kingdom's colonizers by King Phillip II in their 1595 charter of incorporation. As the colony developed, nobility gained a broader social meaning and was claimed by individuals who acquired large amounts of land, by military officials, and by bureaucrats—wealth and power acting as the determinants of intragroup mobility. By comparison with the titled peerage of central Mexico, New Mexico's nobility at best enjoyed the life of a comfortable gentry. Yet, perhaps because of its isolation— and the attendant belief that it was a cultural oasis in a sea of barbarism— New Mexico's aristocracy considered itself second to none. Bearing Old Christian ancestry, harboring pretensions of purity of blood, and eschewing physical labor, it reveled in its rituals of precedence, in ostentatious display of lavish clothing and consumption of luxury goods, in respectful forms of address and titles. Needless to say, such habits were buttressed by force of arms, wealth, and a legal superstructure premised on the belief that the social order was divinely ordained.

Landed peasants who were primarily of mestizo origin but considered themselves "Spaniards" were next in the hierarchy of honor. They had been recruited for the colonization of New Mexico with promises of land, and in 1700 all enjoyed rights to *merced*, a communal land grant consisting of private irrigated farmlands, house plots, and commons for livestock grazing. By 1800, the progressive subdivision of private plots had resulted in parcels too small for subsistence. Under these circumstances, owners of morseled holdings increasingly turned to wage labor. Their ranks were swelled by persons who had not gained access to land as part of their patrimony. Though the land area of New Mexico may seem boundless, it was constrained by limited water sources, by the previous and competing water and land claims of the Pueblo Indians, and by the resistance to geographic expansion offered by hostile tribes.

Lowest in prestige, dishonored and infamous because of their slave status, were the genízaros, a diverse group of Indians who resided in Spanish towns and performed the community's most menial and degrading tasks. Between 1694 and 1849, 3,294 genízaros entered Hispanic households. Early in the seventeenth century, New Mexicans had been granted the privilege of warring against infidel Indians and retaining them in bondage for ten years as compensation for the costs of battle. Though many genízaros remained slaves much longer, they were customarily freed at marriage. Lack of access to land and the development of emotional dependencies on their masters, by whom in most cases they had been raised, meant that even after manumission genízaros had few options for social mobility. Remaining in the household and employment of their former owners was common.

Genízaros (from the Turkish *yeni*, "new," and *cheri*, "troops") were truly New Mexico's shock troops against the infidel. Stigmatized by their former slavery, lacking kinship ties to the European community, and deemed devious because of their lack of mastery of Spanish, the increasing numbers of free genízaros were segregated in special neighborhoods such as Santa Fe's Barrio de Analco or congregated in new settlements such as Belén (1740), Abiquiu (1754), Ojo Caliente (1754), and San Miguel del Vado (1794). All of these genízaro communities—communities now of landed peasants of genízaro origin—were strategically established along the Indian raiding routes and were to serve Spanish settlements as buffers against attack.

The Ideology of Honor

Honor was a polysemic word embodying meanings at two different but fundamentally interrelated levels, one of status and one of virtue. Honor was first and foremost society's measure of social standing, ordering on a single vertical continuum those persons with much honor and differentiating them from those with little. Excellence manifested as territorial expansion of the realm was the monarchy's justification for the initial distribution of honor. Yet, "the claim to honor," as Julian Pitt-Rivers notes, "depends always in the last resort, upon the ability of the claimant to impose himself. Might is the basis of right to precedence, which goes to the man who is bold enough to enforce his claim." The children of the conquistadores gained their parents' honor through ascription and maintained and enhanced it through behavior deemed appropriate to a highly esteemed person.

The second dimension of honor was a constellation of virtue ideals. Dividing the community horizontally along prestige-group boundaries, honor-virtue established the status ordering among equals. Definitions of virtue were gender-specific. Males embodied honor (the sentiment of honor) when they acted *con hombría* (in a manly fashion), exercised authority over family and subordinates, and esteemed honesty and loyalty. Females possessed the moral and ethical equivalent of honor, *vergüenza* (shame), if they were timid, shy, feminine, virginal before marriage and afterwards faithful to their husbands, discreet in the presence of men, and concerned for their reputations. Infractions of the rules of conduct dishonored men and were a sign of shamelessness in women. Shamelessness accumulated around the male head of household and dishonored both the family as a corporate group and all its members.

The maintenance of social inequality was central to the way in which status and virtue were defined to interact, the aim being the perpetuation of the nobility's preeminence. An aristocrat of however low repute was always legally more honorable than the most virtuous peasant. Because precedence at the upper reaches of the social structure guaranteed more material and symbolic benefits, it was usually among the nobility and elites that the most intense conflicts over honor-virtue occurred. Family feuds and vendettas were frequently the way sullied reputations were avenged and claims to virtue upheld.

Consensus seems to have existed among New Mexicans of Hispanic origin regarding the behavior deemed virtuous and worthy of honor. Among the nobility and the peasantry alike, men concerned for their personal and familial repute, judged by how well they resolved the contradictory imperatives of domination (protection of one's womenfolk from assault) and conquest (prowess gained through sullying the purity of other men's women), hoped to minimize affronts to their virtue, thereby maintaining their status. Female seclusion and a high symbolic value placed on virginity and marital fidelity helped accomplish this aim.

Yet only in aristocratic households, where servants and retainers abounded, could resources be expended to ensure that females were being properly restrained and shameful. The maintenance of their virtue was made easier because genízaro women could be forced into sexual service. As slaves they were dishonored by their bondage and could therefore be abused without fear of retaliation, for as one friar lamented in his 1734 report to the viceroy, Spanish New Mexicans justified their rapes saying: "an Indian does not care if you fornicate with his wife because she has no shame [and] . . . only with lascivious treatment are Indian women conquered."

Inequalities in power and status kept peasant men from honorably challenging aristocrats. Both because of this disparity in status and because of the excesses of the nobility in asserting their virility, ideals of female virtue were as intensely cherished by peasants. Manuel Alvarez, the United

States consul in Sante Fe, alluded to this when he wrote in 1834: "the honorable man (if it is possible for a poor man to be honorable) has a jewel in having an honorable wife." Among the peasantry, gender prescriptions undoubtedly had to be reconciled with the exigencies of production and reproduction of material life. The required participation of all able household members in planting and the harvest meant that there were periods when constraints on females of this class were less rigorously enforced. Juana Carillo of Santa Fe admitted as much in 1712 when she confessed enjoying the affections of two men her father had hired for their spring planting. Again, in households where men were frequently absent, such as those of soldiers, muleteers, shepherds, and hunters, cultural ideals were less rigid. The fact that females supervised family and home for large parts of the year, staved off Indian attack, and cared for the group's public rights meant that it was difficult for them to lead sheltered and secluded lives. It was not uncommon for these women to lament that they had been assaulted, raped, or seduced while their husbands or fathers were away from home.

Honor and Marriage

Marriage was the most important ritual event in the life-course, and in it the honor of the family took precedence over all other considerations. The union of two properties, the joining of two households, the creation of a web of affinal relations, the perpetuation of a family's symbolic patrimony—its name and reputation—were transactions so important to the honor-status of the group that marriage was hardly a decision to be made by minors. The norm in New Mexico was for parents to arrange nuptials for their children with little or no consideration of their wishes. Filial piety required the acceptance of any union one's parents deemed appropriate or advantageous.

The 1786 marriage of Francisco Narpa and Juana Lorem in Sandia provides a glimpse of the familial motivations involved in an arranged union. Appearing before the provincial ecclesiastical judge to explain how he had married, Francisco reported: "Having agreed with Juana Lorem that we wished to marry, I asked her grandmother Tomasa Cibaa, and with her permission and that of her relatives, I married." Juana Lorem had a slightly different understanding of the events that led up to her marriage to Francisco. She told the judge, "It is totally false that I agreed to marry the said Francisco. I never wanted to marry the said Francisco. But for fear of my grandmother Tomasa Cibaa I contracted the marriage." Finally, Tomasa Cibaa explained: "I ordered my granddaughter Juana to marry the said Francisco Narpa because he is moderately wealthy, and it is true that I pressured Juana to appear before the priest [for the matrimonial investigation] and say nothing that might provoke questioning." The details of this marriage surface as part of an ecclesiastical investigation into the allegation that the union was incestuous. Francisco had fathered a child by Maria Quieypas, Juana's mother, and therefore his marriage to Juana was invalid. The marriage was annulled, dotal and patrimonial property were confiscated, the three were publicly flogged, and Narpa was exiled from New Mexico.

Of course, I do not wish to suggest that arranged marriage was an inflexible rule. The extent to which parental preference for arranged marriage could be enforced was mediated both by the person's status and by each family's particular fertility history. The number of children in a family, their birth order, and their sex dictated the options available to parents to secure their son or daughter an acceptable or advantageous spouse. These and other variables also conditioned the range of filial responses possible— whether a son or daughter acted as if bound by duty or sentiment or resisted or attempted to manipulate the situation so as to appease everyone's concerns.

From a father's point of view, a round of poker is an excellent metaphor for the way in which limited resources (the patrimony) were manipulated to maximize the gains associated with marital alliance. Pierre Bourdieu has applied this metaphor to the marriage of a family's children. Success at enhancing and perpetuating the family's status is based not only on the hand one is dealt (whether the nuptial candidate is an only child, the eldest of several sons, or the youngest of many daughters) but also the skill with which one plays it (bids, bluffs, and displays). The patrimony was the material resource a father had to apportion among its claimants at strategic moments to maximize reproductive success. Although legally every legitimate child in New Mexico was entitled to an equal share of this wealth, practice varied by class. Aristocratic holders of large landed estates preferred male primogeniture as a way of keeping their property intact. The eldest son, as the heir to the household head's political rights over the group and the person responsible for the name and reputation of the family, was the individual to whom a disproportionate amount of parents' premortem resources was committed. As first in importance, even if preceded by older sisters, he could not suffer a misalliance without lowering the entire family's public rating and diminishing the possibilities of securing honorable partners for his unmarried brothers and sisters. Therefore, he was the child of whom parents expected the most and the child disciplined most severely to ensure obedience but allowed the greatest excesses in other matters. He was also perhaps the most predisposed to bow to duty.

If the eldest son had married well and the family's position had thus been attended to, filial participation in the marriage process was tolerated in subsequent cases. Because younger sons were unlikely to fare as well in the acquisition of marital property and could expect only enough money and movable goods to avoid misalliance, fathers might be more open to their suggestions regarding eligible brides.

Daughters of the nobility were a potential liability on the marriage market, dissipating the material and symbolic patrimony by having their dowries absorbed into their husbands' assets. Every attempt would be made to dispose of nubile females as quickly as possible and at minimal expense. If a daughter experienced a prenuptial dishonor, such as the loss of her virginity, additional resources would have to be committed to secure her an appropriate mate. Thus large amounts of time and energy were spent ensuring that a maiden's sexual shame was being maintained. Undoubtedly, the result was that a woman's freedom to object to a marriage, to express her desires in spouse selection, was more limited than that of her brothers.

Peasants enjoying rights to communal land grants practiced partible inheritance. Sons were given their share of the family's land when they took a bride and were assigned a certain number of *vigas* ("beams"—a way of dividing the space in a house) in the parental home. If space limitations prohibited such a move, assistance was given in the addition of rooms to the house or the construction of a separate edifice in the immediate vicinity. For females, premortem dowries usually consisted of household items and livestock. Daughters seldom received land rights at marriage because parents fully expected the husband's family to meet this need. The authority relations springing from this mode of property division meant that parental supervision over spouse selection and its timing was as rigidly exercised as among the nobility.

For landless freed genízaros, the institution of marriage itself was of no consequence. Many preferred concubinage, as they held no property to transmit and the alienation from their Indian kin that accompanied enslavement made the issue of perpetuation of family name irrelevant. Wage earners and landless peasants were in a similar situation with regard to marriage. Once children were old enough to leave the familial hearth in search of a livelihood, parental control over their behavior all but ceased. Their only concern in the timing of marriage, if in fact they chose matrimony for cultural reasons, was the necessity to accumulate a nest egg with which to establish a conjugal residence.

Marriage and the Church

The settlement of the Kingdom of New Mexico was a joint venture of church and state. In all the remote areas of the Spanish empire in which civilization was to be brought to the Indians, it was by the religious orders, through the institution of missions, that the task was accomplished. Acting as defenders of the Indians, as guardians of community piety and morality, and as a counterpoint to the power of the state, the church at one and the same time legitimated and buttressed the colonial system and challenged certain tenets of its rule. Nowhere was this tension among the authorities of God, of the family head, and of the state clearer than on the issue of marriage.

Until 1776, the Catholic church enjoyed exclusive jurisdiction over the ritual, sacramental, and contractual aspects of matrimony. Ecclesiastical law, articulated as a theory of impediments to marriage, was dominated by two concerns: the prohibition of incest and the determination of the exercise of free will. The latter principle drew on the Roman legal tradition that a nuptial contract was valid only if the parties had given free and absolute consent. The use of persuasion and coercion to arrange marriages of children could place patriarchs in direct confrontation with the church and its clerics.

Arranged marriage was a complex issue for the church. Scripture and canon law were fraught with ambiguities and contradictions on the matter. Christian ideology reinforced the honor code regarding the obedience and personal subordination children owed their parents. "Honor your father and mother," ordered the fourth commandment. "Children, obey your parents in the Lord," enjoined St. Paul in his Epistle to the Ephesians (5:22). The church maintained that the law of nature bound parents and children in a relationship that entailed reciprocal rights and obligations. The authority of man over his wife, children, and servants emanated from God's power over creation, and therefore his was the right to guide and discipline children as necessary. Filial submission, St. Paul promised, would be reciprocated with paternal love, protection, and guidance.

But the vexing question clerics were obliged to ask, in the case of marriage, was when paternal guidance and filial obedience simply became coercion. The issue was of some importance because forced marriages, or those contracted under duress, were invalid. Matrimony was the sacramental union of free will based on mutual consent. Ideally it was the work of God, and "what God has joined together, let no man separate."

The autonomy of individual will, responsibility, and conscience in undertaking marriage was central to Catholic thought. In arranged marriages, in which conflicts between obedience to parents and obedience to one's conscience existed, the will of the individual was to take precedence. The scriptural basis for limits on the authority of the father and the freedom of Christ's message rested in the following: "Call no man your father upon the earth: for One is your Father, which is in heaven" (Matthew 23:9). And again (Matthew 10:34–37):

> Think not that I am come to send peace on earth: I came not to send peace, but a sword. For I am come to set a man at variance against his father, and the daughter against her mother, and the daughter-in-law against her mother-in-law. And a man's foes shall be they of his own household. He that loveth father or mother more than me is not worthy of me: and he that loveth son or daughter more than me is not worthy of me.

A mechanism for the determination that a person was marrying freely existed in canon law. If the slightest hint of coercion surfaced, the local priest had the power to remove the candidate from his/her home for isolation from parental pressures. Once the person's wishes became known, the priest was legally bound either to marry the person, even against parental wishes, or to prohibit a forced union. Don Salvador Martínez of Albuquerque, for example, availed himself of ecclesiastical intervention when he sought Vicar Fray Manuel Roxo's help in his 1761 matrimonial bid for Doña Simona Baldes. Though Martínez had twice asked for Doña Simona's hand in marriage, his proposals had been ignored. Moved by the evidence, the vicar sequestered Doña Simona, who admitted she wanted to be Martínez's bride. The marriage occurred despite parental objections, which may have been due to a gross age difference. Don Salvador was a 62-year-old widower; Doña Simona was only 19.

The freedom that the Catholic church might grant the sexes in the selection of conjugal mates formed the legal foundation for the subversion of parental authority, but, as the experience of all areas of the Spanish colonial empire testifies, the law and its execution were two very different matters. It was not uncommon for clerics charged with the interpretation and execution of canon law to enforce it selectively or to bend its dictates to avoid misalliances or subversion of the social order. If a friar believed an arranged marriage was a good match, he might uphold parental prerogatives and rationalize that the natural authority of a father over his children was in full accord with the will of God.

A variant of such an alliance between priest and parents occurred in Santa Fe in 1710. María Belasquez and Joseph Armijo appeared before Fray Lucas Arebalo that year claiming that her parents would not allow her to marry Joseph. They asked the friar to take María into his custody so that she could express her "true" wishes. María was sequestered but was returned to her father shortly after Joseph left the rectory. Joseph immediately appealed to the provincial eccesiastical judge, who agreed that Fray Lucas had not upheld the marriage canons of the Council of Trent. The two were sequestered anew and were finally joined in wedlock after affirming their desire to be husband and wife.

From the evidence in the ecclesiastical archives, "absolute" legal liberty to choose a spouse meant, in fact, freedom to select a mate from *within* one's class and ethnic group. No examples exist in the Archives of the Archdiocese of Santa Fe of clerics' sanctioning a cross-class marriage over parental objections. The church might subvert the particular authority of parents, but it would not subvert the social order at large. . . .

Social Change

From the years following the reconquest to the early 1770s, the Kingdom of New Mexico was peripheral to the empire. Isolated on the northern margins of New Spain, the colony's only link to "civilization" was a yearly mule train to Mexico City, which traveled over several thousand miles of territory inhabited by hostile Indians. New Mexico contained no significant mineral deposits, its population's material culture was rudimentary, and its cash-crop production (wheat, cotton, corn, pine nuts) was insignificant. In fact, had the Franciscan order not pleaded passionately before the crown for the privilege of converting New Mexico's Indians, colonists might never have been sent there in the first place.

The isolation of the province slowly began to crumble in the 1760s. Frightened by the increasing levels of Russian, Anglo-American, and French encroachment into Texas, New Mexico, and California, King Charles III ordered a series of economic, military, and administrative reforms, commonly known as the Bourbon reforms, to safeguard the territory.

The reform project began in 1765 when the Spanish Royal Corps of Engineers was sent to the northern frontier of New Spain to map the area thoroughly, to identify its mineral and hydraulic resources, to assess the feasibility of textile production, to propose methods for increasing agricultural production, and to outline the military changes necessary to fortify the frontier. On the basis of the expedition's recommendations, northern New Spain was reorganized in 1776 into one military and administrative unit called the Internal Provinces. New presidios were constructed to ward off foreign attack, and vigorous campaigns were staged to subdue the "Apaches," who made trade and communication difficult. It was precisely in this period that permanent settlements were finally established in California, the first mission being built in 1769 at San Diego.

The crown believed that New Mexico could be retained as part of the empire only through fuller integration into the market economy centered in Chihuahua. To achieve this aim, trade and travel restrictions were abolished, New Mexican products were given sales tax exemptions, and agricultural specialists, veterinarians, and master weavers were sent to the area to upgrade local production and improve the competitive position of the kingdom's products. Within a few years the frequency of mule trains to and from Chihuahua increased, money began to circulate more widely, and new colonists from north-central Mexico migrated into the area.

Imperial economic reforms coincided with a period of demographic growth in New Mexico, which resulted in intense land pressure. Between 1760 and 1820, the Spanish and mixed-blood population of New Mexico grew from 7,666 to 28,436. By the 1780s, many of the land grants to the initial colonists were insufficient for subsistence. A few new *mercedes* were conceded in the late 1780s, but not enough to meet the population's needs. Governor Fernando de la Concha noted this in his 1796 report to the commandant of the Internal Provinces and estimated that there were 1,500 individuals without land to till. The inevitable upshot of this situation was the expansion of wage labor. A comparison of the occupational structures of the kingdom in 1790 and 1827 reflects this expansion of wage laborers. In 1790, Albuquerque had an adult working population of 601. Farmers constituted 65 percent (391), 25 percent (151) were craftsmen, and 10 percent (58) were day laborers. By 1827, 610 persons were listed as full-time workers: 66 percent (397) were farmers, 14 percent (85) craftsmen, and 19 percent (113) day laborers. The 1790 census of Santa Fe listed 413 individuals with occupations. Farmers represented 85 percent (350), craftsmen 7 percent (28), and day laborers 8 percent (34). By 1827, of 846 workers, 55 percent (467) were farmers, 12 percent (101) craftsmen, and 31 percent (264) day laborers. An expansion of the day-laborer category in both size and proportion also occurred in Santa Cruz during this period. The end result of the Bourbon reforms and the land pressure that accompanied them was the expansion of socially autonomous forms of labor and increased mobility for a significant portion of the population.

To complete the picture of changes that occurred in the last quarter of the eighteenth century, we must also examine church-state relations as they affected New Mexico. During the reign of Charles III many of the formal aspects of the Patronato Real, the partnership between church and state that had been so effective in the colonization of the Americas, were abolished. The religious orders, perceived as independent and powerful because of their relationship to the indigenous population, were first to lose their privileged status. In New Mexico, where the Franciscan friars and the area's governors had battled incessantly since the 1600s over the extent to which each could exploit Indian land and labor, the Bourbon attack on clerical rights put an end to the feud. The missions were gradually secularized; where 30 friars had administered the sacraments in 1760, by 1834 none remained.

The loosening of the Franciscans' grip on the population of New Mexico, part and parcel of the growth of secularism and the diffusion of rationalism throughout Europe and its colonies, bred an indifference toward moral theology, the scriptures, and the authority of priests. One of the first changes one notes in this increasingly secular society is a linguistic change in the ecclesiastical marriage records. Whereas between 1690 and 1790 most individuals married ostensibly "to save my soul," "to serve God and no other reason," or motivated by similar religious convictions, after 1790 nuptial candidates are moved by "the growing desire we mutually have" and by "the urges of the flesh, human wretchedness and the great love we have for each other." Increasingly, individuals mention personal desires such as love as the reason for marriage.

The Bourbon reforms and the growth of a landless population dependent on wage labor for its reproduction had increased social differentiation. This in turn brought into open question the ideological consensus that had formerly existed between the nobility and the landed peasants regarding ascribed honor as a sign of social status premised on family origin and control over means and instruments of production. For free genízaros, mestizos who could not boast of "Spanish" origin, and landless peasants, honor was of little material consequence. Their social status was obtained primarily through individual achievement; under such circumstances patriarchal control over marriage formation was of no functional significance. After all, parental sanction for arranged marriage was effective because familial honor carried with it property and social privileges. Once children were able with their own wages to accumulate the necessary resources to establish a household, and could not in any way count on significant inheritance of property, generational relations were placed on a new footing.

Examining the period from 1690 to 1848, the major change that occurred in marriage formation was an increased preference for unions based explicitly on romantic love over those arranged by parents pursuing economic considerations. This change was not sudden; it was an ongoing process. Love matches were possible from the earliest days of Spanish settlement but occurred infrequently among the landed classes concerned for the perpetuation of their patrimonies. Children had plenty of parental counsels, ballads, folktales, laws, and sermons to make them realize the disastrous consequences of placing desires over reason.

The history of marriage in a colonial social formation such as New Mexico reveals the centrality of patriarchal control for generational, gender, and class forms of domination. Arranged marriages that enhanced honor provided the nobility and the landed peasantry with a tool by which to protect their status in an unequal society. The various ideologies by which gender and class hierarchies were comprehended and legitimated, however, were not monolithic and static. The partnership between the church and state so instrumental in the conquest of Latin America created distinct views on the meaning of marriage. Though the positions of church and state frequently converged, differences between them enabled children to challenge parental authority without danger to the social order. Similarly, the meanings attached to the system of status and prestige varied by class and changed in response to larger economic forces that themselves transformed relations of production and the power relations between church and state. By the 1800s, the material underpinnings of the honor code had been eroded, creating the conditions that allowed individual urges such as romantic love to exert greater influence on marriage formation.

The French in Rural Canada

R. COLE HARRIS

The condition of rural life in the middle-latitude New World colonies of Europe in the seventeenth and to some extent in the eighteenth centuries presented a fundamental geographical contrast with the mother countries that depended less on differences in climate, flora, fauna, or topography than on the availability of land. Indigenous populations, usually hunters and gatherers, could be pushed aside and vast stretches of new territory opened for settlement. If a forest had to be cleared, sod broken, or marshes drained, this racking labour was usually accomplished; farmland became available and, in comparison with European land, it was relatively cheap. Although land was cheap, European markets were far away, and in the seventeenth century European agricultural prices were generally low and falling. Local markets in recently settled colonies were meagre. In these conditions the farmland that Europeans in the seventeenth century slowly won from new middle-latitude settings overseas became less a cog in a commercial economy than a place for ordinary Europeans to live. It was a setting in which European material life and social values would be reproduced but, given the sudden availability of land and the characteristic weakness of the agricultural market, reproduced in drastically simplified and relatively egalitarian societies. In the eighteenth century the rate of European population growth increased, agricultural prices improved, colonial populations grew, and markets for New World grain and animal products became larger and more lucrative. Agricultural land values rose, agriculture became more centrally commercial, and socio-economic differentiation increased as those in position to take advantage of rising land prices and improved markets did so. But even in the eighteenth century there were pockets of New

R. Cole Harris, "The Extension of France into Rural Canada," in *European Settlement and Development in North America: Essays on Geographical Change in Honour and Memory of Andrew Hill Clark*, 27–45, ed. James R. Gibson, 1978. Reprinted by permission of University of Toronto Press.

World settlement where land was relatively cheap and agricultural markets poor. South Africa beyond the Cape was one such setting, much of the westward fringe of New England and the Middle Colonies was perhaps another, and Canada, its tiny population isolated in the interior of a continent and along the climatic margin of wheat cultivation, was a third.

The relationship between society and land in France and in early Canada could hardly have been more different. The France from which a few thousand people emigrated to Canada was densely settled, old, overwhelmingly rural, and profoundly local. There were almost twenty million French people, 90 per cent of them rural; the population density averaged almost forty per square kilometre. Although there had been some fairly recent reclearing of land abandoned during the Hundred Years War, most farmland had been worked for at least four hundred years. Village churches were more likely to be Romanesque than Gothic, and many village houses were also several centuries old. Houses in villages a few miles apart often reflected quite different local styles, each part of a material culture that was the legacy of a long past of a life *in situ*. Whereas intricate networks of cart roads and paths served local areas, ordinary people who did not live close to navigable water were isolated from most outside goods and people by the high cost of overland travel. Life was contained within a web of inherited local custom, some of it codified in *coutumes,* more acquired orally, much transmitted unconsciously by example. Custom differentiated place from place, creating the innumerable *pays* of rural France—those 'medals struck in the image of a people,' the products of retrospective rural societies each living in a restricted territory for a long, long time.

In this old France land was still the basis of wealth and status. Almost everyone who lived in the countryside, even the artisan and the merchant, worked or controlled a little land. The peasants, the great bulk of the people of France, supported not only themselves and their families but also the small minority of prosperous and wealthy Frenchmen. An oppressive royal tax, the *taille,* that bore particularly on the peasantry, furnished half of the national revenue. Peasants' tithes supported abbeys and priories, while seigneurial charges of many kinds supported an increasingly effete nobility whose high living frequently led them into debt to an urban bourgeoisie— the careful managers and unbending creditors to whom many seigneuries were forfeited. Even this increasingly dynamic and powerful bourgeoisie was characteristically tied to land by the country houses it visited in summer, by its revenue from seigneuries and rotures, or by the many loans to peasants and seigneurs that would be turned eventually into cash or land. In this sharply stratified society to be landless was to be virtually without position, a beggar, *déclassé.* Day labourers clung to their garden patches. At the other end of the spectrum the king, as the seigneur from whom all seigneuries were held, was the ultimate landholder. This would not soon be an industrial country; the strength of seventeenth-century France lay in the peasant masses who worked a land that was scarce and valuable, avidly sought, and tenaciously held.

For Frenchmen the interminable Canadian land was wilderness—land without social meaning, without boundaries, and valueless except as it was cleared. The shock of the encounter with such land drove many soldiers and *engagés* (indentured servants) back to France when their terms of service expired. Most of those who stayed in a colony where the labour requirements of the fur trade were soon satisfied took up the lifelong work of clearing and farming as they found French purpose for, and imposed French meaning on, an alien land. There was no reason why they should not think and act in French terms. No radical ideas had propelled them across the Atlantic. Apart from the Indians with whom few settlers were in regular contact, no new population injected different ways of life. Officials administered Canada as an overseas enclave of France. Yet those who farmed along the lower St Lawrence would not reproduce the French rural landscape, if only because in Canada land for agricultural expansion would long be available for the ordinary person. The availability of land broke French rural life out of the restrictions inherent in its fixed landed base and created conditions in which one element of a French legacy—the independent nuclear family on its own land—would be accentuated while others would atrophy.

This basic geographical contrast between a Europe where land was scarce and expensive, and a New World colony where it was not, lasted in Canada through several generations, for whom agricultural markets were poor and agricultural prices were low. There was time to establish a European society within these conditions, time for it to acquire a tradition. The human landscape that began to emerge along the St Lawrence River near Quebec and Montreal in the middle of the seventeenth century was carved out of the fringe of the Canadian Shield in the middle of the nineteenth century. At the heart of this landscape was the farmhouse on a long lot—farm after similar farm in a row along river or road. Each of these farms was the setting for the life of a family, and the circumstances of one family were much like those of another. A setting where land was cheap and markets were poor had provided an admirable base for the expansion of the self-reliant, nuclear household, with very ordinary people establishing families on their own land, and had weakened or eliminated all other elements of the social heritage of French rural life. French rural society had been pared down to a simple remainder not because a fragment of it had crossed the Atlantic but because conditions in rural Canada had exerted strong selective pressures.

The French Background of Immigrants to Canada

Except in Brittany and in parts of the Auvergne, regions from which almost no settlers came to Canada, the nuclear family was the basic unit of French rural life in the seventeenth century. The ideal of rural life, approached by only a few prosperous farmers, was a family secure in its own house and in control of lands yielding enough to avoid debt—in short, a peasant family able to *vivre de la sienne*. For most peasants such independence was quite unrealizable. There were too many people on too little land, agricultural technology was too inflexible, and the exactions of royal treasury, seigneury, and church weighed too heavily on them. Inevitably the ideal was compromised. At worst the family was driven off the land and scattered in a drifting population of beggars. More commonly sons and daughters left home at an early age to become day labourers, apprentices, or servants. In much of France collective constraints on individual agricultural freedom, imposed by the village community, protected the individual family's access to pasture. Access to stubble fields after harvest (*vaine pâture*) and to common pastures and waste lands was closely regulated so that each peasant family might support a cow, perhaps a few sheep. In places, and at times of particular poverty, constraints such as these loomed larger; where life was a little easier the constraints were relaxed, and the family assumed more independence. The primacy of the family could be strikingly expressed on the landscape in the form of the dispersed farmstead, but even where, as in most of France, rural settlement was still agglomerated, the family often closed itself in behind the thick walls of its house, offering a latched door but not a window to the village street and opening out only into its own interior yard. French civil law, too, in all its local variety, built legal walls around the rights and responsibilities of members of the nuclear family.

The essential support of the family was the garden, often tiny, always enclosed, virtually a part of the house to which it was attached; together with farm buildings it went under a single name: *mazure* in Normandy, *mas* in Languedoc. Apart from cereals the garden produced the bulk of the household's foodstuffs—its vegetables, fruits, and poultry, unless they had to be sold to pay debts. In the garden flax, hemp, or even a few vines might be grown, their products intended partly for sale. This crucial, heavily manured plot paid no tithe, only the seigneurial *cens* [quit-rent paid in kind]. For most peasants the garden was more nearly their own land than any other, an enclosed patch where members of the family could plant, harvest, and experiment as they wished. In much of northern France the arable, on the other hand, was worked in a three-course rotation, and individual holdings, scattered unenclosed within large open fields, were subject to the rhythm of the prevailing rotation and were opened to general pasture when the harvest was in. Pastures were few and small, animals scarce, fields underfertilized, and yields low, seldom more than five or six units of grain for each sown, often much less. Most families depended upon the collective regulation of arable and pasture for their survival, and only a prosperous few managed to enclose their land, thereby removing it from some form of collective control. In western France pastures were larger and more numerous, and there were more animals. Here, where standards of living were somewhat higher, many peasants worked their own, enclosed fields, but even the owners of enclosed fields usually depended upon commons in marshes, sparse forests, or wastes nearby. Few peasant families were able to extend the independence that they enjoyed in their gardens over the whole of their agricultural activities. The more prosperous were the more independent. The poor accepted the collective constraints that enabled them, without nearly enough land of their own, to exist on the land.

In all areas and among all peasants it was a struggle to acquire enough land to support the family. Usually the peasantry controlled less than half of the village land, the rest being in the hands of noblemen, churchmen, or the bourgeoisie, who let it to the peasants in various forms of leasehold or sharecropping. The land that the peasants did hold was divided very unequally. In most villages only two or three peasant families controlled enough arable to support a team of horses and a heavy plough. These families of *laboureurs,* well under 10 per cent of the peasantry, held enough land to live on. Most families had far less than the twenty to twenty-five acres that in a three-course rotation, and after many charges, would supply bread for the subsistence needs of a family. These peasants usually depended upon some form of collective control of arable and pasture, and upon supplementary work or rented land. The poorest became artisans, share-croppers, or day labourers working for *laboureurs* or for tenant farmers on the large estates. Those who were a little better off rented land to increase their arable, and a handful of tenant farmers became *gros fermiers* (prosperous tenant farmers) on large estates, and they were the most prosperous of all the peasantry. But these arrangements—the sharecropping whereby the landowner supplied seed, stock, and tools and took half of the product, the renting of leaseholds for usually three, six, or nine years for fixed sums that amounted to about a quarter of the produce, and even the day labouring, which was commonly a means of repaying advances of seed or the use of a team and plough—created their own lines of dependence and, often, their debts. When the harvest was good, the year's charges might be paid; when it was not, debts accumulated, and most peasant families lived under a burden of debt that approached the value of their land and threatened the basis of their livelihood.

Other charges pressed in on the peasant family. Royal taxes—the *taille* and the *gabelle* (salt tax)—took 20 per cent of its gross product. Tithes varied, a tenth here, a twelfth there, usually about 8 per cent and always collected in kind in the field after the harvest. Seigneurial charges varied even more. In Beauvais they were low, about 4 per cent; elsewhere they were usually much higher. In many ecclesiastical seigneuries, and in those cleared relatively recently, *censitaires* (*cens* payers) usually paid a *champart,* an exorbitant charge that amounted to a second tithe. Together all of these charges took a third to a half of the peasant's gross product. In addition, rent for leased land had to be paid, and at least 20 per cent of the grain had to be kept for seed. Even in good years little enough was left.

Living on the edge of misery, deeply in debt, always faced with the spectre of loss of land, the peasant family could count on little outside support. In principle the seigneur was the master of the village, and in the seventeenth century there were still seigneurs who interceded at court on behalf of their peasants, who supported peasant revolts against the crown, and who recruited soldiers from among their dependents. In these cases there were still personal bonds, often of considerable affection, between peasant and seigneur. But the seigneur or his appointee was also judge in the seigneurial court, even of cases in which he was also a plaintiff, and he was invariably a creditor. Especially as the bourgeoisie displaced the older seigneurial nobility, the seigneurial system became increasingly a fiscal system, a source of heavy charges for the *censitaire* and of revenue for the seigneur. The *curé* was usually far closer to the peasants than the seigneur. Cultivating a little land, probably the offspring of a *laboureur,* he was virtually a peasant. In a society of believers he could be the much loved leader of his parish flock, a man who sometimes sided with the peasants against seigneur or royal official, but who could do little to lighten their burdens, and who taught of duty, obedience, and humility. The *assemblée des habitants,* usually the principal men of the village, met after Sunday mass to discuss such issues as church maintenance, common or woodcutting regulations, and, above all, the collection of royal taxes, for the *assemblée* had to appoint local tax assessors and collectors and furnish an annual lump sum to a royal collector. In some areas this village plutocracy exercised considerable power, even serving as a focus for anti-seigneurial feeling. More often it was dominated by the seigneur or his bailiff, but even when it functioned independently the *assemblée* could only apportion burdens originating in circumstances far beyond its control. In such circumstances the peasant family had few defences; there could be little upward mobility and always there was some dropping off as the most vulnerable peasant families slipped into the ranks of the perhaps half-million Frenchmen who wandered and begged.

Death or emigration were other escapes. During the peasant revolts in Normandy in the 1830s some of the dying were said to have assured their *curés* that they died in peace knowing that, finally, they would be exempt from the *taille.* Some two hundred thousand French people worked in Spain. Canada was another alternative, but it was so remote and uninviting that few left with the intention of settling there—a few dozen families, and the women from Paris poor houses sent in the 1660s to be brides. In 1634 Robert Giffard had enticed several families from Mortagne in Perche to his Canadian seigneury of Beauport only by offering each of them a thousand arpents (840 acres) of land and part of the harvest from his own farm in Canada. Most men came to Canada under a temporary contract as soldiers or *engagés.* But such contracts were also escapes that drew if not from the beggars at least from the desperately poor in the lowest strata of the peasantry. The majority of immigrants to Canada were people of this sort. When their contract expired or their regiment was recalled many returned to France, but more than half stayed to form the principal male stock of Canada's rural population. There were also bourgeoisie, clerics, and people of noble blood among the immigrants to Canada. Considered overall, the immigrant population included almost all the elements of French society— minus, perhaps, the upper echelons of each stratum—but the people who settled the countryside came overwhelmingly from among the nearly destitute and virtually landless.

They came from western France, principally from the old provinces of Aunis, Saintonge, and Poitou in the hinterland of La Rochelle, and from eastern Normandy. A good many of the women came from Paris. In the early years, when Rouen was the principal port of embarkation for Canada, about a quarter of the emigrants were Norman. In 1663 they and their children, together with people from adjacent Perche, formed a third of the Canadian population. Later, as commercial connections shifted to La Rochelle and as regiments that had been recruited in the southwest were sent to Canada, most immigrants came from south of the Loire.

These western lands had seen some of the bitterest peasant revolts in seventeenth-century France. In 1639 ten thousand Norman peasants, rising against increases in the *taille* that were forcing more of them off the land and into debtors' prisons, conducted a guerilla war against royal officials and soldiers until they were brutally put down by the king's army. This was a revolt of *nu-pieds*—the desperate poor against the fiscal exactions of the crown—and it originated in the type of people who predominated among those who went to Canada. Like most of France, these western lands were overpopulated. In spite of increasingly severe regulations that reflected the interests of crown and towns, the peasants had depleted the forest so much that in many areas scarcely a tree was over twenty years old. Land values had risen sharply, and nobles and bourgeoisie sought to control, and then to subdivide and sell, common marshes and wastes. The bourgeoisie had penetrated the countryside at the expense of both nobles and peasants. In many villages and parishes the great majority of peasants were landless day labourers, tenants, or sharecroppers on the estates of the bourgeoisie. Yet this was also the area where the deep-seated individualism of the French peasant, centred on the nuclear family, had found its fullest expression. Long before the right was codified in revisions of the *coutume de Normandie* in 1579 and 1585, Norman peasants had the right to enclose, which meant that they could use their land as they wished without the collective constraints of a common three-course rotation and of *vaine pâturage*. Many peasants lived in dispersed farmsteads amid their own fields. In parts of eastern Normandy fewer than 30 per cent of the farm houses were in villages. Even where poverty was most acute and settlement was largely agglomerated, there were prosperous *laboureurs* who lived away from the village on their own land. Along the lower Seine, source of many of the earliest emigrants to Canada, and here and there on the limestone plains nearby, dispersed farmsteads were aligned along riverbank or road while their land stretched behind in *terrior en arête de poisson*.

Rural Settlement in Canada

Most immigrants to Canada came as individuals. In the early years there was an acute shortage of women, but the crown sent almost a thousand women to Canada in the 1660s, and girls in the colony characteristically married at puberty. Later, women married at an average age of twenty or twenty-one, several years under the average age of marriage for their sex in France. These unions created the households of Canada. Even before 1663, when a few seigneurs had brought small groups of immigrants from the same parts of France, only a quarter of Canadian marriages were between people from the same French province. Upsetting the profound localness of French rural life even more than a transatlantic crossing was the mixing from all over western France that took place within the early Canadian household. The effects on accent, tools, diet, clothing, buildings, agricultural methods, and social practices remain to be studied, but there can be no doubt that the overall tendency was towards cultural standardization as the sharp edges of French regional types quickly blurred and merged. And whereas marriage in France took place within sharply defined social categories, this hierarchy of status must have coarsened in Canada because of the initial difficulty of finding any mate, and because of the impossibility among largely destitute people of establishing their precise social fit in a distant society. Men misrepresented themselves to royal officials—calling themselves *laboureurs* when they had been *journaliers* (day labourers) and *journaliers* when they had hardly worked—and they could be equally dissembling when they married.

Most of the *engagés* and demobilized soldiers who married and settled down in Canada became farmers. The fur trade required a small white labour force. Very few people living east of Trois-Rivières ever engaged in it; by 1700 no more than 2 per cent of all Canadian men were in the west in any given year, and by 1710 not more than 12 per cent of them had spent a season there. The towns employed relatively few artisans and labourers. Yet most of the people who settled in Canada did so voluntarily. They had no niche to return to in France, whereas there was land in Canada and the prospect of a farm. With not nearly enough wage labour in the colony to support its population, labour was always expensive; its price, because any employer had to pay enough to counteract the alternative of farming, was a measure of the attraction of land. The royal shipyards in Quebec near the end of the French régime paid several times French wages yet had difficulty holding Canadian workers. 'As he is a Canadian,' wrote the intendant Bigot of a worker who wanted to leave a yard, 'he prefers his liberty to being subject to a clock.'

In the villages of coastal Normandy and along the lower Seine early in the eighteenth century a *journalier* worked four days to earn a single livre. A thousand livres bought two or three arpents of arable land. In Canada at the same date a *journalier* earned one and one-half to two livres a day, and a thousand livres would buy an enormous tract of uncleared land—even an unsettled seigneury—or a farm lot with some fifteen cleared arpents, a one-room cabin, barn, and stable, and sixty arpents of forest. To generalize broadly, wages were at least five times higher in Canada than in France, and the price of cleared land in Canada, even after the high labour cost of clearing it, was five to ten times lower. Uncleared land, valuable in France, was almost worthless in Canada. A parcel of arable land that could be earned by a year's work in Canada might not be earned in a lifetime in France. In Canada almost any man could obtain a forested lot at any time.

Throughout the French régime seigneurs conceded farm lots without initial charge. Because a forested lot would not produce its first small crop until at least eighteen months after clearing began, a destitute immigrant might begin by renting a partially cleared lot that he would pay for with up to a third or half of its harvest. This was a temporary arrangement. The tenant also obtained a lot *en roture.* If crops on his tenancy were good, he might be able to hire a man to begin clearing his own land; at least he could hope to quit the tenancy with the means to survive the first years of clearing. Permanent tenant farmers were uncommon except near Montreal and Quebec and on some seigneurial domains. Sooner or later most immigrants settled on their own farm lots. Sometimes they were no more than forty to fifty arpents in size, more commonly eighty to 120 arpents of land, which in the first years were cleared at a rate of some two arpents annually and then more slowly as farm work demanded more time. After a lifetime of work a man might have thirty or forty arpents of arable and pasture and hold twice as much forest. Often he would have acquired additional lots for his sons, one of whom would take over the family farm, gradually paying off his brothers and sisters for their equal shares in the inheritance.

In this way immigrants who left France in poverty eventually lived on their own land. The long, thin lots fronting on the river were introduced by immigrants from eastern Normandy but the more basic introduction from France was agricultural individualism centred on the nuclear family. After an Atlantic crossing, a period as a soldier or an *engagé,* perhaps a few years as a tenant farmer, and the trauma of clearing the forest, the French peasant's craving for enough land to support a family was satisfied on a farm lot along the St Lawrence River.

Immigrants who crossed the Atlantic to Canada moved towards land but away from markets. The crop varieties and livestock breeds of north-western France that were raised in Canada never penetrated the French market in the seventeenth century, when prices were low, and rarely in the eighteenth century, when prices were better. The West Indies were also remote, twice as far away by water from Quebec as from Boston. Louisbourg, the naval base and fortress built on Cape Breton Island in 1718, provided some market for Canadian agricultural produce, and in the 1720s and 1730s there were fairly regular sales in the West Indies, but in the seventeenth and eighteenth centuries Canada was isolated by a severely continental location from sizeable agricultural markets in the North Atlantic world. Many of the quarter of the Canadian population who lived in the towns kept gardens and livestock, and members of religious orders were supplied directly by domanial farms in church seigneuries. There were regular market days in Quebec, Trois-Rivières, and Montreal. In the fall merchants toured the countryside near Quebec to buy grain. Eventually most habitants sold a little grain and perhaps a calf and some butter every year, but farming developed in Canada within a chronically depressed agricultural market. Wheat prices declined from 1650 to 1720, rising only slowly and irregularly thereafter. Land prices were static and, after a flurry of land trading in the 1660s and early 1670s, there were few sales.

For a time the brutality of the confrontation with the forest obscured both the benefits of cheap land and the constrictions of the market. A Canadian farm of fifteen cleared arpents met the bare subsistence needs of a family. Unless a habitant cleared some of the land while he still lived with his parents, unless he hired labour or bought a partially cleared lot, he and his family would struggle to survive for almost a decade. Such people would fall into debt and would face scurvy each winter. A few might get back to France; many would die. Here, as elsewhere, the initial confrontation of European settlers with the land around the fringe of the Canadian Shield was a devastating experience tempered only somewhat in the early, most bitter years by the availability of fuel, fish, and game. But the habitant was warmer in winter than were most peasants in northwestern France, where wood was so scarce and expensive that bake ovens often burned matted straw. Fish and game, to which French peasants had steadily less legal access and which they poached at greater risk, must have saved many settlers from starvation during their first Canadian winters, and they remained an important part of the Canadian diet long after the stumps had rotted in the first clearings.

If the farm family survived long enough to clear twenty-five or thirty arpents, then certainly by the second farm generation living standards had risen above those of most French peasants. In 1712 the royal engineer Gideon de Catalogne noted that in Canada everybody ate the wheaten bread afforded by only the most prosperous peasants in France; and if Peter Kalm exaggerated when he wrote in 1749 that meat was the dietary staple of rural Canada, his remark does indicate something of the surprise of an educated European, familiar with the almost meat-free diets of most European peasants, at the amount of meat consumed by ordinary people in Canada. Canadian farms themselves reveal the improvement. A farm worked by the son of its first occupant would have thirty or forty arpents of cleared land. It produced one hundred bushels of wheat and some peas, oats, and barley and carried one or two horses, probably a pair of oxen, five or six cows, three or four pigs, some poultry, and a few sheep. There was a kitchen garden, some apple trees, and a sizeable woodlot, and there was access to the river for fishing and to the forest for hunting. This was unspecialized agriculture, characteristic of subsistent farms, but among the French peasantry only a few *laboureurs* and prosperous tenant farmers possessed more.

Yet Canadian farms did not grow much larger. In some Norman parishes a very few *laboureurs* held two hundred arpents of arable and pasture and owned as many as ten work horses and a hundred sheep. Such men were considerable employers of agricultural labour; often they were creditors and money lenders, and their relative wealth and power set them apart in the rural community. No Canadian habitants worked such farms during the French régime, partly because of partible inheritance but principally because there was no market for the output of a larger farm. The function of farming in Canada was to provide for the subsistence of a family; when this need was met, there was little other function. Clearing stopped—only a handful of habitant farms in Canada contained a hundred cleared arpents—and much the same family farm passed from generation to generation. These subsistence farms created no wealth, but the standard of living of most Canadian farmers was comparable to the French *laboureur moyen*—well within the top 10 per cent of the French peasantry. Probably few French peasants aspired to more; they reached the nobility or the urban bourgeoisie only in their fairy tales. After a generation or two, and after much hardship, Canadians had met this limited aspiration. The independence that most French peasants enjoyed in their gardens and craved for in their farms came far closer to being a reality in a colony where there was land to meet a family's subsistence needs.

Higher living standards depended upon available land rather than upon improved techniques. Livestock were as poorly bred as in France; because of the increased use of the forest for forage and browse, manure was even more rarely spread on the arable; and two-course rotations often replaced three. Some habitants planted fields for several years in succession before relegating them to prolonged pasture or fallow—a form of convertible husbandry used on marginal lands in western France. Average seed/yield ratios were as low in Canada as in France, and would likely have been lower but for the high initial yields of newly cleared land. There had been some drift in Canada towards more extensive agricultural practices as cleared land was substituted for scarce labour, but generally the tools and methods of tradition-bound French peasant agriculture in the seventeenth century, little changed since the late Middle Ages, were transplanted in Canada. Applied to more land than most French peasants controlled, they yielded a higher standard of living.

The Canadian habitant's relative position was further enhanced by the absence of royal taxes. Neither the *gabelle* nor the *taille* was assessed in Canada, and the modest royal demand for road work, a *corvée* of two days a year, was long meaningless in a virtually roadless colony. Royal taxes had been discontinued to encourage settlement, not to alleviate the hardships of the common people, but whether or not royal officials clearly understood the change, their absence reflected the difficulty, common to sparsely settled European colonies overseas, of imposing European charges on inexpensive land amid the fluid conditions of new settlement. In the improbable event that royal taxes had been imposed and collected—to have done so would have made Canada an even less populated colony—the Canadian habitant's standard of living would have remained relatively high, for access to land rather than freedom from taxes was the fundamental change in his situation.

The failure of *gabelle* and *taille* to penetrate the countryside of the lower St Lawrence reflects the relative autonomy of the nuclear family in rural Canada. However much the French peasant family valued its independence, it lived within the impinging influence of village, parish, seigneury, town, province, and state. The Canadian habitant's rough ease created a large measure of independence as, to some extent, it did for the families of *laboureurs* in France. In Canada there was another difference. Because there was little market for farm produce there was little commercial pressure on agricultural land. For this reason the whole institutional infrastructure of French rural life was enormously weakened.

The urban bourgeoisie's massive penetration of the French countryside did not take place in Canada. Even in seigneuries near the towns, habitant families held most of the cleared land, and in remote seigneuries they held virtually all of it. Some merchants had a few farm lots and perhaps a seigneury but most of their energy went into the fur trade, and their impact on rural life was negligible. Faced with chronic agricultural overproduction, capital put into the development of large commercial farms was lost unless, as for the domanial farms on some church seigneuries, there was an assured local market. Land speculations were unprofitable. The few farm purchasers were usually families looking for homes rather than merchants looking for profit. Because of high transportation costs, high wages, and official discouragement of colonial manufacturing, sawmilling, gristmilling, and weaving never developed as export industries. Since the Canadian countryside rewarded neither speculations nor entrepreneurship, the bourgeoisie turned its attention elsewhere.

The seigneurial system faced the same difficulty. Except in a few church seigneuries, there were no large farms on seigneurial domains because there was no market for the production. Seigneurial charges were usually lower than in France—approximately 5 to 10 per cent of the habitant's gross income—and many specific charges, including the *champart,* were discontinued. The small population stretched along the St Lawrence River through almost two hundred different seigneuries, most of which remained unprofitable throughout the French régime. Accounts were poorly kept, and rents went uncollected for years. A few seigneuries, particularly Montreal Island which had by far the largest population of any Canadian seigneury and was managed fastidiously by the Sulpicians, began to produce considerable revenues well before the end of the French régime. In them the seigneur or his agents became a considerable presence, and the habitants, like their French counterparts, procrastinated as best they could in the payment of rents. More commonly the French seigneurial system, which even in relatively small French seigneuries required a manager, an attorney and an assistant attorney, a clerk, a sergeant, lieutenants, and even a gaoler, hung over Canada during the French régime in a state of suspended animation. Its legal structure remained essentially intact, but the conditions that would make it profitable and give it life were largely absent until growing population pressure on the seigneurial lowlands of Quebec in the nineteenth century gave it some of its intended teeth.

Parishes also developed weakly, although Roman Catholicism had come with most immigrants to Canada as naturally as the French language. Often the habitants were served by itinerant priests through two or three generations until there were enough people in a given local area to support a *curé*. On occasion they resisted the bishop's plan to establish a *curé*, perhaps because of the cost (although the Canadian tithe was only 1/26th of the grain harvest), perhaps because of the priest's moral censures and increasingly alien French background, and perhaps simply because they did not see the need. In some *côtes* (short lines of settlement) a chapel or church had been built and *fabrique* (church vestry) organized to meet intermittently, long before the *curé* arrived. Such organization strengthened with his coming but never gained the power of the *assemblée les habitants* with which the *fabrique* tended to merge in France. Royal taxes did not have to be apportioned and, except where commons had been laid out in riparian marshes, collective agricultural arrangements did not have to be worked out. Villages were virtually absent. A weak rural economy had not brought them into being, and settlers had seized the opportunity to live on their own farms. Men were expected to serve in the militia, but we cannot yet say how often it drilled or what social role, if any, it played in the countryside.

In all of these ways the heavy French burden of institutional constraints and financial exactions on the nuclear family were lightened in Canada. The family stood more nearly on its own within a civil law, a system of government, and a set of customs, institutions, and social values that had come from France but had lost much of their force or had been differently combined and emphasized in a new setting where land was cheap and markets were meagre. As time passed, clusters of surnames began to appear along the *côtes,* adumbrating the intricate consanguineous ties in the rural society of nineteenth-century Quebec. The *côte* itself became a loose rural neighbourhood, but neither kin nor *côte* ever replaced the social primacy of the nuclear family. Unless he took over the family land, a son would eventually move away and—until early in the nineteenth century, when there was no more land and he was forced into the factory towns of New England, the lumber camps of the Shield, or the slums of Montreal, Trois-Rivières, and Quebec—reproduce the family farm and the relative freedom of his parents.

Rural society in Canada quickly became and long remained remarkably egalitarian. The extremes of the French countryside had been pared down to a common, minimal ease. During the entire French régime in Canada there was not a single really prosperous habitant farmer and hardly, after the first years, a rural family without some cleared land. The great majority of rural families held some thirty to fifty arpents of arable and pasture and a considerable woodlot. Rural Canada had been a clean social slate to which immigrants who settled on the land brought relatively similar backgrounds of poverty. Social differentiation had not been stamped on the countryside from the beginning, and the common exigencies of clearing land and establishing a farm undoubtedly elicited a relatively common response in the first generation of farms along a *côte*. Partible inheritance meant that the sons who took over the family farm took on a debt to his brothers and sisters that perhaps dampened his initiative. In the longer run rural society did not become stratified socially or economically because of the availability of land and the weakness of the commercial economy. Larger farms and genteel living were blocked by inadequate markets. Agriculture became primarily subsistent, clearing stopped when family needs were met, and new *côtes* were opened in response to demographic pressure rather than to increases in the price of wheat. Farm families lived in rough sufficiency, their lives dominated by the seasonal rhythm of the land, not by more powerful people who lived in other ways. Rural life in Canada had not developed the complex, interlocking hierarchy of French social relations. Habitant families worked out their friendships and their feuds, habitant society acquired a folklore derived and modified from French traditions, and many old people must have possessed a deep lore about the ways of the land. These were its complexities. Institutionally Canadian rural society was simple enough: nuclear families spread across the land in small subsistent farms with few and weak institutional constraints on their independence.

Conclusion

The ambition of the ordinary French family to live securely and independently on its own land had found a more common fulfilment in rural Canada than anywhere in France. Farmhouse after small farmhouse lined the St Lawrence River, each on its own land, each much like its neighbour—a simple landscape created by a simple rural society. In a setting where land was accessible but markets were not, the socio-economic complexity of rural France had been pared away until little more than the ordinary nuclear family remained. As long as cheap land was available the self-subsistent independence that had become the way of life of the Canadian habitant family could be perpetuated in *côte* after *côte* as settlement spread through the St Lawrence lowland and into the fringe of the Shield and Appalachian highlands. When land became scarce, as it did early in the nineteenth century, expansion slowed. Land values rose, the young were forced into non-agricultural activities, and society in the older *côtes* became more stratified. In the 1860s an aged Philippe Aubert de Gaspé could still describe the Canadian habitant as *l'homme le plus indépendant du monde*, but when he wrote this the independence of the habitant family was fast nearing its end. After two centuries of agricultural expansion, the safety valve of cheap land along the lower St Lawrence was finally plugged, and the basis of the autonomy of the French-Canadian rural family had been undermined.

Were these Canadian developments put in a Hartzian perspective, it would be said that a French fragment, in this case the poorer peasantry, had worked out its own limited aspirations in a remote colony far from the entrammelling whole of French society.* While it is true that the great majority of immigrants who settled down to farm in Canada came from relatively common backgrounds of poverty in the lower echelons of the French peasantry, the difficulty with Hartz, I feel, is that he assigns far too passive a role to the particular conditions of environment and economy in New World settings. In Canada the facts that land was abundant and

---

* Louis Hartz, *The Founding of New Societies* (New York 1964).

cheap and that the market for agricultural products was poor meant that, whatever seventeenth-century Frenchmen had tried to farm there, the extremes of wealth and poverty of the French countryside would have tended to diminish rapidly and the nuclear family—the basic unit of all French society—would have asserted itself strongly. A society that was a drastic simplification of rural France had emerged in Canada, but the impetus to simplify had come from Canadian conditions rather than from the fragmentation of French society. Some members of the nobility came to Canada and obtained seigneuries, but then neglected them. The members of the bourgeoisie who controlled the commerce of the Canadian towns had not found it worth their while to extend their hold into the countryside. Had agricultural land in Canada been scarce and valuable, and had there been a regular market for Canadian agricultural products, the very immigrants who came to Canada would have created a strikingly different rural society, undoubtedly more stratified and hierarchical, more representative of the socio-economic variety that characterized all parts of rural France.

The social change that took place in rural Canada in the seventeenth century, and that was sustained in French-Canadian rural society until well into the nineteenth century, would take place wherever northwestern Europeans encountered similar conditions. Cheap land had drastically altered the conditions of European rural life, favouring one element of European society and weakening or eliminating the rest. With the safety valve of such land, an egalitarian, family-centred, rural society would be able to reproduce and extend itself generation after generation. Yet Frederick Jackson Turner neglected the influence of the market and, writing before pre-industrial society in Europe had been rigorously studied, he did not understand that frontier conditions had accentuated and simplified a long process of social evolution in Europe. In medieval society ties of heredity and name among the nobility and of village community among the poor had tended to obscure the nuclear family. From late in the Middle Ages this compact, diverse society, in which people of different station lived in intimate social interaction and in which the family was often not a private setting for socialization, was slowly giving way to another in which social life drew back into the nuclear family, supported eventually by a sense of class. By the seventeenth century the sentiment of the family was widespread, and there was a general tendency, where conditions permitted, to push back ties of wider sociability in favour of the intimacy of the family. This massive social reorganization proceeded quite unevenly, more rapidly among the bourgeoisie than among the nobility or the poor, more rapidly in the principal than in the small towns. In the countryside of middle-latitude colonies overseas Europeans inadvertently found a setting where the ordinary family could find an unusually autonomous existence.

In Canada, where for well over a century a tiny population lived with cheap land and poor markets, conditions particularly favoured the self-sustaining family. The social evolution of plantation colonies obviously was different, and in most middle-latitude colonies cheap land and poor markets were not conditions of settlement for several generations. South African rural society is the closest parallel to the French-Canadian; the stock farm on the veld and the small mixed farm along the lower St Lawrence were the same socio-economic response in different physical conditions to the long availability of land in a weak market economy. But by its very extremity rural society in Canada reveals a social tendency inherent in the outreach of Europe to new lands far from European markets where, for a time, land was likely to be much cheaper and markets much poorer than in Europe. In such circumstances the independent, nuclear family would tend to emerge strongly within an egalitarian, family-centred society, a tendency that would be variously checked or modified by any protracted increase in the price of land or improvement in the market.

Y *F U R T H E R   R E A D I N G*

Robert Archibald, "Acculturation and Assimilation in Colonial New Mexico," *New Mexico Historical Review,* 53 (1978), 205–18
John Francis Bannon, *The Spanish Borderlands Frontier, 1513–1821* (1970)
Herbert E. Bolton, "The Mission as a Frontier Institution in the Spanish-American Colonies," *American Historical Review,* 23 (1917), 42–61
———, *Rim of Christendom* (1936)
———, *The Spanish Borderlands* (1921)
Norman W. Caldwell, *The French in the Mississippi Valley, 1740–1750* (1941)
John A. Caruso, *The Mississippi Valley Frontier: The Age of French Exploration and Settlement* (1966)
W. J. Eccles, *The Canadian Frontier, 1534–1760* (1969)
———, *France in America* (1972)
Henry Folmer, *Franco-Spanish Rivalry in North America, 1542–1763* (1953)
Michael V. Gannon, *The Cross in the Sand: The Early Catholic Church in Florida* (1965)
Peter Gerhard, *The Southeast Frontier of New Spain* (1979)
Charles Gibson, *Spain in America* (1966)
Jack D. L. Holmes, *Gayoso: The Life of a Spanish Governor in the Mississippi Valley, 1789–1799* (1965)
Evelyn Hu-DeHart, *Missionaries, Miners and Indians: Spanish Contact with the Yaqui Nation of Northwestern New Spain, 1533–1820* (1981)
Oakah L. Jones, Jr., *Los Paisanos: Spanish Settlers on the Northern Frontier of New Spain* (1979)
John L. Kessell, *Friars, Soldiers, and Reformers: Hispanic Arizona and the Sonora Mission Frontier, 1767–1856* (1976)
Arthur R. M. Lower, *Canadians in the Making: A Social History of Canada* (1958)
John Francis McDermott, ed., *The Spanish in the Mississippi Valley, 1762–1804* (1974)
David J. Weber, ed., *New Spain's Far Northern Frontier* (1979)

Exploration and Land Policy

Y

The Treaty of Paris in 1783, and the Louisiana Purchase only twenty years later, in 1803, allowed the new United States of America to claim vast areas of land, first beyond the Appalachian Mountains and then beyond the Mississippi River. The second event can be considered the point at which the trans-Mississippi West entered United States history. Even as a U.S. delegation to Paris negotiated possible land purchases from France, President Thomas Jefferson initiated plans for an exploratory expedition to the Far West. Starting on May 14, 1804, Meriwether Lewis and William Clark led their "Corps of Discovery" up the Missouri River, across the Rocky Mountains, and down the Clearwater, Snake, and Columbia rivers to the Pacific. On September 23, 1806, they returned to St. Louis. The Lewis and Clark expedition launched a century of western explorations that received national attention and created new popular heroes like John Charles Frémont, Clarence King, and John Wesley Powell. These government-sponsored explorations also demonstrated that the trans-Mississippi would be a region regularly subject to the plans and policies of national officials typically located on the east coast in distant Washington, D.C.

In nineteenth-century exploration and national land policy, eastern expectations sometimes conflicted with western desires. Ultimately, the role of the federal government in the discovery, mapping, and sale of western lands gave way to a demand by many westerners that they control the development of the West. The seeds of today's controversies over who owns the West may be said to have begun with the Land Ordinance of 1785, the Northwest Ordinance of 1787, the Louisiana Purchase of 1803, and the Lewis and Clark expedition of 1804–1806.

Y *D O C U M E N T S*

The three documents reproduced here present different levels of expectation and perception in the act of exploration. The first selection, Thomas Jefferson's instructions to Meriwether Lewis in 1803, reflects nearly pure expectation. The president indicated in great detail what he hopes Lewis and Clark will record during their trek up the Missouri River and across the Rocky Mountains to the Pacific Ocean. In the second document, Meriwether Lewis's entry in the expedition's journals for June 13, 1805, the author describes his attempts to carry out

Jefferson's instructions. At the Great Falls of the Missouri River, near the present-day city of Great Falls, Montana, Lewis wrote of his frustration at trying to convey the beauty of nature through the written word and scientific measurement. Major Stephen H. Long of the government's Topographical Engineers led an expedition west in the summer of 1820. Following the Platte River across present-day Nebraska and then proceeding along the south branch of that river into present-day Colorado, Long's party eventually reached Pike's Peak in mid-July before turning back. His report, reproduced as the third document, appeared under the authorship of Edwin James, the expedition's physician. The map that accompanied this account labeled the area east of the Rocky Mountains as the Great American Desert. Long and James seemed most interested in the agricultural usefulness of the land they explored. Given their expectations, might they have presented the Great Falls of the Missouri very differently from Meriwether Lewis?

Thomas Jefferson's Instructions to Meriwether Lewis, 1803

To Meriwether Lewis, esquire, captain of the first regiment of infantry of the United States of America:

Your situation as secretary of the president of the United States, has made you acquainted with the objects of my confidential message of January 18, 1803, to the legislature; you have seen the act they passed, which, though expressed in general terms, was meant to sanction those objects, and you are appointed to carry them into execution.

Instruments for ascertaining, by celestial observations, the geography of the country through which you will pass, have been already provided. Light articles for barter and presents among the Indians, arms for your attendants, say for from ten to twelve men, boats, tents, and other travelling apparatus, with ammunition, medicine, surgical instruments, and provisions, you will have prepared, with such aids as the secretary at war can yield in his department; and from him also you will receive authority to engage among our troops, by voluntary agreement, the number of attendants above-mentioned; over whom you, as their commanding officer, are invested with all the powers the laws give in such a case.

As your movements, while within the limits of the United States, will be better directed by occasional communications, adapted to circumstances as they arise, they will not be noticed here. What follows will respect your proceedings after your departure from the United States.

Your mission has been communicated to the ministers here from France, Spain, and Great Britain, and through them to their governments; and such assurances given them as to its objects, as we trust will satisfy them. The country of Louisiana having been ceded by Spain to France, the passport you have from the minister of France, the representative of the present sovereign of the country, will be a protection with all its subjects; and that from the minister of England will entitle you to the friendly aid of any traders of that allegiance with whom you may happen to meet.

The object of your mission is to explore the Missouri river, and such principal streams of it, as, by its course and communication with the waters of the Pacific ocean, whether the Columbia, Oregan, Colorado, or any other river, may offer the most direct and practicable water-communication across the continent, for the purposes of commerce.

Beginning at the mouth of the Missouri, you will take observations of latitude and longitude, at all remarkable points on the river, and especially at the mouths of rivers, at rapids, at islands, and other places and objects distinguished by such natural marks and characters, of a durable kind, as that they may with certainty be recognised hereafter. The courses of the river between these points of observation may be supplied by the compass, the log-line, and by time, corrected by the observations themselves. The variations of the needle, too, in different places, should be noticed.

The interesting points of the portage between the heads of the Missouri, and of the water offering the best communication with the Pacific ocean, should also be fixed by observation; and the course of that water to the ocean, in the same manner as that of the Missouri.

Your observations are to be taken with great pains and accuracy; to be entered distinctly and intelligibly for others as well as yourself; to comprehend all the elements necessary, with the aid of the usual tables, to fix the latitude and longitude of the places at which they were taken; and are to be rendered to the war-office, for the purpose of having the calculations made concurrently by proper persons within the United States. Several copies of these, as well as of your other notes, should be made at leisure times, and put into the care of the most trust worthy of your attendants to guard, by multiplying them against the accidental losses to which they will be exposed. A further guard would be, that one of these copies be on the cuticular membranes of the paper-birch, as less liable to injury from damp than common paper.

The commerce which may be carried on with the people inhabiting the line you will pursue, renders a knowledge of those people important. You will therefore endeavour to make yourself acquainted, as far as a diligent pursuit of your journey shall admit, with the names of the nations and their numbers;

The extent and limits of their possessions;

Their relations with other tribes or nations;

Their language, traditions, monuments;

Their ordinary occupations in agriculture, fishing, hunting, war, arts, and the implements for these;

Their food, clothing, and domestic accommodations;

The diseases prevalent among them, and the remedies they use;

Moral and physical circumstances which distinguish them from the tribes we know;

Peculiarities in their laws, customs, and dispositions;

And articles of commerce they may need or furnish, and to what extent.

And, considering the interest which every nation has in extending and strengthening the authority of reason and justice among the people around them, it will be useful to acquire what knowledge you can of the state of morality, religion, and information among them; as it may better enable those who may endeavour to civilize and instruct them, to adapt their measures to the existing notions and practices of those on whom they are to operate.

Other objects worthy of notice will be—

The soil and face of the country, its growth and vegetable productions, especially those not of the United States;

The animals of the country generally, and especially those not known in the United States;

The remains and accounts of any which may be deemed rare or extinct;

The mineral productions of every kind, but more particularly metals, lime-stone, pit-coal, and saltpetre; salines and mineral waters, noting the temperature of the last, and such circumstances as may indicate their character;

Volcanic appearances;

Climate, as characterized by the thermometer, by the proportion of rainy, cloudy, and clear days; by lightning, hail, snow, ice; by the access and recess of frost; by the winds prevailing at different seasons; the dates at which particular plants put forth, or lose their flower or leaf; times of appearance of particular birds, reptiles or insects.

Although your route will be along the channel of the Missouri, yet you will endeavour to inform yourself, by inquiry, of the character and extent of the country watered by its branches, and especially on its southern side. The North river, or Rio Bravo, which runs into the gulf of Mexico, and the North river, or Rio Colorado, which runs into the gulf of California, are understood to be the principal streams heading opposite to the waters of the Missouri, and running southwardly. Whether the dividing grounds between the Missouri and them are mountains or flat lands, what are their distance from the Missouri, the character of the intermediate country, and the people inhabiting it, are worthy of particular inquiry. The northern waters of the Missouri are less to be inquired after, because they have been ascertained to a considerable degree, and are still in a course of ascertainment by English traders and travellers; but if you can learn any thing certain of the most northern source of the Missisipi, and of its position relatively to the Lake of the Woods, it will be interesting to us. Some account too of the path of the Canadian traders from the Missisipi, at the mouth of the Ouisconsing to where it strikes the Missouri, and of the soil and rivers in its course, is desirable.

In all your intercourse with the natives, treat them in the most friendly and conciliatory manner which their own conduct will admit; allay all jealousies as to the object of your journey; satisfy them of its innocence; make them acquainted with the position, extent, character, peaceable and commercial dispositions of the United States; of our wish to be neighbourly, friendly, and useful to them, and of our dispositions to a commercial intercourse with them; confer with them on the points most convenient as mutual emporiums, and the articles of most desirable interchange for them and us. If a few of their influential chiefs, within practicable distance, wish to visit us, arrange such a visit with them, and furnish them with authority to call on our officers on their entering the United States, to have them conveyed to this place at the public expense. If any of them should wish to have some of their young people brought up with us, and taught such arts as may be useful to them, we will receive, instruct, and take care of them. Such a mission, whether of influential chiefs, or of young people, would give some security to your own party. Carry with you some matter of the kine-pox [cowpox]; inform those of them with whom you may be of its efficacy as a preservative from the small-pox, and instruct and encourage them in the use of it. This may be especially done wherever you winter.

As it is impossible for us to foresee in what manner you will be received by those people, whether with hospitality or hostility, so is it impossible to prescribe the exact degree of perseverance with which you are to pursue your journey. We value too much the lives of citizens to offer them to probable destruction. Your numbers will be sufficient to secure you against the unauthorized opposition of individuals, or of small parties; but if a superior force, authorized, or not authorized, by a nation, should be arrayed against your further passage, and inflexibly determined to arrest it, you must decline its further pursuit and return. In the loss of yourselves we should lose also the information you will have acquired. By returning safely with that, you may enable us to renew the essay with better calculated means. To your own discretion, therefore, must be left the degree of danger you may risk, and the point at which you should decline, only saying, we wish you to err on the side of your safety, and to bring back your party safe, even if it be with less information.

As far up the Missouri as the white settlements extend, an intercourse will probably be found to exist between them and the Spanish posts of St. Louis opposite Cahokia, or St. Genevieve opposite Kaskaskia. From still further up the river the traders may furnish a conveyance for letters. Beyond that you may perhaps be able to engage Indians to bring letters for the government to Cahokia, or Kaskaskia, on promising that they shall there receive such special compensation as you shall have stipulated with them. Avail yourself of these means to communicate to us, at seasonable intervals, a copy of your journal, notes and observations of every kind, putting into cypher whatever might do injury if betrayed.

Should you reach the Pacific ocean, inform yourself of the circumstances which may decide whether the furs of those parts may not be collected as advantageously at the head of the Missouri (convenient as is supposed to the waters of the Colorado and Oregan or Columbia) as at Nootka Sound, or any other point of that coast; and that trade be consequently conducted through the Missouri and United States more beneficially than by the circumnavigation now practised.

On your arrival on that coast, endeavour to learn if there be any port within your reach frequented by the sea vessels of any nation, and to send two of your trusty people back by sea, in such way as shall appear practicable, with a copy of your notes; and should you be of opinion that the return of your party by the way they went will be imminently dangerous, then ship the whole, and return by sea, by the way either of Cape Horn, or the Cape of Good Hope, as you shall be able. As you will be without money, clothes, or provisions, you must endeavour to use the credit of the United States to obtain them; for which purpose open letters of credit shall be furnished you, authorizing you to draw on the executive of the United States, or any of its officers, in any part of the world, on which draughts can be disposed of, and to apply with our recommendations to the consuls, agents, merchants, or citizens of any nation with which we have intercourse, assuring them, in our name, that any aids they may furnish you shall be honourably repaid, and on demand. Our consuls, Thomas Hewes, at Batavia, in Java, William Buchanan, in the Isles of France and Bourbon, and John Elmslie, at the Cape of Good Hope, will be able to supply your necessities, by draughts on us.

Should you find it safe to return by the way you go, after sending two of your party round by sea, or with your whole party, if no conveyance by sea can be found, do so; making such observations on your return as may serve to supply, correct, or confirm those made on your outward journey.

On reentering the United States and reaching a place of safety, discharge any of your attendants who may desire and deserve it, procuring for them immediate payment of all arrears of pay and clothing which may have incurred since their departure, and assure them that they shall be recommended to the liberality of the legislature for the grant of a soldier's portion of land each, as proposed in my message to congress, and repair yourself, with your papers, to the seat of government.

To provide, on the accident of your death, against anarchy, dispersion, and the consequent danger to your party, and total failure of the enterprise, you are hereby authorized, by any instrument signed and written in your own hand, to name the person among them who shall succeed to the command on your decease, and by like instruments to change the nomination, from time to time, as further experience of the characters accompanying you shall point out superior fitness; and all the powers and authorities given to yourself are, in the event of your death, transferred to, and vested in the successor so named, with further power to him and his successors, in like manner to name each his successor, who, on the death of his predecessor, shall be invested with all the powers and authorities given to yourself. Given under my hand at the city of Washington, this twentieth day of June, 1803.

THOMAS JEFFERSON,
President of the United States of America.

Meriwether Lewis at the Great Falls of the Missouri, 1805

Thursday June 13th 1805.

This morning we set out about sunrise after taking breakfast off our venison and fish. we again ascended the hills of the river and gained the level country. the country through which we passed for the first six miles tho' more roling than that we had passed yesterday might still with propryety be deemed a level country; our course as yesterday was generally S W. the river from the place we left it appeared to make a considerable bend to the South. from the extremity of this roling country I overlooked a most beatifull and level plain of great extent or at least 50 or sixty miles; in this there were infinitely more buffaloe than I had ever before witnessed at a view. nearly in the direction I had been travling or S. W. two curious mountains presented themselves of square figures, the sides rising perpendicularly to the hight of 250 feet and appeared to be formed of yellow clay; their tops appeared to be level plains; these inaccessible hights appeared like the ramparts of immence fortifications; I have no doubt but with very little assistance from art they might be rendered impregnable. fearing that the river boar to the South and that I might pass the falls if they existed between this an the snowey mountains I altered my course nealy to the South leaving those insulated hills to my wright and proceeded through the plain; I sent Feels on my right and Drewyer and Gibson on my left with orders to kill some meat and join me at the river where I should halt for dinner. I had proceded on this course about two miles with Goodrich at some distance behind me whin my ears were saluted with the agreeable sound of a fall of water and advancing a little further I saw the spray arrise above the plain like a collumn of smoke which would frequently dispear again in an instant caused I presume by the wind which blew pretty hard from the S. W. I did not however loose my direction to this point which soon began to make a roaring too tremendious to be mistaken for any cause short of the great falls of the Missouri. here I arrived about 12 OClock having traveled by estimate about 15 Miles. I hurryed down the hill which was about 200 feet high and difficult of access, to gaze on this sublimely grand specticle. I took my position on the top of some rocks about 20 feet high opposite the center of the falls. this chain of rocks appear once to have formed a part of those over which the waters tumbled, but in the course of time has been seperated from it to the distance of 150 yards lying prarrallel to it and forming a butment against which the water after falling over the precipice beats with great fury; this barrier extends on the right to the perpendicular clift which forms that board [bound? border?] of the river but to the distance of 120 yards next to the clift it is but a few feet

---

Reprinted from *The Journals of the Lewis and Clark Expedition*, Volume 4, 283–87, edited by Gary E. Moulton, by permission of University of Nebraska Press.

above the level of the water, and here the water in very high tides appears to pass in a channel of 40 yds. next to the higher part of the ledg of rocks; on the left it extends within 80 or ninty yards of the lard. Clift which is also perpendicular; between this abrupt extremity of the ledge of rocks and the perpendicular bluff the whole body of water passes with incredible swiftness. immediately at the cascade the river is about 300 yds. wide; about ninty or a hundred yards of this next the Lard. bluff is a smoth even sheet of water falling over a precipice of at least eighty feet, the remaining part of about 200 yards on my right formes the grandest sight I ever beheld, the hight of the fall is the same of the other but the irregular and somewhat projecting rocks below receives the water in it's passage down and brakes it into a perfect white foam which assumes a thousand forms in a moment sometimes flying up in jets of sparkling foam to the hight of fifteen or twenty feet and are scarcely formed before large roling bodies of the same beaten and foaming water is thrown over and conceals them. in short the rocks seem to be most happily fixed to present a sheet of the whitest beaten froath for 200 yards in length and about 80 feet perpendicular. the water after decending strikes against the butment before mentioned or that on which I stand and seems to reverberate and being met by the more impetuous courant they role and swell into half formed billows of great hight which rise and again disappear in an instant. this butment of rock defends a handsom little bottom of about three acres which is deversified and agreeably shaded with some cottonwood trees; in the lower extremity of the bottom there is a very thick grove of the same kind of trees which are small, in this wood there are several Indian lodges formed of sticks. a few small cedar grow near the ledge of rocks where I rest. below the point of these rocks at a small distance the river is divided by a large rock which rises several feet above the water, and extends downwards with the stream for about 20 yards. about a mile before the water arrives at the pitch it decends very rappidly, and is confined on the Lard. side by a perpendicular clift of about 100 feet, on Stard. side it is also perpendicular for about three hundred yards above the pitch where it is then broken by the discharge of a small ravine, down which the buffaloe have a large beaten road to the water, for it is but in very few places that these anamals can obtain water near this place owing to the steep and inaccessible banks. I see several skelletons of the buffaloe lying in the edge of the water near the Stard. bluff which I presume have been swept down by the current and precipitated over this tremendious fall. about 300 yards below me there is another butment of solid rock with a perpendicular face and abot 60 feet high which projects from the Stard. side at right angles to the distance of 134 yds. and terminates the lower part nearly of the bottom before mentioned; there being a passage arround the end of this butment between it and the river of about 20 yardes; here the river again assumes it's usual width soon spreading to near 300 yards but still continues it's rappidity. from the reflection of the sun on the spray or mist which arrises from these falls there is a beatifull rainbow produced which adds not a little to the beauty of this majestically grand senery. after wrighting this imperfect discription

I again viewed the falls and was so much disgusted with the imperfect idea which it conveyed of the scene that I determined to draw my pen across it and begin agin, but then reflected that I could not perhaps succeed better than pening the first impressions of the mind; I wished for the pencil of Salvator Rosa or the pen of Thompson,* that I might be enabled to give to the enlightened world some just idea of this truly magnifficent and sublimely grand object, which has from the commencement of time been concealed from the view of civilized man; but this was fruitless and vain. I most sincerely regreted that I had not brought a crimee obscura** with me by the assistance of which even I could have hoped to have done better but alas this was also out of my reach; I therefore with the assistance of my pen only indeavoured to trace some of the stronger features of this seen by the assistance of which and my recollection aided by some able pencil I hope still to give to the world some faint idea of an object which at this moment fills me with such pleasure and astonishment, and which of it's kind I will venture to ascert is second to but one in the known world. I retired to the shade of a tree where I determined to fix my camp for the present and dispatch a man in the morning to inform Capt. C. and the party of my success in finding the falls and settle in their minds all further doubts as to the Missouri. the hunters now arrived loaded with excellent buffaloe meat and informed me that they had killed three very fat cows about ¾ of a mile hence. I directed them after they had refreshed themselves to go back and butcher them and bring another load of meat each to our camp determining to employ those who remained with me in drying meat for the party against their arrival. in about 2 hours or at 4 OClock P. M. they set out on this duty, and I walked down the river about three miles to discover if possible some place to which the canoes might arrive or at which they might be drawn on shore in order to be taken by land above the falls; but returned without effecting either of these objects; the river was one continued sene of rappids and cascades which I readily perceived could not be encountered with our canoes, and the Clifts still retained their perpendicular structure and were from 150 to 200 feet high; in short the river appears here to have woarn a channel in the process of time through a solid rock. on my return I found the party at camp; they had butchered the buffaloe and brought in some more meat as I had directed. Goodrich had caught half a douzen very fine trout and a number of both species of the white fish. these trout are from sixteen to twenty three inches in length, precisely resemble our mountain or speckled trout in form and the position of their fins, but the specks on these are of a deep black instead of the red or goald colour of those common to the U.' States. these are furnished long sharp

---

* Salvator Rosa, a seventeenth-century Italian landscape painter, generally painted wild, desolate scenes. James Thomson, an eighteenth-century Scottish poet, was a forerunner of the English Romantic movement; his best-known poem was ''The Seasons.''
** A camera obscura, basically a box with a lens mounted on one wall; light entering through the lens would project an image on the opposite wall of the dark box, which an artist could then trace, getting an almost photographic image.

teeth on the pallet and tongue and have generally a small dash of red on each side behind the front ventral fins; the flesh is of a pale yellowish red, or when in good order, of a rose red.—

I am induced to believe that the Brown, the white and the Grizly bear of this country are the same species only differing in colour from age or more probably from the same natural cause that many other anamals of the same family differ in colour. one of those which we killed yesterday was of a creemcoloured white while the other in company with it was of the common bey or rdish brown, which seems to be the most usual colour of them. the white one appeared from it's tallons and teath to be the youngest; it was smaller than the other, and although a monstrous beast we supposed that it had not yet attained it's growth and that it was a little upwards of two years old. the young cubs which we have killed have always been of a brownish white, but none of them as white as that we killed yesterday. one other that we killed sometime since which I mentioned sunk under some driftwood and was lost, had a white stripe or list of about eleven inches wide entirely arround his body just behind the shoalders, and was much darker than these bear usually are. the grizly bear we have never yet seen. I have seen their tallons in possession of the Indians and from their form I am perswaded if there is any difference between this species and the brown or white bear it is very inconsiderable. There is no such anamal as a black bear in this open country or of that species generally denominated the black bear

my fare is really sumptuous this evening; buffaloe's humps, tongues and marrowbones, fine trout parched meal pepper and salt, and a good appetite; the last is not considered the least of the luxuries.

The Stephen Long Expedition's Report of a Frontier Barrier, 1821

Of the country situated between the meridian of the Council Bluff and the Rocky Mountains

We next proceed to a description of the country westward of the assumed meridian, and extending to the Rocky Mountains, which are its western boundary. This section embraces an extent of about four hundred miles square, lying between 96 and 105 degrees of west longitude, and between 35 and 42 degrees of north latitude.

Proceeding westwardly across the meridian above specified, the hilly country gradually subsides, giving place to a region of vast extent, spreading towards the north and south, and presenting an undulating surface, with nothing to limit the view or variegate the prospect, but here and there a hill, knob, or insulated tract of table-land. At length the Rocky Mountains break upon the view, towering abruptly from the plains, and mingling their snow-capped summits with the clouds.

On approaching the mountains, no other change is observable in the general aspect of the country, except that the isolated knobs and table-lands above alluded to become more frequent and more distinctly marked, the bluffs by which the valleys of watercourses are bounded present a greater abundance of rocks, stones lie in greater profusion upon the surface, and the soil becomes more sandy and sterile. If, to the characteristics above intimated, we add that of an almost complete destitution of woodland (for not more than one thousandth part of the section can be said to possess a timber-growth) we shall have a pretty correct idea of the general aspect of the whole country. . . .

Immediately at the base of the mountains, and also at those of some of the insular table-lands, are situated many remarkable ridges, rising in the form of parapets, to the height of between fifty and one hundred and fifty feet. These appear to have been attached to the neighbouring heights, of which they once constituted a part, but have, at some remote period, been cleft asunder from them by some extraordinary convulsion of nature, which has prostrated them in their present condition.

The rocky stratifications, of which these ridges are principally composed, and which are exactly similar to those of the insulated table-lands, are variously inclined, having various dips, from forty-five to eighty degrees.

Throughout this section of country the surface is occasionally characterized by water-worn pebbles, and gravel of granite, gneiss, and quartz, but the predominant characteristic is sand, which in many instances prevails almost to the entire exclusion of vegetable mould. Large tracts are often to be met with, exhibiting scarcely a trace of vegetation. The whole region, as before hinted, is almost entirely destitute of a timber-growth of any description. In some few instances, however, sandy knobs and ridges make their appearance, thickly covered with red cedars of a dwarfish growth. There are also some few tracts clad in a growth of pitch pine and scrubby oaks; but, in general, nothing of vegetation appears upon the uplands but withered grass of a stinted growth, no more than two or three inches high, prickly pears profusely covering extensive tracts, and weeds of a few varieties, which, like the prickly pear, seem to thrive best in the most arid and sterile soil. . . .

In regard to this extensive section of country, I do not hesitate in giving the opinion, that it is almost wholly unfit for cultivation, and of course uninhabitable by a people depending upon agriculture for their subsistence. Although tracts of fertile land considerably extensive are occasionally to be met with, yet the scarcity of wood and water, almost uniformly prevalent, will prove an insuperable obstacle in the way of settling the country. This objection rests not only against the section immediately under consideration, but applies with equal propriety to a much larger portion of the country. Agreeably to the best intelligence that can be had, concerning the country both northward and southward of the section, and especially to the inferences deducible from the account given by Lewis and Clarke of the country situated between the Missouri and the Rocky Mountains above the river Platte, the vast region commencing near the sources of the Sabine, Trinity, Brases, and Colorado, and extending northwardly to the forty-ninth degree of north latitude, by which the United States' territory is limited in that direction, is throughout of a similar character. The whole of this region seems peculiarly adapted as a range for buffaloes, wild goats, and other wild game; incalculable multitudes of which find ample pasturage and subsistence upon it.

This region, however, viewed as a frontier, may prove of infinite importance to the United States, inasmuch as it is calculated to serve as a barrier to prevent too great an extension of our population westward, and secure us against the machinations or incursions of an enemy that might otherwise be disposed to annoy us in that part of our frontier.

E S S A Y S

William H. Goetzmann and Paul W. Gates are award-winning, nationally recognized scholars. Goetzmann, professor of history and American studies at the University of Texas at Austin, received the Pulitzer Prize and the Parkman Award in 1967 for his book *Exploration and Empire: The Role of the Explorer and Scientist in the Winning of the American West*. The first essay is an excerpt from the introduction and first chapter of that book. Gates served on the history faculty at Cornell University from 1936 to 1971. His special interest in the public domain and federal land policy has resulted in a remarkable number of books and articles. In 1986 he was awarded the Western History Association Prize for lifetime achievement. The second essay presents Gates's overview of the government's land policy. Each essay indicates different ways that either eastern or federal perceptions and plans have affected the discovery and development of the West. Gates is especially aware of the continuing confrontation in the United States between these regional and governmental interests.

Exploration and Expectations

WILLIAM H. GOETZMANN

On an August day in 1868 the Union Pacific made an unscheduled stop at Antelope Station in western Nebraska. From one of the ornate parlor cars a dignified, scholarly gentleman stepped out upon the prairie. He was Othniel Charles Marsh, a Yale paleontologist, and he was following up a story that had appeared in an Omaha newspaper to the effect that a railroad well-digger had accidentally unearthed the bones of a prehistoric man out there in Nebraska at a place famous only as a way station on the emigrant route to the West. Marsh's own account of the incident captures some of the excitement he felt that day:

"Before we approached the small station where the alleged primitive man had been unearthed," Marsh remembered, "I made friends with the

From *Exploration and the Empire: The Explorer and the Scientist in the Winning of the American West*, 3–8, by William H. Goetzmann. Copyright © 1966 by William H. Goetzmann. Reprinted by permission of Alfred A. Knopf, Inc.

conductor, and persuaded him to hold the train long enough for me to glance over the earth thrown out of this well, thinking perchance that I might thus find some fragments, at least, of our early ancestors. In one respect I succeeded beyond my wildest hopes. By rapid search over the huge mound of earth, I soon found many fragments and a number of entire bones, not of man, but of *horses* diminutive indeed, but true equine ancestors. . . . Other fragments told of his contemporaries—a camel, a pig, and a turtle . . . perhaps more . . . when I could remove the clay from the other remains secured. Absorbed in this work I took no note of time.''

When ultimately Marsh reboarded the train, he had the first clues to his reconstruction of Protohippus, the miniature three-toed horse of the Pleistocene era. And out of this "find" grew his classic fossil genealogy of the modern horse, one of the most famous pieces of paleontological evidence for the validity of Darwin's theory of evolution through natural selection.

More significantly for the student of exploration, however, Professor Marsh's Antelope Station adventure marked the beginning of the career of still another outstanding explorer of the American West. For Marsh's enthusiasm went far beyond the fossil horse.

"I could only wonder," he wrote, "if such scientific truths as I had now obtained were concealed in a single well, what untold treasures must there be in the whole Rocky Mountain region. This thought promised rich rewards for the enthusiastic explorer in this new field, and thus my own life work seemed laid out before me."

The nature of Marsh's adventure in 1868 and his subsequent view of himself as a Rocky Mountain explorer (despite his obvious tenderfoot background) highlight one of the most important elements in the history of the American West. The country beyond the Mississippi, as we now know it, was not just "discovered" in one dramatic and colorful era of early-nineteenth-century coonskin exploration. Rather it was discovered and rediscovered by generations of very different explorers down through the centuries following the advent of the shipwrecked Spaniard Cabeza de Vaca. And this process of repeated discovery was in itself among the most important factors which shaped the development of culture and civilization in that region.

Usually, however, exploration is not thought of as a process with cultural significance. Rather it is viewed as a sequence of dramatic discoveries— isolated events, colorful and even interesting perhaps, but of little consequence to the basic sweep of civilization. This is because exploration has rarely if ever been viewed as a continuous form of activity or mode of behavior. The words "exploration" and "discovery" are most often and most casually linked in the popular imagination simply as interchangeable synonyms for "adventure." But exploration is something more than adventure, and something more than discovery. According to Webster, the explorer is actually one who "*seeks* discoveries." He is not simply and solely the "discoverer." Instead the accent is upon process and activity, with advances in knowledge simply fortunate though expected incidents along the way. It is likewise not casual. It is purposeful. It is the seeking. It is one form of the learning process itself, and, as the case of Professor Marsh illustrates, it was often a branch of science which resulted in a discovery at a place trod many times over by previous generations of explorers bent on other missions in days gone by.

The importance of viewing exploration as activity rather than as a sequence of discoveries is further underscored when one considers the distinction between the explorer and the discoverer in terms of the concept of *mission*. Discoveries can be produced by accident, as in the case of the fortunate well-digger at Antelope Station. Exploration, by contrast, is the result of purpose or mission. As such, it is an activity which, to a very large degree, is "programmed" by some older center of culture. That is, its purposes, goals, and evaluation of new data are to a great extent set by the previous experiences, the values, the kinds and categories of existing knowledge, and the current objectives of the civilized centers from which the explorer sets out on his quest. If Marsh, for example, had not been a paleontologist trained at Yale and in Europe, he might have looked for different things on his trip out West. He might have kept his eye out for mineral deposits perhaps, instead of waxing enthusiastic over a "big bonanza" in bones. He certainly never would have set off with such zest in search of an ancient America in the form of gigantic dinosaurs, exotic pterodactyls, and his own favorites—the extinct toothed birds. Yet, his exploring activity, peculiar as it was, programmed by an older center of culture, had a lasting importance not only in terms of his startling discoveries, but also in terms of the effect it had on the future course of science and public policy in the West, and on the United States as a whole as Marsh rose to prominence in the worlds of science and government. The same might be said in varying degrees for a whole host of other nineteenth-century explorers of the American West—men who synthesized the new sights they saw in the wilderness into projections or images of what the older centers thought the West ought to be. Thus in various periods the West became the great empty continent, Eldorado or Cibola, a barren waste of heathen savages and Spaniards, the passage to India, an imperial frontier, a beaver kingdom, the Great American Desert, a land of flocks and herds, a pastoral paradise, an agricultural Arcadia, a military and administrative problem, a bonanza of gold and silver, a safety valve, a haven for saints, a refuge for bad men, and ultimately, toward the end of the nineteenth century, an enormous laboratory. And so it went—there were many more such images that it might be possible to point out, each demonstrating in some measure the preconceptions that an older culture and its explorers brought to the search for knowledge in the new environment.

With this in mind, my aim has been to focus upon exploration as a meaningful activity and to trace its complex impact not only upon the history of the West but upon the nation as a whole, particularly as it stimulated advances in science and scientific institutions and the evolution, on a national level, of a public policy for the West as a part of the nation. Much of the story necessarily revolves about the role of the federal government in sponsoring the exploration of the West, since it is clear that, contrary to the myth of the rugged independent frontiersman, a good part of the exploration done in the West was done under federal sponsorship. From the early days of Lewis and Clark down to the formation of the United States Geological Survey, the government explorer in one form or another played a vital role. And even when the agents of exploration were not federal servants, their constant referent was nevertheless the national government, and the aid and protection it might be expected to provide.

In addition, the history of Western exploration can serve as a vehicle for demonstrating in a more subtle way some of the larger consequences of the way the West was won. If the region was settled along lines or according to images projected by the older centers of culture, then in the most precise way it was—to borrow a modern concept usually not thought of as being applicable to the nineteenth century of rugged individualism—"other-directed." Men appear to have gone out West to reconstitute the society they had known on countless frontiers to the East—only of course with themselves at the top instead of at the bottom of the social and economic ladder. Even as they came in conflict with the rapidly changing Eastern and national interests, Western men were still largely prisoners of an emulative society. This in turn was not unique to the frontier West. America itself grew up in this emulative and "programmed" fashion. Thus the explorers reflecting national images and plans, and the Westerners who followed their lead, were all part of an "other-directed" pattern. And this perhaps is the major difficulty in defining Western culture itself, for the West, as the history of its exploration clearly shows, has always been in rapid transition. It is, as Frederick Jackson Turner has pointed out, more of a process than a place. But that process has been as much an Americanization process as it has been one of distinctiveness. Contrary to Turner's hypothesis, the Western experience in the main appears not to have brought distinctiveness as such to bear on the country, but instead has offered a theater in which American patterns of culture could be endlessly mirrored.

Thus in a sense the problem of Western culture becomes the problem of American culture, which is itself the rapidly changing offspring of an older, broader society. The two units represent different degrees of the same complex problem which continues to tantalize and elude historians down to our own day. Exploration, by no means the eccentric activity it is sometimes taken to be, does offer, however, a major clue to the shifting relationship of the regional to the national culture in our recent historical experience.

In its broadest terms, the history of nineteenth-century Western exploration can be seen unfolding through three major periods each characterized by a dominant set of objectives, particular forms of exploring activity, distinctive types of explorers, and appropriate institutions which governed these other factors. The first of these periods began with Lewis and Clark and continued down to approximately 1845. It was an era of imperial rivalry in which even the mountain men and fur traders were self-conscious pawns in an international competition for the West. The second was a period of settlement and investment in which numbers and opportunity—"westering"—

were all that counted and the explorer was largely dedicated to lending a helping hand in the matter of Manifest Destiny. The third period, from 1860 to 1900, was the era of the Great Surveys, a time for more intensive scientific reconnaissances and inventories. It was also a time for sober second thoughts as to the proper nature, purpose, and future direction of Western settlement. Incipient conservation and planning in the national interest became a vogue, signifying that the West had come of age and its future had become securely wedded to the fortunes of the nation. . . .

The exploration of the American West was never an isolated event. It belongs to world rather than to national history, and never more so than in the opening decades of the nineteenth century. When Captain Meriwether Lewis and Lieutenant William Clark of the United States Army crossed the North American continent from the Mississippi River to the Pacific Ocean between May 14, 1804, and September 26, 1806, they brought to a close nearly three centuries of searching, on the part of European and colonial powers, for a Northwest Passage to India. A new country, the United States, had entered the ancient struggle for control of the trade routes to the Orient, but in so doing, thanks to the work of the Great Captains, it had altered the focus of international rivalry, at least for a time, from the far-off Orient to the Western interior of the North American continent itself. Lewis and Clark had discovered no easy route to Cathay. But theirs had been the final stroke that swept away the eighteenth-century geographers' view that one needed only to cross a single height of land—a ridge of the "Stony Mountains," in Jefferson's terms—before one could look upon the broad Pacific with Cathay on its Western shore. Instead their expedition demonstrated to the world at large the great width of western North America and its potential riches in furs, minerals, fishes, and untold other natural resources. Thus they succeeded in making the West itself an object of desire—a virgin wilderness that formed a thousand-mile vacuum between the great powers of the world and the United States, and into which, by whatever laws of imperialistic physics prevailed, they must inevitably rush. It was a vacuum that acted, as one historian has pointed out, like a greatly expanded European political frontier with intense pressures on either side. As such, the explorer became more than a mere curiosity-seeker. When he led his nation and his culture into the Western "vacuum" so richly endowed by nature, the buckskin explorer became a vital factor in international diplomacy. For much of the nineteenth century it was the explorer out in the wilderness as much as the diplomats in London and Paris and Washington who took the lead in establishing, through his increased geographical knowledge and his control of the Indians, the practical limits of each nation's frontier on the edges of the vast terrestrial sea that lay between them.

It was not by accident that Lewis and Clark so changed the focus of international rivalry for the West. Rather it was a function of their unique role as explorers with a broad sense of national purpose. They were not fur traders, for example, nor even strictly speaking men of commerce. Instead both men were soldiers with extensive experience in frontier regions, chosen for their general intelligence and knowledge of wilderness skills, and programmed by an elaborate set of instructions from Thomas Jefferson, who saw their mission in the very broadest terms. In his appeal to Congress for funds, Jefferson described the expedition as a commercial one because it thus fell within the limits of his Constitutional powers. Yet privately Jefferson also saw it as a "literary" undertaking, which in the parlance of the day meant that it was to collect information covering the whole range of natural history from geology to Indian vocabularies. As explorers, Lewis and Clark might almost be considered a logical extension of the American Philosophical Society, which existed to promote the general advancement of science and the useful arts.

The repeated attention given to the details of their overland trip has tended to obscure what is perhaps the most important fact about the Lewis and Clark expedition, and that is the degree to which it was "programmed," or planned in advance, down to the smallest detail by Jefferson and his scientific associates in Philadelphia, particularly Caspar Wistar, Benjamin Rush, Andrew Ellicott, and Robert Patterson. After years of collecting information about the West, and several abortive attempts to launch an expedition, Jefferson, who also had some backwoods experience as a surveyor in his native Virginia, had a very clear idea of the kinds of information the explorers should collect. This was first and foremost geographical information of the wide-ranging, nonspecialized kind that characterized the returns of such an eminent scientific man as Alexander von Humboldt. If Jefferson's famous *Notes on Virginia* can be said to constitute a perfect model of the rational eighteenth-century mind organizing the many facts of physical and human nature into a broadly conceived and generally useful pattern, then in equal measure the same can be said for the instructions given to Lewis and Clark.

They were called upon first of all to explore the Missouri and Columbia rivers to locate "the most direct and practicable water communication across this continent for the purposes of commerce." But they were also to "fix" geographical positions by astronomical observations so that a map of the region could be made. Moreover, they were to study the Indian inhabitants very carefully, including their numbers, their relations with other tribes, "their language, dress and monuments," their economic and military pursuits, their food, clothing, and houses, their diseases and remedies, and their laws and customs. In addition Lewis and Clark were to study the "soil and face of the country," particularly its vegetable production, its animals, its fossils, the existing minerals, including metals, limestone, coal, salts, mineral waters, and saltpeter. They were also to take note of volcanic action and to keep statistics on the weather. In short, though commerce in furs was to be a prime objective, the explorers were to inquire into almost every phenomenon that might prove useful to settlers from the United States. The very strength of Jefferson's instructions was in their broadness and lack of limitations. It was this general approach that called for the study of any and all useful phenomena that set the pattern for much of the early American exploration in the Far West and gave it a tremendous advantage over the more specialized efforts by competing nations. It keynoted what was to be a more flexible and economically mobile American approach to the West. When American explorers, following Lewis and Clark, went out into the West, they characteristically found many more uses for the land than did their counterparts under different flags.

That this was no accident can further be illustrated by a brief glance at the kind of training received by Meriwether Lewis, the nominal head of the expedition. During the summer of 1803 Lewis was in Philadelphia studying natural history with Wistar, Rush, Peale, and other experts. These men also furnished him with advice in the techniques of collecting, and gave him detailed lists of questions to ask the Indians and other people whom he might meet. Part of his time, too, was spent mastering the sextant, the theodolite, and other instruments that were to be used for the careful calculation of longitude and latitude so necessary for the compilation of an accurate map of the unknown region. He also had opportunity to study maps, such as those of John Mitchell and Guillaume De Lisle, in Jefferson's library; and later, in St. Louis, he studied the Spanish maps of Antoine Soulard and the Missouri River charts of John Evans and James Mackay, as well as their journals. In a few short months his head was crammed with the rudimentary outlines of virtually every branch of natural and physical science, and before the expedition got under way, Clark, too, began to master some of these skills. Clark's field notes show, for example, that the bluff frontier soldier had mastered the arts of geography well enough to be able to calculate with some approximate degree of accuracy the probable distance from Camp DuBois to the Pacific Ocean. Thus, despite their apparent use of erroneous maps of the day that indicated an easy progress over a single mountain ridge from the Missouri to the Columbia, Lewis and Clark, before they started, were able to use the longitude calculations of McKenzie, Vancouver, Evans, and others to determine the magnitude of the trek that lay before them. Had they never made the trip at all, they would at least have added this datum to the existing body of geographical knowledge.

It was as carefully trained agents of a civilized and flexible culture, then, that Lewis and Clark set out into the wilderness and injected the United States into the struggle for a national empire. Their journey took them up the Missouri to Fort Mandan, in present-day North Dakota, where they spent the winter of 1804–05. . . . Then they followed the Missouri along its great bend and down to the Three Forks, where they headed up the Jefferson River and crossed over into Montana's Bitterroot Valley via Lemhi Pass, in one of the most critical stretches of the entire trip. From the Bitterroot they made their way northward to the Clearwater and thence to the Columbia. Then they followed the main Columbia to the Pacific, which they reached on November 7, 1805. In one of the most dramatic moments in the history of exploration, William Clark stood one winter day in a slashing rain and carved on a tall yellow pine overlooking the Pacific: "William Clark December 3rd 1805. By Land from the U. States in 1804 and 1805."

It was in imitation of Alexander McKenzie's announcement of his earlier arrival at the shores of the Pacific far to the north on the Bella Coola River, and a conscious challenge to all other nations who wished to lay claim to the Columbia country. Not only had they collected the required data, filled the notebooks and journals demanded by Jefferson, but they also had served as diplomatic agents of the United States in establishing a claim to the Columbia.

After wintering at Fort Clatsop, the first American settlement west of the Continental Divide, they returned over a new route, with Lewis leading one party overland from Lo-Lo Pass via the Sun River to the Great Falls of the Missouri, and Clark swinging southward to explore the Yellowstone River. They were reunited at the junction of the Missouri and the Yellowstone and gradually descended the Missouri to St. Louis, where they arrived on September 26, 1806, to the cheers of a small crowd assembled on the bank of the river. The story of their trip, which has been told many times, needs no recapitulation in detail. Its significance for the later history of American exploration lies in the flexible point of view which they brought to the West and which was to set the pattern for the many expeditions to follow. They had sketched in the broad outline of the continent, and they had brought back collections and data enough to suggest the immense value of the interior to all kinds of American enterprise. In so doing, they altered forever the focus and nature of the imperial struggle for North America.

But despite the fact that Lewis and Clark had made known such essentials as the width of the continent, the existence of numerous ranges of high mountains, the location and description of the major rivers of the Northwest and the rich resources of the whole region, what was eventually to become the American West was still largely a geographical mystery in the immediate years after their return. Not until 1814, with the publication of their report (edited by Nicholas Biddle and Paul Allen), was there even a satisfactory cartographic representation of the whole region south and west of the Missouri River. Instead, for a long time the West remained an immense unknown, whose limits were gradually being defined by the explorers sent out into it by the governments and fur-trading companies along its margins.

American Land Policy

PAUL W. GATES

In attempting to present an overview of American land policy I propose to discuss in the most general terms the acquisition of the public domain, the fundamental constitutional questions relating to it, the divergent points of view of the older states and the newly developing west, the double effect of the various policies adopted, and the prevailing belief, at least until fairly

Paul W. Gates, ''An Overview of American Land Policy,''© 1976 by the *Agricultural History Society*. Reprinted from *Agricultural History*, Vol. 50, No. 1 (January 1976), 213–229, by permission.

recently, that the federal government should divest itself of the ownership of public land and get it into private hands. Finally I hope to show that many of the old disputes about our public land policies are still unresolved and that we are, in a sense, back to square one.

Philadelphia, the center of government in 1787, was host to the Constitutional Convention which met in Independence Hall while, simultaneously, the Congress of the Articles of Confederation was meeting in Carpenters' Hall writing the Northwest Ordinance to provide government for the territory north of the Ohio, After many disputes and petty jealousies had been composed, Virginia, Massachusetts, and Connecticut had surrendered to the national government all or parts of western land claims and the Congress had provided in the Land Ordinance of 1785 a plan for the management and sale of the land. Though the power to own, manage, grant, and otherwise dispose of the public lands was to be one of the most nationalizing factors in the life of the federal republic, that power received slight attention in the new constitution of 1787. It is confined to twenty-six words in Article IV, Section 3: "The Congress shall have Power to dispose of and make all needful Rules and Regulations respecting the Territory or other Property belonging to the United States. . . ." But more detailed powers and restrictions had previously been agreed to during the period of the Confederation.

Virginia had ceded her western land claims in order to secure Maryland's accession to the Articles of Confederation. But Virginia had imposed two restrictions. First, the lands were to be "considered as a *common* fund for the use and benefit of such of the United States as have become, or shall become members of the confederation or federal alliance of the said States, Virginia included, according to their usual respective proportions in the general charge and expenditure, and shall be . . . disposed of for that purpose, and for no other purpose whatsoever. . . ." Second, the ceded territory should be divided into states and admitted into the Union with "the same rights of sovereignty, freedom and independence as the other States. . . ." In accepting Virginia's act of cession, Congress resolved that it should be "recorded and enrolled among the acts of the United States in Congress assembled." Thus it was established that the public lands were the sole property of the United States, that any income derived therefrom was to be shared by all the states in proportion to their representation in Congress, and that the new states were to have the same rights as the original states.

In the Northwest Ordinance of 1787 Congress declared: "The legislatures of these districts or new States, shall never interfere with the primary disposal of the soil by the United States . . . nor with any regulations Congress may find necessary, for securing the title in such soil, to the *bona fide* purchasers. No tax shall be imposed on lands . . . of the United States; and in no case shall non-resident proprietors be taxed higher than residents." Despite these limitations upon the sovereignty of the new states, and the greater one which barred slavery, Congress stated in that same ordinance that the new states should be admitted into the Union "on an equal footing with the original States, in all respects whatever. . . ." These and other inconsistencies and ambivalent positions respecting the public lands were to have a major bearing on the question, "Whose public lands?"

The Congress of the Confederation had found it difficult to resolve questions relating to the public lands over which it had thus obtained jurisdiction because each of the thirteen original states had retained such ungranted or forfeited lands as remained within their boundaries as they exist today. In addition, Massachusetts had retained ownership of present-day Maine and still held a large portion of western New York; Connecticut retained its western reserve in northeastern Ohio; New York still had many ungranted lands; Virginia retained, until 1792, public land in present-day Kentucky; and Georgia had the greatest amount of ungranted land within its present boundaries and did not cede its western land claims until 1802. Sovereignty was associated with the ownership of ungranted lands within a state's boundaries, yet this right was to be denied to new states created out of the public lands. The public land states were never to forget this limitation upon their sovereignty and their representatives were to devote themselves to rectifying the situation while the original states continued to maneuver to induce Congress to carry out the pledge it had made to Virginia that the benefits arriving from the public domain should be shared by all the states in proportion to their federal ratio.

Notwithstanding the restrictions imposed by the Virginia Act of Cession, Congress had provided in the Land Ordinance of 1785 that section 16 in each township, or one thirty-sixth of the land, should be reserved for schools. It thereby established a precedent for the continued violation of the principle that the public lands were being held for the benefit of all the states. When, subsequently, Congress made one grant after another to the western states, resentment in the older states intensified. The Virginia Act of Cession was not the only basis for their claim that the benefits of the public domain should be shared by all. Equally important was the fact that the Revolution had been won by all thirteen original states at much cost to them and that the cession of territory made by Great Britain had been made to the United States.

Thus there developed two major divisions of opinion on public land questions. The one concerned with the sharing of the land or its benefits among the states became essentially an East-West conflict between the thirteen original states, who were supported after a time by some of the older public land states. They were opposed by the newer public land states who felt that the land should be theirs and as their resources produced income it should be reinvested within their boundaries. The second division was similarly sectional, and even more political, with the more conservative eastern states wishing to prevent the public land states of the West from drawing population away from the East, thereby reducing its congressional representation, and also affecting land values and employment costs in the older area.

How was the public domain to be disposed of? In considering this question the Congress of the Confederation and later Congresses had the experience of the mother country and of the thirteen colonies to draw upon.

During this long period of 180 years, great estates of millions of acres had been granted to the Penn, Calvert, Fairfax, and Granville families and smaller holdings, ranging in size from a few thousand to several hundred thousand, even a million, acres had been bestowed on many more influential persons. These estates were farmed by tenants who paid their landlords both rents and services. By the close of the Revolution the largest of these estates had been forfeited or confiscated and there had been a considerable division of properties into smaller holdings for sale, although these changes were far from revolutionary. Some proprietors who had either evaded taking a stand in the Revolution or who had wisely opted for rebellion, managed, like the Schuylers, Livingstons, and Van Rensselaers of New York to retain their holdings. Despite the radicalism of the Declaration of Independence, and the agrarian uprisings of the time, the period of the Confederation was marked by the establishment of additional large private holdings, by Massachusetts in its New York lands, by Virginia in Kentucky, and by Tennessee and Georgia, which all distributed their lands in the most profligate manner. However, estate making was paralleled in the southern colonies by the headright system and in New England the proprietors' grants were soon divided. Consequently freemen in good standing with the authorities were able to acquire small tracts of land, and, generally speaking, the larger holdings were interspersed with small farms. The very liberality of the various land systems had proved to be the principal attraction to settlers from the old world. By 1790 the population of the United States was already 40 percent of that of Great Britain.

After the Revolution neither of these colonial precedents was at first to be followed. The egalitarian ideas of the time, the growing hostility between the owners of large estates and their tenants, and the financial needs of the federal republic sufficiently account for the fact that the United States did not make extensive *grants* of land to influential people (it did make large sales to two influential groups), but neither did it adopt the headright system with its free grants to free men. The public domain was needed for other purposes.

Alexander Hamilton was anxious that the public lands should provide revenues for the heavily indebted young nation. By an act of 1790 the income from land sales was pledged solely to payment of the nation's debts. Hamilton expected that speculators and land companies would be the principal buyers and that they would then retail the land to actual settlers. At the outset, then, Congress created a wide-open land system with no limitation upon the amount of land individuals could buy. Not until the mid nineteenth century were any limitations to be placed on purchases and these proved quite ineffective.

Questions concerning the pricing of land, the speed at which it should be surveyed and opened for settlement, and the treatment to be meted out to squatters who had helped themselves to the public domain soon created that second fundamental division of opinion between East and West previously referred to. Hamilton had hoped for prompt sale of the public land in large blocks. Later, the conservative attitude toward the public lands, favored by Henry Clay and during his early career by Daniel Webster, was that the lands should be surveyed and opened to settlement only when older areas had been well taken up and improved and the land should be offered at prices that would not tend to draw farmers away from these older areas since their leaving might adversely affect land values and also the wages of labor. Moreover, slow extension of surveys and opening the land to settlement would facilitate compact growth, keep management costs down, and assure the early introduction of roads, schools, churches, and local government, and mean good order. But western pressure groups advocated the speedy opening of new land, the conservative policy was breached, the thinly maintained barriers were broken. The frontier of settlement advanced from Florida to Louisiana, and up the Mississippi to Arkansas and Missouri, and from Ohio to Illinois to Michigan, and new territories and states were created. Soon population reached Utah territory, the Oregon country, and California. Before long the Superintendent of the Census was deploring, with a little less than accuracy, that the frontier was gone. The Webster-Hayne argument about what section had done more for the West was futile, for it was the new West, with its vigorous restless representatives, that had demanded the reduction of all barriers and the elimination of the Indians from any area attractive to whites, and they had been successful in wresting from reluctant representatives of the older states concessions in the price of land and in the terms of purchase. They obtained a general prospective Preemption Law for the protection of squatters and a Homestead Law, subsequently supplemented by additional legislation that made free homesteads of various sizes available to settlers who complied with specific requirements.

The sales policies that were in force everywhere up to 1862 and in areas previously declared open to sale until 1889, plus the government's practice of rewarding veterans with bonuses of land, not cash, had the double effect of creating both small properties and numerous extensive speculator holdings, the latter often of choice land. The result was the development of a strong antimonopolist feeling in the West and a land reform movement in the East, initiated by men like George Henry Evans and Horace Greeley who saw in the public lands the means of alleviating the lot of eastern workingmen. But not until 1866 was the principle of land limitation adopted and then only for the five southern states of Arkansas, Alabama, Florida, Louisiana, and Mississippi. Some congressmen supported the act more as a punitive than a reform measure. George W. Julian, an Indiana congressman and the most realistic of the land reformers, hoped that by limiting the 46 million acres of public lands remaining in these states to homestead entries of no more than 80 acres it would be possible to provide farms for the freedmen and landless whites. Unfortunately the lands available for entry under the Southern Homestead Act were covered with long-leaf pine or were sandy barrens not well adapted to farming. The poorer class and the freedmen received little benefit from the Act. Upon the insistence of southern congressmen, who felt that the measure was a shameful discrimination, it was repealed in 1876.

Although the Homestead Act of 1862 was for a time an outstanding success in enabling many thousands of settlers with little capital to become farm owners, the development of large properties continued even after this fundamental change in policy. Its effectiveness in contributing to the creation of farms was limited by the abuse of the settler laws, the use of dummy entrymen, the continuation of the cash-sale system and the extraordinarily generous sharing of the public lands with the railroads and the states which did not allow free homesteads on their part. Not until 1888–1891 did Congress get around to adopting a general limitation of 160 acres upon land entries, by which time 365,000,000 acres or an area ten times the size of Illinois were not open to homesteading and an additional 50,000,000 acres had passed into the hands of speculators waiting for the rise in the value of their holdings.

The federal government's control of the public domain has been a major factor in shaping federal-state relations. From the outset the new states learned to respect the powers of the national government and to look to it for assistance. When a new state was admitted into the Union it was required to write into its fundamental law the famous clause, irrevocable without the consent of the United States, disclaiming all right and title to the unappropriated lands, including the right to tax them, and declaring that the public lands "shall be and remain at the sole and entire disposition of the United States," that nonresident-owned land should never be taxed higher than resident-owned land, and that public land, when sold, should be exempt from taxation for five years. This practice was begun with the admission of Ohio in 1803, made more explicit with the admission of Louisiana in 1812, and somewhat modified by the omission of the tax exemption clause when Michigan was admitted in 1837.

The western states detected these infringements on their sovereignty, which meant that they were not being admitted to the Union on the same basis as the original states but, anxious for statehood, they accepted them. Besides, what the federal government took away with one hand it began returning with the other. New states received the sixteenth section in each township for schools, as the Land Ordinance had provided, and also land for seminaries and a university, the salt springs, and 5 percent of the net proceeds from the sale of public lands within their borders for construction of roads. As time went on, increasingly generous grants were made to states on their admission or, subsequently, for education, for the drainage of wet lands, and for the construction of roads, canals, or railroads. Few factors had a greater influence on breaking down states-rights' parochialism than the federal government's practice of sharing the public lands and the income derived from them with the states. The West learned to look to Washington for assistance with projects it could not yet afford. Constitutional limitations on the power of the federal government to undertake them were evaded with the argument that these gifts of public land to the states would increase the value and hasten the sale of the land that was retained. Yet, despite federal generosity, the attitude of the West on the public land question remained ambivalent. The western states benefited from federal policy and resented it, because public land within their borders was not all their own to manage as they saw fit.

By sharing portions of the public land with the states the federal government obliged them to create their own land-administering agencies. At the outset the public land states were under heavy pressure to make their lands available to settlers or other buyers as speedily as possible. They gave little attention to the possibility of withholding the lands for higher prices so that they would more adequately serve the purposes for which they had been granted. Later on, states were less prodigal in their management policies and were to obtain larger endowments for schools and universities. One could say that by the twentieth century most of the newer states were doing about as well with their lands as the federal government, some even better. Local control over portions of their resources did not always mean that the newer western states permitted self-seeking interest to dictate improvident management and sales policies. Indeed, in the twentieth century, the great giveaway has been more characteristic of federal than of state policies.

At the outset the grants for railroads were made to states which either undertook construction of the lines themselves or conveyed the land to private corporations. In either case, the state had prime jurisdiction over them. When interstate transcontinentals were planned in the eighteen-sixties, Congress granted the land directly to the corporation, which meant that the states could not regulate these railroads, could not tax their lands until they had been sold and the title conveyed to individuals, and could not compel forfeiture of unearned grants so as to open the land to homesteaders. The railroad mileage of the country increased from 9,021 in 1850 to 123,320 by 1895. I have not tried to determine what proportion of this mileage was built with the aid of land grants. It included most of the main lines of the Union Pacific, the Southern Pacific, the Santa Fe, the Burlington Northern, the Rock Island, the Northwestern, the Milwaukee, the Illinois Central, and the Missouri Pacific. Six new states were admitted into the Union between 1850 and 1885. All the rest of the West was divided into rapidly growing territories, from which seven states had been admitted to the Union by 1896. The construction of the railroads and the colonization work they carried on played a vital part in this rapid development. Altogether an area about the size of Texas was granted for railroads. The Association of American Railroads has long devoted much time and energy to an attempt to convince the country that the grants were mostly of mediocre land. They did include desert land, poor grazing land, and barren mountain tops. But they also included choice corn-belt land in Illinois, Missouri, Iowa, and Nebraska, and excellent wheat land in North Dakota, Montana, and Colorado. Some of the richest and most heavily timbered lands in Washington and Oregon passed to railroads, as did oil- and coal-bearing lands today worth billions of dollars. Much of the latter they still retain (or at least the subsurface rights to such land), although the public transportation services these railroads were supposed to supply have dwindled away.

Representatives of the original thirteen states became resentful of the liberality with which Congress was sharing the public domain with the western states, building them up with grants for roads, canals, and railroads which the older states had had to provide for themselves, and drawing their farmers and their labor away to the cheaper and more fertile lands of the West. The older states recalled that it had been agreed the public domain should benefit all the states. It was theirs too, was it not? They were determined to get their share. In 1832 Henry Clay, a native Virginian, who regarded the terms of the Virginia cession as binding on the government, brought forth a bill to distribute the net proceeds from the sale of the public lands among the states in proportion to their federal ratio and with a special bonus allowed to the states in which the land was sold. Jackson vetoed it. The older states then prepared an alternative to Clay's distribution plan. This was the act which directed that the federal surplus, largely derived from public land sales, be deposited with the states, strictly in proportion to their federal ratio. It became law and was in operation only a short time before it was suspended.

A third effort of the older states to share in the proceeds from western land sales reached enactment in the Distribution Act of 1841, but to win support for its adoption they had to accept features they detested: allowing general prospective preemption of settlers on public lands before the public sale and granting 500,000 acres of land to each public land state for the building of internal improvements. Distribution lasted for but a moment but the western gains were permanent.

In the eighteen-fifties, when Congress was granting lands lavishly to the western states for railroads and swampland drainage and was doubling its grants to new states for public schools, representatives from the non-public land states came forth with proposals that they should share directly in the public lands. One measure, which passed the House but not the Senate, would have given 29,250,000 acres to the non-public land states for public schools; the Dix bill, which easily passed Congress but was vetoed by President Pierce, would have given every state large grants in proportion to their size and population for the improvement in the case of indigent insane people; a third measure, the Morrill Land Grant College Act of 1862, gave 30,000 acres of land or scrip (land office money) for each senator and representative to which it was entitled for the establishment of colleges of agriculture and mechanic arts. This marked the high tide of the movement for the older states to share in the public lands. Since it could not be argued that grants for agricultural colleges would increase the sales value of the remaining public lands, as the railroad grants had been expected to do, it is obvious that the Land Grant College Act was a practical recognition and application of the principle of the Virginia cession and a strong step towards a more liberal interpretation of the constitutional powers of the federal government.

Unfortunately, many of the new colleges were to find they had not the resources to support research in the newer agricultural sciences. Farm leaders, realizing the inadequacies of the new institutions, moved on a broad front to secure more federal aid for them. The agricultural college scrip given to the landless states of the East had entitled them or their assignees to land in the public domain states of the West, which strongly resented that fact, particularly as the scrip had been sold chiefly to speculators who thus acquired large holdings cheaply. This time, therefore, it was proposed to ask not for land but for income from public land sales to subsidize research programs in the agricultural sciences. Since the revenues from public land sales ranged from $4 million to $11 million annually between 1886 and 1891 some of it could easily be spared. Accordingly the Hatch Act of 1887 authorized appropriations of $15,000 to support agricultural experiment stations in every state and the Second Morrill Act of 1890 authorized a similar annual sum for the support of the land-grant colleges. (The 1890 Act permitted the establishment of more than one college in each state.) The latter sum was to be increased each succeeding year until the annual grant amounted to $25,000.

Westerners regarded as extremely dangerous to their interests an alternate proposal which Morrill of Vermont, Blaine of Maine, Hoar of Massachusetts, and other eastern senators had previously advanced. It would have required *all* the net proceeds from the public lands, after certain deductions, to be invested and the earnings to be distributed among all the states for education according to their federal ratio. In the end Morrill concluded that it was wiser to ask for half a loaf than to risk all. He therefore substituted for this proposal his second Morrill bill which Congress, in great relief, adopted. By 1890 Congress had moved far and broken down many barriers in supporting agricultural experiment stations and in instituting annual appropriations for state colleges. At the same time Congress had prevented the older states from tying up the entire revenue from public lands for which it was shortly to advocate a purely sectional use.

One of the aspects of past American land policies that is giving us trouble today is the manner in which land has been acquired from the Indians. Colonial and British governments were badgered by land promoters, with and without capital, and by frontier settlers to purchase additional land from Indian tribes. Often such persons, impatient for the land, induced the Indians to make private agreements with them and then tried to get their Indian deeds validated. The controversies that grew out of such negotiations, the terms of which where often unconscionable, and which often failed to recognize the claims of minor bands or other tribes to the territory in question, led the British government to insist that only properly accredited representatives of the government should have any part in negotiations with the Indians. Territory in which they were conceded to have rights was declared closed to white settlers, whose unauthorized intrusions had in the past led to Indian raids and warfare. The government of the United States adopted these same policies but did not succeed in preventing Indian wars. There was constant pressure from the South and West for the acquisition of reserves that had been solemnly guaranteed to the Indians. The fur trade brought white traders into the reservations. Soon the leading traders had the Indians, and particularly the chiefs, so indebted to them that they were able virtually to dominate the treaty negotiations and bring them to the conclusion desired by the whites. Lump-sum payments for the land surrendered by the Indians went to meet their obligations to the traders who could also look forward to profiting from the annuities agreed upon. Choice sites, often reserved for the chiefs at the instance of the traders, were soon acquired by them. It was the traders who were responsible for the introduction of the individual allotment system into the treaties with the Miami, Potawatomie, Choctaw, Creek, and Chickasaw Indians made during the first third of the nineteenth century. Doubtless the traders contributed also to the Dawes Severalty Act of 1887. Despite the restrictions on alienability, the allotments soon passed into the possession of whites and those who were responsible for the Act ought to have been well aware what the results would be. Step by step the Indians were deprived of their land, forced or induced to sign treaties and accept terms of compensation which they now regard as unconscionable. By an Act of 1946 they have been permitted to reopen their claims on the United States Treasury, and have won $524,000,000 in awards, one tenth of which has gone to predominantly white lawyers. But the Indians, having gained a bagatelle, now want to recover possession of lands they were once cheated out of.

Well before 1890 the best of America's arable lands had passed into private ownership. There remained large areas of dry land east of the Rockies in the intermountain country and in the Pacific Coast states. Irrigation had been practiced on a small scale by Indians in the Southwest, and at the missions in California, and the Mormons had resorted to it from their first settlement in Utah. By the end of the century much private capital had been invested, particularly in the San Joaquin valley of California, in reclaiming arid land. Overoptimistic estimates of the amount of water available and inadequate appreciation of the soil problems of irrigated areas had resulted in large losses but had shown the possibilities in semiarid areas if greater financial resources could be obtained for their development, and if more careful planning were done. In 1899 7,528,000 acres in the public land states were irrigated to some extent. Officials of the western railroads, the real estate interests, and boomer people joined together to win government aid—that is federal aid for irrigation schemes. Three main proposals came under discussion. Outright cession of the remaining public lands to the states, which might then mortgage them to raise funds for irrigation projects accessible to water; grants to the states to enable them to experiment on a small scale, possibly on pilot projects that might lead to something bigger; finally, federal subvention of irrigation. Cession which had been raised over and over again by western states (and was to come up again in the twentieth century) seemed out in view of the West's continued failure to win sufficient eastern support for this proposal. Small pilot plants were experimented with under the Carey Act of 1894, which promised as much as one million acres to any state containing desert lands that undertook irrigation projects. Little was accomplished. During the next eight years only 11,321 acres were patented and altogther less than a million acres of potentially irrigable land had been selected by the eleven eligible states.

Representative Francis G. Newlands, borrowing heavily from the past, including experience with Distribution and the two Morrill Acts, won enactment of a bill to create a revolving fund into which should pour all but 5 percent of the proceeds from public land sales in the sixteen western states and territories. The monies were to be used for the construction of irrigation works in the states from which they were derived.

Estimates of the amount of land that could produce crops if water could be provided ranged as high as 120 to 540 million acres, the former figure being that of Major John W. Powell, though all were extremely optimistic and based on no careful consideration. Newlands, at one point, estimated the possible irrigable area to be 70 million acres and later reduced the figure to 60 million. Actually, little more than 33 million acres are today irrigated, and this includes Texas which was not a public land state. The number of farms into which the irrigable lands might be divided ranged as high as three to six hundred thousand. Planners and dreamers—and propagandists of the time—presented the scheme as one outranked in significance only by the Homestead Act of 1862 in its potential for strengthening rural America. The generating of hydroelectric power was not at that time contemplated. However, it was soon apparent that few or no reclamation projects could be financed without attching them to hydroelectric plants and selling the water and the power, for which there was a ready demand for industrial and domestic use. Willy-nilly then, the Newlands Act, the increasing demands of the West for power, and the fact that irrigated land could repay only a small fraction of the cost of the great dams being planned, pushed the government into the development of public power on an immense scale. The planners and dreamers may have thought of establishing a rural Arcadia in the West but today their accomplishments are more commonly judged by the great industrial development and vast urban sprawl on the once desert lands of southern California, and parts of Arizona and New Mexico.

By the late twenties the West was dissatified with the slow progress of water and power projects financed with aid of the revolving fund of the Newlands Act. Actually the fund failed to revolve, again because of poor planning of the projects. Soon western interests were urging that additional appropriations for reclamation and power projects be made out of general funds. The greater part of the more than seven billion dollars expended to date by the Bureau of Reclamation has been supplementary appropriations from general funds. Nothing comparable to this enormous expenditure of public funds, ostensibly for the irrigation of farmland but increasingly to provide at very low rates hydroelectric power and water for domestic and business uses in the West, has been made in any other section of the country. Even the subsidized Tennessee Valley Authority power development in the South is a small venture in comparison with public power in the West.

Despite the generous treatment the West received from the federal government, it remained dissatisfied. Western states continued to feel that the remaining public lands ought to be controlled and managed for their particular benefits. Limits on the alienation of the public domain should not be imposed, the public ranges should be thrown open to all users without limit, efforts to halt timber plundering from public lands should be resisted, and the growing conservationist sentiment of eastern men, whom the West at that time dubbed "sentimentalists," should be fought to the bitter end. What the West wanted was no restrictions on growth. Only western men familiar with the needs of that section of the country should have responsibility for it. Hence the Commissioners of the General Land Office, the registers and receivers of the local land offices, and the House and Senate Committees on the Public Lands, and later members of the Public Land Law Review Commissions should be from the West.

With reluctance westerners had had to accept National Parks and National Forests and controlled Grazing Districts on the public range and administration by a bureaucracy centered in Washington, but they had the political clout to provide in legislation that the income of these agencies from the sale of products and services should be spent in the West. An Act of 1905 appropriated the revenues from the National Forests for "the protection, administration, improvement and extension" of the Forest Reserves but two years later it was provided that 10 percent of such revenues, later increased to 25 percent, should be returned to the states or territories in which they were collected for the support of schools and roads. Step by step other provisions for returning to the states portions of the revenue from the public lands were adopted: 37.5 percent of the income from sales and royalties for coal, oil, and gas taken from the public lands was allocated to the states of origin and 52.5 percent of these revenues to the Reclamation Fund. Approximately the same distribution was made of the income from the enormously rich lands once granted to the Oregon and California Railroad but revested in the United States. Of the income from grazing leases 12.5 percent was allotted to the states and most of the balance was to be spent in improving the range. Despite these generous allocations of funds from the public lands the West was dissatisfied. In its report to the President in 1970, the western-dominated Public Land Law Review Commission urged that in addition the federal government should make payments to the states in lieu of taxes for public land it still holds in the West, the amount ranging from 60 to 90 percent of taxes on privately owned lands.

Western parochialism appeared in a new guise in 1953 when, inspired by powerful oil interests which found state ownership of natural resources superior for them to federal, combined with a little revived government-type philosophy, it overwhelmed the past vigorous nationalism of the section and induced Congress to convey the tidelands to public land states and Texas. Though this action greatly reduced the possible flow of money into the Reclamation Fund, that was not a serious matter for long, since Congress under western pressure had taken to voting it public funds from general revenue in great amounts.

The big questions about our national land policies raised at the outset and debated from that day to this are still unsettled. Whose public land is it? For whose benefit is it to be administered? How should it be managed and by whom? Easterners thought the public domain should benefit the entire Union with special regard to conservation, broadly speaking: westerners thought it should be administered for their benefit. Neither section won completely in the end. The West continues to resent the retention in federal ownership of any land within their boundaries. We seem to be back where we started.

The old debate continues but there is not the same division of opinion between East and West. There are still elements in the West who feel that the federal government should divest itself of the public lands, if not to individuals as in the old days, at least to the states who, they believe, can manage it best. But there are other elements, both East and West, who feel that the federal government should retain what remains of the public domain, husband it carefully, not primarily for revenue purposes as in the old days, but for careful conservation of our national resources—soil, subsoil, water, trees, and minerals. They feel that the federal government will take the larger view and not allow itself to be pressured by exploitative interests to the same extent it has in the past. Others think that the states are more alert to these dangers. The old debate is still going on but in a larger frame of reference. We now take a broader view of the value of our public domain and have a more acute realization of all the ecological and human interests that must be safeguarded.

It may seem futile to try to decide with the benefit of hindsight whether American land policies have been at all times wise. Not one of the policies adopted worked out in accordance with its advocates' objectives (or what they publicly stated as their objectives), speculator accumulations were rarely contained, whatever the intent of the legislation. Adequate classification of the lands was not made before legislation, sometimes unsuited to it, was applied. Administration was not always efficient or even honest. Endless disputes occurred in some areas. Revenues were wasted. Our national decisions about our public domain were taken originally when the new nation had certain needs and was under certain pressures. Her people had already a hundred and seventy years of frontier experience that had permanently marked their attitude toward the land. As a nation we had had our revolutionary experience, and our forefathers, some of them at least, had certain ideological hopes for the future as a nation. Newcomers arrived, drawn hither by various hopes and experience in societies dominated by landlords. The techniques of agriculture and transportation and industry were at any moment at a given stage of development. All these factors influenced our land policies.

In conclusion, may I suggest that while the management of our remaining public domain is still a most serious and important problem, the management of that portion of our territory that has become private property is a more serious problem. In fact, the old distinction between public and private property is losing its sharpness, or is being eroded away, and for the sake of later generations it should be. Has a man a right to destroy good, irreplaceable agricultural land by covering it up with cement or by stripmining it? Can a man do what is most profitable for him with his own? But is it his own in an unlimited sense? Rather has he not received from society in the ownership of land a bundle of rights which society protects but which society may also limit or modify or even take over? Is not the public land that has passed into private hands a trust? Older and more crowded societies than ours have long since been obliged to take this stand and we should come to this point of view also and soon.

Υ *F U R T H E R   R E A D I N G*

John L. Allen, "Geographical Knowledge and American Images of the Louisiana Territory," *Western Historical Quarterly* 2 (1971), 151–70
———, *Passage Through the Garden: Lewis and Clark and the Image of the American Northwest* (1975)
Vernon Carstensen, ed., *The Public Lands: Studies in the History of the Public Domain* (1963)
Samuel T. Dana, *Forest and Range Policy: Its Development in the United States* (1956)
Everett Dick, *The Lure of the Land: A Social History of the Public Lands from the Articles of Confederation to the New Deal* (1970)
Richard Dillon, *Meriwether Lewis: A Biography* (1965)
Iris H. W. Engstrand, *Spanish Scientists in the New World: The Eighteenth-Century Expeditions* (1981)
Dan L. Flores, ed., *Jefferson and Southwestern Exploration: The Freeman and Custis Accounts of the Red River Expedition of 1806* (1984)
Paul W. Gates, *Fifty Million Acres: Conflicts over Kansas Land Policy, 1854–1890* (1954)
———, *History of Public Land Law Development* (1968)
———, *Landlords and Tenants on the Prairie Frontier: Studies in American Land Policy* (1973)
William H. Goetzmann, *Army Explorations in the American West, 1803–1863* (1959)
———, *New Lands, New Men: America and the Second Great Age of Discovery* (1986)
David F. Hawke, *Those Tremendous Mountains: The Story of the Lewis and Clark Expedition* (1980)
W. Eugene Hollon, *The Great American Desert, Then and Now* (1966)
———, *The Lost Pathfinder: Zebulon Montgomery Pike* (1949)
John Jackle, *Images of the Ohio Valley: A Historical Geography of Travel, 1740 to 1860* (1977)
Hildegard Birder Johnson, *Order upon the Land: The U. S. Rectangular Land Survey and the Upper Mississippi Country* (1976)
Gary D. Libecap and Ronald N. Johnson, "Property Rights, Nineteenth-Century Timber Policy and the Conservation Movement," *Journal of Economic History*, 39 (1979), 129–42
Roger L. Nichols and Patrick L. Halley, *Stephen Long and American Frontier Exploration* (1980)
Howard W. Ottoson, ed., *Land Use Policy and Problems in the United States* (1963)
Yasuo Okada, *Public Lands and Pioneer Farmers: Gage County, Nebraska, 1850–1900* (1971)
E. Louise Peffer, *The Closing of the Public Domain: Disposal and Reservation Policies, 1900–1950* (1951)
Roy M. Robbins, *Our Landed Heritage: The Public Domain, 1776–1970* (2nd ed. 1970)
Glen O. Robinson, *The Forest Service: A Study in Public Land Management* (1960)

Malcolm J. Rohrbough, *The Land Office Business: The Settlement and Administration of American Public Lands, 1789–1837* (1968)

James P. Ronda, *Lewis and Clark Among the Indians* (1984)

William D. Rowley, *U. S. Forest Service Grazing and Rangelands: A History* (1985)

Jerome O. Steffen, *William Clark: Jeffersonian Man on the Frontier* (1977)

Victor Westphall, *The Public Domain in New Mexico, 1854–1891* (1965)

Richard G. Wood, *Stephen Harriman Long, 1784–1864: Army Engineer, Explorer, Inventor* (1966)

William K. Wyant, *Westward in Eden: The Public Lands and the Conservation Movement* (1982)

CHAPTER
5

Fur Trade and Commerce

Y

Today thousands of men and women imitate the life of the Rocky Mountain fur trappers by dressing in buckskins and re-creating the lively activities of the frontier trade gatherings called rendezvouses. *The total membership in these "mountain man" clubs outnumbers the people who actually engaged in fur trapping during the first half of the nineteenth century. These enthusiastic re-creators keep alive a romantic image of the fur trade. This unrealistic romance about the trappers' lives burgeoned during their own latter years in the art of Alfred Jacob Miller and the writings of Washington Irving. Before long, a seemingly authentic American character—heroic, wild, and free—had become part of the national imagination. Historical documents and recent scholarship present a more complex picture. The mountain men's endeavors were part of a broader effort at trade and enterprise that had penetrated the plains and Rocky Mountains. American Indians, especially native women, played a vital role, and the larger story involved Indian tribes, mixed-heritage families, and international corporations. Some have argued that the mountain men's apparent search for adventure and freedom should not be reduced to a tale of interracial diplomacy, family enterprise, and corporate competition. Nonetheless, economic motivations are significant factors in explaining why some men took up this life.*

Y *D O C U M E N T S*

An English traveler, George Frederick Ruxton, authored the first two documents. The first, his colorful and romantic account of his experiences among the mountain men, records many details of their work and appearance and examines their language and attitudes toward women. The second selection is from a novel Ruxton wrote that appeared in 1849, the year after he died in St. Louis, Missouri.

In 1857, at age seventy-seven, Austin Grignon told a representative of the State Historical Society of Wisconsin about the French families of the Green Bay area who had engaged in the fur trade. Grignon's account, which appears here as the third document, reveals how frequently the French traders married native and mixed-heritage women. His attitude toward these marriages was more tolerant and less dramatic than Ruxton's. Can this difference be explained by French-Canadian traditions, or should other factors, such as native traditions and patterns of trade, be considered?

The final three documents present different views of trade in the Far West. The fourth selection is an Indian girl's account of an 1841 trip with her father and a large trapping party that traveled through the Great Basin and down the Colorado River. She describes the harsh life of the natives in the desert, the almost casual use of violence, and the occasional trade in captives. In the fifth document, Joseph Thing, employed by the Columbia River Fishing and Trading Company of Boston, writes back in 1834 to two major investors in that enterprise. He discusses his trip to the Rocky Mountains, his impressions of a rendezvous, and his ideas about selling jerked (smoked and dried) buffalo meat. Thing mentions meeting N. J. Wyeth, a young businessman from Cambridge, Massachusetts, who established Fort Hall in present-day southern Idaho. Wyeth wrote the final document in 1834, before leaving on a trip to the Oregon country via the Columbia River. His instructions to Robert Evans, the agent at the fort, reveal in great detail how a trading post should operate. Wyeth's lists of exchange rates, or "tariffs," for Indians and whites illuminate different levels of trade. The Indians were grossly underpaid, relative to whites. For example, fire steels sold for three cents each in St. Louis, but an Indian exchanged three muskrat ("rat") pelts, worth seventy-five cents in white trade, for one steel. The documents by Thing and Wyeth clearly show that many traders had a ready eye for profits and business opportunities. What other motivations might have brought these men out to the Far West?

George Ruxton on Life Among the Trappers, 1847

The trappers of the Rocky Mountains belong to a "genus" more approximating to the primitive savage than perhaps any other class of civilized man. Their lives being spent in the remote wilderness of the mountains, with no other companion than Nature herself, their habits and character assume a most singular cast of simplicity mingled with ferocity, appearing to take their colouring from the scenes and objects which surround them. Knowing no wants save those of nature, their sole care is to procure sufficient food to support life, and the necessary clothing to protect them from the rigorous climate. This, with the assistance of their trusty rifles, they are generally able to effect, but sometimes at the expense of great peril and hardship. When engaged in their avocation, the natural instinct of primitive man is ever alive, for the purpose of guarding against danger and the provision of necessary food.

Keen observers of nature, they rival the beasts of prey in discovering the haunts and habits of game, and in their skill and cunning in capturing it. Constantly exposed to perils of all kinds, they become callous to any feeling of danger, and destroy human as well as animal life with as little scruple and as freely as they expose their own. Of laws, human or divine, they neither know nor care to know. Their wish is their law, and to attain it they do not scruple as to ways and means Firm friends and bitter enemies, with them it is "a word and a blow," and the blow often first. They may have good qualities, but they are those of the animal; and people fond of giving hard names call them revengeful, bloodthirsty, drunkards (when the wherewithal is to be had), gamblers, regardless of the laws of *meum* and *tuum*—in fact, "White Indians." However, there are exceptions, and I *have* met honest mountain-men. Their animal qualities, however, are undeniable. Strong, active, hardy as bears, daring, expert in the use of their weapons, they are just what uncivilised white man might be supposed to be in a brute state, depending upon his instinct for the support of life. Not a hole or corner in the vast wilderness of the "Far West" but has been ransacked by these hardy men. From the Mississippi to the mouth of the Colorado of the West, from the frozen regions of the North to the Gila in Mexico, the beaver-hunter has set his traps in every creek and stream. All this vast country, but for the daring enterprise of these men, would be even now a *terra incognita* to geographers, as indeed a great portion still is; but there is not an acre that has not been passed and repassed by the trappers in their perilous excursions. The mountains and streams still retain the names assigned to them by the rude hunters; and these alone are the hardy pioneers who have paved the way for the settlement of the western country.

Trappers are of two kinds, the "hired hand" and the "free trapper:" the former hired for the hunt by the fur companies; the latter, supplied with animals and traps by the company, is paid a certain price for his furs and peltries.

There is also the trapper "on his own hook;" but this class is very small. He has his own animals and traps, hunts where he chooses, and sells his peltries to whom he pleases.

On starting for a hunt, the trapper fits himself out with the necessary equipment, either from the Indian trading-forts, or from some of the petty traders—coureurs des bois—who frequent the western country. This equipment consists usually of two or three horses or mules—one for saddle, the others for packs—and six traps, which are carried in a bag of leather called a *trap-sack*. Ammunition, a few pounds of tobacco, dressed deer-skins for mocassins, &c., are carried in a wallet of dressed buffalo-skin, called a possible-sack. His "possibles" and "trap-sack" are generally carried on the saddle-mule when hunting, the others being packed with the furs. The costume of the trapper is a hunting-shirt of dressed buckskin, ornamented with long fringes; pantaloons of the same material, and decorated with porcupine-quills and long fringes down the outside of the leg. A flexible felt hat and mocassins clothe his extremities. Over his left shoulder and under his right arm hang his powder-horn and bullet-pouch, in which he carries his balls, flint and steel, and odds and ends of all kinds. Round the waist is a belt, in which is stuck a large butcher-knife in a sheath of buffalo-hide, made fast to the belt by a chain or guard of steel; which also supports a little buckskin case containing a whetstone. A tomahawk is also often added; and, of course, a long heavy rifle is part and parcel of his equipment. I had nearly forgotten the pipe-holder, which hangs round his neck, and is generally a gage d'amour, and a triumph of squaw workmanship, in shape of a heart, garnished with beads and porcupine-quills.

Thus provided, and having determined the locality of his trapping-ground, he starts to the mountains, sometimes alone, sometimes with three or four in company, as soon as the breaking up of the ice allows him to commence operations. Arrived on his hunting-grounds, he follows the creeks and streams, keeping a sharp look-out for "sign." If he sees a prostrate cotton-wood tree, he examines it to discover if it be the work of beaver—whether "thrown" for the purpose of food, or to dam the stream. The track of the beaver on the mud or sand under the bank is also examined; and if the "sign" be fresh, he sets his trap in the run of the animal, hiding it under water, and attaching it by a stout chain to a picket driven in the bank, or to a bush or tree. A "float-stick" is made fast to the trap by a cord a few feet long, which, if the animal carry away the trap, floats on the water and points out its position. The trap is baited with the "medicine," an oily substance obtained from a gland in the scrotum of the beaver, but distinct from the testes. A stick is dipped into this and planted over the trap; and the beaver, attracted by the smell, and wishing a close inspection, very foolishly puts his leg into the trap, and is a "gone beaver."

When a lodge is discovered, the trap is set at the edge of the dam, at the point where the animal passes from deep to shoal water, and always under water. Early in the morning the hunter mounts his mule and examines the traps. The captured animals are skinned, and the tails, which are a great dainty, carefully packed into camp. The skin is then stretched over a hoop or framework of osier-twigs, and is allowed to dry, the flesh and fatty substance being carefully scraped (grained). When dry, it is folded into a square sheet, the fur turned inwards, and the bundle, containing about ten to twenty skins, tightly pressed and corded, and is ready for transportation. . . .

At a certain time, when the hunt is over, or they have loaded their pack animals, the trappers proceed to the "rendezvous," the locality of which has been previously agreed upon; and here the traders and agents of the fur companies await them, with such assortment of goods as their hardy customers may require, including generally a fair supply of alcohol. The trappers drop in singly and in small bands, bringing their packs of beaver to this mountain market, not unfrequently to the value of a thousand dollars each, the produce of one hunt. The dissipation of the "rendezvous," however, soon turns the trapper's pocket inside out. The goods brought by the traders, although of the most inferior quality, are sold at enormous prices:—Coffee, twenty and thirty shillings a pint-cup, which is the usual measure; tobacco fetches ten and fifteen shillings a plug; alcohol, from twenty to fifty shillings a pint; gunpowder, sixteen shillings a pint-cup; and all other articles at proportionably exorbitant prices.

The "beaver" is purchased at from two to eight dollars per pound; the Hudson's Bay Company alone buying it by the pluie, or "plew," that is, the whole skin, giving a certain price for skins, whether of old beaver or "kittens."

The rendezvous is one continued scene of drunkenness, gambling, and brawling and fighting, as long as the money and credit of the trappers last.

Seated, Indian fashion, round the fires, with a blanket spread before them, groups are seen with their "decks" of cards, playing at "euker," "poker," and "seven-up," the regular mountain-games. The stakes are "beaver," which here is current coin; and when the fur is gone, their horses, mules, rifles, and shirts, hunting-packs, and *breeches,* are staked. Daring gamblers make the rounds of the camp, challenging each other to play for the trapper's highest stake,—his horse, his squaw (if he have one), and, as once happened, his scalp. There goes "hos and beaver!" is the mountain expression when any great loss is sustained; and, sooner or later, "hos and beaver" invariably find their way into the insatiable pockets of the traders. A trapper often squanders the produce of his hunt, amounting to hundreds of dollars, in a couple of hours; and, supplied on credit with another equipment, leaves the rendezvous for another expedition, which has the same result time after time; although one tolerably successful hunt would enable him to return to the settlements and civilised life, with an ample sum to purchase and stock a farm, and enjoy himself in ease and comfort the remainder of his days.

An old trapper, a French Canadian, assured me that he had received fifteen thousand dollars for beaver during a sojourn of twenty years in the mountains. Every year he resolved in his mind to return to Canada, and, with this object, always converted his fur into cash; but a fortnight at the "rendezvous" always cleaned him out, and, at the end of twenty years, he had not even credit sufficient to buy a pound of powder.

These annual gatherings are often the scene of bloody duels, for over their cups and cards no men are more quarrelsome than your mountaineers. Rifles, at twenty paces, settle all differences, and, as may be imagined, the fall of one or other of the combatants is certain, or, as sometimes happens, both fall to the word "fire."

Ruxton on the Trappers' View of Women, 1849

The Indian women who follow the fortunes of the white hunters are remarkable for their affection and fidelity to their husbands, the which virtues, it must be remarked, are all on their own side; for, with very few exceptions, the mountaineers seldom scruple to abandon their Indian wives, whenever the fancy takes them to change their harems; and on such occasions the squaws, thus cast aside, wild with jealousy and despair, have been not unfrequently known to take signal vengeance both on their faithless husbands and on the successful beauties who have supplanted them in their affections. There are some honourable exceptions, however, to such cruelty, and many of the mountaineers stick to their red-skinned wives for better and for worse, often suffering them to gain the upper hand in the domestic economy of the lodges, and being ruled by their better halves in all things pertaining to family affairs; and it may be remarked, that, when once the lady dons the unmentionables, she becomes the veriest termagant that ever henpecked an unfortunate husband.

Your refined trappers, however, who, after many years of bachelor life, incline to take to themselves a better half, often undertake an expedition into the settlements of New Mexico, where not unfrequently they adopt a very "Young Lochinvar" system in procuring the required rib; and have been known to carry off, *vi et armis*, from the midst of a fandango in Fernandez, or El Rancho of Taos, some dark-skinned beauty—with or without her own consent is a matter of unconcern—and bear the ravished fair one across the mountains, where she soon becomes inured to the free and roving life fate has assigned her.

American women are valued at a low figure in the mountains. They are too fine and "fofarraw [fancy]." Neither can they make moccasins, or dress skins; nor are they so schooled to perfect obedience to their lords and masters as to stand a "lodge-poleing [sound thrashing]," which the western lords of the creation not unfrequently deem it their bounden duty to inflict upon their squaws for some dereliction of domestic duty. . . .

Killbuck removed the pipe from his mouth, raised his head, and puffed a rolling cloud of smoke into the air,—knocked the ashes from the bowl, likewise made his "medicine"—and [said]

"From Red River, away up north amongst the Britishers, to Heely (Gila) in the Spanish country—from old Missoura to the Sea of Californy, I've trapped and hunted. I knows the Injuns and thar 'sign,' and they knows *me*, I'm thinkin. Thirty winters has snowed on me in these hyar mountains, and a niggur or a Spaniard would larn 'some' in that time. This old tool" (tapping his rifle) "shoots 'center' *she* does; and if thar's game afoot, this child knows 'bull' from 'cow,' and ought to could. That deer is deer, and goats is goats, is plain as paint to any but a greenhorn. Beaver's a cunning crittur, but I've trapped a 'heap;' and at killing meat when meat's a-running, I'll 'shine' in the biggest kind of crowd. For twenty year I packed a squaw along. Not one, but a man y. irst I had a Blackfoot—the darndest slut as ever cried for fofarrow. I lodge-poled her on Colter's Creek, and made her quit. My buffler hos, and as good as four packs of beaver, I gave for old Bull-tail's daughter. He was head chief of the Ricaree, and 'came' nicely 'round' me. Thar was'nt enough scarlet cloth, nor beads, nor vermilion in Sublette's packs for her. Traps wouldn't buy her all the fofarrow she wanted; and in two years I'd sold her to Cross-Eagle for one of Jake Hawkin's guns—this very one I hold in my hands. Then I tried the Sioux, the Shian, and a Digger from the other side, who made the best moccasin as ever *I* wore. She was the best of all, and was rubbed out by the Yutas in the Bayou Salade. Bad was the best; and after she was gone under I tried no more.

"Afore I left the settlements I know'd a white gal, and she was some punkins. I have never seed nothing as 'ould beat her. Red blood won't 'shine' any ways you fix it; and though I'm h—for 'sign,' a woman's breast is the hardest kind of rock to me, and leaves no trail that I can see of. . . . The gal I said *I* know'd, her name I disremember, but she stands before me as plain as Chimley Rock on Platte, and thirty year and more har'nt changed a feature in her face, to me.

"If you ask this child, he'll tell you to leave the Spanish slut to her

Greasers, and hold on till you take the trail to old Missoura, whar white and Christian gals are to be had for axing. Wagh!''

Augustin Grignon on Native Wives for Green Bay Traders, Recorded in 1857

Of some of the early settlers at Green Bay, I must make a more particular mention. My father Pierre Grignon, Sr., was born in Montreal, and early engaged as a *voyageur* with traders in the Lake Superior country, and having saved his wages, he after awhile engaged as a trader on his own account, and located at Green Bay prior to 1763. He had served on some expeditions, probably during the old French war, but I remember no particulars. By his first wife, a Menomonee woman, he had three children, one of them died young from an injury by a fall, another died while at school at Montreal, and the other, Perrish, grew up, and raised a family. By his marriage with my mother, he raised nine children, and died in November, 1795, just before the birth of his youngest, at about the age of fifty-five or sixty years. He was a spare man, six feet in height, of light complexion; a man of bravery, and full of animation, but by no means quarrelsome. He was highly esteemed, and was regarded as strictly upright in all his dealings. He was particularly hospitable, and no year passed but he entertained many of the traders going to, or returning from, their winter trading posts.

Baptist Brunet, from Quebec, must have come to Green Bay about 1775, and at first, for a year, engaged in my father's employ; the next year married a natural daughter of Gautier De Verville by a Pawnee servant woman of Chas. De Langlade. He was only a farmer, but a very good one, and died at Green Bay about 1815.

Amable and Joseph Roy, brothers, and natives of Montreal, found their way to Green Bay not very long after the old French war. Amable Roy married Agate, the daughter of the Sieur Augustin De Langlade, and the widow of M. Souligny; previous to which, he had done something in the Indian trade, and after his marriage, turned his attention to farming. He had no children; his wife died about 1801, willing him all her property, and he died about a year afterwards, and gave his property to young Louis Grignon, who had lived with him from childhood. Joseph Roy had been employed as an *engage,* and married a Menomonee woman, and raised two sons and four daughters, and survived some years after the war of 1812-'15, and his very aged widow was still living but a very few years since. . . .

James Porlier, who came to Green Bay . . . in 1791, proved the most useful man to the settlement of all the French Canadian emigrants who settled there during my day. He was born at Montreal in 1765, and received a good education at a seminary in that city, with a view of the priesthood; but changing his mind, he engaged in his father's employ, who carried on a large business. In 1791, he received from Gov. Alured Clark a commission of Captain-Lieutenant of the militia of Montreal, and the same year left to seek his fortune in the West, coming directly to Green Bay. He engaged at first as a clerk for my father, and thus remained employed for two years; the first winter remaining in the store at Green Bay, and the next he spent at Mr. Grignon's trading post on the St. Croix. He then engaged in the Indian trade for himself, and spent his winters in the Indian country for many years, on the Sauk river on the Upper Mississippi, Buffalo river, Pine river, and several points on the Mississippi and Wisconsin, and continued more or less in the trade as long as he lived.

It was while on the St. Croix, in 1793, that he married Miss Marguerite Griesie, whose father was a Frenchman, the first clerk Pierre Grignon, Sr., had at Green Bay, where he married a Menomonee woman, and afterwards left the country, abandoning his wife and child. Mr. Porlier found Miss Griesie and her mother with a band of the Menomonees spending the hunting season on the St. Crois. . . .

. . . When Brown county was organized, under the American Government, Mr. Porlier was first appointed an Ensign of militia by Gov. Cass in 1819, and three years afterwards a Lieutenant. In September, 1820, he was commissioned by Gov. Cass, Chief Justice of Brown county, as the successor of Matthew Irwin, and by re-appointments continued to serve as Chief Justice till the organization of Wisconsin Territory, in 1836. In 1820, he was also commissioned a Justice of the Peace and County Commissioner; and in 1822, Judge of Probate. He was almost constantly engaged in public service between 1820 and 1836, and yet found time to do something at his old business as a trader. A few years before his death, the right half of his body became partly paralyzed, and he died after two or three days' illness, at Green Bay, July 12th, 1839, at the age of seventy-four years.

Judge Porlier was about five feet, ten inches in height, of medium size, of light complexion, a little bald, very mild, and invariably pleasant to all. The public positions he filled so long and so well, are the best evidences of the esteem for his character, and the confidence reposed in him. Such was his solicitude to fit himself for his judicial position, that he patiently translated from the English, and left in manuscript, the Revised Laws of Michigan Territory, in the French language. His widow survived him about five years; they had several children, three of whom are still living.

Charles Reaume was . . . a native of La Prairie, nearly opposite to Montreal. His family was very respectable, and he enjoyed good educational advantages. He appears early to have left Montreal, and went to Detroit, where he had relatives, among them a nephew named Alexander Reaume, a trader, but if I ever knew the particulars of his career there, I have forgotten. He engaged in the Indian trade, and, like most traders, roamed the forests of the North-West, between the great Lakes and the Mississippi, and, I think, spent several years in this way, and made several journeys to Mackinaw, and at last one to Montreal, where he became united in marriage to a Miss Sanguenette, daughter of a prominent merchant of that city, and a lady of great worth. He now managed to commence business in Montreal, I think merchandizing, and mostly on credit, and by bad management, soon failed; and, naturally proud and haughty, he did not care to remain there, and thus left Montreal, abandoning his wife,—they having no children,—and again turned his face westward. He came directly to Green Bay, as I have always understood; this was in 1792, and he accompanied Mr. Porlier in the fall of that year, and spent the winter with him on the St. Croix river. Returning to the Bay the next spring, he went to Mackinaw, and managed to obtain on credit about six or seven hundred dollars worth of goods for the Indian trade, and brought them to the Bay, where, erecting a trader's cabin, of logs, covered with slabs, chinked and daubed, he opened his small store, and commenced operations. In due time he sold out, ate up, and squandered his little stock, probably as he had done at Montreal; and having no returns to make to the Mackinaw merchants, he was unable to obtain a new supply, and this ended his attempts at merchandizing.

He was a singular man—vain, pompous, and fond of show; and his sense of honor and justice was not very high. He led a jolly, easy life, always getting his share of good things whenever within his reach, and never seemed to have a care or thought for the morrow. . . .

Reaume would often say, that the next spring his wife was coming from Montreal to join him at Green Bay, and he had said the same thing so repeatedly, year after year, that even the Indians made sport of him about it. One day meeting an old Menomonee named Wat-tau-se-mo-sa, or *One-that-is-coming*, Reaume asked him when he was going to get married, remarking to him that he was getting old. "O," said the Indian, "you have been telling us that Mrs. Reaume is coming out this spring, and I am waiting for her arrival, intending to marry her." This little sally very much stirred up Reaume's anger, when he sent back a volley of *sacres*, very much to the Indian's amusement.

An Indian Girl's Story, 1841

My father was a half Mohawk Indian and half American Scotch. He could speak neither English nor French, but a few broken words of the latter. Tho not tall but rather low of stature he was rather wiry and clean built and as brave as ever drew bow on a foe. He was full of the story of the American war and used to tell me how the British ran this way and the Americans ran that way, how the British fought there and the Americans charged here, and sometimes how both ran away leaving the Indians behind them, and he would then dance and sing Indian war songs of the east, songs of chiefs long gone to join the dead.

He used to take an ironical delight in stripping and painting his body with earth of various colors; then, stalking with his horse, wheeling and dashing, reining short and firing across against and with the wind, and gesturing and speaking to the bushes and the birds, rocks and trees as if they understood him. . . .

In a few days we started,* about 150 men designed to trap the Colorado and its wastes to the sea.** On descending the hills of the big Salt Lake some of the precipices were armed in large antlers of pure pendent salt. It was very fine and white.

About twenty Paiute Indians came to our camp. One of them, a large repulsive man, was naked and full armed. Our leader called him a coward and ordered him away from our tents, but he stood leaning on his weapon. He had shortly before murdered a Canadian trapper while his wife, a Paiute woman, was fetching water. On seeing the body of her white man dead she seized her axe to strike the Indian down, but he, being active and strong, shunned the blow, leaping aside and saying, "You love the white man better than your people. 'Tis good for you to go with him," so he killed her and her two little children. I thought he would be shot to pieces, but our hunters from some cause left him to live. A quarrel arose between him and the slain man about a horse. The deceased struck the savage down with his fist and gave him hard blows on the face, which the Indian soon revenged to the last reckoning by killing him and all his family.

We ascended a muddy little stream six days from the Salt Lake. Scattered sage, juniper, nutwood and willow were on our way. The natives were kind to us. Their women were entirely nude save a short skirt of wolf or rabbit skin which dropped from their hips to half their length of thigh. They lived chiefly on wild fowl, roots, berries, fish and bowskin and garter snakes. Their great enemies were the Spaniards of Taos and California, who always when they could, robbed them of their women and children, leaving nothing but the men and the aged women, thus making their desolation more disconsolate. Their captive women were led to breed with their captors and to work them and sell them like cattle. For these reasons they always fled from us until they knew what we were, although some of us were of similar brand.

Passing on for five further days, two Indian women were found digging roots. They were seized and forced to join us. They wept silently and one of them pointed to her breasts, saying her child that sucked them would die if she left him, but our men took no heed of her. Next day her milk was streaming from her dugs and she became seriously sad, sobbing wildly and vehemently for her young, and I was bent on conniving at her escape. We also came upon three forsaken grass tents whose natives fled at our approach except two children, a boy and girl who had no mother, and their father being out hunting the others left them to their fate. The poor motherless things were much frightened and nearly choked from fear, but a little rude tenderness and some food relieved them of their extreme emotion and in a few days their woeful alarm wore off and they became playful. The

---

*from a camp on the Green River in present-day Wyoming
**the Gulf of California

Restorer, time, grew upon them as every day told how glad and brief and bitter are our seasons.

But the poor father, where was he and what a hopeless fire he must have lighted on the night of his return to his dark and grassy home. I sometimes heard a white man pray and observed he always prayed most when scared, but I did not believe that the Father Spirit heeded his prayers.

In this country the Indians make large barriers of network stretching some of them in a square or round or pointed form as suits the shape of the land. The net made of native grass is staked and hung for thousands of yards, some of them twelve to fifteen thousand paces. In night the hares run and frolic against them and hang like fish. In the morning the Divisioner and gatherer are out and the tribe gets each man, woman and child a share. These hares are visited sometimes when very numerous by a most destructive living plague. The sage tick attacks them in terrible numbers and fixing their heads and foreparts deep into the vitals, neck and along the backbone and breast of the suffering hare they suck the blood of the poor creature until they grow surcharged as large as pigeon eggs. . . .

When on serious alarms these Indians escaped for their interior deserts they carried baskets of water with them. These vessels they made water-tight by putting some gum into them with heated little stones. They then rolled the basket and the gum, in a molten state, stuck to the hollows and crevices inside that no leakage was found in them, and they thus made the vessel perfectly tight, keeping the water gush cool while it lasted.

We were now bearing southwest to west daily, the country becoming extremely barren of grass. The sage was sparse and the gravel more sandy. The prickly pears I counted in 8 tribes were grown to the height of a man. We were two weeks without seeing an Indian, no fowl of any kind no hare nor reptile nor insect, a country that appeared to possess no life; a big solemn silence pervaded the refused waste. I thought the Chief of ages denied it any gladness, yet I saw now and then a lonely flower, but whose face I knew not, stand up bravely from the dead-looking waste. We at last struck a small creek and rested our horses, finding good grass for two days. At night we heard distant shots and we fired our guns in return. Four Spaniards came up that had been after us for many days. Seeing our tracks far back their party despatched them to invite us to wait and trade and travel together. They finally came up to us driving a team of mules packed with Spanish blankets and on their way from Texas to California. The men looked poor and were afoot except the master, who was well horsed. They were driving a band of sheep for their food, killing daily in the evening. With them we traveled two weeks and traded some beaver to them for blankets and a little flour. The women were horsed, but all the children that could walk walked barefooted and looked indigent and needy. Some girls there were going, as they said, to California to marry. A large buck goat led their sheep. The strange bearded thing was to me a great curiosity. Forward he walked always alone in advance. When some distance ahead he would stand, look back and bleat. The Spaniards called him San Juan. Poor sheep, I thought it was sad to travel behind him to be killed and eaten every day. The Spaniards had a guitar and a violin and the children, women and men sang and played every evening. They were happy. They had three Indian children they forced from their parents. In such actions causing the deepest woe on earth, they appeared to be callous and utterly feelingless. Being young, their women frequently untied my hair, which was long and fine and stroking it down invited me to go to California and be happy with them, but my native mountains and father were too dear to me to heed their plausible addresses. Our own party sold them the children they stole as already stated from their parent Indians.

Next day after separating we camped close to a high cliff. . . .

Joseph Thing's Letter from the Rocky Mountains, 1834

Mess Tucker & Williams   Hams Fork Rocky Mountains
                                                              June 29th 1834

Gentn

This will inform you of our arrival in the mountains after a tedious march of 53 days on horseback from Independence. . . .

The first five hundred miles of our journey was a fine roling prarre entirely clear of timber or growth of any kind but grass it being in the spring of the year the grass was thick and green which presented the finest view and scenery of any country that I ever saw. there is nothing to obscure the sight of the eye. and as far as we could see it was the same fine green level and rooling country the soil is good and fertile But the want of wood and water is an objection for not settleing this most beautiful country. the Konzas Indians inhabit the lower part of this fine realm who have a treaty with the United States and at the expiration of a time required on by both parties this fine section of country becomes property of the United States government The upper or western part belongs to a tribe of Indians called the Pawnees they also have a similar treaty with our government Those Indians are alike all others idle and negligent except when they are on the hunt which is their delight. the squaws do what work there is done they raise a little corn and live by hunting.

The last section of the country we past through is a rough broaken sandy barren praerie as they call it but it deserves any other name than that of a praerie There is no vegetation on it except a little grass on the rivers Bottom and some bitter sage on the upland But the Buffaloes are in great plenty in this barren region also the Elk the deer and the antelope and hunting is the principal work in the country and the chase is carried on in great earnest and with great vigor and alacrity the blacks the Indians also the Whites are fond of the chase and the Buffaloe Beef is the staple article of food for thousands of Indians and whites. the fur trade is all done by the whites or nearly so they take 7/8ths of all the Beaver that is taken in this wild region and mountainous part of the globe. . . . The mountain companies are all assembled on this river this season for Rendezvous and as crazy a set of men as I ever saw, drinking is the order of the day and trade is then best effected as it seems two or three glasses of grog is the introduction to trade for that is the time men feel the richest and can buy all the worlde in thirty minutes in particular if you will trust them. Work is out of the question and a free and indipendent man is not to be trifled with for freedom goes a great way in the mountains with the white as well as the Indian. The weather in this country is dry it does not rain any after the spring rains are over the whole country suffers for the want of rain. there is no dew here but it is common to see a frost in the morning. and sometimes ice on the water in all months of the year and yet the thermometer at noon will stand at from 75° to 96° and in the morning at 50° and over. it is cold enough for any man to sleep under two Blankets all most every night through the summer.

It is out of the power of man to raise anything that is common in other countries. the frost and the drouth bids defiance to all efforts of agriculture or Industry of the husbandman. it seems to be formed espressly for the Indian who is content when he has as much meat as to supply his family for the day

Capt [Nathaniel Jarvis] Wyeth has been disappointed in his mountain contract for furs But it is my opinion that he will make more out of the goods than he would if they had taken them only it will take longer to make any returns of importance for the Beaver has to be caught instead of taking what he was to have had on our arrival here The mountain Fur Co have dissolved their copartnership and two of them are a going to hunt and trade with us with thirty or more men and we are fitting out a number of free trappers more here, and there is four more that came up with us that will fit themselves out and go down with us and trade their furs with us then we shall fit out about twenty five on wages and Capt Wyeth intends taking charge of them himself which I think will make about seventy five men in all trapping for this company without the Indian trade which will be something in the course of the year I think there is money to be made in this trade if it is well managed if not it will sink it fast I find that there is another chance of making money in this country which I think more of than I do of the fur trade. But both might be carried on with safety and profit and no one has ever attempted it yet or never have thought of it. that is the Jurk Beef trade for the Havanna [Cuba] market. I think I could with 20 men and thirty horses deliver in New Orleans yearly one Hundred tons of the first rate Beef well cured and fit for the Spanish trade and at that port we could always take the advantage of the Havanna market which is most always good at some seasons of the year. the Buffaloe Beef is superior to our northern Beef and ours is superior to the Southern. The cattle are in abundance and cost nothing only hunting and the tallow is also a great article of trade, for the Buffaloes have much heavier tallow[e?] than our oxen at home. This is one of the best climates in the world for making beef it is always dry through the season for making Beef and the Beef is the fattest and sweetest that I ever saw and I am of the impression that it will be a superior article in the Havanna Market. I have made mention of it to Capt Wyeth and he thinks it would be troublesome to get it to market. But I know it can be had on the river but in particular where it can be taken by water in small boats which we can make in the country down the river to steamboat navigation and from thence to market. please to excuse my trembling hand and errors in this attempt to address you. Yours most Respectfully sgd Joseph Thing

N. J. Wyeth's Instructions for the Fort Hall Trading Post, 1834

Instructions to Robert Evans

Fort Hall July 31st, 1834 as a gent. and Partner of the Columbia River Fishing and Trading Co I leave you the following instructions for your government during the time you may remain in charge of Fort Hall:

1st   You will remain untill you are relieved by another superintendent, or untill the expiration of your time of service with the Co unless you are obliged to evacuate by starvation or hostility of the Indians in either of which cases you will endeavor to cash what goods you are obliged to leave securely.

2nd   In trading you will adhere to the Tariff which is annexed and on no account deviate therefrom and you will give no credit to any one

3rd   You will give no supplies to any of your men unless the Co are $20 in their debt by the acts which have been handed you, you will be able to ascertain when this is the case

4th   You will have the animals left here guarded by one man in the day time and put into the Fort at night.

5th   You will keep one centry at night on duty untill your Fort is entirely finished and afterward and if any guard is found asleep you will note it in your Journal and for this and similar purposes you will keep a book in which you will enter all remarkable occurrences.

6th   Saddles and harness you will keep in some secure place in order that those disposed may have as few facilities of deserting as possible.

7th   After my departure you will first bend your attention to lining the Fort completely after which you will build such buildings as are required for store houses and habitations for the men.

8th   If a cash should be made you will be careful not to communicate it to any one

9th   When goods are sold you will make memorandum of the sale in a Book kept for the purpose entering at the same time the articles for which they are sold and to whom

10th   You will say to every white man and Indian that visits the fort that we shall continue to trade new clean robes, rats and beaver, deer, elk and antelope skins dressed, at the prices established in the tariff and shall supply the Fort with goods from time to time.

11th   You may expect a further supply of goods before the closing in of the winter.

12th   You will on all occasions trade meat whether you have a supply or not at the time.

13th   You will if possible trade 200 Upishemays [square pieces of hide] 25 good riding saddles 500 cords 200 par flushy sinews* &c&c

14th   As articles are sometimes called for that you have not got you will keep a memorandum of them so that the deficiency may be supplied.

15th   When people come to the Fort you will exercise as much hospitality as the state of your provisions will admit of the persons in charge of such parties you will invite to your own table and take for their refreshment such articles from the outfit as you deem suitable an account of which you will keep in order that the Goods left in your charge may be all accounted for.

16th   You will divide your men into two messes and appoint a cook for each, yourself will mess alone and your cook will eat after you have done this will make two messes of each 5 in number and yourself and cook in the third

17th   All hands until the work is done and while strangers are at the fort will be called at sunrise at other times one hour afterwards you will have three meals pr day for all hands

18th   You will avoid as much as possible leaving the Fort yourself, and on no occasion leave less than 6 men in the Fort, and always on such occasions one man on guard placed on the highest point of the fort.

19th   You will keep the store locked up at all times except you are in it yourself trust to no one but yourself

20th   You will not allow the men to trade the smallest article themselves but you will trade for them a reasonable quantity of leather for their own use but in no case exceed the price named in the annexed tariff

21st   As soon as I am gone you will plant some turnips at McKays horse pen first taking away all the old dung

22nd   You will from time to time look into the Cash and if you find it damaging you can remove it to one of the Bastions.

23rd   You will when there is any considerable number of Indians in the Fort keep two men in each Bastion into which allow no Indian to go.

24th   All the Pack and riding saddles which I have here you will have covered with raw hide and all Harness kept in order

25th   You will not leave the Fort yourself unless absolutely necessary but send out men to hunt.

26th   You will keep all the Fire Arms which are left with you except the mens personal Arms loaded and in the Bastions and once a Week you will draw the charges and reload them.

27th   After other matters are arranged you will make in the place laid out a Horse Pen large enough for 100 Horses

28th   You will at convenient time clean the slew of brush and reeds.

---

*Par flushy sinews are thin strips from a dehaired and dried buffalo hide called a parfleche. The best sinews usually came from the neck and back.

29th   You will erect a Privy at the place designated.

30th   Next spring you will endeavour to obtain young Antelope and Buffaloe of both sexes

31st   You will sell any or all the Animals I leave here if you can obtain 25 lb of Beaver for them.

32nd   You have left with you an account against Antoine Godins and Messrs Fraeb & I Jervais, in case they come in and pay up their dues you will credit them to a seasonable [reasonable?] amt. provided they have no beaver, but if they have you will require them to hand it over to you for what they take at the same rates as mentioned in their accounts.

32   You will have a flag made of red flannells four yards long which you will put up at 9 ock. and at 3 ock keeping it up half an hour each time and only hoist the Am. flag on particular occasions

33rd   You will endeavor to fill all the empty keegs with tallow and have them covered with green hide

34th   You will not disturb the goods in Cash for Mr. McKay* unless there is danger from water in which case you will make the safest disposition of them in your power, and you will not deliver them except to my order or personally to Mr. M.Kay.

35th   You will assort the powder before trading commences to avoid the bad appearance that it now makes and you will have a sufficient quantity of lead moulded for trading.

36th   You will in trading with the Ind. divide the papers of vermillion, as they are too large.

37th   Have all the large cut beads put up in strings so that you can measure them out in fathoms and then you will trade for beaver or robes only.

38th   You will on first arrival of a village of Indians give two or three of the chiefs a glass of liquor be sure you give this to none but chiefs of villages and on no other occasion give any to any other Indian.

Indian Tariff

For Robes and Beaver give the following articles for Elk skins and meat the same except the cloths, Blankets axes and large cut Beads

  1 Bunch common beads cut
30 Loads Ammunition
20 Loads ammunition 1 Knife
20 Loads ammunition 10 Paper Vermillion
20 Loads Ammunition Bunch small beads
20 Loads ammunition Small piece Tobacco

---

*Thomas McKay was a mixed-heritage free trader who often worked for the Hudson's Bay Company.

20 Loads ammunition ½ doz small Buttons
20 Loads ammunition 3 awls
20 loads ammunition gun worm 1 flint
 1 Fathom largest cut beads for Beaver or Robe
 1 Common Blanket cost $4.25 for Beaver or Robe
 1 Shirt for Beaver or Robe
½ yard Blue cloth for Beaver or Robe
½ yard Scarlet cloth for Beaver or Robe
Rifle 12 Beaver or Robes Fuzil 8 Beaver or Robe

For Rats [muskrats] or Mink give the following Articles

2 Flints
1 Gun worm
1 Awl
1 Fish hook
2 Loads Ammunition
1 Fire Steel for 3
4 Bells for one

For good Upishemays, Dressed Antelope and dear skins give ammunition only and trade only for good ones

10 loads ammunition and trade only good ones
 5 loads ammunition for cords
12 loads ammunition for saddles each

For all unnamed articles fix a price at your own discretion but purchase none only you are oblidged.

Tariff for the Whites

The prices you will find in the Invoice and marked on the goods. Of the Whites you will trade only Beaver Rats & Mink. Paying as follows in goods:

Viz Beaver $6 pr. large skin or $5 pr lb.
    Rats 25¢
    Mink 25¢
Or cash $3.50 pr lb or $5 pr large skin
    Male Beaver in proportion whether paid for in goods or cash

Y E S S A Y S

William R. Swagerty, a historian at the University of Idaho, in the first essay uses a sample of 312 mountain men to present a statistical profile of this distinct population. Swagerty is particularly interested in patterns of marriage and family life. His findings raise important questions about the "independence" of the mountain men, especially in their domestic life. They also underscore the significance of American Indian women in the fur trade. Howard R. Lamar, professor of history at Yale University and a past president of the Western History Association, considers the role of the trader on the western frontier in the second essay. He stresses the importance of mercantile capitalism in the development of the West. For Lamar, the fur trade is but one part of a larger economic story. Both Lamar and Swagerty offer persuasive proof that images of western trade and fur trapping need revision.

Marriage and Rocky Mountain Trappers

WILLIAM R. SWAGERTY

Since the 1830s much ink has been devoted to that special occupational group of 3,000 or so men who participated in one of the more short-lived socioeconomic phenomena in American history—the fur trade of the Far West. In all of our social history, no other category of Americans, with the exception of politicians, has received so much attention as this cadre of often overly romanticized, yet persistently charismatic, group of mythological and real personalities. Described variously as "rangers of the wilderness . . . come[ing] and go[ing] . . . when and where they please," "a 'genus' more approximating to the primitive savage than perhaps any other class of civilized man," "mountaineer[s] [leading] . . . the wild, Robin Hood kind of life, with all its strange and motley populace . . . ," "Knights without fear and without reproach," a "Reckless Breed of Men," squawmen— "rapacious, tough and antisocial," "pathfinders," "expectant capitalists," and most recently "wasteful and exploitative varmints," the mountain men have survived the test of time as a visible historical subculture within American society.

The fraternal nature of that society has been adequately demonstrated in works on the various companies involved and in the individual studies of smaller brigades, outfits, and teams included in LeRoy R. Hafen's multi-volumed *The Mountain Men and the Fur Trade of the Far West*. Furthermore, since 1963, we have seen three statistical analyses of the mountain men. These quantified studies have shown that the typical mountain men were adventuresome young men who entered the trade in the 1820s and 1830s with some capitalistic aspirations—archetypes first romanticized in the nineteenth century. After ten to twenty years as free trappers and traders, most turned to other occupational pursuits during the 1840s and 1850s after the silk hat replaced the felt hat and when formerly "fat years" of trapping turned to hard times with the overexploitation of beaver populations in the West. The vast majority of these men—mostly French-Canadians and Americans from Missouri, Virginia, and Kentucky—stayed on in the West or returned to Missouri whether or not they continued in occupations directly related to the fur trade. During his lifetime, which averaged sixty-four years,

Copyright by Western History Association. Reprinted by permission. The article first appeared as "Marriage and Settlement Patterns of Rocky Mountain Trappers and Traders," by William R. Swagerty. *Western Historical Quarterly*, 11 (April 1980), 159–180.

Decade of Birth*

1740–1760	6 births
1761–1770	8 "
1771–1780	15 "
1781–1790	36 "
1791–1800	57 "
1801–1810	65 "
1811–1820	39 "
1821–1830	5 "
1831–1840	1 "

mean year of birth = 1800
Fehrman mean = 1805

*Based on 232 cases from a sample of 312.

the typical mountain man married in the region of his major activity and fathered an average of three children. Most never achieved financial wealth; on the contrary, the average trapper/trader was quite different from the owners and field partners who attained financial gain in that the former seldom achieved above-moderate success, while the latter failed as a group as often as they succeeded. The group as a whole did turn away from fur trade enterprises in the direction of small farms, ranches, and mercantile interests, but few mountain men accumulated enough capital in their lifetimes for large entrepreneurial businesses.

In the context of what we know about the mountain men, much credit is due to Richard Fehrman for his brief but illuminating statistical review of the 292 biographical sketches in the Hafen series. What we do not know beyond the total number of marriages and a rough arithmetic breakdown of those marriages by ethnicity are the larger occupational, marital, and settlement patterns of Rocky Mountain trappers and traders based on nationality, rank in the trade, company employment, main area of activity in the trade, education—and the relationships between these factors. The purpose of this paper is to refine the statistical portrait of the Rocky Mountain fur trade as first presented by Fehrman and to explore in particular the relationship between nationality and rank in the industry on the one hand and marriage patterns and ultimate settlement patterns on the other.

Like Fehrman I have based my study on the Hafen series subjects, adding twenty men to the series' 292 subjects. My tabulations corroborate his findings on the place of birth, nationality, decade entering the fur trade, and the locale entered. Of the 232 known birthdates from a sample population of 312, the vast majority of men who would enter the trade had been born by 1815. Of the trappers and traders 50.7 percent were Anglo-Americans. Kentucky, Virginia, and the Louisiana Territory (especially the area of Missouri) accounted for approximately 40 percent of all Anglo-American birthplaces. French-Americans and French-Canadians made up 25.7 percent of the total national backgrounds of the mountain men. Of the total, 18.9 percent were born in Canada. Europeans participated to some degree, as

15.5 percent were born across the Atlantic. The largest contributor from abroad was Scotland, whose 5.7 percent of the total was twice that of England or Ireland. Those of African descent were almost unknown in the trade, with the exceptions of James Beckwourth and Edward Rose. Métis, or mixed-bloods, participated, but only to a small degree, while persons of Spanish-American descent born outside of the Louisiana Territory were almost entirely absent. One out of every one hundred trappers and traders was an Indian, demonstrating that this economic frontier was quite different from all previous ones in the history of the fur industry—especially that of Canada, where Indians were the predominant trappers.

St. Louis and Montreal provided the urban depots from which the fur traders and trappers fanned out, with five men leaving St. Louis in the employ of a company for every one out of Montreal. Of those who began their occupation only after arriving in a distinct trapping region, 21.7 percent of the total commenced their careers in the mountains of southern Colorado and northern New Mexico. Of the total, 28.2 percent initiated their careers after arriving by ship to the Pacific Northwest or on the upper Missouri River region.

By 1820, before the rendezvous system had started in the Rockies, 34.4 percent had already worked in the fur trade. Ten years later, or five years after the first rendezvous in 1825 at Henry's Fork of the Green River in present-day Wyoming, 67 percent had entered. By the year of the last major rendezvous in 1840, over 90 percent had entered the trade.

The overwhelming majority of the mountain men surveyed were trappers and traders. These men (63.4 percent of the total or 176 men) by far outnumbered factors,* owners, and field partners (23.9 percent of the total), whose primary responsibilities were financial and administrative. Numbering only 31, men at the lower echelons—hunters, guides, interpreters, and boatmen (12.7 percent of the total)—are underrepresented, indicating that most men who started at the lower rungs of the financial ladder eventually became "free agents" as trappers or traders; however, there is a paucity of information available on those men engaged in transportation and specialized services. Unlike records for the Hudson's Bay Company, the majority of official and personal records for the Rocky Mountain trade contain little information on day laborers and short-term employees, most of whom were illiterate and left no records of their own.

Employment for these men presents problems in analysis, as many worked sporadically for large companies. Statistics indicate that one-third of the total never worked for anyone—thus reinforcing the stereotype of the free trapper as an individualist. Approximately another one-third worked for small independent firms such as the Rocky Mountain Fur Company, the Columbia Fur Company, William H. Ashley's early brigades, or Nathaniel Wyeth's Oregon ventures. The final one-third were employed by the four leading companies—the Missouri Fur Company, the American Fur Company,

---

*agents in charge of trading posts

the North West Company, and the Hudson's Bay Company. Certainly many men overlapped, working for small and/or large firms part of the time and independently at other periods.

Little is known of the educational background of over two-thirds of the sample. Of the 103 known backgrounds, a surprisingly high number—21.4 percent—authored extensive letters and/or journals. Almost one-half of the known cases had a common school education, while 15 percent are listed as illiterate by their contemporaries. Were more cases known, certainly this percentage would be much higher.

Although Fehrman was reluctant to assess the years of activity in the trade due to rapid population movements in and out of the mountains, the average was fifteen years. A majority of the trappers and traders were active during these years in the northern and southern Rockies (54.6 percent), while another 17.5 percent were active primarily in the Northwest Coast region. Upper Missouri men are underrepresented in the sample (11.4 percent), while California (10.7 percent) and the Plains (5.7 percent) seem accurate. The southern Plains in particular were low in productivity of beaver and high in mortality of trappers who contacted Indian tribes of the region.

Marriage data indicates that most trappers had only one wife (1.45 average). By 1834 first marriage had taken place for the majority. Of 312 cases, 182, or 58.3 percent, never married again. Some of these marriages occurred before the husband headed west. However, 106, or 38.9 percent, of 272 first marriages, were with Indian women. Twenty men married mixed-bloods, while forty-four (16.1 percent) wedded Anglo-Americans. Many French-American marriages (9.2 percent) were consummated before the men involved left the St. Louis area; however, only six of the forty-two known Canadians married other Canadians. Fifty-two trappers who frequented Santa Fe married Spanish-American women there or in Taos (19.1 percent of all first marriages and 67.7 percent of all who would eventually settle in the Taos region), while of those who went on to California, only one-half married daughters of the Californios. Over-two thirds of the women entering first marriages with the mountain men had not married previously. Marriages were normally completed (formally and informally) within a year or two after the subject arrived in a major trading region and resulted in high social mobility. Among Indian cultures marriage yielded special trading and status privileges for a trader; among the Spanish-speaking cultures of New Mexico and California, material gains in the form of land acquisition accompanied many unions.

The average marriage lasted fifteen years and produced three children. First marriages terminated at the death of the husband in 41 percent of all cases. One out of three wives died naturally before the husband. Divorce rate is difficult to determine, as many couples simply separated and remarried, whether or not they had been formally married by European standards. 10.2 percent of the mountain men separated from their first wives. This figure—high when compared to national statistics for the nineteenth century—is nevertheless lower than one might expect after reading romantic literature on the group as a whole. Death of the wife while giving birth (5.4 percent)

Indian Wives—First and Second Marriages*

CULTURE	FIRST MARRIAGE TOTAL #	% OF ALL 1ST WIVES	SECOND MARRIAGE TOTAL #	% OF ALL 2ND WIVES
Métis	20	7.4%	3	3.3%
Tribe Unknown	16	5.9%	8	8.9%
Shoshoni	16	5.9%	4	4.4%
Sioux	14	5.1%	6	6.7%
Flathead	10	3.7%	3	3.3%
Arapaho	6	2.2%	1	1.1%
Nez Perce	6	2.2%	4	4.4%
Blackfeet	5	1.8%	2	2.2%
Pawnee	4	1.5%	1	1.1%
Crow	4	1.5%	1	1.1%
Chinook	3	1.1%	0	0.0%
Clatsop	3	1.1%	2	2.2%
Cheyenne	3	1.1%	2	2.2%

*Tribes represented are only those in which three or more women married trappers/traders at first marriage of the latter.

is average for the mid-nineteenth century. However, both of these statistics are misleading, for in 11 percent of all cases, the fate of the first wife is unknown due to activities of the husband elsewhere. This may indicate that as many as one out of every five mountain men left his first wife or vice versa.

Ninety of 272 trappers and traders married again. Over one-half married Indian or mixed-blooded women. Unlike first marriages, in which a noticeable concentration of Shoshoni, Sioux, Flathead, Arapaho, Nez Perce, and Blackfeet wives is found, second wives of native American descent tend to be more geographically diverse. While total percentage of Sioux wives increased slightly, union with Shoshoni, Flathead, and Blackfeet declined. One explanation for this is the fact that many of the trappers married into tribes that were signers of the plains treaties beginning with the Treaty of Fort Laramie in 1851. One of the provisions of that and other treaties negotiated on the plains during the 1850s and 1860s was a clause which gave status (and sometimes land) to traders who had married into the tribe as well as to their mixed-blooded descendants. Another plausible explanation in the geographic shift is the effect of disease upon tribes of the northern Rockies who, beginning with the Blackfeet in 1837, were decimated by smallpox. According to Clyde Dollar, "the Sioux managed to escape with only limited destruction while the Blackfeet, Assiniboin and Pawnee suffered massively." Still a third explanation is simply the shift in population from the northern Rockies to the trading communities of Oregon, California, the Arkansas River, and the Fort Laramie region in the 1840s.

Despite these disruptive factors, the average length of second marriage parallels that of first marriage at fifteen years. Social mobility improved for some mountain men, but more failed to advance compared with first wedlock.

Ethnicity of Third Wife

CULTURE	% OF TOTAL THIRD MARRIAGES	# OF WOMEN
Indian	41.2%	14
Anglo-American	23.5%	8
Métis	17.6%	6
New Mexican of Spanish descent	11.7%	4
French-American	2.9%	1
French-Canadian	2.9%	1

Nevertheless, these marriages seem fairly stable, as 3.5 children were born to the average couple and termination of marriage came primarily through the death of one of the spouses. A larger percentage of women in this category must be classified as abandoned in contrast to first marriages because unknown fate of the wives and divorces approach 25 percent of the total.

Of the men who took a third wife—some thirty-four in all—there seems to be little relationship between ethnicity of wife and motives for marriage. Economic status declined or remained the same in twice as many cases as it improved noticeably. Indian women occupy 41 percent of this group, while Anglos—mainly emigrants or white women back east—account for another 24 percent and Métis for 18 percent. In this post-Mexican War setting, most trappers in former areas of Mexico already had stable marriages, so Spanish American women represented only 11.7 percent of the total. Other factors in third marriages are unreliable, given the small number of cases. Most appear to have terminated by death; however, 35 percent (the highest thus far) ended with the fate of the wife unknown or by divorce. Abandonment of Indian women could have been more significant once the trapping/trading privileges granted by the tribes were no longer needed, but few personal histories bear this out.

Twelve trappers took a fourth wife. Seven of these women were Indians from the Plains, four were New Mexicans of Spanish descent, and only one—the fourth and final wife of Ashley—was an Anglo-American.* Three of these marriages produced one child each, while two others produced two and four children respectively. Of those men in this group, in addition to Ashley, Ceran St. Vrain, Francis Chardon, Robert Newell, Richens Lacy Wootton, and François Payette would not remarry a fifth time. Four mountain men did take fifth wives. Auguste Pierre Chouteau, William S. "Old Bill" Williams, John Newman, and Toussaint Charbonneau comprised this small squad. According to Chardon, writing in 1838 from Fort Clark, Charbonneau— an old man of eighty—took to himself a young wife, an Assiniboin of

---

*Richard M. Clokey's 1980 biography of Ashley, listed in Further Reading, shows that he only had three wives—a fact uncovered after the publication of Swagerty's article.

Total Number of Wives Per Man (n = 312)

STATUS	# OF MEN	%OF TOTAL VALID CASES
Unknown	23	7.4
No Wife	17	5.4
One Wife	182	58.3
Two Wives	56	17.9
Three Wives	22	7.0
Four Wives	6	1.9
Five Wives	4	1.3
Six Wives	1	.3
Seven Wives	1	.3

fourteen years who had been captured by the Arikara the previous summer and bought by Chardon from that upper Missouri tribe. Characteristic of Chardon's journal is his faithfulness in writing events of general human interest; and so he continued, "The Old Gentleman gave a feast to the Men and a glass of grog—and went to bed with his young wife, with the intention of doing his best."

Charbonneau, best known for his marriage to Sacagawea, boasted throughout his life of his many romances and marriages. By 1843, however, he was dead, and his successor in legend remains Beckwourth, who claimed he had dozens of wives but is known only for six. A braggart and more often than not a man accustomed to spinning mountain yarns, Beckwourth had a true rival in Maurice LeDuc, who can be credited with seven documented marriages in his eighty-eight years of life, including a French-Canadian, a Shoshoni, a Flathead, a Ute, a Sioux, and two New Mexicans thirty years his junior.

In sum, 180 Indian women married mountain men formally and informally according to the custom of the country. Eighty-seven Spanish-Americans in California and New Mexico married generally only after the non-Catholics had converted and were baptized. Twenty-eight Métis, a group that was only fully mature in the last years of the Rocky Mountain fur trade, married mostly Indian trappers—Delawares, Shawnees and Iroquois—and other Métis, while 117 American and Canadian women mostly of British and French extractions remained with their own kind. Overall, marriages seem to have been extremely stable given the circumstances of the multicultural social setting of the fur trade years and the seasonal nature of the industry. Of 312 cases, twenty-three men's sexual lives remain a mystery; seventeen either could not find a wife or chose not to marry at all, while those who did were largely monogamous. Of the ninety men who married more than once, thirty (33.3 percent) of them were polygamous at some point, and most of these can be accounted for as normal behavior from the cultural viewpoint of the Indian tribes, in which dual marriages often transpired. A few men did maintain white wives back east and Indian wives in the West, but this was but a small fraction of the total.

Ethnicity of First Wife Compared with Rank of the Husband (243 cases)

RANK	INDIAN		SPANISH DESCENT		AMERICAN		CANADIAN AND EUROPEAN	
	#	%	#	%	#	%	#	%
Owner	6	27.3	4	18.2	12	54.5	0	0.0
Field-partner	8	53.3	1	6.7	5	33.3	1	6.7
Factor	15	62.5	0	0.0	3	12.5	3	12.5
Trader	20	35.0	20	35.1	14	24.6	1	1.8
Guide	4	50.0	0	0.0	1	12.5	1	12.5
Trapper	32	34.4	35	37.6	21	22.6	3	3.2
Interpreter	6	75.0	0	0.0	1	12.5	0	0.0

% = % of that rank who married X ethnic

Nine-hundred and ninety-six children were born of these unions, or 3.7 per man known to have married. This figure becomes 3.2 average per man for the total sample of 312. Although region of major activity does not seem to be critical for large number of wives per man, nationality is important. French-Canadians lead the list with an average of nearly two wives each. Their cousins to the south—French-Americans mainly from Missouri—are a close second with 1.8 wives each. Métis follow a close third, marrying 1.75 times. Anglo-Americans and British-Canadians seem to be parallel to other Anglos not involved in the fur trade during the same period. Each group married an average of approximately 1.3 times.

Statistically there is a significant correlation between rank and nationality of the men in the trade on the one hand and both of these factors matched against the ethnicity of the first wife on the other. Two-thirds of all Anglo-Americans were trappers, owners, or traders, occupying 62.6 percent of all trapping positions, 50 percent of all ownerships, and 46.8 percent of all trader roles. Of this composite group, less than one-third (29.7 percent) took Indians as first wives. An equal number wed other Americans, while 36 percent married women of Spanish-American roots. The last group is especially significant in that of the 360 male foreigners who entered New Mexico and whose names appear in the Catholic Church records between 1820 and 1850, 75 percent of these men married Mexican women. One-half of all these foreigners were from the United States.

French-Americans were predominantly trappers, owners, and traders as well. Nearly three out of every four fall into these categories. However, in terms of the total work force active in the industry, only 8.4 percent of all trappers and 21 percent of all traders were French-American. Nearly one of every three owners can be traced to a French-American family in St. Louis, but the early Spanish and French oligopolies became highly stratified and competitive systems capitalized upon by Anglo-Americans in the peak years of the fur trade. In terms of marriage, 60 percent of all

Nationality of Subject Compared with Ethnicity of First Wife (259 cases)

NATIONALITY	INDIAN		AMERICAN		SPANISH-D.		CANADIAN-EUR.		MÉTIS	
	#	%	#	%	#	%	#	%	#	%
Anglo-American	38	29.7	39	30.5	46	35.9	2	1.6	2	1.6
French-American	24	60.0	9	22.5	6	15.0	1	2.5	0	0.0
French-Canadian	13	41.9	8	25.8	8	25.8	1	3.2	1	3.2
British-Canadian	1	16.7	0	0.0	1	16.7	2	33.3	2	33.3
Métis	5	62.5	0	0.0	0	0.0	0	0.0	3	37.5
European	21	52.5	11	27.5	3	7.5	3	7.5	2	5.0

% = % of men of X nationality who married women of X ethnicity at first marriage

French-Americans took Indians as first wives, while only 15 percent married women of Spanish-American heritage.

Canadians must be divided into British and French, for while the former mainly traded or ran forts and factories, the latter trapped for them or were on their own. About four out of every ten Canadians married Indian women. French-Canadians and French-Americans are both highly underrepresented in the sample for the fur trade as a whole. Men of French derivation made up the rank and file in the industry, but unfortunately very little is known of the lower echelons, many of whom were camp-tenders and freighters.

Europeans are an interesting lot in that three-fourths of them attained the rank of factor or owner. Their total numbers in both of these high levels of the trade were relatively small, but their success is startling, as 22.7 percent of all owners and 44 percent of all factors were Europeans. The lowest rank where discernible numbers of Europeans are concentrated is the level of trader in which about one of every five could trace his birthplace to a home across the sea.

By region, the Pacific Northwest accommodated these foreigners, with one-half marrying Indians at first wedlock and only one-fifth marrying white women. Of the traders, 15 percent married New Mexicans or Californians. These foreigners who settled in the Southwest were largely from the Bordeaux region of France. Had more white women been available in the northern

Occupational Breakdown by Nationality

OF ALL	X% WERE	
Anglo-Americans	77.7%	Trappers, Traders, or Owners
French-Americans	73.7%	Trappers, Traders, or Owners
British-Canadians	75.0%	Traders or Factors
French-Canadians	64.3%	Trappers
Europeans	75.0%	Owners, Traders, or Factors

Rank of Subject by Nationality (267 cases)

RANK	ANGLO-AM.		FR.-AM.		FR.-CANAD.	
Field-Partner	11	50.0%	6	27.3%	0	0.0%
Owner	11	64.7%	2	11.8%	0	0.0%
Factor	5	20.0%	2	8.0%	3	12.0%
Trader	29	46.8%	13	21.0%	2	25.0%
Guide	5	55.6%	1	11.1%	2	22.2%
Trapper	67	62.6%	9	8.4%	18	16.8%
Interpreter	0	0.0%	4	50.0%	2	25.0%

	BR.-CANAD.		MÉTIS		EUROPEAN	
Owner	0	0.0%	0	0.0%	5	22.7%
Field-Partner	0	0.0%	0	0.0%	4	23.5%
Factor	3	12.0%	1	4.0%	11	44.0%
Trader	3	4.8%	0	0.0%	14	22.6%
Guide	0	0.0%	1	11.0%	0	0.0%
Trapper	2	1.9%	2	1.9%	5	4.7%
Interpreter	0	0.0%	2	25.0%	0	0.0%

Rockies and the Pacific Northwest, one wonders how different the pattern would have been for the Scotch and Irish in particular.

Métis, the group usually termed *half-breeds* during the active years of trade, were an isolated social entity. Whereas whites intermarried with Métis women to some degree in the Far West, Métis men married other Métis or Indians, almost without exception. The most diverse occupational group, Métis seldom achieved high rank but spread their talents among trading, interpreting, guiding, and hunting activities.

In short, it seems that Anglo-Americans were the most reluctant to become "squawmen," although one in three did take an Indian wife at first marriage. This is lower than 49.3 percent—the average total percentage for all nationalities taking Indian wives. It is possible that this lower figure reflects racial prejudice on the part of Anglo-Americans; however, the predilections of Anglo-Americans are better known, as this coterie comprises 50.7 percent of the total population surveyed.

A final question not raised in previous statistical surveys of the mountain men is the relationship between marriage patterns and ultimate settlement areas. The economic decline of trapping in the late 1830s generated a decade of uncertainty and economic instability for most trappers and traders. During these transition years, most mountain men chose to stay in the West, congregating in residential communities, many of which had been important trading centers during the better days of trapping. Of those who returned to the St. Louis area—some 16.2 percent of 297—nearly 70 percent had married or would marry Americans as their final wives. About 20 percent of all French-Canadians and French-Americans still alive settled in the area and were joined by 25 percent of all Europeans who had been active further west. Less than a quarter of these "back-trailers" had married Indian women as their last wives. These men continued in mercantilism or became

Last Area of Settlement of the Mountain Men (297 cases)

AREA	NUMBER OF MEN	% TOTAL MNT. MEN
Pacific Northwest	53	17.8%
St. Louis-Kansas City	48	16.2%
California	44	14.8%
Taos Area	41	13.8%
Northern Rockies	38	12.8%
Arkansas River Settlements	24	8.1%
Great Plains	22	7.4%
East of Mississippi River	19	6.4%
Canada	5	1.7%
Elsewhere	3	1.0%
	297	100.0%

professionals or Indian agents for the United States government. Three examples of this reverse movement are Andrew Drips and James Bridger, who settled in Kansas City, and Henry Chatillon, who settled in St. Louis.

Fifty-three mountain men—the largest single aggregate—settled in the Pacific Northwest. Already a somewhat prosperous community since the 1830s, the Willamette Valley became the final resting place for 11 percent of all Anglo-Americans, 63 percent of all British-Canadians, 21 percent of all French-Canadians, 27 percent of all Europeans, and 50 percent of all Métis. Nearly two-thirds of these trappers and traders, including such men as Joseph Meek, Caleb Wilkins, and Robert Newell, lived out the rest of their lives with their Indian wives—mostly Flathead, Clatsop, and Nez Perce—at French Prairie, Champoeg, and Oregon City, turning primarily to farming and ranching for a livelihood.

California attracted a smaller percentage than might be assumed. The Golden State offered early refuge to such men as William Wolkskill, Jacob Leese, and George Yount. However, while 15 percent of the total mountain men chose Pacific shores, the only ethnic group to migrate in large numbers were Anglo-Americans—28.6 percent of the total. One in every five of these settlers never married, and of those who did the vast majority said their last vows of wedlock with Californian Mexicans. Most acquired land before the American takeover, becoming ranchers, vintners, or merchants. Some continued to take pelts in the seasonal sea otter trade. Only 9 percent of all California settlers took Indian wives with them, and none in the sample married a California Indian.

Taos, a persistent residential community of the mountain men since the 1820s, continued to provide homes for forty-one men, or 13.8 percent of the total. Unlike the example of Christopher Carson, who had two Indian wives before marrying Josepha Jaramillo in 1843, most of the permanent settlers of Taos were not "squawmen," at least not at the time of their last marriages. Almost one-half married Spanish-Americans, many of whom represented prominent New Mexican families through which the trappers gained status and land. These men, such as Charles Beaubien, Steven Lee, and Louis Robidoux turned to ranching, mercantilism, and politics after the American takeover. A good number of the Taos residents continued hunting and trapping as a sideline. Some, such as Charles Bent, Steven Lee, and Simeon Turley, would die violent deaths at the hands of the January mob during the Taos Revolt of 1847.

The Arkansas River settlements of Pueblo, Hardscrabble, and Greenhorn were also important residential communities following the drop in the price of beaver. About one-fifth of the twenty-four settlers in the sample who migrated to these communities had Indian wives with them in their final days. Seventeen percent who lived in these small southern Colorado settlements never married at all, but there was a larger group (60 percent) who found mates among the Hispanos of Colorado and northern New Mexico. Occupationally, these old-timers did some farming, but they also carried on their mountain and hunting activities as freighters, horse ranchers, guides, hidehunters and small merchant-traders. Joseph Doyle, Alexander Barclay, and Richens L. Wootton, the latter of whom even domesticated buffalo as a sideline, are exemplary of this life-style. Writing to his brother in London from Hardscrabble in 1845, Barclay summarized the morale of the community:

> Some twenty or thirty whites have collected together on the Arkansas River under the Mountains for the purpose of living by husbandry and have some hundreds head of cattle amongst us. We raise maize, have hogs and chickens, and with the addition of hunting, for there are plenty of deer and antelope and some bear and elk in our vicinity, we pass a life of sufficient though limited enjoyment. Our wants are few, and as we witness no instance of ostentation and luxury in our neighbors, we have nothing to create envy. . . . Indeed, the men who have located here are all those whom the wreck of the mountain trade and hunting parties have left on the surface, unfitted to return to former haunts or avocations, with minds alienated by new connections from home and early friends, and habits transformed by constant excitement and daring adventure from the dull plodding of the sober citizen to the reckless activity and thrilling interest of a border life, open to the aggression of the savage and the pursuit of free will, free trade and free thinking.

Many mountain men went with their families to the reservations designated in the treaties of the 1850s and 1860s. Ninety-one percent of all former trappers and traders who settled on the Great Plains did so with an Indian or Métis family. Representing only 7.4 percent of the total men in the sample, this is nonetheless important, as most of these were traders, such as James Bordeaux and Joseph Bissonette, who had strong social and kinship ties with the tribes of their wives' lineage (in this case, the Sioux).

The final region attracting large numbers of mountain men is also the area most often romanticized in western literature and in film. Thirty-eight trappers stayed in the northern Rockies, two-thirds with their Indian wives and families. Only 13 percent of the total, many who settled in the more remote mountains avoided the mining rushes of the 1860s and 1870s and became isolated recluses. Of the thirty-eight individuals who remained in the region, the largest single occupational groups were those of rancher and guide-interpreter with five each. Understandably, this was the last stronghold for those men who chose to avoid the changing nature of the American West in the period following the Civil War.

Tim Goodale is illustrative of this pattern. In the early 1860s at the age of sixty, he was found living on Boulder Creek, Colorado, in a teepee with his Shoshoni wife, Jenny. She was described by one observer as "a good looking squaw about twenty five years old who spoke good English and was neatly dressed and [was] a clean housekeeper." When the Colorado mining boom inundated the area, Goodale tried guiding for a time but became disenchanted with the miners and their shantytowns. Thus, he packed up his lodge and moved to the Bitterroot Mountains of Idaho with other trappers and their wives who preferred to live in relative isolation.

Very few mountain men followed the example of Tim Goodale. Most settled down in what might be best described as semisedentary retirement in trading communities. Christopher Carson, the archetype of the mountain man in fiction and in fact, provides a case in point. In 1856, while serving as Indian agent to the Utes, Carson reflected that he and Lucien Maxwell had decided to settle down on farms at Rayado, New Mexico, a few years earlier because they ". . . had been leading a roving life long enough and now was the time, if ever, to make a home for ourselves and our children." Like most of his contemporaries, Carson chose to stay active to the end of his life, although he accepted domestic responsibilities and conceded that his days as a trapper were over.

The conclusion to be drawn from a careful reading of the journals, memoirs, and letters of Carson and other members of the "Rocky Mountain College" of trappers and traders is that settling down was far from ideal, for most reminisced of earlier, more preferable days and lifeways. Wootton, better known as "Uncle Dick," summoned up this attitude while dictating his life-story to Howard L. Conard, who published the account in 1890:

> With the removal of the Indians from the country, the disappearance of the game, the abandonment of the stage lines, and the transfer of the freighting business from wagons to railroad trains the era of adventure, I mean real, stirring, thrilling adventure, ended in this portion of the mountain region.
>
> The whole country has thrown off its wildness, so far as the character of its inhabitants is concerned, although eastern people still speak of it as the frontier. Outside of its rugged mountain peaks, its thickly wooded cañons and its natural scenery, the Wild West is no longer wild.
>
> The wildest thing we see out here now-a-days is a cowboy. . . . Pleasure parties roam about over the mountains and instead of being loaded down with firearms and ammunition, as we used to be when we ventured into the same localities, they carry lunch baskets and amateur photographing outfits. . . .

The West had changed dramatically before the eyes of men like Wootton in the second half of the nineteenth century. Unlike the first two waves of trappers and traders who had been born between 1761–1790 and 1791–1810 respectively, many of the third generation of mountain men—born between 1811 and 1825—lived into the Gilded Age. Some witnessed the turning of the calendar into a new century. Yet this group, whose ranks included Wootton, Jim Baker, Seth E. Ward, and William T. Hamilton, were influenced as much by their own memories as by the romantic idealization of their predecessors like Carson, Bridger, and Jedediah Smith. Hamilton, who lived to 1908, claimed at the age of eighty-two that he continued to spend a part of each year trapping in the mountains of Montana, "thankful that I can still enjoy and appreciate the wonderful beauties of nature." When asked why he exposed himself to the danger inherent in leading the life of a trapper, Hamilton replied: "My answer has always been that there was a charm in the life of a free mountaineer from which one cannot free himself, after he once has fallen under its spell."

Charms aside, there was a lure in the fur trade which kept its participants active after the residential trading communities they established were inundated with farmers, miners, cattlemen, and other settlers. One can only speculate what these communities would have become had the plow, the pick, and the spur not replaced the trap and the trade store in the succession of economic frontiers. Of those trappers and traders with Indian families who were building communities throughout the West, Howard Lamar has recently suggested that "had the Americans not come, possibly a line of métis or halfbreeds would have existed from Oklahoma to Saskatchewan."

What this statistical portrait demonstrates beyond the Goetzmann, Carter-Spencer, and Fehrman surveys is that one must be wary of the stereotyping and compartmentalizing of the mountain men which has characterized writing on the subject since the 1830s. Neither a degenerate antisocial misfit who led a reclusive life in the wild nor an "expectant capitalist" who eagerly sought to rise to entrepreneurial positions in American society, the average mountain man was both nomad and urbanite—rugged individualist as well as community participant. As Howard Lamar has phrased it, the era of the mountain men represents ". . . a variety of human beings living in a fascinating world which combined the scavenger-hunting lifestyle with mercantile capitalism." They entered the West with diverse cultural baggage and adjusted quite well to the environment and the requirements of acceptable social behavior among the cultures with which they interacted and intermarried. This was made necessary in part by the seasonal nature of the fur trade, which required a flexibility of attitude and constraint of behavior that has few parallels in the annals of American history. Their sexual habits—perhaps the ultimate criterion for social behavior—clearly reveal a compromise between Euroamerican Christian norms and mores and those of the various Indian cultures of the American West and Midwest.

John Robertson, commonly called "Jack Robinson," illustrates the successful combination of Indian and white life-styles. Born in North Carolina in 1805, Robertson grew up with a rudimentary knowledge of backwoods skills which would prove valuable later. At age eleven he moved with his family to Missouri. By 1831 he had launched a career in the Rocky Mountain fur trade that would last over fifty years when he happened to meet Thomas Fitzpatrick, who needed "greenhorns" for a trip to Santa Fe. After two years with the Rocky Mountain Fur Company, Robertson had managed to save $100, which he sent from the rendezvous at Pierre's Hole to his parents in Missouri. By 1833, he, like many other company employees, struck out on his own with expectations of making enough to become a trader. Despite hardship and near-death at the hands of the Mohave Indians, Robertson managed to save $1,000 by 1837, and the following year he visited the States to see that his money had been wisely invested by William Sublette, another acquaintance from his early days in the Rockies.

Upon returning to the mountains, Robertson married into the Shoshonis and became a prominent small trader on Green River, where he was met in 1839 by Thomas J. Farnham, who wrote:

> Here were the lodges of Mr. Robinson, a trader, who usually stations himself here to traffic with the Indians and white trappers. His skin lodge was his warehouse; and buffalo robes were spread upon the ground and counter on which he displayed his butcher knives, hatchets, Powder, lead, fish-hooks and whiskey. In exchange for these articles he receives beaver skins from trappers, money from travellers and horses from the Indians. Thus, one would believe, Mr. Robinson drives a very snug little business.

By 1843, Robinson had cornered a very lucrative market in the Green River country and had married another Shoshoni after his first wife, Marique, had proven unfaithful and left him with her child by another marriage. Matt Field, the principal chronicler of Sir William Drummond Stewart's party of sportsmen and pleasure-seekers reported that the most fashionable lady of the Rocky Mountains was Margaret, better known as Madam Jack Robinson—"the intelligent lady of one of the trappers." According to Field,

> Her lodge was called the St. Charles Hotel, as it was the popular resort in camp, and in it we always found the best entertainment. Jack himself was a noble fellow, [and] . . . Madam Jack was quite a leader of Snake fashions. The trappings upon her horse did not cost less than three hundred dollars and the amount of beads and bells that hung about saddle, bridle and cupper, was really dazzling to behold. The greatest lady we saw in the Indian country was Madam Jack Robinson.

Whatever activities of entertainment took place in Madam Jack's lodge drew Indian and white alike—and with them, a bundle of money. By 1854, Robertson was said to have accumulated about $75,000—most of which he wisely invested in St. Louis real estate. By 1860, Robertson at age fifty-five was recorded in the United States census of that year as the proud father of William (age thirteen) and the stepfather of Lucile. His settlement (by then named Robertson) was a complex of small cabins which housed a variety of Indians and white traders and their families and was noted as a very respectable ranching community. Located about ten miles south of Fort Bridger, Robertson, Wyoming, remained an important residential community for trappers and their mixed-blood families—housed and fed by

"Uncle Jack," who slowly sold off much of his St. Louis property to provide for the Indian and non-Indian residents of his town. Jack died in 1882, leaving the remainder of his land and money to his mixed-blooded children and grandchildren.

The life and times of Robertson illustrates that a middle road between the Indian and the white worlds was possible—and, in many cases, desirable to one or the other. From the Indian and Spanish-American points of view, the traders and trappers were not destroyers of their respective cultures and lifeways. The process of acculturation need not necessarily imply deculturation. For those cultures accepting the mountain men into their blood lineages, rational choices were made to accommodate outsiders. By 1850, over seven generations of Indian families mainly from the Rockies and the Plains had traded with Euroamerican trappers and traders. By that date, disease and alcohol had taken their toll among many tribes, but territorial prerogatives and control remained natively sovereign in most of the West. The fur trade was a reciprocal system which had to be bicultural and symbiotic in order to succeed in any given region of the West in the period from 1805–1850.

That mountain men were bicultural does not mean that they were colorblind and without prejudices. The very language of their accounts indicates otherwise. Nor can the fur trade era be excluded from the list of factors which demoralized, depopulated, and eventually dispossessed Indian people in the trans-Mississippi West. The mountain men were, nonetheless, more open-minded and sensitive to other cultural viewpoints than any other social group entering the West during the nineteenth century, especially when compared with categories of settlers involved in bonanza mining, railroad construction, homesteading, town building, and ranching. This can be explained in part by the small number in the group compared with those exploiting the resources of other economic frontiers in the West. For the three thousand traders and trappers who were active across a front from Saskatoon in the north to Chihuahua to the south, from St. Louis in the East to Vancouver Island in the West, numbers were part of the game of survival. The ideal and reality of fraternal organization at the level of each small outfit figured heavily in the behavior and survival of the subculture. This "common cause" mentality was especially pervasive in the earlier years of the trade from the opening of the Missouri River on a systematic basis by Manuel Lisa in 1807 through the mid-1830s. It was less apparent in the competitive and tumultuous period of the late 1830s, when the price of beaver plummeted and streams increasingly failed to yield furs due to overharvesting, forcing some men to turn exclusively to the buffalo trade and others to leave the fur trade altogether.

But the spirit of the earlier years was not lost. After the last rendezvous in 1840, when most mountain men were forced to diversify their means of making a living, residential settlement communities provided a viable alternative to going "white" or "native" for those trappers and traders with Indian wives and half-blooded children. If this was the social price a man paid for the courtesies earlier shown to him by the culture into which he married, most men accepted the paternal and marital obligations of their last wedlock, becoming as responsible in the home as they had been on the trapline or at the sutler's store. Revived heroes in our own times, this unique cadre of characters left a more enduring legacy than their own well-known and documented presence and symbolism in western history—their mixed-blooded children, whose history is yet to be written.

The Trader: Myth's Victim

HOWARD R. LAMAR

In April, 1849, a rambunctious young Texas bachelor named Benjamin Butler Harris set out for the California gold mines with a group of friends. Harris chose to take the Southern Trail across Texas, New Mexico, and Arizona to southern California as his route to the new El Dorado. Soon after he started, Harris and his party met fifteen Comanche Indians and five or six Mexican boy herders driving about five hundred Mexican horses and mules to Torrey's trading station on the Brazos. Torrey's Post, some eight miles below Waco, was the most important trading house in the history of the Brazos frontier. Though the firm was backed by New England capital, General Sam Houston was a shareholder.

The Indians came into Harris' camp, where "at night," wrote Harris,

> we had an interchange of amusements. The Indians entertained us with their songs, accompanied with shot shaken in gourds, with war whoops and jumping (which they think is dancing), after which we, in turn, with violin music danced cotillions upon the green prairie, each Indian dancer being the gentleman and each white representing the lady. I, in my cowskin boots, was introduced to a chief as "Miss Harris" and became his partner in the "light fantastic toe" performance. The chief had by way of ornament a skunk's tail fastened to his scalp lock, whose performance was far "louder" than that diffused by any ballroom dude or coquette. What a travesty! What a mocking of calisthenic exercises followed!

The bucks, Harris explained, did not understand the calls and thus "had to be slung and twisted about by their 'lady' partners, jerked this way and that through the figures until at last we gave up in fatigued merriment and retired for the night."

Aside from the enormous Freudian implications of a Texan playing a "lady" to an Indian chief, what is the significance of Harris' meeting with the Comanches? It is that when the festivities were over, some sobering facts about the nature of frontier trade came to light. The Mexican boy herders told Harris and his friends that their entire town had been wiped out by the Comanches and that the horses and mules they had with them were stolen property. It soon became clear that the boys themselves were

From *The Trader on the American Frontier: Myth's Victim*, 13–40, 49–53, by Howard R. Lamar, published by Texas A & M University Press.

captives of the Indians. The gold-seekers wanted to ambush the Indians and kill them in revenge, but one of their leaders, Captain Samuel M. Parry, and David K. Torrey, who was present, said that such an act could start an Indian war. Instead Torrey bought the boys from the Comanches, and one assumes he bought the animals as well, for Harris noted that Torrey regularly bought goods the Indians had stolen from the Mexican settlements.

The episode epitomized the difference in attitudes between the frontier trader and the nontrading American settler. Harris himself reflected the views of Colonel Harvey Mitchell, a Brazos pioneer, who told them at the outset of their journey "to shoot at every Indian we saw and save them the life of misery in subsisting on snakes, skunks and other disgusting objects." Colonel Mitchell was at least right about skunks. Harris saw the traders in an equally unfavorable light. He felt that Torrey's trading posts were "a curse to Mexico—then at peace with us—and a stimulus to robbery and murder of her people. The Torreys and their trade were, if not the prime factor, the spurs to all this ferocious deviltry."

The Torreys, on the other hand, undoubtedly saw the Comanches as customers and probably as human beings. But our mythic image of such traders has been shaped by American cultural norms and by western movies, which portray them as despicable characters cavorting with Indians and supplying them with guns. In film portrayals the trader usually has a lecherous eye for both the white and the Indian heroine. Yet the Torreys were Connecticut Yankees from a prominent Hartford family and during the 1840's assisted Houston in reversing Mirabeau B. Lamar's disastrous Indian policy of hostility toward the Comanches.

While Harris and the rest of us tend to see the Torreys from a settler's point of view, there was, in fact, a trader's point of view, indeed, a trader's world in North America that lasted from 1600 to 1850. That world has been ignored in our histories of the frontier, although we have full accounts of various frontier enterprises such as the fur trade and the Santa Fe trade. But these enterprises are seen as romantic, episodic, temporary, a mere preface to settlement. Both the fur trade and the Santa Fe trade have been seen as a time of adventure, color, and violence before reality sets in. Still, in the history of the trans-Mississippi West the trader and trade relations were the key to Indian-white relations from 1600 to 1850, a period longer than that of our nation's existence.

In re-examining the main determinants of frontier history, I would like to argue that we have neglected a dual tradition of trade and mercantile capitalism by overstressing the mythic figures of explorers, pioneers, and settlers. On the frontier trade meant many things. Our friend Harris, for example, was understandably shocked at the sale of Mexican children, yet he was actually witnessing the variation of a prehistoric trade which had gone on in the Southwest for centuries. When Coronado came to New Mexico in 1540–1541, he found slaves from the Caddoan villages of Kansas living in the Pueblo towns of New Mexico. Soon after Santa Fe was settled by the Spanish, the governors of that province began trafficking in Indian slaves who were sent to work in the mines of Chihuahua. Cabeza de Vaca, who had himself been enslaved by Texas Indians, was delighted when he encountered Indians fleeing from Spanish slave-hunting parties for, said he, "we gave many thanks to God our Lord. Having almost despaired of finding Christians again, we could hardly restrain our excitement."

From the seventeenth century to the 1860's captured Indian slaves did the work in many New Mexican households. The Spanish themselves had plugged into a general trade system that already existed between the Pueblo Indians and the Plains tribes. Central to that exchange were bison products which were bartered for cotton blankets and maize, but slaves were also an item of intertribal trade. One of the centers of the trade was Pecos, but others were to be found at Taos, Picurís, and San Juan as well. By 1630 the governor was sending expeditions into the Texas Panhandle to trade for hides. Since much of the trade was with the eastern Lipan Apaches, the Spanish tried to placate them and gave them a most-favored-nation status. There were periodic violent fights between Spaniard and Indian, but both sides continued to be governed by the trading motive, so much so that it appears the Spanish even let certain Apaches have horses in order to foster the hide trade.

The Apache and Navaho groups living west of the Rio Grande were not treated well, in part because they had nothing to trade. Instead, the Navahos were raided as a source of slaves. Trade with the eastern Apache continued after the Pueblo Revolt of 1680 until they were largely replaced by a rising trade between Spanish *comancheros* and the Comanches. By concentrating on the history of black slavery in the United States, historians have ignored the existence in the Southwest of an older, more classic form of slavery that had existed in Africa, Asia, Greece, and Rome, in which captives were incorporated into households and often became a part of the tribe or nation that had captured them.

Meanwhile the Spanish horse had spread up from New Mexico both onto the Great Plains and into the Great Basin of Utah. One of the tribes on the northeastern edge of the Great Basin who got horses were the ancestors of the Comanches, who then moved from the Rocky Mountains to eastern Colorado. In this same period Pawnee Indians on the eastern side of the central plains secured guns from French traders and spread them westward. These developments eventually caused a new shift in population, for the Comanches and Utes drove the eastern Apache south and the Comanches began trading with New Mexicans at Taos, where they provided Kiowa, Jumano, Pawnee, and Apache slaves to the Spanish and to the Pueblos. A witness in Taos described the trading:

> Here the governor, alcaldes and lieutenants gather together as many horses as they can; here is collected all the ironwork possible, such as axes, hoes, wedges, picks, bridles, machetes, belduques and knives . . . for trade and barter with these barbarians in exchange for deer and buffalo hides, and for Indian slaves, men and women, small and large, a great multitude of both sexes.

When the new Republic of Mexico let American traders come to Santa

Fe and Taos after 1821, a Euro-Indian trading system some two hundred years old was already in operation. Indians were used to traders when Bent's Fort was built on the Arkansas in 1833 and when Torrey's Post in Texas was founded in 1843. As many as 20,000 Indians might gather first at Bent's to trade and then a portion of them might move on to Torrey's. Some of the horses the Indians had might be sent by relay-barter system up to the Sioux tribes in the Dakotas. These posts and those which sprang up on the Missouri were not only the meeting ground for red and white; they were, as John Ewers tells us, an Indian recreation center, a bank, credit union, pawn shop, and even a health and welfare outpost all rolled into one organization. One can almost hear a condescending Indian telling a friend: "We have this little log post down by the riverfront, where you can get excellent drinks. The proprietor, a paleface, charges too much— you know how grasping they are—but man, it's where the action is."

This imaginary scene, full of linguistic anachronisms, is deliberate because one of the first victims of the accounts of the trader's frontier is that the Indian was himself a victim with no ability to trade or get what he wanted. The fact is that the Plains tribes traded with whites from 1700 to 1850 without a notable deterioration of their culture and strength except by disease after the smallpox epidemics of 1837. During this time at least seven generations traded without losing their culture or tribal identity. On the white side traders took pains to find out what the Indians liked and did not like. Fort Union traders on the upper Missouri were upset that the white beads they had ordered were all blue. They reported to their suppliers that the Indians wanted a large trigger guard on the guns so they could be shot by a mittened finger. We also learn that Indians played trade rivals against one another, and that some traders used Indian policemen—a kind of native security or detective agency to keep order at the posts.

Even before the white trading posts came to the Missouri Valley, the Mandan and Hidatsa villages in the vicinity of present-day Bismarck, North Dakota, were the Pecoses and Taoses of the north. There the Mandans sold corn to the Assiniboine Indians in return for meat and hides. Indians to their east sold the Mandans French or British guns at 100 percent markup, which they resold to those west and south of them at another 100 percent markup. Meanwhile, the Crow, having gotten horses from Great Basin tribes, sold Mandan horses at a fantastic markup. In turn the Mandan and other middleman tribes sold the horses at an equally fantastic markup to the Assiniboine or Cree. The concept of the Indian middleman, so well developed in studies of the Iroquois and the fur trade, has not been fully explored as a factor in trade relations with western tribes.

Among other things, trade in horses meant that an elaborate north-south trade network existed in the Great Basin which supplied Shoshonean Indians on its northern edge with so many horses they became sophisticated dealers in trading with tribes to the north and east of them. Some of these groups provided horses that sped Lewis and Clark on their historic journey to the Pacific coast in 1805.

By the nineteenth century a truly great horsetrader had emerged in the

Great Basin: the Ute Chief Walkara, whom the whites called "Walker." This handsome, hawk-nosed leader, who mixed European finery and Indian costume and had so many bells on his horses that his entourage sounded like a rhythm band, organized a band of mounted raiders and fighters from several tribes, some of them traditional enemies, to raid California ranches for horses. These were sold to mountain men and trappers at the Green River rendezvous. In one famous raid Walkara was joined by two mountain men, Thomas ("Pegleg") Smith and Jim Beckwourth. In 1839–1840 his bands divided and he struck simultaneously at many ranches and carried off more than three thousand horses. The bitter Californio ranchers paid him the dubious tribute of being "the biggest horsethief in history." Walkara sold some horses to Jim Bridger; others were sent to Santa Fe.

Walkara believed in diversification, so he raided Digger and Paiute villages for Indian women and children to be sold to New Mexicans. He liked the Mormons and traded with them. He also joined their church for, as other Indians had learned, "praying makes the pot boil." He was refused a white wife when he asked for one, however. When the Mormons stopped the slave trade and Americans came and ended the horse raids, Walkara fell on bad times. But he was impressive in power or out; it seemed appropriate that at his death fifteen horses were slaughtered on his grave.

If Walkara's obsession was horses, that of the Indian tribes of the Pacific Northwest coast was to acquire metal. From the mid-eighteenth century onward they sought iron, steel, and copper with an intensity that amazed observers. The coastal tribes already had a money system of sorts in dentalium shells secured in trade with California Indians. When Spanish vessels visiting the coast left a boat on shore or even a cross, each was smashed to bits for the ironwork it contained. The Spanish chroniclers tell us that the natives objected to inferior iron and small knives. Since the coastal tribesmen practiced slavery, some chiefs employed their slaves to make special trade goods or collect furs that white traders would want. And just as the horse stimulated cultural and economic changes among the emerging Plains tribes, so knives stimulated an artistic and cultural boom in carved wooden objects in the Northwest.

To the northwest, along the shores of Alaska, another kind of exploitation developed in the eighteenth century when Russian merchants engaged in the sea otter fur trade brought the Aleut fishermen, who were adept at catching otter, into a form of indentured servitude. As the Russians pursued the dwindling herds southward, all the way to the islands off southern California, the dutiful Aleut fishermen went with them.

From this bird's-eye view of the vast native-white trading frontiers of the trans-Mississippi West, several basic facts should be clear: first, that exploitative Indian-Indian and Indian-white trade in the West did not begin with American fur traders and Santa Fe merchants, but preceded actual white contact by generations. Second, we should see that the horse and the gun were not simply new tools of warfare and food gathering, but trade items themselves whose presence motivated warfare and intensified the trade impulse to the point that perhaps more human beings were sold into slavery or exploited for reasons of trade than ever before. Although conditions were vastly different in the American South and the American West, there is perhaps a disturbing parallel in the way a desire for profits from tobacco and cotton promoted black slavery, and a desire for trade goods promoted various forms of bonded labor in the West.

Ever since Frederick Jackson Turner wrote his famous essay, "The Significance of the Frontier in American History," in 1893, we have associated the frontier and wilderness with anarchic freedom, virginity, and democracy. But if we look at the trans-Mississippi West in the decade 1830–1840, we discover a lively trade in Mexican and Indian captives in the Southwest, the practice of debt peonage in New Mexico, Indian peonage at the missions and on the ranches of California, the institution of slavery in the Pacific Northwest, the indenture of Aleuts in Alaska, and the impressment of Hawaiian sailors (Kanakas) by American whaling and trading vessels.

As we have noted earlier, one of the foremost practitioners of a raid-and-trade way of life in the mid-nineteenth century were the Comanches. With this fact in mind the theme of Charles W. Webber's novel, *Old Hicks, the Guide* (1848), which Henry Nash Smith so brilliantly analyzed in his book, *Virgin Land: The American West as Symbol and Myth* (1950), is indeed ironic. In *Old Hicks,* Webber depicted harmless Comanches living in Peaceful Valley on the Upper Canadian River. Then whites appeared who misled them into evil ways. But when left alone the Indians and nature were innocent. Webber would probably have seen the white trader as one of the snakes in the Comanche Eden, but the fact is the trader's instinct was there before the whites came.

Long before Webber imagined his Comanche paradise, Thomas Jefferson dreamed that the American continent was truly a virgin land into which man could escape from evil by a proper use of the land to create a yeoman society. Lewis and Clark were to find that it was otherwise, a discovery which Robert Penn Warren has dramatized in his poem, *Brother to Dragons,* when he has Lewis return and say to Jefferson: "You sent me on a lie."

It is not the intention of this essay to equate trade with wickedness, but to suggest that it has always existed in one form or another in the West. Thus, in our periodic re-examinations of the frontier, we should push our accounts of trade back in time and show maps of prehistoric Indian trade centers and routes, and then depict the Spanish, the French, the British, and the American ones. In the process we should take pains to balance those famous places like Fort Vancouver, Fort Laramie, Fort Union, and Bent's Fort with acknowledgments of the existence of Torrey's and Barnard's posts in Texas and other important ones that are not so well known. In such ways we can begin to discover a major medium through which red and white men first and most successfully communicated, for if the customer was not always right or was not always considered civilized, at least each side had to understand the other.

Let us return to the Texas scene for a moment to see what took place after the Comanche and Kiowa were finally defeated in the 1870's and West Texas became a relatively safe place to live in. One of the first consequences was that Spanish Americans from New Mexico spread by the thousands onto the plains of Texas, Oklahoma, and Kansas to go into ranching and trading and eventually into railroad work, which took them to Kansas City, Omaha, and other railroad centers. It was an invisible "new frontier" that gets into cowboy songs but not into the history texts.

Not untypical was the little town of Tascosa in the Texas Panhandle, which consisted of a few stores around a plaza. Before the Comanches' power was broken, they raided Texas herds on the Goodnight-Loving Trail. After their fall, ranches spread into the area, among them the famous LX ranch founded by Bates and Beals, who like the Torrey brothers were on-the-make New England Yankees. They, too, suffered from raids, not from Indians, but from cattle thieves, and especially from Billy the Kid's gang, which rode out from the Pecos Valley to steal cattle and horses to sell to unquestioning ranchers back in New Mexico. At the same time from the eastern plains came the buffalo hunters armed with high-powered rifles. The latter not only wiped out the buffalo; in so doing they wiped out both the Indian's food supply and his basis of trade. While an ancient historic pattern of raid and trade with modern variations was continuing, the principals involved were no longer either Indian or Spanish.

In a recent article entitled "Stereotypes of the Mountain Man," Harvey L. Carter and Marcia C. Spencer drew the intriguing conclusion that their studies of the mountain men led them to believe that 60 percent of the fur traders in the Rocky Mountains were of French, French-Canadian, or French-Indian descent. Such a statement provides the clue for the next distinctive period of the mythic trading frontier in the West. It was Pierre LaClede, a French trader from New Orleans, who, by chance or design, put it all together when he established St. Louis in 1764 as the most successful trading post in the history of the United States. Symbolically, it was located almost on the site of one of the most elaborate and densely populated prehistoric Indian trading centers in the continental United States: Cahokia Mound.

Using St. Louis as a base, La Clede and his capable sons, the Chouteaus, began trading with the Indians west of the Mississippi. René Auguste and his brother Jean Pierre were in the Osage trade and later in the Missouri fur trade. In another generation Pierre Chouteau, Jr., was in the Upper Missouri trade and lead mining while his brother Auguste Pierre traded in frontier Oklahoma, where he lived like a frontier baron in a long palace with retainers and slaves. Some years before the first Americans appeared, Auguste Pierre traded so far into the Great Plains that the Spanish captured him and took him to Santa Fe. By reaching up the Missouri to the Mandan trading center and southwestward to Santa Fe, the French and Spanish traders in St. Louis provide the missing link to the origins of the western American fur trade. They also provided something else: they were bicultural, and perhaps far more than David and John Torrey they understood and accepted their red customers. Auguste Pierre had Indian and white wives. If the customer was not always right, at least his sister was interesting.

The Chouteaus, however, were only one group among many French trading families and individuals operating on the Mississippi Valley frontier.

The French had been trading across the Mississippi River on a two-thousand-mile front since the early eighteenth century. In 1713 Lamothe de Cadillac sent an intrepid Canadian lieutenant, Louis Juchereau de St. Denis, to found Natchitoches (Louisiana) and to trade into Texas and the border provinces of Mexico. St. Denis soon got to the Rio Grande. Two decades later Sieur de la Vérendrye had explored all the way from Canada to the Missouri, and by the 1790's Frenchmen were trying to trade up the Missouri from St. Louis. Even when Americans came to dominate the fur trade after 1820, French traders and trappers continued to operate their own firms and were among the first to penetrate the Gila River region and the Great Basin. And so, like persistent ghosts, the French names haunt the fur trade, begging recognition: Bernard and Sylvestre Pratte; Etienne Provost; Charles Larpenteur; Jean Baptiste Charbonneau, son of Sacajawea; Henri Chatillon, the dashing hunter-guide whom Parkman described so vividly in *The Oregon Trail;* the brothers Robidoux of Taos, and many others.

Their bicultural approach—the classic stance of a frontier trader—was such that on the northern frontier the mixed bloods came to outnumber the pureblooded Indians before the trade era ended. Some went white, some went native, and some formed new communities that were neither white nor Indian and used log cabins and farmed. The change might express itself in the use of new floral as opposed to geometric designs in crafts, or there might be compromises: those farming might still go on an annual buffalo hunt. In these instances trade meant acculturation but not necessarily defeat or deterioration of the tribes. Had the Americans not come, possibly a line of *metis* or halfbreeds would have existed from Oklahoma to Saskatchewan. Again the image of trader as destroyer is belied.

In his recent study of the Canadian frontier, W. J. Eccles has shifted the spotlight from heroes like Champlain and LaSalle to French merchants and trappers, whom he sees as paving the way for the expansion of the frontier. Eccles also finds that in Indian-white relations, Indian diplomacy was consistently better conceived and better executed than that of the European powers. On the other side, it was the French technology of beaver trapping that started the rise of the most farflung enterprise in colonial North America. And it was the French *coureurs de bois* who first adjusted to the Indian and the wilderness and thus became, in effect, the first "mountain men," though they did not operate in mountainous country. In turn they taught the British in Canada how to live in the forest and to take Indian wives.

By now the point should be obvious that the Indians, the French, and the British were all captivated by the life of the fur trade and its often surprising results. Rather than work to overturn it, they celebrated at the completion of the hunt and during the trading whether at a Montreal fair or a wilderness rendezvous. "Yet were I young again," said an old voyageur to Alexander Ross in 1825, "I should glory in commencing the same career again. I would spend another half-century in the same fields of enjoyment. There is no life as happy as a voyageur's life; none so independent; no place where a man enjoys so much variety and freedom as in the Indian country.''

As we come to the American period of trading and trapping on the Western frontier, we find that here the myths center on the nature of the Rocky Mountain fur trade and particularly on the mountain man. The Rocky Mountain system of fur trade has been praised for liberating the trade from the rivers and stationary posts by using horse-mounted brigades of trappers who stayed in the woods and did their trading once a year at wilderness rendezvous. In this system the trappers bypassed the Indian, which increased the red man's hostility and reduced his source of income for trade. The single-minded efficiency of the American fur trade system implied that it was not to be a permanent way of life but a temporary one, and it seems safe to say that even the wildest mountain man expected the plow to push aside the beaver.

The myth of the mountain man is a more complex story. In a series of historical exchanges that sometimes resemble the famous ''when did you stop beating your wife'' question, scholars and writers have argued as to whether the mountain man was, in the words of Harvey Carter, ''a romantic hero, of legendary or epic proportions''; or a daring but degraded character who could not settle and thus fled to the farthest frontier ''where he has sunk to the level of the savage inhabitants and lived a life free of moral restraint and financial responsibilities''; or whether he was, as William H. Goetzmann has described him, an expectant capitalist, hard-driving, ambitious, ''eager to improve his status in society by the acquisition of wealth.''

One need not quarrel with categorizing mountain men and fur traders in this way, but the first two definitions assume the centrality of the wilderness and the fur-trapping experience, and imply—as did contemporary writers like Washington Irving, Lewis Garrard, and George Ruxton—that the fur trade created a special type of freak: a white savage who gloried in anarchic freedom or who liked killing and scalping. It was assumed that, like a specialized dinosaur, they would die when their special environment collapsed. Such reasoning makes it apparent that they have been the major victims of romantic myths about the innocence and wildness of nature, cults about romantic primitivism, the American belief in progress, and a prudish Victorian fear of miscegenation. The very biculturalism that the French traders practiced became in the mountain men either repulsive depravity or extreme romance. The treatment of mountain men by American writers, diarists, and observers in the nineteenth century is as much an index to our cultural norms as Roy Harvey Pearce's account of white response to Indians in his *Savages and Savagism*. Indeed, the taboo against an Indian life style was remarkably similar to the taboos against the way mountain men lived.

It behooves us to find ways by which we can provide the mountain man with a means of escape from his Rocky Mountain wilderness cage. We might ask first about the origins of certain well-known but representative mountain men. Major Andrew Henry and Zenas Leonard were from Pennsylvania. William Ashley, Jim Bridger, and Joe Meek were Virginians.

Thomas Fitzpatrick and Robert Campbell were from Ireland. We find equally diverse origins among the French trappers: Charles Larpenteur was from Fountainbleau in his native France. Antoine Robidoux was French Canadian. Ceran St. Vrain, partner of the Bents, was born of French nobility in Missouri. What made the fur frontier so fascinating was not that they were all alike, but that they came from such diverse sources. It was a leather-clad foreign legion of all types and classes.

Lewis Garrard in *Wah-To-Yah and the Taos Trail* has given us the impression that all social bonds were dissolved in the mountain man's world, that he was the supreme individualist. Yet we find that the five Sublette brothers, the four Bent brothers, Joseph Walker and his brothers, the innumerable Chouteaus, the Robidoux brothers (some six in number), and Joseph Meek and his two brothers were all in the trade, or related trades, together. Not too surprisingly, blood ties counted, but so did marriage ties. Recent prosographical studies of mountain men indicate that 84 percent were married, of which number 36 percent were married to Indians and 34 percent to whites of Mexican extraction, a category nineteenth-century Americans considered nonwhite. What can we deduce from these bare statistics? Since most mountain men left no record and we have but the sketchiest accounts of the wives of those with records, arguments about whether they were degraded or noble seem useless. It does seem reasonable to argue, however, that if we know how frontier trade systems have always worked from time immemorial, and if we know how extended families worked and behaved in preindustrial societies, and if we see how the traditional French bi-cultural approach worked in North America—as well as how a half-breed society functions—we might begin to understand not only the mountain man, but also the trader and the American fur trade itself.

As a further test of the mythic accounts we must also study the nature of hunting and trapping. To comprehend the philosophy of a scavenging existence and the nature of the chase is to comprehend certain forms of frontier violence which arise when human beings come to view other human beings as quarry. Richard Slotkin, in his *Regeneration Through Violence,* has begun to explain this hunting attitude and the sense of power through killing—or through reducing the wilderness—in such a way that it does indeed seem as American as apple pie.

Next, it seems in order to differentiate mountain men not only by background and attitude, but also by age difference and generational attitudes. Major Andrew Henry was born in 1775, and his partner in the Rocky Mountain fur trade, William H. Ashley, was born in 1778. They came from a generation which knew the older systems of the fur trade, and in Missouri they came to know French ways. Ashley, once he was successful, lived grandly like the Chouteaus or a rich fur merchant of Montreal. What might be called a "second generation," born around 1798–1800, included Jedediah Smith, Charles Bent, Joseph Reddeford Walker, James Clyman, and William Sublette. That remarkable group was followed by an equally impressive "third generation" consisting of Jim Bridger, Zenas Leonard, William Bent, Kit Carson, Joe Meek, and Robert Campbell. Still another generation, in which "Uncle Dick" Wootton, Jim Baker, and William T. Hamilton could be found, was born between 1816 and 1822. Reporters interviewing the last three near the end of the nineteenth century have given us some of our most exaggerated accounts of the mountain man.

Finally, one might look at their total careers. The assumption has always existed that the mountain men were locked into a single exciting job, and that when it ended they were left broken and disoriented. The fact is that the hunting-gathering existence can take many forms. It is, so the anthropologists tell us, an efficient and flexible form of survival. At the same time the trader, whether on the frontier or in the city, is also flexible. Jedediah Smith, the greatest of the mountain men, had already switched to the Sante Fe trade when he was killed by Charles Webber's innocent Comanches at a waterhole near the Cimarron. Henry and Ashley were in other businesses besides fur trading. In these men and others we can see a powerful combination of the scavenger-hunter and the mercantile mind which turned them into talented jacks-of-all-trades.

Yet we can never destroy the myth. Despite the fact that many mountain men, including Jedediah Smith, were clean-shaven and wore regular American clothes, the image of Francis Parkman's Henri Chatillon, with his drooping felt hat, fringed deerskin leggings and moccasins, armed with a rifle and a knife, will not go away. Thus we must recognize and analyze what it was in our society after 1822 and down to the present that makes us make them a frontier myth. Part of it can be explained by the Victorian romanticism of the nineteenth century. But a major part stems from the fact that we can still go into the woods today and experience the thrill of hunting, danger, and death. It is simply a variation of the eternal adventure story, American-style.

Meanwhile we are encountering a new mythic mountain man in the popular genre of wilderness movies. As millions see *Jeremiah Johnson, A Man Called Horse,* or the adventures of a family in the wilderness, once again the issue arises: is that life degraded or noble, monstrous or kindly primitive? The point the historian must make is that they were not necessarily either, but rather a variety of human beings living in a fascinating world which combined the scavenger-hunting lifestyle with mercantile capitalism. . . .

As the frontier receded and the trading post and the cattle town disappeared, a new kind of trader appeared: the wholesale commission merchant who supplied army posts or smaller local stores by freight wagon or by train. The bicultural firm of Otero and Seller operated in territorial New Mexico, as did the firm of Charles Ilfeld, a Jewish immigrant in New Mexico. In Arizona two firms, Lord and Williams and Tully and Ochoa dominated the territory's mercantile economy for a time. In San Francisco the powerful Parrott Company supplied firms in Nevada and Arizona. In Wyoming everyone was aware that Senator Francis E. Warren's wholesale company was but the tip of a pyramid of business enterprises. In Montana the Missoula Mercantile Company, founded in the nineteenth century, still exists, as does ZCMI, the century-old department store in Salt Lake City.

When the western trader evolved from scavenger-exploiter to merchant-developer, his customers changed from Indians and frontiersmen to white settlers. It may be more than a half-truth to say that Neiman-Marcus is now serving demanding Texans just as the Torrey Brothers once served the Comanches. However great the change, there was continuity. In 1859, old Louis Vasquez, Jim Bridger's veteran partner at Bridger's Fort, sent his nephew to gold-rush Denver with goods to supply the Pikes Peakers. Jim Beckwourth, black mountain man and once a chief of the Crows, set up a hotel in the Sierras on one of the main roads to the California mines. Jim Baker, one of the wildest looking of mountain men, operated a store at the Green River Crossing of the Mormon Trail, but when gold was discovered in the Pike's Peak region, he set up a store in Denver, built a toll bridge, and ran a ranch before becoming a guide and interpreter for the Ute Indian Agency. Mountain man "Uncle Dick" Wootton ran a trading post in Denver as well as a saloon and hotel before building his famous toll road over Raton Pass.

The story of the merchant-trader runs right to the present in some parts of the West. In 1886 David and William Babbitt, two brothers in the grocery and hardware business in Cincinnati, bought a ranch in Flagstaff, Arizona, on the Atlantic and Pacific Railroad. David and another brother, George, ran a store there while William and brother Charles managed the ranch. By 1889 the Babbitt Brothers Trading Company had expanded into sheep raising, real estate, ice and meat-packing, and had bought the remnant herd of the Aztec Land and Cattle Company. In many ways they were doing what Charles and William Bent were doing at Bent's Fort and Dr. John McLoughlin was doing at Fort Vancouver, Oregon, a half century before. Eventually the Babbitts established branch stores at Holbrook, Winslow, Williams, and Kingman. They also opened Indian trading posts at Red Lake, Willow Springs, and Tuba City. By 1918 the company had automobile dealerships in Phoenix, Tucson, and El Paso. Three of the brothers went into politics as had mountain men Ashley, Sublette, and Joe Meek. By 1960 the Babbitt enterprises included a chain of supermarkets, seven Indian posts, four cattle ranches, and still other operations. A similar story of evolution could be told about two other frontier merchant firms in Arizona: the Goldwater stores and the business enterprises of the late Senator Carl Hayden.

In re-examining the frontier we need to know more about the elusive and flexible frontier trader, his attitudes and his world, for in many instances he was more of a key figure in Indian history than the missionary was. There was, as Meriwether Lewis knew, a fundamental contradiction in Jefferson's dream. The sage of Monticello hoped that the trader would be replaced by the self-sufficient farmer and that the Indian himself would be assimilated and become a farmer. Unlike most of his countrymen, Jefferson even thought that reds and whites should marry so that they would become one people. What he did not understand was that the Indian was Indian and that trade was the one successful means of communication between the world of the Indian and the world of the white. The trader, however hostile, had to know and tolerate two worlds, whereas the farmer did not, for he had no need for the Indian. What Jefferson seemed to deny was that trade itself was exciting, romantic, dangerous—and profitable. Combined with the thrill of the chase it was an inevitable and attractive part of the human condition. The combination was, in fact, a major ingredient of a unique and vigorous emerging American culture. Lewis and Clark were sent to open a passage to India and to spy out new homesteads for American farmers. What they did was to open up new franchise areas for the Indian trade. Frontier and West were, and are, two symbols of the special Indian and trader's world that resulted. And however devastating the outcome, everyone agreed that the beaver was more fun than the plow.

Y FURTHER READING

Lewis Atherton, *The Frontier Merchant in Mid-America* (1939)

Jennifer S. H. Brown, *Strangers in Blood: Fur Trade Company Families in Indian Country* (1980)

Harvey Lewis Carter and Marcia Carpenter Spence, "Stereotypes of the Mountainmen," *Western Historical Quarterly*, 6 (1975), 17–32

Richard M. Clokey, *William H. Ashley: Enterprise and Politics in the Trans-Mississippi West* (1980)

Daniel Francis and Toby Morantz, *Partners in Furs: A History of the Fur Trade in Eastern James Bay, 1600–1870* (1983)

Carolyn Gilman, *Where Two Worlds Meet: The Great Lakes Fur Trade* (1982)

Fred R. Gowans, *Rocky Mountain Rendezvous: A History of the Fur Trade Rendezvous, 1825–1840* (1977)

Conrad E. Heidenreich and Arthur J. Ray, *The Early Fur Trades: A Study in Cultural Interaction* (1976)

Harold Hickerson, "Fur Trade Colonialism and the North American Indian," *Journal of Ethnic Studies*, 1 (1973), 15–44

Theodore J. Karamanski, *Fur Trade and Exploration Opening the Far Northwest, 1821–1852* (1983)

Shepard Krech III, ed., *Indians, Animals, and the Fur Trade* (1981)

——, *The Subarctic Fur Trade: Native Social and Economic Adaptations* (1984)

Calvin Martin, *Keepers of the Game: Indian-Animal Relationships and the Fur Trade* (1978)

Frederick Merk, *Fur Trade and Empire* (1931)

Robert D. Mitchell, *Commercialism and Frontier: Perspectives on the Early Shenandoah Valley* (1977)

Thomas Elliot Norton, *The Fur Trade in Colonial New York, 1686–1776* (1974)

Richard E. Oglesby, *Manuel Lisa and the Opening of the Missouri Fur Trade* (1963)

James Neal Primm, *Economic Policy in the Development of a Western State: Missouri, 1820–1860* (1954)

George Irving Quimby, *Indian Culture and European Trade Goods: The Archaeology of the Historic Period in the Western Great Lakes Region* (1966)

Arthur J. Ray, *Indians in the Fur Trade: Their Role as Hunters, Trappers and Middlemen in the Lands Southwest of Hudson Bay, 1660–1870* (1974)

————, "Reflections on Fur Trade Social History and Métis History in Canada," *American Indian Culture and Research Journal*, 6 (1982), 91–107

————and Donald S. Freeman, *'Give Us Good Measure': An Economic Analysis of the Relations Between the Indians and the Hudson's Bay Company before 1763* (1978)

E. E. Rich, "Trade Habits and Economic Motivation Among the Indians of North America," *Canadian Journal of Economics and Political Science*, 26 (1960), 35–53

Lewis O. Saum, *The Fur Trader and the Indian* (1965)

John E. Sunder, *The Fur Trade on the Upper Missouri, 1840–1865* (1965)

Peter A. Thomas, "The Fur Trade, Indian Land and the Need to Define Adequate Environmental Parameters," *Ethnohistory*, 28 (1981), 359–79

Alan W. Trelease, "The Iroquois and the Western Fur Trade: A Problem of Interpretation," *Mississippi Valley Historical Review*, 49 (1962), 32–51

Robert A. Trennert, *Indian Trade on the Middle Border* (1981)

Daniel H. Usner, Jr., "The Frontier Exchange Economy of the Lower Mississippi Valley in the Eighteenth Century," *William and Mary Quarterly*, 44 (1987), 165–92

Sylvia Van Kirt, *Many Tender Ties: Women in Fur Trade Society, 1670–1870* (1983)

David J. Weber, *The Taos Trappers: The Fur Trade in the Far Southwest, 1540–1846* (1971)

David J. Wishart, *The Fur Trade of the American West, 1807–1840: A Geographical Synthesis* (1979)

W. Raymond Wood and Thomas D. Thiessen, *Early Fur Trade on the Northern Plains: Canadian Traders Among the Mandan and Hidatsa Indians, 1738–1818* (1985)

Mary C. Wright, "Economic Development and Native American Women in the Early Nineteenth Century," *American Quarterly*, 33 (1981), 525–36

Racism and Westward Expansion

Y

The assumption of white Anglo-Saxon cultural superiority infused many histori-cal developments in the nineteenth-century United States. Was this assumption the same as racism? In government policies toward American Indians and Mexi-cans, the possibility of racist motivations has been considered by several histori-ans. Linked with this question is the commitment to national expansion that nineteenth-century Americans often referred to as "Manifest Destiny." Did rac-ism spur white Americans and their national government to remove the Indians from the eastern United States to territories west of the Mississippi, and then to pursue wars of land acquisition against the western Indians and the nation of Mexico? When different cultures collide, are the aggressive acts of the victorious, dominant society too readily considered "racist"? Can other motivations, even good intentions, sometimes explain what happened?

Y *DOCUMENTS*

The first four documents present justifications for and reactions to the policy of Indian removal. In 1835, leaders of a small faction of the Cherokees, represent-ing possibly one thousand of the sixteen thousand tribal members, signed the Treaty of New Echota. Ratified by the U.S. Congress in 1836, this treaty forced the ultimate removal of the Cherokees to the Indian Territory west of the Mis-sissippi River. Not surprisingly, Congressman Charles Eaton Haynes of Georgia, in whose state most of the Cherokee Nation was located, supported a bill to fi-nance the removal mandated by the treaty. His remarks, reprinted as the first document, summarize some of the history of the removal policy. Haynes argues that the Indians need to be removed because of the presence of degrading white neighbors who might overwhelm them. In the second selection, President An-drew Jackson's annual message of 1835, the chief executive communicates a similar perspective. He maintains that the Indians can attain prosperity and prog-ress only if they are separated from whites. Like Haynes, Jackson stresses the benefits to be gained by the native Americans.

    The third document is the statement by the Cherokees' National Council of August 1, 1838—two months before the main body of the tribe left on its forced march, the Trail of Tears. It is an eloquent rebuttal of the Treaty of New Echota and of the removal policy. The Trail of Tears lasted from October 1838 to March 1839. At least two thousand of the sixteen thousand Cherokees died on this journey to the Indian Territory in what is now Oklahoma. In November 1838, Commissioner of Indian Affairs T. Harley Crawford did not know of this high rate of mortality when he wrote about what he considered a humane and benevolent policy of removal. Crawford's report on Indian relations appears as the fourth selection.

The final four documents present opinions about and observations of Mexicans. In the fifth document, dating from early January 1848, Senator John C. Calhoun of South Carolina, the great advocate of black slavery, argues before Congress at the conclusion of the Mexican War that the conquered nation should not be incorporated into the United States. He bases his view on a system of racial hierarchy that placed some Indian tribes above the Mexicans. Later in the same month, Senator John A. Dix of New York spoke to Congress of an inevitable expansion of the United States that he believed dictated the annexation of some of Mexico and its peoples. Dix's prejudiced plea is reprinted as the sixth selection. Both Calhoun and Dix had clear opinions of the undesirable results of mixing the races.

In the seventh document, an excerpt from the 1845 *Emigrants' Guide to California and Oregon,* author Lansford W. Hastings displays a negative view of the Mexicans in Alta California and of their religion. In the final selection, published in 1848, Edwin Bryant, a visitor to California, expresses a more positive and far less judgmental attitude toward the Hispanic Californians than Hastings's. Still, each man reveals deeply felt personal beliefs about class distinctions and racial mixing.

Charles Eaton Haynes on Indian Removal, 1836

When [the Andrew Jackson] administration came into power, seven years ago, it found a partial system of Indian colonization west of the Mississippi in operation; partial, not in withholding its benefits from any tribe which might desire to enjoy them, but only inasmuch as it embraced but a portion of the tribes then residing east of the Mississippi. The principal of these were a portion of the Creeks and Cherokees, to which have been since added the Choctaws and Chickasaws, with numerous smaller bands, together with a treaty in 1832 contemplating the removal of the remaining and greater portion of the Creeks; and, lately, the treaty with the Cherokees, to provide for the fulfilment of which the present appropriation is asked at our hands. Within the last six or seven years, the policy of removing and colonizing the Indians in the States east of the Mississippi, to the westward of that river, in a region remote from the habitation of the white man, has been among the topics of universal and bitter discussion from one end of the Union to the other. Nor on any other subject has the course of General Jackson's administration been more violently or unjustly assailed. And here I take leave to say, that so far from Indian hostilities having been provoked, either by the negligence or injustice of that administration, they may, with much greater justice, be ascribed to the political philanthropy, so loudly and pharisaically displayed by its political opponents; and I will further say, that should war arise on the part of the Cherokees, the sin of it lies not at the door of this administration, or its supporters. It may not be amiss to inquire, briefly, into the history of Indian emigration west of the Mississippi. If I am not greatly mistaken, one of the motives which induced Mr. Jefferson to desire the annexation of Louisiana to the United States was the prospective removal of the eastern Indians to its remote and uninhabited regions.

Certain it is, that in January, 1809, when addressed by a Cherokee delegation on that subject, he encouraged their examination of the country high up on Arkansas and White rivers, and promised to aid them in their emigration to it, if they should desire to remove after having explored it. It is believed that a portion of the tribe did emigrate to that country not long afterwards. Within the first year of Mr. Monroe's administration, the year 1819, a treaty was made with the whole tribe, providing for the emigration of such portion as might wish to join their brethren west of the Mississippi; and if the terms of that treaty had not been materially changed by another entered into in the year 1819, there can be but little doubt that a much larger number would have done so. But it may be answered, that, so far, the Government had not entered upon any general system upon this subject; and that, in the partial emigrations which had then taken place, it rather followed, than attempted to lead, the inclination of the Indians. However this may have been, the whole aspect of the question was changed by the especial message communicated to Congress by Mr. [James] Monroe, on the 27th of January, 1825, in which he stated that it had long occupied the attention of the Government, and recommended a general plan of Indian emigration and colonization west of the Mississippi, accompanied by an elaborate report of the Secretary of War on the subject. But a short period of Mr. Monroe's term of service then remained unexpired; but he did not go out of office until he had communicated to the Senate the treaty of the Indian Spring, of February of the same year, which provided, among other things, for an exchange of territory, and the removal of such of the Creek Indians as might desire it, beyond the Mississippi, and the operation of which treaty was arrested by his successor, in the manner I have already stated.

In 1826, an arrangement was made by the then Chief Magistrate for the removal of a portion of the Creeks to the west of the Mississippi; and in 1828, a treaty with the Cherokees of the west, which looked to the same object. Thus it appears, that, although by the act of Congress passed in May, 1830, and the treaties concluded with the Choctaws in 1830, with the Creeks in 1832, the Seminoles in 1834, and more recently with the Cherokees, and within the same period with many smaller bands, the scheme of Indian emigration and colonization west of the States and Territories beyond the Mississippi has been enlarged and systematized, its germe has a much earlier date, and the whole was recommended by Mr. Monroe in 1825. . . . It might, therefore, on the score of time and the authority of high names, be considered worse than useless to explain or defend it. But as this is the last time that I propose ever to discuss this subject, I hope I may be permitted to present a few considerations, derived from experience and the nature of things, why this system is best, both for the whites and the Indians, and especially for the latter. The races are as separate and distinct as color, character, and general condition, could well make them; the one possessing the arts and knowledge of cultivated life—the other the rude, unpolished nature of the savage. The consequence might, therefore, be naturally expected, that it is impossible that they should constitute one community with any thing like practical equality between them. Nor has experience in the slightest degree disappointed the deductions which a sound logic would have derived from these considerations. I have been told, and am in no way disposed to doubt it, that for many years past the remnants of Indian tribes still lingering in most of the old States of this Union have been treated with kindness and humanity. But of what avail have been all the efforts of ages to elevate their character and improve their condition? Alas! that character has continued to descend to the lowest depths of degradation, and that condition to unmitigated misery. Thus has it always been with the Indians, when surrounded by a white population; and thus it must always be, until the laws of nature and society shall undergo such change as can only be produced by the impress of the Deity. Nor can there be difficulty in explaining it. The poor Indian, (and in such condition he is indeed poor,) of inferior and degraded cast, associates with none of the white race, but such as are qualified to sink him into still deeper degradation. What, then, should be done to save the remnant from the moral pestilence which would inevitably await them, if relief and salvation shall be delayed until these causes shall be bought to operate upon them? There is no remedy but to remove them beyond the reach of the contamination which will surely come over them, if permitted to remain until they shall be surrounded by the causes to which I have adverted.

Andrew Jackson on Indian Removal, 1835

The plan of removing the aboriginal people who yet remain within the settled portions of the United States to the country west of the Mississippi River approaches its consummation. It was adopted on the most mature consideration of the condition of this race, and ought to be persisted in till the object is accomplished, and prosecuted with as much vigor as a just regard to their circumstances will permit, and as fast as their consent can be obtained. All preceding experiments for the improvement of the Indians have failed. It seems now to be an established fact that they can not live in contact with a civilized community and prosper. Ages of fruitless endeavors have at length brought us to a knowledge of this principle of intercommunication with them. The past we can not recall, but the future we can provide for. Independently of the treaty stipulations into which we have entered with the various tribes for the usufructuary rights they have ceded to us, no one can doubt the moral duty of the Government of the United States to protect and if possible to preserve and perpetuate the scattered remnants of this race which are left within our borders. In the discharge of this duty an extensive region in the West has been assigned for their permanent residence. It has been divided into districts and allotted among them. Many have already removed and others are preparing to go, and with the exception of two small bands living in Ohio and Indiana, not exceeding 1,500 persons, and of the Cherokees, all the tribes on the east side of the Mississippi, and extending from Lake Michigan to Florida, have entered into engagements which will lead to their transplantation.

The plan for their removal and reestablishment is founded upon the knowledge we have gained of their character and habits, and has been dictated by a spirit of enlarged liberality. A territory exceeding in extent that relinquished has been granted to each tribe. Of its climate, fertility, and capacity to support an Indian population the representations are highly favorable. To these districts the Indians are removed at the expense of the United States, and with certain supplies of clothing, arms, ammunition, and other indispensable articles; they are also furnished gratuitously with provisions for the period of a year after their arrival at their new homes. In that time, from the nature of the country and of the products raised by them, they can subsist themselves by agricultural labor, if they choose to resort to that mode of life; if they do not they are upon the skirts of the great prairies, where countless herds of buffalo roam, and a short time suffices to adapt their own habits to the changes which a change of the animals destined for their food may require. Ample arrangements have also been made for the support of schools; in some instances council houses and churches are to be erected, dwellings constructed for the chiefs, and mills for common use. Funds have been set apart for the maintenance of the poor; the most necessary mechanical arts have been introduced, and blacksmiths, gunsmiths, wheelwrights, millwrights, etc., are supported among them. Steel and iron, and sometimes salt, are purchased for them, and plows and other farming utensils, domestic animals, looms, spinning wheels, cards, etc., are presented to them. And besides these beneficial arrangements, annuities are in all cases paid, amounting in some instances to more than $30 for each individual of the tribe, and in all cases sufficiently great, if justly divided and prudently expended, to enable them, in addition to their own exertions, to live comfortably. And as a stimulus for exertion, it is now provided by law that "in all cases of the appointment of interpreters or other persons employed for the benefit of the Indians a preference shall be given to persons of Indian descent, if such can be found who are properly qualified for the discharge of the duties."

Such are the arrangements for the physical comfort and for the moral improvement of the Indians. The necessary measures for their political advancement and for their separation from our citizens have not been neglected. The pledge of the United States has been given by Congress that the country destined for the residence of this people shall be forever "secured and guaranteed to them." A country west of Missouri and Arkansas has been assigned to them, into which the white settlements are not to be pushed. No political communities can be formed in that extensive region, except those which are established by the Indians themselves or by the United States for them and with their concurrence. A barrier has thus been raised for their protection against the encroachment of our citizens, and guarding the Indians as far as possible from those evils which have brought them to their present condition. Summary authority has been given by law to destroy all ardent spirits found in their country, without waiting the doubtful result and slow process of a legal seizure. I consider the absolute and unconditional interdiction of this article among these people as the first and great step in their melioration. Halfway measures will answer no purpose. These can not successfully contend against the cupidity of the seller and the overpowering appetite of the buyer. And the destructive effects of the traffic are marked in every page of the history of our Indian intercourse.

Some general legislation seems necessary for the regulation of the relations which will exist in this new state of things between the Government and people of the United States and these transplanted Indian tribes, and for the establishment among the latter, and with their own consent, of some principles of intercommunication which their juxtaposition will call for; that moral may be substituted for physical force, the authority of a few and simple laws for the tomahawk, and that an end may be put to those bloody wars whose prosecution seems to have made part of their social system.

After the further details of this arrangement are completed, with a very general supervision over them, they ought to be left to the progress of events. These, I indulge the hope, will secure their prosperity and improvement, and a large portion of the moral debt we owe them will then be paid.

Statement of the National Council of the Cherokees, 1838

AQUOHEE CAMP, *August* 1, 1838.
Whereas, the title of the Cherokee people to their lands, is the most ancient, pure, and absolute known to man; its date is beyond the reach of human record; its validity confirmed and illustrated by possession and enjoyment antecedent to all pretence of claim by any other portion of the human race:

And whereas, the free consent of the Cherokee people is indispensable to a valid transfer of the Cherokee title; and whereas, the said Cherokee people have neither by themselves, nor their representatives, given such consent; it follows that the original title and ownership of said lands still vest in the Cherokee nation unimpaired and absolute:

Resolved, therefore, By the national committee and council, and people of the Cherokee nation, in general council assembled, That the whole Cherokee territory, as described in the first article of the treaty of 1819, between the United States and the Cherokee nation, still remains the rightful and undoubted property of the said Cherokee nation. And that all damages and losses, direct or incidental, resulting from the enforcement of the alleged stipulations of the pretended treaty of New Echota, are in justice and equity chargeable to the account of the United States.

And whereas, the Cherokee people have existed as a distinct national community, in the possession and exercise of the appropriate and essential attributes of sovereignty, for a period extending into antiquity beyond the dates and records and memory of man:

And whereas, these attributes, with the rights and franchises which they involve, have never been relinquished by the Cherokee people, but are now in full force and virtue.

And whereas, the natural, political, and moral relations subsisting among the citizens of the Cherokee nation towards each other, and towards the body politic, cannot in reason and justice be dissolved by the expulsion of the nation from its own territory by the power of the United States' Government:

Resolved, therefore, By the national committee and council, and people of the Cherokee nation, in general council assembled, That the inherent sovereignty of the Cherokee nation, together with the constitution, laws, and usages of the same, is, and by the authority aforesaid, is hereby declared in full force and virtue, and shall continue so to be, in perpetuity, subject to such modifications as the general welfare may render expedient.

Resolved, further, That the Cherokee people, in consenting to an investigation of their individual claims, and receiving payment upon them, and for their improvements, do not intend that it shall be so construed as yielding or giving their sanction or approval to the pretended treaty of 1835: nor as compromitting, in any manner, their just claim against the United States hereafter, for a full and satisfactory indemnification for their country, and for all individual losses and injuries.

And be it further Resolved, That the principal chief be, and he is hereby authorized to select and appoint such persons as he may deem necessary and suitable for the purpose of collecting and registering all individual claims against the United States, with the proofs, and to report to him their proceedings as they progress.

RICHARD TAYLOR,
President National Council.
GOING SNAKE,
Speaker of Council.

STEPHEN FOREMAN, *Clerk Nat. Committee.*

Capt. Brown,	Richard Foreman,	Samuel Christee,
Toonowee,	William,	Kotaquaskee,
Katelah,	Howestee,	Yoh-natsee,
Ooyah Kee,	Beaver Carrier,	Samuel Foreman.

Signed by a Committee in behalf of the people.

T. Hartley Crawford's Report on Indian Affairs, 1838

WAR DEPARTMENT,
Office of Indian Affairs, November 25, 1838.

SIR: In compliance with your directions, the following report is made of the transactions of this office for the last year.

The most striking feature of the peculiar relations that the Indians bear to the United States is their removal to the west side of the Mississippi—a change of residence effected under treaties, and with the utmost regard to their comfort that the circumstances of each admitted. The advance of white settlements, and the consuming effect of their approach to the red man's home, had long been observed by the humane with pain, as leading to the speedy extinction of the weaker party. But it is not believed that any suggestion of the policy now in a course of execution was authoritatively made prior to the commencement of the present century. Since, it has repeatedly, and at various intervals, received the sanction of the Chief Magistrates of the United States, and of one or the other House of Congress; without, however, any definite action, previous to the law passed eight years ago. Treaty engagements had been previously made for their removal West with several of the tribes; but the act referred to was a formal and general recognition of the measure, as desirable in regard of all the Indians within any State or Territory east of the Mississippi. Whatever apprehensions might have been honestly entertained of the results of this scheme, the arguments in favor of its adoption, deduced from observation, and the destructive effects of a continuance in their old positions, are so far strengthened by the success attendant upon its execution as to have convinced all, it is thought, of the humane and benevolent tendency of the measure. Experience had shown that, however commendable the efforts to meliorate a savage surrounded by a white population, they were not compensated to any great extent by the gratification which is the best reward of doing good. A few individuals in a still smaller number of tribes have been educated, and profited by the opportunities afforded them to become civilized and highly respectable men; but the mass has retrograded, giving by the contrast greater prominency to their more wisely judging brethren. What can even the moral and educated Indian promise himself in a white settlement? Equality he does not and cannot possess, and the influence that is the just possession of his qualities in the ordinary social relations of life is denied him. Separated from deteriorating associations with white men, the reverse will be the fact. A fair and wide field will be open before him, in which he can cultivate the moral and intellectual virtues of the human beings around him, and aid in elevating them to the highest condition which they are capable of reaching. If these views are correct, the reflection is pleasant that is derived from the belief that a greater sacrifice of feeling is not made in their removal than falls to the lot of our fellow-citizens, in the numerous changes of residence that considerations of bettering their condition are daily producing. Indeed, it cannot be admitted to be so great; for, while the white man moves west or south, accompanied by his family only, the Indians go by tribes, carrying with them all the pleasures of ancient acquaintance, common habits, and common interests. It can scarcely be contended that they are more susceptible of suffering at the breaking up of local associations than we are; for, apart from their condition not favoring the indulgence of the finer feelings, fact proves that they sell a part of their possessions without reluctance, and leave their cabins, and burial-places, and the mounds and monuments which were the objects of their pride or affection, for a remote position in the same district. For whatever they have ceded to the United States they have been amply compensated. I speak not of former times, to which reference is not made, but of later days. The case of the Cherokees is a striking example of the liberality of the Government in all its branches. By the treaty, they had stipulated to remove west of the Mississippi within two years from its ratification, which took place on 23d May, 1836. The obligations of the United States, State rights, and acts by virtue of those rights, and in anticipation of Cherokee removal, made a compliance with this provision of the treaty indispensable at the time stipulated, or as soon thereafter as it was practicable without harshness. To ensure it, General [Winfield] Scott was despatched to their late country, and performed a delicate and difficult duty, embarrassed by circumstances over which there is no human control, with great judgment and humanity.

John C. Calhoun on Incorporating Mexico, 1848

Sir, we have heard how much glory our country has acquired in this war. I acknowledge it to the full amount, Mr. President, so far as military glory is concerned. The army has done nobly, chivalrously; they have conferred honor on the country, for which I sincerely thank them.

. . . Now, sir, much as I regard military glory; much as I rejoice to behold our people in possession of the indomitable energy and courage which surmount all difficulties, and which class them amongst the first military people of the age, I would be very sorry indeed that our Government should lose any reputation for wisdom, moderation, discretion, justice, and those other high qualities which have distinguished us in the early stages of our history.

. . . It is without example or precedent, either to hold Mexico as a province, or to incorporate her into our Union. No example of such a line of policy can be found. We have conquered many of the neighboring tribes of Indians, but we never thought of holding them in subjection—never of incorporating them into our Union. They have either been left as an independent people amongst us, or been driven into the forests.

I know further, sir, that we have never dreamt of incorporating into our Union any but the Caucasian race—the free white race. To incorporate Mexico, would be the very first instance of the kind of incorporating an Indian race; for more than half of the Mexicans are Indians, and the other is composed chiefly of mixed tribes. I protest against such a union as that! Ours, sir, is the Government of a white race. The greatest misfortunes of Spanish America are to be traced to the fatal error of placing these colored races on an equality with the white race. That error destroyed the social arrangement which formed the basis of society. The Portuguese and ourselves have escaped—the Portuguese at least to some extent—and we are the only people on this continent which have made revolutions without being followed by anarchy. And yet it is professed and talked about to erect these Mexicans into a Territorial Government, and place them on an equality with the people of the United States. I protest utterly against such a project.

Sir, it is a remarkable fact, that in the whole history of man, as far as my knowledge extends, there is no instance whatever of any civilized colored races being found equal to the establishment of free popular government, although by far the largest portion of the human family is composed of these races. And even in the savage state we scarcely find them anywhere with such government, except it be our noble savages—for noble I will call them. They, for the most part, had free institutions, but they are easily sustained amongst a savage people. Are we to overlook this fact? Are we to associate with ourselves as equals, companions, and fellow-citizens, the Indians and mixed race of Mexico? Sir, I should consider such a thing as fatal to our institutions. . . .

I come now to the proposition of incorporating her into our Union. Well, as far as law is concerned, that is easy. You can establish a Territorial Government for every State in Mexico, and there are some twenty of them. You can appoint governors, judges, and magistrates. You can give the people a subordinate government, allowing them to legislate for themselves, whilst you defray the cost. So far as law goes, the thing is done. There is no analogy between this and our Territorial Governments. Our Territories are only an offset of our own people, or foreigners from the same regions from which we came. They are small in number. They are incapable of forming a government. It would be inconvenient for them to sustain a government, if it were formed; and they are very much obliged to the United States for undertaking the trouble, knowing that, on the attainment of their majority—when they come to manhood—at twenty-one—they will be introduced to an equality with all the other members of the Union. It is entirely different with Mexico. You have no need of armies to keep your Territories in subjection. But when you incorporate Mexico, you must have powerful armies to keep them in subjection. You may call it annexation, but it is a forced annexation, which is a contradiction in terms, according to my conception. You will be involved, in one word, in all the evils which I attribute to holding Mexico as a province. In fact, it will be but a Provincial Government, under the name of a Territorial Government. How long will that last? How long will it be before Mexico will be capable of incorporation into our Union? Why, if we judge from the examples before us, it will be a very long time. Ireland has been held in subjection by England for seven or eight hundred years, and yet still remains hostile, although her people are of kindred race with the conquerors. A few French Canadians on this continent yet maintain the attitude of hostile people; and never will the time come, in my opinion, Mr. President, that these Mexicans will be heartily reconciled to your authority. They have Castilian blood in their veins—the old Gothic, quite equal to the Anglo-Saxon in many respects— in some respects superior. Of all nations of the earth they are the most pertinacious—have the highest sense of nationality—hold out longest, and often even with the least prospect of effecting their object. On this subject also I have conversed with officers of the army, and they all entertain the same opinion, that these people are now hostile, and will continue so.

But, Mr. President, suppose all these difficulties removed; suppose these people attached to our Union, and desirous of incorporating with us, ought we to bring them in? Are they fit to be connected with us? Are they fit for self-government and for governing you? Are you, any of you, willing that your States should be governed by these twenty-odd Mexican States, with a population of about only one million of your blood, and two or three millions of mixed blood, better informed, all the rest pure Indians, a mixed blood equally ignorant and unfit for liberty, impure races, not as good as the Cherokees or Choctaws?

We make a great mistake, sir, when we suppose that all people are capable of self-government. We are anxious to force free government on all; and I see that it has been urged in a very respectable quarter, that it is the mission of this country to spread civil and religious liberty over all the world, and especially over this continent. It is a great mistake. None but people advanced to a very high state of moral and intellectual improvement are capable, in a civilized state, of maintaining free government; and amongst those who are so purified, very few, indeed, have had the good fortune of forming a constitution capable of endurance.

John A. Dix on Expansion and Mexican Lands, 1848

Sir, no one who has paid a moderate degree of attention to the laws and elements of our increase, can doubt that our population is destined to spread itself across the American continent, filling up, with more or less completeness, according to attractions of soil and climate, the space that intervenes between the Atlantic and Pacific oceans. This eventual, and, perhaps, in the order of time, this not very distant extension of our settlements over a tract of country, with a diameter, as we go westward, greatly disproportioned to its length, becomes a subject of the highest interest to us. On the whole extent of our northern flank, from New Brunswick to the point where the northern boundary of Oregon touches the Pacific, we are in contact with British colonists, having, for the most part, the same common origin with ourselves, but controlled and moulded by political influences from the Eastern hemisphere, if not adverse, certainly not decidedly friendly to us. The strongest tie which can be relied on to bind us to mutual offices of friendship and good neighborhood, is that of commerce; and this, as we know, is apt to run into rivalry, and sometimes becomes a fruitful source of alienation.

From our northern boundary, we turn to our southern. What races are to border on us here, what is to be their social and political character, and what their means of annoyance? Are our two frontiers, only seven parallels of latitude apart when we pass Texas, to be flanked by settlements having no common bond of union with ours? Our whole southern line is conterminous, throughout its whole extent, with the territories of Mexico, a large portion of which is nearly unpopulated. The geographical area of Mexico is about 1,500,000 square miles, and her population about 7,000,000 souls. The whole northern and central portion, taking the twenty-sixth parallel of latitude as the dividing line, containing more than 1,000,000 square miles, has about 650,000 inhabitants—about two inhabitants to three square miles. The southern portion, with less than 500,000 square miles, has a population of nearly six and a half millions of souls, or thirteen inhabitants to one square mile. The aboriginal races, which occupy and overrun a portion of California and New Mexico, must there, as everywhere else, give way before the advancing wave of civilization, either to be overwhelmed by it, or to be driven upon perpetually contracting areas, where, from a diminution of their accustomed sources of subsistence, they must ultimately become extinct by force of an invincible law. We see the operation of this law in every portion of this continent. We have no power to control it, if we would. It is the behest of Providence that idleness, and ignorance, and barbarism, shall give place to industry, and knowledge, and civilization. The European and mixed races, which possess Mexico, are not likely, either from moral or physical energy, to become formidable rivals or enemies. The bold and courageous enterprise which overran and conquered Mexico, appears not to have descended to the present possessors of the soil. Either from the influence of climate or the admixture of races—the fusion of castes, to use the technical phrase—the conquerors have, in turn, become the conquered. The ancient Castilian energy is, in a great degree, subdued; and it has given place, with many other noble traits of the Spanish character, to a peculiarity which seems to have marked the race in that country, under whatever combinations it is found—a proneness to civil discord, and a suicidal waste of its own strength.

With such a territory and such a people on our southern border, what is to be the inevitable course of empire? It needs no powers of prophecy to foretell. Sir, I desire to speak plainly: why should we not, when we are discussing the operation of moral and physical laws, which are beyond our control? As our population moves westward on our own territory, portions will cross our southern boundary. Settlements will be formed within the unoccupied and sparsely-peopled territory of Mexico. Uncongenial habits and tastes, differences of political opinion and principle, and numberless other elements of diversity will lead to a separation of these newly-formed societies from the inefficient government of Mexico. They will not endure to be held in subjection to a system, which neither yields them protection nor offers any incentive to their proper development and growth. They will form independent States on the basis of constitutions identical in all their leading features with our own; and they will naturally seek to unite their fortunes to ours. The fate of California is already sealed: it can never be reunited to Mexico. The operation of the great causes, to which I have alluded, must, at no distant day, detach the whole of northern Mexico from the southern portion of that republic. It is for the very reason that she is incapable of defending her possessions against the elements of disorder within and the progress of better influences from without, that I desire to see the inevitable political change which is to be wrought in the condition of her northern departments, brought about without any improper interference on our part.

An Emigrants' Guide Describes the Mexicans in California, 1845

The entire population of Upper California, including foreigners, Mexicans and Indians, may be estimated at about thirty-one thousand human souls, of whom, about one thousand are foreigners, ten thousand are Mexicans, and the residue are Indians. By the term foreigners, I include all those who are not native citizens of Mexico, whether they have become citizens by naturalization, or whether they remain in a state of alienage. They consist, chiefly, of Americans, Englishmen, Frenchmen, Germans and Spaniards, but there is a very large majority of the former. The foreigners are principally settled at the various towns, and upon the Sacramento; those of whom who, are located at the latter place, consist almost entirely of our own citizens. The foreigners of this country are, generally, very intelligent; many of them have received all the advantages of an education; and they all possess an unusual degree of industry and enterprise. . . .

The Mexicans differ, in every particular, from the foreigners; ignorance and its concomitant, superstition, together with suspicion and superciliousness, constitute the chief ingredients, of the Mexican character. More indomitable ignorance does not prevail, among any people who make the least pretentions to civilization; in truth, they are scarcely a visible grade, in the scale of intelligence, above the barbarous tribes by whom they are surrounded; but this is not surprising, especially when we consider the relation, which these people occupy to their barbarous neighbors, in other particulars. Many of the lower order of them, have intermarried with the various tribes, and have resided with them so long, and lived in a manner so entirely similar, that it has become almost impossible, to trace the least distinctions between them, either in reference to intelligence, or complexion. There is another class, which is, if possible, of a lower order still, than those just alluded to, and which consists of the aborigines themselves, who have been slightly civilized, or rather *domesticated*. These two classes constitute almost the entire Mexican population, of California, and among them almost every variety and shade of complexion may be found, from the African black, to the tawny brown of our southern Indians. Although there is a great variety, and dissimilarity among them, in reference to their complexions, yet in their beastly habits and an entire want of all moral principle, as well as a perfect destitution of all intelligence, there appears to be a perfect similarity. A more full description of these classes, will be found, in what is said, in reference to the Indians, for as most of the lower order of Mexicans, are Indians in fact, whatever is said in reference to the one, will also be applicable to the other. The higher order of the Mexicans, in point of intelligence, are perhaps about equal, to the lower order of our citizens, throughout our western states; but among these even, are very few, who are, to any extent, learned or even intelligent. Learning and intelligence appear to be confined, almost entirely, to the priests, who are, generally, both learned and intelligent. The priests are not only the sole proprietors, of the learning and intelligence, but also, of the liberty and happiness of the people, all of which they parcel out to their blind votaries, with a very sparing hand; and thus it is, that all the Mexican people are kept, in this state of degrading ignorance, and humiliating vassalage. The priests here, not only have the possession of the keys of the understanding, and the door of liberty, but they also, have both the present and ultimate happiness, of these ignorant people, entirely at their disposal. Such at least, is the belief of the people, and such are the doctrines there taught by the priests. At times, I sympathize with these unfortunate beings, but again, I frequently think, that, perhaps, it is fortunate for the residue of mankind, that these semi-barbarians, are thus *ridden* and restrained, and if they are to be thus priest ridden, it is, no doubt, preferable, that they should retain their present *riders*.

Edwin Bryant's View of Hispanic Californians, 1848

The permanent population of that portion of Upper California situated between the Sierra Nevada and the Pacific, I estimate at 25,000. Of this number, 8,000 are Hispano-Americans, 5,000 foreigners, chiefly from the United States, and 12,000 christianized Indians. There are considerable numbers of wild or Gentile Indians inhabiting the valley of the San Joaquin, and the gorges of the Sierra, not included in this estimate. They are probably as numerous as the Christian Indians. The Indian population inhabiting the region of the Great Salt Lake, Mary's river, the oases of the Great Desert Basin, and the country bordering the Rio Colorado and its tributaries, being spread over a vast extent of territory, are scarcely seen, although the aggregate number is considerable.

The Californians do not differ materially from the Mexicans, from whom they are descended, in other provinces of that country. Physically and intellectually, the men, probably, are superior to the same race farther south, and inhabiting the countries contiguous to the city of Mexico. The intermixture of blood with the Indian and negro races has been less, although it is very perceptible.

The men, as a general fact, are well made, with pleasing, sprightly countenances, and possessing much grace and ease of manners, and vivacity of conversation. But hitherto they have had little knowledge of the world and of events, beyond what they have heard through Mexico, and derived from the super-cargoes of merchant-ships and whalemen touching upon the coast. There are no public schools in the country—at least I never heard of one. There are but few books. General Valléjo has a library with many valuable books, and this is the only one I saw, although there are others; but they are rare, and confined to a few families.

The men are almost constantly on horseback, and as horsemen excel any I have seen in other parts of the world. From the nature of their pursuits and amusements, they have brought horsemanship to a perfection challenging admiration and exciting astonishment. They are trained to the horse and the use of the lasso, (*riata,* as it is here called,) from their infancy. The first act of a child, when he is able to stand alone, is to throw his toy-lasso around the neck of a kitten; his next feat is performed on the dog; his next upon a goat or calf; and so on, until he mounts the horse, and demonstrates his skill upon horses and cattle. The crowning feat of dexterity with the *riata,* and of horsemanship, combined with daring courage, is the lassoing of the grisly bear. This feat is performed frequently upon this large and ferocious animal, but it is sometimes fatal to the performer and his horse. Well drilled, with experienced military leaders, such as would inspire them with confidence in their skill and prowess, the Californians ought to be the finest cavalry in the world. The Californian saddle is, I venture to assert, the best that has been invented, for the horse and the rider. Seated in one of these, it is scarcely possible to be unseated by any ordinary casualty. The bridle-bit is clumsily made, but so constructed that the horse is compelled to obey the rider upon the slightest intimation. The spurs are of immense size, but they answer to an experienced horseman the double purpose of exciting the horse, and of maintaining the rider in his seat under difficult circumstances.

For the pleasures of the table they care but little. With his horse and trappings, his sarape and blanket, a piece of beef and a *tortilla,* the Californian is content, so far as his personal comforts are concerned. But he is ardent in his pursuit of amusement and pleasure, and those consist chiefly in the fandango, the game of monte, horse-racing, and bull and bear baiting. They gamble freely and desperately, but pay their losses with the most strict punctuality, at any and every sacrifice, and manifest but little concern about them. They are obedient to their magistrates; and in all disputed cases decided by them, acquiesce without uttering a word of complaint. They have been accused of treachery and insincerity. Whatever may have been the grounds for these accusations in particular instances, I know not; but judging from my own observation and experience, they are as free from these qualities as our own people.

While the men are employed in attending to the herds of cattle and horses, and engaged in their other amusements, the women (I speak of the middle classes on the ranchos) superintend and perform most of the drudgery appertaining to housekeeping, and the cultivation of the gardens, from whence are drawn such vegetables as are consumed at the table. These are few, consisting of *frijoles,* potatoes, onions, and *chiles.* The assistants in these labors are the Indian men and women, legally reduced to servitude.

Υ ESSAYS

Reginald Horsman, of the University of Wisconsin—Milwaukee, and Francis Paul Prucha of Marquette University, also in Milwaukee, may share the same city, but they do not share the same view that racism may have determined nineteenth-century government policy toward the Indians. Horsman is well known for his books and articles on American expansionism. His 1981 study, *Race and Manifest Destiny,* is the source of the first essay that follows. The second selection, Prucha's essay, is a direct response to a 1975 article by Horsman that prefigured some of the arguments in the 1981 book. Prucha has written prolifically on U.S. Indian policy. His magnum opus in this field, *The Great Father,* published in 1984, received the Billington Prize of the Organization of American Historians. Prucha has served as president of the Western History Association and in 1987 received that organization's award for lifetime achievement.

David J. Weber, a professor of history at Southern Methodist University, is widely admired for his studies of the Spanish borderlands and the northern frontiers of Mexico. His essay, the third selection here, considers stereotypes and raises the possibility that stereotyping, rather than racism, explains Anglo-American attitudes toward Mexicans. Can Weber's approach be applied successfully to the analysis of white attitudes toward Indians?

Racial Destiny and the Indians

REGINALD HORSMAN

Between 1815 and the mid-1850s an American Anglo-Saxon ideology was used internally to bolster the power and protect the status of the existing population and externally to justify American territorial and economic expansion. Internally it was made quite clear that the American republic was a white Anglo-Saxon republic; other white races would be absorbed within the existing racial mass while nonwhite races would be rigorously excluded from any equal participation as citizens. Externally American pressure on adjacent territories was justified by the argument that only the American Anglo-Saxons could bring the political and economic changes that would make possible unlimited world progress. These arguments were used to justify the annexation of sparsely populated areas and the economic penetration of areas that were heavily populated with ''inferior'' races. The latter were not annexed, because the strong belief that inferior peoples should not be allowed to participate equally in the American system of government was accompanied by a continuing belief that colonial possessions would corrupt the republic. Some in the United States still argued that other peoples could be taught to enjoy republican freedom, but they were outnumbered by those who maintained that many other races were incapable of substantial accomplishments. The United States shaped policies which reflected a belief in the racial inferiority and expendability of Indians, Mexicans, and other inferior races, and which looked forward to a world shaped and dominated by a superior American Anglo-Saxon race.

Between 1815 amd 1850 the American Indians were rejected by the

Reprinted by permission of the publishers from *Race and Manifest Destiny: The Origins of American Anglo-Saxonism,* 189–207, by Reginald Horsman, Cambridge, Massachusetts: Harvard University Press, Copyright © 1981 by the President and Fellows of Harvard College.

white American society. Before 1830 there was a bitter struggle as those who believed in the Enlightenment view of the Indian as an innately equal, improvable being desperately defended the older ideals, but year by year the ideas of those who felt the Indians were expendable were reinforced by a variety of scientific and intellectual arguments. Indian Removal represented a major victory for ideas which, though long latent in American society, became fully explicit only after 1830. Political power was exercised by those who believed the Indians to be inferior, who did not wish them to be accepted as equals within American society, and who expected them ultimately to disappear. In shaping an Indian policy American politicians reflected the new ruthlessness of racial confidence.

The eighteenth-century transatlantic view of the Indian as an innately equal, fully improvable being did not, of course, disappear from American thinking. For two decades after 1815 this view had major defenders. Even after that time missionaries, reformers, and other friends of the Indian hoped for Indian transformation, and the rhetoric of government leaders was frequently couched in terms of improvability. But there is considerable evidence to show that after 1830 neither the mass of the American people nor the political leaders of the country believed that the Indians could be melded into American society.

The eighteenth-century image of the Indian as a "noble savage" also persisted into the middle of the century, though in modified form. Major American writers—Cooper, Hawthorne, Thoreau, Melville—and their minor followers, while blending harsher tones into their portraits, viewed the Indian as a tragic and in some ways noble figure—and certainly as far more human than the bestial savage portrayed in so many frontier descriptions. Even William Gilmore Simms, for all his rampant expansionism, retained the older literary image of the Indian in much of his writing.

On a popular level, however, this literary image of the Indian as a complex, tragic figure was to a large extent offset by the widespread, horror-laden captivity literature and by the novels of figures such as Robert Montgomery Bird, who depicted the Indian as an expendable wild beast. When Bird published his *Nick of the Woods* in 1837, he admitted that his literary portrait of the Indians was in "hues darker than are usually employed by the painters of such figures. The North American savage has never appeared to us the gallant and heroic personage he seems to others." Yet while the literary view of the Indian was mixed, there was a common assumption that the Indian was doomed to inevitable extinction. A tone of regret for a being who could not be saved permeated creative writing on the Indian in the years until 1850.

The scientific attack on the Indian as inferior and expendable, which burgeoned from 1830 to 1850, gave many Americans the authoritative backing they needed for long-assumed beliefs. Frontiersmen were as pleased to accept the scientific condemnation of the Indians as slaveowners were to accept scientific attacks on the blacks. The dominant scientific position by the 1840s was that the Indians were doomed because of innate inferiority, that they were succumbing to a superior race, and that this was for the good of America and the world. The impotence of the federal government in the face of the massacres of California Indians in the 1850s has to be viewed against the widespread intellectual and popular view that the replacement of an inferior by a superior race was the fulfillment of the laws of science and nature.

Although the idea of removing Indians to distant, unwanted western lands had been suggested after the Louisiana Purchase in 1803, this suggestion originally involved Indians who wished to retain their existing way of life. Indians who resisted assimilation were at times encouraged to remove beyond the Mississippi, but those who were showing signs of accepting the outward forms of white civilization were encouraged to perpetuate themselves upon the land, farm it, bequeath it to their heirs, and transform their way of life. Indian Removal as developed between 1815 and 1830 was a rejection of all Indians as Indians, not simply a rejection of unassimilated Indians who would not accept the American life-style.

The expansion of the United States in the years after 1815 rapidly brought intense pressure on federal commitments to the Indians. As settlers poured into the eastern half of the Mississippi Valley, the demand for land reached unprecedented heights. In the South settlers lured by the rich cotton lands in Georgia, Alabama, and Mississippi spread rapidly over all available areas, and Indian settlements were threatened by white frontiersmen anxious to make their fortunes. The condition of the Indians in the eastern half of the country was disputed at the time and has been disputed since; one reason is the wide variation that existed among tribes from the Great Lakes to the Gulf. The Indians of Ohio, Indiana, and Illinois were in no condition to resist the pressure from white settlers. After decades of war and white contact they were easy to dispossess and to confine on smaller and smaller areas of land. Few Indians were established in successful farming communities on the white pattern; many were demoralized and drifting, with tribal structures shattered, game disappearing, and little hope of survival.

The South was much different. Although there can be considerable disagreement as to the proportion of Indians who had even outwardly conformed to white cultural patterns, and even more difficulty in deciding on the degree of acculturation, there is no doubt that in the states of Georgia, Tennessee, Alabama, and Mississippi there were many Indians who had gone part way in fulfilling Jeffersonian hopes for their transformation. Indeed, until different arguments were needed in the 1820s to justify a different policy, federal officials frequently testified to Indian "progress" in the South, notably among the Cherokees. There were literally thousands of Indians in the southern states who were capable of remaining on the land and even prospering. They were not destitute, they were not disorganized, and they were not doomed to inevitable extinction.

In the years after 1815, even within the context of an Enlightenment Indian policy, a good case could be made for the removal of the remaining Indians from the states of Ohio, Indiana, and Illinois. The assimilation policy had achieved very little success, and it could be argued that the remaining Indians were doomed unless they were removed. This was not the case in the South, and after 1815 the main arguments concerning removal revolved around the states of Tennessee, Georgia, Alabama, and Mississippi. Most white Americans in those areas were simply unwilling to allow Indians, whether transformed or not, to retain land and to achieve equality with white settlers. This accelerated the national process of regarding the Indian simply as an inferior savage who blocked progress. What had been an instinctive reaction of frontiersmen fighting for land was soon to become a majority point of view among Americans and their governmental officials.

When in the years following the War of 1812 Secretary of War William H. Crawford made it clear by word and treaty that the government hoped to keep the Indians on the lands they possessed east of the Mississippi River, and that he wished to assimilate these Indians within American society, he stirred widespread resentment among Tennesseans and other Southerners who wished to obtain all the good land in their region. In 1816 Governor Joseph McMinn of Tennessee indicated that he believed the time was approaching when the federal government should eliminate all general Indian claims within his state by ending tribal ownership. Individual Indians should be able to retain land and pass it on to their heirs. This was not to mean full acceptance into American society, for McMinn suggested that these Indians should be given "all the rights of a free citizen of color of the United States." It soon became apparent that the breaking up of tribal lands was intended to simplify the removal of all Indians from the state, not to promote the assimilation of individuals.

In January 1817 the Senate Committee on Public Lands endorsed the general policy of exchanging Indian lands east of the Mississippi for lands to the west of that river, but insisted that this should be done by the voluntary consent of the tribes. This plan became the cornerstone of Indian policy in the new administration of President James Monroe. His secretary of war, John C. Calhoun, emphasized in the following years that the administration was anxious to effect a voluntary removal of the Indians to the west side of the Mississippi. The policy was a failure because it satisfied neither whites nor Indians. The whites wanted more forceful action by the federal government, and the Indians wanted to stay where they were. Those Indians who had used white "civilization" efforts to expand their own earlier agricultural base had no reason to want to move; they emphasized that they were doing what they had repeatedly been told to do before 1812, and that their lands had been guaranteed to them by the federal government.

Even had the Indians been prepared to cede their tribal lands, the idea of private Indian land ownership was doomed by the unwillingness of the southern whites to accept Indians on a basis of equality. McMinn had suggested giving Indians who remained the rights of "a free citizen of color." Georgia made it clear that she wanted no Indians at all—whether living on tribal land or on private property. In the 1820s the focus of the Indian controversy shifted to Georgia. At the time of the 1802 agreement by which Georgia had ceded her western land claims, the federal government had agreed to extinguish Indian claims within the state. By 1820 Georgia was infuriated that rather than removing the Creeks and the Cherokees the federal government had encouraged permanent occupancy by its civilization program.

In December 1821 the House of Representatives appointed a select committee to consider Georgia's problems under the 1802 agreement. George Gilmer, a representative from that state, proposed this step, resisted efforts to have the question sent to the standing committee on Indian affairs, and chaired the special committee. When the committee reported early in 1822, it argued that the executive had violated the rights of both Georgia and Congress—the former because of the granting of lands in Georgia to Indians as individuals, the latter because of the agreement that the Indians could become citizens. For the federal government to conform to its 1802 agreement with Georgia, the committee reported, "it will be necessary for the United States to relinquish the policy which they seem to have adopted with regard to civilizing the Indians, and rendering them permanent upon their lands, and changing their title by occupancy into a fee-simple title, at least in respect to the Creek and Cherokee Indians."

The idea of removing most of the Indians by allowing some of them to remain as private property owners was unacceptable to Georgia, and, under pressure from that state, Congress in 1822 and 1823 urged the executive to eliminate not only tribal but also individual Indian land claims within the state. The appropriation of fifty thousand dollars to buy out lands granted to Indians in fee simple since 1814 caused particularly bitter debate, for this was a direct rejection and repudiation of the assimilation and incorporation policies pursued since the 1790s. The total acreage involved was less than twenty-three thousand, but the Indians were not allowed to retain even this tiny portion of the huge Georgia domain. After an initial defeat, the House passed the appropriation by a vote of fifty-eight to thirty; these Indians were to be removed because they were Indians, not because they held huge tribal lands or because they had refused to assume white ways.

In its last two years the Monroe administration was beset by an almost continual crisis in Indian affairs; Tennessee, Georgia, Alabama, and Mississippi were all pressing the federal government to remove the Indians from their states. The Indian tribes for the most part wanted to remain where they were. Those who had achieved the greatest success in assimilation would be the most hurt by removal westward. They had followed Jefferson's injunctions to assume white ways; they were now to be thrown off their land. Faced by the intransigence of the southern states, the executive moved toward the idea of removing all the eastern Indians who were in the path of white settlement.

Sentiment in Georgia became more extreme in these years, particularly after the election of George M. Troup as governor. When the Cherokees in the fall of 1823 again refused to cede lands, Troup asked the Georgia legislature to demand action by the federal government. This it did, and Troup told Calhoun that the wrongs done to Georgia "must be repaired by an Act of decisive character." The Georgia delegation in Washington attacked the policy of the executive in such violent terms that Monroe in a cabinet meeting said that "he had never received such a paper." It was ruefully asked in the meeting what had kindled "this raging fever for Indian lands."

Governor Troup made it obvious that it was not merely a question of obtaining satisfaction for Georgia under the terms of the 1802 agreement, and that he was not advocating removal from Georgia merely that Indians should be welcomed within the republican fold in a less crowded area. In 1824 he attacked the whole concept of the amalgamation of the Indians within American society: "the utmost of rights and privileges which public opinion would concede to Indians, would fix them in a middle station, between the negro and the white man; and that, as long as they survived this degradation, without the possibility of attaining the elevation of the latter, they would gradually sink to the condition of the former—a point of degeneracy below which they could not fall; it is likely, before they reached this, their wretchedness would find relief in broken hearts."

The extent of the federal dilemma was revealed clearly by the cabinet discussions of February and March 1824. What swayed Monroe and the cabinet was the white unwillingness to have Indians in their states, not any philanthropic aim to save the Indians from degradation and extermination. The situation of the Indians in the Northwest, where some friends of the Indians were suggesting removal to save them, was not a major consideration in the creation of a federal removal policy. The executive and Congress shaped a policy in response to southern pressure. Calhoun made it quite clear in the cabinet at the end of February that the main problem was not those Indians who had failed to respond to white civilization but those who had succeeded. "The great difficulty," he argued, "arises from the progress of the Cherokees in civilization. They are now, within the limits of Georgia, about fifteen thousand, and increasing in equal proportion with the whites; all cultivators, with a representative government, judicial courts, Lancaster schools,* and permanent property." The Cherokees were not in danger because they had failed to adapt to white ways; they were in danger because of a Georgian greed for land, the unwillingness of most whites to accept Indians within their society, and the failure of the federal government to honor its previous commitments.

At the end of March Monroe informed Congress of his dilemma. He said he had attempted to fulfill the terms of the 1802 compact with Georgia, but that the Indians were resisting further cessions of land, even though their happiness and security would be promoted if they could be persuaded to move. Congress now joined Georgia in attacking the policy of the executive branch. A select committee appointed to deal with Monroe's message consisted of Georgian John Forsyth as chairman and an additional membership of two other Georgians, one North Carolinian, and one South Carolinian. Not surprisingly the committee urged that Indian claims in Georgia should, if necessary, be extinguished by force.

In January 1825 the executive presented Congress with a comprehensive

---

* The Lancaster plan used student monitors to carry on instruction.

removal plan. The eastern Indians were to be removed to the region west of Arkansas and Missouri and to the region west of Lake Michigan. The latter suggestion was later abandoned as Wisconsin became more desirable to speculators and settlers. This new land in the West was to be a "permanent" home, and Indian civilization was to be encouraged. Although the federal government had stated what it wanted, dilemmas remained. The question of the use of force had still not been resolved, and the morality of removal was still being questioned in Congress. Congress was badly split on these issues, and in 1825 and 1826 the vague Monroe-Calhoun removal plans could not obtain a general supporting vote in the House.

The new administration of President John Quincy Adams clearly revealed the hardening of attitudes toward the Indians at the national level. Adams himself was not deeply committed on either side of the Indian question, although he was inclined to believe that the Indians could not stay in the East and were probably doomed wherever they were located. James Barbour, his secretary of war until 1828, thought as a Jeffersonian at a time when Jeffersonian dreams were vanishing. His initial and rather naive hope was that the Indians could be given individual plots of land and incorporated as private individuals in the states where they lived. Georgia had already rejected this solution, and in the cabinet in December 1825 Secretary of State Henry Clay candidly told Barbour why any plan for incorporating individual Indians within white society was not acceptable. Clay, who in his public statements often attacked the ruthlessness involved in American expansion, argued that "it was impossible to civilize Indians; that there never was a full-blooded Indian who took to civilization. It was not in their nature. He believed they were destined to extinction, and, although he would never use or countenance inhumanity towards them, he did not think them, as a race, worth preserving. He considered them as essentially inferior to the Anglo-Saxon race, which were now taking their place on this continent. They were not an improvable breed, and their disappearance from the human family will be no great loss to the world. In point of fact they were rapidly disappearing, and he did not believe that in fifty years from this time there would be any of them left." Over the next twenty years American scientists, supposedly on the basis of empirical evidence, resoundingly endorsed Clay's conclusions. John Quincy Adams tells a good deal about his own opinions, as well as those of Barbour, with his comment that "Governor Barbour was somewhat shocked at these opinions, for which I fear there is too much foundation."

Faced by a divided cabinet and intransigent states, Barbour was forced to modify his plans, and he suggested to the cabinet that the Indians should be removed, but that they should be brought to civilization and incorporated into the union by combining them in a separate territory west of the Mississippi. Barbour was to make it quite clear later that he had no real faith in this plan, which had been forced upon him. The cabinet accepted the plan, not out of conviction, but because it was the only politically acceptable one. On the day Barbour reluctantly proposed it to the cabinet, Adams commented about the Indians that "I fear there is no practicable plan by which they can be organized into one civilized, or half-civilized, Government. Mr. Rush, Mr. Southard, and Mr. Wirt all expressed their doubts of the practicability of Governor Barbour's plan; but they had nothing more effective to propose, and I approved it from the same motive." Clay was absent due to illness on this occasion, but his views were already well known to Barbour.

Barbour's experience in dealing with Adams's cabinet makes it quite clear that Indian Removal was not an effort to civilize the Indians under more favorable circumstances, which was how the Jacksonians justified the measure; rather it was an act to allow white Americans to occupy all the lands they wanted east of the Mississippi River. The settlers wanted all of the land and none of the Indians. Many friends of the Indian objected to the new policy, but they were not in sufficient numbers to exert decisive political influence. The only friends of the Indian who supported removal from the beginning were those, like Isaac McCoy, who worked among the demoralized and disorganized northwestern tribes, and who thought removal might save those Indians from simply disappearing under the white advance. Other friends of the Indian eventually supported removal when they had no other choice.

When Barbour in February 1826 sent his plan for an Indian territory beyond the Mississippi to the House Committee on Indian Affairs, he publicly reflected on the inconsistencies of the policy he was proposing. He pointed out that as long as the desire for land "continues to direct our councils" every humane attempt to better the condition of the Indians would fail. After persuading the Indians to farm, he said, the government now desired to expel them: "They see that our professions are insincere; that our promises have been broken; that the happiness of the Indians is a cheap sacrifice to the acquisition of new lands." We tell the Indians they can have new desirable lands, he said, but they ask us "What new pledges can you give us that we shall not again be exiled when it is your wish to possess these lands?" Barbour knew that no honest pledge could be given. The tide of the white population will flow, he wrote, until arrested "by the distant shores of the Pacific."

Barbour found himself in a politically impossible position in the late 1820s. In March 1827 he told Jeremiah Evarts, secretary of the American Board of Commissioners for Foreign Missions, that "one great argument in favor of removal of the Indians is that they *cannot remain where they are,* on account of the determination of the States of Georgia, Alabama, and Mississippi that they *shall not.*" Barbour thought that state cupidity would not be resisted permanently by the federal government. He was right. Barbour had no faith in his own plan for a territorial government west of the Mississippi, and even that acknowledgment of possible ultimate Indian equality was to prove unacceptable to Congress.

Support for Indian Removal became broader in the late 1820s as the inability of the federal government to resist southern state pressure became obvious. The only question left was who would grasp the nettle and force the Indians to accept the removal policy. That Thomas A. McKenney, who headed the Office of Indian Affairs within the War Department, and Lewis Cass, of major importance for Indian relations in the Old Northwest, should in the late 1820s have moved from a position of opposing to supporting removal is hardly surprising. They were both servants of a government that for over ten years had urged the necessity of removal and was near the point of abandoning the Indians to the states. The federal government was bowing before southern state pressures, causing confusion and despair among the southern Indians, and then was using this confusion and despair as a justification for removal.

Isaac McCoy, who had long supported removal as in the best interests of the northwestern Indians he served, admitted that general removal "was agitated chiefly for the purpose of obtaining other ends than the welfare of the Indians." Even those politicians who regretted what was happening to the Indians and offered to help McCoy in doing what he could for Indian improvement, had no faith in what they were doing. McCoy later said that they "frankly told me they believed the Indian race was destined to become extinct. It was our duty to adopt all feasible measures for their preservation, but all would fail." Much missionary support for the removal of the southern Indians came when all else had failed and when the federal government had tossed the Indians to the wolves. By that time the missionaries could do little but shepherd their flocks beyond the Mississippi.

The election of Jackson in 1828 sealed the fate of the southern Indians. Since 1814 Jackson had been anxious to clear the Indians from the southern states. After the War of 1812 his presence as a commissioner to negotiate Indian treaties had regularly been requested in the South. The states knew well that he would do all that was possible to obtain land. He was determined to have removal. As president he made it known through Secretary of War John Eaton that he would no longer protect the Indians against the southern states who wanted their lands. Georgia, Alabama, Mississippi, and Tennessee had all given Jackson crushing popular majorities in the 1828 election. Once Jackson was elected the southern states could extend their jurisdiction over the Indian lands within their borders. Neither John Marshall at the Supreme Court nor the missionaries among the Indians could save them.

The general removal bill debated before Congress in the spring of 1830 disavowed the use of force, but it was well understood that the Indians would have no choice. They would either remove or be left to the mercies of the southern states. The bill was bitterly fought, and the opposition repeatedly pointed out the moral failure of federal policy. Edward Everett stated it simply and accurately: "It is the object of this bill to appropriate a sum of money to cooperate with the States in the compulsory removal of the Indians." Opposition speaker after speaker pointed out that the southern Indians would now be forced out, that they would suffer in the act of removal, and that the white population would eventually sweep over the new lands that were to be permanently guaranteed. All this was true. When the removal bill passed by a narrow majority, every possible means was used by the Jackson administration to implement the measure. If pressure and bribery would not work, then private allotments were made; it was well understood that the private allotments would pass swiftly into the hands of the whites. Many Indians resisted to the last, citing the earlier federal guarantees of their lands and their progress in civilization. It was of no avail. The southern states got what they wanted—the Indians, civilized or not, were removed.

Lewis Cass, who had long worked among and dealt with the Indians, became under Jackson an ardent advocate of removal. In a long article in 1830 he argued that there seemed to be an insurmountable obstacle in the habits or temperaments of Indians which prevented their adapting to American ways; the differences were such as to designate them "as a distinct variety of the human race." Cass attacked "Rousseau and the disciples of his school," who had persuaded themselves of the inferiority of civilized to savage life. "The Indians," wrote Cass, "are entitled to the enjoyment of all the rights which do not interfere with the obvious designs of Providence, and with the just claims of others." Existing relations with the Indians had "resulted from our superiority in physical and moral power."

Jackson spent no sleepless nights over Indian Removal. He was confident, as those who supported him were confident, that Providence was guiding the hand of the American race, and that the same Providence which had blessed the United States with good government, power, and prosperity had provided that inferior peoples should yield their "unused" domain to those who through its use could benefit themselves and the world. "What good man," asked Jackson in his second annual message in December 1830, "would prefer a country covered with forests and ranged by a few thousand savages to our extensive Republic, studded with cities, towns, and prosperous farms, embellished with all the improvements which art can devise or industry execute, occupied by more than 12,000,000 happy people, and filled with all the blessings of liberty, civilization, and religion?" A member of Congress who supported removal asked, "What is history but the obituary of nations?" He wanted to know if the United States should "check the course of human happiness—obstruct the march of science—stay the works of art, and stop the arm of industry, because they will efface in their progress the wigwam of the red hunter, and put out forever the council fire of his tribe?"

The reality of Indian Removal was seen quite clearly in the 1830s by observers unconcerned with the main Washington debate. Thomas Dew in his 1832 work defending slavery took it for granted that this removal of the Indians was a temporary expedient, and that the American population would soon press once again over the Indian borders. He used the expulsion and assumed future disappearance of the Indians as an argument to defend the expediency and morality of black slavery: more Indians would have been saved, he argued, if they had been enslaved. Tocqueville quickly perceived the shallowness of government promises of a permanent Indian home and future civilization beyond the Mississippi. He said that "the central government, when it promises these unhappy people a permanent asylum in the West, is well aware of its inability to guarantee this." The Creeks and the Cherokees had appealed to the central government against state oppression, Tocqueville said, but the federal government had determined to let a few tribes perish rather than shatter the union. "It is impossible," he said, "to destroy men with more respect to the laws of humanity."

While the eastern Indians moved west beyond the Mississippi, discussions of Indian matters in Congress revealed both the unwillingness of the majority to accept the Indians as equals, and the extent to which a sense of Anglo-Saxon racial destiny and of irreversible distinctions between races was beginning to invade the popular consciousness. James W. Bouldin of Virginia argued that the Indians could not survive in competition with Anglo-Saxons. The Indians, he said, were "a noble, gallant, injured race," which has "suffered nothing but wrong and injury from us, since the Anglo-Saxon race (borrowing an expression of Mr. [John] Randolph, my predecessor, which seems to have become popular) first landed in this country." The solution was to remove them, because otherwise they would disappear. The blacks had grown in number in America only because they were enslaved and under the protection of "the Anglo-Saxons."

The effort to create a formal Indian territory on the usual territorial model, with a degree of self-government and with the purpose of allowing Indians to emerge as equal citizens, was consistently blocked in Congress. The idea particularly stirred the fears of southern Congressmen, who saw the possibility of a dangerous precedent. William Archer of Virginia admitted that it "might be because he was a Southron," but he feared provision for the eventual admission of Indians to the American union would lead to far more serious questions—the possibility of the admission of Cuba, Haiti, and the free colony of blacks in Canada.

As the mistreatment of the Indians was increasingly justified by arguments of their inferiority, some members of Congress, even outside of the Northeast, challenged this new view of Indian deficiencies. Ambrose Sevier of Arkansas said that "there were many individuals of the several tribes, and especially since the establishment of the Choctaw Academy in Kentucky, who were as intelligent as nine tenths of the members of this House." John Tipton of Indiana attacked the whole notion that the Indians were incapable of improvement: "With regard to mental ability, we have no reason to believe they would suffer by a comparison with any other people . . . it would be preposterous to suppose that a whole nation of people were destitute of capacity to improve their condition . . . Are they not human beings, possessing all the passions of rational men, and all the powers of thought which belong to the human mind?" Tipton went to the heart of the matter when he said that it was natural that Americans should look for the causes of Indian disappearance among the Indians rather than among the whites, but this was a false search.

Indian resistance to the rapid appropriation of their lands was used to condemn them further as semihuman savages. Anglo-Saxon aggression was hailed as manly, Indian resistance was condemned as beastly. This was particularly the case in discussing the fighting in Florida in the late 1830s and early 1840s, for here escaped slaves mingled with Indian warriors to complicate the fears of the Southerners. David Levy of Florida argued as the pioneers of western Pennsylvania and Tennessee had argued at the time of the American Revolution. He stressed Indian atrocities, even holding up a barbed spear point taken from the body of a child, and saying, in words reminiscent of Hugh H. Brackenridge, "let us hear no more, I pray, from any quarter, of sympathy for these Indians. *They* know no mercy. They are demons, not men. They have the human form, but nothing of the human heart. Horror and detestation should follow the thought of them. If they cannot be emigrated, they should be exterminated." The Indian, said William A. Graham of North Carolina, like the wild animals could not be tamed: "You might as well expect the red man to change the color of his skin as his habits and pursuits."

To some southern Congressmen the Florida hostilities, rather than being an effort to dispossess Indians from areas desired by whites, simply became a confrontation between the colored and the white races of the earth. Thomas Hart Benton talked in the Senate of the desolation of forty-one thousand square miles in Florida—"made so by the ravages of the colored races upon the white!" The blacks, he argued, had combined with the Indians to commit wholesale atrocities, and he told a northern senator who had expressed sympathy for the Indians that his sympathy was misplaced— he should realize that "it is his own white race which has been the sufferer in Florida; and that the colored races have exulted in the slaughter and destruction of men, women, and children, descended, like the Senator himself, from the white branch of the human race." The conflict was no longer viewed as that of civilization against savagery, as in the eighteenth century; it was becoming the white race against the colored races.

By the 1840s the friends of the Indian felt overwhelmed by the new tendencies and were very much on the defensive. Daniel Webster had written in 1838 that the Whig members of Congress who had "taken an interest in seeing justice done to the Indians are worn out and exhausted. An Administration man, come from where he will, has no concern for Indian rights." Those friends of the Indian who still believed that the Indians were capable of attaining equality with the white race were in a difficult position in the 1840s and 1850s. Many missionaries were still hopeful that the Indians could be saved by being transformed, and commissioners of Indian affairs often maintained the rhetoric and optimism of an older generation, but most Americans and their politicians had rejected the Indians as equal fellow citizens.

Faced by unfavorable political realities and by the widespread dissemination of the scientific view that the Indians were inherently inferior, the friends of the Indian spent much of their time trying to defend the Indian capacity for improvement and trying to combat the view that the Indians were doomed to extinction. Isaac McCoy in 1840 attacked the idea that any race of man had been brought into existence with "some innate self-destroying principle," but he acknowledged that "lectures on the manners and customs of the Indians, whether consisting of encomium or censure, usually wind up with a prediction of the utter extinction of the race." Thomas McKenney in 1846 admitted that Indian Removal had not created a haven for the Indians. He said all past experience showed that the United States would seek to dislodge the Indians again unless relations between the United States and the Indian tribes took a new form. His object in asking for a new course of action, he said, was to defend them from adverse judgments and to declare them *"human."* Except for their color and their lack of superior advantages, they were in all respects like white Americans.

When Lewis Henry Morgan in 1851 defended the capacity of the Indians for improvement and argued that education and Christianity would be their only salvation, he was quite frank in admitting the general state of the public mind on this question. "The frequent attempts which have been made to educate the Indian, and the numerous failures in which these attempts have eventuated," he said, "have, to some extent, created a belief in the public mind, that his education and reclamation are both impossible." Morgan stressed that the existing system of federal Indian policy was "evidently temporary in its plans and purposes." It was designed, he argued, for the least possible inconvenience rather than "reclamation" and eventual citizenship: "The sentiment which this system proclaims is not as emphatic as that emblazoned upon the Roman policy towards the Carthaginians— *Carthago est delenda,*—'Carthage must be destroyed:' but it reads in not less significant characters—*The destiny of the Indian is extermination.* This sentiment, which is so wide-spread as to have become a general theme for school-boy declamation, is not only founded upon erroneous views, but it has been prejudicial to the Indian himself." By 1850 the American public and American politicians had for the most part abandoned any belief in potential Indian equality. They now believed that American Indians were doomed because of their own inferiority and that their extinction would further world progress.

The experience of the United States with the Indians in the first half of the nineteenth century helped to convince many Americans that American expansion might mean the eventual extinction of inferior races that lacked the innate ability to transform their way of life. The American public and American politicians had developed their own racial theories alongside, and even before, those of American intellectuals. They were pleased to gain confirmation of their beliefs from the scientists, but they often articulated ideas about Indian inferiority that received scientific proof only at a later date. As American hopes of creating a policy based on Enlightenment ideals of human equality failed, and as they relentlessly drove the Indians from all areas desired by the whites, Americans transferred their own failure to the Indians and condemned the Indians racially. By 1850 only a minority of Americans believed that transformed Indians would eventually assume a permanent, equal place within American society.

Scientific Racism and Indian Policy

FRANCIS PAUL PRUCHA

United States policy toward the Indians cannot be treated in a vacuum, set apart by the historian (consciously or unconsciously) from the main currents of American thought. Prominent ideas of the age had significant influence—or at least, to state the proposition negatively, Indian policy did not go counter to prevailing sentiments and attitudes. It is difficult, to be sure, to determine prevailing attitudes and ideas. Works like those of Perry Miller, Russel B. Nye, and Rush Welter, for example, are not completely satisfactory when used as background for Indian policy in the pre–Civil War period. And in fact, it probably is not a good idea to set up a paradigm against which Indian policy is then projected. A thorough study of Indian policy, in the light of the intellectual currents it reflected, may in the long run help us to test the completeness and accuracy of accepted analyses of the American mind, for intellectual historians sometimes jump to unwarranted conclusions about the effect on practice of the ideas they discover in the writings of a period.

Within this larger context, one can investigate the relationship between official Indian policy (as formulated by the federal government—President, Congress, and Indian Office) and philosophical and scientific views of race in the nineteenth century. Were there pervasive views of race upon which Indian policy was built? Did federal policy toward the Indians reflect changing scientific findings about inherent racial characteristics? Or did federal officials ignore or reject the work of the scientists and rely instead on other, more traditional views?

These questions have been discussed in a recent article by Reginald Horsman, "Scientific Racism and the American Indian in the Mid-Nineteenth Century." Horsman notes the work of the "American School" of ethnology in the 1840s and 1850s, especially the writings of Samuel G. Morton, George R. Gliddon, Josiah C. Nott, and Ephraim G. Squier. He describes their theories of separate species for the different races, each separately created and innately superior or inferior to the others, and speaks of the "pervasive influence" of this new racism and "its success in the popular mind." Dismissing the arguments of the 1840s made by supporters of attempts to civilize the Indians as "the rhetoric and optimism of an older generation," he concludes:

> It seems that by the middle of the nineteenth century science itself had endorsed the earlier popular feeling that the Indians were not worth saving and envisaged a world bettered as the all-conquering Anglo-Saxon branch of the Caucasian race superseded inferior peoples. The American School of ethnologists in the eyes of many had made nonsense of the long-reiterated claim that given time the Indians were fully capable of absorbing American civilization and assimilable on an equal basis. The people of the United States now had scientific reasons to account for Indian failures and to explain and justify American expansion.

Horsman is not alone in this kind of sweeping (and largely unsubstantiated) generalization. Most important are the similar statements in Thomas F. Gossett's widely used book *Race: The History of an Idea in America.*

Reprinted from *Indian Policy in the United States: Historical Essays,* 180–197, by Francis Paul Prucha, by permission of the University of Nebraska Press. Copyright © 1981 by the University of Nebraska Press.

Gossett, like other writers on racism in the United States, is concerned primarily with attitudes and findings about blacks, and the Indians appear in many cases only incidently or lumped together with "other nonwhite races." But he does have a chapter on "The Indian in the Nineteenth Century" in which he makes a number of remarkable assertions, including the following:

> The nineteenth century was obsessed with the idea that it was race which explained the character of peoples. The notion that traits of temperament and intelligence are inborn in races and only superficially changed by environment or education was enough to blind the dominant whites. The Indians suffered more than any other ethnic minority from the cruel dicta of racism. The frontiersman, beset with the problem of conquering the wilderness, was in no mood to understand anything about the Indians except that they were at best a nuisance and at worst a terrible danger. The leading thinkers of the era were generally convinced that Indian traits were racially inherent and therefore could not be changed. The difference between the frontiersmen's view of the Indians and that of the intellectuals was more apparent than real. In general, the frontiersmen either looked forward with pleasure to the extinction of the Indians or at least were indifferent to it. The intellectuals were most often equally convinced with the frontiersmen that the Indians, because of their inherent nature, must ultimately disappear. They were frequently willing to sigh philosophically over the fate of the Indians, but this was an empty gesture.

Similar statements appear in the writings of Russel B. Nye, woven into a rather loose discussion of views about the Indians:

> The anthropology of the times assumed that race was a determining factor in people's destiny; color, character, and intelligence went together; certain traits were inherent in certain races, nor could they be substantially altered by either education or environment. Some races were better than others, the Indian and Negro being lowest in the scale.

> The idea of the Indian as irremediably savage was the commonly accepted basis for thinking about him for the first half of the nineteenth century.

> It was generally agreed that the Indian's racial inheritances made it impossible to civilize him.

There is little doubt that whites in the nineteenth century, including the officials of the Indian Office and other policy makers, considered Indian *cultures* inferior to their own, for the cultural pluralism of today was not a viable idea at the time. The question, however, is not about the culture of the Indians but about their innate racial inferiority. Were the Indians judged to be biologically—as a race—inherently inferior, and if so, did this view affect Indian policy? The statements of Horsman, Gossett, and Nye jar strangely with fundamental documents on the formulation and underpinnings of Indian policy in the nineteenth century and with widespread patterns of belief.

We can look at the problem first in the Jeffersonian period. The Enlightenment thought reflected by Thomas Jefferson and contemporary thinkers had no place for ideas of racial inferiority in regard to the Indians. Those men believed in the unity of mankind. "We shall probably find," Jefferson wrote of the Indians in his *Notes on the State of Virginia,* "that they are formed in mind as well as in body, in the same module with the 'Homo sapiens Europaeus.'" They believed that mankind passed, inexorably, through stages of society, from savagism, through barbarism, to civilization. Jefferson expressed this view in a striking comparison of geographical states with temporal ones.

> Let a philosophic observer commence a journey from the savages of the Rocky Mountains, eastwardly towards our seacoast. These [the savages] he would observe in the earliest stage of association living under no law but that of nature, subsisting and covering themselves with the flesh and skins of wild beasts. He would next find those on our frontiers in the pastoral state, raising domestic animals to supply the defects of hunting. Then succeed our own semi-barbarous citizens, the pioneers of the advance of civilization, and so in his progress he would meet the gradual shades of improving man until he would reach his, as yet, most improved state in our seaboard towns. This, in fact, is equivalent to a survey, in time, of the progress of man from the infancy of creation to the present day.

The Jeffersonians were environmentalists, holding that conditions and circumstances of life made men what they were and that by changing the environment man's culture would be changed. There was no room in this optimistic framework for innate, racial inferiority not amenable to perfecting influences. And in practice the men of the Enlightenment sought ways to bring about the transformation in Indian society which they believed possible and inevitable. Washington and Jefferson, and their secretaries of war, Knox and Dearborn, promoted the civilization of the tribes by the introduction of agriculture and domestic arts, and the trade and intercourse laws made provision for these measures. Success, they thought, was assured. Dearborn expressed his opinion to the Creek agent in 1803: "The progress made in the introduction of the arts of civilization among the Creeks must be highly pleasing to every benevolent mind, and in my opinion is conclusive evidence of the practicability of such improvements upon the state of society among the several Indian Nations as may ultimately destroy all distinctions between what are called Savages and civilized people."

In the second, third, and fourth decades of the century, these philanthropic sentiments were still strong, but Enlightenment thought had in fact been mixed with, or perhaps it would be more accurate to say replaced by, another strain of thought, which for want of a better term can be called evangelical Christianity. The views about the nature of the Indians and the possibility of their transformation held by the rationalists and by the churchmen were much the same if not identical. But the basis was different. One built on the rationalism of the Enlightenment, on the laws of nature discovered in God's creation by rational men. The other was a product of a new surge of evangelical religion that came with the turn of the century, a new missionary spirit, a revivalism that was to be a dominant mark of Protestant Christian America for a full century or more. The faith of Christians was less easily dislodged by new scientific discoveries than was the rationalism of Jeffersonians.

Indicative of the new force was the establishment in 1810 of the American Board of Commissioners for Foreign Missions in Boston to evangelize the heathen—including the American Indians—and the Board's founding of a school for the Cherokees at Brainerd in 1816. It may be unfair to single out one missionary society, for Methodists and Baptists and Quakers and Episcopalians all at about the same time began or renewed their efforts to convert and civilize the Indians of the United States. However we mark the beginnings, official Indian policy and Indian missionary activities of these Protestant churches joined in a close partnership that lasted until the end of the century. So firmly entrenched was this religious missionary approach to Indian affairs that it could not be easily disrupted; it was the chief reason why Indian policy development was so frequently, if not universally, a reform movement.

There is evidence, from the first years of the new nation, of government-missionary cooperation, which harked back to colonial Christian enterprises among the Indians. Even Secretary of War Henry Knox, on whom depended much of the initial formulation of Indian policy, looked to missionaries to supply the aid the government wanted to provide the Indians in leading them to civilization. But the key man in developing missionary-government activity in Indian affairs in the early nineteenth century was Thomas L. McKenney, who, with his appointment as superintendent of Indian trade in 1816, began a lifetime of interest in and influence on Indian policy. McKenney, of Quaker background, can hardly be considered a man of the Enlightenment. He was a *Christian* humanitarian, for whom the civilization and Christianization of the Indians was of great moment. He was unequivocal in his stand on the equality of the red race and the reasons for his opinion. In a letter to Christopher Vandeventer in 1818, asking for a copy of a manuscript by Lewis Cass on Indian relations, McKenney said: "I will be gratified, I am sure, with a perusal of Gov. Cass's view of our Indian relations. I hope he has considered them as Human Beings,—because, if he has not, I shall believe the good book is profane to him, which says, 'of *one blood,* God made all the nations to dwell upon the face of the earth.' And were this not satisfactory an Anatomical examination would prove it—And it might be an affair of Mercy to let *skeptics* have a few Indians for dissection."

McKenney was a tireless instigator of missionary efforts for the Indians, and he made his Indian trade office a continuing center for planning and prodding. His big effort was persuading Congress to appropriate money for the education and civilization of the Indians. His success in getting the "civilization fund" established in 1819 was a great missionary and humanitarian victory. The use of the fund, determined by Secretary of War Calhoun, was dependent upon "benevolent societies," that is the missionaries, who were already at work in Indian education and for whom the federal funds were a tremendous inducement to expand their Christian enterprises.

When McKenney was appointed by Calhoun in 1824 to head the Indian

Office established in the War Department, he did not change his views about the inherent equality—and therefore capabilities—of the Indians, nor did he weaken his drive to provide them with the means to transcend their savage state and quickly assume the characteristics of the white Christian society of which McKenney and other humanitarians were so proud. In his first report he noted the laudatory reports from the superintendents of the Indian schools in operation and remarked:

> They certainly demonstrate that no insuperable difficulty is in the way of a complete reformation of the principles and pursuits of the Indians. Judging from what has been accomplished since the adoption by the Government, in 1819 of the system upon which all Schools are now operating and making due allowance for the tardy advancements of the first 2 or 3 years, which are for the most part consumed in the work of preparation and in overcoming the prejudices and apprehensions of the Indians, there is good reason to believe, that an entire reformation may be effected, (I mean among the tribes bordering our settlements, and to whom those benefits have been extended,) in the course of the present generation.

McKenney's immediate successors in the Indian Office were of the same mind. This is not surprising, for there were few questions in humane and rational men's minds about the fundamental equality of all men and the possibility, by proper education, of bringing the children of the forest up to the high cultural level of the whites.

The removal question, which dominated much of the public discussion of Indian affairs in the decade after 1825, did not upset the consensus. The question of the speed at which civilization was progressing, to be sure, was much argued, and the deleterious effects of proximity to the vices of white society much debated, but neither side doubted the innate capability of the Indian. The antiremoval crusade, led and dominated to a large degree by the evangelical humanitarians of the American Board of Commissioners for Foreign Missions, was, as might be assumed, the more vocal on the point of Indian capabilities. "I believe, sir," Senator Theodore Frelinghuysen declared in Senate debates in 1830, "it is not now seriously denied that the Indians are men, endowed with kindred faculties and powers with ourselves; that they have a place in human sympathy, and are justly entitled to a share in the common bounties of a benignant Providence. And, with this conceded, I ask in what code of the law of nations, or by what process of abstract deduction, their rights have been extinguished?" Senator Asher Robbins, of Rhode Island, declared with equal vehemence: "The Indian is a man, and has all the rights of man. The same God who made us made him and endowed him with the same rights; for 'of one blood hath he made all the men who dwell upon the earth.'"

There was considerable argument in support of removal on the basis of unfavorable reports about the Indians' conditions and progress in civilization. But Wilson Lumpkin, of Georgia, the chief spokesman for removal, admitted: "I entertain no doubt that a remnant of these people may be entirely reclaimed from their native savage habits, and be brought to enter into the full enjoyment of all the blessings of civilized society. It appears to me, we have too many instances of individual improvement amongst the various native tribes of America, to hesitate any longer in determining whether the Indians are susceptible of civilization.''

Then, about 1840, the almost universal agreement about the nature of the Indians and their origin faced a dramatic challenge from the American School of ethnology. The cranial measurements of [Samuel George] Morton, the somewhat flamboyant antics of [George R.] Gliddon, and the propagandistic publications of [Josiah C.] Nott brought to the public an alternative view of the Indians, and one wrapped in the mantle of science.

Unable to reconcile accepted timetables of human history, based on a reading of the Bible, with the diversity of human races, the purveyors of the new doctrine opted for polygenesis—the separate creation of the races as distinct species. Once it was admitted that the blacks and the Indians were different species from the Caucasians and that not all members of the human race were descended from Adam, it was easy to conclude that some races were inherently inferior to others. In the world of practical affairs, the new scientific doctrines could furnish support for the slave status of the blacks and the dispossession and extinction of the Indians.

The question, of course, is precisely this: Did the scientific findings in fact dominate the American mind, and did the formulators of public policy with regard to the nonwhite races accept and then act upon the theories?

In the case of the blacks we can rely upon the judgment of the most thorough and careful student of scientific racism before the Civil War, William R. Stanton. In his study, *The Leopard's Spots,* he concludes that in neither the North nor the South were the scientists' conclusions about the inferiority of blacks accepted as a basis for action. The scientists themselves were not tied together by any desire to support slavery but by an antireligious sentiment. ''The conscious extrascientific bond which linked many of these men together,'' Stanton says, ''was not sympathy for Southern institutions but anticlericalism and antibiblicism.'' He continues: ''The doctrine [of diverse origins] was soothing to the cultural nationalism of the times, yet the response of the North might have been anticipated. The doctrine lent comfort to slavery and so could not be accepted as a guide to conduct. Northerners rejected in this context the Jeffersonian ideal that science should be the guide of political life and the arbiter of social problems.''

The South, presented with the opportunity to ground the defense of slavery on a scientific basis, turned away. ''Southerners,'' says Stanton, ''discerned in the doctrine of multiple origins an assault upon orthodox religion (a shrewd enough interpretation) and chose to hold fast to the latter. . . . The Bible did lend considerable support to slavery, but so did science. Opting for the Bible was the mark of the South's already profound commitment to religion. Heretofore this had not necessarily been an anti-intellectual position. But when the issue was clearly drawn, the South turned its back on the only intellectually respectable defense of slavery it could have taken up.'' The practical effect for slavery was negative; ''the lasting significance of the American researches in ethnology before the Civil War must be sought in the history of science."

A similar conclusion is reached by John S. Haller, Jr., who wrote: "The South was too fundamentalist and New England too moralistic to meet on scientific terms which were unbiblical and unemotional. . . . The stance of the North and South was basically Christian, biblical, and monogenist. The scientific argument of diverse origins, by reason of its generally more anti-biblical approach, moved more and more out of the public eye and back into the closed circle of a few scientific savants."

So much for blacks. But did the doctrines of diverse origins and inferiority of races play a different role in Indian affairs? Can we conclude with Horsman that "the American School of ethnologists in the eyes of many had made nonsense of the long-reiterated claim that given time the Indians were fully capable of absorbing American civilization and assimilable on an equal basis"? Is Gossett correct in concluding that "the notion that traits of temperament and intelligence are inborn in races and only superficially changed by environment or education was enough to blind the dominant whites," that "the Indians suffered more than any other ethnic minority from the cruel dicta of racism"?

The answer is emphatically "no." If, for example, we take the commissioners of Indian affairs as representative of federal policy makers in the heyday of the American School, we find a uniform—and in some cases a very strong—adherence to traditional positions. There are few indications that they were aware of the new scientific theories. If the scientific racism is adverted to at all, it is rejected. The notion that the Indians were men, different from whites because of the conditioning factors of their savage or barbaric culture, but susceptible of reformation and complete civilization, was the fundamental basis of what the commissioners said and did. Although the exigencies of Indian removal in the 1830s disrupted the education and civilization programs, these humanitarian measures were picked up with new enthusiasm in the decades of the 1840s and 1850s. A few typical examples will make this clear.

T. Hartley Crawford, commissioner from 1838 to 1844, was not an easy enthusiast about Indian civilization. He was well aware of past failures, of the slow and tedious climb from savagery to civilization, and he felt that it was impossible without radically changing the ways of the Indians. Individual allotments of land, manual training schools (for girls as well as for boys), and persistence on the part of Christian teachers were all essential. At times he almost seemed to despair, but at the end of his term he spoke unequivocally. "Some of . . . [the] tribes," he wrote in 1843, "the most incredulous must admit, are fairly launched on the tide of civilization. The fact of Indian capability to become all that education and Christianity can make man is incontestably established." And the following year he reported: "The condition of the Indian race, as connected with the United States, is, in the general, one of improvement, and slow but sure approaches to civilization, very distinctly marked, in my judgment. It is proved, I think, conclusively, that it is in no respect inferior to our own race, except in being less fortunately circumstanced.''

William Medill, Crawford's successor, took a hard line on the necessity of teaching Indians to forsake the chase and take up agriculture: "Thus by slow but sure means may a whole nation be raised from the depths of barbarism to comparative civilization and happiness." Indians in the Pacific Northwest he reported on very favorably. "Through the benevolent policy of various Christian churches," he noted, "and the indefatigable exertion of the missionaries in their employ, they have prescribed and well adapted rules for their government, which are observed and respected to a degree worthy of the most intelligent whites. . . . Under these circumstances, so promising in their consequences, and grateful to the feelings of the philanthropist, it would seem to be the duty of the government of the United States to encourage their advancement, and still further aid their progress in the paths of civilization." He spoke of forcing the Indians to resort to labor, "and thus commence the transition from a state of barbarism and moral depression, to one of civilization and moral elevation."

Orlando Brown, who served only a year as commissioner, declared in 1849: "A great moral and social revolution is . . . now in progress among a number of the tribes, which, by the adoption of similar measures in other cases, might be rapidly extended to most, if not all, of those located on our western borders; so that, in a few years, it is believed that in intelligence and resources they would compare favorably with many portions of our white population." He ended with high optimism: "There is encouraging ground for the belief that a large share of success will, in the end, crown the philanthropic efforts of the Government and of individuals to civilize and to christianize the Indians tribes. . . . [I]t is now no longer a problem whether [the Indians] are capable of self-government or not. They have proved their capacity for social happiness, by adopting written constitutions upon the model of our own, by establishing and sustaining schools, by successfully devoting themselves to agricultural pursuits, by respectable attainments in the learned professions and mechanic arts, and by adopting the manners and customs of our people so far as they are applicable to their own condition. To insure such gratifying results with tribes but recently brought within the jurisdiction of the United States, we have but to avail ourselves of the experience of the past."

Commissioner Luke Lea spoke strongly in the same vein. "The history of the Indian furnishes abundant proof that he possesses all the elements essential to his elevation," he wrote in 1851; "all the powers, instincts, and sympathies which appertain to his white brother; and which only need the proper development and direction to enable him to tread with equal step and dignity the walks of civilized life. . . . That his inferiority is a necessity of his nature, is neither taught by philosophy, nor attested by experience." Lea admitted, however, that "prejudice against him originating in error of opinion on this subject" had been "a formidable obstacle in the way of his improvement."

Another pre–Civil War example was George W. Manypenny. He was not overly sanguine, for he noted the slowness of the Indians' progress toward civilization, but there is nothing in his reports to indicate that he thought ultimate success was impossible. "Much has been effected," he said in 1853, "but far more remains to be done, to secure and accomplish the full and complete regeneration of this singular and interesting race within our borders; but the object is a noble one, and in all respects deserving of the attention and energies of the government of a great Christian people." Manypenny saw many drawbacks to Indian progress—including "erroneous opinions and prejudices in relation to the disposition, characteristics, capacity, and intellectual powers of the race"—but he himself did not despair. "I believe," he said, "that the Indian may be domesticated, improved, and elevated; that he may be completely and thoroughly civilized, and made a useful element of our population."

Crawford, Medill, Lea, Brown, and Manypenny clearly did not accept the view of the Indian proposed by Morton, Gliddon, Squier, and Nott. They did not subscribe to the racist positions of *DeBow's Review* and the *Democratic Review*. Their viewpoints and their actions (especially in regard to education for the Indians) continued to follow the pattern of evangelical Christianity of the first decades of the century.

Moreover, they consciously aligned themselves with the missionaries to the Indians, relying on the churches in large part for the program of education and civilization they espoused. This partnership was explicitly acknowledged by William Medill in 1847:

> In every system which has been adopted for promoting the cause of education among the Indians, the Department has found its most efficient and faithful auxiliaries and laborers in the societies of the several Christian denominations, which have sent out missionaries, established schools, and maintained local teachers among the different tribes. Deriving their impulse from principles of philanthropy and religion, and devoting a large amount of their own means to the education, moral elevation and improvement of the tribes, the Department has not hesitated to make them the instrument, to a considerable extent, of applying the funds appropriated by the government for like purposes. Their exertions have thus been encouraged, and a greater degree of economy at the same time secured in the expenditure of the public money.

The commissioners, of course, were not alone in ignoring scientific racism nor in their understanding of the Indian and their hopes for his future. They no doubt felt reinforced by the opinions of men who knew the Indians from long contact and study.

Henry R. Schoolcraft, the longtime agent to the Chippewas and one of America's noted ethnologists, was disgusted with Nott and Gliddon's book, *Types of Mankind*. "Well," he remarked in 1854, "if this be all, that America is to send back to Europe, after feasting on her rich stores of learning, science, philosophy & religion for three centuries, it were better that the Aborigines had maintained their dark empire of pow pows & jugglers undisturbed."

Thomas L. McKenney, appearing on the lecture circuit in the 1840s with lectures on the "origin, history, character, and the wrongs and rights of the Indians," held firm to monogenesis.

> I am aware [he said] that opinions are entertained by some, embracing the theory of multiform creations; by such, the doctrine that the whole family of man sprang from one original and common stock, is denied. There is, however, but one source whence information can be derived on this subject— and that is the Bible; and, until those who base their convictions on Bible testimony, consent to throw aside that great land-mark of truth, they must continue in the belief that "the Lord God formed *man* of the dust of the ground, and breathed into his nostrils the breath of life, when he became a living soul." Being thus formed, and thus endowed, he was put by his Creator in *the* garden, which was eastward, in Eden, whence flowed the river which parted, and became into four heads; and that from his fruitfulness his species were propagated.

The propagation of the entire human race from "an original pair," McKenney asserted, "is a truth so universally admitted, as to render any elaborate argument in its support superfluous." Since the Eden of Adam and Eve was not in America, the Indians could not have been indigenous to America. McKenney believed that the Indians were of Asiatic origin and had migrated to the New World by way of the Bering Strait. He argued that in his lectures against those who said that the Indian was irreclaimable.

The pioneer anthropologist Lewis Henry Morgan, too, seemed unaffected by the stir of scientific racism. Morgan's solution for the Indian problem was not destruction but assimilation. The Indians, he wrote in 1845, "must prepare to be incorporated into the great brotherhood of American nations as equal citizens; perhaps even be engrafted on our race. I sincerely hope this may be the result." His famous *League of the Iroquois* was intended, he wrote in the first sentence, "to encourage a kindlier feeling towards the Indian, founded upon a truer knowledge of his civil and domestic institutions, and of his capabilities for future elevation." Morgan argued in 1852 that inequality among men was not innate, but rather social and artificial.

Horsman ends his study at 1859 and leaves the impression that by mid-century America had accepted the racist doctrines of the scientists, that the decades of the 1840s and 1850s were a watershed, which the men in the Office of Indian Affairs were a bit slow to cross ("repeating the old rhetoric") but which they would ultimately and inevitably reach. This might be a possible interpretation if one stops at mid-century (although it seems clear that the commissioners were not merely repeating old rhetoric), but it is not possible if one looks at the nineteenth century as a whole. In the first place, the polygenesis doctrines of the American School, on which they rested the diversity of human species and the inferiority of the nonwhite races, were rendered outmoded by the evolutionary theories of Charles Darwin. Morton and Nott and their friends turned out to be scientific oddities, their cranial measurements relegated to the attic like the phrenology with which they flirted. But, more significantly, the Indian policy of the post–Civil War decades continued the optimism and doctrines of Indian perfectibility with which we have been dealing.

The dominance of evangelical Protestant views in Indian policy after the Civil War was, if anything, stronger than it had been before. Three of the commissioners of Indian affairs—Nathaniel G. Taylor, E. P. Smith, and Thomas Jefferson Morgan—were ordained Protestant ministers, and others, like Hiram Price, were prominent laymen in their churches. The Board of Indian Commissioners, established in 1869, was almost a Protestant church body. The assignment of Indian agencies to missionary societies was an abdication by the government of fundamental Indian Office duties, which were thrust into the hands of churchmen and the agents they selected. And when, after 1880, the dominant influence on Indian policy reform came from new reform organizations like the Boston Indian Citizenship Committee, the Women's National Indian Association, the Indian Rights Association, and the Lake Mohonk Conference of the Friends of the Indian, professedly Christian philanthropists were in the saddle.

Scientific racism of the period from 1865 to 1900 was less clearly marked toward the Indians than toward the blacks. For "colored races," it was argued, evolution had been slowed or stopped, leaving the Caucasian alone to continually progress. But this line of thought was not reflected in Indian policy formulation. Two examples will suffice.

Commissioner of Indian Affairs Nathaniel G. Taylor (1865–69) was the leader in the campaign to keep Indian affairs in civilian hands and out of the hands of the military. In his annual report of 1868 he presented a remarkable example of the doctrine of efficient causality in regard to civilizing the Indians. He asked the question, How can our Indian tribes be civilized? And he answered, in part:

> History and experience have laid the key to its solution in our hands, at the proper moment, and all we need to do is to use it, and we at once reach the desired answer. It so happens that under the silent and seemingly slow operation of efficient causes, certain tribes of our Indians have already emerged from a state of pagan barbarism, and are to-day clothed in the garments of civilization, and sitting under the vine and fig tree of an intelligent scriptural Christianity.

The example he pointed to was that of the Five Civilized Tribes, which only a short time before had been pagans and savages.

> But behold the contrast which greets the world to-day! The blanket and the bow are discarded; the spear is broken, and the hatchet and war-club lie buried; the skin lodge and primitive tepe have given place to the cottage and the mansion; the buckskin robe, the paint and beads have vanished, and are now replaced with the tasteful fabrics of civilization. Medicine lodges and their orgies, and heathen offerings, are mingling with the dust of a forgotten idolatry. School-houses abound, and the feet of many thousand little Indian children—children intelligent and thirsting after knowledge—are seen every day entering these vestibules of science; while churches dedicated to the Christian's God, and vocal with His praise from the lips of redeemed thousands, reflect from their domes and spires the earliest rays and latest beams of that sun whose daily light now blesses them as five Christian and enlightened nations so recently heathen savages.

"Thus the fact stands out clear, well-defined, and indisputable," Taylor declared, "that Indians, not only as individuals but as tribes, are capable of civilization and of christianization."

The commissioner then reached his point: "Now if like causes under similar circumstances always produce like effects—which no sensible person will deny—it is clear that the application of the same causes, that have resulted in civilizing these tribes, to other tribes under similar circumstances, must produce their civilization." He pointed to localization of members of the tribe in limited areas, attention to agriculture and pastoral pursuits, and the teachings of Christian missionaries.

A second example is Thomas Jefferson Morgan, who was the epitome of the reforming spirit of the 1880s and 1890s. While he was commissioner of Indian affairs, he delivered an address in Albany on Indian education, which he entitled *A Plea for the Papoose*. It was a sort of fantasy, in which he spoke what he thought Indian infants would say if they could speak. It is a long statement of his belief in the unity of mankind and in the importance of environment. The Indian children had a "kinship with us," he said. "They, too, are human and endowed with all the faculties of human nature; made in the image of God, bearing the likeness of their Creator, and having the same possibilities of growth and development that are possessed by any other class of children."

Morgan noted that many people had treated the Indians badly. "The term 'savage' is often applied to them as carrying with it a condemnation of them as inhuman beings," he wrote; "bloodthirsty, gloating in war, rejoicing in revenge, happy in creating havoc, and irreconcilably hostile to all that is noble, true and good. But if the Indian babies could speak for themselves, they would say that whatever of savagery or brutishness there has been in the history of their people has been due rather to unfortunate circumstances, for which they were not always responsible, than to any inherent defect of nature. Under proper conditions the Indian baby grows into the cultivated, refined Christian gentleman or lovely woman, and the plea for the papoose is that this humanity shall be recognized. Indian nature is human nature bound in red."

He repeated this idea again and again. "All human babies inherit human natures," he insisted, "and the development of these inherent powers is a matter of culture, subject to the conditions of environment. The pretty, innocent papoose has in itself the potency of a painted savage, prowling like a beast of prey, or the possibilities of a sweet and gentle womanhood or a noble and useful manhood. Undoubtedly," he admitted, "there is much in heredity. No amount of culture will grow oranges on a rose bush, or develop a corn-stalk into an oak tree. There is also, undoubtedly, much in the race differences between the Mongolian and the Caucasian, and between these and the African and the Indian, yet the essential elements of human nature are the same in all and in each, and the possibilities of development are limited only by the opportunities for growth and by culture forces. We are all creatures of culture."

To be sure, Morgan and his friends in the reforming groups did not think that the Indians on their reservations should be allowed to stop the onward march of Anglo-Saxon civilization. But it seems clear that it was Indian culture that they condemned, not the innate qualities of the Indians, which they believed should be shaped by education and proper environment. There is just too much evidence, both before and after the Civil War, to permit the conclusion that "it was generally agreed that the Indian's racial inheritances made it impossible to civilize him." The effect of scientific racism on the formulation of Indian policy in the nineteenth century was, indeed, practically nil.

Anglo-American Stereotypes of Mexicans

DAVID J. WEBER

Many nineteenth-century, Anglo-American visitors to what is today the Southwestern United States (defined for present purposes as the four border states of Alta California, Arizona, New Mexico, and Texas), depicted the Mexican residents of that area in the most unflattering terms. Mexicans were described as lazy, ignorant, bigoted, superstitious, cheating, thieving, gambling, cruel, sinister, cowardly half-breeds. As a consequence of their supposed innate depravity, Mexicans were seen as incapable of developing republican institutions or achieving material progress. These opinions of Mexicans, some of which endure to the present, are familiar to most Southwesterners and can be found in the writings of many early Anglo-American writers. One example will suffice. Thomas Jefferson Farnham, a New England attorney who toured Alta California in the early 1840s, described the *californios* thus:

> There never was a doubt among Californians that they were at the head of the human race. In cowardice, ignorance, pretension, and dastardly tyranny, the reader has learned that this pretension is well founded.
>
> Thus much for the Spanish population of the Californias; in every way a poor apology of European extraction; as a general thing, incapable of reading or writing, and knowing nothing of science or literature, nothing of government but its brutal force, nothing of virtue but the sanction of the Church, nothing of religion but ceremonies of the national ritual. Destitute of industry themselves, they compel the poor Indian to labor for them, affording him a bare savage existence for his toil, upon their plantations and the fields of the Missions. In a word, the Californians are an imbecile, pusillanimous, race of men, and unfit to control the destinies of that beautiful country. . . .
>
> No one acquainted with the indolent, mixed race of California, will ever believe that they will populate, much less, for any length of time, govern

---

David J. Weber, " 'Scarce more than Apes': Historical Roots of Anglo American Stereotypes of Mexicans in the Border Region," in David J. Weber, ed., *New Spain's Far Northern Frontier: Essays on Spain in the American West, 1540–1821*, 295–304 (Albuquerque: University of New Mexico Press, 1981), 180–197.

the country. The law of Nature which curses the mulatto here with a constitution less robust than that of either race from which he sprang, lays a similar penalty upon the mingling of the Indian and white races in California and Mexico. They must fade away. . . .

Not all Americans who came to the Mexican frontier shared Farnham's passionate contempt for Mexicans, but many did and they expressed their feelings in no uncertain terms. Charles Bent, a merchant who became prominent in New Mexico in the 1830s and 1840s and took a Mexican woman as his common-law wife, wrote that "the Mexican character is made up of stupidity, obstinacy, ignorance, duplicity, and vanity." Noah Smithwick, who settled in Texas in 1827, later recalled that "I looked on the Mexicans as scarce more than apes." This image of Mexicans as subhuman creatures was shared by a Santa Fe trader who preferred not to consider Mexicans as part of "humanity," but to classify them separately as "Mexicanity."

If Anglo Americans had portrayed individual Mexicans in a negative fashion, we might think little of it, for surely there were Mexicans, just as there were Anglo Americans, who fit the description. When such characterizations are applied to an entire people, however, they clearly are no longer based on empirical evidence and cannot be regarded as valid generalizations. Sweeping generalizations, which either have no basis in fact, or which are based on "overgeneralizations of facts," are known as stereotypes. Negative stereotypes are, of course, an obstacle to communication and understanding for they are usually expressions of prejudice which, as Walter Lippmann once put it, "precedes the use of reason."

Stereotypes need not always be negative, of course. In describing Mexicans as a peculiarly depraved people, for example, early Anglo-American writers, who were almost always males, frequently took pains to exempt Mexican women from their disparaging remarks. Hence, the negative stereotype applies to the male half of the Mexican population; the feminine half has enjoyed a positive image. "The men of northern Mexico," wrote one early American settler in Arizona, "are far inferior to the women in every respect." Similarly, an English visitor to Alta California in 1842 concluded that women were "by far the more industrious half of the population."

Male visitors to the Mexican frontier, who usually had not seen a woman for several months, were frequently impressed with the beauty, kindness, and flirtatiousness of Mexican women. In forming this positive stereotype, American males allowed their hormones to overcome their ethnocentrism. Indeed, one visitor to New Mexico put aside his characteristic chauvinism to pronounce Mexican women "more beautiful" than their counterparts in the United States. Another young American traveler in New Mexico carried a stereotype to its extremes by asserting that "women is women the whole world over, no matter where she is found."

Americans found some things to dislike about Mexican women, to be sure, but in general their high regard for Mexican women stands in sharp contrast to their contempt for Mexican men. Francis Parkman, traveling in the far West in 1846, revealed this dichotomy in American thinking clearly if unconsciously when he termed Mexican women "Spanish" and Mexican men "Mexicans."

How did a negative stereotype of Mexican males develop? There are many approaches to that question which cannot be explored in a brief paper. As a historian, I would like to suggest that the answer has larger dimensions than usually suggested by Southwestern writers. One popular explanation, implied more often than it is stated, is that a negative stereotype of Mexicans developed as a result of the contacts made between Mexicans and Anglo Americans in the border region in the two and a half decades before the so-called Mexican War.

There is no doubt that Anglo Americans' first significant contact with Mexicans occurred in the border region. Anglo-American trappers, traders, and settlers first entered Texas, New Mexico, and Alta California in the 1820s, after Mexico achieved independence from Spain and relaxed restrictions against foreigners. The Anglo Americans who entered northernmost Mexico in the 1820s, 1830s, and 1840s, it is said, came to know an area of Mexico that was backward politically, economically, and culturally. Thus, it has been suggested, Anglo Americans formed a mistaken notion of what *all* Mexicans were like on the basis of contact with relatively *few* Mexicans in the border region.

Writers who have taken this position have found support from a contemporary Mexican visitor to the frontier, General Manuel Mier y Terán, who, after inspecting Texas in 1828, reported to President Guadalupe Victoria:

> It would cause you the same chagrin that it has caused me to see the opinion that is held of our nation by these foreign colonists [i.e., Anglo Americans], since, with the exception of some few who have journeyed to our capital, they know no other Mexicans than the inhabitants about here, and excepting the authorities . . . the said inhabitants are the most ignorant of negroes and Indians.

As literary historian Cecil Robinson summed up the situation, "Early American writers and chroniclers in dealing with Mexico generally mistook a part for the whole thing."

I would like to suggest that no such mistake occurred. On the contrary, many Anglo-American writers held a contemptuous view of Mexican males wherever they encountered them. General Mier y Terán, for example, would have been even more chagrined had he known the private views that Stephen Austin expressed about Mexicans during a visit to Mexico City in 1822–23. Austin wrote that: "the people are bigoted and superstitious to an extreem [*sic*], and indolence appears to be the general order of the day." "To be candid the majority of the people of the whole nation as far as I have seen them want nothing but tails to be more brutes than the apes."

It could be said that Austin's previous experience in Texas had predisposed him to dislike Mexicans wherever he found them. This was not the case with Joel Roberts Poinsett, who never set foot in what is today the Southwest. In 1822 Poinsett visited Mexico for the first time, traveling to Mexico City by way of Vera Cruz. In his well-known *Notes on Mexico,* Poinsett pronounced Mexicans in general to be lazy. The Indians and mixed-bloods were "indolent," he said, and the "lazy" creoles "are not remarkable for their attainments, or for the strictness of their morals." He described the upper class as a complacent, self-satisfied group. The clergy, Poinsett said, had too great an influence in society, and the people were superstitious. Just as visitors to the frontier would note. Mexicans practiced terrible vices of gambling and smoking, and gave little thought to the future. Poinsett found the people to be generally ugly, and one can only wonder if this was because he had also discovered them to be "swarthy." Compared to most of his contemporaries, Poinsett's observations tended to be sophisticated. The well-traveled Poinsett showed some awareness of his prejudices and tried, but often failed, to avoid overgeneralizing.

More typical was another visitor to Mexico in 1822 whose notes, describing a journey from Tampico to Mexico City, appeared in the appendix to Poinsett's work. This anonymous traveler dismissed all Mexicans with the characteristic stereotype:

> Their occupation seems to consist, principally, in removing fleas and lice from each other, drinking pulque [homemade liquor], smoking cigars, when they can, and sleeping.

On a return visit to Mexico in 1825, Joel Poinsett brought with him a young secretary, Edward Thornton Tayloe, another person who had had no previous contact with Mexicans. Tayloe quickly judged the residents of Mexico City, including the upper class, to be superstitious and lazy. Not as gallant as some of his contemporaries, Tayloe singled out upper-class women, especially, as "idle and useless." "They can do naught but eat, sleep, smoke or talk, or visit the theatre." The Mexicans, Tayloe wrote, were ignorant, vicious, thieving, and incapable of governing themselves as republicans. In fact, Mexicans had no virtues whatsoever. "Should I attempt to find them out," Tayloe wrote, "I fear I shall fail."

These remarks by a necessarily small sample of Anglo-American visitors to Mexico City in the early 1820s, seem to indicate that Anglo Americans did not, as Cecil Robinson said, mistake "a part" of Mexico "for the whole thing." A negative stereotype of Mexicans was articulated very early, almost as soon as foreigners began to get a good look at Mexico City after 1821. The relative uniformity of the stereotype suggests the possibility that the observers were making valid generalizations—that Mexicans were lazy, ignorant, bigoted, superstitious, cheating, thieving, gambling, cruel, sinister, cowardly half-breeds, incapable of self-government or material progress. Yet, a closer look at American thought suggests that the stereotype was based not so much on direct observation or experience with Mexicans, but was in large part an extension of negative attitudes toward Catholic Spaniards which Anglo Americans had inherited from their Protestant English forebears.

During the colonial period, English colonists on the Atlantic Coast had almost no contact with Mexicans or other Latin Americans. Nonetheless, seventeenth-century Protestant New Englanders, such as Samuel Sewall and Cotton Mather, took a jaundiced view of Catholic Latin America, based largely on what they had read in literature from England. Sewall believed that Mexican culture was doomed to fall before a triumphant Protestantism and hoped that Mexico would hasten the process by revolting against Spain. Mather took the trouble to learn Spanish in order to write a missionary tract for Spaniards in the New World, designed "to open their eyes and be converted . . . away from Satan to God."

Anti-Spanish views inherited from England were far more complex than simple anti-Catholicism, however. The English colonists also believed that Spanish government was authoritarian, corrupt, and decadent, and that Spaniards were bigoted, cruel, greedy, tyrannical, fanatical, treacherous, and lazy. In attempting to respond to these charges, Spanish historians have found it convenient to give them a pejorative label: the Black Legend. Not surprisingly, in defending themselves from the "blackening" effect of this "Legend," Spaniards have often gone to the other extreme of white-washing Spain of all faults, giving rise to what Spain's detractors called a White Legend.

The origins of the Black Legend are complex. Some of its roots lie in the New World where Spanish conquistadors have been viewed as the apotheosis of evil. Interestingly, Spain's enemies drew much of their inspiration from the self-critical writings of Spaniards themselves, most notably Bartolomé de las Casas, who was widely read in England and in her American colonies. In this literature, Spaniards were depicted as grasping adventurers who came to the New World, not to seek liberty or better homes for their families as did the English, but to search for treasure and to live in idleness on the sweat of enslaved aborigines. This image remained alive. In 1821, the same year that Mexico won independence from Spain, Henry Clay told Congress that if Anglo Americans moved into Texas "it will be peopled by freemen and sons of freemen, carrying with them our language, our laws, and our liberties." Should Texas remain part of Mexico, however, Clay warned that "it may become the habitation of despotism and slaves, subject to the vile domination of the Inquisition and of superstition."

For our purposes, suffice it to say that Mexicans, the descendants of the Spanish conquistadors, inherited the reputation of their forefathers. As Phillip Wayne Powell recently put it: "We [Anglo Americans] transferred some of our ingrained antipathy toward Catholic Spain to her American heirs."

Powell is one of the few historians to take note of this connection between the Black Legend and anti-Mexicanism, but one does not need to read too carefully in the writings of Anglo-American visitors to the Mexican frontier to find evidences of the Black Legend. One of the most explicit statements comes from young Lewis Garrard, who visited New Mexico during the Mexican War. After briefly characterizing the New Mexican males as alternatively "servile," and "villainous," he explained the reason for their depravity in terms which show clearly the influence of the Black Legend. "The extreme degradation into which they are fallen," Garrard observed, "seems a fearful retribution on the destroyers of [the] Aztec Empire."

In addition to the Black Legend, Anglo Americans found one other element to despise in Mexicans—racial mixture. Color-conscious Anglo Americans were nearly unanimous in commenting upon the dark skin of the "swarthy" Mexican *mestizos* who, it was generally agreed, had inherited the worst qualities of Spaniards and Indians, resulting in a "race" still more despicable than that of either parent group. In suggesting that Anglo Americans were racists, I am not trying to ignore the racist nature of Mexican society. We do not have time to elaborate on this matter and for present purposes I simply want to suggest that a belief in the Black Legend, combined with a belief in the inferiority of mixed-bloods, enabled Anglo Americans to predict erroneously what Mexicans would be like (that is, to construct a stereotype) even before coming into significant contact with them. Not surprisingly, the Anglo Americans' expectations were fulfilled.

Anglo-American stereotypes of Mexicans, then, did not originate in the border region. Indeed, as early as 1822 the Mexican minister in Washington recognized that Anglo Americans viewed Mexicans as "inferiors." There can be little doubt, however, that the growing number of travelers, merchants, trappers, and settlers who entered northernmost Mexico after 1821 nourished the stereotype and through writing and conversation, encouraged its growth throughout the United States.

To understand better the nature of Anglo American stereotypes of Mexicans, let us examine how one of its components functioned—that is, the frequent charge that Mexicans were lazy.

Disparaging remarks regarding Mexicans' lack of initiative were widespread, and were especially abundant in literature describing the border region. Typical was a visitor to San Antonio who observed in 1837 that "The life of the Mexican here is one of unconcerned indolence and ease. As long as he is satisfied with a bare living for the present, there is no reason that he should give himself much trouble about the future." Many writers expressed their disdain for Mexicans' work habits in more colorful terms. Albert Pike, visiting New Mexico in 1831, found the *nuevo mexicanos* "a lazy gossiping people, always lounging on their blankets and smoking the cigarrillos—living on nothing and without labor." How Mexicans lived on nothing, Pike does not trouble himself to explain. An American resident of California told his readers that "you might as well expect a sloth to leave a tree, that has one inch of bark left upon its trunk, as to expect a Californian to labor, whilst a *real* glistens in his pocket." Richard Henry Dana likened laziness in California to an endemic disease, terming it "California Fever," which, he said, might spare the first generation but which, "always attacks the second." As an enduring monument to the laziness of Mexicans, there is said to be a gravestone somewhere in California which bears the inscription: "Aquí reposa Juan Espinosa. Nunca en su vida hizo otra cosa." ("Here rests Juan Espinosa. Never did he do anything else.")

Contemporary accounts of the laziness of Mexican frontiersmen are abundant, then, and even include accusations made by officials from Mexico

City and Mexican or Spanish-born clergy who had their own reasons for labeling the frontiersmen lazy. Some historians have taken these contemporary accounts at face value and perpetuated the stereotype of Mexican indolence. Yet, it is not only possible to refute the charge that Mexican frontiersmen were lazy, but there is reason to suppose that Mexicans on the frontier were energetic pioneers who worked as hard, if not harder, than their compatriots in the more "civilized" areas of central Mexico. With the exception of Alta California, it was more difficult to exploit Indian labor on the frontier than in central Mexico; frontiersmen had to work with their own hands. For example, the *encomienda* (a system of distributing Indian labor), was unsuccessful and short-lived in the Borderlands, operating only in seventeenth-century New Mexico. Hard work by colonists from Mexico was necessary in some areas of the frontier to provide defense against hostile Indians. Moreover, hard work was probably rewarded on the frontier, where there seems to have been greater social mobility than in central Mexico.

The idea that Mexican frontiersmen were industrious has been suggested by historians such as Silvio Zavala and France Scholes, and anthropologist Miguel Leon-Portilla. It was also mentioned by contemporaries such as Miguel Ramos Arizpe in Texas, Pedro Bautista Pino in New Mexico, Alexander von Humboldt, the German savant and traveler, and Zebulon Montgomery Pike, the "lost pathfinder." Pike, for example, termed the inhabitants of New Mexico "the bravest and most hardy subjects in New Spain," because of "their continual wars with the savage nations who surround them," because of their isolation from the rest of New Spain, and because they lacked gold and silver, a source of easy wealth.

It is possible, then, that Mexicans on the frontier were not lazy and were perhaps even harder working than their countrymen to the south. Nevertheless, Anglo-American visitors generally described frontier Mexicans as lazy. How can this be explained? The Black Legend, which identifies Spaniards as lazy, offers part of the explanation. An understanding of Anglo American attitudes toward racial mixture also adds to the explanation, for Anglo Americans generally regarded persons of mixed blood as lazy. In 1844, for example, Thomas Jefferson Farnham, described the complexion of upper class Californians as "a light clear bronze; not white . . . not remarkably pure in any way; a lazy color." Still a third explanation needs to be considered. Psychologists tell us that we stereotype ethnic groups in part because "in them we may perceive our own shortcomings." According to Maurice Janowitz and Bruno Bettelheim, "ethnic hostility is a projection of unacceptable inner strivings onto a minority group." The ethnic group, in other words, becomes our alter ego. Examined in this context, the Anglo-American observation that Mexicans were lazy may tell us more about the rigorous work ethic of nineteenth-century Americans than it does about Mexican culture.

The fact that many Anglo Americans blamed the economic and cultural under-development of Mexico's far northern frontier on the "indolent" character of the Mexican settlers not only reveals a bias, but is simplistic.

Better explanations for underdevelopment could have been found by looking into historical, geographical, and economic circumstances that contributed to the relative backwardness of the region. Indeed, had they looked more closely, Anglo Americans might have found that underdevelopment was not as much a result of the supposed laziness of Mexican frontiersmen, but instead, the frontiersmen's lack of initiative was a result of underdevelopment and of peculiar frontier conditions. As one astute Franciscan, José Señán, summed up the situation of the *californios;* "I have good reason to accuse the settlers of laziness, but there is equally good reason to excuse them in large part. Their lack of enthusiasm for their work is not surprising, inasmuch as they regard most of it as fruitless." In a province dominated by the military, Señán explained, a settler was prohibited from selling grain or other surplus crops to anyone except the quartermaster at "absurdly low prices" fixed by law, "while being charged exorbitantly for whatever goods he can procure." Clothing, farm implements, and household goods were in short supply and soldiers had first preference at purchasing them. Even if the settlers had cash, then, "there would be no place to spend it." The situation in Texas was similar, according to Fray Mariano Sosa, who saw the lack of a market for agricultural goods as destroying "incentive to raise larger or better crops."

Whereas some padres blamed the military system for economic stagnation and lack of incentive among the frontier settlers, some settlers, especially in California, criticized the padres for monopolizing Indian labor and the best lands.

Those who truly understood the rugged conditions of life on the frontier and the legal restrictions on trade and commerce, then, were not so quick to label frontiersmen lazy. Indeed, some knowledgeable officials expressed admiration for the frontiersmen's tenaciousness and initiative. As Governor Manuel Salcedo wrote of the *tejanos* in 1809: "one . . . marvels at how the most of them cultivate their lands without the necessary farming tools, . . . how some have built houses without artisans . . . how in this poverty they have been able to dress themselves and their families."

For most Anglo-American observers, however, there was no need to look too closely for explanations of lack of economic progress on the Mexican frontier. The stereotype of Mexican laziness constituted a sufficient explanation. Historians of the border region need to be reminded, then, that Anglo Americans did not necessarily see what they said they saw. This contention may be unprovable, but it is not unreasonable. A stereotype, psychologist Gordon Allport tells us, "may interfere with even the simplest rational judgments."

This discussion of the historical roots of Anglo-American stereotypes is not solely of academic interest, for stereotypes have had a profound impact on Mexican–United States relations and on the treatment of Mexicans and Mexican Americans in the United States. The stereotype of the inferior Mexican lay behind the arrogant sense of cultural and political superiority, known in United States history as Manifest Destiny, that led to the United States seizure of half the Mexican Republic in 1846–47. The stereotype of the inferior Mexican has been used to the present to justify efforts to "Americanize" Mexicans in the Southwestern United States, substituting their "folkways," with "superior" Anglo-American culture. Stereotypes have also helped Anglo Americans rationalize their exploitation and mistreatment of Mexican and Mexican-American workers in the fields and factories of the border region. Those who seek to improve the economic conditions of Mexicans in United States, or to make relations between Mexicans and Anglo Americans more harmonious, need to be reminded that deeply rooted stereotypes stand as a formidable obstacle to progress. We have come a long way since Noah Smithwick thought that Mexicans were "scarce more than apes," but we have not come nearly far enough.

Y *FURTHER READING*

Eugene H. Berwanger, *The Frontier Against Slavery: Western Anti-Negro Prejudice and the Slavery Extension Controversy* (1967)

Robert E. Bieder, "Scientific Attitudes Toward Indian Mixed-Bloods in Early Nineteenth Century America," *Journal of Ethnic Studies*, 8 (1980), 17–30

Ray A. Billington, *The Far Western Frontier, 1830–1860* (1956)

Gene M. Brack, "Mexican Opinion, American Racism, and the War of 1846," *Western Historical Quarterly*, 1 (1970), 161–74

——, *Mexico Views Manifest Destiny, 1821–1846: An Essay on the Origins of the Mexican War* (1975)

Seymour V. Connor and Odie B. Faulk, *North America Divided: The Mexican War, 1846–1848* (1971)

Arnoldo De Leon, *They Called Them Greasers: Anglo Attitudes Toward Mexicans in Texas, 1821–1900* (1983)

Arthur H. DeRosier, Jr., *The Removal of the Choctaw Indians* (1970)

Richard Drinnon, *Facing West: The Metaphysics of Indian-Hating and Empire-Building* (1980)

Daniel J. Garr, "A Rare and Desolate Land: Population and Race in Hispanic California," *Western Historical Quarterly*, 6 (1975), 133–48

William H. Goetzmann, *When the Eagle Screamed: The Romantic Horizon in American Diplomacy, 1800–1860* (1966)

Norman A. Graebner, "Lessons of the Mexican War," *Pacific Historical Review*, 47 (1978), 325–42

Michael D. Green, *The Politics of Indian Removal: Creek Government and Society in Crisis* (1982)

Klaus, J. Hansen, "The Millenium the West, and Race in the Antebellum American Mind," *Western Historical Quarterly*, 3 (1972), 373–90

Robert F. Heizer and Alan F. Almquist, *The Other Californians: Prejudice and Discrimination under Spain, Mexico, and the United States to 1920* (1971)

Thomas R. Hietala, *Manifest Destiny: Anxious Aggrandizement in Late Jacksonian America* (1985)

Reginald Horsman, *Expansion and American Indian Policy, 1783–1812* (1970)

——, *The Frontier in the Formative Years, 1783–1815* (1970)

Robert W. Johannsen, *To the Halls of the Montezumas: The Mexican War in the American Imagination* (1985)

Ernest M. Lander, Jr., *Reluctant Imperialists: Calhoun, the South Carolinians and the Mexican War* (1980)

David J. Langum, "Californios and the Image of Indolence," *Western Historical Quarterly*, 9 (1978), 181–96

Robert M. McCluggae, "The Senate and Indian Land Titles, 1800–1825," *Western Historical Quarterly,* 1 (1970), 415–25

Frederick Merk, *Manifest Destiny and Mission in American History: A Reinterpretation* (1963)

David M. Pletcher, *The Diplomacy of Annexation: Texas, Oregon, and the Mexican War* (1973)

Philip Wayne Powell, *Tree of Hate: Propaganda and Prejudices Affecting United States Relations with the Hispanic World* (1971)

Francis P. Prucha, *American Indian Policy in the Formative Years: The Indian Trade and Intercourse Acts, 1790–1834* (1962)

———, "Andrew Jackson's Indian Policy: A Reassessment," *Journal of American History,* 56 (1969), 527–39

James A. Rowley, *Race and Politics: "Bleeding Kansas" and the Coming of the Civil War* (1969)

Michael Paul Rogin, *Fathers and Children: Andrew Jackson and the Subjugation of the American Indian* (1975)

Ronald N. Satz, *American Indian Policy in the Jacksonian Era* (1975)

Bernard W. Sheehan, *Seeds of Extinction: Jeffersonian Philanthropy and the American Indian* (1973)

Robert Shulman, "Parkman's Indians and American Violence," *Massachusetts Review,* 12 (1971), 221–39

Raymond W. Stedman, *Shadows of the Indian: Stereotypes in American Culture* (1982)

Joe A. Stout, Jr., *The Liberators: Filibustering Expeditions into Mexico and the Last Thrust of Manifest Destiny* (1973)

Norman M. Tutorow, *Texas Annexation and the Mexican War: A Political Study of the Old Northwest* (1978)

Alden T. Vaughan, "From White Man to Redskin: Changing Anglo-American Perceptions of the American Indian," *American Historical Review,* 87 (1982), 917–53

Charles Vevier, "American Continentalism: An Idea of Expansion," *American Historical Review,* 65 (1960), 323–35

Herman J. Viola, *Thomas L. McKenney: Architect of America's Early Indian Policy, 1816–1830* (1974)

Albert K. Weinberg, *Manifest Destiny: A Study of Nationalist Expansion in American History* (1939)

Walter L. Williams, "United States Indian Policy and the Debate over Philippine Annexation: Implications for the Origins of American Imperialism," *Journal of American History,* 66 (1980), 810–31

Mary E. Young, *Redskins, Ruffleshirts, and Rednecks: Indian Allotments in Alabama and Mississippi, 1830–1860* (1961)

Overland Migration and Family Structure

Y

Two dramatic episodes of the 1840s and 1850s in the settling of the trans-Mississippi West have become major case studies for family history: the overland migration to California and Oregon, and the Mormons' establishment of their Great Basin "kingdom." Each event is associated with a certain seemingly unique institution—on the one hand, the wagon trains of the overlanders, and on the other, the polygamous marriages of the Mormons. In each situation, the lives of women, men, and children are known to have been affected, but the ways in which their lives may have changed are not so clear.

An older, somewhat idealized image of the overland experience had men and women emerging as strong, independent pioneers with every step westward. Here the influence of Frederick Jackson Turner's ideas is obvious. The Mormon story has been more problematic. Older scholarship certainly projects images of suffering and heroism—the flight from persecution in Illinois, the hand-cart battalions crossing the plains, the success with agriculture in the Utah desert— but the enigma of polygamy has always loomed. In the nineteenth century, Mormon men's practice of taking more than one wife seemed as immoral an act to social reformers as the owning of black slaves in the South.

Recent scholarship has shifted its focus away from the heroic acts of overland pioneers and the religious peculiarity of Mormon polygamy to consider the daily lives of the women and families who traveled the trails west or established homes as part of a plural marriage. This new scholarly emphasis reflects the influence of social history and women's studies on efforts to understand the western experience.

Y DOCUMENTS

The first two documents are the personal accounts of overlanders. In the first document, Kitturah Belknap's description of her preparations to leave Iowa for Oregon reveals the numerous tasks that began well before a family took to the trail. In her Iowa homestead on the Des Moines River, Belknap bore four children, three of whom died. During her 1848 overland trip, while pregnant, she cared for her surviving four-year-old. After reaching Oregon, she gave birth to five additional children, two of whom died from typhoid fever. Belknap lived until 1913, to the age of ninety-three. The second selection comprises two letters written by the thirteen-year-old Virginia Reed in 1846–1847. Her story relates the harrowing ordeal of the Donner party, an overland saga that included acts of cannibalism. The site of this tragedy is now marked by a monument near the interstate highway that traverses the Sierra Nevada.

The third, fourth, and fifth documents are comments on polygamy. Sir Richard Burton, the English explorer and ethnographer, traveled extensively in the Islamic world and in Africa. His attitude was that of a cultural sophisticate who enjoyed examining peculiar practices of exotic people. After visiting Salt Lake City, he tried to explain why polygamy had become estblished among the Mormons; his ideas are reprinted here as the third document, dated 1860. He avoids the moral outrage of most other mid-nineteenth-century visitors but not the assumed superiority of most other British travelers. In the fourth selection Helen Mar Whitney, a true believer and defender of the Mormon faith, espouses some attitudes about women's role in marriage that seem most appropriate in the era of Sir Richard Burton's monarch, Queen Victoria. The final document is a version, collected in 1932, of the folk song "Brigham, Brigham Young," which was in oral circulation in the latter decades of the 1800s. It serves as an example of the humor that was used to criticize the Mormon practice of plural marriage and the behavior of married women in general. The image of shrewish, quarreling wives was a popular humorous view of marriage that predated Mormon polygamy by centuries, as Shakespeare's play *The Taming of the Shrew* (1593) attests.

Kitturah Belknap Prepares for the Trip to Oregon, 1847–1848

We found the folks all excitement about Oregon. Some had gone in the spring of 1847. Four families of our connection and many of the neighbors but they had not been heard from since crossing the Missouri River. All was excitement and commotion. Our home was sold waiting our return to make out the papers. It was all fixed up for us to live with Father Belknaps as the man wanted the house on our place. Ransom's and Father's had not been sold yet. It did not suit me to live with them so I told them it was out of the question. For the first time since our marriage I put my foot down and said "will and won't" so it was arranged for us to go on Rant's place and live in their house till it was sold. I knew it would use me and the little sick baby up to be in such a tumult. There was nothing done or talked of but what had Oregon in it and the loom was banging and the wheels buzzing and trades being made from daylight till bedtime so I was glad to get settled.

My dear little girl, Martha, was sick all summer and October 30 she died, one year and one month old. Now we have one little puny boy left. So now I will spend what little strength I have left getting ready to cross the Rockies.

Will cut out some sewing to have to pick up at all the odd moments for I will try to have clothes enough to last a year.

November, 1847. Have cut out four muslin shirts for George and two suits for the little boy (Jessie). With what he has that will last him (if he lives) until he will want a different pattern.

The material for the men's outer garments has to be woven yet. The neighbors are all very kind to come in to see me, so I don't feel lonely like I would. They don't bring any work, but just pick up my sewing, so I think I will soon get a lot done. Then they are not the kind with long sad faces but always leave me with such pleasant smiling faces that it does me good to think of them and I try not to think of the parting time but look forward to the time when we shall meet, to part no more.

Now I will begin to work and plan to make everything with an eye to starting out on a six month's trip. The first thing is to lay plans and then work up to the program. The first thing is to make a piece of linen for a wagon cover and some sacks. Will spin mostly evenings while my husband reads to me. The little wheel in the corner doesn't make any noise. I spin for Mother Belknap and Mrs. Hawley and they will weave. Now that it is in the loom I must work almost day and night to get the filling ready to keep the loom busy. The men are busy making ox yokes and bows for the wagon covers and trading for oxen.

Now the new year has come and I'll write (1848). My health is better and I don't spend much time with housework. This is my program. Will make a muslin cover for the wagon as we will have a double cover so we can keep warm and dry; put the muslin on first and then the heavy linen one for strength. They both have to be sewed real good and strong. I have to spin the thread and sew all those long seams with my fingers then I have to make a new feather tick for my bed. I will put the feathers of two beds into one tick and sleep on it.

February. The linen is ready to go to work on and six two bushel bags all ready to sew up. That I will do evenings by the light of a dip candle for I have made enough to last all winter after we get to Oregon. Now my work is all planned so I can go right along. Have cut out two pairs of pants for George (homemade jeans). A kind lady friend came in today and sewed all day on one pair then took them home with her to finish. Another came to buy some of my dishes and she took two shirts home to make to pay for them.

Now it is March and we have our team all ready and in good condition. Three good yoke of oxen and a good wagon. The company have arranged to start on the 10th of April. I expect to load up the first wagon. George is practicing with the oxen. I don't want to leave my kind friends here but they all think it best so I am anxious to get off. I have worked almost day and night this winter. I have sewing about all done but a coat and vest for George. He got some nice material for a suit and had a tailor cut it out and Aunt Betsey Starr helped me two days with them so I am about ready to load up. Will wash and begin to pack and start with some old clothes on and when we can't wear them any longer we will leave them on the road.

I think we are fixed very comfortable for the trip. This week I will wash and pack away everything except what we want to wear on the trip.

April 5th. This week I cook up something to last us a few days till we get used to camp fare. Bake bread, make a lot of crackers and fry doughnuts, cook a chicken, boil ham, and stew some dryed fruit. There is enough to last us over the first Sunday so now we will begin to gather up the scatterings. Tomorrow is Saturday and next Tuesday we start so will put in some things today. Only one more Sunday here. Some of the folks will walk to meeting. We have had our farewell meeting so I won't go. I don't think I could stand it so George stays with me and we will take a rest for tomorrow will be a busy day.

Monday, April 9th, 1848. I am the first one up. Breakfast is over and our wagon is backed up to the steps. We will load at the hind end and shove the things in front. The first thing is a big box that will just fit in the wagon bed. That will have the bacon, salt and various other things. It will be covered with a cover made of light boards nailed on two pieces of inch plank about 3 inches wide. This will serve us for a table. There is a hole in each corner and we have sticks sharpened at one end so they will stick in the ground. Then we put the box cover on, slip the legs in the holes and we have a nice table. When it is on the box George will sit on it and let his feet hang over and drive the team. It is just as high as the wagon bed. Now we will put in the old chest that is packed with our clothes and things we will want to wear and use on the way. Then there is the medicine chest. There will be cleats fastened to the bottom of the wagon bed to keep things from slipping out of place.

There is a vacant place clear across that will be large enough to set a chair. Will set it with the back against the side of the wagon bed and there I will ride. On the other side will be a vacancy where little Jessie can play. He has a few toys and some marbles and some sticks for whip stocks and some blocks for oxen. I tie a string on the stick and he uses my work basket for a covered wagon and plays going to Oregon. He never seems to get tired or cross (but here I am leaving the wagon half packed and getting off on the journey).

The next thing is a box as high as the chest that is packed with a few dishes and things we won't need till we get thru. And now we will put in the long sacks of flour and other things. The sacks are made of homemade linen and will hold 125 pounds. There are four sacks of flour and one of corn meal. Now come the groceries. We will make a wall of smaller sacks stood on end; dried apples and peaches, beans, rice, sugar and coffee, the latter being in the green state. We will brown it in a skillet as we want to use it. Everything must be put in strong bags; no paper wrappings for this trip.

There is a corner left for the washtub and the lunch basket will just fit in the tub. The dishes we want to use will all be in the basket. I am going to start with good earthen dishes and if they get broken I have tin ones to take their place. Have made four nice little table cloths so am going to live just like I was at home. Now we will fill the other corner with pick-ups. The ironware that I will want to use every day will go in a box on the hind end of the wagon like a feed box.

Now we are loaded all but the bed. I wanted to put it in and sleep out but George said I wouldn't rest any so I will level up the sacks with some extra bedding, then there is a side of sole leather that will go on first, then two comforts and we have a good enough bed for anyone to sleep on. At night I will turn my chair down to make the bed a little longer. All we will have to do in the morning is put in the bed and make some coffee and roll out.

The wagon looks so nice. The nice white cover is drawn down tight to the side boards with a good ridge to keep from sagging. It's high enough for me to stand straight under the roof with a curtain to put down in front and one at the back end. Now its all done and I get in out of the tumult. Now that everything is ready I will rest a little then we will eat a bit. Mother Belknap has made a pot of mush and we are all going to eat mush and milk to save the milk that otherwise would have to be thrown out. Then we have prayers and then to bed.

Tuesday, April 10, 1848. Daylight dawned with none awake but me. I try to keep quiet so as not to wake anyone but pretty soon Father Belknap's voice was heard with that well-known sound, "Wife, wife, rise and flutter," and there was no more quiet for anyone. Breakfast is soon over. My dishes and food for lunch are packed away and put in the proper place. The iron things are packed in some old pieces of old thick rags. Now for the feather bed; I nicely folded the two ends together and lay it on the sacks. The covers are folded and the pillows laid smoothly on, reserving one for the outside so if I or the little boy get sleepy we have a good place to lie. Now my chair and the churn and we will be all done.

Our wagon is ready to start. I get in the wagon and in my chair busy with some unfinished work. Jessie is in his place with his whip starting for Oregon. George and the boys have gone out in the field for the cattle. Dr. Walker calls at the wagon to see me and give me some good advice and give me the parting hand for neither of us could speak the word "farewell." He told me to keep up good courage and said, "Don't fret; whatever happens don't fret and cry for courage will do more for you than anything else." Then he took the little boy in his arms and presented to him a nice Bible with his blessings and was off.

Virginia Reed Writes of the Donner Party's Ordeals, 1846–1847

Independence rock* July[th] 12   1846

My Dear Couzin   I take this opper tuny to Write to you to let you know that I am Well at present and hope that you are well. We have all had good helth—We came to the blue—the Water was so hye we had to stay thare 4 days—in the mean time gramma died. she be came spechless the day before she died. We buried her verry decent   We made a nete coffin

---

* on the Oregon Trail, east of South Pass

and buried her under a tree we had a head stone and had her name cutonit, and the date and yere verry nice, and at the head of the grave was a tree we cut some letters on it the young men soded it all ofer and put Flores on it We miss her verry much evry time we come in the wagon we look up at the bed for her We have came throw several tribs of indians the Caw Indians the saw the shawnees, at the caw viliage paw counted 20050 Indians We diden see no Indians from the time we left the cow viliage till we come to fort Laramy the Caw Indians are gong to War With the crows we hav to pas throw ther fiting grounds the sowe Indians are the pretest drest Indians thare is Paw goes a bufalo hunting most every day and kils 2 or 3 buffalo every day paw shot a elk som of our compan saw a grisly bear We have the thermometer 102°—average for the last 6 days We selabrated the 4 of July on plat at bever criek several of the Gentemen in Springfield gave paw a botel of licker and said it shoulden be opend tell the 4 day of July and paw was to look to the east and drink it and thay was to look to the West an drink it at 12 oclock paw treted the company and we all had some leminade. maw and pau is well and sends there best love to you all. I send my best love to you all We hav hard from uncle cad severe times he went to california and now is gone to oregon he is well. I am a going to send this letter by a man coming from oregon by his self he is going to take his family to oregon We are all doing Well and in hye sperits so I must close yur letter. You are for ever my affectionate couzen

Virginia E. B. Reed

Napa Vallie
California
May 16th 1847

My Dear Cousan   May^{the} 16   1847

I take this oppertunity to write to you to let you now that we are all Well at presant and hope this letter may find you all well to My dear Cousan I am a going to Write to you about our trubels geting to Callifornia; We had good luck til we come to big Sandy thare we lost our best yoak of oxons we come to Brigers Fort & we lost another ox we sold some of our provisions & baut a yoak of Cows & oxen & they pursuaded us to take Hastings cut of over the salt plain thay said it saved 3 Hondred miles, we went that road & we had to go through a long drive of 40 miles With out water or grass Hastings said it was 40 but i think it was 80 miles We traveld a day and night & a nother day and at noon pa went on to see if he coud find Water, he had not bin gone long till some of the oxen give out and we had to leve the Wagons and take the oxen on to water one of the men staid with us and others went on with the cattel to water pa was a coming back to us with Water and met the men & thay was about 10 miles from water pa said thay git to water that night, and the next day to bring the cattel back for the wagons any [and] bring some Water pa got to us about noon the man that was with us took the horse and went on to water We wated thare thought Thay would come we wated till night and We thought we start and walk to Mr doners wagons that night we took what little water we had and some bread and started pa caried Thomos and all the rest of us walk we got to Donner and thay were all a sleep so we laid down on the ground we spred one shawl down we laid doun on it and spred another over us and then put the dogs on top it was the couldes night you most ever saw the wind blew and if it haden bin for the dogs we would have Frosen as soon as it was day we went to Miss Donners she said we could not walk to the Water and if we staid we could ride in thare wagons to the spring so pa went on to the water to see why thay did not bring the cattel when he got thare thare was but one ox and cow thare none of the rest had got to water Mr Donner come out that night with his cattel and braught his Wagons and all of us in we staid thare a week and Hunted for our cattel and could not find them so some of the companie took thare oxons and went out and brout in one wagon and cashed the other tow and a grate manie things all but what we could put in one Wagon we had to divied our propessions out to them to get them to carie them We got three yoak with our oxe & cow so we [went] on that way a while and we got out of provisions and pa had to go on to callifornia for provisions we could not get along that way, in 2 or 3 days after pa left we had to cash our wagon and take Mr. graves wagon and cash some more of our things well we went on that way a while and then we had to get Mr Eddies Wagon we went on that way awhile and then we had to cash all our our close except a change or 2 and put them in Mr Brins Wagon and Thomos & James rode the 2 horses and the rest of us had to walk, we went on that way a Whild and we come to a nother long drive of 40 miles and then we went with Mr Donner

We had to Walk all the time we was a travling up the truckee river we met that and 2 Indians that we had sent out for propessions to Suter Fort thay had met pa, not fur from Suters Fort he looked very bad he had not ate but 3 times in 7 days and thes days with out any thing his horse was not abel to carrie him thay give him a horse and he went on so we cashed some more of our things all but what we could pack on one mule and we started Martha and James road behind the two Indians it was a raing then in the Vallies and snowing on the montains so we went on that way 3 or 4 days tell we come to the big mountain or the Callifornia Mountain the snow then was about 3 feet deep thare was some wagons thare thay said thay had atempted to cross and could not, well we thought we would try it so we started and thay started again with thare wagons the snow was then way to the muels side the farther we went up the deeper the snow got so the wagons could not go so thay packed thare oxons and started with us carring a child a piece and driving the oxons in snow up to thare wast the mule Martha and the Indian was on was the best one so thay went and broak the road and that indian was the Pilot so we went on that way 2 miles and the mules kept faling down in the snow head formost and the Indian said he could not find the road we stoped and let the Indian and man go on to hunt the road thay went on and found the road to the top of the mountain and come back and said they thought we could git over if it did not snow any more well the Woman were all so tirder caring there Children that thay could not go over that night so we made a fire and got something to eat & ma spred down a bufalorobe & we all laid down on it & spred somthing over us & ma sit up by the fire & it snowed one foot on top of the bed so we got up in the morning & the snow was so deep we could not go over & we had to go back to the cabin & build more cabins & stay thare all Winter without Pa we had not the first thing to eat Ma maid arrangements for some cattel giving 2 for 1 in callifornia we seldom thot of bread for we had not had any since [blot, words not readable] & the cattel was so poor thay could note hadley gitup when thay laid down we stoped thare the 4th of November & staid till March and what we had to eat i cant hardley tell you & we had that man & Indians to feed well thay started over a foot and had to come back so thay made snow shoes and started again & it come on a storme & thay had to come back it would snow 10 days before it would stop thay wated tell it stoped & started again I was a goeing with them & I took sick & could not go—thare was 15 started & thare was 7 got throw 5 Weman & 2 men it come a storme and thay lost the road & got out of provisions & the ones that got throwe had to eat them that Died not long after thay started we got out of provisions & had to put Martha at one cabin James at another Thomas at another & Ma & Elizea & Milt Eliot & I dried up what littel meat we had and started to see if we could get across & had to leve the childrin o Mary you may think that hard to leve theme with strangers & did not now wether we would see them again or not we could hardle get a way from them but we told theme we would bring them Bread & then thay was willing to stay we went & was out 5 days in the mountains Elie giv out & had to go back we went on a day longer we had to lay by a day & make snow shows & we went on a while and coud not find the road & we had to turn back I could go on verry well while i thout we wer giting along but as soone as we had to turn back i coud hadley git along but we got to the cabins that night I froze one of my feet verry bad & that same night thare was the worst storme we had that winter & if we had not come back that night we would never got back we had nothing to eat but ox hides o Mary I would cry and wish I had what you all wasted Eliza had to go to Mr Graves cabin & we staid at Mr Breen thay had meat all the time & we had to kill littel cash the dog & eat him we ate his head and feet & hide & evry thing about him o my Dear Cousin you dont now what trubel is yet a many a time we had on the last thing a cooking and did not now wher the next would come from but there was awl wais some way provided

there was 15 in the cabon we was in and half of us had to lay a bed all the time thare was 10 starved to death there we was hadley abel to walk we lived on litle cash a week and after Mr Breen would cook his meat we would take the bones and boil them 3 or 4 days at a time ma went down to the other caben and got half a hide carried it in snow up to her wast it snowed and would cover the cabin all over so we could not git out for 2 or 3 days we would have to cut pieces of the loges in sied to make a fire with I coud hardly eat the hides and had not eat anything 3 days Pa stated out to us with providions and then came a storme and he could not go he cash his provision and went back on the other side of the bay to get compana of men and the San Wakien got so hye he could not crose well thay Made up a Compana at Suters Fort and sent out we had not ate any thing for 3 days & we had onely a half a hide and we was out on top of the cabin and we seen them a coming

O my Dear Cousin you dont now how glad i was, we run and met them one of them we knew we had traveled with them on the road thay staid thare 3 days to recruet a little so we could go thare was 20 started all of us started and went a piece and Martha and Thomas giv out & so the men had to take them back ma and Eliza James & I come on and o Mary that was the hades thing yet to come on and leiv them thar did not now but what thay would starve to Death Martha said well ma if you never see me again do the best you can the men said thay could hadly stand it it maid them all cry but they said it was better for all of us to go on for if we was to go back we would eat that much more from them thay give them a littel meat and flore and took them back and we come on we went over great hye mountain as strait as stair steps in snow up to our knees litle James walk the hole way over all the mountain in snow up to his waist he said every step he took he was a gitting nigher Pa and somthing to eat the Bears took the provision the men had cashed and we had but very little to eat when we had traveld 5 days travel we met Pa with 13 men going to the cabins o Mary you do not nou how glad we was to see him we had not seen him for months we thought we woul never see him again he heard we was coming and he made some seet cakes to give us he said he would see Martha and Thomas the next day he went to tow days what took us 5 days some of the compana was eating from them that Died but Thomas & Martha had not ate any Pa and the men started with 12 people Hiram O Miller Carried Thomas and Pa caried Martha and thay wer caught in [unreadable word] and thay had to stop Two days it stormed so thay could not go and the Bears took their provision and thay weer 4 days without anything Pa and Hiram and all the men started one of Donner boys Pa a carring Martha Hiram caring Thomas and the snow was up to thare wast and it a snowing so thay could hadley see the way they raped the chidlren up and never took them out for 4 days & thay had nothing to eat in all that time Thomas asked for somthing to eat once those that thay brought from the cabins some of them was not able to come and som would not come Thare was 3 died and the rest eat them thay was 10 days without any thing to eat but the Dead Pa braught Thom and pady on to where we was none of the men was abel to go there feet was froze very bad so they was a nother Compana went and braught them all in thay are all in from the Mountains now but five they was men went out after them and was caught in a storm and had to come back thare is another compana gone thare was half got through that was stoped thare sent to their relief thare was but   families got that all of them got   we was one

O Mary I have not wrote you half of the truble we have had but I hav Wrote you anuf to let you now that you dont now whattruble is   but thank the Good god we have all got throw and the onely family that did not eat human flesh   we have left every thing but i dont cair for that   we have got through but Dont let this letter dishaten anybody and never take no cutofs and hury along as fast as you can

My Dear Cousin

We are all very well pleased with Callifornia partucularly with the climate   let it be ever so hot a day thare is all wais cool nights   it is a beautiful Country   it is mostley in vallies it aut to be a beautiful Country to pay us for our trubel geting there   it is the greatest place for catle and horses you ever saw   it would Just suit Charley for he could ride down 3 or 4 horses a day and he could lern to be Bocarro that one who lases cattel the spanards and Indians are the best riders i ever say   thay have a spanish sadel and woden sturups and great big spurs the wheel of them is 5 inches in diameter and thay could not manage the Callifornia horses witout the spurs, thay wont go atol if they cant hear the spurs rattle   they have littel bells to them to make them rattle   thay blindfold the horses and then sadel them and git on them and then take the blindfole of and let run and if thay cant sit on thay tie themselves on and let them run as fast as they can and go out to a band of bullluck and throw the reatter on a wild bullluck and but it around the horn of his sadel and he can hold it as long as he wants

a nother Indian throws his reatter on its feet and throws them and when thay git take the reatter of of them they are very dangerous   they will run after you then hook there horses and run after any person thay see   thay ride from 80 to 100 miles a day & have some of the spanard have from 6 to 7000 head of horses and from 15 to 16000 head Cattel   we are all verry fleshey   Ma waies 10040 pon and still a gaing   I weigh 80 tel Henriet if she wants to get Married for to come to Callifornia   she can get a spanyard any time   that Eliza is a going to marrie a a spanyard by the name of Armeho and Eliza weighs 10070 We have not saw uncle Cadon yet but we have had 2 letters from him   he is well and is a coming here as soon as he can   Mary take this letter to uncle Gurshon and to all tha i know to all of our neighbors and tell Dochter Meniel and every girl i know and let them read it   Mary kiss little Sue and Maryann for me and give my best love to all i know to uncle James and Lida and all the rest of the famila and to uncle Gurshon aunt Percilla and all the Children and to all of our neighbors and to all she knows   so no more at present

pa is yerbayan [Yerba Buena]

My Dear casons
Virginia Elizabeth B Reed

Sir Richard Burton Examines Mormon Polygamy, 1860

The literalism with which the Mormons have interpreted Scripture has led them directly to polygamy. The texts promising to Abraham a progeny numerous as the stars above or the sands below, and that "in his seed (a polygamist) all the families of the earth shall be blessed," induce them, his descendants, to seek a similar blessing. The theory announcing that "the man is not without the woman, nor the woman without the man," is by them interpreted into an absolute command that both sexes should marry, and that a woman cannot enter the heavenly kingdom without a husband to introduce her. A virgin's end is annihilation or absorption, *nox est perpetua una dormienda;* and as baptism for the dead—an old rite, revived and founded upon the writings of St. Paul quoted in the last chapter,—has been made a part of practice, vicarious marriage for the departed also enters into the Mormon scheme. . . . The Mormons . . . see in the New Testament no order against plurality; and in the Old dispensation they find the practice sanctioned in a family, ever the friends of God, and out of which the Redeemer sprang. Finally, they find throughout the nations of the earth, three polygamists in theory to one monogame.

The "chaste and plural marriage" being once legalised, finds a multitude of supporters. The anti-Mormons declare that it is at once fornication and adultery—a sin which absorbs all others. The Mormons point triumphantly to the austere morals of their community, their superior freedom from maladive influences, and the absence of that uncleanness and licentiousness which distinguish the cities of the civilised world. They boast that if it be an evil they have at least chosen the lesser evil, that they practise openly as a virtue what others do secretly as a sin. . . . Like its sister institution Slavery, the birth and growth of a similar age, Polygamy acquires *vim* by abuse and detraction; the more turpitude is heaped upon it, the brighter and more glorious it appears to its votaries.

There are rules and regulations of Mormonism—I cannot say whether they date before or after the heavenly command to pluralise—which disprove the popular statement that such marriages are made to gratify licentiousness, and which render polygamy a positive necessity. All sensuality in the married state is strictly forbidden beyond the requisite for ensuring progeny,—the practice, in fact, of Adam and Abraham. During the gestation and nursing of children, the strictest continence on the part of the mother is required— rather for a hygienic than for a religious reason. The same custom is practised in part by the Jews, and in whole by some of the noblest tribes of savages; the splendid physical development of the Kaffir race in South Africa is attributed by some authors to a rule of continence like that of the Mormons, and to a lactation prolonged for two years. . . .

Besides religious and physiological, there are social motives for the plurality. As in the days of Abraham, the lands about New Jordan are broad and the people few. . . . To the unprejudiced traveller it appears that polygamy is the rule where population is required . . .

The other motive for polygamy in Utah is economy. Servants are rare and costly; it is cheaper and more comfortable to marry them. Many converts are attracted by the prospect of becoming wives, especially from places where, like Clifton, there are sixty-four females to thirty-six males. The old maid is, as she ought to be, an unknown entity. Life in the wilds of Western America is a course of severe toil: a single woman cannot perform the manifold duties of housekeeping, cooking, scrubbing, washing, darning, child-bearing, and nursing a family. A division of labour is necessary, and she finds it by acquiring a sisterhood. Throughout the States whenever a woman is seen at manual or outdoor work, one is certain that she is Irish, German, or Scandinavian. The delicacy and fragility of the Anglo-American female nature is at once the cause and the effect of this exemption from toil. . . .

For the attachment of the women of the Saints to the doctrine of plurality there are many reasons. The Mormon prophets have expended all their arts upon this end, well knowing that without the hearty co-operation of mothers and wives, sisters and daughters, no institution can live long. They have bribed them with promises of Paradise—they have subjugated them with threats of annihilation. With them once a Mormon always a Mormon. I have said that a modified reaction respecting the community of Saints has set in throughout the States; people no longer wonder that their missionaries do not show horns and cloven feet, and the Federal officer, the itinerant politician, the platform orator, and the place-seeking demagogue, can no longer make political capital by bullying, oppressing, and abusing them. The tide has turned, and will turn yet more. But the individual still suffers: the apostate Mormon is looked upon by other people as a scamp or a knave, and the woman worse than a prostitute. Again, all the fervour of a new faith burns in their bosoms, with a heat which we can little appreciate, and the revelation of Mr. Joseph Smith is considered on this point as superior to the Christian as the latter is in others to the Mosaic Dispensation. Polygamy is a positive command from heaven. . . .

Another curious effect of fervent belief may be noticed in the married state. When a man has four or five wives with reasonable families by each, he is fixed for life: his interests, if not his affections, bind him irrevocably to his New Faith. But the bachelor, as well as the monogamic youth, is prone to back-sliding. Apostasy is apparently so common that many of the new Saints form a mere floating population. He is proved by a mission before being permitted to marry, and even then women, dreading a possible renegade with the terrible consequences of a heavenless future to themselves, are shy of saying yes.

Helen Mar Whitney Defends Plural Marriage, 1884

Women, I willingly admit, are the weaker sex, and that men should lead, but how many of them are really capable of leading or governing? How many of them have caused the wife of his bosom to hide her face in very shame—the woman whom he had promised to love and to cherish till death did them part, but was too utterly selfish to make any sacrifice to insure her comfort or happiness, or that of his offspring. Such will indulge their appetites, and every pernicious and unhallowed lust must be gratified at the risk of her poor heart's breaking. Though this may be a slow process, it is murder nevertheless, and their offspring are receiving the legacy— handed down by a profligate father with the certainty of transmitting the same to the coming generations, who have been sinned against in having to take up with feeble and diseased frames, and no constitutions to begin life with. Thus human life is being shortened. Various and complicated diseases are continually multiplying, which baffle the understanding and skill of the most learned physicians. These diseases and defects are too often laid at the mother's door. There are laws laid down which should not be violated, and the greatest crimes have become so common that the world thinks little or nothing of them. Thousands of delicate women are united to men who show them not the least consideration—she being his "property" he can take license and she thereby becomes the most wretched of slaves. But through this patriarchal order (deride it as they may) is to come the emancipation of womankind, which has been decreed, as well as the restoration of all the human family who have not sinned against all hope of their redemption. That it is a trial, no sensitive woman nor sensible man will deny, but what is the whole of life if not a trial, and what righteous movement or reform was ever yet inaugurated, without human suffering to some degree?

But those who think that men have no trials in the plural order of marriage, are greatly deceived. The wives have far greater liberty than the husband, and they have the power to make him happy or very unhappy. For this cause, among others, there are not many men who are willing to take upon themselves these extra burdens and responsibilities, even for the sake of a higher glory hereafter. It certainly takes considerable religion and faith to stimulate a man who loves a quiet, easy-going life, to take up this cross, even with the hope of a future crown. . . .

There are few to be found in the world whose piety, purity of life and unselfish acts can be compared with the greater portion of these men and women of the covenant, who through faith and righteousness have gained power with God to go forth conquering and to conquer. They have more joy and pride in being descendants of the royal family of Abraham, who with his wives and children were so highly honored of God, than in all that earth and mortals could bestow. Could more of the eventful histories of our women be published they would furnish volumes of interesting reading— equal, I think, to any novels, with just this difference, they would be truths instead of fiction. They would show what women are capable of doing and that we have some leading spirits who have few, if any, equals. At all events they are bound to make a mark in the world, many thanks to their traducers for helping to bring them into notice. . . .

I have traveled considerably in Utah during the past two years and have had many opportunities of learning the minds of "Mormon" women upon the plural wife system. I know that there are scores who will endorse what I have expressed. I also testify that the ones who live up to the golden rule in this principle find blessings in it, even in this life. Instead of being man-worshipers, remaining in the same old grooves in which the human family have been at a stand still, or tending downward through many generations, we are rising above our earthly idols, and find that we have easier access to the throne of grace. Our Father says He will not accept of a divided heart. There can be no evil in a thing that inspires prayer, drives selfishness from the heart and lengthens the cords of human feelings, leading one to do greater deeds of kindness outside of his or her own little circle. Those who are so narrow minded as to think of no one's comfort and pleasure but their own, are not capable of enjoying any great amount of eternal glory. We can never enjoy anything to its fullest extent until we have first tasted of its opposite. But if a wife and mother does her part, is true to her husband and teaches her children to walk in the true path, holding out faithful to the end, all she suffers will but add greater laurels to her crown in the world to come. And the future happiness of such, could they obtain even the slightest glimpse of it, would repay them, and they would be willing, even anxious to endure all that was possible to make them deserving of that pure and unalloyed bliss of which I solemnly testify that I have had a foretaste.

I have not written with "the pen of the fanatic," but with the heart "of a woman," who is in earnest, and does not "prefer the glory of man above the glory of God."

"Brigham, Brigham Young", An Anti-Mormon Folk Song, Collected in 1932

Old Brigham Young was a Mormon bold,
    And a leader of the roaring rams,
And a shepherd of a heap of pretty little sheep,
    And a nice fold of pretty little lambs.
And he lived with five and forty wives
    In the city of Great Salt Lake
Where they woo and coo as pretty doves do
    And cackle like ducks to a drake.

Chorus:
Brigham, Brigham Young;
    'Tis a miracle he survives,
With his roaring rams, his pretty little lambs,
    And five and forty wives.

Number forty-five was about sixteen,
    Number one was sixty-three,
And among such a riot how he ever keeps them quiet
    Is a right-down mystery to me.
For they clatter and they claw, and they jaw, jaw, jaw,
    Each one has a different desire;

It would aid the renown of the best shop in town
　To supply them with half what they require.

Old Brigham Young was a stout man once
　But now he is thin and old,
And I love to state, there's no hair on his pate
　Which once wore a covering of gold.
For his youngest wives won't have white wool
　And his old ones won't take red,
So in tearing it out they have taken turn about
　Till they've pulled all the wool from his head.

Now his boys sing songs all day,
　And his girls they all sing psalms;
And among such a crowd he has it pretty loud
　For they're as musical as Chinese Gongs.
And when they advance for a Mormon dance,
　He is filled with a greatest surprise,
For they're sure to end the night with a tabernacle fight
　And scratch out one another's eyes.

There never was a home like Brigham Young's,
　So curious and so queer,
For if his joys are double he has a terrible lot of trouble,
　For it gains on him year by year.
He sets in his state and bears his fate
　In a satisfied sort of way;
He has one wife to bury and one wife to marry
　And a new kid born every day.

Now if anybody envies Brigham Young,
　Let them go to Great Salt Lake,
And if they have leisure to examine at their pleasure
　They'll find it's a great mistake.
One wife at a time, so says my rhyme,
　Is enough for the proudest don,
So e'er you strive to live lord of forty-five
　Live happy if you can with one.

ϒ *E S S A Y S*

The late John D. Unruh, Jr., was a professor of history at Bluffton College in Ohio before his untimely death at age thirty-nine in 1976. His monumental study of the overland trails experience, *The Plains Across,* was published posthumously in 1979. It won numerous awards, including the Billington Award of the Organization of American Historians. The excerpt presented here as the first selection is from Unruh's concluding chapter, which emphasizes themes developed earlier in his book, especially those of the cooperation and support that developed among the overlanders and the real dangers that they faced. John Mack Faragher teaches social and frontier history at Mount Holyoke College in Massachusetts. His 1979 book *Women and Men on the Overland Trail* received the

Organization of American Historians' Turner Prize. A chapter from this work, republished here as the second essay, analyzes the different daily tasks men and women undertook during the journey west. Faragher's feminist interpretation of this division of labor presents a different image of the overland experience from Unruh's.

In the third and final essay, Lawrence Foster, a professor in the School of Social Sciences at the Georgia Institute of Technology, raises important questions about how the lives of Mormon women in early Utah may be understood. Foster considers the positive features that some women may have found in polygamy. Faragher's and Foster's ways of viewing women's lives seem very different, especially if one asks how each would consider the concept of exploitation.

The Traveling Community of the Overlanders

JOHN D. UNRUH, JR.

The emigration experience was ever changing; each travel year evidenced distinctive patterns, unique dramas of triumph and tragedy, new contributions to the mosaic of western development.

For example, it seems axiomatic to distinguish between abnormally wet and abnormally dry years along the trails, since climatic fluctuation had a far-reaching impact upon the overland journey. In 1844 unseasonable rains created such havoc with stream crossings that it took one large company fully two and a half weeks to ford a single swollen creek. Indeed, that traveling group needed sixty-one days to penetrate 200 miles west of the Missouri River. But exceptionally rainy weather had commensurate advantages: 1853 California-bound travelers enjoyed far easier desert crossings because they found grass growing where overlanders had never seen it before.

Differentiation must also be made between years when most emigrants outfitted with considerable care and years such as 1850, when they recklessly took so little that they set the stage for catastrophic starvation. Viewing the overland emigrations in historical perspective similarly requires differentiating between years when disease was infrequent (such as the early 1840s) and the gold rush years, when thousands of emigrants fell victim to cholera epidemics; between years when family groups dominated the trails and the early gold rush years, when the route was thronged with unaccompanied men; between years when the pace of travel was slower and the gold rush years, when the hurry-up atmosphere was so prevalent that many travelers discarded even such standard expressions of compassion as delaying the journey for several days so that a dangerously sick or injured comrade might have a better chance to recover. Thus the 1849 Pioneer Line, which had rashly promised to deliver its passengers to the California

John D. Unruh, Jr., "The Overlanders in Historical Perspective," in *The Plains Across: The Overland Emigrants and the Trans-Mississippi West, 1840–60*, 379–381, 385–390, 408–412, University of Illinois Press, 1979.

gold fields in sixty days, had no time for such niceties. The wagon in which a young Marylander lay at death's door kept bouncing westward. It was ominously followed by two trainmen bearing picks and shovels with which to dig the diseased forty-niner's grave without a moment's delay.

The inexorable growth of supportive facilities, so closely intertwined with the accelerating numbers of westbound pioneers, further negates the usefulness of a "typical year" approach in explaining the westward movement. Overland travel was radically altered by the Mormon hegira to the Salt Lake Valley, by the advent of profit-seeking merchants and entrepreneurs, and by the gradual extension of government services westward to the Pacific. By the early 1850s, for example, the Latter-Day Saints' "halfway house" could furnish the traveler with everything from provisions, wagons, or draft animals to bathhouses, barbershops, and law courts for the adjudication of severed traveling agreements. The optimistic entrepreneurs who bridged rivers and constructed trading posts from one end of the overland trail to the other transformed the character of overland travel at the same time that they made it more expensive. Similarly revolutionizing the nature of the overland journey were the diverse traveler-oriented activities of the federal government: exploration, survey, road construction, postal services, the establishment of forts, the dispatching of punitive military expeditions, the allocation of protective escorts for emigrant caravans, the negotiation of Indian treaties designed to insure the safety of emigrant travel.

The constantly changing pattern of overland travel was evident in many other ways. The California gold rush accelerated the amount of eastbound trail traffic. Trail improvements contributed to significant reductions in the amount of time required to travel the overland route, whether westbound or eastbound. Similarly, it is clear that the Indian "threat" to overlanders was a feature of the 1850s far more than of the 1840s, and that travelers were much more likely to have serious problems west of South Pass than on the early portion of the journey. And it was only a few years before the appearance of reasonably reliable overland guidebooks made the employment of mountaineer guides unnecessary. The need for relying upon a guidebook for route directions, in turn, was quickly rendered superfluous by the heavy trail travel, which indelibly marked the overland route even for the most inept greenhorn—west of St. Joseph the "heavy beaten track" was measured at forty-five paces across in 1852. Not even at the Missouri River jumping-off points did static conditions prevail, since emigrants increasingly gravitated northward toward Council Bluffs–Omaha as their point of departure.

Once the overlanders began traveling westward, they discovered growing settlements initially associated with bridges, trading posts, forts, or stage stations and thus also a direct outgrowth of the overland emigrations. During the 1840s overlanders had regularly remarked that they were leaving "civilization" to launch out into the "wilderness" once they had crossed the Missouri River. By the mid-1850s such phraseology was no longer appropriate, since the westbound emigrant now traveled for hundreds of miles past farms and through towns. The massive amounts of humanitarian relief furnished by Oregon and California in order to ease the travel hardships along the last several hundred miles of the overland trails likewise altered the perceptions with which travelers approached the transcontinental journey. Indeed, the rapidity with which momentous change had come to the Far West was most clearly evidenced by the fact that California had achieved statehood in 1850 and Oregon in 1859. During the early 1840s, in contrast, westbound pioneers did not even know whether they were going to be able to remain citizens of the United States. . . .

Portraying the overland emigrations in historical perspective further requires an awareness that changing travel conditions must be complemented with an appreciation of the long-neglected factors of cooperation and community. Contrary to prevailing media stereotypes, the overland emigrants did not go west in isolation, each small company alone on the trail with only its ingenuity and heroism to see it through. Even in the early 1840s, before the trails had become so crowded that it was sometimes necessary to stop early to secure a decent campsite, the quantity of trail traffic was astounding: eastbound and westbound emigrants, fur-trapping caravans, traders, hunting and sightseeing parties, missionaries, army units, trade-eager Indians. The overland trip was never as isolated an enterprise as legend would have it. During the California gold rush the trails were transformed into wide and busy highways. Polluted with travel debris, they were often so dusty that overlanders donned goggles to see, and so crowded that traveling partners and relatives became separated in the vast multitudes passing east and west.

Moreover, for too long the antebellum West has been portrayed only negatively as a wilderness barrier of trackless deserts, impassable mountains, bloodthirsty Indians, and savage wild beasts—all of which the courageous little bands of overlanders had to conquer singlehandedly before they reached the paradises on the Pacific. The West, of course, *was* an obstacle to overland travel. But it was also a help, and so too were its inhabitants. Over a quarter of a million successful overland emigrants in a twenty-year time span conclusively attest to the fact that western terrain, climate, and inhabitants posed no insurmountable obstacle to overland travel. The overlander never strayed far from the life-sustaining rivers angling sequentially westward from the Missouri: the Platte, Sweetwater, Snake, Columbia, Humboldt, Carson, and Truckee. If the emigrant outfitted carefully, commenced his journey as soon as the prairie grasses sustained grazing, maintained reasonable hygiene, treated the Indians fairly, respectfully, and strictly, and followed a routine of deliberate daily travel interspersed with regular days of rest, there was little reason to fear the overland trip. Indeed, there was a certain rhythm to successful trail travel. Most emigrants eventually learned that a pell-mell dash westward was a flirtation with disaster. Western weather and landscape could not be bludgeoned into submission, at least not with animal power. Overland travel had to be synchronized with climate and terrain.

The positive contribution of western flora and fauna to successful overland travel is self-evident. Overland emigrants were totally dependent on grass and water for survival, with wood or buffalo chips only slightly less important. Forty-niner Bernard Reid, at an encampment near South Pass where his company found "excellent wood, water and grass," termed these essentials "the emigrant's trinity of good things." Saleratus secured at places like Soda Springs served as an effective substitute for yeast or baking soda during the course of the journey. The West also offered supplemental food. Thousands of hungry overlanders feasted on the buffalo, elk, deer, duck, and other wild game that emigrant marksmen shot, on fish that emigrant anglers took from rivers and streams, on berries and herbs that travelers found near the trails. A great many buffalo, however, were killed not for food but for "sport." It was a rare company of overlanders which did not temporarily forget all trail discipline at their first sighting of a buffalo herd and go racing off in reckless pursuit. The passing overlanders began the senseless assault on the great bison herds which ultimately led to their near extinction. Isaac Foster was one of a handful of diarists who expressed concern at the wanton destruction: ". . . the valley of the Platte for 200 miles presents the aspect of the vicinity of a slaughter yard; dotted all over with skeletons of buffalos; such waste of the creatures that God has made for man seems wicked, but every emigrant seems to wish to signalize himself by killing a buffalo." The ramifications of this nonconservationist outlook on the part of the majority of overlanders were correctly assessed the following year by John Steele after he passed twelve buffalo left to rot: "Such destruction of game doubtless enrages the Indians against the whites."

For virtually all overlanders the western Indians were akin to the buffalo in symbolizing danger and adventure. The first trail encounter with Indians invariably resulted in a long diary entry or a lengthy paragraph in the next letter home, complete with an analysis of Indian character, demeanor, apparel, and customs, and rife with speculation on the nature of future encounters. While fascinated emigrant diarists were not always condemnatory in their attitudes toward the Indians, they rarely acknowledged the positive Indian contribution to overland travel. On examination, however, the much-maligned "savage Indians" of folklore prove to have been of considerable assistance to passing overlanders, particularly during the 1840s before the boom in supportive facilities set in. That Indian begging and thievery were traveling nuisances cannot be denied, but it is also clear that the extent of Indian attacks on overland caravans has been greatly exaggerated. In fact, there is considerable evidence that the fatal trail confrontations which did occur were usually prompted by emigrant insults and disdain for Indian rights, as well as by indiscriminate and injudicious chastisement meted out by the U.S. Army. Notwithstanding the fact that nearly 400 emigrants were killed by Indians in the first twenty years of overland travel, Indian tribes provided overlanders with information, foodstuffs, clothing, equipment, horses, canoeing and swimming skills, traveling materials, and other assistance. Indians, like the West they inhabited, should henceforth be regarded more positively as helpful assistants to overland travelers and not only negatively as barriers.

Just as the overlander who succeeded in the transcontinental trek found it necessary to harmonize his travel with the land and its long-term inhabitants, a successful journey required cooperation with eastbound and westbound colleagues on the trail. Indeed, in describing the overland emigrations it is appropriate to speak of the "traveling community." Emigrants shared information and commiserated about frightening trailside rumors, they forwarded letters, cooperated in erecting rude bridges across streams, and exulted in meeting fellow lodge members. They combined forces to hunt strayed or stolen cattle, to chastise marauding Indians, or to hear and pass judgment upon cases of trailside criminal activity. They sold surplus foodstuffs and traveling supplies, generously aided their less fortunate comrades, and regularly shared meals with those who had temporarily become separated from their traveling company while seeking strayed stock, admiring the landscape, or napping by the side of the trail. Those who still possessed wagons at the end of the journey often transported the baggage of those forced to abandon their conveyances; physicians were on call to those in distress for miles around. When all else failed, there was always someone's debris to fuel a campfire or assuage hunger. On the closing stages of the journey emigrants came to rely so much upon relief and assistance from the settlers of Oregon and California that when it was not forthcoming in the anticipated amounts they occasionally grumbled in dissatisfaction. Forty-niner Elisha Perkins testified to the pervasiveness of this cooperative outlook:

> When we left the frontier we were told great stories about the selfishness & want of feeling among the Emigrants that the hardships and uncertainties of the journey had soured what 'milk of human kindness' they might have possessed. I wish to bear my testimony against this slander. Never have I seen so much hospitality & good feeling anywhere exhibited as since I have been on this route. Let any stranger visit a camp no matter who or where, & the best of everything is brought out, he is fed, & caressed almost universally. If at meal time the best pieces are put on his plate & if the train has any luxuries they are placed before him. Nor have I seen any man in trouble, deserted, without all the assistance they could render. There are of course individual exceptions to all this, & such men are known to almost every train following.

That westbound and eastbound travelers, particularly during the gold rush, did not always conclude their journey in company with the companions with whom they had started is less important to an understanding of the emigrations than is this persistence of emigrant interaction. Believing that there was security in numbers, particularly during the 1840s, the emigrants had carefully grouped together prior to starting. Sometimes these were informal traveling associations, while on other occasions constitutions and bylaws were carefully drafted. Once en route it was not unusual for overlanders to switch to another company more congenial to their traveling speed or outlook on life. As new friends were made, old traveling partnerships were scrapped and new ones inaugurated.

The subsequent formation and long history of the California and Oregon pioneer organizations are further evidence of the camaraderie which prevailed among those participating in the great collective adventure of overland travel, an experience which broke down barriers of religion, politics, and place of birth. Perhaps this nationalizing, democratizing quality of overland travel was seen most clearly in the traveling groups of the early 1840s and in the passenger trains of 1849 and 1850, where many total strangers suddenly joined forces with little alternative but to pull together if their journey was to be successful. Traveling in a sixty-man outfit incorporating groups from Mississippi, Tennessee, Illinois, and Ohio, David Dewolf remarked that "we are a mixed up multitude but we all get along fine. Some of them get in a spur now & then but soon get over it. This trip binds us together like a band of brothers."

Another interesting characteristic of the traveling community was the fluidity with which personal possessions changed hands throughout the journey. In 1843, for example, James Nesmith traded guns twice in one day. A horse he had purchased en route from a Snake Indian he subsequently exchanged with a Chinook brave for a canoe. William Chamberlain's 1849 trading activity was considerably more energetic. After beginning by exchanging tents with a Fort Kearny soldier and trading his lantern for butter with some Mormon travelers, he got down to serious swapping at Fort Laramie by exchanging mules with a Cincinnati emigrant. Three days later he traded his new mule for a pony; two weeks later at the Green River he swapped the pony for a mule with a French trader (paying $10 extra); four days later "Peg-leg" Smith, another trader, got the mule and $20 in exchange for an Indian pony. A month later Chamberlain was once again riding a mule. He had owned at least six different riding animals during the course of his overland journey. Other emigrants, growing tired of their wagons or teams (sometimes even before they had begun their journey), would seek out someone willing to swap and move forward with a different vehicle powered by a different type of animal.

Yet another intriguing facet of the traveling community was the unique way in which emigrants came to recognize their fellow travelers by the mottoes emblazoned on their wagon covers. While many overlanders merely affixed their names and place of origin to their canvas tops, countless emigrants revealed their personalities through the slogans they displayed, or at least so some of their traveling colleagues thought. The artistically inclined decorated their wagon covers with huge images of buffalo, eagles, oxen, giraffes, and lions, as well as with the ubiquitous elephant. The more reflective counseled "Patience and Perseverance," "Never Say Die," and "Westward the Tide of Emigration Rolls." In the early 1840s political slogans such as "54° 40' or Fight" and "Oregon, the Whole or None" were much in evidence.

The gold rushers were the most creative sloganeers. Their word plays on gold were to be expected ("Gold Hunters," "Gold or a Grave," and "With my wash bowl on my knee"), as were variations on the trail password "*Have You Seen the Elephant?*" Also not unusual were such allusions to song and sweetheart as "Sweet Sallie," "Our Sal," or "Flora." Less predictable were such gems as "Davy Crockett through by day light," "*Bob Tail* Company *East Beat*," "Be sure you are right and let him rip," and "Brest for doze dat spect noting for dey will not be disappointed."

The "Tornado Train," "Prairie Bird," "Albatross," "Merry Suckers," and "Passia Bird" also attracted attention; and surely no one missed the "Hell Greasers," "Red Rover," the "Pirate," or the "Ass." When such a familiarly marked wagon came into view the overlander felt like welcoming an old friend—and was also able to conveniently gauge whether he was keeping up with the flow of travel.

Examples further illustrating the collective nature of the emigrating experience abound, but few are more persuasive than the experience related by Margaret Windsor, a young girl traveling overland in 1852. During the last 500 miles of the journey Margaret cared for a baby whose mother had died en route. At each campground Margaret would seek out a woman to nurse the infant. She was, she later recalled, never once refused. Additional evidence of this collective community can be seen in the many travelers who contributed generously to a fund enabling the victim of an accidental shooting in 1850 to receive continuing treatment and be transported back to his home.

The significantly changing nature of overland travel and the crucial role of cooperative assistance emerge, therefore, as the key factors in understanding the antebellum overland emigrations. . . .

Finally, viewing the overland emigrations in historical perspective requires a reconsideration of the dangers attendant to the journey. While there was a great deal of potential disaster associated with an overland trip during the antebellum era, it remains a moot point whether the mortality rate on "the plains across" much exceeded the average death rate among Americans resisting the call of the frontier to remain at home. Estimates of trail mortality have varied widely, ranging as high as 30,000 emigrant deaths for the 1842–59 period. Although overall estimates rarely fall below 6 percent of those starting west (a figure accepted by Mattes in the most recent assessment of mortality on the overland trail), this writer believes that a 4 percent rate of trail mortality comports more closely with the available evidence.

Whatever the actual percentage, one fact is clear: the actual dangers of the overland venture have been considerably misrepresented by the myth-makers' overemphasis on Indian treachery. The less than 400 emigrants killed by Indians during the antebellum era represent a mere 4 percent of the estimated 10,000 or more emigrant deaths. It follows that disease and trail accidents were far more to be feared by the prospective overlander than were the native inhabitants of the West.

Disease was far and away the number one killer, accounting for nearly nine out of every ten deaths. Although the emigrant was never completely safe from the scourge of epidemic disease, the initial portion of the trail to Fort Laramie, otherwise the easiest segment of the journey, occasioned the most disease-induced deaths. During her trip to Oregon in 1852, for example, Cecelia Adams carefully recorded in her diary the locations of 401 new graves, speculating that she had seen only one-fifth of the fresh graves. Slightly over half of the burials had occurred east of Fort Laramie, nearly three-fourths prior to Fort Hall, and the last 21 percent beyond Fort Boise. Considering the hasty burials so characteristic on the trip, grave-counting was often a doubly depressing task, as John Clark, an 1852 tabulator, explained: "The Sign for a new grave was to See their feet with old Shoes or boots on Sticking up through the Sand at other places you Saw the old hat & dusty garments that had been thrown away & quite a number had been So lightly Covered with Sand or Sod the Kiotes had drawn them partly out & Eat of the Carcase this is a coman occurance on the plain."

Diarrhea, tuberculosis, smallpox, mumps, and a host of other illnesses downed travelers, but the chief afflictions were cholera, mountain fever, and scurvy. In 1850 and again in 1852, at least 2,000 overlanders died of the dreaded cholera, most before reaching Fort Laramie. Raging epidemically in the American West between 1848 and 1855, Asiatic cholera killed with exceeding quickness. It felled entire families, decimated large caravans, and lined the trail with individual and mass graves. One 1852 traveler enumerated fifty-two graves at a single encampment. Perilous as cholera was on the trail, the emigrant was scarcely any more susceptible than he would have been back in the settlements. In St. Louis alone more than 4,000 citizens fell victim to cholera during 1849. John H. McBride was not entirely in error in reassuring his wife in an 1850 letter from Fort Laramie, "There is less sickness probably among the emigrants en route for California than among the same number of men at their homes East."

Once beyond Fort Laramie the overlanders entered the zone where they encountered what was commonly termed "mountain fever." Either Rocky Mountain spotted fever or Colorado tick fever, the disease was less virulent than cholera but deadly enough. If the travelers shook off mountain fever, as most ultimately did, the last portion of the journey found them most susceptible to scurvy as months without sufficient fruits and vegetables began to take their toll. Again, deaths were infrequent but suffering was widespread. These major trail diseases were all so inadequately understood that even the presence of many physicians and pseudo-physicians in the emigrations was of little consequence in prompting greater concern with sanitation, hygiene, and diet. The Mormons, by contrast, whose passages to Salt Lake City were invariably better organized and included a higher percentage of females, succumbed less frequently to diseases on their north side of the Platte River trail.

Since no section of the overland trail was accident-free, prudent emigrants never relaxed their vigilance, for carelessness was second only to disease as a hazard of cross-country travel. Perhaps one of the most persuasive factors in convincing overlanders that the prevailing notion of the Great American Desert needed considerable refinement was the extraordinarily high incidence of drownings and near drownings during the course of the trip. One of the most unexpected facets of the "overland" journey was that death by water claimed almost as many victims during the antebellum era as did the much-feared Indians—perhaps as many as 300, at least 90 in 1850 alone. Drownings commenced at the crossing of the Missouri River even before the trip had fairly begun, and continued at virtually every stream and river crossing on the entire length of the Oregon-California Trail. Most drownings occurred in the Platte River, particularly at the Fort Laramie crossing, where approximately nineteen overlanders drowned in 1850, and at the North Fork some 130 miles beyond the fort, where at least twenty-eight were lost in 1849 and twenty-one in 1850. The Green River crossing was another particularly treacherous stretch of water which claimed at least thirty-seven victims in 1850. In the mid-1840s the notoriously dangerous Columbia River had provided the motivation for several of the attempts to fashion ancillary routes into the Willamette Valley. Even the seemingly tame Humboldt River reaped its share of careless travelers—at least nine in 1850.

Drownings continued year after year, reaching their apex during the crowded conditions of the gold rush, when, despite the presence of bridges and semi-safe ferries, impatience, poverty, and/or parsimony led many travelers to attempt their own crossings, often with disastrous results. But men—and drowning victims were almost exclusively male—were lost also while patronizing ferryboats, while swimming and bathing, while crossing stock over a river to forage on better grass. One inebriated 1853 emigrant misjudged rain-swollen Buffalo Creek for a slough, drove his wagon in, and was never seen again. While accidental drownings usually claimed men in individual mishaps, small groups were also lost, invariably following the capsizing of a raft. On one such 1850 occasion at the Green River, nine out of the ten men aboard drowned.

Almost every emigrant diarist records either a drowning witnessed personally, a report of one or more drownings shortly before or after their own successful passage of a river, or one or more narrow escapes. Even when an emigrant barely escaped while attempting to ford a river, the outcome was often catastrophic. Orange Gaylord witnessed an 1850 mishap at the Green River, where an emigrant lost his wagon, provisions, and belongings. Obviously, the impact of the many "near misses" upon the traveling community was significant, as were the family tragedies occasioned by many of the drownings. In the space of less than twenty-four hours in 1847, for example, two women were widowed and nine children rendered fatherless by drownings at a Snake River crossing.

After drownings the commonest cause of fatal accidents was careless handling of the fantastic arsenal of firearms the overlanders carried west with them. Jacob Snyder's largest single expenditure in 1845 was for armaments: more than he spent on his wagon, or his mule, or his cattle, or even his food for the entire journey. Jessy Thornton reported in 1846 that their seventy-two-wagon train of 130 men, 65 women, and 125 children possessed 104 pistols, 155 guns, 1,672 pounds of lead, and 1,100 pounds of powder. William Kelly's description of their twenty-five-man company's weaponry characterized men marching off as to war—which is what some emigrants expected the journey to be: ". . . but we were well equipped, each man carrying in his belt a revolver, a sword, and bowie-knife; the mounted men having besides a pair of holster-pistols and a rifle slung from the horn of their saddles, over and above which there were several double and single-shot guns and rifles suspended in the waggons, in loops, near the forepart, where they would be easily accessible in case of attack."

"Pawnee," writing from his Fort Kearny vantage point, witnessed so many companies like Kelly's that he appropriately termed the forty-niners "walking arsenals," and wryly suggested that "arms of all kinds must certainly be scarce in the States, after such a drain as the emigrants must have made upon them.'' Even the government helped foster this mania for armaments. According to Texas senator Thomas S. Rusk, the rationale for the 1849 congressional authorization of $50,000 for the sale of weapons at cost was that the westbound emigrants should not go forth without adequate "means of defence.'' The Secretary of War's notice specifying how the emigrants could procure their desired firearms was widely publicized in newspapers. The cut-rate prices for rifles, muskets, carbines, pistols, and ammunition remained in effect during 1850.

It really did not matter that guidebook writers like Joseph Ware and Lansford Hastings admonished emigrants to treat their dangerous weapons with care; or even that several prudent joint-stock companies incorporated careful restrictions in their constitutions about when and where guns could be discharged and how they should be carried. The overlanders had to learn from bitter experience, as Hastings's own 1842 company had done. Their guns had been carried capped and primed until one of their number had been accidentally killed. The correctness of Hastings's analysis that they had been "mere sophomores in the great school of experience" was demonstrated yearly on the plains, beginning in 1841 with the fatal shooting of emigrant James Shotwell, who tried to remove his gun from a wagon—muzzle first.

The bloodshed was most pronounced in 1849 and 1850. Forty-niners reaching the jumping-off points by boat from St. Louis had been recklessly spending their days in target practice, shooting at deer, hogs, dogs, and most anything else they saw. William Kelly noted that only at mealtimes did the "unintermitting fusilade" stop. Careless gun handling in the outfitting posts resulted in accidental shootings almost daily. Once out on the plains the mayhem quickly peaked. William Kelly's well-prepared company lost their first man while fording the Big Blue River, after he had attempted to draw his loaded gun from his wagon—muzzle first. The thirteen buckshot passing through his body killed him instantly. Andrew Orvis, after himself having been accidentally shot in the hip and seeing several men killed and maimed, commented that "hundreds of guns and pistols" had been accidentally discharged. Several overlanders acknowledged that they were much more frightened of carelessly handled guns in their own trains than they were of any hostile Indians. The validity of their observations was borne out by the steady stream of patients treated for bullet wounds at the Kearny and Laramie army hospitals, as well as by the grave markers beside the trail.

Men's and Women's Work on the Overland Trail

JOHN MACK FARAGHER

The routines of farm life and the sexual division of farm labor were translated smoothly into the work of the trail. By contrast, in all-male parties the assignments of trail duty were a source of conflict. As Noah Brooks remembered,

At the onset none knew who should drive the oxen, who should do the cooking, or whose ingenuity would be taxed to mend broken wagons or tattered clothing. Gradually, and not altogether without grumbling and objection each man filled his own proper place. . . . Indeed, the division of labor in a party of emigrants was a prolific cause of quarrel. . . . We saw not a little fighting in the camps of others who sometimes jogged along the trail in our company, and these bloody fisticuffs were invariably the outcome of disputes over the divisions of labor.

Likewise Rebecca Ketcham, traveling without family in a volunteer party of men and couples, noted after almost two months on the trail and considerable shifting of jobs, "I believe the day's work is pretty regularly laid out now."

For family parties this division of labor was more easily accomplished; it was assumed that men would drive the oxen and mend the wagons, that women would cook and sew. We might expect that the extraordinary conditions of the trip would have disturbed the standard patterns, but as both men and women recorded in the diaries, journals, and reminiscences of the emigration, from the preparations for the journey right through to arrival on the Pacific Coast, responsibilities were apportioned in strict adherence to the traditional sexual division. . . .

On the trail, men's work was narrowed to one principal task—getting the wagons and the family safely through to the coast. Thus men were concerned almost exclusively with transportation: the care of wagons and stock, driving and droving, leadership and protection of the family and party. On a normal day of travel the men of each family were up between four and five in the morning to cut out their oxen from the herd and drive them to the wagon for yoking and hitching. The wagon and running gear had to be thoroughly checked over. After breakfast the wagons pulled out, often in single file, but frequently drivers spread themselves out to avoid the choking dust thrown up by the hooves and wheels to the front. Normally a man drove each wagon. Since many parties had some additional loose stock, some men herded and drove the stock to the rear of the line. A good morning march began by seven and continued until the noon hour, when drivers pulled up, unhitched their oxen, set the stock to grazing, and settled down for the midday meal the women produced. After an hour or so for lunch and rest, the men hitched up the oxen again and picked up the line of march.

Driving and droving were strenuous and demanding occupations. Some men drove their wagons while sitting on the wagon perch, but most drove by walking alongside the oxen; a few men owned horses they rode along the trail, but most walked. "Of course riding was out of the question. We

John Mack Faragher, "Men's and Women's Work on the Overland Trail," from *Women and Men on the Overland Trail*, 66–87, with deletions 66–71, 1979. Reprinted by permission of Yale University Press.

had one horse, but he was reserved for emergencies, and nobody but a shirk would think of crawling into a wagon, loaded down as it was with the necessities of life, unless sickness made it impossible for him to walk.'' Walking the fifteen or so miles of trail each day was, in the best of conditions, enough to tire any man. Conditions, of course, were not always the best. Soaring midday summer temperatures on the shadeless plains sapped the strength. The mornings, on the other had, especially in the high plains and mountains, were sometimes frigid. '' 'Tis dredful cold,'' Agnes Stewart scratched early on May 17, 1853, ''Oh, the wind goes to a person's heart. I will shiver to death. I feel for the men gathering the cattle and yoking them up. It was so cold for them, and no warm breakfast.'' Driving, and especially herding the cattle, meant eating large portions of dust. ''It has been immensely disagreeable for the drivers today for a Northwest wind drove the dust in clouds into their faces, as they walk besides their teams. Am glad that I am not an ox driver.'' The sun and wind decreed another common fate, painful chapped skin. ''I feel well except my lips, they have been sore ever since I left Council Bluffs; but one half of the Emigrants share the same fate, something I had never heard of before.''

The most common obstacles were the rivers. By the 1850s many crossings were served by ferries, and as long as the emigrants could afford the toll, the only inconvenience was the wait. At other times and places, however, oxen and wagons had to be driven down steep embankments and across the flow, and the danger of quicksand bogs or rapid currents that could sweep away goods, stock, or men lurked in even the shallowest of streams. Consequently men took the greatest care at crossings. Women and children frequently shuttled over on horseback or raft. Sometimes men labored to build rude bridges or ferries for the wagons. Most often they double- or triple-teamed the oxen and drew each wagon across. At any rate, it was slow, frustrating, demanding work. Along the road wagons could always break down; axles especially were prone to snap with all the jolting. Only a lucky man did not have to jerry-rig or abandon a wagon along the road.

By the late afternoon the normal demands of most days had so tired the men that sleep could not be resisted. ''A drowsiness has fallen apparently on men and beast; teamsters fall asleep on their perches and even when walking by their teams, and the words of command are now addressed to the slowly creeping oxen in the soft tenor of women or the piping trebel of children, while the snores of the teamsters make a droning accompaniment.'' ''It is with the greatest effort we can keep awake. Even Mr. Gray sometimes nods with the lines in his hands,'' Rebecca Ketcham wrote in her journal. ''We can all, as soon as we stop, lie down on the grass or anywhere and be asleep in less than no time almost.''

In the evenings the stock sometimes had to be driven a distance for grazing. ''The men of the company divided into two bands. The elderly ones were detailed to stay with the wagons; keeping one or two horses with them while the others, taking with them the other horses, drove the cattle up the creek valley, searching for food.'' After a hard day's drive in 1853, George Belshaw and some other men from his party ''took the

Cattle and Horses about one mile to feed and watched them all night. I fealt well but it is hard fateage loosing so much rest and Driving the teams through the Day and to manage so large a company and get them along as fast as I can."

Belshaw was, as he noted, captain of his train. For those men in the advance guard there was added responsibility. George complained in a letter to his brother, Henry, "They have elected me captain. I have taken them across one stream and it keeps me very busy all the time to pick the camping places for them and attend to everything, besides, and lead them along, as you know some of them are very slow so I have to urge them up. I do not get to bed until ten or eleven, and have to be up at daylight. I have my hand full, but you know I will persevere for a better climate."

Guard duty was another responsibility that fell to men. The duty rotated, two or three men splitting the night's watch, protecting the stock from wolves or Indians, preventing a sudden stampede. Guard duty was probably the most hated male chore but one—chasing lost stock. A slipshod night's watch could halt a party for days as the men roamed the prairie, often unsuccessfully, in search of the stock. Men measured their success in units of forward progress: the mileage they calculated and noted in their daily journals. A setback of days because of lost stock was, in these terms, a frustrating failure.

There was a distinctive dialectic to men's work on the trail. The heads of household had overall responsibility for movement. It was men who had made the decision to move, it was men who determined the route, direction, and speed of travel, it was men who would make the sometimes fateful decisions to turn back or move on, it was men upon whom fell the burden of repairing faulty or broken equipment. In short, it was men who provided the leadership for the emigration: men would take the credit, and they had to accept the blame. This responsibility bore heavily upon husbands and fathers as they led their wives and children into hardships they had not fully anticipated. There is, of course, no way to measure their burden; we can be sure, however, that it took its toll of energy, vitality, and good humor.

The physical work of men was organized so as to provide compensations for this heavy burden of responsibility. While the wagons were rolling, men worked at peak capacity. Time and again in men's accounts of their trips, they took spiteful aim at the few shirking able-bodied males who dared to hitch a ride on one of the wagons. A man worked the trail from the time the oxen were yoked in the morning until they were herded in the evening; a person who did not work at this full capacity and with this constancy was simply not a man. But when the wagons were parked once more, the oxen and cattle set out to graze, and the guard was posted, men were off duty. There were occasional jobs to be done, of course, and men were still in command, to be sure, but in the evening they acted out their responsibilities at a leisurely pace, intermingling work with the pleasures of food, relaxation, and company. Men bore final responsibility, but they enjoyed a rhythm of long periods of hard work punctuated by periods of rest.

Women's trail work was structured around the men's: women were the working support of the trail's labor system. In the first instance, women enjoyed little overall responsibility for the direction or outcome of the emigration. They were not called upon to participate in making the critical decisions; indeed, a wife had probably played almost no role in the decision to emigrate in the first place. The lack of overall responsibility, however, was accompanied by a demanding work schedule that made adult women the most fully and materially responsible members of the family. The men's work schedule required that a woman tend to the needs of her family when the wheels stopped turning for the day. The need to work did not disappear when the men went off duty; work merely changed its character. Randall Hewitt put it most bluntly: "Having ladies do the 'housework' everything went along smoothly." Amelia Knight confirmed this view from a distinctively feminine perspective. Her husband was upset at having lost three hired hands who had decided to pack through alone; Amelia saw it differently. As she confided in her diary, "I am pleased, as . . . I shall have three less to wait on."

On the other hand, in contrast to men, women were not at liberty to relax while their opposite numbers worked. After all, who could relax while bumping and jogging along in a wagon? More to the point, during the hours of travel women were either working or on call, available to lend a hand, do a critical job, or take over for an ailing male. When the overriding principle of the trail was to "keep moving," could an able body simply stand by? Women's work, then, was a reflex of men's: a rhythm of long hours on call to substitute and supplement the work of men, punctuated by shorter periods of intense activity.

First we shall look at work that belonged distinctively to women. They regularly began the trail day by getting up around four, an hour to half an hour before the men, to stoke the fire and put up kettles of water to begin breakfast. If there was a cow along, wives milked her before breakfast. James Clyman arose early one morning to write in his journal as the women prepared breakfast and noted that other than the breakfast bustle there was no other activity "except Sleeping which is performed by the male part of the camp to the greatest perfection." By the time coffee had been boiled, bacon fried, beans warmed, and bread baked, all of which required a good hour's work, the men had arisen to hear the report from the last guard, brought in the oxen, and were ready for their meal.

Cooking in the open was a new experience for most women. As Lodisa Frizzell wrote, "it goes so much 'agin the grane' at first." "Eliza soon discovered that cooking over a campfire was far different from cooking on a stove or a range." "Two forked sticks were driven into the ground, a pole laid across, and the kettle swung upon it." Pots were continually falling into the fire, and families soon became accustomed to ashen crust on their food. In the absence of tables, all preparation was on the ground. This "requires me to stoop considerably. All our work here requires stooping. Not having tables, chairs or anything it is very hard on the back." The weather rarely cooperated, especially in the early morning. "Everything was soaked with water and dry wood so scarce that our women could scarcely make coffee or fry meat." "Rainy this morning; very disagreeble getting breakfast," Cecelia Adams complained in her diary, and she noted a few weeks later that she "could not raise enough fire to cook breakfast." James Clyman, ever an admiring observer of women, committed to his journal the story of "one young lady which showed herself worthy of the bravest undaunted pioneer of west, for after having kneaded her dough she watched and nursed the fire and held an umbrella over the fire and her skillet with the greatest composure for near 2 hours."

After breakfast the women washed the tinware, stowed away the cooking equipment and food, and packed up while the men readied the wagons. After several hours on the road there was a brief stop at noon. Then, while the men relaxed, the women brought out the lunch, usually prepared the night before, and the party enjoyed a cold meal and a few minutes of rest. After the women had again packed up their gear, the wagons pushed off once more for the remainder of the afternoon.

By evening everyone was ready for camp. After one particularly rough day of moving their wagons across a cold stream, the Burns party moved into camp. "Our campfire was soon burning brightly and in a few minutes we sat down to a nice warm supper prepared by Mrs. W. P. Burns, which was eaten with relish." For men, the evening was the reward for a hard day's labor; for women, who prepared the reward, unpacking the wagons was the prelude to four or five hours of sustained work. Rebecca Ketcham lamented these relentless demands: "To ride on horseback, rain or shine, tired or sick, or whatever might be the matter, then as soon as we get into camp, go to work!"

The fire had to be kindled and water brought to camp. If the travelers were lucky, the camp was close by a spring. The fear of mosquitoes, unhealthy vapors, or hidden Indians, however, kept them away from the covered, low-lying river bottoms, so water had to be hauled, usually by women. Collecting fuel for the fire was also women's work. Presumably if wood had had to be chopped, men would have done it, but there being no trees, women cooked with sagebrush, cottonwood twigs, or buffalo chips, which they gathered. James Reed, writing in his diary, noted that "the women and children are now out gathering 'Buffalo Chips' to burn in order to do the cooking." Some women complained about having to handle and cook with dried dung, but necessity, of course, prevailed. Because there was frequently not enough kindling in the vicinity of camp for both the evening and morning fires, women collected chips as they traveled. "We always had a sack of them hanging on the side of the wagon on the plains. We used to average about ten miles a day and I believe that I ran an extra five miles trying to gather feed for our toothless ox or buffalo chips for our evening fire."

Despite the primitive surroundings, women continued to practice mid-western culinary arts. Judging from the diary notations of menus, women worked mightily to overcome the limit imposed by hauling weights. In addition to the basics—cooking bacon, beans, and coffee—women milked, made butter and cheese, boiled and mashed potatoes, made gravies, stewed dried fruit, made bread, biscuits, pies, and cakes, puddings of bread, rice, or cracker, and even prepared preserves and jellies from wild berries and fruit gathered along the way. The cooking continued past the dinner hour and into the late evening as food for the next day's breakfast and lunch was prepared: "Everybody is in bed but Agnes and myself i believe and we would be there to but we have wait til the apples are stewed enough."

Camp was just like home in one respect—there was plenty of housework. After dinner the beds had to be made up, wagons cleaned out, and provisions taken out to air to prevent mildew. There were always clothes to mend or socks to knit. "I visited the tents of our fellow-travelers and found the ladies busily employed, as if sitting by the fireside which they had so recently left. . . . Mrs West, a lady of seventy, and her daughter Mrs Campbell, were knitting."

Except for rinsing out a few garments in the evening, however, the family washing piled up; women waited for a day when the wagons might stop over near an ample supply of water. Washing "was not done always on Monday to the annoyance of our excellent housekeepers who at home had been accustomed to thus honoring 'blue Monday.' " The wagons made frequent, unavoidable stops for one reason or another, and women invariably used these occasions to wash. "Came to a creek so high we could not cross, camped, the women to washing and the men to examining their provisions." "It is agreed to stay in this camp until tomorrow to rest the cattle. Water and grass are both fine. The women are going to wash. It is the best chance we have had for a long time, wood and water are plenty and convenient." "One of the company broke the axletree of his wagon, then camped, the women washed." "Still at Bridger. Here we have a good time for washing, which we women deem a great privilege." For parties that had agreed to "rest" on Sundays, the day was turned to washing, but under the pressures of time few parties could observe the Sabbath strictly. If there had been no occasion to stop over for two or three weeks, women demanded a chance to wash; or, as George Belshaw put it, "the women ruled and would wash." In most parties women spent a full day washing about every two weeks.

Washing began early. "The banks of the small rivulet was lined at an early hour after breakfast with fires, kettles, washtubs, and piles of unwashed linen, showing conclusively that a general lustration was to be performed by the female portion of our party." If there was fuel to spare, water was heated, but generally women had to be content to suds their harsh soap in hard, cold water. A day of sun, wind, soap, and water could be a painful combination. "Camilia and I both burnt our arms very badly while washing. They were red and swollen and painful as though scalded with boiling water. Our hands are blacker than any farmer's, and I do not see that there is any way of preventing it, for everything has to be done in the wind and sun."

With all this, there were the children to be watched, although the burden of other responsibilities made child care a relatively low priority. Notes on children are rare in the accounts of men and women, and when they do appear, children are the accompaniment to other work. "In getting up a steep bank after we had forded a stream I had to carry a heavy stone to block the wheels . . . , and carry and pull along the children at the same time." "Descending the mountain, which was steep and difficult, the men having to steady the wagons down while we women carried and led our children." At most times children fended for themselves, the older boys working with the men, the older girls appointed as nursemaids to the younger ones. The ultimate responsibility, however, resided with the mothers.

In parties with more than one able-bodied woman, women divided up their responsibilities just as the men did. Women would commonly take turns cooking. However, as Helen Carpenter complained to her diary, even with help from sisters and children

> the plain fact of the matter is *we have no time for sociability*. From the time we get up in the morning, until we are on the road, it is hurry scurry to get breakfast and put away the things that necessarily had to be pulled out last night—while under way there is no room in the wagon for a visitor, nooning is barely enough to eat a cold bite—and at night all the cooking utensils and provisions are to be gotten about the camp fire and cooking enough done to last until the next night.
>
> Although there is not much to cook, the difficulty and inconvenience of doing it, amounts to a great deal—so by the time one has squatted around the fire and cooked bread and bacon, and made several dozen trips to and from the wagon—washed the dishes (with no place to drain them) and gotten things ready for an early breakfast, some of the others already have their night caps on—at any rate its time to go to bed.
>
> In respect to women's work the days are all very much the same. . . . Some women have very little help about the camp, being obliged to get the wood and water (as far as possible), make camp fires, unpack at night and pack up in the morning—and if they are Missourians they have the milking to do, if they are fortunate enough to have cows.
>
> I am lucky in having a Yankee for a husband, so I am well waited on.

Most women, of course, were from Missouri and its midwestern environs and had the worst of it by Mrs. Carpenter's description.

Indeed, despite Mrs. Carpenter's disclaimer for Yankee men, men assisted in only the most unusual of circumstances. In some parties men did the cooking during storms and very bad weather. And most husbands, like Jessy Thornton, took over when their wives fell sick; Thornton only asked that Nancy "not scold me for my blunders." There were other instances where husband and wife both hired into a party to do the cooking, or where women were relieved of cooking when a man hired on as trail cook.

Men, however, made inept domestic helpers. The experience of single men again places the family experience in perspective.

"How do you like it overland?"

His mother she will say;
"All right, except for cooking,
Then the devil is to pay.

For some won't cook, and others can't,
And then it's curse and damn;
The coffe pot's begun to leak,
So has the frying pan.

John A. Johnson was one of the many who followed his heart to the goldfields in 1849, leaving his wife Almire and their children behind. In a rich series of letters written home, he discussed among many other things the cooking arrangements in his party of five men. "It would no doubt be interesting to hear how we manage matters in camp as to cooking, etc.," he wrote. "All of us seem to understand cooking as well as our wives and are anxious to try their hands." A few weeks later he added: "We have, as I said before, several excellent cooks in our company. Some crack on making one thing and some another and really we get along very well in this respect. Today each mess made a pot-pie; I had the honor of officiating at our mess; it was good of course."

Perhaps inspired by his success at Sunday dinner, his confidence was building; a week later he wrote that

> yesterday our mess . . . proposed that if I would act as cook on the road I would be relieved from every other kind of work and further that I need not stand guard at night. I said *I would do it* and it was unanimously agreed to; so that I need not harness or touch a mule, or do any other work on the road, save preparing the food, which to me, you know, will not be burdensome as I have a rather natural taste for that kind of work and they all think so. . . . The beauty of my berth is that I can walk, ride in the wagon or on a mule all day as I please and after supper go to bed and *sleep all night* while others have to watch or stand guard two hours every other night and are consequently exposed to danger if there be any dangers at any time for Indians.

A friend of the family traveling with the male party wrote to Johnson's wife as if to address her suspicions about her husband's newfound capacity for the wifely role: "He is decidedly the best cook in the camp. He goes about it rather awkwardly but really I don't think his wife can beat him at making bread."

Johnson's tenure as trail cook was all too predictable. A week later he wrote home again: "I have given up the office of chief cook and take my turn with the rest and my portion of other duties. I had rather do so as it is more slavish work than I had anticipated and by far the hardest post to occupy. I found I was working all the time during our halts while others were at least a portion of the time resting. I could not get time to write a letter or a note—as for guarding, my turn will not come oftener than once in two and perhaps three nights and then only two hours at a time with some eight or ten others."

Where families, not single men, made up the parties, women were only too glad to replace men at the campfire. Men's clumsiness with domestic details was an object of feminine scorn. "Mr Gray does most of the cooking," Rebecca Ketcham noted, "and it is most amusing to see some of his operations." Lucy Cooke traveled all the way to Salt Lake with a hired male cook but went on to California the next season without male domestic assistance: "It's so nice to have women folks manage the cooking; things look so much sweeter." "We are in a camp tonight with a small company of emigrants among whom are several ladies," Frances Sawyer wrote. "These, like myself, were engaged in helping to cook supper, and I have no doubt, but that they all enjoyed it heartily as I did." She was, undoubtedly, correct. Camp housework was "more slavish" than even experienced farm women might have expected. It was "by far the hardest post to occupy" but accepted by women, nonetheless, as their responsibility.

What about the work women did during the hours of travel? The picture that emerges from men's and women's accounts is fuzzy and indistinct, reflecting a confusion as to what was normative in the actual situations that developed out on the trail. Men were supposed to be the drivers of the wagons and stock, and clearly the leaders of the march; women were to enjoy the privilege of riding in the wagons. Both men and women agreed on this division of labor, and during the early weeks on the trail most people conformed to this ideal. Certainly men rarely rode the wagons, and women frequently did. This distinction between riding and walking was so basic that it came close to a role-defining division between the sexes.

> Mrs Ridgley said that her back ached riding all day in a wagon that jolted you to pieces every time you hit a stone. She didn't see how that poor woman in the wagon in back of the deacon's could get along, with a cross baby. And if one was a man one wouldn't have to sit cramped up all day and every day.
>
> In mild defense of his sex Mr Ridgley would reply that it wasn't exactly easy to walk halfway across the continent alongside of a team of oxen with a yoke of steers in the center that you had to keep watching continually. At which his good wife would smile a little wearily. *She* knew who had the hardest part of the bargain, etc.

If there was a formulaic quality to this conjugal debate it was because this behavior was taken to be standard for men and women. Essentially the haggling was about the respective virtues of the sexes themselves.

In fact, this was not the full picture. Women walked too, and many women walked most of the time. We have already noted women gathering fuel as they walked. As the emigrants matured with the march, they could see how every extra pound lessened the distance a team could haul, so "the women would walk to lighten the load" and even "would push to help the poor teams up the hills." There is cause for believing that by the time the journey was well under way women walked as a matter of course. The difference remained that women could ride when they tired of the walk, while men could not. When they did choose to ride, women busied themselves with mending or knitting.

When teamsters fell sick or were otherwise incapacitated, women, of course, substituted. Emergencies—stranded wagons, prairie fires, Indian scares—also called on women to carry out male duties. This is not surprising. More unexpected, perhaps, is that many women took a regular turn at driving both the wagons and the stock. As we have seen, men only rarely took over the women's work. Women, however, regularly performed certain details of what were men's responsibilities. "Mrs Burnett and myself drove and slept alternately during the day," Peter Burnett recalled. "I drive a great deal now, as I am very fond of handling the lines," Frances Sawyer wrote in her journal. In their diary accounts women were more likely than men to note women's work with the stock; fewer than a fifth of the men's diaries mention women driving, compared to a full third of the women's. Yet women themselves seemed a bit reluctant to admit this discrepancy in the conventional division of labor. "The two-horse spring wagon was our bed room and was driven by the Major," Margaret Haun wrote, and then added "and in good stretches of the road by myself." Susan Angell declared that their mule-drawn wagon was "driven by my husband"—certainly a clear statement, except that later, in passing, she added the important qualifier that she "took turns in driving the mule teams during each day." These women stated the normative as if it were the actual situation; the truth only came out in elaboration. Their values prevented them from writing simply, "My husband and I drove the wagon." These indications suggest that the work of women during the traveling hours violated normative standards of work.

There was, of course, a social life in the camps. Young people frequently got together for singing and sometimes dancing around the campfires. "The young ones of our party are all assembled around a blazing fire, from which sounds of mirth and hilarity come floating on the evening breeze." Special occasions, like the Fourth of July or a stopover at Fort Laramie or Fort Bridger, might generate an evening of merrymaking. But women were mostly just too busy for evening entertainments. If they were able to end their domestic duties a little early, women too gathered around the campfires, but mostly in feminine groups. "High teas were not popular but tatting, knitting, crocheting, exchanging recepts for cooking beans or dried apples or swapping food for the sake of variety kept us in practice of feminine occupations and diversions." For their part, the menfolk spent their evening hour "lolling and smoking their pipes and guessing, or maybe betting, how many miles we had covered during the day."

Quite simply, women had little extra time, although men found time for a variety of leisure activities. Fishing and swimming were common at the rivers and occasional ponds. Randall Hewitt remembered men producing "greasy, well-thumbed packs of cards," and games of euchre, old sledge, and pinochle were "something for amusement constantly."

The most popular male pastime, however, was hunting. Nearly every man hunted whenever he could. When the wagons stopped for a wash day, men would hunt. "We shall not move today. The women will wash and the men will hunt," John Zeiber wrote in his diary. The captain's order for the day in one 1844 train was "a rest for the cattle, wash day for the women, and a day to hunt for the men." Although captains' orders in general soon fell out of favor, the priorities remained the same. Moreover, despite expert advice as to the folly of stopping the march for a hunt, men who otherwise stressed the importance of continual movement above all else would stop their wagons, saddle all available mounts, and head out for the kill at the slightest sign of a distant buffalo herd. When the cry "Buffalo!" was raised, excitement pulsed from one man to the next; Minto's captain, "General" Cornelius Gilliam, "called loudly for his horse. . . . He slung himself into the saddle, and turning his face to the train called in a raised voice, 'You boys with the teams camp where there is wood and water, and you that can get horses and guns mount and follow me.' He did not speak to any particular officer, and in the ardor of the hunter seemed to have forgotten the responsibility of the general." When the buffalo appeared, many men left their responsibilities behind with the women. As her party moved across buffalo country, Cecelia Adams noted in her diary that "our boys are on the chase most of the time."

Men had this opportunity for play, and play it was. The amount of usable food produced by these masculine sorties was dismally low. Edward Parrish recorded that his comrades had killed buffalo enough for 40,000 pounds of meat but left nearly all for the birds; the hunters had neither the time, the equipment, nor the inclination for butchering. "God forgive us for such waste and save us from such ignorance," Parrish pled. Burnett offered sound advice: "When you reach the country of buffalo, never stop your wagons to hunt, as you will eat up more provisions than you will save." Hunting could not, then, be justified as a working activity. Nor did very many men seem to feel, as Parrish did, that it required such a justification. Most simply felt as George Belshaw: "Fine sport was this for all the Boys."

There was no comparable play activity for women outside of their working time. Hunting was but a glaring example of the contrasting ways in which men and women employed their time on the trail. Men worked within a pattern of activity/inactivity geared for functional efficiency; periods of maximum exertion were matched by periods of rest and relaxation. This pattern was in literal accord with the principal function of the trip; indeed, men could and did see themselves as the motive force itself, since it was principally men's labor that drove the wagons. In addition, men had the prerogative of leadership, including the option of stopping the train. Women's work, on the other hand, was at the mercy of the march and its male leadership. Unable to rest during the long hours on the road, often called upon to lend a crucial hand during the day, women finally shifted into high gear in the evenings, precisely when the men and the wagons lay still.

Hunting well illustrates a second characteristic distinction between the work of the sexes. In their roles as leaders of the march, men had to work together with other men. As we have seen, cooperation, whether in trains or informally, was at a premium for the length of the march. It was during the moving hours that cooperation was most in demand: agreeing and holding to the line and pace of the march, agreeing to a camping time and place, assisting one another in the difficult stretches. Men were the representatives of the parties and families, and security was dependent upon their ability to communicate and cooperate. Collective games, storytelling, singing and dancing—all shaped mainly by the male participants—were important ways of building and sustaining social cooperation. Hunting together was another important way. The buffalo hunters returning from their successful (albeit wasteful) foray, Minto remembers, "made a jolly party going back to camp, as the man who led the way, walking beside his mule, Joseph Watt, started us singing"—an archetypal scene of male camaraderie. Women's work confined wives to the family circle. There was little chance, as Helen Carpenter said, to visit while traveling, and in the evening women were all but bound to the domestic fires.

These distinctions could ordinarily be contained by family dynamics habituated to the everyday differences between men's and women's work. Women, as we have seen, were used to working beyond the boundaries of "sun to sun." There was a difference on the trail, however, which produced some significant conflict. On their simple farms, men and women were engaged in common work with an internal character. Here on the trail the work of men and women diverged: men fixed exclusively on outward goals—the stock, grass and water, mileage, the destination, future planning—compatible with their working goals. Women, because of the repetitive features of their work, found it more difficult to achieve this outward perspective.

Phoebe Judson articulated this divergence of the sexes:

> During the week our men had been very busily employed. . . . Saturday night found them very tired and much in need of physical rest, so they lolled around in the tents and on their blankets spread on the grass, or under the wagons out of the sunshine, seeming to realize that the "Sabbath was made for man." But the women, who had only been anxious spectators of their arduous work, . . . not being weary in body, could not fully appreciate physical rest, and were rendered more uneasy by the continual passing of emigrant trains all day long. . . . To me, much of the day was spent in meditating over the past and in forebodings for the future.

Reams of testimony could be marshaled to demonstrate the physical exhaustion of women, so we can only assume that Mrs. Judson's memory was faulty. The anxiety she remembered feeling, however, was real enough and pervaded nearly every woman's account of her experience. The immediate source of this anxiety was the divergent goals and work patterns of men and women on the trail. On a deeper level, however, these divergences themselves were part and parcel of significant cultural distinctions between men and women. The conflict between sexual styles we see revealed in the analysis of the division of labor found more fundamental expression on the level of values, beliefs, expectations, and emotions.

Polygamy and Mormon Women

LAWRENCE FOSTER

I

The Mormon attempt to establish polygamy in Utah and adjacent areas in the Intermountain West during the last half of the nineteenth century constitutes the largest, best organized, and most controversial effort to radically restructure marriage and family life in nineteenth-century America. While other alternatives to monogamy in this period, such as the systems of the celibate Shakers and the free-love Oneida Perfectionists, directly affected only a few thousand individuals at most, polygamy ultimately became the family ideal for more than one hundred thousand Latter-day Saints who placed their indelible cultural imprint on much of the American West. In setting up their Great Basin kingdom the Mormons skillfully and systematically sought to create an autonomous religious and cultural order based on American and biblical models. Polygamy became an integral part of that larger effort between 1852, when the Mormons in Utah first publicly announced that they were practicing it, and 1890, when, under intense federal pressure, they began to give up the practice.

Few aspects of Mormon polygamy have been more controversial than its impact on women. During the nineteenth century hostile external observers attacked the practice as a "relic of barbarism," a system of institutionalized lust that degraded women, destroyed the unity of the family, and led inevitably to unhappiness, debaucheries, and excesses of all kinds. Nineteenth-century Latter-day Saints were equally vigorous in defending their marital practices, arguing that plural marriage and the Old Testament patriarchal model on which it was based actually strengthened family and kinship ties, led to the rearing of righteous children in the best families, and allowed women greater freedom in choosing the men they really wanted to marry. More recently, both Mormon and non-Mormon scholars have attempted to treat polygamy with greater objectivity, to show how it functioned in pioneer Utah and what it meant to the people who participated in it. Through the use of demographic studies, literary analyses, oral histories, group biographies, and a variety of other methods, these writers have highlighted key questions raised by this extraordinary effort to introduce new forms of marriage and family relations in nineteenth-century America.

Based on current research and available manuscript materials, it is now possible to move beyond simple polemics and begin to understand the complex ways in which polygamy affected relationships between men and women in the Great Basin region. Although polygamy had been secretly taught and practiced by Mormons at least as early as 1841 in Nauvoo,

Lawrence Foster, "Polygamy and the Frontier: Mormon Women in Early Utah," *Utah Historical Quarterly*, 50 (Summer 1982), 268–289. Slightly abridged and reprinted by permission of the author and publisher. All rights reserved.

Illinois, not until the difficult exodus to the relative isolation of the Inter-mountain West were the Latter-day Saints free to set up their unorthodox marriage system without constant external interference. During the years between 1847, when the Mormons first arrived in Utah, and 1877, when Brigham Young died, polygamy became an integral part of Mormon life in the Great Basin region and profoundly influenced the experiences and activity of women there.

The problems and challenges of life under polygamy in Utah are described in numerous diaries, journals, letters, and other first-hand accounts by Mormon women. Perhaps the finest presentation of the range of women's experiences under polygamy is found in the reflections of Jane Snyder Richards, first wife of the Mormon apostle Franklin D. Richards and herself active in many capacities on behalf of her family and the women of Utah. In 1880 in an interview entitled "The Inner Facts of Social Life in Utah," Mrs. Richards spoke candidly about her experiences and feelings with the non-Mormon Mrs. Hubert Howe Bancroft who was helping her husband collect information for his monumental history of Utah. Although Mrs. Richards was far from a typical Mormon wife and mother, her interview and other writings sensitively portray many of the characteristic features of early polygamy as well as the complex adjustments necessary to make polygamy work, even in an unusually good relationship. Observing Mr. and Mrs. Richards together, Mrs. Bancroft wrote:

> He seems remarkably considerate and kind and speaks of her with gratitude and pride, and that he wanted her to enjoy this little visit to California for she has suffered so much affliction and so many hardships. . . . his attentions and kind consideration for her are very marked. She is certainly very devoted to him, and I am imagining this trip and the one they have just returned from in the East, as a sort of honey-moon in middle life.

. . .

Underlying the entire interview between Mrs. Bancroft and Mrs. Richards was an awareness of the intense personal commitment and the difficult personal renunciations involved in the practice of polygamy, especially for women and, most especially, for the first wife. Romantic love was sharply undercut by the new arrangements. Jane Richards spoke of her initial "re-pugnance" when she first learned of polygamy in Illinois; how "crushed" she felt when her husband first approached her about the possibility of taking another wife; and of her unhappiness when he married three new wives in Utah after he had returned from an extended mission to England. Like many other Mormon women, Mrs. Richards was only able to accept polygamy because she convinced herself that it was essential to her salvation and to that of her husband. She found that in practice polygamy "was not such a trial as she had feared" and that she and the other wives were able to cooperate effectively. On several occasions during the interview Mrs. Richards appeared to be trying to reassure herself that her husband was motivated by a sense of religious duty and not by any lustful desires. Mrs.

Bancroft concluded her record of the interview by observing that on the whole it seemed to her that Mormon women considered polygamy

> as a religious duty and schooled themselves to bear its discomforts as a sort of religious penance, and that it was a matter of pride to make everybody believe they lived happily and to persuade themselves and others that was not a trial; and that a long life of such discipline makes the trial lighter.

Other diary and journal accounts, interviews with individuals who lived in polygamous families, and recent quantitative analyses show that religious commitment was, indeed, the primary reason that most Mormon women—and most men as well—gave for entering into plural marriage. Only a sense of the cosmic importance of their endeavor was enough to convince thousands of individuals to accept or adopt practices radically at variance with all that they had ever been taught. As the Mormon mother Annie Clark Tanner, who grew up in a polygamous household and became a plural wife herself, declared:

> I am sure that women would never have accepted polygamy had it not been for their religion. No woman ever consented to its practice without great sacrifice on her part. There is something so sacred about the relationship of husband and wife that a third party in the family is sure to disturb the confidence and security that formerly existed.
>
> The principle of Celestial Marriage was considered the capstone of the Mormon religion. Only by practicing it would the highest exaltation in the Celestial Kingdom of God be obtained. According to the founders of the Mormon Church, the great purpose of this life is to prepare for the Celestial Kingdom in the world to come. The tremendous sacrifices of the Mormon people can only be understood if one keeps in mind this basic otherworld philosophy.

Although polygamy was especially difficult for women, it also required significant renunciations from the men who took on the responsibility of marrying plural wives. Since polygamists such as Franklin Richards were typically of a higher religious and economic status than the average member, they were frequently called away from home on church business for extended periods of time so that they had relatively little opportunity to be with their families. Furthermore, even when such Mormon polygamists were at home, they faced complex problems of family management that made significant expression of romantic love difficult. Like other serious polygamists, Franklin Richards had to try to avoid favoritism toward his plural wives if he were to maintain family harmony; he had to try to make an equitable distribution of his time, money, and affections when he was not away on church business. Jane Richards remembered how even her husband's most sincere efforts to treat his wives equally led to frustration and heartache. Even with the best of will, individuals who had been socialized into monogamous norms found the necessary transition to the new patterns of relationships in polygamy difficult.

Given the complexities of polygamy and the renunciations that it entailed, it is not surprising to find that plural marriage was far from universally practiced in the Great Basin. Using a sample of more than 6,000 prominent Mormon families, Stanley Snow Ivins estimated that at most only 15 to 20 percent were polygamous. Using a subsample of 1,784 polygamous men, Ivins found that a large majority, 66.3 percent, married only the one extra wife considered necessary for the highest exaltation in the celestial kingdom. Another 21.2 percent married three wives, and 6.7 percent went so far as to take four wives. The remaining group of less than 6 percent married five or more women. The limited incidence of polygamy may also have been due in part to the limited number of available women. At no time during Utah territorial history did the total number of women outnumber the men. Finally, according to Ivin's figures, the rate at which new polygamous marriages were established was always in an overall decline after the early 1856–57 peak. Sporadic increases in the rate of entry into polygamous marriages occurred during times of internal or external crisis, when polygamy served as a rallying point through which Mormons could prove their loyalty to the church, but continued exhortation and group pressure appear to have been necessary to sustain the practice.

Although plural marriage may well have been less than appealing to many men and women, such arrangements can be viewed in context as part of the necessary subordination of individual desires to long-term group goals that underlay Mormon success in the rapid settlement and development of the Intermountain West. Sexual impulses were sublimated into the arduous group enterprise of settling Utah and building up a Zion in the wilderness. As the historian Leonard Arrington has observed—"Only a high degree of religious devotion and discipline, superb organization and planning, made survival possible" in early Utah. Mormon men, particularly the leading Mormon men who were most often polygamists, had to be willing to move flexibly on church assignments as the demands of the group required. By partially breaking down exclusive bonds between a husband and wife, and by undercutting direct emotional involvement in family affairs in favor of church business, polygamy may well have contributed significantly to the long-range demands of centralized planning and the rapid establishment of a new religious and communal order.

II

Polygamy obviously required difficult renunciations and tended to undercut, though by no means to eliminate, emotional attachments based on romantic love. Yet polygamy also had certain positive features that gave it staying power. In a rather impressionistic survey of 110 plural marriages, the sociologist Kimball Young concluded that 53 percent were highly or reasonably successful, 25 percent were of moderate to doubtful success, and 23 percent were unsuccessful. Other evidence, which will be indicated below, also suggests positive features that could be present in polygamous marriages. What were some of the possible compensatory aspects of plural marriage for women, and how did they adapt to the demands of the new arrangements?

How did polygamy in some instances encourage women to develop self-reliance and independence?

The status advantages of being a plural wife have seldom been seriously considered. Non-Mormon critics of polygamy have almost invariably assumed that since they would have felt degraded under plural marriage, plural wives must also have felt degraded. Plausible though this might seem, little internal Mormon evidence supports such a view. Life certainly did hold special trials for plural wives, but at least until the 1880s, being a plural wife brought higher status through association with the most influential men and through a sense of serving as a religious and social model for others. First wives such as Jane Richards who married under monogamous expectations often had considerable difficulty in adjusting, but many plural wives had other reactions. In some cases, first wives actively encouraged a reluctant husband to take a plural wife so that they could both reach the highest state of exaltation in the afterlife or for other more pragmatic economic or personal considerations. Viewed as an honorable and desirable practice, plural marriage could give women a sense of pride and significance within the Mormon community.

The almost cosmic importance attached to home and family life was a major factor determining woman's status in the Great Basin region. Children were highly valued by Mormons. Like outside converts, children provided an essential work force to help in settling the new land and in building up an essentially agrarian economy in Utah. One polygamous wife emphasized the extreme importance that Mormons placed on childbearing and child rearing:

> Our children are considered stars in a mother's crown, and the more there are, if righteous, the more glory they will add to her and their father's eternal kingdom, for their parents on earth, if they continue righteous, will eventually become as Gods to reign in glory. Nothing but this, and a desire to please our Father in heaven, could tempt the majority of Mormon men or women either, to take upon themselves the burdens and responsibilities of plural marriage.

In terms strikingly familiar to those used by their Victorian contemporaries, Mormons stressed the positive and vital social role that women could play in the family and, by extension, in the larger community, which in the Mormon case was generally coterminous with the family. As one observer has noted, "Polygamy seemed to introduce no outstanding change in how Mormon women viewed themselves in their home role; the family was often treated in the same sentimental tones used by those who lauded the monogamous family.

The Mormon emphasis on the mother-child relationship served compensatory emotional functions for women whose husbands were often absent. Jane Richards, like many other plural wives, indicated that her primary emotional involvement was with her children, rather than with her husband. Similarly, Mrs. S. A. Cooks, who became a Mormon despite her aversion to polygamy, described how Heber C. Kimball's first wife, Vilate, had advised an unhappy plural wife that "her comfort must be wholly in her children; that she must lay aside wholly all interest or thought in what her husband was doing while he was away from her" and simply be as "pleased to see him when he came in as she was pleased to see any friend." In short, the woman was advised to maintain an emotional distance from her husband in order to avoid psychic hurt. Mrs. Cooks concluded: "Mrs. Kimball interested herself very much in the welfare of other's wives and their children to see that there was plenty of homespun clothing etc. for all; and set a noble example to others situated as she was."

The strong stress on ties of sisterhood between plural wives also served an important compensatory emotional function when the husband was absent. Informal female support networks and cooperation among women developed, especially during crisis periods such as those associated with childbirth, economic hardship, and bereavement. Mormon "sister-wives," as they were sometimes called, often literally were blood sisters. Of Vicky Burgess-Olson's sample, for instance, 31.2 percent of the plural marriages included at least one pair of sisters. Although such sororal polygamy was a departure from Old Testament standards and led to erroneous allegations that the Mormons practiced "incest," such arrangements made much practical sense. If two sisters were married to the same man, they could more easily adjust to each other in the marriage than total strangers could.

The popular semi-novelistic American stereotype of the plural wife as living in a Mormon "harem" had almost no basis in fact. Far from secluding women from the world, polygamy and the cohesive Mormon village community with which it was associated could lead some women to participate actively in the larger society. The non-Mormon historian Gail Casterline has noted:

> As in New England colonial families, the Mormon wife seemed to move with relative ease and frequency between home, neighborhood, and church; the Mormon village plan of settlement allowed a variety of social contacts outside the immediate family. Wives were not cloistered or excluded from the larger society as in a harem, although husbands did seem to have a possessive attitude on the issue of their womenfolk associating with Gentiles.

Women's independence was stimulated in a variety of ways by the social conditions of frontier Utah and by the practice of polygamy. With husbands frequently away on church missions, wives and their children tended to be thrown back on their own resources and on those of their immediate relatives and friends. Jane Richards said that her husband

> was away so much she learned to live comfortably without him, as she would tell him to tease him sometimes; and even now he is away two thirds of the time as she is the only wife in Ogden, so that she often forgets when he is home, and has even sat down at meals forgetting to call him. She says she always feels very badly about it when it happens, but that he was more necessary to her in her early life.

Mrs. Bancroft added: "And yet she is a very devoted wife, and he is remarkably attentive to her. To see them together I would never imagine either had a thought but the other shared.''

Other accounts also stressed this same tendency of polygamy practice to encourage women's independence. After stating that ''Plural marriage destroys the oneness of course'' and that it ''is a great trial of feelings,'' Mary Horne noted that the practice got her away from being ''so bound and so united to her husband that she could do nothing without him.'' She became ''freer and can do herself individually things she never could have attempted before; and work out her individual character as separate from her husband.'' Evidently in some cases women also were grateful for the possibility polygamy offered for freedom from male sexual demands; as Mary J. Tanner noted: ''It is a physical blessing to weakly women.'' And the feisty Martha Hughes Cannon, who was the first woman state senator in the United States and the fourth wife of a polygamist, argued that a plural wife was in a better position than a single wife: ''If her husband has four wives, she had three weeks of freedom every single month.''

While this might be the kind of ''freedom'' that some wives would wish to be freed *from,* it does suggest how polygamy and the exigencies of life in the Great Basin region could force women into new roles and break down certain sex stereotypes, at least temporarily. In the absence of their husbands, women and their children ran farms and businesses. Some early census reports even went so far as to identify plural wives as ''heads of households.'' Burgess-Olson's sample showed that in polygamous marriages, husbands and wives exercised approximately equal responsibilities in financial management, while in her monogamous sample, men held greater control. By the late nineteenth century a relatively large class of professional women, many of them plural wives, had developed in Utah. Women dominated the medical profession, for instance, and a sizeable number worked as teachers and writers.

Brigham Young and other early church leaders recognized the necessity of making use of female talent in establishing and maintaining the group in the sometimes hostile environment of the Great Basin. Mormon leaders encouraged education for women from the very early settlement period, as indicated by the establishment of the University of Deseret as a coeducational institution in 1850. Women voted earlier in Utah than in any other state or territory in the United States, including Wyoming. And, somewhat ironically in view of the non-Mormon attacks on the degradation polygamy supposedly caused women, the efforts of Mormon women in the 1870s and 1880s to organize themselves to support plural marriage against external attacks served as a significant means of increasing their political awareness and involvement.

One major forum for women's expression in the church was the Relief Society. Originally founded in 1842, the Relief Society was organized ''under the priesthood after a pattern of the priesthood'' to support a variety of activities, including the building of a temple, charitable work, and cultural betterment. During the troubled period that followed Joseph Smith's death, the Relief Society became largely inactive, but with the reestablishment of the society in the mid-1850s under the leadership of Eliza R. Snow, it went on to play an important role in Utah economic, social, and cultural life.

Perhaps the most impressive achievement of the women of Utah in the late nineteenth century was the publication of the *Woman's Exponent*. Although it was not officially sponsored or financed by the church, this largely woman-managed, -supported, and -produced newspaper served as the major voice for Mormon women's concerns during its publication between 1872 and 1914. The *Exponent* was the second periodical expressly for women to appear in the trans-Mississippi West. A respectable and well-produced periodical by any standards, the *Exponent* spoke highly for the literacy and intelligence of its women contributors and designers. The wide-ranging historical and literary concerns of this publication were by no means limited to sectarian matters.

As suggested by its masthead slogan: "The Rights of the Women of Zion, The Rights of the Women of All Nations," the *Woman's Exponent* provided an important forum for the discussion of many problems of "woman's sphere." Expressing an almost feminist awareness at times, the *Exponent* devoted much attention to the universally inequitable position of women in politics, education, and the professions. Even marriage was not put forward as an absolute imperative for women. In the *Exponent*'s wide-ranging discussion of issues, only polygamy, then one of the key elements of Mormon self-definition as a group, failed to receive a critique. Overall, the *Woman's Exponent* portrayed Mormon women as individuals of character, intelligence, and high aspirations. It served an important identity-building function and helped to reinforce pride and unity among the women of the church.

As Casterline observed:

> The reinstitution of the ancient custom of polygamy may have in its own subtle ways served as a liberating force for women. This may have occurred by default, with restless or dissatisfied plural wives looking for places to direct their energies, or it may have occurred through the necessity of a wife's supporting her family. Some women may have welcomed polygamy as a great boon, as it decreased some of the demands and divided the duties of the wife role, allowing them more time to develop personal talents. By these quirks in its machinery, plural marriage did in some cases provide a working method for women to achieve independence from men.

III

Despite certain positive or at least mitigating features such as those mentioned above, polygamy was obviously a more demanding way to organize marriage than monogamy. Even under the best of circumstances, developing and sustaining an optimal relationship among husband, wives, and children in polygamous families was difficult. How did Mormon families deal with the inevitable tensions that arose in plural marriages? Although the studies of James E. Hulett, Jr., Kimball Young, and Vicky Burgess-Olson reveal great differences in the ways conflict situations were mananged in both monogamous and polygamous families, the general rule was to try to deal with problems within the home as much as possible. As Jane Richards noted: "It is making confidants of other women in their domestic disturbances that has brought about most of the trouble in polygamy, and the less people gossip, the better off they are." In the practice of polygamy, as in other aspects of social life in Utah, great stress was placed on unity and consensus, on the avoidance of public expressions of hostility. This emphasis may well help account for the impressive degree of external order and social harmony described by many of the more open-minded visitors to Utah in the nineteenth century.

Even with good will and sincere effort, attempts to salvage a relationship could fail. In such cases the possibility of separation or divorce always remained. Jane Richards was quite frank in noting, for instance, that when her husband first talked with her in Illinois about the possibility of taking another wife, she told him that he should do what he felt he had to do and that "if she found they [she and the new wife] could not live without quarreling, she should leave him." This never became necessary for her, but she noted that others had taken such steps: "If a marriage is unhappy, the parties can go to any of the council and present their difficulties and are readily granted a divorce."

How representative were Jane Richards's informal observations on nineteenth-century Mormon attitudes toward divorce? This topic has only recently begun to be investigated, but a few preliminary observations may be made. One initial point of reference is Utah territorial divorce policy. The Utah divorce law of February 4, 1852, was one of the most liberal in the country. For instance, a divorce could be granted not only to a person who "is a resident of the Territory" but also to a person who "wishes to become one." Presumably this proviso allowed the Mormon church flexibility in dealing rapidly with converts who had separated from an unbelieving spouse and who needed to be reintegrated as quickly as possible into the new Mormon society. In addition to the usual causes, a divorce could be granted to the plaintiff in cases in which the defendant was guilty of "absenting himself without reasonable cause for more than one year." If liberally applied, such a provision could be used to terminate unsatisfactory relationships in which missionaries were gone for extended periods of time. Finally, the territorial law contained an omnibus clause allowing divorce "when it shall be made to appear to the satisfaction of the court, that the parties cannot live in peace and union together, and that their welfare requires a separation."

The Utah divorce law cannot necessarily be assumed to represent Mormon church policy, since marriage and divorce—particularly polygamous marriage and divorce, which were not directly recognized in territorial law—were handled primarily through church courts and procedures. Instead, the primary function of the divorce law probably was to provide maximum flexibility for Mormons in handling their own unorthodox arrangements. What, then, was the Mormon church's policy on divorce? The official stand was a highly complex one. In theory, divorce was strongly discouraged. Marriage was viewed in the light of eternity as a vital part of life that brought out the finest aspects of human relationships. Brigham Young and other early leaders repeatedly inveighed against divorce, particularly when requested by the man. Using rather salty language, Young could suggest, for example, that one man had made his bed and would have to lie in it. Declarations such as the following were typical: "It is not right for men to divorce their wives the way they do. I am determined that if men do not stop divorcing their wives, I will stop sealing."

Yet, if men were discouraged from divorcing their wives, women were given remarkable freedom in seeking a divorce for themselves in unsatisfactory situations. Young himself once publicly offered to give a divorce to any of his wives who did not want to live with him any longer. He could declare that "he liked a woman to live with her husband as long as she could bear with him and if her life became too burdensome then leave and get a divorce." In an important sermon in the Salt Lake Tabernacle on October 8, 1861, Brigham Young further developed the argument about when a woman could leave a man lawfully. He said that if a woman became alienated in her feelings and affections from her husband, then it was his duty to give her a bill of divorce and set her free. Men must not have sexual relations with their wives when they were thus alienated. Children born of such alienated unions were properly seen as "bastards," not the product of a full marriage relationship.

This line of argument is strikingly similar to the 1842 argument put out in Illinois in *The Peace Maker*, the first defense of polygamy ever printed under Mormon auspices. According to that pamphlet, whose authorship and significance have been hotly debated, the only "biblical" (i.e., legitimate) grounds for divorce was the alienation of a wife's affections from her husband. If a man became dissatisfied with his wife he could not legitimately divorce her if she remained loyal to him, since that would be an irresponsible shirking of family duties. Instead, his option in such a case was to take additional wives, while maintaining the first and her children. This approach is essentially the same as early Utah practice. Women had the primary initiative in determining when to terminate a relationship, while the husband could not easily divorce his wife if she were opposed. No stigma was attached to the remarriage of a divorced woman; indeed, such remarriage was normally assumed. Thus, in Utah, women could find through easy divorce and remarriage the opportunity for what amounted to a sort of de facto serial polygamy (though Mormon writings never spoke in such terms), while their husbands were allowed to take additional wives if they wished.

The relationship of polygamy and divorce in early Utah may also be easier to understand as a result of the recent recovery of records of 1,645 divorces granted during the Brigham Young period (1847–77). Although these records have not yet been thoroughly analyzed, the bulk of the cases appear to have involved plural marriages. Since the entire population of Utah numbered only 86,786 in 1870 (with a high percentage of the population consisting of unmarried children and youths), the divorce rate might appear rather high. Support for such a conclusion is also suggested by D. Michael Quinn's listing of Mormon church leaders and their wives between 1832 and 1932. A simple analysis of his data shows that the 72 church leaders who practiced plural marriage had a total of 391 wives, with 54 divorces, 26 separations, and 1 annulment. For perspective, one should note that at least some of these divorces were those of apparently nonconjugal wives whose marital ties were only symbolic. The extent to which the divorce situation in Utah and surrounding areas of Mormon settlement differed from that of other frontier areas also needs to be investigated.

To understand the significance of this data on divorce, it must be placed within the larger context of the development of plural marriage and other early Mormon social institutions. Plural marriage appears never to have become fully institutionalized during the relatively brief period when it was publicly practiced in Utah. Joseph Smith's revelatory mandate promulgating polygamy in 1843 had required that polygamy be introduced, but it did not specify exactly how it was to be practiced after it was introduced. Later Mormon leaders apparently also claimed no special inspiration on exactly how the system was to be regulated, except to continue to insist, as Joseph Smith had, that all plural marriages must be sanctioned and sealed by the central church authorities.

The wide variation in polygamy practice has been noted by scholars. James E. Hulett, Jr., one of the earliest serious students of Mormon polygamy, observed that he had "expected to find a variety of behavior but not so great a variety." No fully standardized patterns of handling the needs of polygamous families for things such as shelter, food, clothing, and amusement appear to have developed, although there were tendencies toward such standardization. For example, plural wives sometimes lived together under one roof, sometimes had separate houses adjoining each other, and sometimes lived in entirely different locations. Hulett argued that Mormon society of the period continued to remain basically monogamous in its norms and that "except for the broad outlines, the local culture provided no efficient and detailed techniques for control of the polygamous family; each family in a sense had to develop its own culture." Although Hulett's sample was primarily taken from the period of extreme stress in the late nineteenth century when polygamy was under heavy attack, scholars who have focused on the period when polygamy was more openly practiced have also found significant variation in the ways polygamous families were organized.

The primary reason that polygamy never became fully standardized in Utah was the short period of time that it existed before the intense anti-polygamy persecution of the late nineteenth century led the Mormon church to discontinue the practice. Had there been greater time for the new cultural patterns to develop free of external pressure, plural marriage probably would have continued to adapt itself to the changing conditions of the Great Basin region. Just how the new marriage practices would eventually have stabilized will now never be known, however. After the mainstream of the Mormon church broke decisively with polygamy practice at the turn of the century, a small number of dissidents did continue to practice polygamy, but the church as a whole moved on to find new ways of expressing its underlying family ideals through monogamous marriage. Today, somewhat paradoxically, Mormons are among the most "traditional" of any group in their attitudes toward family life and the role of women.

IV

What is the significance of this extraordinary nineteenth-century Mormon experiment with plural marriage? Was the effort simply a freakish American sideshow, a rather unpleasant and unappealing aberration, or does it raise larger issues that are of concern today?

As the largest and best sustained attempt in nineteenth-century America to create an alternative to monogamous marriage and family life, Mormon polygamy does suggest larger issues worthy of further exploration. At the most basic level, investigations such as those of Ivins, Burgess-Olson, Smith and Kunz, and others are needed to show how monogamous and polygamous Mormon marriages in early Utah differed from each other. To what extent were the distinctive features of nineteenth-century Mormon family life due to the existence of polygamy and to what extent were they a product of the broader Mormon drive for cultural and religious autonomy? How did the life experiences of monogamous wives differ from those of first wives or of subsequent wives in polygamous families?

A second area worthy of further investigation is a comparison of the experiences of Mormon plural wives with the experiences of other women on the frontier or in the larger Victorian society. Recent research by Maureen Ursenbach Beecher, for instance, suggests that at least in the economic sphere, Mormon women were largely indistinguishable from other women in the frontier West. Similarly, Mormon women appear to have been remarkably closely in touch with general currents of thought and practice in Victorian society. At times, in fact, they seem to have been in advance of popular trends. In what ways were Mormon women in contact with the larger society, and what role did polygamy play in that contact?

Finally, Mormon polygamy of the nineteenth century raises comparative and cross-cultural questions of much significance for the present. The problems of women acting as heads of single-parent families, for example, bear much resemblance to the problems of women in some polygamous families. The issue of easy divorce and its effect on family life are also worthy of comparison. And, of course, the Mormon experience provides an American example of polygamy that could be compared with polygamy as it functions in non-Western societies today, as studied by anthropologists such as Remi Clignet.

These and other questions may fruitfully be investigated by using the nineteenth-century Mormon experience as a reference point. Perry Miller could as easily have been speaking of the Mormons as of the New England Puritans when he wrote of their experiment as an "ideal laboratory": "It was relatively isolated, the people were comparatively homogenous and the forces of history played upon it in ways that can more satisfactorily be traced than in more complex societies. Here is an opportunity, as nearly perfect as the student is apt to find, for extracting certain generalizations about the relationship of thought or ideas to communal experience." Scholars have only begun to make use of the rich Mormon experience to understand the nature and significance of women's varied experiences in nineteenth-century America.

Y *F U R T H E R   R E A D I N G*

William A. Bowen, *The Willamette Valley: Migration and Settlement on the Oregon Frontier* (1978)
Claudia Bushman, ed., *Mormon Sisters: Women in Early Utah* (1976)
Jessie L. Embry, *Mormon Polygamous Families* (1987)
John Mack Faragher, *Sugar Creek: Life on the Illinois Prairie* (1986)
Lawrence Foster, *Religion and Sexuality* (1981)
Boyd Gibbons, "The Itch to Move West: Life and Death on the Oregon Trail," *National Geographic,* 170 (1986), 147–77
LeRoy R. Hafen and Ann W. Hafen, *Handcarts to Zion* (1960)
Harlan Hague, *The Road to California: The Search for a Southern Overland Route, 1540–1848* (1978)
Robert V. Hine, *Community on the American Frontier: Separate but Not Alone* (1980)
Julie Roy Jeffrey, *Frontier Women* (1979)
David Rich Lewis, "Argonauts and the Overland Trail Experience," *Western Historical Quarterly,* 16 (1985), 285–305
Merrill J. Mattes, *The Great Platte River Road: The Covered Wagon Mainline via Fort Kearney to Fort Laramie* (1969)
Ruth B. Moynihan, "Children and Young People on the Overland Trail," *Western Historical Quarterly,* 6 (1975), 279–92
Sandra L. Myres, *Ho for California! Women's Overland Diaries From the Huntington Library* (1980)
———, *Westering Women and the Frontier Experience* (1982)
Linda Kay Newell and Valeen Tippetts Avery, *Mormon Enigma: Emma Hale Smith* (1984)
David M. Potter, ed., *Trail to California: The Overland Journal of Vincent Geiger and Wakeman Bryarly* (1945)
John Phillip Reid, *Law For the Elephant: Property and Social Behavior on the Overland Trail* (1980)
Glenda Riley, *Women and Indians on the Frontier* (1984)
Lillian Schlissel, *Women's Diaries of the Westward Journey* (1982)
Wallace Stegner, *The Gathering of Zion: The Story of the Mormon Trail* (1964)
Annie Clark Tanner, *A Mormon Mother* (1976)
Richard S. Van Wagoner, *Mormon Polygamy: A History* (1986)

Miners and Cowboys

Y

The Overland Trails and Mormon Utah may tell a tale of women, men, and families in the West, but the mining rushes and cattle drives are overwhelmingly a story of masculine endeavor. Although women and children were not absent from ranch houses and mining camps, the popular image of the lives of western miners and cowboys centers almost exclusively on males. It would be a mistake, however, to see these male figures as white Anglo-Americans. Western miners and cowboys were racially and culturally pluralistic. The California gold fields in the 1850s attracted an abundance of Asians, Polynesians, native Americans, Afro-Americans, Latin Americans, and Europeans. The cowboys of the 1870s and 1880s were black (Afro-American), bronze (Mexican and Mexican-American), white (Anglo-American), or very white (British).

A hearty spirit of economic opportunity—wildcat capitalism at its most vigorous—created the mining rushes and cattle drives. Nonetheless, only a few cattle barons and mining tycoons emerged with fortunes made in the West. Most cowboys and miners became wage laborers. Each group had significant episodes of labor organizing and armed clashes, although the 1883 cowboy strike in the Texas Panhandle did not approach the violence at the Coeur d'Alene, Idaho, mines in 1892 or the labor war that raged in 1913–1914 around the mines at Ludlow, Colorado.

The status of miners and cowboys as laborers, combined with each group's racial and ethnic diversity, calls up questions of economic exploitation and social discrimination. Ultimately we must wonder how good a life most cowboys or miners enjoyed in the West.

Y *DOCUMENTS*

The episodes described in the first three documents provide vivid glimpses into miners' lives. In the first document, dated 1848, Henry Bigler, a Mormon employed by John Sutter to help build a mill, gives a detailed memoir of the initial discovery of gold that brought a worldwide rush of miners to California. Granville Stuart, who went on to be an important cattleman in Montana, spent several months in the California gold fields in 1852–1853. The second selection is his account of how newcomers got started panning for gold. Note his description of an outbreak of violence between Chinese miners and California Indians. The third document, comprising the report of the Chinese consul at New York and a memorial from 559 Chinese miners, describes the killings that occurred in Rock Springs, Wyoming, in 1885 when white miners rampaged against Chinese residents of the mining town.

The final two documents present information about cattle raising and a cowboy's life. The first of these is an excerpt from James S. Brisbin's 1881 book of advice, *The Beef Bonanza, or How to Get Rich on the Plains,* in which he boasted that high profits might be gained from investing in cattle. His book is only one of myriad publications, past and present, that have advised Americans on how to make a fortune. Obviously, both cattlemen and miners were willing to grab for wealth. Charles Siringo was a working Texas cowboy who never became wealthy, although, like Henry Bigler, Granville Stuart, and the Chinese miners of Rock Springs, he had his dreams. Siringo wrote several books about his life as a cowboy and about his later career as a Pinkerton detective. The last document is an excerpt from his first book, *A Texas Cow Boy, or Fifteen Years on the Hurricane Deck of A Spanish Pony* (1885). It describes his interaction with black horsemen and cowboys, as well as his preparation for a cattle drive north.

Henry Bigler's Account of Gold at Sutter's Mill, 1848

My journal tells me it was on the afternoon of the twenty-fourth day of January, 1848, while I was at my drill busy preparing to put in a blast when Marshall as usual went to see Wimmer and the Indians who were at work towards the lower end of the race. Then he sent a young Indian for Brown to send him a plate. At this time Brown and one of the Indians were whipsawing in the mill yard. Brown was the top sawyer. He jumped from the saw pit, remarking at the same time that he wondered what Marshall wanted with a tin plate and went to the shanty and gave the Indian a plate. Just before we quit work, he [Marshall] came up and said he believed he had found a gold mine. Some said there was no such good luck, but very little anyway was said at that time about it. He did not show us anything. Neither did he say he had any, but went off up to his own house on the side of the mountain. But before we went to bed, he came in and commenced talking with us, saying he believed he had found gold near the lower end of the race and, if I remember right, he told us that he tried to melt some and could not do it, and he spoke to Brown and me saying, "Brown I want you and Bigler to shut down the head gate early in the morning; throw in a little sawdust, rotten leaves, and dirt and make all tight and I'll see what there is in the morning."

Accordingly the next morning we did as he told us while Marshall went alone down in the race, and we went in for our breakfast, and after we had breakfasted and come out, Brown to his sawing, Stephens to hewing, I to my drilling, every man at his own job, Marshall came up carrying his old white hat in his arm looking wonderfully pleased and good natured. There was a heavy smile on his countenance. Some of the boys said they knew in a minute as soon as they saw him that something was the matter. As he came up he said, "Boys, by G———d I believe I have found a gold mine" and set his hat on the work bench that stood in the mill yard. Every man gathered instantly around to see what he had and there, sure enough, on the top of the hat crown (knocked in a little) lay the pure stuff; how much I do not know, perhaps half an ounce, maybe more, from the smallest particle up to the size of a kernel of wheat or larger. The most of it was in very thin small flakes. The coarse were more round and in little cubes. In fact in most all shapes. Every man fully expressed his conviction believing firmly it was gold although none of us had ever seen gold before in its native state. Azariah Smith pulled out a five-dollar piece (part of his soldier money) and we compared the dust with it. There seemed to be no difference as to color or weight, only that the coin looked a little brighter and rather more white. This we accounted for because of the alloy in it. Marshall turned about, and we all followed him, and in looking close, we could find particles here and there on the base rock and in seams and crevices. Conjectures were it must be rich, and from that time the fever set in and gold was on the brain. We, however, only spent a short time when every man went to work at his regular day labor; but gold was the talk.

Granville Stuart in the California Gold Camps, 1852–1853

We spent a week at Sam Neal's ranch in the Sacramento valley, but as every meal we ate cost each of us one dollar James and I determined to leave and go up into the mountains to the gold mines. We went sixteen miles up in the foothills to a little village on the ridge between the west branch of Feather river and Little Butte creek. This little village was known as Butte Mills, because there was a sawmill near by run by water power from Little Butte creek, but it soon got its proper and well deserved name of Dog Town, for although there were only ten houses, there were sixteen fully developed dogs. From the edge of town one looked down into the West branch, where its waters flowed in a cañon a thousand feet deep, which in the course of about a million years it had worn down through talcose slate. This stream had been rich in placer gold, and was still being worked by many miners. James and I looked it over, but it was all claimed, and as we knew absolutely nothing about mining, we thought we had best hunt for some place that was easier to work than a small river that was full of large boulders, over which the water dashed and foamed.

We became acquainted with two young men, Wyatt M. Smith, eighteen years of age and Fountain J. Sweeney, age nineteen years, and being about our ages we were soon fast friends. They told us about six miles up Little Butte creek, there were some gulches (ravines) known as "Tom Neal's dry diggins," that they thought were rich, and they proposed to us to go up there and go in with them in mining. They had been in California for about a year, and already knew a little about how to mine. We thought it a good chance to learn from them and accepted their kind offer. They already had some tools, and a part of a kitchen outfit to cook with. James and I bought some additional things and rolling up our blankets, with an extra shirt apiece, took them on our backs and started for the "diggins." Thus we entered upon a new, strange, and untried life. . . .

At Dog Town we knew a man who in daytime followed the occupation of a crevice miner, and at night that of a professional gambler. In the morning he would put a little lunch in his pocket and taking a small pick and a gold pan, and crevice spoon, he would go down into the deep cañon of the West branch and carefully scan its shores along near the water; searching for the fissures or cracks in the bedrock which often contained sand and gravel forced into them in past ages, and in among which was usually considerable gold. When he found one of these crevices he would dig its contents up loose with his little pick and then scrape it all out carefully with his crevice spoon, and put it into the shallow circular iron pan, always called, "a little gold pan," which he would then take to the edge of the water, and squatting down begin to wash the sand and fine gravel by a circular motion that would gradually carry it out over the edge of the pan, leaving the gold in the bottom. He told us he had been crevicing for over two years and that he had learned where to look for favorable places to hunt for rich crevices, but was not always successful. We asked him what were his usual gains in a day. He said that the first year he would frequently find two or three ounces of gold a day and some lucky day considerably more, but for the past year he could only average one ounce a day for the mines were now more carefully worked. One day he returned to town about noon and joyfully showed me a beautiful bright nugget of pure gold that he had just found. It weighed six and one-fourth ounces and was worth one hundred dollars. He said it was the largest nugget that he had ever found, but that he had found several of from one to five ounces. . . .

In July, 1853, some Concow Indians, whose village was over on the North fork of Feather river, came over to the West branch and killed two Chinamen who were mining there and wounded two others. These Indians, in common with all those living on the western slope of the Sierra Nevada, were not allowed by the miners to have firearms and the Chinamen were killed with bows and arrows. Considerable numbers of Chinamen were by this time in California, mostly all engaged in mining on claims worked out and abandoned by white men. The Indians disliked them because they thought them other kinds of Indians, but I never heard of them killing any others, although they often robbed them. The West branch Chinamen brought their dead up to Dog Town for burial and their wounded excited much feeling against the Indians. The result was that the white miners offered to go and drive the murderers out of that part of the mines, if the Chinamen would go with them and carry their food and blankets, which they gladly agreed to do. My recollection is that sixteen well armed men went, accompanied by twelve Chinamen carrying food and blankets. The Indians discovered their approach and fled like deer, the miners firing on them as they ran. I think only two were killed and several wounded. A few of the Chinamen carried shot guns and when the miniature battle began the men said the Chinamen were widely excited and would shut both eyes and fire both barrels of their shot guns at once, the recoil nearly knocking them down, while the buckshot from their guns went tearing through the tops of the oak trees. The men said they were in greater danger from the Chinamen than from the Indians, because they did not know how to handle firearms. The little army was absent three days. I thought at the time that most of them were ashamed of the raid after it was over. The Indians moved and I never heard of them making any trouble afterwards. Brother James happened to be in Dog Town when the foray started and went with it. I was up at our diggings and knew nothing of it until he got back. The grateful Chinamen sent to San Francisco and presented each of their white allies with a large embroidered red silk handkerchief and a quart of brandy.

In the winter of 1852 after the rains began, the roads became so bad and the Sacramento valley was mostly flooded so that no food supplies could be brought up to Dog Town for over a month. Fortunately there was food enough of all kinds except flour. We had none of that for over two weeks, but we had beans and bacon and squirrels. When the pack train got in with the flour the packers swore that they would not make another trip that winter and demanded fifty dollars per one hundred pounds. We thought it well to buy a sack (fifty pound sacks were unknown until three years later) rather than to do without for the remainder of the winter and did so. By the time we had eaten half of it two pack trains loaded with flour arrived and the price fell to twelve cents a pound. Nearly all the flour used in California that winter came from Chile, South America. It had a yellow color and was first class. Large quantities of beans were also brought from there. In fact if these two articles had not been brought from Chile everybody would have been reduced to meat straight.

In the spring of 1853 we grew tired of our diggings because we were entirely dependent on the rains for water and determined to seek a better place to mine. So James, Rezin Anderson, and I took our respective rolls of bedding on our backs and our rifles on our shoulders and started for Rabbit creek in Sierra county. We went by way of Morrison's ravine, then across Feather river at the ferry, then up the slope between Feather and Yuba rivers, stopping one night at Forbestown, first known as "Boles Dry Diggins," then up the ridge to "Mountain cottage," where we entered the snow of the Sierra Nevadas. We found the snow constantly becoming deeper, but here was a well beaten pack trail.

We arrived at Rabbit creek when the snow was sixteen feet deep. All the miners' cabins had steps cut in the snow down to the doors. There being no stoves, all cabins had open fireplaces, the chimneys of which were made to extend six or seven feet above the roof, so as to get to the surface of the snow. These chimneys gave plenty of air and the snow kept it so warm that the doors were open all day. The mines were all deep gravel channels from twenty-five to one hundred and twenty-five feet deep on the mountain spurs and ridges, and were worked by hydraulic pipes in which the water was piped down into the cuts and thrown against the banks which were composed of white quartz gravel and sand. These immense gravel beds were once ancient river beds before the mountains and ridges were upheaved, and all contained enough fine gold to pay richly for washing them away by hydraulic process. Through lines of sluice boxes the sand and gravel was dumped into the surrounding cañons which drained into the North fork of the Yuba river. Here the claims were two hundred feet square. No man could have more than one claim. All the claims along the water front were being worked so we located ours further back, but had to wait for those in front to wash their claims before we could work ours. Every mining district in California in those days had their own laws made by the miners and by them enforced. As we could not work our mines at once we went to work in a nearby mine where the gravel was forty feet deep. Part of us worked on day shift and the others on night shift.

We would work all week, but on Saturday night the miners would get up a stag dance, there being very few women in the camp. There were two fiddlers, one played first violin and the other played second. The first player was left handed but he was a good one and such fun as we would have.

Chinese Accounts of the
Killings at Rock Springs, 1885

CHINESE CONSULATE-GENERAL,
San Francisco, Cal., October 5, 1885.
Sir: I have the honor to state that in compliance with your excellency's instructions, I proceeded with Col. F. A. Bee, Chinese counsul at San Francisco, and Mr. Tseng Hoy, interpreter, to Rock Springs, where we arrived on the 18th September, 1885, for the purpose of investigating the present condition of our countrymen in the latter place, and of ascertaining the facts connected with the recent riot that took place there against them.

As soon as we reached Rock Springs we ordered the remains of those Chinese killed in the riot to be disinterred and examined. We had fourteen coffins dug up, on opening which we found some bodies entire, some parts of bodies, the bones of separate bodies, and promiscuous heaps of bones; and we also dug up the remains of one without a coffin. Inquiring of the coroner at Rock Springs, he stated that since the 3d of September he had examined and interred nineteen persons, and I found that the Union Pacific Railroad Company had interred the remains of two. Besides five entire bodies, the remains of eight others were recognizable, while the bones of eight others were found wrapped up in separate bundles. We had, therefore, exhumed in all the remains of twenty one persons. . . .

Omitting those whose wounds have healed since the riot, I find that there are fifteen Chinese more or less severely wounded, several of whom, it is feared, will die, and several be disabled for life. . . .

With reference to the property destroyed by the mob, I find that every one of the surviving Chinese has been rendered penniless by the cruel attack. There are three reasons why the Chinese so completely lost their property: 1st, most of them when fleeing had no time to gather up their money, and those that did carry money with them were forcibly deprived of it by the mob; 2d, what they left in their houses was either plundered or burnt; 3d, the huts which they built for themselves were completely destroyed.

Since the riot took place it has been impossible for them to secure even a torn sheet or any article of clothing to protect them from the cold, or even the crumbs from the table to satisfy their hunger, or even a plank or mat to rest their bodies on. These poor creatures, numbering hundreds, are all hungry and clothed in rags. They look worn out and frightened, and most of them forlorn and absent-minded. Words fail to give an idea of their sufferings, and their appearance is a sad one to human eyes to witness.

Upon making inquiries as to the past, I found that the Chinese so savagely and unmercifully deprived of their property had been in Rock Springs, some for over ten years, others for a shorter time, for the purpose of working in mines or on railroads. Some of the Chinese locating at Rock Springs were afterwards joined by their fathers, brothers, or other relations, all settling themselves there as colonists, while others came with their goods for the purpose of peddling or trading. In the course of time they had built for themselves more than seventy huts, and the Union Pacific Railroad Company had also built more than thirty camp houses for its employés, thus forming quite a town. This town is now nothing but a mass of ruins.

The total value of the property lost belonging to over seven hundred persons is only about $147,000, this being an average of only a little more than $200 for each. I have concluded that no one has made any fraudulent claim.

. . . I beg to inclose for your consideration . . . a copy of the memorial addressed to me while at Rock Springs by five hundred and fifty-nine Chinese.

I am, your obedient servant,

HUANG SIH CHUEN,
Chinese Consul at New York.

ROCK SPRINGS, WYO., *September 18, 1885.*

Hon. HUANG SIH CHUEN,
Chinese Consul:

YOUR HONOR: We, the undersigned, have been in Rock Springs, Wyoming Territory, for periods ranging from one to fifteen years, for the purpose of working on the railroads and in the coal mines.

Up to the time of the recent troubles we had worked along with the white men, and had not had the least ill-feeling against them. The officers of the companies employing us treated us and the white men kindly, placing both races on the same footing and paying the same wages.

Several times we had been approached by the white men and requested to join them in asking the companies for an increase in the wages of all, both Chinese and white men. We inquired of them what we should do if the companies refused to grant an increase. They answered that if the companies would not increase our wages we should all strike, then the companies would be obliged to increase our wages. To this we dissented, wherefore we excited their animosity against us.

During the past two years there has been in existence in "Whitemen's Town," Rock Springs, an organization composed of white miners, whose object was to bring about the expulsion of all Chinese from the Territory. To them or to their object we have paid no attention. About the month of August of this year notices were posted up, all the way from Evanston to Rock Springs, demanding the expulsion of the Chinese, &c. On the evening of September 1, 1885, the bell of the building in which said organization meets rang for a meeting. It was rumored on that night that threats had been made against the Chinese.

On the morning of September 2, a little past 7 o'clock, more than ten white men, some in ordinary dress and others in mining suits, ran into Coal-pit No. 6, loudly declaring that the Chinese should not be permitted to work there. The Chinese present reasoned with them in a few words, but were attacked with murderous weapons, and three of their number wounded. The white foreman of the coal-pit, hearing of the disturbance, ordered all to stop work for the time being.

After the work had stopped, all the white men in and near Coal-pit No. 6 began to assemble by the dozen. They carried fire-arms, and marched to Rock Springs by way of the railroad from Coal-pit No. 6, and crossing the railroad bridge, went directly to "Whitemen's Town." All this took place before 10 o'clock a. m. We now heard the bell ringing for a meeting at the white men's organization building. Not long after all the white men came out of that building, most of them assembling in the bar-rooms, the crowds meanwhile growing larger and larger.

About 2 o'clock in the afternoon a mob, divided into two gangs, came toward "Chinatown," one gang coming by way of the plank bridge, and the other by way of the railroad bridge. The gang coming by way of the railroad bridge was the larger, and was subdivided into many squads, some of which did not cross the bridge, but remained standing on the side opposite to "Chinatown;" others that had already crossed the bridge stood on the right and left at the end of it. Several squads marched up the hill behind Coal-pit No. 3. One squad remained at Coal-shed No. 3, and another at the pump-house. The squad that remained at the pump-house fired the first shot, and the squad that stood at Coal-shed No. 3 immediately followed their example and fired. The Chinese by name of Lor Sun Kit was the first person shot, and fell to the ground. At that time the Chinese began to realize that the mob were bent on killing. The Chinese, though greatly alarmed, did not yet begin to flee.

Soon after, the mob on the hill behind Coal-pit No. 3 came down from the hill, and joining the different squads of the mob, fired their weapons and pressed on to Chinatown.

The gang that were at the plank bridge also divided into several squads, pressing near and surrounding "Chinatown." One squad of them guarded the plank bridge in order to cut off the retreat of the Chinese.

Not long after it was everywhere reported that a Chinese named Leo Dye Bah, who lived in the western part of "Chinatown," was killed by a bullet, and that another named Yip Ah Marn, resident in the eastern end of the town, was likewise killed. The Chinese now, to save their lives, fled in confusion in every direction, some going up the hill behind Coal-pit No. 3, others along the foot of the hill where Coal-pit No. 4 is; some from the eastern end of the town fled across Bitter Creek to the opposite hill, and others from the western end by the foot of the hill on the right of Coal-pit No. 5. The mob were now coming in the three directions, namely, the east and west sides of the town and from the wagon road.

Whenever the mob met a Chinese they stopped him, and pointing a weapon at him, asked him if he had any revolver, and then approaching him they searched his person, robbing him of his watch or any gold or silver that he might have about him, before letting him go. Some of the rioters would let a Chinese go after depriving him of all his gold and silver, while another Chinese would be beaten with the butt ends of the weapons before being let go. Some of the rioters, when they could not stop a Chinese, would shoot him dead on the spot, and then search and rob him. Some would overtake a Chinese, throw him down and search and rob him before they would let him go. Some of the rioters would not fire their weapons, but would only use the butt ends to beat the Chinese with. Some would not beat a Chinese, but rob him of whatever he had and let him go, yelling to him to go quickly. Some, who took no part either in beating or robbing the Chinese, stood by, shouting loudly and laughing and clapping their hands.

There was a gang of women that stood at the "Chinatown" end of the plank bridge and cheered; among the women, two of them each fired successive shots at the Chinese. This was done about a little past 3 o'clock p. m. . . .

Some of the rioters went off toward the railroad of Coal-pit No. 6, others set fire to the Chinese houses. Between 4 o'clock and a little past 9 o'clock p. m. all the camp houses belonging to the coal company and the Chinese huts had been burned down completely, only one of the company's camp houses remaining. Several of the camp houses near Coal-pit No. 6 were also burned, and the three Chinese huts there were also burned. All the Chinese houses burned numbered seventy-nine.

Some of the Chinese were killed at the bank of Bitter Creek, some near the railroad bridge, and some in "Chinatown." After having been killed, the dead bodies of some were carried to the burning buildings and thrown into the flames. Some of the Chinese who had hid themselves in the houses were killed and their bodies burned; some, who on account of sickness could not run, were burned alive in the houses. One Chinese was killed in "Whitemen's Town" in a laundry house, and his house demolished. The whole number of Chinese killed was twenty-eight and those wounded fifteen.

James S. Briskin on How to Make Money Raising Cattle, 1881

I have been a resident of the West for twelve years, and my official duties have called me during that time into nearly every state and territory between the Missouri and the Pacific Coast. Almost every valley, hill, mountain, and pass of which I have written has been ridden over by me on horseback, and I have observed everywhere the unbounded capacity of the West, not only for stock-growing, but farming, mining, and manufacturing. To me the West is a never ceasing source of wonder, and I cannot imagine why people remain in the overcrowded East, while so many lands and chances are to the west of them. The West today is not what it was yesterday, and it will not be tomorrow what it is today. New discoveries, new developments, and improvements are constantly being made, and a new West is springing up.

The West! The mighty West! That land where the buffalo still roams and the wild savage dwells; where the broad rivers flow and the boundless prairie stretches away for thousands of miles; where new states are every year carved out and myriads of people find homes and wealth; where the poor, professional young man, flying from the overcrowded East and the tyranny of a moneyed aristocracy, finds honor and wealth; where the young politician, unoppressed by rings and combinations, relying upon his own abilities, may rise to position and fame; where there are lands for the landless, money for the moneyless, briefs for lawyers, patients for doctors, and above all, labor and its reward to every poor man who is willing to work. This is the West as I have known it for twelve years, and learned to love it because of its grateful return to all those who have tried to improve it. Its big-hearted people never push a young man back, but generously help him on, and so, by being great themselves, have learned how to make others great. "Where can I raise the best stock?" "Where had I best settle?" "Where can I buy the cheapest and best land?" "Where will I be safe?" These are questions asked every day by people all over the East. In vain do they look into books and newspapers for answers to their inquiries; they are not to be found; at least, not truthful ones. I do not suppose I can supply all the information required, but I can give my impressions, which shall at least have the merit of being honest. I believe Kansas and Iowa are the best unsettled farming states; Nebraska is the best state for farming and stock-raising combined; Colorado is the best state for sheep-growing, farming, and mining; Wyoming is the best territory for cattle-growing alone; Montana is the best territory for cattle-growing and mining.

It does not matter where the emigrant settles in the West, so he comes; and he will almost anywhere soon find himself better off than if he had remained in the East. . . .

Estimate of Profits of a Cash Capital of $25,000 Invested in Cattle for Five Years

AUGUST, 1879, FIRST YEAR		
Buy 500 yearling steers, @ $7.00		$ 3,500
500 two-year-olds, @ $12.00		6,000
500 three-year-olds, @ $20.00		10,000
Expenses: horses, camp outfit, ranch, and incidentals		5,500
		$25,000

AUGUST, 1880, SECOND YEAR		
On hand, two-year-olds	500	
three-year-olds	500	
beeves	500	
	1,500	
Sell 500 beeves, average 1,000 lbs., @ 3 cts. per pound		$15,000
Expenses	$2,500	
10 percent interest on capital	2,500	
		$5,000
		$10,000
Buy 1,000 yearlings, @ $7.00		7,000
$3,000 surplus capital funds		$ 3,000

AUGUST, 1881, THIRD YEAR		
On hand, two-year-olds		$ 1,000
three-year-olds		500
beeves		500
		2,000
Sell 500 beeves, @ $30.00		$15,000
Expenses	$2,500	
Interest	2,500	
		5,000
		$10,000
Buy 800 two-year-olds, @ $12.00		9,600
$400 to surplus capital fund		$400

AUGUST, 1882, FOURTH YEAR		
On hand, three-year-olds		1,800
Beeves		500
		2,300
Sell 500 beeves, @ $30.00 per head		$15,000
Expenses and interest		5,000
		$10,000
Buy 500 three-year-olds, @ $20.00		10,000

AUGUST, 1883, FIFTH YEAR		
On hand, beeves	2,300	
Sell 2,300 beeves, @ $30.00		$69,000
Expenses	$5,000	
Interest	2,500	
		7,500
		$61,500
Deduct original capital		25,000
Net profit in five years		$36,500

This would leave a capital to begin new with greater than the original, besides the ranch, horses, etc., still on hand; the $3,000 surplus-capital fund could have been invested in cows to hold the range. The above estimate is based upon the supposition that $25,000 capital had been borrowed for four years at 10 per cent interest.

Buying yearling steers and selling beeves keeps the capital more in hand, and a class of cattle that can be forced on the market with better results to the seller; and if yearlings or two-year-olds can be bought in lots to suit the purchaser, this kind of trade will show enormous profits. A herd of:

2,000 yearlings @	$ 7.50	
2,000 two-year-olds, @	12.00	
2,000 three-year-olds, @	18.00	
6,000 will cost, say		$75,000
Expense of herding		6,000
Interest, at 10 per cent		7,500
End of first year		$13,500
Sell 2,000 beeves, @ $30.00		$60,000
Deduct interest and herding		13,500
Balance		$46,500
Buy 2,000 yearlings, @ $7.00		14,000
		$32,500

This gives at the beginning of the second year: first, the same number and grade of cattle; second, 10 per cent interest on original capital; and third, $32,500 net profits. This will more than double the capital in three years, besides paying 10 per cent interest, all losses, and expenses. In a few years it will be a difficult matter to find a vacant range in Wyoming, Nebraska, or Montana suitable for or capable of sustaining 5,000 head of cattle. The watercourses are fast being taken up or squatted upon by small herders or branches of large herds.

If $250,000 were invested in ten ranches and ranges, placing 2,000 head on each range, by selling the beeves as fast as they mature, and all the cows as soon as they were too old to breed well, and investing the receipts in young cattle, at the end of five years there would be at least 45,000 head on the ten ranges, worth at least $18.00 per head, or $810,000. Assuming the capital was borrowed at 10 per cent interest, in five years the interest would amount to $125,000, which must be deducted; $250,000 principal, and interest for five years, compounded at 25 percent per annum, would only be $762,938, or less than the value of the cattle, exclusive of the ranches and fixtures. I have often thought if some enterprising persons would form a joint-stock company for the purpose of breeding, buying, and selling horses, cattle, and sheep, it would prove enormously profitable. I have no doubt but a company properly managed would declare an annual dividend of at least 25 per cent. Such a company organized with a president, secretary, treasurer, and board of directors, and conducted on strictly business principles, would realize a far larger profit on the money invested than if put into mining, lumber, iron, manufacturing, or land companies. Nothing,

I believe, would beat associated capital in the cattle trade, unless it would be banking, and stock-raising would probably fully compete with even banking as a means of profit on capital invested in large sums. . . .

I have often been asked to write something about the great cattle herds of Texas. As yet we have but few herds in the West, the business being too new. An owner with 10,000 or 12,000 head in Wyoming or Montana would be considered a large grower, but such a person in New Mexico or Texas a few years ago, when I was there, would have been called but a small herder. I do not think the herds South are as large or numerous now as they were five years since, and the business is gradually drawing off North to the plains, which are the natural homes of the future cattle kings of America. Texas, in 1867, had 2,000,000 oxen and other cattle, exclusive of cows. In 1870 it was estimated the number had increased to 3,000,000, exclusive of cows, and of these there were 80,000 in the state returned by the county assessors. The enormous total of 3,800,000 cattle in one state may well excite our astonishment. Of these, one-fourth were beeves, one-fourth cows, and the other two-fourths, yearlings and two-year-olds. The increase each year was 750,000 calves, and of the older cattle there were on hand at one time 1,900,000 young cattle, 950,000 cows, and 950,000 beeves. These cattle were scattered along the Nueces, Guadalupe, San Antonio, Colorado, Leon, Brazos, Trinity, Sabine, and Red rivers. Colonel Richard King, on the Santa Catrutos River, was one of the largest owners. His ranch, known as the Santa Catrutos Ranch, contained nineteen Spanish leagues of land, or about 84,132 acres. The Santa Catrutos River and its tributaries water this immense ranch, and on it were grazing 65,000 head of cattle, 10,000 horses, 7,000 sheep, and 8,000 goats. One thousand saddle horses and three hundred Mexicans were kept constantly employed in herding, sorting, and driving the stock. The number of calves branded annually on this ranch were 12,000 head, and the number of beeves sold about 10,000. Near Goliad, on the San Antonio River, is located Mr. O'Connor's ranch. Some years ago he had 40,000 head of cattle, and branded annually 11,700 calves. The sales of beeves amounted to from $75,000 to $80,000 per year. Mr. O'Connor commenced cattle-raising with 1,500 head, for which he paid $8,000, in 1852.

Mr. Kennedy's ranch on the Río Grande and Nueces contained 142,840 acres. A fertile little peninsula jutted into the Gulf, and was surrounded on three sides by water. The other side was closed with plank, the whole line of fence being thirty miles long. Every three miles there was a little ranch by the fence and a house for the Mexican herders. On the ranch there were 30,000 head of cattle, besides an immense number of other stock.

There were many other large ranches on the Río Grande, Nueces, Guadalupe, San Antonio, Colorado, Leon, Brazos, Trinity, Sabine, and Red rivers. Mr. John Hitson had 50,000 head of cattle on a ranch in Pinto County, on the Brazos. He drove 10,000 head North annually and employed 300 saddle horses and 50 herders to take care of his cattle. Twenty years ago he was working by the day on a Texas farm. John Chisholm had 30,000 head; Mr. Parks, 20,000; James Brown, 15,000; Martin Childers, 10,000 head, Robert Sloan, 12,000; Mr. Coleman, 12,000; Charles Rivers, 10,000; and many others, from 8,000 to 20,000 head. These were some of the cattle princes of Texas. Of the 1,000 men who owned 3,000,000 head of cattle, it is said not one hundred commenced with large means. Texas is fast becoming an agricultural state, and in a few years more most of the great herds there will be transferred to the plains of the West, the natural grazing grounds of the nation.

Among the great drivers North are John Hitson, who brings up from Texas to the Plattes every year 7,000 to 8,000 head; John Chisholm, 6,000; James Patterson, 8,000; George F. Reynolds, 5,000; Charles Goodnight, 5,000; John Anderson, 3,000; W. P. Black, 2,000; C. C. Campbell, 3,000; Robert White, 2,000; Samuel Goldstone, 2,000; Henry Martin, 2,000; and many others, from 1,000 to 4,000 head. The whole number of cattle driven North from Texas annually cannot be less than 100,000 to 150,000. The superior advantages of the Northern climate over the South for cattle has become so generally known as to need no comment.

Charles Siringo Returns to Texas, 1880

Before starting out on my little journey of only eleven hundred miles, I bought a pack-saddle and cooking outfit—that is, just a frying pan, small coffee pot, etc. I used the mare for a pack animal and rode Whisky-peet. I had just six dollars left when I rode out of Nickerson [Kansas].

I went through Fort Reno and Fort Sill, Indian territory and crossed Red river into Texas on the old military road, opposite Henrietta.

When within ten miles of Denton, Texas, on Pecan creek, Whisky-peet became lame—so much so that he could scarcely walk. I was stopping over night with a Mr. Cobb, and next morning I first noticed his lameness.

I lacked about twenty-five cents of having enough to pay Mr. Cobb for my night's lodging that morning. I had sold my watch for five dollars a short while before and now that was spent.

Whisky-peet being too lame to travel, I left him with Mr. Cobb while I rode into Denton to try and make a raise of some money.

I tried to swap my mare off for a smaller animal and get some boot, but every one seemed to think that she had been stolen; I being so anxious to swap.

I rode back to Mr. Cobb's that night in the same fix, financially, as when I left that morning.

The next day I made a raise of some money. Mr. Cobb and I made a saddle swap, he giving me twenty dollars to boot. He and I also swapped bridles, I getting four dollars and a half to boot. One of his little boys then gave me his saddle and one dollar and a half for my pack-saddle, which had cost me ten dollars in Nickerson. I then had lots of money.

Whisky-peet soon got over his lameness, having just stuck a little snag into the frog of his foot, which I succeeded in finding and pulling out before it had time to do serious damage, and I started on my journey again.

On arriving in Denton that time, a negro struck me for a horse swap right away. I got a three year old pony and six dollars in money for my mare; the pony suited just as well for a pack animal as the mare.

The next day after leaving Denton, I stopped in a negro settlement and won a fifty-dollar horse, running Whisky-peet against a sleepy looking grey. I had up twenty dollars in money and my Winchester, a fine silver mounted gun. I won the race by at least ten open feet, but the negroes tried to swindle me out of it.

While riding along that evening three negroes rode up and claimed the horse I had won. They claimed that the parties who bet him off had no right to him, as they just had borrowed him from one of them to ride to the Settlement that morning. I finally let them have him for twenty dollars.

I went through the following towns after leaving Denton: Ft. Worth, Clenborn, Hillsborough, Waco, Herrene, Bryant, Brenham and Columbus; besides scores of smaller places.

I rode up to mother's little shanty on Cashe's creek after being on the road just a month and twelve days.

To say that mother was glad to see me would only half express it. She bounced me the first thing about not coming back the next fall after leaving as I had promised. I had been gone nearly four years. . . .

I put in the winter [1880] visiting friends, hunting, etc. I had sold my cattle—the mavricks branded nearly four years before—to Mr. Geo. Hamilton, at the market price, from five to ten dollars a head, according to quality, to be paid for when he got his own brand put on to them. Every now and then he would brand a few, and with the money received for them I would buy grub and keep up my dignity.

About the first of March I received a letter from Mr. Rosencrans, one of D. T. Beals' partners, stating that Mr. Beals had bought his cattle in middle Texas instead of southern as he had expected, and as he had told me in Chicago. "But," continued the letter, "we have bought a herd from Charles Word of Goliad, on the San Antonia River, to be delivered at our Panhandle ranch and have secured you the job of bossing it. Now should you wish to come back and work for us, go out and report to Mr. Word at once."

The next day I kissed mother good-bye, gave Whisky-peet a hug, patted Chief—a large white dog that I had picked up in the Indian Territory on my way through—a few farewell pats on the head, mounted "Gotch"—a pony I had swapped my star-spangled winchester for—and struck out for Goliad, ninety miles west. Leaving Whisky-peet behind was almost as severe on me as having sixteen jawteeth pulled. I left him, in Horace Yeamans' care, so that I could come back by rail the coming fall. I failed to come back though that fall as I expected, therefore never got to see the faithful animal again; he died the following spring.

A three days' ride brought me to Goliad, the place where Fannin and his brave followers met their sad fate during the Mexican war. It was dark when I arrived there. After putting up my horse, I learned from the old gent Mr. Word, who was a saddler, and whom I found at work in his shop, that his son Charlie was out at Beeville, gathering a bunch of cattle.

Next morning I struck out for Beeville, thirty miles west, arriving there about four o'clock in the afternoon.

About sun-down I found Charles Word, and his crowd of muddy cow-punchers, five miles west of town. They were almost up to their ears in mud, (it having been raining all day,) trying to finish "road-branding" that lot of steers before dark. The corral having no "chute" the boys had to rope and wrestle with the wild brutes until the hot iron could be applied to their wet and muddy sides.

When I rode up to the corral, Charlie came out, and I introduced myself. He shook my hand with a look of astonishment on his brow, as much to say, I'll be—if Beals mustn't be crazy, sending this smooth-faced kid here to take charge of a herd for me! He finally after talking awhile told me that I would have to work under Mr. Stephens, until we got ready to put up the Beals herd—or at least the one I was to accompany. He also told me to keep the boys from knowing that I was going to boss the next herd, as several of them were fishing for the job, and might become stubborn should they know the truth.

I went on "night-guard" after supper and it continued to rain all night, so that I failed to get any sleep; but then I didn't mind it, as I was well rested.

The next day after going to work, was when I caught fits though, working in a muddy pen all day. When night came I didn't feel as much like going on guard as I did the night before. A laughable circumstance happened that morning after going into the branding-pen.

As the pen had no "chute" we had to rope and tie down, while applying the brand. The men working in pairs, one, which ever happened to get a good chance, to catch the animal by both fore feet as he run by which would "bump" him, that is, capsize him. The other fellow would then be ready to jump aboard and hold him until securely fastened. There being only seven of us to do the roping that morning, it of course left one man without a "pard," and that one was me. Each one you see is always anxious to get a good roper for a "pard," as then everything works smoothly. Mr. Word told me to sit on the fence and rest until Ike Word, an old negro who used to belong to the Word family, and who was the best roper in the crowd, returned from town where he had been sent with a message.

It wasn't long till old Ike galloped up, wearing a broad grin. He was very anxious to get in the pen and show "dem fellers de art of cotching um by boaf front feet." But when his boss told him he would have to take me for a "pard" his broad grin vanished. Calling Mr. Word to one side he told him that he didn't want that yankee for a "pard," as he would have to do all the work, etc. He was told to try me one round and if I didn't suit he could take some one else. Shortly afterwards while passing Mr. Word old Ike whispered and said: "Dogon me if dat yankee don't surprise de natives!'' When night came, and while I was on herd, old Ike sat around the camp fire wondering to the other boys "whar dat yankee learned to rope so well.'' You see Mr. Word had told the boys that I was from the Panhandle, and old Ike thought the Panhandle was way up in Yankeedom somewhere, hence he thinking I was a yankee. A few days after that though, I satisfied old Ike that I was a thoroughbred.

Mr. Word bought a bunch of ponies, new arrivals from Mexico, and among them was a large iron-grey, which the mexicans had pointed out as being "Muncho Deablo.'' None of the boys, not even old Ike, cared to tackle him. So one morning I caught and saddled him. He fought like a tiger while being saddled; and after getting it securely fastened he threw it off and stamped it into a hundred pieces, with his front feet, which caused me to have to buy a new one next day. I then borrowed Mr. Stephens' saddle, and after getting securely seated in it, raised the blinds and gave him the full benefit of spurs and quirt. After pitching about half a mile, me, saddle and all went up in the air, the girths having broken. But having the "hackimore" rope fastened to my belt I held to him until help arrived. I then borrowed another saddle, and this time stayed with him. From that on, old Ike recognized me as a genuine cow-puncher.

We finally got that herd, of thirty-seven hundred steers, ready for the trail; but the very night after getting them counted and ready to turn over to Mr. Stephens the next morning, they stanpeded, half of them getting away and mixing up with thousands of other cattle.

Mr. Stephens thought he would try a new scheme that trip up the trail, so he bought a lot of new bulls-eye lanterns to be used around the herd on dark, stormy nights, so that each man could tell just where the other was stationed by the reflection of his light.

This night in question being very dark and stormy, Stephens thought he would christen his new lamps. He gave me one, although I protested against such nonsense.

About ten o'clock some one suddenly flashed his bulls-eye towards the herd, and off they went, as though shot out of a gun.

In running my horse at full speed in trying to get to the lead, or in front of them, me, horse, bulls-eye and all went over an old rail fence— where there had once been a ranch—in a pile. I put the entire blame onto the lamp, the light of which had blinded my horse so that he didn't see the fence.

I wasn't long in picking myself up and mounting my horse who was standing close by, still trembling from the shock he received. I left the lamp where it lay, swearing vengeance against the use of them, around cattle, and dashed off after the flying herd.

When daylight came I and a fellow by the name of Glass, found ourselves with about half of the herd, at least ten miles from camp. The rest of the herd was scattered all over the country, badly mixed up with other cattle. It took us several days to get the lost ones gathered, and the herd in shape again.

After bidding Stephens and the boys who were to accompany him, adieu, to meet again on Red River where he was to wait for us, we pulled for Goliad to rig up a new outfit, horses, wagon, etc.

The horses, Word bought out of a mexican herd which had just arrived from Old Mexico. He gave eighteen dollars a head for the choice, out of several hundred head.

Being all ready to start for Kimble County, two hundred miles northwest, where the herd was to be gathered, Mr. Word turned the outfit over to me, while he went around by stage.

⋎ *E S S A Y S*

In the first essay, Randall E. Rohe, who teaches geography at the University of Wisconsin—Waukesha, traces the diffusion of Chinese miners across the West after the California gold rush. He outlines a pattern of enterprise and economic opportunity that has been obscured by studies of racial discrimination against the Chinese. The second selection, by the late Kenneth W. Porter, a historian who for many years taught at the University of Oregon, examines the daily life of black cowboys. Like Rohe's essay, his article describes the relative equality of social and economic opportunity. Most telling is Porter's comparison of the situation for blacks in the post–Civil War South with their opportunities as cowboys. Porter nonetheless accepts the existence of limitations as to how far blacks could advance in the cattle business. Does Rohe perceive such limitations for the Chinese? To what extent must we still recognize that the quality of life for black cowboys or Chinese miners, or their chances for economic betterment, were compromised by racism?

Chinese Miners in the Far West

RANDALL E. ROHE

The best available statistics suggest that the major gold rushes in the American West attracted from 10,000 to 100,000 persons per year. Each gold rush clearly reflected its importance, world or regional, in the origin of its participants, and while the foreign element formed a noticeable portion of some gold rushes, Americans invariably comprised the primary component of any goldfield population. But American dominance of the goldfields often ended or considerably lessened with the end of the flush production period, usually the placer period.

With the exhaustion of the rich surface placers, came an increasing necessity for the employment of capital on a large scale and corporate methods to work the deep diggings. As a result, hired labor became the rule in most types of mining and many of the original miners turned to other occupations or moved to new mining regions. Almost ritually, in area

Randall E. Rohe, "Chinese Mining in the Far West, 1850–1890," *Montana the Magazine of Western History*, 32 (Autumn 1982), 2–19 with minor abridgements. Reprinted by permission of the Montana Historical Society.

after area, men of foreign birth replaced the original miners, following close upon the initial rush and early halcyon period. In the placer areas, it was the Chinese who usually supplanted the original miners. A government report in 1871 noted:

> Very few Chinese engaged in lode mining. The Chinese almost completely restricted themselves to placer mining, especially working areas abandoned by whites and reworking tailings. In some quartz mines and stamp mills, however, the Chinese did supply the labor for "certain inferior purposes such as dumping cars, surface excavation, etc."

As yields declined, almost every placer region of note received its complement of Chinese, and they became, in fact, a ubiquitous feature of the mining West.

The omnipresence of the Chinese on the mining frontier is well known, but their role in mining, except in California, is sparsely and inadequately understood. The dynamics and direction of the Chinese movement through the mining regions of the West need examination as well. Most existing studies fail to examine the factors that influenced the magnitude and timing of their migrations, and no work attempts to depict cartographically, Chinese activities on the mining frontier. More than one writer has equated the Chinese arrival with a mining district's decline, describing them as a useful index of wornout mines and low-level technology or as harbingers of decline. But this commonly held view may be in error. Chinese migration may have corresponded to a technological change, as mining moved from an individual, labor-intensive operation to a corporate, capital-intensive one. The generalization that the Chinese movement into mining occurred immediately after the flush production period seems based largely on the pattern of California and the Northwest. Does the history of the Chinese experience in the remainder of the West lend further support to this generalization?

The vast majority of works on the Chinese stress prejudice and discrimination, perhaps to the point of overstatement. Of all the minority groups that participated in the mining frontier the Chinese certainly received the harshest and most inequitable treatment, but studies emphasizing racial discrimination may overlook the importance of Chinese actions on the frontier. Economic competition is the commonly given reason for the harassment felt by the Chinese. But did the Chinese compete with white miners or complement them? Moreover, what in fact did most Chinese do on the western mining frontier?

California Beginnings

Before the California goldrush, Chinese immigration to the United States was almost negligible, but soon, like others attracted to the goldfields, the Chinese came in numbers. On February 1, 1849, fifty-four Chinese resided in California; by January 1, 1850, the number had reached 791; and by the end of 1850 it had passed 4,000. After 1850–1851, Chinese immigration increased dramatically. Internal turmoil and economic instability in China provided the "push," gold in California, the "pull." In 1851, 2,400 to 2,700 Chinese arrived and a year later, the peak period of Chinese immigration, between 18,000 and 20,000 Chinese reached California. The immigration of 1852 brought the number of Chinese in California to about 25,000, a nearly four-fold increase in population in one year.

The bulk of the Chinese emigration to California depended on a credit-ticket system, which paid their passage in turn for a stated term of labor. Six Chinese companies or district associations, headquartered in San Francisco with branch offices in Sacramento and Stockton, administered this system in accordance with Chinese laws. Up to 1854, the majority of Chinese came from about fifteen of seventy-two districts in Kwangtung Province in southern China. Eventually, twenty-one districts in Kwangtung Province supplied 99 per cent of all the Chinese immigrants to the United States. With minor exceptions, Hongkong served as point of departure.

The long crossing lasted forty-five to sixty days, sometimes longer. Under cramped conditions, meager provisions, primitive sanitary facilities, and poor ventilation, it is surprising how many survived the Pacific crossing. Chinese immigrants landed in San Francisco and often remained but a few days there before boarding steamers that transported them to Sacramento, Stockton, Marysville, and other points on the Sacramento and San Joaquin Rivers. In these towns, agents of the Six Companies directed the indentured immigrants to points throughout the mining region. This pattern of Chinese migration was the result of several factors: fluctuations in the economy, how long the migrants might stay, and the changing population level as new arrivals came to the United States. All of this was within the framework of the Six Companies.

Only a few Chinese reached the gold region immediately following Marshall's discovery [at Sutter's mill]. In 1850, Chinese constituted only about 500 out of 57,787 miners in California. As Chinese immigration increased, however, the number of Chinese in the goldfields rose significantly. Beginning in 1851, contemporary writers, like the following, mentioned the increasing presence of Chinese in the goldfields:

> Followed up the Yuba at the foot of the mountains about three miles to Missouri Bar. Found a great many Chinese rocking with cradles, making from three to eight dollars a day.

The large immigrations of 1852–1854 coincided with a mass entry into mining. As the *San Francisco Herald* reported in 1852:

> The Chinese hive has swarmed here [Middle Fork of Yuba] as elsewhere this Spring [1852]—at least 5000, off and on have visited the locality.

> Among the rush of miners into our country [Shasta] . . . we observed our Oriental friend "John" frequently multiplied.

Within two years of their heaviest immigration, the Chinese had penetrated to practically every mining district in California. In fact, the Chinese already dominated some districts, and as early as 1855 contemporary newspapers placed the number of Chinese miners in California at 20,000.

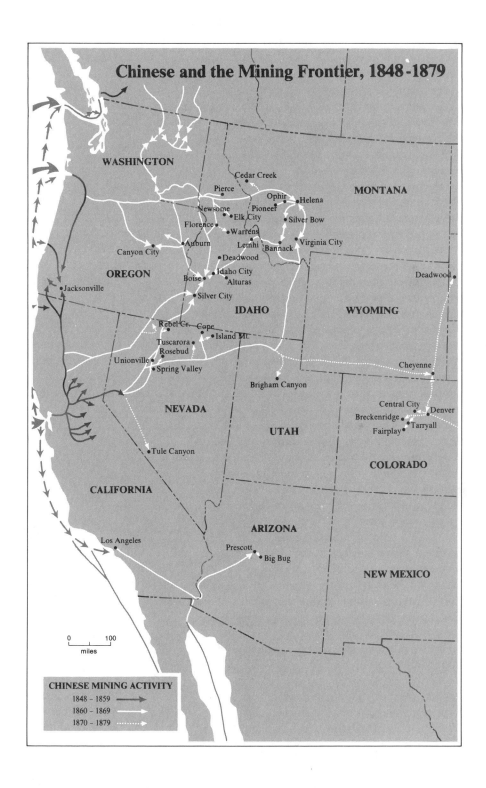

Chinese and the Mining Frontier, 1848-1879

WASHINGTON

MONTANA

Cedar Creek
Pierce
Ophir • Helena
Newsome Pioneer
Elk City • Silver Bow
Florence • Warrens
Auburn Lemhi Virginia City
Canyon City Bannack
Deadwood

OREGON
Boise • Idaho City
Jacksonville Alturas
Silver City Deadwood

IDAHO WYOMING

Rebel Cr.
Cope
Tuscarora • Island Mt.
Rosebud Cheyenne
Unionville
Spring Valley

NEVADA Brigham Canyon

Central City
UTAH Breckenridge • Denver
Fairplay • Tarryall

Tule Canyon COLORADO

CALIFORNIA

ARIZONA

Los Angeles
Prescott
Big Bug
NEW MEXICO

0   100
miles

CHINESE MINING ACTIVITY
1848 – 1859
1860 – 1869
1870 – 1879

The Chinese generally set up camps near their claims along the streams they worked, with small tents and brush wickiup-type structures serving as houses. In 1850 there were few large settlements of Chinese, but later groups of one hundred or more Chinese miners banded together in short-lived villages throughout the mining region. Some established their own settlements, while others occupied camps deserted by white miners. In 1852, almost one-third of the Chinese lived in large camps and only a few hundred resided in localities with large foreign, non-Chinese populations; the Chinese tended to band together.

Some California towns restricted Chinese residents to specific districts or sections of their municipalities; other towns achieved the same result by *de facto* custom. Wherever the Chinese resided, however, the tight, almost self-segregated, nature of their settlements was dominant, providing the Chinese a measure of protection and the ability to retain their culture and social institutions. Characteristic of the larger Chinese settlements was the presence of a joss house or temple. In California, the towns of Weaverville, Shasta, Yuba, Placerville, Coloma, Grass Valley, and many others contained "Chinatown" sections. One of the largest Chinese mining settlements, Chinese Camp, had a population of 2,000 and was located near Sonora.

By the end of the 1850s, Chinese represented perhaps a quarter of the state's miners. During this period, Chinese turned almost exclusively to mining as an occupation. In February 1859, for example, the *Sacramento Daily Union* reported that 75 per cent of the Chinese population of California were employed in mining. Census enumerators in 1860 found that 24,282 Chinese out of a total Chinese population of 34,935 worked as miners, and two years later some 30,000 of the 48,391 Chinese in the state worked as miners. A year later, probably the peak of Chinese mining, 80 to 85 per cent of the Chinese population engaged in mining.

Within a few years, however, many Chinese left mining regions. The burden of the Foreign Miners' Tax, coupled with numerous outrages perpetrated upon them, drove the Chinese from the California mines. In 1867, only 35 per cent to 50 per cent of the more than 50,000 Chinese in California engaged in mining. Yet, as mining declined as an occupation among Chinese, they still had a significant presence in California's goldfields because the number of white miners declined even faster. An exodus of white miners to the Northwest goldfields in the 1860s left the Chinese as the largest single ethnic or national group of miners. By 1870, Chinese accounted for over half of the total mining population and according to one report, they accounted for three-fifths of the miners in 1873.

Over the course of the 1870s, however, the total number of Chinese miners continued to decrease. They either followed the mining frontier or found other employment in towns. By 1876, less than 12,500 Chinese miners remained and the decline persisted, leaving only 10,024 in 1880. Yet, mining ranked second only to common laboring as the major occupation of the Chinese, well above most other occupational categories. In 1884, the number of Chinese miners rose to 15,000, but that figure represented only approximately 15 per cent of the Chinese population. Five years later, Chinese miners constituted less than a third of the mining population, and after the turn of the century, their proportion dropped to only about 15 per cent.

As a general rule, the Chinese worked for themselves or Chinese companies, although there is documentation of white and Chinese miners working side-by-side and even co-operating in joint ventures. Especially during the early years, most Chinese worked as independent miners and were never a significant portion of the labor employed by white companies. Over the years, however, whites employed more and more Chinese so that by the late 1880s whites had nearly one-third of California's Chinese miners in their employ. Whites paid Chinese $1.00 to $1.25 a day in the 1860s, increasing it to $1.75 to $2.00 by the 1870s.

For their own protection, Chinese miners often worked together in groups of a dozen or more. Their equipment, in the 1860s, consisted of little more than shovels, picks, pans and cradles. Diarist Alpheus Richardson described what was probably a typical California Chinese placer operation in 1852 near Bidwell Bar:

> This morning as we was [*sic*] about to start several Chinamen passed along the road with their mining tools such as cradles, picks, pans and shovels, all tied to the middle of a pole and a man at each end of the pole. This is the way—two and two with their implements and with broad brimmed hats, short breeches, wooden shoes, pipe in the mouth, and long hair plaited and laying down on their backs—quite a show for a green Californian. . .

Chinese miners continued to use the cradle or rocker* long after their white counterparts had abandoned it. Its long employment by the Chinese was probably because of its cheapness and portability. For the Chinese, mobility was important, especially when hostility from whites forced them to move quickly from one mining district to another. The long use of the rocker also seems to have forestalled the Chinese from using larger, more sophisticated equipment. A description in 1850 of Chinese miners building river dams for mining purposes demonstrates their involvement in relatively large-scale operations early on, but most Chinese miners did not improve beyond the use of the rocker until after whites had departed and Chinese formed mining companies of their own.

The Chinese mining companies of the early 1860s typically consisted of fewer than five workers and were co-operative ventures for river mining. This type of mining involved building dams, ditches and flumes to divert streams from their natural beds, enabling miners to work sands in the streambeds. Chinese miners normally constructed wing dams in these operations. On the American River, where river mining began in California, the Chinese dominated river mining activity by 1859, and within four years they had inherited the greater part of the river claims in the entire state. As a government report commented in 1875:

> The river-bars, once noted for their great yield are now nearly exhausted.

---

* a long, wooden box mounted on rockers, used to wash gold-bearing soils

Having ceased to pay the demands of white labor, this class of mining has been abandoned to the patient and plodding Chinese, who are still engaged on the banks and bars of the Yuba in washing ground which has been worked three or four times by white labor. Their system of operation is to turn rivers from their beds by means of long flumes and run the dirt through boxes.

The main exception to the Chinese monopoly in river mining was in the "Northwest Mines" where whites were still a significant force in this form of mining through the 1880s. But here as well, the Chinese acquired more and more of a monopoly so that as late as 1890 the State Mineralogist reported that Chinese held numerous river claims and several thousand of them were using wing dams. The old wing dams on the Feather, Yuba and American rivers were gone by 1890, the mineralogist wrote, "except where small companies of Chinese are at work."

The typical Chinese river mining operations in the late 1880s and 1890s consisted of a company of four to ten men using derricks, dams, pumps, and ditches along with traditional placer tools. Yuba River operations were described by census enumerators in 1890 as a small but profitable enterprise:

There were about 100 Chinese employed in river mining on the North Yuba river, which flows by the town of Downieville, scattered, in about a dozen companies, 10 miles each way from the town. The average time worked each year is 120 days, in 1889 probably 150, and the aggregate product between $35,000 and $45,000 annually. About half of this is sold at the bank of Messrs. Scammon & Co., at Downieville; the other half to a Chinese buyer in the same town or taken direct to San Francisco. The aggregate amount of capital invested by the Chinese in their operations is not more than $25,000. The plant consists of temporary dams in the river, one or more water wheels, and Chinese rotary pumps, derricks, ditches and sluices to each claim.

Although the river mining activities of the Chinese attracted considerable attention, most Chinese companies during the 1865 to 1880 period worked in hydraulic mining, with a few working drifts. Chinese avoided drift mining except when employed by whites, as in 1884 when nearly 200 worked for whites in drifts near Oroville on the Feather River. A court decision that outlawed dumping mine tailings into streams halted much hydraulic mining, but a leading engineering publication claimed that this did not stop the Chinese.

Most of these mines are operated under leases obtained by the Chinese, who, through recourse to their peculiar methods, manage to escape arrest, or, if arrested, manage, by these same methods, to keep their leased claims, and also those they purchase, running all the same.

Some Chinese worked for whites in hydraulic operations, such as in Siskiyou County, California, in the early 1890s where half of the miners were Chinese. Whites employed Chinese in hauling away large boulders. The Chinese moved these large rocks with slings attached to poles and then neatly stacked them in piles near mining sites; many of these stacks remain today as physical reminders of Chinese involvement in California hydraulic mining.

North to Oregon

From California, many Chinese followed the advance of the mining strikes in the Northwest, where they duplicated patterns established in the Golden State. As production declined and original miners moved on to new areas or claims, the Chinese came. From mining region to mining region, singly or in groups, the Chinese usually travelled by foot, occasionally by mule or horseback, and sometimes by stage. It was in the Northwest that the Chinese established a base for their further movement into the Rocky Mountains.

Control remained in the hands of the "Six Companies." Commercial agents or storekeepers in constant contact with the headquarters of their district companies directed the movement. Perhaps as early as 1852, the Chinese reached the goldfields of southwestern Oregon. Apparently, the number of Chinese remained small until 1856, but in the next year, the *Oregonian* alleged that:

> The Chinamen are about to take the country. There are from one thousand to twelve hundred in this county [Josephine] engaged in mining. They are buying out the American miners, paying big prices for their claims.

In the summer of 1859, the *Sacramento Daily Union* reported the dominance of Chinese in some Oregon mining areas, but the census of 1860 gave Oregon a total of only 425 Chinese, although 370 of them did work as miners. Through the 1860s, the number of Chinese in the goldfields of southwestern Oregon continued to increase. "Many of the mining districts in this county [Jackson]," the *Oregon Sentinel* reported, "are fast being filled up with Chinamen. There are at least 100 on Jackass Creek, 175 on Applegate, 60 on Sardine Creek, 30 on Kiota Creek and 15 or 20 on the bars of Rogue River." Another writer described what seemed to be a great increase of Chinese in the Rogue River Valley.

> We observed in squads, the ubiquitous Chinamen, moving from mining locality to mining locality, fleeing from the kicks of one to the cuffs of the other, with no fixed abiding place to be called his permanent home.

As early as 1864, and probably earlier, the Chinese dominated some districts. "Chinese are working over many old diggings," the *Daily Oregonian* noted in 1868, "and along the bars of Rogue river these people may be seen in numerous places employing their patient industry in washing out the gold which white labor has neglected as too small pay." Rossiter Raymond, who compiled a government report on western mining districts, noted in 1869 that Chinese mainly worked the once very productive mines of southwestern Oregon, and the decennial census in the following year indicated that southwestern Oregon accounted for over a quarter of the Chinese in the state. The dominance of the Chinese in the mines of southwestern Oregon continued in the 1870s and 1880s, as Raymond reported:

> The western districts, once the scene of a busy placer mining industry, have relapsed into comparative idleness, though the ancient diggings are still reworked here and there by Chinese.

From California and Oregon, the Chinese followed the advance of mining into British Columbia in 1858 when news of gold on the Fraser River filtered southward. . . .

To Idaho's Owyhee District

The Chinese advancement into Idaho began in 1864. That year newspapers noted the presence of Chinese along the Snake River and the South Fork of the Clearwater. At first, the Chinese encountered hostile resistance, but as each district declined more and more claims transferred from white to Chinese ownership. Oro Fino was the first. After considerable opposition, the claim holders at Oro Fino favorable to Chinese labor gained the ascendancy and finally in September 1864, the miners of the Oro Fino District adopted a resolution to invite the Chinese into that camp. The *Walla Walla Statesman* immediately perceived the significance:

> Heretofore the miners have very generally prohibited Chinamen from working the mines of the upper country, by their local district laws, but it is apparent that those laws will not exclude them much longer.

> As the mining camps become less productive and laborers follow up the richest diggings, it may be safely assumed that other mining localities will shortly follow the example of Oro Fino in the motion of introducing Chinese labor. . . . it will not be long before that whole upper country will be overrun with them.

The prophecy proved true. Within the next few years, the Chinese appeared in almost every mining district of northern Idaho. In early 1865, one newspaper reported that the estimate of the Chinese agents of the movement of Chinese into the "upper country" during the coming season ranged from 2,000 to 5,000. Two years later, several newspapers commented on the great number of Chinese in some of the northern districts.

The movement of Chinese did not stop at the northern mines. In the middle sixties, the Chinese extended southward into the mining districts of central Idaho, reaching the Owyhee District in the spring of 1865. As early as May of that year, the *Idaho World* noted that:

> Our camp [Silver Creek] is likely to be taken, subdued and occupied by the celestial. A large gang lately arrived here, and hundreds more are on their way. . . .

The comments of this contemporary proved remarkably correct. Almost within a year, the omnipresence of the Chinese in the Owyhee District led the *Owyhee Avalanche* to comment that "Almost every abandoned claim or gulch in which the color of gold can be found has its gang of Chinamen at work.'' In 1867, the *Walla Walla Statesman* expected over 500 Chinese to work just Jordan Creek.

Almost simultaneously with Chinese activities in the Owyhee District came their advance into the Boise Basin. The first Chinese miners in the Boise Basin, only fifty or sixty, arrived in 1865. *The Idaho World*, on November 11, 1865, reported large numbers of Chinese crowding into the Basin, and a week later the newspaper predicted the intended introduction of thousands of Chinese into Idaho the next spring. They would, according to the *World*, ''buy up all the old, good-for-nothing claims in the country.'' It was another prediction time proved correct; two years later the *Idaho World* announced the probable presence of fully 5,000 Chinese in the Basin in the ensuing mining season. The real figure probably was closer to 2,000, but by 1868 the Chinese accounted for fully one-third of the mining population in the vicinity of Idaho City. The next year the Chinese population of Boise County reached 3,000, compared to a white population of about 7,000, and Idaho City contained ''about as many Chinese as whites.'' The Chinese, by 1870, held the greater portions of the creek and gulch claims of the Boise Basin. The same year saw the introduction of Chinese labor into the Warren District, which attracted some 1,200 Chinese in the space of only two years. These Chinese, according to a government report, ''monopolized the gravel workings, going over the mining grounds a second and a third time.''

The discoveries of 1863–1864 in the Kootenay of British Columbia and in Montana, coupled with declining production, drew many miners away from the northern Idaho districts. Mining district laws against Chinese miners, which had been poorly enforced anyhow, became more relaxed, and finally, on January 11, 1866, the Idaho territorial legislature passed an act allowing the Chinese to mine on payment of a license fee of five dollars per month. These conditions accelerated the movement of Chinese into Idaho in the latter 1860s.

The census of 1870 disclosed that the Chinese represented almost a third of the people in Idaho and, even more revealing, the census showed that the Chinese constituted almost 60 per cent of the miners. Rossiter Raymond, in his mining report of 1872, estimated that ''Probably two-thirds of all the claims now worked are in the hands of Chinese.'' His report for the following year graphically reiterated the dominance of the Chinese in the goldfields of Idaho:

> For every well paying claim worked by white men, we find at present probably not less than five or six which return profit only to Chinamen, and a few camps are almost exclusively worked and owned by them.

The census of 1880 showed a decrease in the number of Chinese, although they continued to engage chiefly in mining and to dominate many placer areas. The exodus of Chinese from Idaho continued through the 1880s; the census of 1890 disclosed that 2,007 Chinese remained, with perhaps 40 per cent of them working as miners.

Mining areas in northeastern Oregon's Blue Mountains, opened in 1861–1864, represented a contemporaneous extension of Idaho mining activity. As the placer yield declined in northeastern Oregon in the late 1860s, the Chinese became prominent, expanding successively into the John Day, Powder River and Burnt River Districts in 1866, 1867, and 1868. By the end of the decade, they predominated, sometimes to the extreme, in many of the mining districts of the Blue Mountains. In 1868, for instance, the North Fork of the John Day contained some 200 Chinese, "they having bought up nearly all the old river claims." Rossiter Raymond, in his report for 1870, evaluated their importance in these districts:

> Meager returns from Canon City and neighboring districts indicate a somewhat increased production . . . mainly by reason of the influx of Chinese, who succeed . . . by their superior patience and economy [to] continue the production of gold in many localities where it would otherwise cease. . . .

Chinese miners, over the next two decades, continued to increase in the mining districts of northeastern Oregon, but by the 1890s the attraction of mining for the Chinese declined. Many left the mines and northeastern Oregon or turned to other occupations.

Into the Montana Rockies

Almost immediately following the Chinese advancement into Idaho and adjacent Oregon, came their expansion into Montana. As early as 1866, the *Walla Walla Statesman* reported the arrival of Chinese near Virginia City for the purpose of mining. A year later they had extended their field of operation to Helena. James W. Taylor, in a government report describing the conditions of mining in Montana for 1867, noted:

> The bulk of the auriferous treasure is now exhausted . . . the placers once worked over, are said to be exhausted . . . the diggings now fall into the hands of the Chinese, who patiently glean the fields abandoned by the whites.

The latter 1860s brought increasing mention of Chinese entrance into mining. Of the approximately 800 Chinese in Montana in 1868, about 60 per cent of them worked as miners. A contemporary estimate set the Chinese population for 1869 at between 2,000 and 3,000, although the census of 1870 reported slightly less than 2,000 Chinese in the territory. As in other states and territories, mining employed the overwhelming majority of Chinese. The census listed over 70 per cent of Montana's Chinese as miners, even though they accounted for only slightly more than 20 per cent of all miners.

Newspapers and the Mining Commissioner's Reports of the 1870s noted the presence of Chinese in many of the placer areas. Despite their widespread presence, however, the total Chinese population apparently remained small. The census of 1880 recorded less than 2,000 Chinese in Montana. During the 1880s the Chinese continued to increase and spread throughout the territory, with the result that by 1885 almost every placer district in the major mining counties contained some Chinese, notably Deer Lodge, Lewis and Clark, Jefferson, Choteau, Meagher, Beaverhead, Madison, and Gallatin counties. Although the census in 1890 gave the number of Chinese in Montana as 2,532, perhaps only a little more than 10 per cent of them worked as miners.

Of the Northwestern states, Washington attracted the fewest Chinese. The meager placers of the state offered only limited opportunities for mining, but Chinese miners worked throughout central Washington, in the mining districts of the Wenatchee Mountains, and along the Yakima, Wenatchee and Columbia rivers. . . . A Corps of Engineers report in 1881 mentions Chinese miners all along the Columbia as far as Rock Island. The upper portions of the river especially contained large numbers of Chinese, sometimes engaged in rather substantial mining operations, as a government report noted:

> There are quite a number of Chinamen engaged in mining on the river bars. . . . In some instances the Chinamen have put in flumes several miles in length and constructed quite extensive works to obtain the precious metal.

Through the middle 1880s, the Columbia region continued to attract some Chinese, but few of them continued mining in Washington by the end of the decade. The census for that year recorded 3,260 Chinese, but probably less than 7 per cent of these worked as miners.

Colorado and the Southwest

Unlike the other major placer areas of the West, those of Colorado did not receive an influx of Chinese immediately following its flush production period. Even when the Chinese did arrive, their numbers remained relatively insignificant. Probably the quite limited extent of its placers, compared to those of California, Idaho, and Montana, primarily accounted for the restricted Chinese migration to Colorado. . . .

Shortly after the Chinese achieved a notable, if somewhat limited, presence in Colorado their advance reached still farther eastward. In 1875 the Chinese arrived in the newly discovered goldfields of the Black Hills, although they did not engage in mining until 1878. A year later the *Engineering and Mining Journal* reported Chinese reworking several claims along lower Whitewood Gulch; in 1880 Chinese worked a dozen or so of the fifty claims in Deadwood and Whitewood Gulches. The Black Hills, however, attracted relatively few Chinese. Census reports in 1880 and 1890 gave Dakota Territory some 200 Chinese and only a few were miners. The relatively limited placer deposits of the Black Hills, the declining appeal of mining as an occupation, and probably, too, the always present discrimination toward the Chinese explain the fewer Chinese miners in the Dakotas.

On a much smaller scale than the Chinese advance into the Northwest and the Rocky Mountains was their parallel movement into the Southwest. The first contingent of Chinese to reach the Southwest arrived in 1856; that year Chinese laborers worked on a mining ditch at Gold Canyon near Dayton, Nevada. Recognizing the possibilities of mining, some fifty Chinese began working the claims abandoned (or thought unproductive) by whites. Although the Chinese formed the majority of miners working the Gold Canyon placers by 1859, their numbers remained small.

The building of the Virginia and Truckee, and the Central Pacific railroads, however, brought many more Chinese to Nevada, and with the completion of these railroads some of the unemployed Chinese turned to mining and spread throughout the northern half of the state. The Chinese population stood at 3,152 in 1870, with 240 of these working as miners, or only approximately 8 per cent of the Chinese population and 3 per cent of all miners. Ten years later Nevada's Chinese population reached its peak at 5,416, although probably less than 10 per cent worked as miners and they accounted for less than 10 per cent of all miners. Despite the small percentage of Chinese miners, the Chinese did dominate some districts, such as the Spring Valley (or Paradise) District where the Director of the Mint reported that "seventy-five or eighty Chinamen were profitably working the old Placer mines" in 1883. Between 1884 and 1895, an estimated 3,000 Chinese worked the Spring Valley District in north central Nevada. The Chinese population of Nevada had declined to less than 3,000 by 1890, of which perhaps 15 per cent found employment as miners. Their population decline continued during the 1890s and by the turn of the century only 1,352 Chinese remained in Nevada, very few of which were miners.

Several factors combined to retard and limit the Chinese advancement throughout much of the Southwest. The placers there generally proved to be widely scattered and not particularly rich. Scarcity of water also limited mining operations. The presence of potentially hostile Indians, at least initially, proved an important factor in parts of the Southwest. Anti-Chinese discrimination, likewise, played its usual role. But in many parts of the Southwest it was competition from Mexicans that proved to be the major factor.

In most of the Southwest, it appears that Mexicans served as counterparts to the Chinese. As with the Chinese in the rest of the West, Mexicans in the Southwest worked the less valuable deposits or those areas worked out and abandoned by white miners. New Mexico and Arizona especially attracted large numbers of Mexicans. The placers along the Colorado River in Arizona provide a typical example of the Mexican role in mining in the Southwest. "For several years these Colorado placers," Hubert Howe Bancroft wrote in 1889, "attracted a crowd of Californians . . . but as a rule the dry washing processes were too tedious for the permanent occupation of only but Mexicans and Indians."

During the 1860s, Mexicans gained control of more and more of the placer areas of the Southwest. The major placer districts of Arizona were described in 1871 as dominated by Mexican miners. Little change took place in the next ten years and a description of placer mining in Arizona in 1881 still emphasized the omnipresence of Mexicans:

Gold placers have also been found in many portions of the Territory, which after yielding large amounts . . . were abandoned. . . . Considerable quantities of gold are, however, still obtained from them by individual enterprise of Mexicans.

During the same period, the *Engineering and Mining Journal* reported of the major placer areas of New Mexico, "all the districts have been worked for some years, mostly by Mexicans."

Despite stiff competition from Mexicans, the Chinese did participate in placer mining in both Arizona and New Mexico. The first Chinese perhaps reached Arizona in 1869. Within a few months, the *Arizona Miner* reported an influx of Chinese miners near Prescott:

> The flight of ye Chinamen is Big Bugwards. Two, three and four cents to the pan were found by one of them recently. The finder sent word to his fellow countrymen in Prescott, who . . . resolved to start immediately. . .

Apparently, the number of Chinese engaged in mining in Arizona and New Mexico until the 1890s was few. They probably reached their peak in the late 1890s and just after the turn of the century. Of the two states, the placers of Arizona received by far the greatest number of Chinese.

Chinese and Gold

Of all the ethnic groups represented in the placer areas of the West, perhaps none proved more ubiquitous and significant than the Chinese. They excelled in saving gold, especially fine gold, under difficult conditions. They complemented rather than competed with white miners; competition between whites and Chinese miners was generally in terms of hired labor and was probably more implied than real. Many times the movement of independent Chinese miners into a mining district was encouraged. As the rich, surface placers declined and the original miners moved on, the Chinese almost without fail replaced them, and this movement of Chinese brought about a new concentration of miners in areas abandoned by whites. In effect, the Chinese slowed population declines by settling recently abandoned mining areas, and maintained gold production in those same areas.

During their first decade in the West, most Chinese worked in the mines, about 75 per cent of them by the early 1860s. By the 1870s they had spread to almost every major placer area in the West, and the late 1860s and early 1870s, in fact, probably marked the peak of Chinese mining activity. In 1870 mining employed less than a third of the Chinese population, but the Chinese represented over 25 per cent of all miners, and in some individual states the Chinese accounted for one-half to almost two-thirds of all miners. Over the next two decades the Chinese in increasing numbers turned away from mining, so that by 1890 they probably represented less than a tenth of all miners in the West. By the end of the century, the Chinese had for the most part abandoned mining; in fact, by this date, most had died, returned to China, moved east, or settled in the larger cities of the West Coast.

The amount of gold recovered by the Chinese will never be known, and the meager statistics available preclude even an educated guess. More than one government official lamented the impossibility of getting any details on Chinese mining operations or the amount of gold they produced. The Chinese were very secretive and seldom mined at only one location for any extended time. Most of the gold passed into the hands of Chinese merchants and a good part of it went on to China. A few scattered references, like the following, are all we have.

> The reports from sixty four placer claims in Grant County [Oregon, 1870] eleven . . . worked by white men with paid labor, and the remainder by Chinese . . . show for the former a yield of $4 per day per hand, and for the latter only $1.30. There is no doubt that the Chinese have in this case concealed the actual amount of their production, reporting an aggregate of about $126,000, when the real amount must have been at least twice as great.

Contrary to the prevailing opinion of the day, the Chinese did not send all of their gold to China and they were an important factor in the economic development of many areas.

> Colville [Washington] feels the loss of her Chinamen, they having been the principal consumers of her productions. They worked and took out . . . on the Columbia and Pend Oreille rivers, where white men would not work, and nearly every dollar they made was money put into circulation, and the benefit of which would never have been felt had it not been for them.

The Chinese paid their share of taxes—miner's taxes, property taxes, poll taxes, and other assessments—and they received none of the services their tax money provided. They made significant purchases of mining equipment and mining claims.

Almost without exception, the Chinese appeared on each successive mining frontier. The Chinese role in mining, despite their omnipresence, remains largely unexamined. The majority of existing works have stressed the discrimination and prejudice felt by the Chinese almost to the point of distorting reality. Many of the generalizations on the Chinese require re-examination. The low level technology (rocker syndrome) attributed to the Chinese needs restatement; many examples of extensive Chinese mining operations exist. The influx of Chinese into a district did not necessarily correspond with a district's decline. Often it coincided with the exhaustion of the rich surface placers and the change-over methods that enabled the working of lower-grade deposits.

Hopefully researchers will move away from the overworked theme of anti-Chinese discrimination and investigate other aspects of the Chinese experience on the western mining frontier. Details in the diffusion of Chinese miners throughout the West in the late nineteenth-century, for example, need clarification, and little is known of Chinese mining activities in south-western states and smaller western mining areas.

The distribution of Chinatown settlements in the mining West and their morphology, layout, location within mining towns, and more, need examination. How distinctive was the cultural landscape of the Chinese and what were its characteristics? And there are numerous other questions that must be asked. Do Chinese place names suggest the location and intensity of Chinese mining activity in the West? Apparently, the Chinese purposely introduced and spread a particular plant species—"Trees of Heaven" (*Ailanthus altissima*)—in the West. Why did they plant these trees and does the present range of the trees have any bearing on the extent of Chinese mining activity in the West? Why did the Chinese avoid lode mining, or did they avoid it completely? And, finally, what role did the Chinese play in labor conflicts in the lode mining industry in the last two decades of the nineteenth-century?

Chinese mining in the American West is not what we have previously thought it to be. Because we do not know enough about the Chinese mining communities, generalizations are hazardous, but there is no question that much remains to be discovered about Chinese in the mining West. As perhaps the most important of ethnic groups involved in western gold mining, the Chinese deserve a full re-examination.

The Labor of Negro Cowboys

KENNETH W. PORTER

The range-cattle industry in its various aspects, and in its importance to the United States and particularly to the Great Plains for the post–Civil War generation, has been the subject of numerous studies. This industry was rendered possible by such factors as vast expanses of grazing land, projected railroad lines across the Missouri and onto the Great Plains, the rise of heavy industry and the consequent demand for beef of less-than-high quality by the meat-hungry industrial population. But like the steel, mining, packing, and other industries, it also needed a labor force—workers with special abilities and qualities—for although the cowhand or cowboy possibly was no more than a "hired man on horseback," he was a hired man with skills in riding, roping, and branding which could not be easily acquired. Most of his working hours were spent in such routine tasks as riding the range and turning back drifting steers; rounding up, branding, and castrating calves; selecting beeves for the market; and, even on the "long drive," jogging along and daily "eating dirt" on the flanks or in the rear of a few thousand "cow critters." But he also needed the inborn courage and quick thinking to use these skills effectively while confronting

Kenneth W. Porter, "Negro Labor in the Western Cattle Industry, 1866–1900," *Labor History*, 10 (Summer 1969), 346–353, 354–364, 367–368, 370–374. Reprinted by Permission.

an enraged bull, swimming a milling herd across a flooded river, or trying to turn a stampede of fear-crazed steers.

But the general public, under the influence of decades of "Western" movies and, more recently, television shows has come to regard the cowboy's workaday activities as altogether secondary to fighting off hostile Indians, pursuing rustlers and holding "necktie parties" for them, saving the rancher's daughter from Mexican raiders, and engaging in quick-draw gunfights in dusty streets. From similar sources this same public has also learned that cowboys, with the exception of an occasional low-browed villain or exotic and comic-accented *vaquero,* were all of the purest and noblest Anglo-Saxon type, as in Owen Wister's *The Virginian.*

In reality, as George W. Saunders of the Texas Trail Drivers Association has authoritatively estimated, of the fully 35,000 men who went up the trail from Texas with herds during the heroic age of the cattle industry, 1866–1895, "about one-third were Negroes and Mexicans." This estimate is closely confirmed by extant lists of trail-herd outfits which identify their members racially. These lists also demonstrate that Negroes out-numbered Mexicans by more than two to one—slightly more than 63 percent whites, 25 percent Negroes, and slightly under 12 percent Mexicans.

The racial breakdown of individual outfits, of course, varied widely. Some were nearly all of one race, such as the 1874 outfit which was all-Negro, except for a white boss, or the 1872 outfit which consisted of a white trail-boss, eight Mexicans, and a Negro; but more typical were the two 1877 outfits composed, respectively, of seven whites and two Negro cowboys, and a Negro cook; and seven whites, two Negroes, and a Mexican hostler. Many outfits had no Mexicans at all, but it was an exceptional outfit that did not have at least one Negro and enough outfits were nearly all Negro, or a third or more Negro, to bring the number up to the estimated twenty-five percent of the total. A trail-herd outfit of about a dozen men would on the average consist of seven or eight whites, including the trail boss, three Negroes—one of whom was probably the cook, while another might be the horse wrangler, and the third would simply be a trail hand—and one or two Mexicans; if a Negro was not the wrangler, then a Mexican often was. Needless to say, this is not the typical trail outfit of popular literature and drama.

The racial make-up of ranch outfits, with their seasonal and day-by-day fluctuations, was not so well recorded as that of the trail-herd outfits, but available information indicates that ranch hands, in Texas at least, were white, Negro, and Mexican in proportions varying according to locality and to ranchowner tastes; probably the overall proportions differed little from those of trail outfits. A ranch in the Indian Territory during the late 1890s, for example, was staffed by eight cowhands, two of whom were Negroes. Negro cowhands were particularly numerous on the Texas Gulf Coast, in the coastal brush east of the Nueces and at the mouth of the Brazos and south of Houston, and parts of the Indian Territory; in some sections they were in the majority, and some ranches worked Negroes almost exclusively.

Negro trail drivers swarmed west and north with herds from the Texas "hive" and, though most returned, a few remained as ranch hands as far north as Wyoming, the Dakotas, and even Canada and as far west as New Mexico, Arizona, and even California and Oregon.

Wranglers

Negroes occupied all the positions among cattle-industry employees, from the usually lowly wrangler through ordinary hand to top hand and lofty cook. But they were almost never, except in the highly infrequent case of an all-Negro outfit, to be found as ranch or trail boss.

Negroes and also Mexicans were frequently wranglers, or *remuderos*— in charge of the saddle horses not immediately in use—usually regarded as the lowliest job in the cattle industry, except for the boy who sometimes served as wrangler's assistant. There were exceptions, however, including some Negro wranglers who became "second in authority to the foreman" in a few camps. Such wranglers were "horse men" in the highest sense: capable of detecting and treating illness and injury, selecting the proper horse for each job, and taking the ginger out of unruly animals. Among these wranglers-extraordinary were Nigger Jim Kelly, the horsebreaker, horsetrainer, handyman, and gunman of the notorious Print Olive; and the famous John Chisum's "Nigger Frank," "who spent a lifetime wrangling Long I horses" and whom a white cattleman declared "the best line rider and horsewrangler I ever saw."

Cowboys

The majority of Negroes on the ranch or "long drive" were neither wranglers nor yet authoritative cooks (of whom more later). They were top hands or ordinary hands who, on the long drive, rode the point, the swing, the flank, or the drag, according to their experience and ability. The point—the position of honor—was at the front of the herd where the steers were strongest, most restless, and most likely to try to break away. There the most experienced top hands rode. Farther back, the cattle were somewhat less troublesome, while in the rear, where the tired beasts were comparatively easy to manage, could be found the fledgling cowboys of the drag, "eating the dust" of the entire herd. Negroes rode in all these positions.

These Negro cowboys, whether on ranch or trail, were generally regarded as good workers, who got along well with others and who took pride in their work. A white Texan, a former cowboy and rancher, went so far as to write that "there was no better cowman on earth than the Negro."

Old, experienced Negro cowhands frequently served as unofficial, one-man apprentice systems to white greenhorns. This was particularly true, of course, when the fledgling was the employer's son or relative. Will Rogers, for example, got his first lessons in riding and roping from a Cherokee Negro employee of his father. Almost any young would-be cowboy who showed the proper spirit, however, might have the good fortune to be "adopted" and "showed the ropes" by one of these black veterans, who would sometimes take on the inexperienced boy as partner when white cowboys were unwilling to do so. Charles Siringo, later famous as a cowboy-detective-author, recalled that Negro cowboys again and again came to his rescue when, in his reckless cowboy youth, his life was threatened by a mad steer, a wild bronc, and even a hired assassin.

Negro cowhands confronted all the dangers and met all the tests of the long trail. One poorly clad cowboy froze to death in his saddle during a "Norther" rather than give up and go in to the chuckwagon. Stampedes were an ever-present danger, and experienced Negroes were frequently prominent in attempting to prevent or control them. Indeed they were also often among the few cowboys who stayed with the herd when others threw in their hands.

Crossing the wide, deep, frequently flooded rivers was even more dangerous than stampedes. According to a white ex-cowboy, "it was the Negro hand who usually tried out the swimming water when a trailing herd came to a swollen stream"—either because of his superior ability or because he was regarded as expendable. But whether or not this statement is valid, it probably would not have been made had not Negroes frequently demonstrated their ability to cope with the problems of river crossings. Numerous anecdotes about such crossings tell of Negro cowhands saving themselves by their own efforts, being assisted to dry land by white cattlemen and, on more than one occasion, saving their lives.

Negroes not only often showed courage and quick thinking in extricating themselves and others from the danger of swollen rivers, but in at least one case also displayed ingenuity superior to that of a great trail boss. In 1877 Ab Blocker, "the fastest driver on the trail," had reached the Platte River, which was spanned by a bridge of sorts, but the wild longhorns had never seen a bridge and refused to cross it. It looked as if, after all, they would have to swim the herd when a Negro hand suggested—and his suggestion was adopted—that they should drive the chuckwagon slowly across, followed by old Bully, an ox; the lead steers would follow Bully and the rest of the herd would trail them.

Riders and Ropers

Although every top hand had to be a skillful rider and roper, some were so outstanding as to be considered "bronco busters" and/or ropers *par excellence* rather than as merely uncommonly able cowboys. Numerous references suggest that Negroes and Mexicans were widely regarded as particularly expert in both these capacities—the Mexicans especially noted for their prowess with the *reata* (or lasso). Mexicans were also, correctly or not, blamed for cruelty toward animals and consequently fell into disrepute as horsebreakers, whereas the Negroes maintained and even advanced a reputation which went back to antebellum days.

A white ex–cowpuncher-writer states that Negroes were hired largely for their ability to cope with bad horses which the white cowhands did not want to tackle. "The Negro cow hands of the middle 1880s . . . were usually called on to do the hardest work around an outfit. . . . This most often took the form of 'topping' or taking the first pitch out of the rough horses of the outfit. . . . It was not unusual for one young Negro to 'top' a half dozen hard-pitching horses before breakfast." Andy Adams, the cowboy-author and a man who was far from being a Negrophile, declared that the "greatest bit of bad horse riding" he ever saw was performed by a dozen Negro cowboys who were assigned to ride a dozen horses which the white cowpunchers of their outfit were afraid to tackle. But each of the Negroes stayed on his horse till the animal was conquered.

The list of Negro bronc riders—the comparatively few whose names have survived—is still a long one. A few of the better known, partly because they attracted the attention of published writers, were the following: Isam, Isom, or Isham Dart of Brown's Hole, "where Colorado, Wyoming, and Utah cornered," who, although now remembered principally as a reputed rustler, was also "numbered among the top bronc stompers of the Old West"; Nigger Jim Kelly, whom oldtime cowboys considered the peer of any rider they had seen in the United States, Canada, or the Argentine; a mulatto named Williams in the Badlands of South Dakota, who was a horse-trainer rather than a horsebreaker and whose methods won the admiration of Theodore Roosevelt; and Jim Perry, the famous XIT cook, who was even better known as "one of the best riders and roper ever to hit the West."

While most of the famous riders were bronco busters only as one aspect of their work as cowhands, some, including a number of Negroes, were officially recognized as ranch horsebreakers, and a few were full-time or nearly full-time professionals. Perhaps the most famous of the professionals was Matthew (Bones) Hooks of the Panhandle—remembered, after his retirement from horsebreaking to Pullman-portering, for having once taken off his jacket and cap and laid aside his clothes brush, to mount and break an outlaw which no one had been able to ride, while his train stood in the station.

Other Negro cowhands were particularly renowned as ropers, such as Ab Blocker's Frank, who was, according to a white cowboy, "the best hand with a rope I ever saw," and whose roping skill once saved his employer from an angry steer; Ike Word, according to Charles Siringo, "the best roper" at a roundup near Beeville, Texas; Jim Simpson, "about the best roper" on his part of the Wyoming range; and, more recently, the Negro rancher Jess Pickett who, according to a white neighbor, was "the world's best roper."

Naturally enough, many of the famous Negro riders, such as Isom Dart and Jim Perry, were almost or quite as renowned as ropers. One of the most spectacular at both riding and roping was "Nigger Add," "one of the best hands on the Pecos," who would as a matter of course "top off" several bad horses of a morning. Walking into a corral full of tough broncs, he would seize any one he chose by the ear and nose, lead him out of the bunch, and then show him who was boss. As a roper he was even more sensational, and had the unusual technique of roping on foot, a practice which would have killed an ordinary man. He would tie a rope around his hips, work up to a horse in the corral or in the open pasture, rope him around the neck as he dashed by at full speed, and then, by sheer strength and skill, flatten the horse out on the ground where a lesser man would have been dragged to death. Indeed, the prowess of such Negro riders, horsebreakers, and horse-trainers was so outstanding as to contribute to the commonly held belief of the time that there was some natural affinity between Negroes and horses. . . .

Cowboy Cooks—Men of Parts

High in the hierarchy of cow-country employees was the ranch or trail cook, who ranked next to the foreman or trail boss and, in camp, ruled supreme over an area of sixty feet around the chuckwagon. In addition to culinary skill—including the ability to prepare a meal in a blizzard, cloudburst, or high wind—the cook also had to be an expert muleskinner or bullwhacker, capable of driving two or three yoke of oxen or a four-mule team attached to the chuckwagon over the most difficult terrain, including flooded rivers. He could do more than anyone else to make life pleasant and many a cowboy selected an outfit because of the reputation of its cook. In compensation for duties which few men could satisfactorily perform, the cook normally was paid from $5 per month more than the ordinary cowhand up to even twice as much.

The cowboy cook was also commonly credited with other qualities less essential and certainly less endearing than the ability to cook and drive the chuckwagon. He was frequently something of a despot; bad-tempered, hard-featured, and unlovely. "As tetchy as a cook" is still a ranch byword. He was often an old "stove-up" cowpuncher who resented having to "wait on" cowboys still in their prime, "just kids" in his opinion. He often was also a "hard character," and frequently had a drinking problem. Finally, as one authority has stated, cooks were seldom good riders.

The above description of the cowboy-cook is synthesized from the reports of numerous observers on cooks of all races and backgrounds in all parts of the cow-country. Some of these qualities doubtless applied to most of them, and all to some of them. But numerous accounts of Negro cow-country cooks suggest that the traditional "hard character" pattern fitted them much less than it did whites. The cow-country cook of the Texas and Texas-influenced range, if not typically a Negro, was at least very frequently one. To be sure, the historian of the cowboy-cook writes: "Most bosses preferred a native white cook. . . . Some Negroes were good cooks, but were usually lazy, and, too, white cowboys refused to take orders from them." This statement, however, is not confirmed by the literature of the cattle country, which strongly suggests that many if not most cattlemen were in agreement with the trail boss who wrote: "For cooks I always preferred darkies."

The primary reason for this preference is probably that Negroes simply were on the average better workers than the available whites. They could, of course, occasionally be lazy, stupid, careless, dishonest, and many whites were excellent cooks, but the cow-camp menus on record seem to have been disproportionately the work of Negro cooks. Good cooks occasionally supplemented the filling but somewhat monotonous diet of biscuits, "sow-belly," beef, molasses, and coffee by carrying a gun in the wagon and, between dishwashing and starting the next meal, hunted deer, turkey, and other game. An extraordinary cook who took full advantage of such opportunities was a thirty-year-old Negro named Sam who, in 1878, prepared for an outfit on Pease River what one of its members years later described as "about the most luscious eating. . . . I have ever enjoyed . . . an oven of buffalo steaks, another . . . of roast bear meat, better than pork, a frying pan full of the breast of wild turkey in gravy of flour, water, and grease, . . . antelope ribs barbecued on a stick over the coals." Sometimes he would roast a turkey in its feathers in a pit. He also cooked wild plums, stewing them or making them into a cobbler. Small wonder that the cowboys of his outfit always saw to it that he had plenty of wood. Sam was merely one of a galaxy of Negro cow-country cooks, each with his specialty— Dutch oven-baked peach pies, "cathead biscuits," "son-of-a-gun stew," etc.

The cook was frequently in sole charge not merely of the kitchen but of the ranch house itself, and on the long drive was of course frequently left alone to protect the chuckwagon and its contents in any emergency, whether crossing a river or encountering Indians. A Negro cook distinguished himself in an episode of 1877 in which the other members of his outfit played no very heroic roles. Four white men and three Negroes were working cattle in Coleman County, Texas, when Indians suddenly swooped down upon them. All took refuge in a cave except "old Negro Andy, the cook," who stayed by the wagon, fought off the Indians, and saved the supplies.

By and large, Negro cooks managed their kitchens or chuckwagon, dealt with Indians, and accomplished their culinary feats without the "crankiness" which was almost as much standard equipment for cow-country cooks as was their "starter" for salt-rising bread. Some white cooks manifested such behavior to an almost psychopathic extent, and some Negro cooks lived up to the tradition, to be sure, but more typical were those remembered for opposite qualities. Jim Perry was not only a fine cook but also "the best Negro who ever lived"; Sam "always had a cheerful word or a cheerful song"; etc. Frank Dobie believes that Negro and Mexican cooks were notably above average in their tendency to be "providers by nature" and in their readiness to go out of their way to furnish extra services, from medicinal supplies to home-made remedies. When, for example, a young cowboy drank alkali water, and "wasn't feeling too good," Jim Simpson, the Negro cook, told him to roll a can of tomatoes in his slicker for both food and drink; the acid from the tomatoes would help neutralize the alkali.

The Negro cook often possessed other skills beyond the culinary. So many Negro cooks, in fact, were noted riders and ropers that something of a pattern emerges. The wild-game cook extraordinary, Black Sam, was such a good rider that "frequently one of the boys would get him to 'top' a bad horse." Jim Perry of the XIT was not only the best cook that ever lived, according to a white hand, but he was also the best rider as well. Jim Simpson, roundup cook and fiddler, who had come up from Texas in the 1880s with a herd of longhorns, was at one time also "about the best roper" in that part of the Wyoming range. When an associate of one of the famous Blockers expressed some doubt about his roping ability, Blocker told his Negro cook, "Goat," to wipe the dough off his hands and get a rope and a horse. Blocker swung a regular "Blocker loop" on the first cow, which picked up her front feet, and the cow pony did the rest. "Goat" similarly roped and threw the next cow, Blocker the third, and so on, until they had roped about twenty, never missing.

Negro cooks often left the chuckwagon for the saddle in an emergency. "Doc" Little, who had risen from cowboy to volunteer cook's assistant to full-time cook, "always remained the good cowboy" and in the event of a stampede was usually the first on a horse. The same was said of the Slaughter cook, "Old Bat." When a drove of 500 horses stampeded, taking the *remuda* with them, including the *remudero's* own picketed horse, the Negro cook threw himself on the trailing rope and "went bumping along for about a hundred yards" before he could stop the animal. He then mounted and took the lead in rounding up the herd.

All cowboys . . . were expected to be able to "sing" in order to soothe the restless cattle. Just as they were expert riders and ropers, Negro cooks were frequently singers, musicians, and even composers. Although hard-worked, they were about the only men in an outfit with the opportunity to carry and play a musical instrument. "The Zebra Dun," a song about a supposed greenhorn who surprised everyone by riding an outlaw horse, is said to have been composed by Jake, who worked for a Pecos River ranch. One chuckwagon cook who supplemented his menu with deer and turkey which he shot himself, also sang and played the guitar. Another, Old Bat, the Slaughter cook, played both the fiddle and the fife. Jim Perry, the XIT cook, was not only the best cook, the best rider, and the best Negro in the world, but also the best fiddler. Jim Simpson, Negro cook and roper of the Wyoming range, was also the regular fiddler for the Saturday night dances. Big Sam, cook and rider, played the banjo and sang until someone stepped on the instrument, whereupon the bunch bought him a fiddle on which he would play such songs as "Green corn, green corn, bring along the demijohn." But the Negro cook-musician who made the most spectacular appearance on the cow-country stage was Gordon Davis, who led Ab Blocker's trail herd through Dodge City while mounted on his left wheel ox, fiddle in hand, playing "Buffalo Gals."

Negro cooks, in addition to riding and roping, singing and playing, sometimes possessed skills so various as to be unclassifiable. The Negro cook, "Old Lee," was "handy as a pocket shirt, ready to do anything, and with the 'know-how' for almost anything that showed up, from cooking to horsewrangling to mending saddle leathers and boots." One of the most versatile of Negro cooks was John Battavia Hinnaut ("Old Bat"), probably the most useful man on the Slaughter spread. Although primarily and officially a roundup cook, he was a first-class ranch-hand, a musician, an expert teamster and coachman, an Indian fighter, a mighty hunter, and also served as the boss's valet, practical nurse, and bodyguard.

That the Negro cow-country cook frequently possessed unusual abilities was due in part to limitations imposed because of racial discrimination. He was much more likely than the average white man to have been brought up about the kitchen and stables of a plantation or ranch and there, at an early age, to have become acquainted with cooking and horses. He was less likely to regard kitchen chores as somehow beneath him. The unusually able and ambitious white cowboy could look forward to possible promotion to foreman or trail boss; the Negro of equal ability knew he had little chance of attaining such a position. To become a ranch or roundup cook was about as much as could be expected. Age, inexperience, or physical handicap might preclude a white man from any ranch job outside of the kitchen; but for the superior Negro cowboy to preside over a chuckwagon or ranch kitchen meant an increase in pay and prestige.

Foremen and Trail Bosses

The Negro cowhand, however able, could, as we have seen, rarely rise to a position higher than chuckwagon or ranch-house cook. The principal obstacle to his becoming a ranch foreman or trail boss was a general belief that a Negro simply did not possess the qualities necessary for such a position. But even if a ranch owner or group of cattlemen were confident that a Negro had the necessary intelligence, initiative, and general capacity, there was always the practical consideration that such a man, even if in charge of an all-Negro outfit, would on occasion have to deal with white foremen and trail bosses who might refuse to recognize his authority, and that expensive trouble might ensue. A Negro, however great his ability, thus had difficulty in attaining greater authority than could be exercised over a chuckwagon or kitchen. The phenomenal success of Ora Haley, who for three decades was the dominant figure in the range-cattle business of Northwestern Colorado, is said to have been partly due to his Negro top hand Thornton Biggs, who although he "taught a whole generation of future range managers, wagon bosses, and all-round cowpunchers the finer points of the range-cattle business," himself "never became a range manager or even a foreman." The fairer-minded recognized the handicaps under which their Negro cowhands labored. Jim Perry, redoubtable cook, rider, and fiddler of the XIT ranch, once wryly remarked: "If it weren't for my damned old black face I'd have been boss of one of these divisions long ago." "And no doubt he would have," a white employee commented.

And yet a very few Negroes of exceptional ability, and sometimes under unusual circumstances, did make the grade. There was the master West Texas rider and roper, "Nigger Add" or "Old Add" who, by 1889 if not earlier, was the LFD's range boss, working "South Texas colored hands almost entirely." One of his qualifications was that he was a "dictionary of earmarks and brands" but probably more important was his universal popularity among cattlemen from Toyah, Texas, to Las Vegas, New Mexico. Nigger Add's outfit consisted "almost entirely" of Negroes—and one wonders who the exceptions were. Probably they were Mexicans.

But did any Negro break through the color line to direct outfits including at least some whites? A leading authority on the cow country doubts that it could have happened. Nevertheless at least one Negro, it seems, through sheer ability and force of character was able to defy the tradition that the white man always gives the orders and the black man obeys. Al Jones was a six-footer with a proud carriage and finely chiseled features of a somewhat "Indian" type. He went up the trail no less than thirteen times, and four times—once was in 1885—he was trail boss, directing Negroes, Mexicans, and sometimes white men. As a trail boss he was resourceful and decisive, but probably needed an abundance of tact to get the job done.

Paradoxically, the race prejudice which prevented more than a very few Negro cowhands from rising to the status of foreman or trail boss may have spurred able and ambitious Negroes into taking up land, acquiring cattle, and setting up as independent small ranchers, whereas, lacking the incentive such an obstacle provided, they might have remained satisfied with a position as ranch foreman. But the story of the Negro rancher belongs to the history of petty capitalism rather than to labor history.

Henchmen, Bodyguards, "Bankers," and Factotums

Some especially able and trustworthy cow-country Negroes fulfilled roles for which there was no equivalent among white cowhands; as confidential assistants, factotums and, when it was necessary to transport large sums of money, bodyguards and "bankers."

Colonel Charles Goodnight wrote of Bose Ikard, his right hand man: "I have trusted him farther than any living man. He was my detective, banker, and everything else." Bose would sometimes have on his person proceeds from his employer's cattle sales amounting to as much as $20,000, since it was reasoned that a thief would be unlikely to search a Negro's belongings.

John Slaughter's "Old Bat" played a similar role. Officially a roundup cook, he could also do almost any ranch work, but his major importance was as a general factotum in anything connected with Slaughter's personal needs—valet, practical nurse, and, above all, bodyguard. When Slaughter was on a cattle-buying trip, Bat always went along to guard the approximately $10,000 in gold which Slaughter usually carried in his money belt, watching while his employer slept. When Slaughter went into Mexico, where silver was preferable, Bat had charge of a mule loaded with "dobe" dollars. His fitness as bodyguard was demonstrated in action against the Apache and when, with another Negro, he stood at Slaughter's side and helped beat off an attack by Mexican bandits.

Print Olive's handyman and bodyguard was Nigger Jim Kelly—wrangler, horsebreaker, gunman—who in the fall of 1869 accompanied his boss back from Fort Kearney, Nebraska, their saddlebags stuffed with currency and gold, and who in 1872, with a quick well-aimed bullet, saved Print's life after he had been shot three times and was about to be killed.

Still another formidable Negro henchman was Zeke, a giant "two-knife" Negro, who in 1879 accompanied Colonel Draper to Dodge City on a cattle-buying trip with a paper-wrapped bundle of $5,000 in currency. Finally, there was "Old Nep." The famous "Shanghai" Pierce may have thought more of him, according to Frank Dobie, than of anyone else; for thirty-five years Neptune Holmes used to accompany Shanghai on his cattle-buying expeditions, leading a mule loaded with saddlebags which bulged with gold and silver and on which he would pillow his head at night.

Where large sums of money were involved, and courage and loyalty in protecting and defending it was needed, prominent cattlemen such as Goodnight, Slaughter, Olive, and Pierce, characteristically preferred to depend on Negro bodyguards.

Wages

For a generation and more, cow-country Negroes distinguished themselves as riders and ropers, cooks and bodyguards, as well as in the more common and still highly necessary positions of wranglers, ordinary cowboys, and top hands. What compensation, financial and psychological, did they receive for their services? And how did their wages, working, and living conditions, and opportunities for advancement and a "good life," compare with those of white hands of corresponding abilities and of Negroes outside the cattle country?

In view of the racial situation which then prevailed throughout the United States, particularly in the South and West, it can be assumed that Negro cowmen encountered discrimination and segregation. The question therefore is not: Did discrimination and segregation exist? But rather: What was their extent and character? And how uniform were they? For although racism was general, it did vary from region to region, from state to state, and even from community to community. It also varied from period to period, probably increasing rather than diminishing during the years in question.

Racial discrimination in the cattle country falls into several categories: wages and working conditions on the job; personal and social relations on the ranch or on cattle trails; and in town or at the end of the cattle trail.

Discrimination was probably least evident on the job. As to wages, cow-punching was, of course, by no means a highly paid occupation, regardless of race. Wages of various categories of cowhands varied widely not only from year to year and from region to region, but even within the same year and region and sometimes within the same outfit as well. Wages were generally low, but increased somewhat from the 1860s into the 1890s and were higher on the Northern Range than in Texas and Kansas. An ordinary hand in the South received from a minimum $15 per month immediately after the Civil War, to $20–$30 through the late 1860s, 1870s, and into the

1880s, to as much as $45 in the 1890s. An experienced top hand would receive $5 or $10 per month more than a less experienced man, and trail hands were paid somewhat more than ordinary ranch hands. Especially experienced trail hands, below the rank of trail boss, occasionally drew double wages of as much as $60 or even $75; but a "green" boy would receive half-wages of $10–$15. The wages of trail bosses and foremen normally ranged during this period from $100 to $150. Cooks' salaries, as we have seen, might be as little as that of a top hand or as much as double an ordinary cowhand's, but customarily were $5 or $10 more than those of the best-paid cowhand in the outfit. In the North, cowhands usually got about $10 a month more than those in the South. In all cases compensation included food and, in the case of ranch hands, sleeping accommodations, such as they were.

Strange though it may seem, there is no clear-cut evidence that Negro cowhands were generally or seriously discriminated against in the matter of wages, though this was obviously so with Mexicans, who sometimes received one half to one third that of white cowboys earning $20–25. "Teddy Blue," to be sure, says of the Olive outfit, for which he worked in 1879, that they hated Mexicans and "niggers" but "hired them because they worked cheaper than white men." He gives no details, however, and the notoriously violent Olives may have been no more typical in their wage policy than in their conduct generally. On the other hand, one trail boss stated: "I have worked white Americans, Mexicans, and Negroes and they all got just the same salary." Wages were so much under the control of the individual employer that no doubt Negroes were sometimes discriminated against; but such discrimination seems not to have been characteristic and, when it occurred, was never nearly as serious as that to which Mexicans were subjected. . . .

Living Conditions

Discrimination and segregation off the job, whether on the ranch or the cattle trail, would have been difficult. Hendrix insists on at least partially segregated eating facilities when he describes the Negroes as "topping" the white hands' horses while the whites ate breakfast—presumably the Negroes ate at the "second table"—and he also states that the Negroes "had their own dishes"! But one can hardly imagine the independent and even cranky chuckwagon cook actually taking the trouble to segregate the dishes! Hendrix may have been reading back into the 1870s and 1880s the pattern of race relationships which he considered proper in his own times.

Actually, firsthand accounts of ranch and cattle-trail life indicate about as much segregation as prevailed on Huckleberry Finn's and the "Nigger Jim's" raft before the appearance of "The King" and "The Duke." The sleeping arrangements were usually such as to defy any idea of racial segregation. Ranchowner, trail boss, Negro and white cowhands—particularly in bad weather—frequently not only slept in the same shack or tent but also shared the same blankets. The one case of such segregation I have encountered occurred on a Wyoming ranch in 1885 when an Irish cook (sex not specified) refused to allow a Negro bronc buster to sleep in the bunkhouse. But when white women began to appear, those extreme manifestations of racial "integration" belonging to the womanless world of the cattle trail and the wintering camp yielded to a more formal and conventional pattern of conduct. When a highly respected Negro cowboy, in the midst of a blizzard, was permitted to sleep on the kitchen floor of a shack in which a camp manager was living with his wife it was regarded by the Negro as an example of extreme condescension or of humanity or both. . . .

Recreation and Social Life

The Negro cowboy engaged in the same amusements as the white—on a basis ranging from apparently complete integration to rigid separation. The extent of this segregation depended upon how well the parties knew one another and, more important, upon whether or not the whites included women.

To understand the character and degree of this segregation, and the way in which it was regarded by both whites and blacks, one must remember that the white men and women of the cow country were largely Southerners, or Westerners with a Southern exposure, while the Negroes, if not former slaves, were usually the children of ex-slaves. Both whites and Negroes were thus acquainted, by personal experience or recent tradition, with racial *discrimination* far more severe than anything practiced in the post-bellum cow country, even though racial *segregation* under slavery was less rigid than it became during the late nineteenth century.

When ranch work was slack, particularly in the winter, the hands sometimes held a dance, either a "bunkhouse 'shindig' " in which the participants were all males or a "regular dance" with girls from neighboring ranches or from town if one was close enough. On these occasions the Negro hands had the opportunity to shine, as musicians or dancers or both. Although serving as musicians at either type of dance, they were more conspicuous as dancers in the womanless bunkhouse affairs. Indeed, they might not appear on the dance floor with white women, though, singly or in groups, they might present dancing exhibitions as part of the entertainment.

Segregation in a cattle town, where the Negro cowhand was more of a stranger and white women were present, was much more clearcut than on the familiar ranch. But even here the restrictions were not always as rigid as one might perhaps expect. On the town's streets and among members of the same outfit, segregation might be non-existent. A French baron, returning in 1883 from a visit to the Black Hills, was astonished to see a group of cowboys throwing the lasso and wrestling in front of the door to the hotel bar, with a Negro participating "on a footing of perfect equality." Consequently, he naively assumed that "race prejudice had disappeared," but had the cowboys *entered* the bar this illusion would probably have vanished, even though the region was the Northern Range, not Gulf Coast Texas.

Even in Texas, however, segregation in the saloons was apparently informal. Whites, it seems, were served at one end of the bar, Negroes at the other. But should a white man and a Negro choose to drink and converse together in the "neutral zone" between the two sections probably no objection would be raised. The gunman and gambler Ben Thompson once undertook to "integrate" a San Antonio saloon at the point of a revolver, forcing the bartender to permit the Negroes to "spread out" from their crowded corner into the vacant space at the "white" end of the bar. His friends charitably assumed that he was suffering from a nervous breakdown, but since, upon an earlier occasion, Thompson had shot a white bully who was trying to force a Cherokee-Negro cowboy to down a beer mug full of whiskey, he may actually have been in part influenced by a fleeting impulse to defend the underdog.

If the Negro, however, moved from the saloon to a restaurant, he would encounter a completely segregated situation, partly because of the symbolic value attached to sitting down and eating together—as opposed to standing up at the same bar—but principally because women might be guests in the dining room or cafe. In a town without a colored restaurant, the Negro might have food handed to him at the back door of a cafe—perhaps he might even be permitted to eat in the kitchen—but more probably would, like many white cowboys, prefer to purchase groceries and eat sitting on a hitching rail.

Negroes, of course, were not lodged in "white" hotels—unless they were in attendance on prominent white cattlemen—but cowboys, black and white, usually felt that they had better use for their money than to spend it on hotel rooms. They preferred to spread their "hot rolls" in a livery stable or some other sheltered spot.

The most rigorously segregated cow-town establishments, at least so far as Negro cowhands were concerned, were brothels staffed with white prostitutes. However, the larger cow-towns at least, such as Dodge City, were also equipped with *bagnios* occupied by "soiled doves of color," while smaller communities usually had a few "public women" of color who operated independently. The rule that Negroes must not patronize white prostitutes did not of course bar relations between white cowhands and colored women.

The cow-town gambling-house, on the other hand, was apparently entirely unsegregated. A gambler who intended to separate a Negro trail hand from his wages through the more than expert use of cards and dice could hardly do so without sitting down with him at the same card or crap table.

The Negro cowhand was accustomed to a degree of segregation and apparently did not resent it—at least not to the extent of risking his life in defiance of the practice. Clashes between Negro cowhands and whites were exceedingly rare. When racial encounters occurred in cattle towns, the Negroes involved were almost always colored soldiers.

Conclusion

Without the services of the eight or nine thousand Negroes—a quarter of the total number of trail drivers—who during the generation after the Civil War helped to move herds up the cattle trails to shipping points, Indian reservations, and fattening grounds and who, between drives, worked on the ranches of Texas and the Indian Territory, the cattle industry would have been seriously handicapped. For apart from their considerable numbers, many of them were especially well-qualified top hands, riders, ropers, and cooks. Of the comparatively few Negroes on the Northern Range, a good many were also men of conspicuous abilities who notably contributed to the industry in that region. These cowhands, in their turn, benefitted from their participation in the industry, even if not to the extent that they deserved. That a degree of discrimination and segregation existed in the cattle country should not obscure the fact that, during the halcyon days of the cattle range, Negroes there frequently enjoyed greater opportunities for a dignified life than anywhere else in the United States. They worked, ate, slept, played, and on occasion fought, side by side with their white comrades, and their ability and courage won respect, even admiration. They were often paid the same wages as white cowboys and, in the case of certain horsebreakers, ropers, and cooks, occupied positions of considerable prestige. In a region and period characterized by violence, their lives were probably safer than they would have been in the Southern cotton regions where between 1,500 and 1,600 Negroes were lynched in the two decades after 1882. The skilled and handy Negro probably had a more enjoyable, if a rougher, existence as a cowhand than he would have had as a sharecropper or laborer. Bose Ikard, for example, had a rich, full, and dignified life on the West Texas frontier—as trail driver, as Indian fighter, and as Colonel Goodnight's right-hand man—more so undoubtedly than he could ever have known on a plantation in his native Mississippi.

Negro cowhands, to be sure, were not treated as "equals," except in the rude quasi-equality of the round-up, roping-pen, stampede, and river-crossing—where they were sometimes tacitly recognized even as superiors—but where else in post–Civil War America, at a time of the Negro's nadir, did so many adult Negroes and whites attain even this degree of fraternity? The cow country was no utopia for Negroes, but it did demonstrate that under some circumstances and for at least brief periods white and black in significant numbers could live and work together on more nearly equal terms than had been possible in the United States for two hundred years or would be possible again for nearly another century.

Y *F U R T H E R   R E A D I N G*

E. C. Abbott ("Teddy Blue") and Helena Huntington Smith, *We Pointed Them North* (1939)
Andy Adams, *The Log of a Cowboy* (1903)

Lewis Atherton, *The Cattle Kings* (1961)

Floyd C. Bard, *Horse Wrangler: Sixty Years in the Saddle in Wyoming and Montana* (1960)

Gunther Barth, *Bitter Strength: A History of the Chinese in the United States, 1850–1870* (1964)

Ronald C. Brown, *Hard-Rock Miners: The Intermountain West, 1860–1920* (1979)

David Dary, *Cowboy Culture: A Saga of Five Centuries* (1981)

J. Frank Dobie, *Cow People* (1964)

Philip Durham and Everett L. Jones, *The Negro Cowboys* (1965)

Robert R. Dykstra, *The Cattle Towns* (1968)

Joe B. Frantz and Julian E. Choate, Jr., *The American Cowboy: The Myth and the Reality* (1955)

William S. Greever, *The Bonanza West: The Story of the Western Mining Rushes, 1848–1900* (1963)

Gene M. Gressley, *Bankers and Cattlemen* (1966)

J. S. Holliday, *The World Rushed In: The California Gold Rush Experience* (1981)

William H. Hutchinson, "The Cowboy and the Class Struggle, or, Never Put Marx in the Saddle," *Arizona and the West*, 14 (1972), 321–30

Teresa Jordan, *Cowgirls: Women of the American West* (1982)

Rudolph Lapp, *Blacks in Gold Rush California* (1977)

Richard E. Lingenfelter, *Hardrock Miners: A History of the Mining Labor Movement in the American West, 1863–1893* (1974)

David E. Lopez, "Cowboy Strikes and Unions," *Labor History*, 18 (1977), 325–40

Ralph Mann, *After the Gold Rush: Society in Grass Valley and Nevada City, California, 1849–1870* (1982)

Stuart Creighton Miller, *The Unwelcome Immigrant: The American Image of the Chinese, 1785–1882* (1969)

Rodman Wilson Paul, *California Gold* (1947)

————, *Mining Frontiers of the Far West, 1848–1880* (1963)

Jean-Nicolas Perlot, *Gold Seeker* (1985)

Paula Petrik, *No Step Backward: Women and Family on the Rocky Mountain Mining Frontier, Helena, Montana, 1865–1900* (1987)

Alexander Saxton, *The Indispensable Enemy: Labor and the Anti-Chinese Movement in California* (1971)

Peter K. Simpson, "The Social Side of the Cattle Industry," *Agricultural History*, 49 (1975), 39–50

Charles A. Siringo, *Riata and Spurs: The Story of a Lifetime Spent in the Saddle as Cowboy and Ranger* (1927)

Duane A. Smith, *Rocky Mountain Mining Camps: The Urban Frontier* (1967)

Clark C. Spence, *Mining Engineers and the American West: The Lace Boot Brigade, 1849–1933* (1970)

Vivian H. Whitlock, *Cowboy Life on the Llano Estacado* (1970)

Donald E. Worcester, *The Chisholm Trail: High Road of the Cattle Kingdom* (1980)

Mark Wyman, *Hard Rock Epic: Western Miners and the Industrial Revolution, 1860–1910* (1979)

Otis E. Young, Jr., *Black Powder and Hand Steel: Miners and Machines on the Old Western Frontier* (1976)

Paul E. Young, *Back Trail of an Old Cowboy* (1983)

Western Violence

Υ

*Was violence in the post–Civil War West greater than or distinctive from vio-
lence in the rest of the United States at that time? Is part of the legacy of frontier individualism a higher propensity for violent action? Is violence within the
United States a product of regional or national character? These questions are
provocative and disturbing. Western history certainly has a record of violence.
Yet it should be remembered that the most violent episode of American history—
the Civil War—was fought, with only minor exceptions, east of the Mississippi
River valley. Westerners killed, but never on the scale of this North-South
conflict.*

    *Still, the history of violence in the West has its stories of mayhem and
slaughter, many involving attacks on Indian villages. It also has numerous
characters like Butch Cassidy and Jesse James, whose willingness to resort to
violence for illegal gain did not preclude their elevation to the status of folk
hero. Other westerners, among them George Armstrong Custer and Billy the
Kid, gained lasting fame through violent action and dramatic death. The ac-
claim accorded these individuals as either outlaws or fallen heroes reveals that in
the West, and indeed in the nation as a whole, many people approved of certain kinds of violence.*

Υ *D O C U M E N T S*

The first two documents present accounts of violence between Indians and
whites. At dawn on November 29, 1864, one thousand territorial volunteers under the command of Colonel John M. Chivington attacked the camp of some five
hundred sleeping Cheyennes on the banks of Sand Creek in what is now Colorado. The Cheyenne leaders, Black Kettle and White Antelope, believing that a
peace treaty was in effect, had already turned in their arms at Fort Lyon. The
soldiers slaughtered men, women, and children indiscriminately and mutilated
their bodies. At least one hundred and fifty Indians died in what is known as the
Sand Creek Massacre. Robert Bent's testimony about this event, reprinted as the
first document, was given to a special congressional committee that investigated
the affair.

    On June 25, 1876, Lieutenant Colonel George Armstrong Custer divided his command of the Seventh Cavalry. The troops that followed him along the bluffs above the valley of the Little Big Horn were overwhelmed by a superior force of Sioux, Arapahos, and Northern Cheyennes in one of the great disasters of American military history. The exact details of the battle and of Custer's death remain controversial. The excerpt republished here as the second document comes from the *Helena Daily Herald* of July 15, 1876. It gives Lieutenant James Bradley's description of the field after the battle and the Crow scout Curley's account of the battle itself. Some historians have questioned the validity of Curley's testimony in the light of his tale of miraculous escape at the end. They believe that he may have put a far greater distance between himself and the field of battle before the fighting started.

The third selection, comprising three ballads that look at the violent lives and deaths of some outlaws, reveals that lawbreakers may indeed be recognized as folk heroes. The ballad of Jesse James, well known for its reference to his betrayal by "that dirty little coward," also gives fanciful details of Frank and Jesse's outlaw life, including the claim that Jesse, like Robin Hood, was a friend to the poor. The ballad of Cole Younger recounts with folkloric directness some dramatic events that took place in 1876 in Northfield, Minnesota. There, after a failed bank robbery, the three Younger brothers—Cole, Jim, and Bob—were captured, while their cohorts, the James brothers, escaped. The ballad of Gregorio Cortez must properly be sung in Spanish. It is based on events in Texas in 1901 in which an Anglo sheriff was killed while attempting to arrest Cortez in a case of wrongful accusations of horse stealing exacerbated by bungled translations by the sheriff's assistant. For ten days over five hundred miles of Texas territory, Cortez eluded the Texas Rangers and local posses. He was finally arrested near the Mexican border. Four years of trials and eight years in prison followed. The ballad focuses on Cortez's dramatic flight, in which this lone Mexican escaped posses that sometimes numbered more than three hundred men.

The death of Jesse James produced not only folk songs but also something akin to pulp fiction. The anonymous account presented here as the fourth document appeared in 1882, the year of James's death. Its title page read, "Jesse James: The Life and Daring Adventures of this Bold Highwayman and Bank Robber and His No Less Celebrated Brother Frank James together with the Thrilling Exploits of the Younger Boys, written by *** (one who dare not NOW disclose his identity). The Only Book containing the Romantic Life of Jesse James and his Pretty Wife who clung to Him to the Last." The final document, a report in the June 15, 1894, *Weekly Elevator* of Fort Smith, Arkansas, on the death of Bill Dalton, is not as breathlessly presented. It nonetheless demonstrates that other outlaws also came to a violent end.

Robert Bent on the Sand Creek Atrocities, 1864

I am twenty-four years old; was born on the Arkansas river. I am pretty well acquainted with the Indians of the plains, having spent most of my life among them. I was employed as guide and interpreter at Fort Lyon by Major Anthony. Colonel Chivington ordered me to accompany him on his way to Sand creek. The command consisted of from nine hundred to one thousand men, principally Colorado volunteers. We left Fort Lyon at eight o'clock in the evening, and came on to the Indian camp at daylight the next morning. Colonel Chivington surrounded the village with his troops.

When we came in sight of the camp I saw the American flag waving and heard Black Kettle tell the Indians to stand round the flag, and there they were huddled—men, women, and children. This was when we were within fifty yards of the Indians. I also saw a white flag raised. These flags were in so conspicuous a position that they must have been seen. When the troops fired the Indians ran, some of the men into their lodges, probably to get their arms. They had time to get away if they had wanted to. I remained on the field five hours, and when I left there were shots being fired up the creek. I think there were six hundred Indians in all. I think there were thirty-five braves and some old men, about sixty in all. All fought well. At the time the rest of the men were away from camp, hunting. I visited the battle-ground one month afterwards; saw the remains of a good many; counted sixty-nine, but a number had been eaten by the wolves and dogs. After the firing the warriors put the squaws and children together, and surrounded them to protect them. I saw five squaws under a bank for shelter. When the troops came up to them they ran out and showed their persons to let the soldiers know they were squaws and begged for mercy, but the soldiers shot them all. I saw one squaw lying on the bank whose leg had been broken by a shell; a soldier came up to her with a drawn sabre; she raised her arm to protect herself, when he struck, breaking her arm; she rolled over and raised her other arm, when he struck, breaking it, and then left her without killing her. There seemed to be an indiscriminate slaughter of men, women, and children. There were some thirty or forty squaws collected in a hole for protection; they sent out a little girl about six years old with a white flag on a stick; she had not proceeded but a few steps when she was shot and killed. All the squaws in that hole were afterwards killed, and four or five bucks outside. The squaws offered no resistance. Every one I saw dead was scalped. I saw one squaw cut open with an unborn child, as I thought, lying by her side. Captain Soulé afterwards told me that such was the fact. I saw the body of White Antelope with the privates cut off, and I heard a soldier say he was going to make a tobacco-pouch out of them. I saw one squaw whose privates had been cut out. I heard Colonel Chivington say to the soldiers as they charged past him, "Remember our wives and children murdered on the Platte and Arkansas." He occupied a position where he could not have failed to have seen the American flag, which I think was a garrison flag, six by twelve. He was within fifty yards when he planted his battery. I saw a little girl about five years of age who had been hid in the sand; two soldiers discovered her, drew their pistols and shot her, and then pulled her out of the sand by the arm. I saw quite a number of infants in arms killed with their mothers.

James Bradley on
Custer's Disaster
on the Little Bighorn, 1876

THE VALLEY OF DEATH
PARTICULARS OF THE MASSACRE OF
CUSTER'S COMMAND

*   *   *

THE UNWRITTEN CHAPTER

*   *   *

"CURLEY," A CROW SCOUT, THE
ONLY SURVIVOR OF THE BATTLE,
TELLS THE STORY

*   *   *

NOT UNTIL THEIR AMMUNITION WAS
GONE WERE OUR TROOPS BUTCHERED

*   *   *

A LARGE NUMBER OF INDIANS KILLED

*   *   *

Lieut. Jas. H. Bradley, of the 7th infantry, who commanded the scouts under Gibbon on the recent march from the Yellowstone to the Little Horn [sic] and return, arrived in this city last night and left for Fort Shaw this morning. He left the command one week ago to-day, in camp near Fort Pease, and everything was quiet. Our reporter interviewed Lieut. Bradley, who very kindly gave us a description of the Little Horn disaster, but more particularly the account of Custer's battle and massacre, which has not heretofore been published. It would be in place at this juncture to state that Lieut. Bradley, with his scouts, on the morning of the 27th of June, crossed to the opposite side of the Little Horn from which the command was marching, and deployed out through the hills in skirmish line. (The evening previous three Crow scouts had reported to the Lieutenant that Custer's regiment of cavalry had been cut to pieces. This report was not credited by Terry and Gibbon; yet it was known that they were approaching the Indian village, and the scouts were, if possible, unusually vigilant and active.) About 9 o'clock, a scout reported to Lieut. Bradley that he saw an object which looked like a dead horse. The Lieutenant found it to be a dead cavalry horse, and, going a few yards further on, to the brow of a hill, looking into the valley below, a terrible scene was presented to view. It was literally strewn with the dead of the gallant Seventh Cavalry. Lieut. Bradley rode hurriedly over the field, and in a few minutes time counted *one hundred and ninety-seven* dead bodies. Custer fell upon the highest point of the field; and around him, within a space of five rods square, lay forty-two men and thirty-one horses. The dead soldiers all lay within a circle embracing only a few hundred yards square. The Lieutenant immediately reported to Gibbon, which was the first intelligence of the battle received. A few moments later a scout arrived from Reno's command, asking for assistance, and Terry and Gibbon pushed forward to the rescue.

Not a single survivor of Custer's command was found, and even up to the time General Terry made out his official report to General Sheridan it was supposed that the last soul had perished. But when the command returned to the Yellowstone they found there a Crow scout named "Curley," who, as verified by Major Reno, rode out with Custer on that fatal day. He alone escaped, and his account of the battle we give below. It is interesting, as being the only story of the fight ever to be looked for from one who was an actual participant on Custer's side—Curley being, in all human probability the only survivor of his command. . . . Curley is not well informed, as he was himself concealed in a deep ravine, from which but a small part of the field was visible.

The fight appears to have begun, from Curley's description of the situation of the sun, about 2:30 or 3 o'clock p.m., and continued without intermission until nearly sunset. The Indians had completely surrounded the command, leaving their horses in ravines well to the rear, themselves pressing forward to attack on foot. Confident in the great superiority of their numbers, they made several charges on all points of Custer's line; but the troops held their position firmly, and delivered a heavy fire, and every time drove them back. Curley says the firing was more rapid than anything he had ever conceived of, being a continuous roll, like (as he expressed it) "The Snapping of the Threads in the Tearing of a Blanket."

The troops expended all the ammunition in their belts, and then sought their horses for the reserve ammunition carried in their saddle pockets.

As long as their ammunition held out, the troops, though losing considerably in the fight, maintained their position in spite of all the efforts of the Sioux. From the weakening of their fire towards the close of the afternoon the Indians appeared to believe that their ammunition was about exhausted, and they made a grand final charge, in the course of which the last of the command was destroyed, the men being shot, where they laid in their positions in the line, at such close quarters that many were killed with arrows. Curley says that Custer remained alive through the greater part of the engagement, animating his men to determined resistance; but about an hour before the close of the fight received a mortal wound.

Curley says the field was thickly strewn with the dead bodies of the Sioux who fell in the attack—in number considerably more than the force of soldiers engaged. He is satisfied that their loss will exceed 300 killed, beside an immense number wounded. Curley accomplished his escape by drawing his blanket about him in the manner of the Sioux, and passing through an interval which had been made in their line as they scattered over the field in their final charge. He says they must have seen him, as he was in plain view, but was probably mistaken by the Sioux for one of their own number or one of their allied Arapahoes or Cheyennes.

Three Ballads of Outlaw Heroes: Jesse James, Cole Younger, and Gregorio Cortez

Jesse James

Jesse James was a lad that killed a-many a man;
He robbed the Danville train
But that dirty little coward that shot Mr. Howard
Has laid poor Jesse in his grave.

Poor Jesse had a wife to mourn for his life,
Three children they were brave,
But that dirty little coward shot Mr. Howard
Has laid poor Jesse in his grave.

It was Robert Ford that dirty little coward,
I wonder how he does feel,
For he eat of Jesse's bread and he slept in Jesse's bed,
Then laid poor Jesse in his grave.

Jesse was a man a friend to the poor,
He never would see a man suffer pain;
And with his brother Frank he robbed the Chicago bank
And stopped the Glendale train.

It was his brother Frank that robbed the Gallatine bank,
And carried the money from town;
It was in this very place that they had a little race,
For they shot Captain Sheets to the ground.

They went to the crossing not very far from there,
And there they did the same;
With the agent on his knees he delivered up the key
To the outlaws Frank and Jesse James.

It was on Wednesday night the moon was shining bright,
They robbed the Glendale train;
The people they did say for many miles away,
It was robbed by Frank and Jesse James.

It was on Saturday night Jesse was at home
Talking with his family brave,
Robert Ford came along like a thief in the night
And laid poor Jesse in his grave.

The people held their breath when they heard of Jesse's death,
And wondered how ever he came to die
It was one of the gang called little Robert Ford,
He shot poor Jesse on the sly.

Jesse went to his rest with his hand on his breast;
The devil will be upon his knee
He was born one day in the country of Clay
And came from a solitary race.

This song was made by Billy Gashade,
As soon as the news did arrive,
He said there was no man with the law in his hand
Who could take Jesse James when alive.

Cole Younger

I am a highway bandit man, Cole Younger is my name
Though many a depredations have brought my life to shame
A-robbing of the Northfield bank was a shame I'll never deny
I'm doomed a poor prisoner, in the Stillwater Jail I lie.

'Tis one of the high, bold robberies the truth to you I'll tell
A Californee miner whose fate to us befell
Saying, "Hand your money over and make no long delay,"
A trick that I'll be sorry of until my dying day.

Then we left good old Texas, that good old lone star state,
Out on Nebraskee prairies the James boys we did meet
With knives, guns, and revolvers we all sit down to play
A good old game of poker to pass the time away.

Out on Nebraskee prairies the Denver came along
Says I to Bob, "Let's rob her as she goes rolling on."
Killed the engineer and fireman, conductor 'scaped alive
Their bodies now lie moulding beneath Nebraska's skies.

We saddled up our horses and northward we did go
To the God forsaken country called Minnesot-ee-oh
I had my eye on the Northfield bank when brother Bob did
    say,
"Cole, if you undertake that job, you'll always curse the day."

We stationed out our pickets and up to the bank did go
It was there upon the counter I struck my fatal blow
Saying, "Hand your money over and make no long delay
For we're the noted Younger boys, and 'low no time to stay."

The cashier being a true Westfield, refused our noble band
It was Jesse James that pulled the trigger that killed that
    faithful man
In vain we searched for the money drawers while the battle
    raged outside
Until we saw our safety was a quick and desperate ride.

It was Charlie pitched off by his post, Doc Wheeler drew his
    gun
He shot poor Charlie through the heart, who cried, "My God,
    I'm done."
Again Doc Wheeler drew his gun, results of which you'll see
Well, Miller he fell from his horse in mortal agony.

Come boys, and ride for life and death; there's hundreds on
    our trail
The Younger boys were doomed to fate and landed right in jail
They've taken us to the Stillwater Jail to worry our lives away
The James boys they can tell the tale of that eventful day.

Gregorio Cortez

En el condado del Carmen
miren lo que ha sucedido,
murió el Cherife Mayor,
quedando Román herido.

In the county of El Carmen
Look what has happened;
The Major Sheriff died,
Leaving Román badly wounded.

Otro día por la mañana,	The next day, in the morning,
cuando la gente llegó,	When people arrived,
unos a los otros dicen:	They said to one another,
—No saben quién lo mató.	"It is not known who killed him."
Se anduvieron informando	They went around asking questions,
como tres horas después,	About three hours afterward;
supieron que el malhechor	They found that the wrongdoer
era Gregorio Cortez.	Had been Gregorio Cortez.
Ya insortaron a Cortez	Now they have outlawed Cortez,
por toditito el estado,	Throughout the whole state;
que vivo o muerto lo aprehendan	Let him be taken, dead or alive;
porque a varios ha matado.	He has killed several men.
Decía Gregorio Cortez	Then said Gregorio Cortez,
con su pistola en la mano:	With his pistol in his hand,
—No siento haberlo matado,	"I don't regret that I killed him;
al que siento es a mi hermano.	I regret my brother's death."
Decía Gregorio Cortez	Then said Gregorio Cortez,
con su alma muy encendida:	And his soul was all aflame,
—No siento haberlo matado,	"I don't regret that I killed him;
la defensa es permitida.	A man must defend himself."
Venían los americanos	The Americans were coming;
que por el viento volaban	They seemed to fly through the air;
porque se iban a ganar	Because they were going to get
tres mil pesos que les daban.	Three thousand dollars they were offered.
Tiró con rumbo a Gonzales,	He struck out for Gonzales;
varios cherifes lo vieron,	Several sheriffs saw him;
no lo quisieron seguir	They decided not to follow
porque le tuvieron miedo.	Because they were afraid of him.
Venían los perros jaunes,	The bloodhounds were coming,
venían sobre la huella,	They were coming on the trail,
pero alcanzar a Cortez	But overtaking Cortez
era seguir a una estrella.	Was like following a star.
Decía Gregorio Cortez:	Then said Gregorio Cortez,
—¿Pa' qué se valen de planes?	"What is the use of your scheming?
Si no pueden agarrarme	You cannot catch me,
ni con esos perros jaunes.	Even with those bloodhounds."
Decían los americanos:	Then the Americans said,
—Si lo alcanzamos ¿qué haremos?	"If we catch up with him, what shall we do?
Si le entramos por derecho	If we fight him man to man,
muy poquitos volveremos.	Very few of us will return."

Reprinted from *"With His Pistol in His Hand": A Border Ballad and Its Hero*, 158–161, by Americo Paredes, 1958, by permission of the University of Texas Press.

Se fué de Brownsville al rancho,
lo alcanzaron a rodear,
poquitos más de trescientos,
y allí les brincó el corral.

From Brownsville he went to the
   ranch.
They succeeded in surrounding him;
Quite a few more than three
   hundred,
But there he jumped their corral.

Allá por El Encinal,
según lo que aquí se dice,
se agarraron a balazos
y les mató otro cherife.

Over by El Encinal,
According to what we hear,
They got into a gunfight,
And he killed them another sheriff.

Decía Gregorio Cortez
con su pistola en la mano:
—No corran, rinches cobardes,
con un solo mexicano.

Then said Gregorio Cortez,
With his pistol in his hand,
"Don't run, you cowardly rangers,
From just one Mexican."

Tiró con rumbo a Laredo
sin ninguna timidez:
—Síganme, rinches cobardes,
yo soy Gregorio Cortez.

He struck out for Laredo
Without showing any fear,
"Follow me, cowardly rangers,
I am Gregorio Cortez."

Gregorio le dice a Juan
en el rancho del Ciprés:
—Platícame qué hay de nuevo,
yo soy Gregorio Cortez.

Gregorio says to Juan,
At the Cypress Ranch,
"Tell me the news;
I am Gregorio Cortez."

Gregorio le dice a Juan:
—Muy pronto lo vas a ver,
anda y dile a los cherifes
que me vengan a aprehender.

Gregorio says to Juan,
"You will see it happen soon;
Go call the sheriffs
So they can come and arrest me."

Cuando llegan los cherifes
Gregorio se presentó:
—Por la buena sí me llevan,
porque de otro modo no.

When the sheriffs arrive,
Gregorio gave himself up,
"You take me because I'm willing,
But not any other way."

Ya agarraron a Cortez,
ya terminó la cuestión,
la pobre de su familia
la lleva en el corazón.

Now they have taken Cortez,
Now matters are at an end;
His poor family
Are suffering in their hearts.

Ya con ésta me despido
a la sombra de un ciprés,
aquí se acaba cantando
la tragedia de Cortez.

Now with this I say farewell,
In the shade of a cypress,
This is the end of the singing
Of the ballad about Cortez.

The Death of Jesse James, 1882

*The end of the play—The curtain falls—The lights turned
down, and the King of American bandits makes a hasty exit!*

On the morning of April 3d, 1882, Jesse James "died with his boots on."
That it was a cowardly assassination I am forced to admit, but in writing
of one that I knew well I have but this to say: he would have done the

same to anyone whom he for one moment suspected! He would have killed the man and *inquired into the facts afterwards!* St. Joseph, Missouri, was the scene of his "taking off," and the Ford boys were "in at the death!"

He was shot down by two men who were in his confidence, and who had planned a raid for that very night. After the Blue Cut robbery in September, 1881, James was in hiding at his mother's house at Kearney, near Kansas City. He remained there for a few weeks and kept very quiet. Some time in November he went to St. Joseph and established himself in a little shanty in the southeastern part of the city. His wife, who was devotedly attached to him, and who is young and pretty, went with him. Although there had long been a price upon the heads of the James boys, Jesse paid no attention to it. His many hairbreadth escapades had made him oblivious to danger. Instead of going to Texas, as had been his custom when hunted down too closely, he remained in Missouri, only taking care to keep out of sight. He had been living very quietly in "Saint Jo," always kept himself well armed to guard against surprise, and his shanty was a regular arsenal.

After the shooting it was learned that Jesse had been planning another desperate raid, with the help of two brothers named Robert and Charles Ford. Just who these men were was not then known. It was believed they had been engaged in robberies with him before, but they claimed that they had been on his track for a long time, with the intention of capturing him and claiming the heavy rewards offered by the express companies, that have suffered from his depredations, and the State authorities. However that may be they were in his confidence. Charles had been at his house for several weeks, and Robert came a week or ten days before the assassination. These two men were the ones who shot down their chief without giving him a second's warning. James always wore a belt stuffed full of revolvers of the latest pattern. They were always loaded and he never took a step without them. If the Ford brothers had given him cause for the slightest suspicion he would have shot them down without hesitation. He had often treated detectives who had tried to gain his confidence in just that manner, and he would not have hesitated to do it again. It was thought for this reason that the Fords had been with him before and were well known to him, and it is not impossible that they became frightened at the general breaking up of the band and the many arrests, and sought to cover their own tracks and make themselves right at the same time with the authorities by taking the life of the great outlaw.

At 9 o'clock on the morning of April 3d, 1882, the great outlaw and the two Fords were together in a front room in Jesse James' house. Unconscious of danger James unbuckled his belt and threw it on the bed preparatory to washing himself. He was unarmed. Jesse got upon a chair to arrange a picture. The brothers had determined to kill him and get the reward and this was their chance.

They exchanged glances and silently stepped between the pistols and their victim. Both drew their pistols. The click of the hammers fell on the ear of Jesse, and he was turning his head evidently to see what caused the warning sound when Robert, the youngest brother, sent a bullet crashing through his brain. The murdered bandit fell backward without a cry and rolled in his death agony on the floor.

Jesse's wife, who was in the next room, ran in and saw the two brothers scaling the fence and making off. Hardly had the shot been fired when there was a piercing scream. The dead man's wife flung herself upon the prostrate body and gave way to her grief in a flood of tears. The Fords gave themselves up and were hurried away to the court house and a guard immediately put on duty. The news spread like wildfire. The house was surrounded by excited people and hundreds of persons talked about the bloody deed on the streets. The body was taken in charge by the police and photographed. Persons who had known the outlaw were allowed to view the remains. They declared that there was no doubt this time and at last the great bandit had been killed. The face is fine-looking and intelligent and would not be taken for that of a cruel murderer. The house was searched and found to contain a quantity of firearms and ammunition. In the stable was several splendid horses.

An Arkansas Newspaper on the Killing of Bill Dalton, 1894

BILL DALTON, THE BANDIT, KILLED

AT ELK, I.T., WHILE TRYING TO

ESCAPE FROM DEPUTY MARSHALS.

Bill Dalton, the notorious desperado and bandit, met his death on the 8th inst. at Elk, I.T. [Indian Territory]. C.L. Hart, a deputy marshal of the Paris district, fired the shot that sent the spirit of the outlaw to its home.

Last Friday afternoon a man named Wallace, accompanied by two women, rode into Ardmore and bought $200 worth of goods, for which they paid cash. Wallace, being a dissolute sort of a fellow, and known to be generally short of cash, his movements attracted attention. After purchasing the goods he went to the express office and called for a package which was given to him. This caused his arrest by the officers, who had been watching him, and the package upon being broken open was found to contain several gallons of whiskey. From the parties arrested and the incautious remarks the woman dropped the officials concluded the liquor was intended for the Longview bank robbers, who were thought to be camped near Elk, a small town 25 miles northwest of Ardmore. A posse of United States deputy marshals, consisting of D.E. Booker, S.F. Gladsay, S. Leatherman, E. Roberts, W.B. Freeman, M. Glover and Ross Hart, started for the freebooters' rendezvous. The Wallace place, where they had reason to believe their gang was in hiding, was surrounded by the posse about 8 a.m. that day, and while the men were taking their positions Dalton was seen to come out and look around and immediately return. The officers on the east side were discovered by him through a window or by some woman in the house, and, pistols in hand, he jumped through a window on the north and started to run east. Hart was less than thirty yards from the house and called on him to halt. Dalton half turned around, tried to take aim while running, and just then the officer shot. Two jumps in the air were the only motions made. His pistol fell from his hand, and with a groan he sank to the ground, and Hart ran up and asked him what he was doing there, but he was too near dead to reply.

The remains were taken to Ardmore, where they were viewed by thousands of people. Dalton's wife was one of the women who had been captured, and she identified the corpse as that of her husband. Cole Dalton and another brother of the outlaw called on the following day and made the identification more complete. The body will be sent to California for burial.

The house in which Dalton was staying was searched and a large lot of letters and notes found which had been addressed to the outlaw. Considerable evidences were found which prove that he was the leader of the bank robbery at Longview, Texas. Considerable money was found in the house, besides $275 on the body of Dalton. This was given to his wife.

The black hair of the corpse at first led to doubts as to whether Dalton had been killed. These doubts were removed during the process of embalming where it was discovered that the hair had been dyed.

Y ESSAYS

Richard White, a talented historian at the University of Utah is best known for his work in ethnohistory and environmental studies. In the first essay, he considers whether western outlaws may be viewed as a social movement in the spirit of the "social bandits" described by the European historian E. J. Hobsbawm. Did these outlaws fight for a better world even as they broke the law? White's careful analysis shows the limitations of such assumptions. His essay goes on to explain how historical reality gave way to popular perceptions of the bandit and western hero. In the second selection, Roger D. McGrath, an independent historian who often teaches at the University of California—Los Angeles, closely examines western violence by comparing the historical records from the 1860s into the 1880s for two mining camps, Bodie and Aurora, located in the mountains on either side of the border between present-day California and Nevada. He then compares crime rates in eastern cities with those in his two frontier communities. Whether such rates may be validly compared has troubled some historians. Yet McGrath's conclusions about the nature and frequency of violence on the mining frontier are keenly focused. Still, one may ask whether there are forms of violence, especially against women and children in the domestic setting, that may not be readily found in nineteenth-century records. Whatever the case, McGrath questions older assumptions about the high frequency of violence in the West, just as White challenges assumptions about outlaws as social bandits.

Outlaw Gangs and Social Bandits

RICHARD WHITE

Americans have often regarded western outlaws as heroes. In popular culture—legend, folksongs, and movies—the American West might as well be Sherwood Forest; its plains and prairies teem with what E. J. Hobsbawm has called social bandits. Driven outside the law because of some act sanctioned by local conventions but regarded as criminal by the state or local authorities, the social bandit has been forced to become an outlaw. Members of his community, however, still consider him an honorable and admirable man. They protect him and are ready to reassimilate him if persecution by the state should stop. The social bandit is a man who violates the law but who still serves a higher justice. He robs from the rich and gives to the poor and only kills in self-defense or just revenge. As long as he observes this code, he is, in myth and legend, invulnerable to his enemies; he can die or be captured only when betrayed by friends.

In the American West, stories of this kind have gathered around many historical outlaws: Jesse James, Billy the Kid, Cole Younger, Sam Bass, John Wesley Hardin, Bob Dalton, Bill Dalton, Bill Doolin, and more. These men exert a surprising fascination on a nation that takes some pride in due process and the rule of law and where the standard version of western settlement is subordination of "savagery" to law and civilization. These bandits, however, exist in more than legend; as actual outlaws many enjoyed substantial amounts of local support. Such outlaws must be taken seriously as social bandits. Their appeal, while complex, is not mysterious, and it provides insights not only into certain kinds of western settlement and social conditions but also into basic paradoxes of American culture itself.

The tendency to justify certain outlaws as decent, honorable men despite their violation of the law is, in a sense, unique only because these men openly were bandits. In other ways social bandits fit into a continuum of extralegal organizations, such as claims clubs, vigilantes, and whitecaps*— prevalent throughout the United States but most common in the West. In certain situations the differences between social bandits (criminals) and vigilantes (law enforcers) were not great, and although this may offend certain modern law and order sensibilities, it is a mistake to impose such contemporary distinctions on nineteenth-century conditions.

In the American West during this period, concepts of legality, extra-legality, and illegality became quite confusing. Well into the late nineteenth century public law enforcement remained weak, particularly in rural areas where a variety of extralegal organizations supplemented or replaced the constituted authorities. Members of claims clubs, vigilantes, and whitecaps, of course, proclaimed their allegiance to community norms and saw themselves as establishing order, not contributing to disorder. On many occasions they were probably correct. Often, however, the line between extralegal organizations who claimed to preserve order and extralegal gangs accused of creating disorder was a fine one indeed. Claims clubs using threats of violence or actual violence to gain additional public land for their members,

Copyright by Western History Association. Reprinted by permission. The article first appeared as "Outlaw Gangs of the Middle Border: American Social Bandits," by Richard White. *Western Historical Quarterly,* 12 (October 1981), 387–408.

* a type of vigilante group that sprang up in many different areas of the country toward the end of the nineteenth century and that was given to violence with racist overtones—e.g., flogging blacks in northern Texas and anti-Mexican actions in southern Texas

even when this involved driving off legitimate claimants, vigilante committees whose targets might only be economic or political rivals, or whitecaps who chose to upgrade the moral tone of the community through beatings and whippings may not be outlaws, but distinguishing them from criminals on moral or legal grounds is not very compelling. In the West, *criminal* could be an ambiguous term, and vigilantes often became the armed force of one racial, class, or cultural group moving against other groups with opposing interests. In such cases vigilantes often provoked retaliation, and local civil war resulted. American history is full of such encounters, ranging from the Regulator/Moderator conflicts of the colonial Carolina backcountry, through the anti-Mormon movements of the American frontier, to the Johnson County War of 1892.

Social bandits, however, did not represent this kind of organized opposition to vigilantes. They, too, arose where law enforcement was distrusted, where criminal was an ambiguous category, and where the legitimacy of vigilantism was questioned. Where social banditry occurred, however, the vigilantes and their opponents did not form two coherent groups, but instead consisted of numerous, mutually hostile factions. Regulator/Moderator struggles represented broad social divisions; social bandits thrived amidst personal feuds and vendettas.

Three gangs that seem most clearly part of a western social bandit tradition are the James-Younger gang of western Missouri and its lineal successors led by Jesse James (1866[?]–1882), the Dalton gang of Oklahoma Territory (1890–1892), and the Doolin-Dalton gang of Oklahoma Territory (1892–1896). Such a list is purposefully narrow and is not meant to be exclusive. These are only the most famous gangs, but an examination of them can establish both the reality of social banditry and the nature of its appeal.

Social bandits are almost by definition creations of their supporters, but this support must be carefully defined. Virtually all criminals have some people who aid them, since there will always be those who find profit and advantage in doing so. Social bandits, too, may have supporters who are essentially confederates. What separates social bandits from ordinary criminals, however, is the existence of large numbers of other people who aid them but who are only technically implicated in their crimes. Such people are not themselves criminals and are willing to justify their own actions in supporting outlaws on grounds other than fear, profit, or expediency. When such people exist in large enough numbers to make an area a haven for a particular group of outlaws, then social banditry exists. For the James-Younger, Dalton, and Doolin-Dalton gangs, this support had three major components: the kinship networks so important to western settlement in general, active supporters, and those people who can be termed passive sympathizers.

That two of these three gangs organized themselves around sets of brothers—the James brothers, the Younger brothers, and the Dalton brothers—is perhaps the most striking illustration of the importance of kinship in social banditry. Centered on blood relations, the James-Younger gang and, to a much lesser extent the Dalton gang depended on relatives to hide them, feed them, warn them of danger, and provide them with alibis. The James brothers recruited two of their cousins—Wood and Clarence Hite—into the gang, and even the Ford brothers, who eventually murdered Jesse, were recruited because they were related by marriage to Jim Cummins, another gang member. Only the Doolin-Dalton gang lacked widespread kin connections, and this forced them to rely more heavily on other forms of support, which were, however, common to all the gangs.

Besides kinspeople, the gangs drew on a larger group of active supporters who knew the outlaws personally and who duplicated many of the services provided by relatives of the bandits. The James-Younger gang recruited such supporters largely from among neighbors and the ex-Confederate guerrillas who had ridden with them in the Civil War. Such "friends of the outlaws" were, according to the man who broke the gang—William Wallace—"thick in the country portions of Jackson County," and many people in the region believed that no local jury would ever convict members of the James gang.

Similar support existed in Oklahoma. The Daltons—Bob, Emmett and Grat—had possessed "many friends in the territory" and had found aid not only among farmers but also on the ranches along the Cimarron River, in the Creek Nation, and in the Cheyenne-Arapaho country. The Doolin-Dalton gang apparently built on this earlier network of support. Frank Canton, who as undersheriff of Pawnee County pursued the Doolin-Dalton gang, distinguished their active sympathizers from the twenty-five to thirty confederates who fenced stolen goods for the outlaws.

> The Dalton gang and especially Bill Doolin had many friends among the settlers south of Pawnee along the Cimarron River, and along the line of Pawnee County. There is no doubt that Doolin furnished many of them money to buy groceries to live upon when they first settled in that country and had a hard struggle for existence. They appreciated his kindness even though he was an outlaw with a price upon his head, and there were plenty of people who would get up at the hour of midnight if necessary to ride to Bill Doolin to warn him of the approach of officers when they were seen in that vicinity.

U.S. Marshal Evett Nix, too, complained that "protectors and friends" of the Doolin-Dalton gang "were numerous." The small town of Ingalls in Payne County became a particularly notorious center of sympathy for the gang. Three deputy marshals died in the disastrous raid officers made on the town in 1893, and when a posse pursued the bandits into the surrounding countryside, local farmers misdirected the deputies. The frustrated officers retaliated by arresting a number of local citizens for aiding the outlaws. Probandit sentiment persisted in the region into 1894 when a local newspaper reported that Bill Doolin was openly "circulating among his many friends in the Sooner Valley" and pointedly remarked that deputy marshals had been absent from the area as usual. Years later, when the state erected a monument to the deputies who fell at Ingalls, at least one old local resident complained that it had been erected to the "wrong bunch." In the case of all three gangs, the network of primary supporters remained localized. The James-Younger gang in its prime drew largely on Clay, Jackson, and Ray counties in Missouri, while the Daltons and the Doolin-Dalton gang relied heavily on people in Payne, Kingfisher, and Pawnee counties, as well as ranchers in the neighboring sections of the Indian nations and the Cherokee strip.

The final category of popular sympathy for outlaws was probably at once the largest, the least important in terms of the bandits' day-to-day activities, and yet the most critical in the transformation of the outlaws into local heroes. This third group consisted of passive sympathizers—people who probably had never seen an actual outlaw, let alone ever aided one. Their sympathy, however, was quite real, and given a chance they publicly demonstrated it. They mourned Jesse James, "lionized" Bill Doolin after his capture, flocked to see Frank James after his surrender, packed his trial, and applauded his acquittal. Such sympathizers appeared even in Coffeeville, Kansas, where the Dalton gang tried to outdo the James-Younger gang by robbing two banks at once. The result was a bloody debacle—the death of most of the gang and the killing of numerous citizens. Yet within days of the fight, some people openly sympathized with the outlaws on the streets of Coffeeville.

The mere existence of support, however, does not explain the reasons for it. The simplest explanation, and one advanced by many anti-outlaw writers, was that the bandits' supporters acted from fear. This is not very persuasive. While arguing that fear brought support, many popular writers have often simultaneously incorporated major elements of the bandits' legends into their own writings. They paradoxically argue against a sympathy that they themselves reflect. Such sympathy seems an unlikely product of fear, and there is little evidence for the reign of terror by these gangs reported by outside newspapers for Missouri in the 1870s and Oklahoma in the 1890s. Both Dalton and Doolin-Dalton gang members were welcomed to the country dances and other community affairs in Oklahoma that they attended. Certainly they had become locally notorious, but fear was not the dominant note in their notoriety. In Payne County, for example, a Stillwater grocer fortuitously named Bill Dalton capitalized on outlaw Bill Dalton's fame in an advertisement with banner headlines proclaiming that:

> Bill Dalton's Gang Are After You And If You Can Give Them A Trial You Will Be Convinced That They Keep The Freshest & Best Goods In The City At The Lowest Prices.

Feared killers are not usually relied on to promote the sale of groceries. Finally, if fear was the only cause of the bandits' support, it is hard to explain the continued expression of public sympathy after the outlaws were dead or imprisoned and no one had much to fear from them anymore.

A social bandit cannot survive through terror alone, and these bandits did not. They had ties to the local community predating their life of crime, and during their criminal careers social bandits reinforced those local ties.

Gangs that did not have such connections or did not maintain them remained parasites whose lack of shelter and aid condemned them to destruction. The social bandits needed popular support; they could not undercut it by indiscriminately robbing the inhabitants of the regions in which they lived and operated. Those outlaws who simply preyed on local communities were hunted down like the stock thieves of Indian Territory. No one romanticized, and rarely even remembered, Dock Bishop and Frank Latham, or the more notorious Zip Wyatt-Ike Black gang, for example. The social bandits avoided such a fate by concentrating their robberies on railroads and banks. Thus, they not only avoided directly harming local people, but they also preyed upon institutions that many farmers believed were preying on them.

Beyond this, social bandits often did assist their supporters in at least small ways. There is no need to accept the numerous romantic stories of gallant outlaws paying the mortgages on the farms of poor widows to grant them an economic role in their local communities. Bill Doolin may very well have helped poor settlers through some hard times with groceries and small gifts; the Dalton and Doolin-Dalton gangs certainly did provide oysters and refreshments for local dances, and such small kindnesses were also probably practiced by the James-Younger gang. What was probably more significant to their supporters in chronically cash-short economies, however, was that all these gangs paid very well for the horses, feed, and supplies they needed. Their largess won them friends.

If fear fails as an explanation for what appears to be legitimate social banditry, then the next logical recourse is to the interpretation E. J. Hobsbawm offered to explain European bandits. According to Hobsbawm, social banditry is a premodern social revolt—a protest against either excessive exploitation from above or against the overturn of traditional norms by modernizing elements in a society. It is quintessentially a peasant protest. Hobsbawm mentioned Jesse James himself as following in this European tradition. The shortcomings of a literal reading of Hobsbawm are obvious. Jesse James could not be a peasant champion because there were no American peasants to champion. Yet Hobsbawm's analysis might be retrieved by reinterpreting the western outlaws more generally as champions of a "traditional" society against a "modern" society.

Such evidence as can be recovered, however, indicates that this interpretation, too, is badly flawed. Both the outlaws and their supporters came from modern, market-oriented groups and not from poor, traditional groups. The James-Younger gang had its origins in the Confederate guerrillas of the Civil War who were recruited from the economic and social elite of Jackson and neighboring counties. Usually guerrillas were the "elder offspring of well-to-do, slave holding farmers." The chief members of the James-Younger gang were ex-guerrillas with similar origins. Colonel Henry Younger, the father of the Younger brothers, owned 3,500 acres of land in Jackson and Cass counties before the Civil War. His wife was a daughter of a member of the Missouri legislature. The father of Jesse and Frank James was a Baptist minister who in 1850 owned a 275-acre farm. Their stepfather was a physician who resided with their mother on a Missouri farm worth

$10,000 in 1870, and their uncle, George Hite, Sr., was said, probably with some exaggeration, to have been worth $100,000 before losing heavily in the tobacco speculation that forced him into bankruptcy in 1877.

Many of the gang's other supporters enjoyed similar social standing. Joseph Shelby, the Confederate cavalry leader, and members of the large Hudspeth family all aided the James-Younger gang, and all were prosperous farmers with sizable landholdings. The jury that acquitted Frank James of murder was composed of twelve "well-to-do thrifty farmers," and Clay County, in the heart of the bandit country, was "one of the richest counties in the state," inhabited by a people who were "well-dressed, well-to-do, and hospitable." These substantial farmers and speculators seem an unlikely source for premodern rebels or as leaders of a revolt of the rural poor.

Members and supporters of the Dalton and Doolin-Dalton gangs were not so prosperous, but then these gangs did not have such a firmly established rural region to draw upon. The Daltons were, by most accounts, an ordinary midwestern farm family. Three Dalton brothers became farmers; one was a deputy marshal killed in the line of duty; the other four eventually became outlaws. Bill Doolin was a ranch foreman and, according to local residents, a "respected citizen" before becoming a bandit. Bitter Creek Newcomb, Little Bill Raidler, and Dick Broadwell all had middle-class origins in families of merchants and farmers, and Raidler had supposedly attended college. The remainder of these two gangs included equal numbers of previously honest cowboys and small-time thugs and drifters without close family connections. Supporters of the Oklahoma gangs also apparently spanned class lines, ranging from small-scale farmers to large-scale ranchers like Jim Riley, who was locally considered well-to-do.

Neither class nor traditional values seem to be significant factors in the support of bandits, but the tendency of supporters to live in rural rather than urban regions suggest a third possible explanation of social banditry as an exotic appendage of the agrarian revolt of post–Civil War America. Some evidence, taken in isolation, seems to support such a connection with rural radicalism. Both local boosters and government officials interested in attracting capital attacked the gangs. They blamed them for discouraging investment and immigration. Governor Crittenden and Senator Carl Schurz of Missouri, for example, defended the assassination of Jesse James in ridding the state of "a great hindrance to its prosperity and as likely to give an important stimulus to real estate speculation, railroad enterprise, and foreign immigration."

On the other side, positions taken by some of the bandits after their careers were over make them appear to be radicals. Frank James credited his robberies with maintaining local prosperity because they had frightened eastern capital out of Jackson County and thus kept it free of mortgages. And in 1897 he declared: "If there is ever another war in this country, which may happen, it will be between capital and labor, I mean between greed and manhood, and I'm as ready to march now in defense of American manhood as I was when a boy in the defense of the South. Unless we can stop this government by injunction that's what we are coming to." Frank

James was not alone in his swing to the left. James Younger became a socialist while in prison.

Put in context, however, all of this is considerably less compelling. While active criminals, none of the bandits took radical political positions. Nor did agrarian groups show much sympathy for the bandits. Contemporary writers pointed out that politicians and capitalists stole far more than bandits, and individual farmers aided the gangs, but organized agrarians did not confuse banditry with political action. The leading agrarian party in Missouri in the 1870s—the People's party—although it attacked banks and monopolies, also denounced lawlessness, particularly that of the James-Younger gang. It is also instructive to remember that the Farmers Alliance, which eventually spawned the Populist party, started out as a group to combat horse theft. The Populists themselves showed no more interest in banditry as a variant of political action than had the People's party of Missouri. In any case, if banditry were political in nature and inspired by agrarian resentment against banks and railroads, it is hard to explain why support for bandits was largely confined to Oklahoma in the 1890s while Populism spread all over the South and West.

A better explanation of social banditry is possible. It begins with the peculiar social conditions of western Missouri in the 1860s and 1870s and Oklahoma in the 1890s that allowed social bandits to emerge as variants of the widespread extralegal organizations already common in the West. The exceptional situations prevailing in both Missouri and Oklahoma encouraged popular identification with the outlaws whom local people supported not because of their crimes but rather because of certain culturally defined masculine virtues the outlaws embodied. In each locale there were good reasons to value such virtues. This emphasis on the bandits as symbols of masculinity, in turn, made them accessible to the larger culture at a time when masculinity itself was being widely worried over and glorified. The bandit's virtues made him a cultural hero and embarked him on a posthumous career (of a very conservative sort) which is far from over yet. All of this requires considerable explanation.

Public support of bandits can obviously exist only in areas where belief in the honesty and competency of public law enforcement has been seriously eroded. This was the case in both postwar Missouri and Oklahoma in the 1890s. In the Missouri countryside, ex-Confederates hated and feared Union sheriffs, who they believed used their offices to settle old scores from the war, and they regarded the state militia, called up to maintain order, as plunderers and freebooters. Wartime antagonisms and turmoil faded in time, but when the Pinkertons attacked the home of Zerelda Samuel, mother of the James boys, blowing off her arm and killing her young son—the half-brother of Jesse and Frank—they rekindled hatred of the authorities. Governor Crittenden's subsequent solicitation of assassins to kill Jesse only deepened the prevailing distrust of the equity and honesty of law enforcement.

In Oklahoma settlers similarly distrusted U.S. deputy marshals, whom they often regarded as little better than criminals themselves. During the land rush, deputies used their office unfairly to secure the best lands and later spent much of their time arresting farmers who cut timber on the public domain or on Indian lands and prosecuting settlers who happened to be found with small amounts of whiskey in the Indian nations. Farmers believed that deputies sought only the fees they collected by persecuting "poor defenseless claim holders." On at least two occasions in the late winter and spring of 1893, resentment ran high enough for armed groups to attempt to attack deputy marshals and free their prisoners.

Although newspapers praised their bravery when they died in the line of duty, living marshals merited much less sympathy. Local newspapers rarely praised crimes social bandits committed, but they commonly ridiculed and denounced the lawmen who pursued them. In April of 1894, for example, the *Pond Creek Voice* reported that deputy marshals riding past the garden of an old woman who lived near the Cimarron River had mistaken her scarecrow for an outlaw and had riddled it with bullets before riding off in panic to report their ambush by the Doolin-Dalton gang. When Bill Dalton was actually killed, the *Stillwater Gazette* reported that it would come as a great relief to the deputy marshals "who have made it a practice to ride in the opposite direction from where he was every time they got him located." In the eyes of many people, the deputy marshals were simply another group of armed men, distinguished mainly by their cowardice, who rode around the territory posing a threat to life and property. The transition of the Dalton brothers from deputy marshals and possemen to open criminals was no fall from grace. Indeed, it may have gained the brothers support in some areas.

This distrust of law enforcement is particularly significant in the light of the widespread disorder existing in both areas. Following the Civil War, robbery and murder continued to occur in northwestern Missouri with appalling frequency. Gangs of ex-guerrillas from both sides pillaged and sought revenge for wartime acts; committees of public safety organized, and vigilantes remained active until the mid-1870s. Numerous armed bands, each protecting its own interests, clashed in the countryside. Legal protection was often unavailable. All this was not merely the last gasp of the Lost Cause; it was not a simple reflection of Union/Confederate divisions. Many local ex-Confederates, for example, opposed the James-Younger gang. The Confederate background of the outlaws certainly won them some sympathy, but only within the local context of chaotic, factional disorder.

The situation in Oklahoma in the 1890s was a remarkably similar mixture of predation, personal vengeance, and vigilantism. With the demand for Oklahoma land exceeding its availability, the government resorted to one of the most astonishing systems of distributing resources ever attempted by a modern state. Settlers in Oklahoma raced for their land. The races were spectacular, colorful, and virtually impossible to police. Numerous people—the "sooners"—stole over the line ahead of the starting time to stake claims. Sooners only increased the inevitable conflicts among people who claimed to have arrived first at a desirable plot of land. In the end the land rushes sowed a crop of litigation and violence. Even if nothing else divided a community, bitter factional struggles for land were sure to persist for years. In Payne County, the center of support for the Doolin-Dalton gang, the county attorney claimed, perhaps with some exaggeration, that there were fifty murders as the direct result of land claim cases in the early years. Such murders involved the leading citizens of Payne County. The first representative of Payne County to the Oklahoma legislature and speaker of the assembly, I. N. Terrill, terminated his political career in 1891 by murdering a man in a land dispute.

Given the distrust of local law enforcement, protection in such disputes often demanded organization and violence. In 1893, for example, the *Oklahoma State Capital* reported the presumed lynching of three sooners by a local vigilante committee. Apparently both sides—the alleged sooners and the vigilante committee—were armed and resorting to violence. Such actions, the reporter contended, were common: "Reports are coming in every day of white cap whippings and terrorizing and it is nothing to see the sooner pulling out every day, claiming that they have been threatened with hanging by vigilant committees if they did not go." The large numbers of horse and cattle thieves who had long existed in a sort of parasitic relationship with the large cattle operations and who now turned to stealing from settlers only increased the level of private violence.

The situation in Oklahoma was, however, more complicated than extralegal groups enforcing the laws against thieves and sooners. There was some ambiguity about what constituted theft. For example, Evan Barnard, an ex-cowboy and settler in Oklahoma who wrote one of the best of western memoirs, defended stock theft by his friend, Ranicky Bill: "He was generous and big-hearted . . . if he knew any settler who was hungry, he did not hesitate to rustle beef, and give it to the starving people. In the early days of Oklahoma, a man who did that was not such a bad person after all." According to Barnard, such attitudes were shared by many settlers. When it became clear that the large ranchers would lose their leases on Indian lands, the homesteaders moved in to steal wood, fencing, and stock. All the old-time cattlemen, Barnard contended, would admit that the "settlers were good rustlers." In practice *sooner, rustler, vigilante,* and *outlaw* were ambiguous terms; very often they were only pejorative names for those whose interests were not the same as other citizens.

In both Missouri and Oklahoma, pervasive lawlessness and widespread distrust of public law enforcement divided the countryside not into two clearly opposing groups, but rather into innumerable local factions. Conditions were ripe for factional violence and social banditry. A rather detailed example from Oklahoma is perhaps the best way to illustrate how tangled the relationship of gangs, vigilantes, and other armed groups could become; how supposed, and even demonstrated, criminal behavior might not cost people public sympathy; how private violence could be deemed not only necessary but admirable; and how social bandits garnered support in such situations.

In 1889, Evan Barnard, his friend Ranicky Bill, and other ex-cowboys banded together before the run for Oklahoma Territory to secure and protect land claims. It was a necessary precaution because "just staking a claim did not hold it." Barnard drove one man from his claim by flourishing a winchester and a six-shooter and telling him it was "a hundred and sixty acres or six feet, and I did not give a damn which it was." Bravado was not sufficient to drive off two other challengers, however; for them, Barnard had to demonstrate "the backing I had among the cowboys." This backing was available regardless of the merits of any specific case. One of Barnard's friends failed to secure a claim, but visits from Barnard's associates persuaded the legitimate claimant to sell out to him for $75. The claimant left but declared: " 'If I had half the backing that you have, I would stay with you until hell froze over'. . . . He left the claim and Ranicky Bill remarked, 'hits sure hell to get things regulated in a new country.' " Ranicky Bill himself had to stop a contest on his claim by shooting up his opponent's camp. Private force clearly was both a necessary supplement to, and a substitute for, legal right.

Such bullying understandably stirred up resentment against Barnard and his friends, and some regarded them as sooners, which they were not. When these accusations were compounded by charges that Ranicky Bill was a horse thief, the vigilantes struck. They attacked Ranicky Bill's cabin, and although he escaped, the vigilantes threatened to hang Barnard and another neighbor. Ranicky Bill surrendered to authorities to clear himself, but his real protection came from thirty cowboys who gathered a day after the incident and offered to help him. Later, vigilantes seized another neighbor and twice hoisted him off the ground with a rope that cut into his neck. He refused to confess and was released, but now the entire neighborhood armed against the vigilantes, who ceased their operations.

According to Barnard, none of those accused by the vigilantes were thieves, but other incidents narrated in his book indicate how thoroughly such accusations were tied up in land disputes and factional quarrels. Friends and neighbors of Barnard apparently did steal a team of horses and other property from a claim jumper named Sniderwine during a land dispute. They considered this a legitimate means of driving him from his claim and probably perjured themselves to protect each other.

In such an atmosphere, the organization of settlers into armed groups or gangs for protection seems to have been common. The argument made by an actual stock thief to a new settler that in Oklahoma a man's legal rights and property were worthless without friends sometimes led to the corollary that if you were going to be denounced and attacked for supposed crimes, then you might as well have the "game as the name." And in practice, personal quarrels with each side denouncing the other as sooners and thieves sometimes left local newspapers totally unable to sort out the merits of the case. Personal loyalties and personal qualities in these situations took on larger than normal significance. Law, theft, and even murder became ambiguous categories; strong men who protected themselves and aided their friends could gain local respect transcending their separate criminal activities.

This respect for strong men who could protect and revenge themselves is the real heart of the social bandits' appeal. It is precisely this personal element that gang members and their supporters chose to emphasize. What distinguished social bandits and their supporters (as it distinguished peasant social bandits and theirs) from radicals and revolutionaries was their stubborn refusal to envision the social problems enmeshing them in anything but personal terms. The James and Younger brothers claimed they were hounded into banditry by vindictive Union men who would not leave them alone after the war. They fought only for self-preservation and revenge, not for a social cause. Supporters of Jesse James justified each of his murders as an act of vengeance against men who had attacked his comrades or family. Indeed, the chief propagandist for the James brothers, Missouri newspaper editor John Edwards, made personal vengeance the underlying theme of all their actions from the Civil War onward. Edwards distinguished the guerrillas from regular soldiers by saying these men fought not for a cause but to avenge assaults against themselves and their families. Personal defense and revenge, he claimed, dominated the entire career of the James and Younger brothers. Whether such a claim is accurate or not matters less than that it was credible. When John Edwards claimed these brothers were merely strong men seeking to defend their rights, the appeal could be felt deeply by those who knew that neither they nor the authorities could protect their own rights and property.

The Daltons' grievances, like those of the James and Younger brothers, were personal. They said they became outlaws because the federal government would not pay them for their services as deputy marshals and the express companies had falsely accused them of robbery. They were not radicals who fought against the system itself; they fought against what they regarded as its corruption by their enemies. Emmett Dalton declared that "our fights were not so much against the law, but rather against the law as it was then enforced." At least two members of the Dalton gang asserted that their criminal careers began with land problems, and Bill Doolin, like Cole Younger before him, claimed it was only the personal vindictiveness of his enemies and the corruption of the authorities that stopped him from surrendering. Many of the supporters of the outlaws agreed with these assertions of persecution, and movements for full or partial amnesty for the gangs were common.

Given social conditions in Oklahoma and Missouri, there was a decisive allure in strong men who defended themselves, righted their own wrongs, and took vengeance on their enemies despite the corruption of the existing order. Such virtues were of more than nostalgic interest. In praising bandits, supporters admired them more for their attributes than their acts. Bandits were brave, daring, free, shrewd, and tough, yet also loyal, gentle, generous, and polite. They were not common criminals. Lon Stansbery, who knew Bill Doolin from the 3-D ranch, was, for instance, forthright about the bandits' heroic stature and masculine virtue:

> The outlaws of that day were not hijackers or petty thieves, and some of them had hearts, even though they were outlaws. They always treated women with respect and no rancher was ever afraid to leave his family on the ranch on account of outlaws. While they would stand up and shoot it out with men, when women were around, they were the first to take off their Stetsons and act like real men.

And Red Orrington, a deputy marshal, called the Daltons "four of as fine fellows as I ever knew," brave men who went on the scout (the local term for banditry) for "love of adventure."

From the initial exploits of the James-Younger gang until the death of Bill Doolin, appraisals of the outlaws' character by their supporters, while sometimes allowing for an understandable laxity in regard to the sixth and eighth commandments, remained strong and consistent in their praise. The James and Younger brothers were "brilliant, bold, indefatigable roughriders," and in the words of an amnesty resolution introduced in the Missouri legislature, "brave . . . generous . . . gallant . . . honorable" men. The Daltons were "big hearted and generous" in every way, "like the average western man," while Bill Doolin was a "naturally . . . kind-hearted, sympathetic man." A contemporary diary from Ingalls comments that the Doolin-Dalton gang was "as a rule quite (*sic*) and peaceable," even though they moved about heavily armed, and residents later remembered them as "well behaved . . . quiet and friendly," a description close to an Oklahoma school-teacher's memory of the Daltons as "nice and polite." Some supporters proclaimed them innocent of their crimes, others merely excused them, but all demanded sympathy not so much for the crime as for the criminal. Again it must be emphasized that what is being praised here is not lawlessness per se. Outlaw stories go out of their way to detach the social bandit from the ordinary criminal. Thus, in one story Bill Doolin turns a common thief who tried to join his gang over to a deputy marshal, since "they would have no men in their outfit who would rob a poor man or any individual." John Edwards also took pains to distinguish the James-Younger gang from common criminals.

> There are men in Jackson, Cass, and Clay—a few there are left—who learned to dare when there was no such word as quarter in the dictionary of the Border. Men who have carried their lives in their hands so long that they do not know how to commit them over into the keeping of the laws and regulations that exist now, and those men sometimes rob. But it is always in the glare of day and in the teeth of multitude. With them booty is but the second thought; the wild drama of the adventure first. These men never go upon the highway in lonesome places to plunder the pilgrim. That they leave to the ignobler pack of jackals. But they ride at midday into the county seat, while court is sitting, take the cash out of the vault and put the cashier in and ride out of town to the music of cracking pistols.

And the *Ardmore [Oklahoma] State Herald* made the connections between the Doolin-Dalton gang and Robin Hood explicit:

> Their life is made up of daring. Their courage is always with them and their rifles as well. They are kind to the benighted traveler, and it is not a fiction that when robbing a train they refuse to take from a woman.
>
> It is said that Bill Doolin, at present the reigning highwayman, is friendly to the people in one neighborhood, bestowing all sorts of presents upon the children. It is his boast that he never killed a man.

This is as fully a romantic figure as Robin Hood ever cut.

Such Robin Hood descriptions only echoed those of the James-Younger gang twenty years before.

By the 1890s, in Oklahoma at least, the standards of how proper social bandits should behave seemed clear enough for the *Oklahoma State Capital,* a paper with little sympathy for outlaws, to lecture Bill Dalton on his duties as the heir of a great tradition. Bill Dalton, in an interview with a local reporter only the week before, had claimed he was considering teaming up with Frank James to open a saloon in Chicago to take advantage of their fame and the World's Fair. The saloon never materialized, and Bill Dalton had left Guthrie without paying his board bill. The *State Capital* had complained:

> There is supposed to be honor among thieves. Men who presume to be great in any calling avoid the common faults of men. There is a heroism even in desperadoes, and the people admire an ideal type of that class. The James and Younger brothers are remembered as never having robbed a poor family or assaulted an unarmed man. Even the "Dalton boys"— they who really stood up to their "knitten" and looked down the muzzles of Winchesters—did brave and not ignoble deeds. But Bill Dalton—"Board Bill" Dalton—has besmirched the family escutcheon. The brothers, dead, when they hear what he has done, will turn over in their graves and groan— "Oh, Bill."

Bill Dalton's future specialization in bank and train robbery and his violent death presumably redeemed the family honor.

Social bandits thus did exist in a meaningful sense in the American West, yet their actual social impact, confined as it was to small areas with extreme conditions, was minor. They never sought social change, and the actual social evolution of Missouri and Oklahoma owes little to them. Nevertheless, their impact on American culture has been immense. The social bandits who metaphorically rode out of Missouri and Oklahoma into America at large quickly transcended the specific economic and political conditions of the areas that produced them and became national cultural symbols. The outlaws were ready-made cultural heroes—their local supporters had already presented them in terms accessible to the nation as a whole. The portrait of the outlaw as a strong man righting his own wrongs and taking his own revenge had a deep appeal to a society concerned with the place of masculinity and masculine virtues in a newly industrialized and seemingly effete order.

Practically, of course, the outlaw as a model of male conduct was hopeless, and early popularizers of the outlaws stressed that although their virtues and qualities were admirable, their actions were inappropriate. Edwards portrayed the James and Younger brothers as men born out of their time, and Zoe Tilghman (whose book ostensibly denied the outlaws were heroic) claimed the Oklahoma bandits were cowboys "who could not bring their natures to the subjection of such a change from the wild free life to that kind that came to surround them. They were the venturesome spirits of the old Southwest and could not be tamed.''

Those who seriously worried about masculine virtue in the late nineteenth and early twentieth centuries romanticized toughness, loyalty, bravery, generosity, honor, and daring, but sought to channel it into muscular Christianity or college football, not into robbing banks and trains. The outlaws' virtues were cherished, but their actions were archaic and antisocial. In this paradox of accepted virtue without an appropriate arena in which to exist lay the real power of the outlaws' appeal. The outlaw legend, rather than the childish solutions of reformers who sought to provide for the development of "masculine" virtues through organized sports or the dangerous solutions of chauvinists who praised war, retained the complexity, ambivalence, and paradoxes of a personal experience in which accepted male virtue had little relevance to an industrialized, bureaucratized world.

Ambivalence saved Jesse James and the mythical western hero that sprang from his legends from becoming Frank Merriwell on a horse. The position of the western hero reflects the paradoxical position most Americans occupy in an industrialized capitalist society. The traits and acts of the outlaw become symbols of the larger, structural oppositions—oppositions of law and justice, individualism and community, nature and civilization—never adequately reconciled in American life. Assimilated into the classic western, the social bandit becomes the western hero—a figure of great appeal. The western is not the simple-minded celebration of the triumph of American virtue over evil that it is so often ignorantly and unjustly presumed to be; instead it is the opposite. It plays on the unresolved contradictions and oppositions of America itself.

The entire structure of the classic western film poses the hero between contrasting values both of which are very attractive: private justice and the order provided by law, individualism and community, nature and civilization. The hero, posed between the oppositions, remains ambivalent. Like the actual social bandit, the western hero never attempts to change the structure itself, but rather tries to achieve a reconciliation through his own courage and virtue. Western heroes personify culturally defined masculine virtues of strength, self-reliance, and honor in a world where they have ceased to be effective. More often than not the hero fails or only partially succeeds in his task and like the epitome of the classic western hero, Shane, is left wounded and out of place in a world he has himself helped to create. In the hero's dilemma, viewers recognize their own struggle to reconcile the cultural irreconcilables that society demands of them—individualism and community responsibility, personal dominance and cooperation, maximum productivity and respect for nature. The bandit and the western hero are social failures, and this paradoxically guarantees them their cultural success. It is as a cultural symbol that Jesse James would survive and thrive even though "that dirty little coward, that shot Mr. Howard [had] laid poor Jesse in his grave.''

Violence on a Mining Frontier

ROGER D. MCGRATH

The trans-Sierra frontier [in California] was unmistakably violent and lawless, but only in special ways. Whereas bank robbery, rape, racial violence, and serious juvenile crime seem not to have occurred, and robbery, theft, and burglary occurred relatively infrequently, shootings and shoot-outs among roughs, badmen, and miners were fairly regular events. Vigilantism visited Aurora once and Bodie three times, and warfare between Indians and whites was a bloody reality—mostly for Owens Valley ranchers and the Second Cavalry—during Aurora's boom years. Thus the violence and lawlessness that the trans-Sierra frontier experienced was generally confined to a few special categories and did not directly affect all activities or all people. The old, the young, the unwilling, the weak, and the female—with the notable exception of the prostitute—were, for the most part, safe from harm. If, as many popularly assume, much of America's crime problem stems from a heritage of frontier violence and lawlessness, then it is ironic that the crimes most common today—robbery, theft, burglary, and rape—were of no great significance and, in the case of rape, seemingly nonexistent on the trans-Sierra frontier.

Robbery was as often aimed at stagecoaches as at individuals. There were eleven robberies and three attempted robberies of stages during Bodie's boom years and possibly an equal number during Aurora's heyday. At the same times there were ten robberies and three attempted robberies of individuals in Bodie and a somewhat smaller number in Aurora. When highwaymen stopped a stagecoach, they usually took only the express box and left the passengers unmolested. Passengers often remarked that they had received only the most courteous treatment from the highwaymen. Only twice were passengers robbed. In the first instance the highwaymen later apologized for their conduct, and in the second instance the robbers were drunk.

Stage robberies were almost exclusively nighttime events. Only one occurred during the day. The stages carrying the great bullion shipments were not the targets of the highwaymen. The highwaymen had no desire to tangle with the two or more shotgun messengers who always rode on the bullion stages, preferring instead to prey on the unguarded coaches. Only once did messengers and highwaymen exchange gunfire—a messenger was wounded and a highwayman killed—and in that instance they met by chance. Several of the highwaymen lived in San Francisco and crossed into the trans-Sierra country only to rob stages. Not more than three highwaymen were ever apprehended, and only two of those were convicted of robbery. The only deterrent to stage robbery seems to have been the shotgun messengers.

Next to stagecoach robbery, bank robbery is probably the form of robbery most popularly associated with the frontier West. Yet, although

Roger D. McGrath, "The Heritage of the Trans-Sierra Frontier," in *Gunfighters, Highwaymen & Vigilantes,* 247–260, University of California Press. © 1984 The Regents of the University of California. Reprinted by permission.

Aurora and Bodie together boasted several banks, no bank robbery was ever attempted. Most of the bankers were armed, as were their employees, and a robber would have run a considerable risk of being killed. If highwaymen were unwilling to stop the messenger-guarded stages, then who would wish to take the even greater risk of robbing a bank?

There were only ten robberies and three attempted robberies of individuals—other than those robbed as part of a stage holdup—in Bodie during its boom years, and there seem to have been even fewer in Aurora during its heyday. Nevertheless, the few robberies that did occur outraged the citizens and in Bodie provoked talk of vigilantism. In nearly every one of these robberies the circumstances were so similar as to be interchangeable: The robbery victim had spent the evening in a gambling den, saloon, or brothel; he had revealed in some way that he had on his person a tidy sum of money; and he was staggering home drunk late at night when the attack occurred.

Again, it would seem that in both Aurora and Bodie more robberies might have occurred if the citizens had not gone about armed and ready to fight. It is revealing that nearly all robbery victims were staggering drunk when attacked. A man in anything resembling a sober state was simply too dangerous to rob. The presence of police officers patrolling the streets at night may also have deterred some robbers, although no officer in Bodie ever made an arrest of a robber or came to the rescue of a robbery victim, and several officers were dismissed from duty for alleged cooperation with robbers.

Bodie's total of twenty-one robberies—eleven of stages and ten of individuals—over a five-year period converts to a rate of 84 robberies per 100,000 inhabitants per year. On this scale—the same scale that the Federal Bureau of Investigation uses to index crime—New York in 1980 had a robbery rate of 1,140, Miami 995, Los Angeles 628, San Francisco–Oakland 521, Atlanta 347, and Chicago 294. Equaling Bodie's rate of 84 was Santa Rosa, California. The lowest rate of robbery among U.S. cities was Bismarck, North Dakota's 7.5. The rate for the United States as a whole, including small towns and rural areas, was 243. Thus Bodie, even with its stagecoach robberies included, had a robbery rate significantly below the national average in 1980.

Unfortunately, it is impossible to compare Bodie's rate of robbery—or rates of any other crimes—directly with those of eastern towns during the nineteenth century. All crime studies of the eastern towns are based on numbers of arrests and not on numbers of offenses. It is generally conceded that, except in the case of murder and manslaughter, numbers of offenses are many times greater—often four or five or more—than numbers of arrests. Bodie's experience certainly confirms this. For the great majority of offenses in Bodie there were no arrests.

Nevertheless, comparisons can be made by extrapolation of the numbers of arrests. For example, Boston's robbery arrest rate for the years 1880 through 1882 was 23. If four robberies were committed for every one arrest—a ratio based on FBI statistics for 1980—then Boston's robbery rate was 92. During the same years Salem, Massachusetts, had a robbery arrest rate of 13, giving it a robbery rate of 52. Thus it would seem that Boston and Salem had robbery rates roughly comparable—considering the estimation and projection involved—to Bodie's rate of 84. But it would also seem, since stagecoach robberies accounted for about half of Bodie's robberies, that the individual was more likely to be robbed in Boston or Salem than in Bodie.

Just as the heavily armed messengers prevented robbery of the bullion stages, and the armed citizenry discouraged robbery of individuals, the armed homeowner and merchant discouraged burglary of home and business. Between 1877 and 1883, there were only 32 burglaries—17 of homes and 15 of businesses—in Bodie. Again, Aurora seems to have had fewer still. At least a half-dozen attempted burglaries in Bodie were thwarted by the presence of armed citizens. The newspapers regularly advocated shooting burglars on sight, and several burglars were, in fact, shot at. Moreover, Bodieites, even when not armed, were willing to fight intruders.

Bodie's five-year total of 32 burglaries converts to an average of 6.4 burglaries a year and gives the town a burglary rate of 128 on the FBI scale. In 1980 Miami had a burglary rate of 3,282, New York 2,661, Los Angeles 2,602, San Francisco–Oakland 2,267, Atlanta 2,210, and Chicago 1,241. The Grand Forks, North Dakota, rate of 566 and the Johnstown, Pennsylvania, rate of 587 were lowest among U.S. cities. The rate for the United States as a whole was 1,668, or thirteen times that for Bodie. Boston's burglary arrest rate from 1880 through 1882 was 87, and Salem's was 54. A conversion factor of 7—a figure based on FBI data—gives these towns burglary rates of 609 and 378, rates three to five times greater than that for Bodie.

Theft was not a major problem in Aurora or Bodie. Bodie had some forty-five instances of theft, and most of the theft was for firewood and blankets. Included in this total of forty-five thefts are six instances of horse theft. Only two horse thieves were ever caught, and they were punished far less severely than would traditionally be supposed; one of them was sentenced to serve six months in the county jail, and the other to serve one year in the state penitentiary. Although there were thousands of head of cattle to the west of Aurora and Bodie in the Bridgeport Valley and to the south in the Owens Valley, cattle rustling, except for Indian depredations during the warfare of the 1860s, did not exist.

Bodie's forty-five instances of theft give it a theft rate of 180. In 1980 Miami had a theft rate of 5,452, San Franciso–Oakland 4,571, Atlanta, 3,947, Los Angeles 3,372, New York 3,369, and Chicago 3,206. Lowest theft rates among U.S. cities were those of Steubenville, Ohio, at 916, and Johnstown, Pennsylvania, at 972. The rate for the United States as a whole was 3,156, more than seventeen times that for Bodie. Boston's theft arrest rate for 1880 through 1882 was 575, Salem's 525. A conversion factor of 6—a factor consistent with the FBI data—gives the towns theft rates of 3,450 and 3,150.

Thus Bodie's rates of robbery, burglary, and theft were dramatically lower than those of most U.S. cities in 1980 and were as low as or significantly lower than those for Boston and Salem from 1880 through 1882. Even if four or five times as much robbery, burglary, and theft occurred in Bodie but went unreported in the newspapers and unrecorded in the jail register and court records, Bodie would still have had rates dramatically lower than those for most U.S. cities in 1980. In comparison with nineteenth-century Boston and Salem, Bodie's rate of theft would still be many times lower, its burglary rate about equal, and its robbery rate higher. Aurora seems to have had rates lower than Bodie—the available evidence so indicates—but because of the incomplete nature of the sources such a conclusion must remain speculative.

Institutions of law enforcement and justice certainly were not responsible for the low rates or robbery, burglary, and theft. Rarely were any of the perpetrators of these types of crime arrested, and even less often were they convicted. Many law officers had less than zealous attitudes about their work, and some operated on both sides of the law; gang-leader John Daly and several of his men served as officers in Aurora, and several Bodie officers may have cooperated with robbers. When a man *was* arrested, chances were good that he would not be convicted. Because so few men were convicted of these crimes, it does not seem that the normal punishment—imprisonment in jail or the penitentiary—could have served as much of a deterrent.

The citizens themselves, armed with various types of firearms and willing to kill to protect their persons or property, were evidently the most important deterrent to larcenous crime. Full employment may also have served as something of a deterrent. Aurora, where few were without jobs, seems to have had slightly less larcenous crime than Bodie, where many suffered periodic unemployment. Perhaps the most intangible of the possible deterrents was the optimistic attitude of Aurorans and Bodieites. They had hope. And while men have hope, no matter what their circumstances are, they are less likely to commit crime.

Aurora and Bodie women, other than prostitutes, suffered little from crime or violence. In Bodie from 1878 through 1882 there were only some thirty violent encounters between men and women, and prostitutes were involved in twenty-five of them. When women fought women, prostitutes accounted for thirteen of seventeen fights. Only a handful of either of these types of violent encounters had serious consequences. Just one resulted in death, and in that case the woman was a former prostitute and her murderer was insane. There was also one woman who died from the effects of an abortion, and another who nearly died from a clubbing.

A very obvious double standard existed in Bodie. While the "decent" women were treated with the greatest deference, prostitutes were socially ostracized and generally shown no respect. Newspapers often treated beatings of prostitutes humorously, and the attitude of police and judges was only slightly better. Men who assaulted prostitutes were usually arrested for their attacks, but their punishments were far less severe than if they had assaulted "respectable" women. The double standard extended even to the graveyard. Prostitutes who died in Bodie were buried outside the fence of the graveyard.

The greatest threat facing women in Bodie was suicide. Six women killed themselves during the town's boom years, and four others tried to do so. The six deaths give Bodie an extraordinarily high female suicide rate of 24. From 1868 through 1872 Philadelphia had a female suicide rate of only 2.0, and the United States during the 1970s had female suicide rates that all fell between 6 and 7; in 1978 the rate for females was 6.3. The difference between Bodie's rate and those of nineteenth-century Philadelphia and the United States today would be even greater if the figures were based only on populations of women rather than on total populations. Women normally represent about half of the population; in Bodie they made up only some 10 or 12 percent. Accounting for this difference would give Bodie an astounding female suicide rate of 100 or more. Prostitutes contributed disproportionately to the high rate. While they constituted considerably less than half of the female population, they committed half of the suicides.

Bodie women were six or seven times more likely to kill themselves than were Bodie men. The opposite was true in Philadelphia during the 1870s; for every one woman who killed herself more than five men took their own lives. The opposite is also true in more recent times. During the 1970s (the ratio is much the same for the 1950s and 1960s) males in the United States killed themselves at a rate three times that of females.

Although Bodie's female suicide rate was extraordinarily high, there was nothing unusual about the methods the women employed to kill themselves. Two shot themselves to death, and the other four overdosed on some type of drug or ingested poison. Much the same holds true today. In 1978, for example, some 36 percent of female suicides were committed with guns, and about 41 percent with drugs or poison.

If suicide was a serious threat to women, rape and robbery were not. Only one woman, a prostitute, was robbed in Bodie, and there were no reports of women having been robbed in Aurora. There were also no reported cases of rape in either Aurora or Bodie. This does not necessarily mean that rape did not occur, since rape is a crime that has traditionally been underreported. Nevertheless, there was not even one report of rape, and there is nothing to suggest that rape may have occurred. On the other hand, there is a considerable body of evidence that indicates that women, other than prostitutes, were only rarely the victims of crime and were generally treated with the utmost respect. There were two cases reported in which attempted rape was alleged. In neither of these cases, both involving prostitutes, did testimony of witnesses support the allegations.

Aurora's and Bodie's records of no rapes and thus rape rates of zero were not matched by nineteenth-century Boston or Salem. From 1880 through 1882 Boston had a rape arrest rate of 3.0 and Salem 4.8. A conversion factor of 2.6—a figure consistent with FBI data in 1980—gives the towns rape rates of 7.8 and 12.5. Nor are Aurora's and Bodie's rates matched by any U.S. city today, although in 1980 Johnstown, Pennsylvania, had a rate of only 5.7. Close behind were Steubenville, Ohio, at 6.2; Bismarck, North Dakota, at 6.3; and Lancaster, Pennsylvania, at 6.4. At the other end of the scale was Los Angeles with more than five thousand rapes in 1980 and a rate of 75.4. Miami had a rate of 67.0, San Francisco–Oakland 64.0, Atlanta 62.3, New York 43.3, and Chicago 30.0. The rape rate for the United States as a whole in 1980 was 36.4.

Juvenile crime is not even mentioned in Aurora; in Bodie it was almost entirely of the youthful prank and malicious mischief variety. The most frequent complaint against the teen-age roughs in Bodie was their use of obscene language. Their drinking, smoking—mostly tobacco but occasionally opium—and gambling were also causes of complaint. They committed a few petty thefts and burglaries, but no violent crimes. By contrast, youth today commit a significant percentage of the violent crime in the United States. In 1980, 9 percent of the arrests for murder, 15 percent of those for rape, and 30 percent of those for robbery were of persons under the age of eighteen. Moreover, there is simply no comparison between Bodie's gang of teen-agers who loitered at the corner of Green and Wood streets and today's youth gangs. In Los Angeles county alone, youth gangs were responsible for 351 homicides in 1980.

Aurora and Bodie had sizable populations of Chinese and smaller but also significant populations of Mexicans, yet there was no racially motivated violence in either town. Moreover, Chinese and Mexicans seem to have been treated no differently by the legal system than were other Aurorans and Bodieites. In the one case in which white witnesses and Chinese witnesses gave contradictory testimony, the jurors accepted the word of the Chinese over that of the whites. Attorneys made themselves available to the Chinese and Mexicans, and Patrick Reddy, Bodie's ablest lawyer, defended Sam Chung, the Chinese badman, more than once. When convicted of crimes, Chinese and Mexicans suffered penalties similar to those meted out to other Bodieites, and non-Mexican whites were punished no differently for their crimes against minorities than if they had committed them against anyone else. Despite this seemingly equal treatment, Mexicans and especially Chinese often preferred to avoid dealing with the justice system. Mexicans, as the murder of John Hackwell, the attempted murder of John Wheeler, and the attempted kidnapping of Sam Chung demonstrated, sought to personally avenge what they thought to be wrongs. Chinese let the secret societies handle most of Chinatown's problems. The authorities quickly learned that if both the victim and the perpetrator of a crime were Chinese, they could expect little or no cooperation, even from the victim himself.

The Chinese and Mexicans carried guns and knives, as did nearly everyone else on the trans-Sierra frontier, and were not averse to using them. Minority crime was not greatly different from that committed by the majority. The most spectacular difference, at least in Bodie, was the tong warfare of the Chinese. The Chinese were involved in a disproportionate number of burglaries and thefts, instances of selling liquor to Indians, and fights over and assaults on women. Mexicans also sold more than their share of liquor to Indians and committed a disproportionate number of horse thefts.

In Aurora and Bodie then, Chinese and Mexicans were not the targets of racially inspired violece. Women were not the victims of rape nor, for the most part, any kind of assault. And larcenous crime was of no great importance. In most ways the towns were not violent or lawless places. But when it came to men fighting men, Aurora and Bodie were unmistakably violent. Fistfights were nightly occurrences and gunfights were not infrequent. Some of these fights resulted from disputes over property and women; a few, from political differences; a handful, from domestic quarrels or arguments between neighbors; but most, from disputes over who was the better man, affronts to personal honor, careless insults, and challenges to pecking order in the saloon. For the most part, the parties involved in these fights were willing participants. Many of them belonged to that class of western frontiersmen known as badmen: proud, confident, and recklessly brave individuals who were always ready to do battle and to do battle in earnest. But most of them were simply miners, teamsters, carpenters, and woodchoppers.

Thirty-one Bodieites and no fewer than seventeen Aurorans were shot, stabbed, or beaten to death, mostly in fights, during the boom years. Because the record for Aurora is incomplete, it is very possible that more than seventeen Aurorans were victims of homicide. The large majority of these killings would fall today into the FBI's category of murder and nonnegligent (voluntary as opposed to accidental) manslaughter. Of Bodie's thirty-one killings probably twenty-nine qualify for such categorization. This would give Bodie a murder and nonnegligent manslaughter rate of 116 on the FBI scale. Aurora, with sixteen of its seventeen recorded killings qualifying, would have a rate of 64.

No U.S. city today comes close to matching Bodie's rate of 116 or even Aurora's 64. In 1980 Miami led the nation with a rate of 32.7. Las Vegas, Nevada, was a distant second at 23.4, followed closely by Los Angeles at 23.3. New York had a rate of 21.0, Chicago 14.5, Atlanta 14.4, and San Francisco–Oakland 11.7. A half-dozen cities had rates of zero. The rate for the United States as a whole in 1980 was 10.2, a rate less than one-eleventh that for Bodie.

Nor do eastern cities during the nineteenth century seem to have had rates more than a fraction of Bodie's. From 1880 through 1882 Boston had a murder and manslaughter (Boston police did not consistently distinguish between negligent and nonnegligent manslaughter) arrest rate of only 3.8 while Salem recorded a 0.0. Since murder and manslaughter are two crimes for which arrests usually equal or occasionally even exceed offenses, there was probably little difference between Boston's and Salem's rates of arrest and rates of offenses. From 1874 through 1880 Philadelphia had a homicide rate of 3.7, and its overall rate for the second half of the nineteenth century was 3.0.

Aurora and Bodie seem to have been matched in homicide rates only by other western frontier towns. Although studies have not been done that calculate homicide rates for other frontier towns, a look at the numbers of homicides that did occur in several of the towns suggests that their rates were, like those for Aurora and Bodie, very high. Virginia City had eight homicides during the year and a half following its founding in 1859. In 1876, the year of its birth, Deadwood had four homicides. Ellsworth, one of the

Kansas cattle towns, had eight homicides during the twelve months following its establishment in 1867, and Dodge City, the queen of the cattle towns, had nine in its first year, 1872–1873. Since the populations of all these towns were small—never more than two or three thousand during the first year—their homicide rates would seem to have been very high. By contrast, Oakland, California, a western but by 1870 no longer a frontier town, had only two homicides during the entire first half of the 1870s, and its population was more than 11,000 in 1870 and nearly 25,000 in 1875.

Several factors would appear to be responsible for the high rates of homicide in Aurora and Bodie. First, the towns' populations were composed mostly of young, healthy, adventurous, single males who adhered to a code of conduct that required a man to stand and fight, even if, or perhaps especially if, it could mean death. Courage was admired above all else. Ironically, these men had come to the West for a materialistic end—to strike it rich—and yet their value structure emphasized the nonmaterialistic values of honor, pride, and courage. Alcohol played a major role as well. These men imbibed prodigious quantities of whiskey. Sobriety was thought proper only for Sunday school teachers and women.

If the character of the men and their consumption of alcohol made fighting inevitable, then their side arms often made fighting fatal. While the carrying of guns probably reduced the incidence of robbery, burglary, and theft, it undoubtedly increased the number of homicides. Although a couple of homicides resulted from beatings and a few from stabbings, the great majority resulted from shootings. With or without the gun, Aurorans and Bodieites would still have fought, but without the gun their fights would not have been so deadly.

The citizens of Aurora and Bodie were generally not troubled by the great numbers of killings, nor were they very upset because only one man was ever convicted by the courts of murder or manslaughter. They accepted the killings and the lack of convictions because those killed, with only a few exceptions, had been willing combatants, and many of them were roughs or badmen. The old, the weak, the female, the innocent, and those unwilling to fight were rarely the targets of attacks. But when they *were* attacked—and murdered—the reaction of the citizens was immediate and came in the form of vigilantism.

Contrary to the popular image of vigilantes as an angry, unruly mob, the vigilantes in both Aurora and Bodie displayed military-like organization and discipline and went about their work in a quiet, orderly, and deliberate manner. The vigilance committees that were formed after the murder of William Johnson in Aurora and Thomas Treloar in Bodie—the Citizens' Safety Committee and the Bodie 601—had as members some of the towns' leading citizens as well as the support of the local newspapers. In both towns the vigilantes waited until the coroner's jury had rendered a verdict before they acted. At no time did any officer of the law attempt to interfere with the actions of the vigilantes. Moreover, the after-the-fact investigations of the vigilantes by the grand jury in Aurora and the coroner's jury in Bodie resulted in nothing more than justifications of vigilantism.

The Citizens' Safety Committee and the Bodie 601 fit the model of "socially constructive" committees of vigilance. In each case they were supported by a great majority of the townspeople, including the leading citizens; they were well regulated; they dealt quickly and effectively with criminal problems; they left the towns in more stable and orderly conditions; and when opposition developed, they disbanded. The committees made no attempt to interfere with the regular institutions of law enforcement and justice in matters that were unrelated to the killings of Johnson and Treloar. Unlike some other vigilante movements, most notably San Francisco's Committee of Vigilance of 1856, the vigilantes in Aurora and Bodie had no political motives.

The vigilance committees were organized, not because there were no established institutions of law enforcement and justice, but because those institutions had failed, in the eyes of the vigilantes, to provide justice. That was not greatly troubling when the homicide victim was a rough or a badman or a man who had chosen to fight, but it was unacceptable when the victim was an innocent party. While killers were invariably arrested and charged with murder, most were discharged after an examination in justice court. In Bodie some forty men were arrested for murder (on three different occasions more than one man was arrested for the same murder) but only seven of these men eventually went to trial in superior court. The rest were either discharged after an examination in justice court or not indicted by the grand jury. Of the seven who were tried all but one—the insane Job Draper—were found not guilty.

Defense attorneys were surprisingly capable, and one, Patrick Reddy, was unquestionably brilliant. Reddy defended two men in justice court examinations and five men in superior court trials on charges of murder. Although the evidence against his clients appeared incontrovertibly damning on two occasions and strong on four others, Reddy never lost a case. One strategy commonly employed by Reddy, and by other defense attorneys, was delay. Since the population of the mining towns was largely transient, a postponement of a trial often meant the loss of prosecution witnesses. The tactic Reddy and the others employed most often to cause delays was disqualification of jurors. In one case Reddy managed to disqualify the entire jury. Jurors were difficult to replace. Aurorans and Bodieites found an endless number of excuses for not serving as jurors, and the county sheriffs regularly mentioned the trouble they had in producing the requisite twelve good and true men. For this reason judges refused to excuse potential jurors if they were familiar with a particular case and instead dismissed them only if they thought they could not be fair-minded.

Defense attorneys also had an important advantage over their colleagues who represented the state. Prosecutors in criminal cases had to prove, as they have to today, not only that the preponderance of the evidence indicated that a defendant was guilty but that the defendant was guilty beyond a reasonable doubt. Moreover, all twelve jurors had to be so convinced. Defense attorneys often were able to place a reasonable doubt in the mind of at least one member of the jury and have a mistrial declared. This usually meant months of delay. The first two murder trials of Chinese badman Sam Chung, for example, ended in hung juries. When he was tried a third time, a full year after the murder, one key prosecution witness had died and another had left the state. Chung was found not guilty.

Also working to the advantage of the defense was the attitude of Aurorans and Bodieites. They thought that a man was fully justified in killing another man if that other man had threatened the first man's life. This held true even if some time had elapsed between the threat and the murder, as the murders of William Carder in Aurora and Jack Myers in Bodie demonstrated. Since the men of the trans-Sierra frontier were known to be men of their word, there was no such thing as an idle threat. Also, since fights were serious business and often proved fatal, any move that a man made during a confrontation which the other man involved in the dispute might interpret as a move for a gun justified that other man's drawing his gun and firing.

If the attitude of the people and the law itself stacked the odds in favor of the defense, so too did the attorneys themselves. The most capable attorneys, such as Patrick Reddy, John McQuaid, and Thomas Ryan, were in private practice and not, except when pressed into service, in the employ of the state. The defense attorneys regularly outshone the prosecutors. Patrick Reddy's performances in court were legendary. Known for his devastating cross-examinations of prosecution witnesses, he was also known to quote the law to the prosecutors, a tactic that brought roars of approval from spectators and left prosecutors chagrined. On the trans-Sierra frontier murder convictions were hard to come by.

Two forms of violence and lawlessness existed in Aurora which were unknown in Bodie, political violence and warfare between Indians and whites. Political violence in Aurora was due entirely to the California-Nevada boundary dispute and the Civil War. The editors of Aurora's two newspapers, one Unionist and the other Copperhead, bore the brunt of this violence. They were both shot once and threatened many times, not by mobs, as occurred elsewhere in California during the Civil War, but by individuals. Aurora was a border town, both literally and figuratively, and political divisions ran deep during the Civil War years. Republican and Democratic clubs were organized almost as soon as the town was established, and there was even a group of Confederate sympathizers who, for a time, held regular meetings and rallies. Fistfights over political disputes were common, and voting frauds and other irregularities were not unknown.

Unlike Aurora, Bodie experienced no politically inspired acts of violence or lawlessness. Bodieites generally paid little attention to national politics—the Civil War was only a memory—and almost none to local politics—the California-Nevada boundary had been established. The only political issue that consistently aroused large numbers of Bodieites, at least Irish Bodieites, was England's continued occupation of Ireland and her oppression of the Irish. Bodie boasted a local chapter of the Land League of Ireland, and the chapter's meetings regularly filled the Miners' Union Hall to overflowing.

Warfare between Indians and whites occurred on the trans-Sierra frontier only during Aurora's boom years. This warfare cost the lives of no fewer than two hundred Indians and thirty whites; perhaps another hundred Indians and whites were wounded. It was not the activities of the miners that precipitated the warfare but those of the ranchers. It is conceivable that the miners and the Indians could have lived together in amity. Once the cattlemen began stocking the range lands of the trans-Sierra, however, warfare was inevitable. Cattle grazing meant less forage for the indigenous animals, whose numbers began to decline as the numbers of steers increased, and the destruction of native plants, whose seeds and roots were the staple of the Indian diet. The Indians of the arid and inhospitable trans-Sierra country had always suffered from a precarious food supply. With white encroachment that food supply was reduced even further, and the Indians had little choice but to prey on cattle and become beef eaters or starve. When a cowboy riding herd in the Owens Valley shot an Indian cattle rustler, the warfare began.

The Indians of the trans-Sierra country fought much as Indians fought elsewhere in the American West. They excelled at hit-and-run raiding and laying ambushes, but had no unity of command, logistical support, or sense of strategy. They were, after all, family men fighting in defense of their homeland, not professional soldiers. They were nearly always outgunned, and they suffered continually from food shortages. Destruction of Indian food caches, a favorite tactic of the whites, was tantamount to destroying the Indians themselves.

The warfare saw cruelty and savagery on both sides. Indians tortured their white (and in one case black) captives to death and gave no quarter to white noncombatants, including women and children. Whites shot down Indian women and children on more than one occasion and twice summarily executed Indian prisoners. If both the Indians and the whites were responsible for cruelty and savagery, ultimate responsibility for the conflict lay with the whites. They were trespassers on Indian lands. They were the invaders, the aggressors. From the perspective of the whites, however, there appeared to be ample room for settlement. They did not comprehend that the Indians were already, as required by the needs of a hunting and gathering people, making maximum use of the land. Nor did the whites comprehend that stocking the range lands with cattle would force the Indians either to drastically alter their way of life or to fight against encroachment by whites. Most Indians chose to fight.

By the time of Bodie's boom most of the Indians of the trans-Sierra frontier had been removed to reservations. A few small bands still roamed the hills, but it was almost impossible to eke out an existence. Woodchoppers had denuded most hillsides of trees and with them the pine nut, a staple of the Indian diet. Some three dozen Indians lived in Bodie, but they were not important figures in violence or lawlessness. For the most part they were pathetic alcoholics who would occasionally ransack a cabin, commit a theft, or get in a fight, usually with another Indian or a Chinese. When drunk they spent much of their time in jail for "safe keeping," as the authorities termed it. The Indian had been robbed of his land, his culture, and his identity, all within the span of a few years, and the results were devastating.

The violence and lawlessness that visited the trans-Sierra frontier most frequently and affected it most deeply, then, took special forms: warfare between Indians and whites, stagecoach robbery, vigilantism, and gunfights. These activities bear little or no relation to the violence and lawlessness that pervade American society today. Serious juvenile offenses, crimes against the elderly and weak, rape, robbery, burglary, and theft were either nonexistent or of little significance on the trans-Sierra frontier. If the trans-Sierra frontier was at all representative of frontiers in general, then there seems to be little justification for blaming contemporary American violence and lawlessness on a frontier heritage.

The experience of the trans-Sierra frontier also demonstrates that some long-cherished notions about violence, lawlessness, and justice in the Old West—especially those created by motion pictures and, still worse, television—are nothing more than myth. Probably the most glaring example of myth conflicting with reality is that of the gunfighter. Film and television imagery suggests that a quick draw was the critical factor in a gunfight and that shooters were deadly accurate. In Aurora and Bodie the critical factor was not a quick draw but accuracy, and although some gunfighters were deadly accurate—from fairly long range Irish Tom Carberry shot one man between the eyes and another in the heart—most were not. Shooters missed their targets more often than they hit them, and there were fights in which six-shooters were emptied at close range with no one being hit. There were many reasons for the inaccuracy of a shooter. The fights often occurred in crowded saloons where a shooter's arm was bumped or grabbed, the lighting was dim, the shooter was often intoxicated, and guns malfunctioned and misfired.

Shooters normally carried their guns not in a holster but in a pocket or tucked into a waistband. While the revolver most often used was a Colt, the popular model during Bodie's heyday was not the Peacemaker but the Lightning, and fifteen years earlier during Aurora's boom it was the Navy or Dragoon. Gunfights were almost always between private citizens; lawmen were rarely involved. Only once did a lawman—Richard O'Malley in Bodie—participate in a one-on-one gunfight with another man.

Other film and television images also contradict reality on the trans-Sierra frontier. Indians never launched attacks on soldiers, civilians, or stagecoaches which could prove costly to themselves. The Indian did not risk suffering great losses. Bank robbery did not occur, and stagecoaches carrying great bullion shipments were not stopped by highwaymen. Guards on stages—the shotgun messengers—exchanged gunfire with highwaymen only once. Women, even prostitutes, rarely ventured into saloons. For the most part, the saloon was an all-male preserve. Alcohol was not the only popular intoxicant. Opium was plentiful and widely used, and addiction to opium, among whites, was not rare. Prostitutes were often addicted to both alcohol and opium.

Institutions of law enforcement and justice were well established, and defendants were entitled to every protection that they receive today. Defense attorneys were highly capable and sophisticated and won acquittals for most of their clients. Horse thieves were not hanged; they were sentenced to short jail or prison terms. Although minorities were certainly the objects of some abuse and varying degrees of social ostracism, they were treated equally and fairly by the criminal justice system. Jailbreaks were rare— only one in Bodie and two in Aurora. Vigilantism was the product not of hysterical torch-waving mobs but of highly organized and disciplined bodies of men. Lawmen did not take heroic stands against vigilantes; they stood aside or cooperated. The murderers hanged were not sniveling cowards at the end but brave men.

The trans-Sierra frontier, then, did not give us the basis for much of the motion picture and television portrayal of the Old West, nor does it seem to have fathered the violence and lawlessness that plagues America today. But it certainly did give us warfare between Indians and whites, highwaymen, prostitutes and gamblers, opium smokers, vigilantes, pistol-packing women, a Chinese tong battle and a Chinese badman, a brilliant one-armed lawyer who never lost a case, a gang of badmen, and gunfighters aplenty.

Υ *F U R T H E R   R E A D I N G*

Ralph K. Andrist, *The Long Death: The Last Days of the Plains Indians* (1964)

Larry D. Ball, *The United States Marshals of New Mexico and Arizona Territories, 1846–1912* (1978)

David Bodenhamer, "Law and Disorder on the Early Frontier: Marion County, Indiana, 1823–1850," *Western Historical Quarterly,* 10 (1979), 323–36

Allan G. Bogue, "The Iowa Claim Clubs: Symbol and Substance," *Mississippi Valley Historical Review,* 45 (1958), 231–53

Richard Maxwell Brown, *Strain of Violence: Historical Studies of American Violence and Vigilantism* (1975)

Jack Burrows, "John Ringo: The Story of a Western Myth," *Montana the Magazine of Western History,* 25 (1980), 2–15

Anne M. Butler, *Daughters of Joy, Sisters of Misery: Prostitutes in the American West, 1865–90* (1985)

Lew L. Callaway, *Montana's Righteous Hangmen: The Vigilantes in Action* (1982)

John G. Cawelti, *The Six-Gun Mystique* (1971)

Harry Sinclair Drago, *The Great Range Wars* (1970)

Johnny France and Malcolm McConnell, *Incident at Big Sky* (1986)

Lawrence M. Freidman and Robert V. Percival, *The Roots of Justice: Crime and Punishment in Alameda County, California, 1870–1910* (1981)

Wayne Gard, *Frontier Justice* (1949)

Robert V. Haynes, *A Night of Violence: The Houston Riot of 1917* (1976)

Eugene W. Hollon, *Frontier Violence: Another Look* (1974)

W. Turrentine Jackson, "Wells Fargo: Symbol of the Wild West?" *Western Historical Quarterly,* 3 (1972), 179–96

Philip D. Jordan, *Frontier Law and Order* (1970)

William A. Keleher, *Violence in Lincoln County, 1869–1881* (1957)

Thomas C. Leonard, "Red, White and Army Blue: Empathy and Anger in the American West," *American Quarterly*, 26 (1974), 179–89

Daniel F. Littlefield, Jr. and Lonnie E. Underhill, "The 'Crazy Snake Uprising' of 1909: A Red, Black, or White Affair?" *Arizona and the West*, 20 (1978), 307–24

Nyle H. Miller and Joseph W. Snell, *Great Gunfighters of the Kansas Cowtowns, 1867–1886* (1967)

Earl Mottram, "The Persuasive Lips: Men and Guns in America, the West," *Journal of American Studies*, 10 (1976), 53–84

Dallin H. Oaks and Marvin S. Hill, *Carthage Conspiracy: The Trial of the Accused Assassins of Joseph Smith* (1975)

Bill O'Neal, *Encyclopedia of Western Gunfighters* (1969)

Frank Richard Prassal, *The Western Peace Officer: A Legacy of Law and Order* (1972)

Joseph G. Rosa, *The Gunfighter: Man or Myth?* (1969)

Robert J. Rosenbaum, *Mexicano Resistance in the Southwest: "The Sacred Right of Self Preservation"* (1981)

Julian Samora et al., *Gunpowder Justice: A Reassessment of the Texas Rangers* (1979)

Robert M. Senkewicz, *Vigilantes in Gold Rush San Francisco* (1985)

William A. Settle, Jr., *Jesse James Was His Name . . .* (1966)

Glenn H. Shirley, *West of Hell's Fringe: Crime, Criminals, and the Federal Peace Officers in Oklahoma Territory* (1977)

Richard Slotkin, *Regeneration Through Violence: The Mythology of the American Frontier, 1600–1860* (1973)

C. L. Sonnichsen, *Pass of the North* (1968)

George R. Stewart, *Committee of Vigilance: Revolution in San Francisco, 1851* (1964)

Robert M. Utley, *High Noon in Lincoln* (1987)

——, *The Indian Frontier of the American West, 1846–1890* (1984)

Paul I. Wellman, *A Dynasty of Western Outlaws* (1961)

John P. Wilson, *Merchants, Guns, and Money: The Story of Lincoln County and Its Wars* (1987)

John R. Wunder, "Chinese in Trouble: Criminal Law and Race on the Trans-Mississippi West Frontier," *Western Historical Quarterly*, 17 (1986), 25–42

——, *Inferior Courts, Superior Justice: A History of the Justices of the Peace on the Northwest Frontier, 1853–1889* (1979)

CHAPTER
10

Reservations and Homesteads

Y

The attempts at farming the interior lands of the trans-Mississippi West make for one of the great sagas of the region's history. The farmers whose destination was Oregon or California migrated on overland trails but were rewarded with good soil and adequate—sometimes overabundant—rainfall at the end of their journey. In contrast, the farmers who tried to settle on the central and northern plains often traveled west by railroad, not wagon train. Yet only their trip was easier than the overlanders' journey. Harsh winters, irregular precipitation, and swarms of grasshoppers made many give up. Still, promises of better acreage for sale by railroad companies, as well as offers of "free" land from the federal government, brought new swarms of settlers. Even agricultural science inflated farmers' hopes. The technique of dry farming (using only rain—no human-introduced irrigation—to water crops) developed by land-grant universities in the West, persuaded many individuals that the high-plains areas across the northern tier of western states would support family agriculture. The first two decades of the twentieth century saw a rush of homesteaders to these northern areas. Many either failed before 1920 or were dragged under by the agricultural depression that started in that decade.

Ironically, during the same period in which so many farmers went bust, the federal government insisted that most Indian reservations be broken up and that individual native families take up farming on 160-acre allotments. The "surplus" reservation lands went to non-Indian farmers. The total loss of Indian lands is astounding. From the passage of the General Allotment Act of 1887, sponsored by Senator Henry Dawes of Massachusetts, to 1934, when federal legislation ended the policy, American Indians lost approximately 60 percent of their 138 million acres of reservation land.

Hardship and failure plagued farmers in the interior West. Why, then, did so many men and women try to make a life as farmers in this region?

Y*DOCUMENTS*

The first five documents present memories of homesteading and farming. The first selection, spanning 1877–1900, considers the early attempts at agriculture on the Indian reservations. John Stands-in-Timber, a traditionalist and one leader of the Northern Cheyennes, recounts the problems of learning to plow. In the same selection, Ella C. Deloria, a Yankton Sioux scholar and educator, recalls how farming disrupted traditional patterns of life. The second document gives the reminiscences of a Danish father and son. The Jorgensens moved from Waupaca, Wisconsin, to Dagmar, Montana, in 1906. The father, Jorgen, wants to live with fellow Danes, whereas the son, Otto, sees the move west as a great American adventure. In the third selection, Rufus Jones remembers the effort to find a dryland farm in north-central Montana in 1913. He admits that although neither he nor his brother Earl are farmers, they are nevertheless eager to find any acreage that seems suitable to their inexperienced eyes. In the fourth document, dated 1913, Elinore Stewart is full of enthusiasm for women taking up home-steads in Wyoming. Her words, contained in a letter to a friend, convey the seemingly realistic dreams that lured so many onto the land. In the fifth reading, dated 1916, Catharine Calk McCarty describes how cattle from a nearby ranch wandered onto her land. Her resolution of this problem shows that a lone home-steader could still find neighborly support and cooperation.

The final three documents depict more clearly negative views of farming. The parody folk song "Idaho Land" appeared in a 1917 book that extolled dry farming in north-central Montana. The lyrics lament the excessive dryness of farms in southern Idaho. The ultimate result for Montana farmers is highlighted in the last two documents: W. M. Black's plea in 1921 to Governor Joe Dixon, and Montana farmer Edward J. Bell's careful accounting of his family's efforts at dry farming from 1911 to 1923. Bell concludes that modern techniques of agricul-ture might have brought success to his family's farm in eastern Montana. His optimism at the end of the piece also demonstrates that for many farmers, hope returns with one good harvest.

John Stands-in-Timber and Ella C. Deloria
Recall the Early Days of Reservation Farming, 1877–1900

[John Stands-in-Timber:] The government started the Indians raising gardens as soon as they surrendered. Some had gardens of corn and other crops. . . . They had forgotten how, though they all used to garden in the old days before they hunted buffalo. Now they were learning about new crops as well, things they had never seen before. The Dull Knife people got to Oklahoma in 1877 about the time the watermelons ripened, and when the Southern Cheyennes gave them some they cut them up and boiled them like squash. They did not know you could eat them raw. But later when they planted their own they put sugar with the seeds. They said it would make them sweeter when they grew.

When they reached Tongue River every man was supposed to have a garden of his own. A government farmer went around to teach them. And many of them worked hard, even carrying buckets of water from the river by hand. One man, Black White Man, wanted to raise cotton. He had seen it in Oklahoma. He plowed a piece of ground and smoothed it up, and

Reprinted from John Stands-in-Timber and Margot Liberty, *Cheyenne Memories*, 276–78, by permission of Yale University Press. Copyright © 1967 by Yale University Press.

when it was ready he took his wife's quilt and made little pieces from the inside and planted them with a garden hoe. When his wife missed the quilt, she got after him. He was afraid to tell her, but finally he said, "I got it and took out the cotton and planted it. We will have more quilts than we need, as soon as it grows."

When they first learned to plow in Oklahoma the farmer told them to get ready and come to a certain place and he would show them. They did not understand. They thought "Get ready" meant fancy costumes and not their new pants and shirts. So everybody had feathers on their heads and necklaces and leggings and fancy moccasins. It looked like a dance, not a farming lesson. And all the women and children went along to see them.

The farmer told one man to grab the handles while he started ahead with the team. But the plow jumped out of the ground and turned over, and the Indian fell down. But he tried again, and by the time they got back around he was doing pretty well. Then they all tried. At last they came to one man who had been watching closely. When he started off the dirt rolled right over and he went clear around that way, and the criers started announcing, "Ha-aah! See that man!" The women made war cries and everybody hollered just as if he had counted coup.

Another time when they practiced plowing down there, one man plowed up a bull snake and the next man plowed up a rattlesnake, and after that they were all afraid to go.

In Montana they began to help each other. The government issued plows to quite a few men, and in Birney the Fox Military Society used to plow together as soon as the frost was out. They would all gather at the farthest place up the river and work together until that was done, and then move to the next. They had seven or eight plows and it went faster that way. Besides, it was more fun.

One year they decided to finish every garden in ten days, and any member who did not show up would be punished. Everything was fine for several days, until they got to Black Eagle's place. And Looks Behind never came. The rest of them finished plowing for Black Eagle and Medicine Top and Broken Jaw. Then they all got on their horses, and us kids followed them to the Medicine Bull place on Tie Creek and there was Looks Behind, fixing his fence.

They all yelled and fired their guns, and galloped by and hit him with their quirts. There were twenty or thirty of them. Looks Behind had a shovel and at first he was going to fight, but he took it. Afterwards he could hardly talk. They made him get on his horse and go back and start plowing right away.

[Ella C. Deloria:] At length there came the time when individual allotments of land were made. Families were encouraged to live out on them and start

---

Reprinted from *Speaking of Indians*, 60–63, by Ella C. Deloria. Copyright 1979, Dakota Press, University of South Dakota.

to be farmers forthwith. Equipment for this, as well as some essential furniture, was given the most docile ones by way of inducement. But again, it wasn't easy to make the spiritual and social adjustment. The people were too used to living in large family groups, cooperatively and happily. Now, here they were in little father-mother-child units (with an occasional grandparent, to be sure), often miles from their other relatives, trying to farm an arid land—the very same land from which, later on, white farmers of Old World tradition and training could not exact even a subsistence living. Enduring frightful loneliness and working at unfamiliar tasks just to put himself ahead financially were outside the average Dakota's ken. For him there were other values. The people naturally loved to foregather; and now the merest excuse for doing so became doubly precious. For any sort of gathering it was the easiest thing to abandon the small garden, leave the stock to fend for themselves, and go away for one to four weeks. On returning, they might find the place a wreck. That was too bad; but to miss getting together with other Dakotas was far worse.

After a time, however, they were making better, larger houses—neater, too, with the logs planed so as to fit closer and requiring less of the mud chinking that was always coming loose in the first cabins. The doors and windows fitted better, there were floors, and the roofs were of boards. The people began to make ingenious adaptations of some elements in their old life to the new. For instance, at one period they transferred the art decorations of the tipi to the loghouse. Out of G.I. muslin they made very large wall coverings, a carry over from the dew curtain of a tipi and called by the same term, *ozan*. On these they painted beautiful designs and made lively black and white drawings of historical scenes of hunting or battles or peacemaking between tribes, and courtship scenes, games, and such like activities of the past. People went visiting just to see one another's pictographs and to hear the stories they preserved. I barely remember one such wall covering which had been given to be sold, the proceeds to be used for missionary work. My father brought it home, and my mother had it hung so that the teachers at the school might see it. It was large enough to cover most of two sides of our fourteen by fifteen foot dining room in the rectory. This interesting mode of decoration passed out quite suddenly when it became the fashion, perhaps about 1908, to build frame houses.

My impression is that the women took special pride in caring for their new homes and new furniture. Once my mother took me along to call on Nancy Gall, daughter of the famous chief, and we found her vigorously scrubbing her pine floor to a brilliant yellow and cleaning house generally. "I promised the *tiwaheawanyaka* [guardian-of-the-family] to do this every Floorwashing Day [Saturday], and I have never missed yet!" she explained, rising from her knees to greet my mother.

A salute right here to the government field matrons, those guardians-of-the-family! Attached to the agency staffs, they did a great deal of good in helping the women to a fine start and inspiring them to learn. It was a pity they were withdrawn, for, in a way, they were the most constructive influence exerted by government at that period. They were no Home Ec. Ph.D's, that's true. They were only sensible, motherly women, usually elderly, with *hearts that were right*. And that, I think, is nearly enough in practical work with so called backward peoples. Feeling their warmth and sympathy, the people responded well in numerous cases and spoke of them later on with respectful gratitude. Among other things, those women taught the Dakota housewives to make "lung bread," as yeast raised bread was named because of the air holes. Formerly only baking-powder dough was known, but now there was a definite preference for the new kind. The field matrons taught many. Others made long journeys to our mission to be taught there.

I can imagine the delight of the husbands when their wives wished to make the trip. With what sudden alacrity they must have stepped around, getting the team hitched to the wagon! To their monotonous new life, it was a welcome break to get together with other men also camping around the mission for one reason or another. "We are here while *winunhca* learns how to make lung bread." So they would account for themselves, temporarily happy again, as they sat in circles upon the ground to smoke the endless pipe and talk about past glories.

They needed those breaks, poor things! It was they who suffered the most from the enforced change, whether they realized it or not. It was their life primarily that was wrecked; it was their exclusive occupation that was abruptly ended. The women could go right on bearing children and rearing them. They could cook, feed their families, set up and strike camp unaided, pack and unpack when on a trip. Even embroidery, exclusively a woman's art, was not cut off suddenly. It tapered away as the buffalo and deer skins on which the work was done became more and more scarce. By slow degrees, meanwhile, they could learn other work and were able to make the shift more easily.

The man was the tragic figure. Frustrated, with his age old occupation suddenly gone, he was left in a daze, unable to overcome the strange and passively powerful inertia that stayed him from doing anything else. And so he sat by the hour, indifferent and inactive, watching—perhaps envying— his wife, as she went right on working at the same essential role of woman that had been hers since time immemorial. In such a mental state, what did he care that unsympathetic onlookers called him "lazy Indian" and accused him of driving his wife, like a slave, while "he took his ease"! As though he enjoyed it! If, as he sat there, someone had called, "Hey! There's a herd of buffalo beyond that hill! Come quick!" he would have sprung into life instantly again. But, alas, no such thing would ever happen now. All he could do, or thought he could do, on his "farm" was to water the horses mechanically, bring in fuel and water, cut a little hay, tend a little garden. He did it listlessly, almost glad when the garden died on his hands for lack of rain. His heart was not in what he was doing anyway—until something human came up: a gathering of the people, where he could be with many relatives again; or a death, when he must go to help with the mourning; or a cow to be butchered, reminiscent of the hunt; or time to go to the agency for the biweekly issue of rations. That he must not miss. For him and his family, that was what still gave meaning to life.

Kinship continued strong, in spite of the dispersion, and the people had all the time in the world now for honoring each other, and for the giving of courtesy food and goods with still the same fervor. This was, in a way, the golden age for giving, for there was more to do with—yards of G.I. goods, numerous items of rationed foods (as if they didn't all have the same amounts to begin with!), and beautiful silver dollars, ideal gifts to seal a handshake—sometimes with a murmured, "My relative, with this I shake your hand," but, just as often, transferring it from palm to palm without a word.

Going after rations involved several days, with pleasant camps en route, depending on how far away a family lived from the agency. Traveling in company, as in olden days, packing a tipi and other essential equipment and starting out leisurely, and at the last arriving to form one great camp circle once more for three or four precious days—that was living! The intervening times were waiting times. Drawing rations was almost incidental.

Jorgen and Otto Jorgensen Remember the Decision to Homestead in Montana, 1906

[Jorgen:] One would think that we would have been satisfied to settle down where we were but such was not the case. We had constantly longed for fellowship with other Danes in a Danish congregation in a Danish settlement with a Danish school. There was a Danish Church in Waupaca [Wisconsin] but that was a distance of seven miles away. Our neighbors were all native Americans. Most of them were uneducated and not too intellectual. They were congenial and friendly enough but we got little satisfaction or enjoyment from fellowship with them. The language was a handicap too because Kristiane [his wife] had not had as good an opportunity to learn it as I who had mixed with other people more. She could make herself understood alright but has since improved a great deal. She reads English books quite well but when it comes to writing I have to do it.

In the meantime we had managed to get all the land under cultivation that I was able to handle without hired help. All we had to do was to plant potatoes in the spring, dig them up in the fall, and haul them to town during the winter which was a little too tame an existence. I have mentioned two reasons why we wanted to move but there was a third. The older girls were growing up, and what if one of them should come home some day with one of these individuals with a foreign background and present him as her sweetheart. This was unthinkable. (Strangely enough after we came to Montana one of the girls actually did come and present an American as her sweetheart but he was a high class individual. He was a lawyer who later became district judge for Sheridan and other counties.)

When E. F. Madsen's call came in "Dannevirke" in 1906 to establish a Danish colony in eastern Montana, I immediately said, "That's where we are going,'' and Kristiane immediately agreed. I think people thought we were crazy to abandon what was, as far as people could tell, the comfort and security we had for insecurity and a cold, harsh climate. ''You'll freeze to death out there,'' they said and related terrifying experiences of people who had succumbed in snowstorms. But it didn't seem to make much of an impression on us. I was past 50 years of age and if we were to build up another farm it was time to get started.

E. F. Madsen from Clinton, Iowa had been out in Montana on October 6, 1906 to find a place for a new Danish colony and had selected the place where it now is located in the northeast corner of Montana about 25 miles from the Canadian line and close to the Dakota boundary. Madsen named it ''Dagmar.'' It's full name is ''Dronning Dagmar's Minde'' (Queen Dagmar's Memorial), and is the first such colony in the United States. The land is fertile with smooth rolling prairies. The land was not surveyed but could be claimed by anyone over 21 years of age under Squatter's right. The 160 acres allowed was later increased to 320 acres. . . .

[Otto:] My first recollection of any talk of moving or living anywhere else but where we were, was the folks, setting at the kitchen table one night—it must have been in 1906. Mother was fidgeting with something or other on the table, listening to Pa read aloud from the weekly Danish publication, *Dannevirke,* with a bright, faraway look in her eyes; and when he had finished, she said: ''Skul' vi?'' (should we?) We kids sat around, I for one, with open mouth, sensing something special was in the wind, and when the word Montana was mentioned,—MONTANA!! Montana to me was a magic word! That's where Falsbuts' were going to go! And Falsbuts' boys had thoroughly briefed me on what could be expected there: buffalo, cowboys, and wild horses—Oh boy! Free land, homesteads, Montana and the West! No one has any idea of what those magic words could conjure up in a 10-year-old boy's mind!

As I have grown older, I have often wondered what prompts the pioneering spirit in some people and leaves others completely devoid of it.

As the folks became serious about the matter, the idea crystallized, as was evidenced by the preparations such as a new cookstove, a swell big kitchen range, new harnesses, etc. It was now ''for sure'' that the big adventure was about to become a reality. But it was not until the spring of 1908 that all the difficulties of such an undertaking were overcome. Selling the farm, auction sale, getting the cash, etc. We didn't sell much—everything was stuffed into the immigrant-car, (special homeseekers rates) and when I say ''stuffed'' I mean just that! Cows and calves, chickens, pigs, horses, dogs, (no cats). All household goods, all the farming implements, wagons, mower, hayrake, and hayrack. The hayrack was used to double-deck the chickens above the cows.

I have often wondered what Pa's reactions were to all this. He never showed anything, outwardly. I remember when we left the farm for the last time, and we were about to get into the wagon. He was buttoning his coat with one hand and with the other, reached down to stroke the big old gray tom-cat, which was to be left behind; and he said, ''Kitty, Kitty!'' I was dumbfounded, for I had never seen him do a thing like that before. He straightened up and looked around at the good new house and big new red barn; and in his slow, easy-going and deliberate way, climbed into the wagon. I have often wondered what his innermost thoughts were at that moment. But like so many thousands before him who have pulled up stakes for the unknown future in the West, he left little room for sentiment. In tribute to my father, I think this was his staunchest moment. Of course, the die was cast; the decision had been made some time before, which also took courage—but the final last look at the fruits of 12 to 14 of his best years, brought from him no outward sign of regret. Nor did he, I'm glad to say, ever live to regret it. To turn his back on all this, against the advice of well-meaning neighbors and friends; and at the age of 51 years, take a family of eight children out into the un-tracked prairies fifty miles from the railroad and "nowhere" with measly small capital, took courage and fortitude, to say the least. That kind of spirit and courage, I'm afraid, is fast becoming a thing of the past in these United States.

Rufus Jones on the Rush for Dryland Farms in Montana, 1913

About 1910 I learned that the U.S.A. was betting a half section of dry land that you couldn't live on and make a living from it for three years. Having a desire to become a farmer, Earl [his brother] and I decided that we would take that bet. Mabel and I sold our little home on Eighth Street for which we had worked so hard that we might have money to get to Montana and have money to live on until the first crop came. We sure had no idea how much it would take!

In the spring of 1913 Earl and I went to Montana to locate a homestead. We bought tickets for Great Falls as the Great Northern gave the most glowing description of that part of the state. Arriving and after looking around we decided we didn't like the looks of the land, and besides the homesteads were all taken for twenty miles around. We went to Helena not knowing any more about Helena than we had known about Great Falls and found that the land there had been homesteaded, too. Anyway when we asked for tickets to Helena they told us the train had left an hour before and the next train would leave day after tomorrow. We figured we just wouldn't wait that long so we took the train to Lewistown in the Judith Basin. We repeated the same questions and received the same answers as before. Homesteads near all taken.

In Lewistown we met Francis Chevanne, who was also from Des Moines. He had been in Montana for three years and had a homestead up in Denton County. He advised us to try up around Grass Range. There was no railroad to Grass Range so we hired a couple of saddle horses and early the next

Reprinted from Rufus M. Jones Papers, Toole Archives, Small Collections 33, Maureen and Mike Mansfield Library, University of Montana.

morning we started up over the Judith Mountains. About half way up we came across a road gang and asked the way to Grass Range. One of the men said, "You all just stay on this road, don't get offen it and in about six hours you'll be there." When we reached the top it began to hail and rain, with a strong wind. The horses turned tail and started back toward Lewistown and not being horsemen we went back in spite of anything we could do. By the time we got back to Lewistown the sun was shining. We still couldn't get a room so Francis took us to his room, had a cot put in and gave us his bed. We went to bed at five thirty P.M. I don't think we ever paid him for the room.

Next day I went to the Land Office to inquire about land. I got to talking to a Spanish War Veteran who said, "I'm not supposed to give out any information but I hear there is a lot of good land that has just been opened up along the Milwaukee Railroad, north of Bascom and Hibbard, east of Melstone." We took the train to Harlowtown, waited there about four hours and got one into Melstone.

That night I bumped into Fred Wilson, a locator and also a veterinarian who agreed to pick us up the next afternoon at Sumatra and take us out to his place for the night and would show us some very fine land the next day. His fee for locating us was to be fifty dollars each. We slept that night on the kitchen floor with a very thin sugan comforter* under us. Early the next morning we started to look the country over.

Wilson had picked up another prospect the night before so there were three of us. Wilson hitched up a team with some difficulty as one of the horses, a range horse, had only been hitched up once before. He put on her, what he called a war bridle with a sash cord as a controlling devise and gave me the end of the rope, saying, "If she begins to act up and I say 'cull' give the rope a big jerk." However she didn't act up and by the time we got home she seemed to be a well broken horse. Wilson took us north and northeast clear up to Breed Creek. This third prospect was hard to please and very particular. We called him the *Bo Hunk*. Earl and I not being farmers were more easily satisfied, except, for the fact that all the land he showed us was gumbo, covered with scrubby sage brush and very little grass. We figured if the good lord couldn't make grass grow we would hardly be able to raise wheat or corn. As a last resort he showed us section 4, township 11, range 32. Earl and I thought that would do us being only a mile from the Rattlesnake Springs which never went dry.

Being late afternoon, we returned to his place and had our supper, expecting to go to Sumatra the next morning to file. About ten o'clock that night Bo Hunk took the door knob in his hand, for what we supposed was obvious reasons, but instead of coming back in the house he hightailed it for Sumatra on foot. I don't know to this day whether he filed on any of the land he had seen or not. He could have as he knew the legal description of several sections.

---

*a heavy patchwork comforter weighing about four pounds

Elinore Stewart Advocates
Homesteading for Women, 1913

January 23, 1913.

DEAR MRS. CONEY,—

When I read of the hard times among the Denver poor, I feel like urging them every one to get out and file on land. I am very enthusiastic about women homesteading. It really requires less strength and labor to raise plenty to satisfy a large family than it does to go out to wash, with the added satisfaction of knowing that their job will not be lost to them if they care to keep it. Even if improving the place does go slowly, it is that much done to stay done. Whatever is raised is the homesteader's own, and there is no house-rent to pay. This year Jerrine [her daughter] cut and dropped enough potatoes to raise a ton of fine potatoes. She wanted to try, so we let her, and you will remember that she is but six years old. We had a man to break the ground and cover the potatoes for her and the man irrigated them once. That was all that was done until digging time, when they were ploughed out and Jerrine picked them up. Any woman strong enough to go out by the day could have done every bit of the work and put in two or three times that much, and it would have been so much more pleasant than to work so hard in the city and then be on starvation rations in the winter.

To me, homesteading is the solution of all poverty's problems, but I realize that temperament has much to do with success in any undertaking, and persons afraid of coyotes and work and loneliness had better let ranching alone. At the same time, any woman who can stand her own company, can see the beauty of the sunset, loves growing things, and is willing to put in as much time at careful labor as she does over the washtub, will certainly succeed; will have independence, plenty to eat all the time, and a home of her own in the end.

Experimenting need cost the homesteader no more than the work, because by applying to the Department of Agriculture at Washington he can get enough of any seed and as many kinds as he wants to make a thorough trial, and it does n't even cost postage. Also one can always get bulletins from there and from the Experiment Station of one's own State concerning any problem or as many problems as may come up. I would not, for anything, allow Mr. Stewart [her husband] to do anything toward improving my place, for I want the fun and the experience myself. And I want to be able to speak from experience when I tell others what they can do. Theories are very beautiful, but facts are what must be had, and what I intend to give some time.

Here I am boring you to death with things that cannot interest you! You'd think I wanted you to homestead, would n't you? But I am only thinking of the troops of tired, worried women, sometimes even cold and hungry, scared to death of losing their places to work, who could have plenty to eat, who could have good fires by gathering the wood, and comfortable homes of their own, if they but had the courage and determination to get them.

I must stop right now before you get so tired you will not answer. With much love to you from Jerrine and myself, I am

Yours affectionately,

Elinore Rupert Stewart.

Catharine Calk McCarty and Her Cattlemen Neighbors, 1916

My homestead home, a log house, on the side of a hill on the open range with its dirt floor and dirt roof, seemed a haven that next summer when the hot winds, parching the land as well as the face, seemed never to end. At the back of the house, where the shadows were longest, a hole in the ground, about two feet deep and four feet in diameter served as the "icebox." The water, carried up the hill from my brother's well, and kept covered in the icebox, seemed very cool. . . .

My brother was not on the homestead that summer. Colonel, my dog, followed Tramp and me wherever we went. The old saying, a horse and a dog are man's best friends, I found was true.

As the hot days of July, 1916, neared their end, the wheat as well as the oats were turning yellow. One morning I was awakened by Colonel barking as though something was wrong. Opening the door, stepping out into the morning sun just coming over the hill, I saw a large herd of range cattle pushing against the wire fence around the crop.

This is serious—in a day our crop will be gone and all the feed for winter, I thought. Saddling Tramp and taking my revolver I attempted to round up the cattle. I was not very adept at this. The cattle sensed it. In despair, I shot into the air; this really got them going, and with Colonel helping, the cattle were driven what seemed a long ways away, and I hoped they would not find their way back. Hurrying home, I fed Colonel and Tramp, ate my breakfast, dinner and supper in one.

The next day, at daylight the cattle were back. This continued for several days. Shooting in the air and the dog barking seemed to be the only way I could get them moving.

One day when my three-meals-in-one was over, two strange men rode up, came to the door, introduced themselves, and said, "We are representatives of the local stock association. Are you the lady shooting cattle?"

"No," I replied, "I am not shooting cattle. I am just driving them away from that little crop. Every day I think they will lose their way but every morning, there they are."

"Aren't you shooting at them? That's illegal. The stockmen cannot put up with that. The sheriff will serve notice on you if you don't stop."

"I cannot drive them; the only way I can get them away is to shoot in the air."

"You can't do that," they cried. "We are a committee to notify you that this will have to stop."

"Fine," I said, "if I stop shooting at your cattle, you'll have to help." By that time, they were drinking some coffee. "I'm just a forlorn homesteader trying to protect a little crop while my brother is away. You both have mowers, haven't you, and men, and horses? Well, how about coming here, cutting the crop, and putting up a corral?"

They looked at me.

"If you don't want me to run your cattle, you'll have to cut the crop," I laughed.

They looked at each other. Finally one of them said, "By golly, maybe we could do that."

I said, "Well, if you do that, I'll cook the best dinner I can. You'll have to come early, as those cattle will push in the fence and one hundred head of cattle can do a lot of eating."

We talked awhile about the cattle business, what luck they were having, and how the range had been taken up; and if I were going to shoot and run their cattle, they would not weigh anything in the fall. "They will be nothing but drags if we ever get them to market," they cried.

I listened very attentively, wondering, "Will they really do this? Will they be here tomorrow?" They left with a grin.

Sure enough, next morning, at daylight they were back with a mower and hay rake. There were two men, one mowing, one raking, and two others putting up a corral, taking the wire and posts from the fence. "How wonderful of them," I kept saying to myself.

I cooked everything I had on hand. Making some lemon pies, with lemons and eggs taken from the "icebox" at the back of the cabin, hot biscuits, and the last of some ham and beans, jam, and anything else I could find. I got them filled up. I tried to show them what good sports I thought they were, and how much I appreciated their help, telling them that they were not at all like stockmen who hate honyockers, as homesteaders were called.

They left with mower, hay rake, horses, and bid me a very friendly farewell. I looked at the hay in the corral and the herd having a good feed on the stubble left on the field. That night I slept soundly, way into the next day. No more riding at daybreak, shooting, running cattle. Those days were over.

Shortly I had word from Mr. Hetherington, who seemed to be head of the local stockmen and dominated the association. He wanted to see me. I was afraid that he would want pay for the men who worked and for his rake and mower. I heard he was crippled with rheumatism and I decided to face the lion in his den. I found the way to his home, one day after a long ride. When I knocked at the door, Mrs. Hetherington opened it, and I introduced myself.

"Oh yes," she greeted me, "Mr. Hetherington thought you would be coming one of these days." She brought me into the room where a large man, with shaggy greying hair and heavy eyebrows, sat on a chair.

"Did you want to see me?" I meekly asked.

He fairly shouted, "I sent for you, didn't I? I wanted to see the red-headed girl who rides around shooting cattle."

"But, Mr. Hetherington," I began.

"No, I know. When the local association sent two men to order you to stop shooting and running cattle, what did the weak fools do? Nothing to make you stop, but you talked them into bringing our machinery, horses, and men, cutting your crop, and even building a corral for that handful of hay."

"Did you want to see me?" I began again.

"Yes, I wanted to see what you looked like," he bellowed. Then he threw back his head and laughed and laughed. "This is the best joke on us I ever heard, stockmen cutting honyocker's hay. If it gets around, we'll be the laughing stock of the country."

I laughed, too. Mrs. Hetherington came in with coffee and cake, and we talked and talked. I told him what fine men I thought stockmen are, not at all like homesteaders pictured them, and that my brother hopes in the future to join their crowd.

We parted friends. During that summer, some of the stockmen now and then rode by the house to see how everything was. I thought that the resentment they bore to homesteaders was highly exaggerated.

"Idaho Land," A Parody Folk Song, 1917
(to the tune of *Beulah Land*)

I've reached the land of wind and heat
Where nothing grows for man to eat;
This awful dust and scorching heat,
In all the world is hard to beat.

Chorus: Oh, Idaho land,
        Oh, Idaho land,
As on the alkali beds I stand,
I look across the sage-brush plains
And wonder why it never rains
Till Gabriel blows his trumpet sound
And says the rain has all gone 'round.

The farmer goes out to his corn,
I never saw him look so lorn,
He is amazed, he's almost shocked
To find the corn amid the stalk.

The people here are all one race;
Starvation stares us in the face;
We do not live, we only stay—
We are too poor to move away.

W. M. Black's Plea for
Aid for Montana Farmers, 1921

SHELBY, MONTANA
JULY 28, 1921

HON. JOSEPH M. DIXON,
HELENA, MONTANA

MY DEAR SIR:

I have been requested by several responsible persons in this vicinity to place the following situation before you. . . . Owing to continued crop failures due to drouth, cut worms, and grasshoppers in this county and the counties adjacent to this along the main line of the G.N. Ry. a large majority of the people are in very hard circumstances. They have very little to eat and will have very little to wear to keep them from suffering when cold weather approaches. They will also find it almost impossible to obtain fuel in sufficient quantities to keep comfortable. A survey of the situation reveals that several families at present are not getting enough to eat.

I know of three families right now, Governor, where there are a father and mother and from two to four minor children, and either the father or the mother is unable to work owing to illness or infirmity, the children are too young to take care of themselves. In one instance, the mother is almost an invalid, she has three children, the father cannot leave her. . . . All they have had to eat for the past two months has been potatoes, last year's crop, bread and eggs. They sold what little butter one cow made in order to buy a little sugar and syrup. The children are almost naked, and are indeed a pitiable sight. Other instances might also be cited, some better than this, others worse. One family of eight, the mother an invalid, only one cot in the single room shack, the oldest child about twelve years of age, no chairs or dishes, only tin plates and spoons. The father is working on the railroad section but cannot meet expenses.

The Red Cross has an agent here, a man, but he does not seem to grasp the situation. . . . A woman could do much better for the reason that she could visit these homes and have personal, heart to heart talks with the mothers in the homes. Many of these people feel proud and in many instances do not feel like soliciting aid, altho they are in dire need. Those of us who are more fortunate believe that a wider and better movement should be set on foot in order to take care of these unfortunate people, and at least these small children. They are really the ones who are suffering. They need more for the upbuilding of their bodies than the food they are now obtaining. They will become our future citizens.

Immediate aid for some is required in the line of food and clothing. A system of relief which can be extended as it is required should be instituted for what will be required in winter weather. We understand that work can be obtained over in Washington on small tracts of land, which may also be rented. But these farmers cannot leave in many instances; some have not the railroad fare. But many could leave and obtain work if they had the transportation. Others might find work in the localities in this State where crops are good if there was a system of finding where this work could be had, and some means of getting the man there. These people are all American born largely, and feel that it is their fault that they are in the condition they now find themselves and do not like to ask for aid. . . .

Now Governor, I have written at length on this as I feel deeply about it. I know these people personally, some are my neighbors. I believe a more extended action should be taken by the Red Cross, or some such organization for this relief. . . .

We feel that the present representative of the Red Cross . . . has not grasped fully the situation which exists. Many of these people donated eagerly what they could from their small living during the war . . . and now, owing to no fault of theirs, they are certainly entitled to relief.

YOURS RESPECTFULLY,

W. M. BLACK

The Bell Family Tries Dry Farming, 1911–1923

I became aware of the crop reporting service of the U.S. Department of Agriculture when my father was appointed crop reporter for Wibaux County. Two or three others in different parts of the county sent him their observations once a month. He consolidated these with his own estimates for a county report to Helena and had me do the clerical work. I was much impressed at being allowed to use franked envelopes requiring no postage but with a $300 fine for misuse of them. As a result of this service we received the monthly crop report from Washington, the weekly newsletter from Helena and could request other publications of the Department. Partly because of this activity we kept some records of our own operations.

During the first five years on the farm our wheat averaged about 15 bushels an acre. That was considerably less than the 23 bushel average for Montana for the same period. All our wheat was on spring or fall plowing as we had not yet learned about summer fallowing. Prices for wheat at Wibaux ranged from about 65 cents to one dollar a bushel. These yields and prices now seem extremely low but we thought our income for those years was fairly satisfactory.

In 1916, when the state had an average yield of 19 bushels an acre of wheat, we got only six or seven because of the rust in our area. The price that year was around $1.50 a bushel and we would have made a killing had it not been for the rust.

In 1917, we harvested 1,021 bushels of wheat from 158 acres and 132

Reprinted from *Homesteading in Montana: 1911–1923. Life in the Blue Mountain Country,* 57–60, by Edward J. Bell, Jr. 1975. Courtesy of Montana State University, Bozeman, MT 59715.

bushels of flaxseed from 19 acres. At wartime prices of $2.05 a bushel for wheat and $3.02 for flaxseed, our returns from these crops were about $2,500. We also sold a few steers. My mother got $5.00 a week from eggs and butter but that was for only part of the year. The weather in 1917 was not as good as we had hoped. Summer showers passed us by and we had some hail damage on our southwest corner.

In 1918 we again complained that rains were not coming our way. Wheat yielded about six bushels an acre compared with six and a half the year before. We had about 200 bushels of flaxseed which sold for $3.30 a bushel and about 800 bushels of wheat at $2.00 a bushel giving us $2,260 from the sale of grain. All our spring wheat that year was Marquis, a new variety that had replaced the old Haynes Bluestem after the rust epidemic of 1916.

In 1919 my father and I decided to go all out for production. Returns from the previous two years of high prices had been very disappointing but dryland farmers always think next year will be better. We planted over 300 acres of wheat and rye and about 50 acres of feed grains.

We had an open winter and got an early start in the spring, but were delayed by snow in late March and early April. The fall and winter had been dry. A little precipitation in May raised our hopes temporarily, but no rain fell after that. The oats failed to germinate; we had little or no garden and wheat prospects dwindled.

Then came the grasshoppers. We got a circular from the Agricultural Experiment Station at Bozeman and used their formula in mixing poisoned bran. After spreading the bran over our fields we saw hordes of insects coming from the draws and rangeland over too wide an area for us and our neighbors to cover. In the circular from Bozeman we also found a diagram for a catching machine. Papa made one and I caught 100 bushels of grasshoppers. At the end of each round the box was full of hoppers. For a scoop I used a square five-gallon oil can with the top cut out. Dry grasshoppers were hard to get from the catcher box into a sack. I finally hauled a tub of water to the field and used a hand sprayer to wet the insects, after which they were easier to manage.

We put the hoppers in the 100-bushel grain tank, resting on posts behind the granary. It was clear that we would have no other use for the grain wagons that year. When the tank was full I quit catching. This operation didn't really benefit the wheat as the damage had already been done, but it was better than to sit around and worry when there wasn't anything else to do. The folks used the hoppers for chicken feed that winter. By the middle of July the grasshoppers had disappeared. We thought this was partly due to parasites and partly because there wasn't anything left for the grasshoppers to eat.

In spite of all this, we had a little wheat at harvest time. The 20 acres of summer fallow was full of Russian thistles but tall enough to use the binder. Other wheat was too short for the binder but Papa made a header by extending the elevator canvas on our eight-foot binder. We made header boxes from a couple of bundle racks and got two neighbor boys to drive the teams. By harvesting around the edges of the draws and other places where any wheat had survived, we were able to cut 200 acres.

The feed grains were complete failures and we got only six loads of rye hay from the 25 acres planted the fall before. I mowed the grass on the hill tops and in the draws. These were places where we had not cut hay in former years when other native grasses were available. We also put up two stacks of Russian thistle hay.

Our 200 acres of wheat yielded 425 bushels of which 99 bushels came from 20 acres of spring wheat on land that had been summer fallowed the year before. This was our first experience with summer fallow.

There wasn't any income that year from the sale of grain because we needed to save the wheat for seed. My father sold a few steers and for a while Mother had a little money from eggs and butter. They also ground some wheat in the feed mill and used it for breakfast food. The bank continued to make loans for current expenses. Averill and Papa spent a rather frustrating winter bringing the cattle through on Russian thistles and the meager amount of other hay and straw. I was a senior in high school then.

In the period 1920–1923, yields were better but prices broke sharply in the fall of 1920 and continued to decline. In view of the depressed situation it was decided that Averill and I should get our college education as soon as possible. During his freshman year, 1920–1921, he found that we could support ourselves while going to college. The folks stuck it out until the 1923 failure of the Wibaux County Bank. This took all their property, because my father was a director with double liability on his stock. Then they also moved to Bozeman where they spent the rest of their lives.

Our operations were small in the light of present-day standards. We never had a tractor and the big team hitch was unknown to us. Six horses on a two bottom gang plow were the most we ever hooked up at one time. We never were able to get the crop seeded as early as it should have been, and when we did find out about summer fallow, we never seemed to be able to plow the ground early enough. Plowing for fallow was usually delayed until the land was dry and the weeds full grown.

Averill became known as M.A. Bell and was an authority on dryland farming methods. As superintendent of the Northern Montana Research Center at Havre, he conducted experiments in all phases of wheat improvement and cultivation. Timeliness of operations, proper summer fallow tillage and variety improvement were among the things he emphasized. On one occasion I heard him hark back to our experiences on the Wibaux County farm. The discussion was about control of excess wheat production. He said in effect, "If you really want to reduce production, go back to the old Haynes Bluestem variety, plow the fallow in July and seed the crop in late May and you won't have any surplus." This was by way of emphasizing the importance of what had been discovered by agronomists and farmers since our first attempts at dryland farming.

In the first essay, Thomas R. Wessel of Montana State University, whose published works have examined Indian-white relations, discusses the government policy of converting Indians into independent farmers. He shows that many Indian agents at the turn of the century recognized that stock raising was better suited than crop agriculture to the northern plains; but the necessary changes in policy did not follow. In the second selection, Mary W. M. Hargreaves, professor emeritus of history at the University of Kentucky and a past president of the Agricultural History Society, examines the lives of farm women on the northern plains. She recognizes the loneliness and hardship that many faced, but she also sees a pattern of necessary adaptation and renewed commitment since 1940. A somewhat different story is presented in the third essay, by Gilbert C. Fite, professor emeritus of history at the University of Georgia and a past president of the Agricultural History Society and both the Western and the Southern History associations. Fite considers the lives of his own grandparents and parents in South Dakota. Through their story, he shows the hard decisions and occasional prosperity of Dakota farmers. He stresses that although his grandparents may have ultimately lost their land, they did enjoy a reasonable standard of living while they farmed. Fite concludes that farming in the late nineteenth and early twentieth centuries helped raise new generations of Americans, who ultimately left the land.

Farming on the Northern Plains Reservations

THOMAS R. WESSEL

Between 1880 and 1910 the federal government pursued one of the most intense and persistent efforts in social engineering the nation had witnessed. The government's goal was no less than the transformation of an entire race. Driven by righteous self-confidence and firm in their convictions, government officials and private reform groups initiated a program to convert the American Indians from savage warriors to sedentary farmers. While the program of acculturation and eventual assimilation contained several lines of attack on tribal society, teaching the Indians farming underpinned the effort.

Farming's virtues appealed to reformers for a variety of reasons, not the least of which was the existence within the boundaries of the reservations of large tracts of land already available for the enterprise. Scattering the tribesmen on individual farms over a large territory would erode their communal attachments. Moreover, farming conjured up a vision of hard work, individual self-reliance, thift and rectitude fundamental to most reformer's ideal of Christian citizens.

After 1880 a farming future for American Indians became an article of

Thomas R. Wessel, "Agent of Acculturation: Farming on the Northern Plains Reservations, 1880–1910," © 1986 by the *Agricultural History Society.* Reprinted from *Agricultural History,* Vol. 60, No. 2, (Spring 1986), 233–245, by permission.

faith for reformers and government officials alike. Among true believers it was a faith neither subject to examination nor mitigated by context. If any of the reformers recognized the dramatic changes occurring in American agriculture in the late nineteenth century none considered how that change might affect their reforming zeal, or alter their vision of the Indians' future.

By 1880 most American farmers had already abandoned the parochial Jeffersonian model of independent self-sufficiency toward becoming petty capitalists producing for national and international markets. The dislocations wrought in farming had already led to farm protests that continued to characterize American farming through the end of the century. Farmers' loud and sometimes violent collective efforts to salvage their position in American society was in stark contrast to the tranquility reformers envisioned and government officials demanded for the American Indians.

Probably no government effort to work such a transformation on the American Indians encountered more environmental and human obstacles than on the northern plains of the Dakotas and Montana. In the early 1880s few reservation agents in the field expressed any optimism about educating Indians as farmers. All had for a decade or more insisted that the Dakotas were fit only for stock-raising. Montana agents lamented that since the tribes could still find buffalo north of the Missouri River, there was no point in starting agricultural programs. Besides, they noted, Montana was only good for grazing in any event.

Agents in the West advanced two reasons for their reluctance to enter into farming operations. The climate and soils of the Dakotas and Montana did not lend itself to crop agriculture and the Indians were not prepared to undertake the task. J. C. O'Connor, the Agent at Grand River, summarized most agents' attitude in 1872 when he reported that "The Indians wish to enter into stock-raising and this undertaking is best suited to both their habits and the character of the country." Theodore M. Koues, the Agent at Cheyenne River, conceded the possibility of eventually establishing the Indians as farmers, but not very quickly. "In giving up the chase," Kouse noted, "stock-growing would seem to be the most natural occupation for them to engage in. This is an intermediate step to agriculture. . . ." Kouse's comment anticipated the position of most Dakota and Montana agents in the early 1880s and anticipated the nation's most prominent writer on Indian culture.

In 1878 Lewis Henry Morgan published his *Ancient Society*. In *Ancient Society*, Morgan developed a grand scheme to explain man's rise to civilization. He postulated a series of advancements based on human subsistence patterns that in simplified form described movement from savage hunters to barbarous herdsmen to civilized farmers. Morgan noted that some American Indians had reached a level of barbarism that included some primitive agriculture in their subsistence. The Plains Indians from his own observations (he had travelled among the Plains Indians in Kansas earlier in the century and had visited Fort Benton, Montana Territory in 1858) clearly were only at low levels of barbarism. Any attempt to teach these Indians crop farming, Morgan insisted, was doomed to failure. To leap across the evolutionary threshold was beyond human capacity. "We have overlooked," Morgan wrote in a letter to *The Nation* in 1878, "the fact that the principal Indian tribes have passed by natural development out of the condition of savages into that of barbarians. In relative progress they are now precisely where our own barbarous ancestors were when by the domestication of animals, they passed from a similar into a higher condition of barbarism, though still two ethnical periods below civilization."

Morgan's insistence that the rise of man to civilization traced an immutable line through the stages of development caught the fancy of many self-appointed experts on the human condition. The next year General Nelson Miles repeated Morgan's admonition in the *Review of Reviews* and a decade later William Graham Sumner echoing Morgan chastized the government for its persistent efforts to teach farming to the western Indians.

Reformers and most government officials were, however, too impatient to wait on Morgan's system for the Indians to evolve into individual farmers. Throughout the 1880s the newly formed Indian Rights Association, and a succession of Commissioners of Indian Affairs and Secretaries of the Interior pressed for increased agricultural training and the ultimate allotment of the reservations into model homesteads. Few western reservation agents, even if inclined, could overtly resist the pressure to conform to Washington's dictates.

With the emphasis in Washington clearly bent on crop agriculture, agents in the field moved to align themselves with the prevailing wisdom of their superiors, some nearly apologizing for their earlier apostasy. Agent Jacob Kauffman reported in 1880 from Fort Berthold that "the government has located these Indians in the latitude of 49' 35' where so small proportion of land is susceptable of cultivation, with soil thin, rough, rocky and unfit for cultivation except along the river, in narrow strips, that in my judgement the white man with all his superior intelligence and experience, would utterly fail to make a living farming." Eight years later Fort Berthold's agent, Abram J. Gifford was ecstatic over farming. "Every family," he wrote, "has settled upon an allotment of land and has commenced a life leading to complete independence, and all are engaged more or less, as they are able, in farming, adding continually each year to their improvements. . . ."

By 1890 even failing at farming on the Fort Berthold reservation was apparently a blessing. That year the Agent reported that the "Progress in this department [agriculture] is not the most flattering, owning chiefly to the difficulties presented by extremely dry climate. That they have acquired sufficient interest in farming to feel disappointed at the failure of a crop is, I think, an important point gained."

Valentine McGillycuddy, the long-time agent at Pine Ridge, was slower to convert, but was enthusiastic for crop farming by mid-decade. McGillycuddy noted in 1880 that "agriculture as compared with the above [stock-raising] had its disadvantages, considering the people, climate and country we have to deal with. . . ." "Hence in my judgement," McGillycuddy wrote, "our Indians will naturally become producers, first as stock raisers, and in course of time, by degrees, become farmers." Just three years later, McGillycuddy was not so sure. "Theoretical experts on the Indian question," he commented, "appear to have recently discovered that our Indians are natural born herders. The theory is good, but the practice fails, and for the following reason: the horse is good to ride on, and the cow is good to eat." By 1885 McGillycuddy was announcing that "the amount of farming has fully quadrupled during the past year and the yield has been very good. . . ." By the end of the decade agents such as James McLaughlin at Standing Rock, felt the need to proclaim that "I have always advocated an agricultural life rather than a pastoral one for Indians in their transitional state, as the former means a fixed abode with domestic cares which tend to civilize while the life of a stock-grower is more that of a nomad in following his herd."

The agents had discovered that ending overt resistance to crop farming for the Indians had positive benefits. Few ever thought they had sufficient staff to maintain order on the reservations. A chance to add to that staff was not lightly ignored even if the additional staff was for an enterprise in which they had little confidence. Likely few agents had any intention of utilizing additional farm employees to teach Indians farming, at least, not as a major responsibility. Most western agents remained wedded to developing a livestock industry on the reservations even if their reports and the Indian Office's directives suggested otherwise.

Typically in the 1880s reservations on the northern plains were self-contained communities. Even after the government reduced the size of the Dakota and Montana reservations in the late 1880s they remained formidable units. The Blackfeet reservation was over two million acres while most of the Dakota reservations were over 2.5 million acres. The population under the agents control in Montana and Dakota numbered between two and five thousand people on each reservation.

By 1880 the staffing pattern at a reservation agency was firmly fixed. Along with the resident agent most reservations employed a chief clerk/bookkeeper, a physician, a carpenter, a blacksmith, a farmer and a number of laborers. Generally, the work of most of the staff kept them near the agency. The reservation farmer raised food stuffs for the employees and for the agency stock including the agency's beef herd. The beef herd provided meat for the Indians' weekly ration. On some reservations the agency farm was attached to a boarding school where the principal purpose was to raise food for the school. By 1885 most agents had divided the reservations into farming districts, as few as two on the Blackfeet reservation and as many as five at Pine Ridge. Each district was under the supervision of an additional farmer with one employee designated as the farmer-in-charge. Occasionally, the agent acted as the farmer-in-charge such as at Standing Rock. Dividing the reservation into districts was accompanied by the moving of the Indian population to the district sites away from the central villages near the agency office. The district offices in effect became sub-agencies duplicating at that level the same activities once centralized in the agent's office. The arrangement satisfied the need as agents saw it, breaking the tribe into controllable groups under the farmers' supervision, but did little to advance the cause of agriculture among the Indians.

Before 1885 the reservation agent generally appointed the farmer. More often than not, the farmers were related to the agent or a business associate. Their ability or commitment to farming was coincidental. In 1882 at Fort Berthold the agent's son acted as the government farmer. Agent Kauffman also employed his daughter on the reservation. The three Kauffmans held claims to 1600 acres south of Fort Stevenson and according to government inspector B. B. Benedict spent as much time on their claim as on the reservation. The farmer at the Crow Agency was the agent's cousin and the son of a local contractor building houses on the reservation. One inspector noted that there was no wheat grown on the Crow reservation, but they had a threshing machine that lay in ruins.

Even agent McGillycuddy, one of the more respected agents, was not above a kind of nepotism. His farmer/clerk was Frank Stewart. Stewart had been raised in the McGillycuddy home in Minnesota and used the McGillycuddy name until taking employment on the reservation. The farmer at Rosebud was a former business partner of the agent and according to one inspector was not a farmer, but worked on the reservation as a carpenter. The assistant farmer was a storekeeper. Inspector Robert Gardner complained that the farmer at the Cheyenne River reservation was never around. On this particular inspection in 1882 the farmer, Frank Anderson, was working to recover some strayed cattle "to the utter neglect of any attention to agency Indians toward farming." When later the inspector asked Anderson to explain his duties, Anderson replied he issued rations, helped put up hay for the agency herd and went from camp to camp to see that peace was maintained. When asked what he did toward teaching farming to Indians, Anderson honestly replied, nothing. The agency farmer at Standing Rock was also unavailable to a visiting Inspector in 1880. He was tending bar at the local trader's store.

After 1885 the election of the first Democratic administration since 1856 led to wholesale changes in personnel on the western reservations, but no discernible change in teaching farming to Indians. Beginning that year, the Office of Indian Affairs increased farmer appointments on the reservations. While nepotism declined, politically inspired appointments increased. Inspector E. D. Banister complained in 1886 that the farmer at Fort Berthold, Edward Lyke knew nothing about farming. Nevertheless, Lyke remained in his position until 1889. The additional farmer at Fort Berthold apparently did little farming either. The inspector noted that Governor Louis K. Church of Dakota Territory had requested the appointment.

Certainly, the increase in government farmers on the Dakota and Montana reservations had little effect in establishing anything like commercial crop farming among the Indians. Acres devoted to crop farming did increase, but for the most part the effort was in expanded vegetable gardening and hay fields. In 1890 the Blackfeet reservation recorded no cultivation although the agent listed 210 acres under cultivation in 1880, some devoted to wheat. At Pine Ridge the acres cultivated increased during the decade from 1,800 to 3,425 acres, but purchases at Pine Ridge of farm equipment consisting principally of mowing machines and sulky rakes suggested most of the land was for winter stock feed. A similar purchase at Standing Rock mostly of hay forks and scythes along with garden tools suggested the increase there of from 1142 to 5000 acres cultivated was not intended to enhance commercial farming. Much the same pattern existed at Rosebud and Cheyenne River. Some effort to establish small grain agriculture did occur at Fort Berthold. Out of the 890 acres cultivated 550 were devoted to wheat. It was apparently the only reservation that included reapers among its equipment purchases in the 1880s.

Undoubtedly, the severe droughts of the latter half of the 1880s inhibited the development of crop agriculture, but little change occurred in cropping patterns during the 1890s. Vegetable production increased substantially along with corn, with very little wheat grown and on some reservations none recorded at all. The exception again was Fort Berthold where 8500 bushels of wheat were harvested along with 3200 bushels of corn and 4700 bushels of vegetables. Given the adult male population of the reservations ranging from barely over 500 at the Blackfeet reservation to over 1300 at Rosebud, even a crude conversion of bushels to acres suggests individual acreages probably numbered only about one to three acres. Nevertheless, the number of government farmers during the 1890s increased on the reservations from a total of 239 to 329 for all reservations in the country. Nearly all of the Dakota and Montana reservations increased the number of farmers on the agency staff during the decade.

Even had agents assigned government farmers the task of teaching farming and the weather, and the Indians had cooperated, the instability in the farmer corps mitigated against successful efforts. The turn-over rate among government farmers remained high for most of the period. At Fort Berthold eleven men held the position of farmer-in-charge between 1885 and 1900. One, the first, lasted four years; some, however, lasted as little as two months. For most, one season or less exhausted the attractions of North Dakota. At Pine Ridge between 1884 and 1892 nine men acted as the farmer-in-charge. After 1892 Pine Ridge dispensed with a head farmer but employed five additional farmers, each in charge of a district. At Rosebud no farmer-in-charge remained in the job for longer than fourteen months before 1895. Frank Robinson then held the position for six years. Eleven men held the position at Cheyenne River, with all but three serving no longer than fourteen months.

The most stable reservations were in Montana. At Blackfeet two men served as farmer-in-charge between 1890 and 1901. At Crow five men held the position between 1885 and 1889, one for eighteen months and one for three weeks. (That is not a record; on one reservation the farmer lasted eleven days.) For the next eight years, W. H. Steele acted as the farmer-in-charge at Crow. He was dismissed in 1897 when an Interior Department Inspector discovered Steele was preoccupied with acting as a purchasing agent for nearby ranchers and ran a hotel just over the reservation border. At Crow and Blackfeet crop farming was associated with irrigation development in the 1890s. In both cases, however, the Indian Service employed irrigation experts to develop the system and teach the Indians necessary operations. The government farmers appeared to have had little to do with the enterprise.

While the retention rate among farmers-in-charge was low, it was even lower among additional farmers who presumably had the principal responsibility to teach farming to the Indians. It was not unusual for the entire corps of additional farmers to turn over nearly every year. At Crow during the time of W. H. Steele thirty men held the five positions in a seven-year period.

The fact remained that most agents, and farmers followed the orders from their agent, continued to believe that the northern plains was grazing country. After the experience of the drought years of the 1880s most again explicitly pressed for increased stock issues as the basis of a cash economy for the Indians with cultivation restricted to winter stock feed and gardening. The agents valued the government farmers, but as assistant agents to help maintain control of the reservation population. What farming the agents and farmers encouraged was subsistence gardening intended to provide a vegetable supplement to the weekly ration and as one inspector put it, so the Indians would stay at home.

Throughout the 1890s Dakota and Montana Agents and increasingly, Interior Department inspectors, advocated stock raising as the only suitable enterprise for the reservations. Few supported crop agriculture except on those reservations where irrigation was already underway. For the Dakotas, Interior Department inspectors insisted that money spent on farming was wasted; the money should be spent on cattle. By 1896 McLaughlin, since 1893 an Interior Department inspector, noted in his report that "insufficient rainfall together with blighting hot wind and protracted droughts discourages agricultural pursuits. They are usually unremunerative in this country." He also noted that the Indians at Standing Rock were all "more or less in stock raising" with some Indians owning as many as 60 head of cattle. The past year the agency had purchased over one and three-quarter million pounds of gross beef from the reservations' stockmen and expected that figure to increase in the coming years.

The persistence of drought and the availability of Indian funds generated from land sessions persuaded the Office of Indian Affairs to purchase stock cattle even while preparing to divide the reservations into individual allotments. In 1880 nearly all cattle on the Dakota and Montana reservations were part of the agency herd and used as the source of beef ration. That year only 66 government cattle grazed on the Fort Berthold range, with 68 at the Blackfeet agency. On the larger reservations such as Pine Ridge the agent listed 1500 head, with 500 at Standing Rock and 2,600 at Cheyenne River. By 1890 Cheyenne River counted 9000 head of cattle, 9,400 at Pine Ridge and 4,560 at Standing Rock. Fort Berthold had increased to 160 head and the Blackfeet agent reported 850 head of cattle. Over the next decade the numbers increased substantially with Blackfeet reporting 12,000 head, over

12,000 at Standing Rock, over 15,000 at Cheyenne River and 42,316 at Pine Ridge.

Certainly, by the turn of the century western agents seemed to have won the debate over crop farming or stock raising on the northern plains reservations. They had employed farmers and then diverted their work to other reservations tasks and avoided significant expenditures in crop farming. While western agents could dissemble about farming, they could not resist the rush for allotment on the northern plains reservations.

Congress had passed the Dawes Severalty Act in 1887 as the center piece of its assimilation program. The government applied allotment sparingly over the next decade, but moved vigorously to divide the reservations into individual holdings after 1900. Allotment was a complicated process involving surveying of the reservations, the establishment of enrollment lists and the filing of selections before the Department of the Interior issued trust patents. Generally, the process took from eight to ten years to complete and on some reservations such as the Blackfeet nearly seventeen years. Consequently, the effect of allotment on stock raising was not immediately apparent. Most reservations continued to increase their cattle herds between 1900 and 1910 although disputes over grazing leases and grazing permits retarded the efforts of many Indian stockmen.

In the meantime the Office of Indian Affairs moved to improve its farmer corps. Responding to complaints of incompetent farmers, the government had already in 1892 insisted that prospective government farmers had to have spent at least five years "immediately previous to such employment practically engaged in the occupation of farming." Complaints nevertheless continued. In 1899 one Interior Department inspector complained that the farmer at Crow Reservation was a Democrat with a hatred for gold Republicans, "foisted on the government through the operation of the Civil Service Law." A more common complaint, however, appeared in an article by George Bird Grinnell the same year. "Often," Grinnell wrote, "the agency farmers, whose immediate duty it was to instruct the people in the pursuit of civilization, do anything rather than that. They putter around the agency, or they are stablemen, or they work in the blacksmith shop, or put up new buildings, or paint and whitewash old ones, or spend much of their time at butchering and the issue, do anything, in fact, except to teach the Indians farming." Grinnell was quite right, but the government farmers were not independent employees. They did the work the agent assigned.

In 1902 the Indian Office appointed Levi Chubbuck as Inspector of Farm and Farming Organizations. The Indian Office assigned Chubbuck the task of invigorating the farmer corps and promoting crop agriculture on the reservations. Chubbuck spent most of his time in the southwest where he became an apostle of irrigation. For the northern plains he became an early proponent of dry farming techniques and urged government farmers and agents to make contact with the land grant colleges and experiment stations in the region. Apparently, Chubbuck's mission met with some success. In 1909 several government farmers attended the Dry Farming Congress at Billings, Montana, and expressed considerable enthusiasm for the new methods. In 1910 in a further effort to up-grade the quality of reservation farmers the government required successful completion of an examination for eligibility for appointment.

The year 1910 proved a crucial turning point for Indian agriculture on the northern plains reservations. By that year allotment had led to the loss of large tracts of Indian land to white settlement and the break-up of natural grazing ranges on the land left to the Indians. Dry-land farming techniques accepted in 1910 proved no more successful for Indian farmers than they did for white farmers. Another twenty years would pass before sufficient understanding of the plains environment developed successful small grain culture in the region and then not on tracts the size of the most generous allotment. Another twenty years would pass before the government considered livestock again and moved to combine many allotments into grazing districts on the Mizpaw-Pumpkin Creek model. In the meantime, government farmers continued to act as subagents and the Indians of the northern plains were soon left without a farming economy, without cattle, without much of their land and for many without hope.

Women Homesteaders on the Northern Plains

MARY W. M. HARGREAVES

A saying was current during the settlement of the North American Plains that "this was a great country for men and horses, but hell on women and cattle." Cattle might well have been added to the front segment of the grouping, as we have been repeatedly advised by land-use planners down to the present day. But what of women, the fourth element in the adage?

By 1870 the ratio of women to men had already significantly exceeded one to two in Kansas, Nebraska, and the Dakotas. To the west, however, in the high plains and the mountainous Territory of Colorado women did not attain that proportion until nearly 1880, and in Montana and Wyoming not until nearly 1890. The settlement of the Greeley Colony in Colorado, of agricultural communities near mining centers in all three of these Territories, and of railroad towns along four transcontinental routes across the region accounts for this early incursion of women in the predominantly male domain of the mining and livestock frontiers. The number of women did not approximate 200,000 in Kansas until the decade of the seventies, in Nebraska until around 1880, in Colorado until the mid nineties, in the Dakotas until around 1905, and in Montana until about 1915. In Wyoming there are less than 166,000 women today. Women came on to the plains as an accompaniment of the expansion of agricultural development.

Mary W. M. Hargreaves, "Women in the Agricultural Settlement of the Northern Plains," © 1976 by the *Agricultural History Society*. Reprinted from *Agricultural History*, Vol. 50, No. 1 (January 1976), 179–189, by permission.

For those who came first, to the mining camps, the cattle towns, and even the remote ranches, there was a status role which offset many of the hardships. Charles Howard Shinn's account of the California mining camps points to this aspect: "Men often travelled miles to welcome 'the first real lady in camp.' A New-England youth of seventeen once rode thirty-five miles, after a week's hard work in his father's claim, to see a miner's wife who had arrived in an adjoining district. 'Because,' he said, 'I wanted to see a home-like lady; and, father, do you know, she sewed a button on for me, and told me not to gamble and not to drink. It sounded just like mother.' " As Shinn reported the prevailing attitude: "Women were queens, children were angels."

The delightful account of open-range ranch life by Nannie T. Alderson, *A Bride Goes West,* supports this view. Living in Indian country in southeastern Montana, at first up the Rosebud River valley, later up the Tongue, and finally on Muddy Creek—all a hundred miles or so from town life at Miles City—Mrs. Alderson in nearly fifteen years, from 1879 to 1893, was left unguarded only twice; and she noted such protection as generally applicable to western women on ranches. Cowboys taught her to cook and cooperated in the domestic chores of meal preparation. She at first sent the laundry to an Indian woman; but, balking at ten cents a piece, and a week's bill that totaled $10.80, she undertook to acquire the art of washing clothes—but never learned to cope with the problem of hard water. The Alderson cowboys soon "bragged on" her yeast rolls and her expertise in "foxing" breeches, but she obviously had not been brought to the West for her domestic skills. We merely invert her phrase in commenting: "Women, like rivers, were few, and they gained in importance proportionally."

Robert Dykstra reminds us that cow-town housewives, "legendary pillars of frontier moral uplift," had "little collective influence" in the politics of Kansas reform during the early years. "The gradual domestication of cattle town society" triumphed only "as family groups gradually infiltrated the demographic structure." But women of the suffrage movement at the turn of the century viewed the western experience somewhat differently. They could then point to the first four states which had given women the vote: Wyoming, in 1869; Colorado, in 1893; Utah, in 1896, after the Territorial vote extended in 1870 had been abrogated under the Edmunds-Tucker Act of 1887; and Idaho, too, in 1896. In Montana tax-paying women might vote on questions of taxation (1889). But in Kansas, under legislation of 1887, the vote for women was restricted to municipal elections, a limited privilege denied to women of rural areas. Kansas women, who had won this concession only after tremendous effort, attributed the achievements of their sisters in the mountain states to the scarcity of population—and, one might add, the relatively greater scarcity of female population—which minimized their potential influence. Women of the agricultural frontier waited long years before their impact in "the demographic structure" took form as the right to general suffrage.

Proponents of woman suffrage in the states under farming development saw the opposition of foreign immigrants as their principal obstacle. The promotionalism that attracted large groups of settlers from a culture alien to that which had generated the liberalization of women's status in the area to the west retarded the democratizing influence on this last American frontier. In Kansas full suffrage was not accorded women until 1912, in Montana, not until 1914, in the Dakotas and Nebraska, not until passage of the federal amendment. The status role of women on the plains dwindled as the numbers of their sex increased in the early years of the twentieth century. Meanwhile the trials of their life in the area were not appreciably lessened.

Loneliness was, by all accounts, the most oppressive of those hardships. That isolation was a general problem of farm life had been a particular concern in the organization of the Patrons of Husbandry, or Grange, lodges, even before the depression of the mid 1870s led to reorientation of that movement toward political and economic issues. The continuing influence of the Grange, with expanded membership in older agricultural regions after 1880, rested upon its social and educational services. The organization of farmers' institutes in the 1870s and the enactment of the Smith-Lever and Smith-Hughes agricultural extension and vocational training programs of 1914 and 1917 represented a continuing recognition of the problem of rural isolation. In all these programs, and remarkably so in the early growth of the Grange, social contact for farm women was emphasized. That the People's Party, or Populists, of the 1890s was the only major political party generally identified with woman suffrage reflected the importance attached to the role of women in an appeal addressed primarily to rural concerns.

Nannie Alderson, the rancher's bride, thought her life more lonely than that of a farmer's wife, who could count upon the men coming in from the fields for regular meals; but she forgot that cowhands were more numerous than husbands, that she had many contacts growing out of ranch hospitality, which dwindled as wayside taverns sprang up with agricultural settlement, and that many women homesteaded alone—one estimate placed the proportion of land held by women as high as a third in the Dakotas in 1887. As mechanized farming developed on the plains, farm size increased and farm spacing became increasingly dispersed—from the 160-acre plots of the prairies, to the 320-acre units of the benchlands after 1909, to the 640-acre stock-farming tracts after 1916, to the 1,000-acre tractor farms and the 10,000-acre ranches of modern times.

Loneliness was measured in a variety of terms—by the years since the writer had been to town, the days or weeks between mail delivery, the miles from the nearest neighbor, the distance to go to borrow a book, the high excitement of a seasonal social activity, or the sorrow at sending a child away to secondary school in town. Large families compensated in a measure for loneliness; but they added to it, too, when the weary mother found she could no longer cast off family burdens for even infrequent excursions from home. Loneliness was the mood epitomized in Faye Cashatt Lewis's title for her volume describing life in Tripp County, South Dakota, in 1909—*Nothing to Make a Shadow*.

Those women who lived to write reminiscences tell of the salubrious climate which forestalled much illness but always recount, too, the alarms of childbirth remote from doctors and the horror of accidents or serious disease when a day's travel, perhaps by railroad, delayed hospitalization. Grace Fairchild, the "Frontier Woman" depicted in an account of settlement in western South Dakota from 1902 to 1940, bore nine children, six of them in less than eight years, with the help of neighbor women and, on several occasions, the services of a doctor homesteading twelve miles to the east. Nannie Alderson went to town for delivery of her first two babies but, with the responsibility for their care, could not leave the ranch when the last two were born, and an inexperienced midwife almost killed one of them. Mrs. Alderson herself nearly died on another occasion when she suffered a miscarriage. The climax of Dale Eunson's narrative of life *Up on the Rim,* twenty miles northwest of Billings, was the night his mother sent him, at age seven, out into a blizzard to summon help because her baby was arriving early.

Where doctors could be found in the region, they were too frequently alcoholics who had been driven from practice in the East. A Dr. Roberts, of *Alberta Homestead,* in the period from 1906 to 1912, was a rarity among the settlers—though unlicensed to practice in Canada, he traveled one March a round trip of forty miles ten times to care for a typhoid case. Even with his professional skill at hand the Robertses were forced to carry their sick boy forty miles by horse and wagon to obtain antitoxin for diphtheria. For ordinary ills women on the plains dispensed home remedies— onions, epsom salts, kerosene, and whiskey.

That migraine appears as a recurrent complaint in several accounts of women's life in the region suggests the accumulation of tensions. Women developed obsessive fears in this environment—for Nannie Alderson, fear that her husband would be injured in a horse fight (a premonition, perhaps, of the manner of his death years later when they had moved to town); for Sara Roberts, fear of prairie fire, not an irrational terror when during late summer and early fall flames lighted the sky halfway around the horizon; for most women, fear that some member of the family would be lost while traveling at night or in a blizzard. Mrs. Lewis, envisioning the worst in the children's report of rescuing a colt from a well, burst into tears: "It might have been one of the children in the well! There are so many dangers in this country; more that [*sic*] we ever knew about before we came."

The persistent wind and the coyotes' howls were unnerving. Faye Lewis found the latter "like nothing so much as a despair encompassing all eternity." While Mrs. Alderson expressed delight in the cosy camaraderie of a winter fireside, with cowboys and husband confined in close quarters, more often women complained of the overcrowding in small claim shacks, built with perhaps only one door and a single window, too dark for reading or sewing through the long winter months. Sara Roberts chafed at the confinement: "This weather and being cut off from everybody is almost too much for me." Even Mrs. Alderson's account is liberally salted with self-reproach for gloom.

Women in rural areas everywhere in the early years of the twentieth century continued to perform tasks from which urban women had begun to break away in the 1870s. Farmers' wives kept the chickens, milked the cows, planted and tended the gardens, churned the butter, baked the bread, salted the meat, brined the kraut and corn, canned and preserved the fruit and vegetables, sewed the women's clothing and much of the men's, cooked the meals, washed and ironed, cleaned and decorated the house, and occasionally helped in the fields. On the plains women did all these chores and more—they served as midwives and nurses for ailing neighbors, circulated petitions to get schools established, and provided lodging and meals for transients and for some drifters who were not so transient.

And plains women worked in a physiographic setting where scarcity of water and wood complicated domestic as well as agricultural occupations. Water at shallow levels was generally brackish and in many areas so difficult to reach that wells were inconveniently located, if, indeed, they could be provided. In the dry-farming country of northern Montana and western South Dakota water of satisfactory quality for drinking often ranged from 200 to 500 feet in depth. There it could be obtained only by drilling, which cost, in 1914, a dollar a foot, with an additional 25 cents to a dollar for casing, plus the charge for a pump, windmill, or gasoline engine. Use of cisterns for catching rainwater was widespread, and hauling of water in barrels was common in some districts as late as the 1920s. Nannie Alderson's problems in laundering were not exceptional. Grace Fairchild spoke grimly of the alkaline water found west of the Missouri in South Dakota: "Anybody who drinks such water and isn't accustomed to it will get as sick as a poisoned pup."

Houses in a land of scarce timber were roughly structured. Everett Dick, in *Sod-House Frontier,* has described the dreariness, the dampness, and the dirtiness of a sod house or dugout, where soil particles and straw "kept dropping on everything in the house," roof and walls leaked rivulets as snows melted or rains came, and floors became quagmires. Nannie Alderson, as a bride, received special consideration when her floors were sheeted with wagon canvas. Such dwellings did afford warmth in winter, as the Robertses testified when they resorted to a sod house after they found their log structure too cold for Alberta weather. By the eighties, Dick notes, a large proportion of the claim shacks were made of frame covered with tar paper and chinked with mud. Grace Fairchild complained that, with the warping of the cottonwood siding and the drying of the mud filler, they were always in need of repair. And Jessie Eunson knew well the torments of the nether regions as she pickled cucumbers under a July sun beating upon tar paper.

Women tried to make such dwellings attractive by whitewashing the exterior, plastering walls with multiple coats of mud, and lining the interior with muslin or bright calico. But snakes in the kitchen as an accompaniment of such rough construction terrified more than one of the housewives who have recounted their experiences. Most reporters also noted problems of combating lice and bedbugs.

Perhaps the women who have written such accounts were more literate, better educated, more concerned for the refinements of the life they had known to the east than the average frontier settler. But common parlance asserted and limited evidence sustains the view that those who carried the agricultural advance beyond the hundredth meridian were very often school-teachers, clerks, artisans, unemployed widows, or "old maids"—city folk. A survey of the occupational backgrounds of 550 homesteaders in the north central Montana "triangle" in 1922, when already several years of drought had driven out the more easily disheartened, revealed that only 51 percent had been farming before they came to the region. Over a quarter of the tenants listed in the North Dakota *Census* of 1920 lacked previous farm experience. The lure of speculative profits to be gleaned from the last of the dwindling public domain attracted an unusually large number of settlers whose hands were uncalloused. Land Office regulations which permitted leave of absence from the claim through the winter months and completion of entry after only three summers of farming encouraged schoolteachers to vacation as homesteaders. Grace Fairchild, noting that single women could file claims but not the married, commented: "It always looked to me as if the government was run by men and all the laws were made for them. So women had to take up claims before they got married." Or after their husbands died. In the Fairchilds' case, her widowed mother filed an adjoining claim, lived on it just long enough to complete entry, and then transferred it to expand the Fairchild holding.

But even more committed agricultural pioneers carried with them to the frontier cultivated tastes expressed by the inclusion of pianos, organs, Haviland china, silver candelabra, and similar symbols of gracious living as freight in homesteaders' boxcars. Gradually women of the plains relinquished most of these treasures, as they lost, too, their hopes of finding quick wealth in farming ventures. They shared the discouragements when promising crops were destroyed by hail or early frost, and the anxiety when weeks of drought stunted grain. A good yield could mean income for home improvements—a wood floor, a shingled roof, an additional room. But those who settled the Dakotas during the first decade of the twentieth century learned by 1910 and 1911 of the perils of agriculture beyond the line of semiaridity. Many of those who broke the benchlands of Montana during the second decade abandoned the struggle during the years of drought and cascading grain prices from 1917 to 1924. Farmers on the plains found that increased capital expenditures were needed for larger land units, machinery with which to practice a more extensive type of operation, and livestock to permit diversification of the enterprise. Accumulation of reserves sufficient to maintain the business through several years of low or even negative return emerged as a dictum of successful management if one were to survive in the area. Household refinements had to wait.

Purchase of an automobile or truck might be justified as a necessary farm expense—it could be used to speed the delivery of supplies to the farm and of crops to town. The impact of the automobile in breaking the isolation of rural life was revolutionary. But household conveniences were much slower in coming. While the introduction of gasoline pumps and, around 1915, of pneumatic-pressure systems facilitated the installation of indoor plumbing, the cost was prohibitive for most plains settlers through the lean years that continued until 1940. A survey in 1935 of six South Dakota counties, selected to represent farming areas across the state, showed that at least three-fourths of the households were still dependent on an outside water supply; only one-fifth had electricity; only 12 percent, central heating. Jones and Perkins Counties, on the plains just west of the Missouri River, ranked at the bottom in material standard of living. Lawrence County, adjacent to a lumbering center, still had many log cabins; sod houses were yet common in Perkins. And in the latter area "soddies" were even then being constructed.

Census reports for North Dakota in 1945 show electricity in only 13 percent of the farm dwellings of Pierce County, on the hundredth meridian, and 25 percent of those in McKenzie, a ranching and irrigated farming center on the western border. Running water was indicated for only 5 percent of the Pierce County homes and 9 percent of those in McKenzie. Running water was then available in 10, 12, up to 15 percent of the farmhouses in the earlier settled areas of southwestern North Dakota, lands developed along the Northern Pacific route shortly after the turn of the century; but in the northwestern counties the percentages still stood at 3 to 6 percent.

Medical facilities also remained limited. In 1940 five west-river counties of South Dakota had only one doctor. One entire county and parts of twelve others—all in the trans-Missouri region—lacked access to a hospital within a radius of fifty miles. Dentists—Nannie Alderson had found toothache one of her greatest tribulations—were still in 1940 concentrated in the larger towns and cities.

For women, life in the agricultural development of the northern plains continued rigorous. Small wonder that during the drought years of the thirties the proportion of emigrants from the region was more female than male. A 1935 survey of those who had left South Dakota showed that the women were better educated than the men—a reflection of the general fact that girls on the farms achieved more schooling than boys; but the survey also indicated that women who were college graduates were more likely to emigrate than men of comparable education. Of the college-educated women migrants who remained in the state, none had married farmers, and only two of the twenty-six who had left the area were associated with occupations identified as agricultural.

The characteristics of the outmigration shifted by the end of the thirties, when military service and wartime job opportunities contributed to an exodus of men. At the same time, the improved quality of life in the area with the development of rural electrification and improved transportation appears to have enhanced the attractions of the region for women. While the male population of the Dakotas and Wyoming has declined since 1940, the number of women on the plains has increased everywhere but in North Dakota. By 1960 there were more women than men in Kansas, Nebraska, and Colorado, and by 1970 in Montana and South Dakota, as well.

The women whose reminiscences have told so much of the hardships of early settlement on the plains almost always expressed delight in the climate, the scenery, and the springtime awakening of nature. Occasionally, like Jessie Eunson's, their enthusiasm converted projects for a temporary venture into a serious farming commitment. Elinore Pruitt Stewart, who in 1913 proudly completed her entry on a claim in western Wyoming, saw homesteading as "the solution of all poverty's problems." While warning that "persons afraid of coyotes and work and loneliness had better let ranching alone," she argued that "any woman who can stand her own company, can see the beauty of the sunset, loves growing things, and is willing to put in as much time at careful labor as she does over the washtub, will certainly succeed; will have independence, plenty to eat all the time, and a home of her own in the end." Not many women adjusted to this life so well as Grace Fairchild, who took over farm management with a flexible awareness that old programs must be modified to fit a new land. But the increasing proportion of women in the region today indicates that they generally have made the necessary adaptations. The changes which have fostered the shift in commitment since 1940 are another chapter.

A Family Farm Chronicle

GILBERT C. FITE

During the last quarter century, historians have talked and written a good deal about doing history from the bottom up. Historians, it was said, had been too much enamored with society's elites. To better understand our history, these critics insisted that we needed to look at the lives and activities of common men and women. Furthermore, scholars argued, local records which more fully revealed the life of the common people should be explored in depth. Dusty county court house basements with their land, tax, assessment, mortgage, and other records became a favorite place to dig into the lives of ordinary individuals.

Not having any great theory of history to propound and wanting to be in one of the main streams of current American historiography, I decided to talk about one of those common men who settled on the Dakota frontier. Moreover, the information on this pioneer farmer has come almost exclusively from those county records which dirty your hands and ruin your eyes. The fact that the individual whose farming career I intend to discuss happens to be my maternal grandfather, makes this exercise no less legitimate as a study of common, ordinary citizens.

The free and cheap land of the American West drew people like a powerful magnet. Unlike a magnet that draws and holds metals to it in a firm and lasting grasp, many Americans were held by the land only temporarily. Rather than realizing their Jeffersonian dreams of establishing a successful

Copyright by Western History Association. Reprinted by permission. The article first appeared as "Failure on the Last Frontier: A Family Chronicle" by Gilbert C. Fite. *Western Historical Quarterly,* 18 (January 1987), 5–14.

farm and living a happy, contented life under their own vine and fig tree, they were battered and defeated by nature and ruined by economic conditions over which they had no control. Many western pioneers on the last frontier filed on government land in a spirit of hope and optimism only to find that natural and man-made barriers defeated their hopes and aspirations.

One such man was Benjamin Franklin McCardle. Born in Virginia in 1862, he was the son of Samuel McCardle, who moved to Mason County, West Virginia where the family lived in 1880. After holding jobs in different parts of the state, in the spring of 1888, Frank, as he was generally known, struck out for the West. After a journey of some twelve hundred miles, he arrived at Wessington Springs in Jerauld County, Dakota Territory. He must have made the last part of the journey on foot or by stage because the railroad did not reach this village of about three hundred people in east-central Dakota until 1903.

By the time McCardle, now twenty-six years old, arrived on that prairie-plains frontier, the Great Dakota boom had burst. During 1883 and the spring of 1884, thousands of settlers had flocked to the region between the James and Missouri Rivers in search of free land. But by 1886 drouth, poor farm prices, and marketing problems had brought shock and discouragement to many of those optimistic pioneers. Territorial Governor Gilbert A. Pierce reported in 1886 that the year had been less than prosperous for many settlers. In translation the Governor's political rhetoric really meant that times were very hard. Conditions got worse in 1887 and 1888, the year McCardle arrived. The drouth was so bad in 1889 in parts of Dakota Territory that thousands of farmers were overwhelmed by want and destitution. Many accepted public charity, while others left Dakota to escape starvation and complete ruin.

McCardle, then, reached the Dakota frontier at a most unfavorable time. But he was determined to establish himself in the community. There was still some government land that could be filed on, and relinquishments could be purchased cheap from settlers who were discouraged and ready to leave. McCardle, however, made no immediate effort to obtain land. He had no capital to begin farming, even on free land. Thus, he obtained a job on the farm of H. G. Gilbert, who lived in Harmony township a few miles northwest of Wessington Springs.

That same year Mary E. Alguire, a young woman who had been born in New York state in 1862, settled with her foster family in Jerauld County. After being orphaned she was raised by the A. S. Fordham family, with whom she traveled to Dakota. Mary Alguire got a job as a housekeeper with the J. R. Eddy family, who lived not far from the Gilberts where Frank worked. Frank and Mary, the hired girl and hired man of neighboring farmers, soon became acquainted and were married in the fall of 1890. In December 1889, just a few months before her marriage, Mary had homesteaded on a quarter section of land five miles west and four north of Wessington Springs. Like many other homesteaders, she managed to fulfill the legal residence requirement, although she did not live on the homestead for any substantial period of time.

In 1891, a few months after their marriage, the young couple moved to Dale township in the east-central part of the county. They rented a farm located on the southwest quarter of section twenty-six. Their first daughter, Mary Jane, was born there on 5 September 1891. The McCardles lived on this rented farm for two years.

Meanwhile, Frank filed a timber culture claim on a quarter section two miles north of where he was living. Most of the 160 acres lay just above the Firesteel Creek flat, an area extending back from the mostly dry creek bed some three-fourths of a mile and which grew abundant salt grass. The soil on the flat was a dark gumbo which, when wet, stuck to a person's feet and to buggy and wagon wheels. The upland part of the McCardle land had a sandy base in which crops usually failed when moisture was short. The average rainfall in Jerauld County, which was situated on the ninety-ninth meridian, was eighteen to twenty inches a year, which meant that crop production was marginal. The one good thing about the McCardle land was that it had an abundant supply of underground water only fifteen to twenty feet below the surface. A windmill standing over a shallow well could supply unlimited amounts of water for household and livestock needs.

Frank and Mary moved to their tree claim late in 1892 or early in 1893. In November 1892 another daughter, Frances Hazel, arrived. Frank got to his own farm in time to meet the assessor, whose report—in the middle of 1893—showed how this young farmer, his wife, and growing family were faring on government land. The McCardles had 2 cows and 2 calves, and 2 other cattle, but no additional livestock. These 2 "other cattle" were probably a team of oxen. A year earlier, when he was still on his rented farm, he had reported 4 working oxen to the assessor. The McCardles had no hogs or chickens. At least they reported none to the assessor. The assessed value of their personal property was only $15.

The same year that McCardle moved to his tree claim, the Panic of 1893 set off a long and severe depression. Farm prices dropped drastically, and, to make matters worse, in 1894 much of the Great Plains fell victim to extreme drouth and heat. Many farm families had a difficult time eking out a living of any kind. There are no diaries, letters, or account books which reveal how the McCardles weathered the hard times of the 1890s, but, like many unnamed pioneers, they somehow managed to survive. They even added slightly to their personal property, as well as to their family. In March 1895 a son, Lincoln Elwood, was born. A few months later when the assessor called, he could record that the McCardles owned 4 horses, 4 cows, 2 calves, and 2 hogs. Their taxes on personal property, however, went unpaid even though they amounted to only $4.87.

Times continued to be hard, and the McCardles made little economic progress. It was not until 1899 that Frank and Mary McCardle began to increase their personal property substantially, especially in the form of livestock. By that time they owned 8 horses, 1 stallion, 3 cows, 50 sheep, and 7 hogs. While the value of their agricultural machinery was assessed at only $15, this was three times what it had been listed at two or three years earlier. By 1900 McCardle's sheep herd reached a little over 400 head. Considering the time, the McCardles were doing rather well compared to many of their neighbors. Between 1890 and 1900 several hundred farmers in Jerauld County had given up and called it quits. The number of farms in the county dropped from 790 to 487, or by about 300 in that depression-filled decade.

After farming for ten years, McCardle actually appeared to be on the road to becoming a successful family farmer and livestock man. Moreover, the family finances received a boost in February 1901 when his wife sold her homestead for $500. In September 1902 Frank received the patent for his farm from the United States Land Office.

It was not long, however, before the McCardles were wrestling with a common problem that plagued most frontier farmers—lack of capital. On 23 November 1904, just a few days after McCardle's land had been registered in the Land Patent Record, he borrowed $900 at six percent interest secured by a mortgage on his land. The loan was to run for five years. He also borrowed another $54 which was to be repaid in a similar period. In his case the lender took out the interest in advance so McCardle received $45 which was to be repaid at $9 a year. He paid off the small loan within a few months, but when the $900 mortgage was due in 1909 he was unable to meet his obligation. Consequently, on 1 December 1909 he borrowed $1,000 from the South Dakota School Fund at five percent interest and paid off his old note. The new loan was due in 1913. It is not clear whether McCardle did not have the money to pay off his mortgage, or whether he preferred refinancing, but he renewed his loan from the School Fund in 1913 and again in 1916. In other words, McCardle managed to extend his borrowing until June 1921 when payment would be due. From 1909 to 1921 he borrowed money to pay off previous loans.

Although McCardle continued in debt, he greatly improved his economic condition in the first two decades of the twentieth century. He benefited from that more prosperous period to which farmers sometimes referred as the Golden Era of American Agriculture. Farm commodity and land prices both rose sharply during those years. By 1910 McCardle had 11 head of horses and mules, 65 head of cattle and calves, 6 hogs and a fair supply of agricultural implements. He had been able to build a comfortable five-room house and a large stock barn. He sent his two daughters to Wessington Springs Seminary, a secondary and junior college institution which had been established by the Free Methodist Church in the 1880s. The furnishings in the McCardle home were adequate. He even bought a piano for his daughter, Mary. The assessed valuation of his personal property was nearly $1,000, and his quarter section of land was on the tax rolls at $1,333, up from $475 in 1902.

Things got even better for the McCardle family during the next decade. Although there were occasional drouths in the area, McCardle raised enough feed for his livestock and built up his assets. He also improved his standard of living. McCardle was one of the few farmers in the area who had an automobile as early as 1914. By 1915 he was one of the leading livestock raisers in Dale township. He owned 156 cattle and had become a well-known horse and mule trader. His personal property was assessed at $6,776. Higher prices generated by the outbreak of war in Europe were bringing a taste of genuine prosperity to this established farmer, who was now far removed from his hard-scrabble pioneer days. By 1917 his personal property was valued at $8,861, which included nearly 200 head of cattle, a large number for any farmer in that community.

A quarter century after they began farming on a rented quarter section of land, Frank and Mary McCardle seemed to have achieved the dream of many Americans, that of owning their own farm and enjoying a decent, middle-class standard of living. With hard work, fair management, and some luck, they had moved from bare subsistence with scarcely any property, to a comfortable living, and land and personal property worth between $30,000 and $40,000. Surely he was better off than if he had stayed in West Virginia and found work in the coal mines or steel mills.

Like most farmers Frank McCardle wanted more land. He needed additional acreage for his growing livestock herds, and he hoped to leave a farm to each of his three children. What could be more a part of the American dream than to leave a good inheritance to his son and daughters? So, in 1911, he began to buy land. In that year he purchased 160 acres in an adjoining section. Four years later he bought 320 acres next to his home place. He also acquired what was known as a short quarter of 128 acres some three miles from the home farm. By 1917 he owned 768 acres, including the 160 acres he had acquired under the Timber Culture Act. The average size farm in Jerauld county in 1920 was 404 acres, making McCardle's holdings nearly double the county average.

Meanwhile, his daughters did not wait around for their prospective inheritances. In the summer of 1916, Hazel and her husband Arthur Shoff, and McCardle's oldest daughter, Mary, headed for northwest South Dakota to find land of their own. Their search took them to Perkins County, about seventy-five miles from the Montana border. The Shoffs and Mary McCardle first bought a quarter section from James B. Carter of Baker, Montana. The land was located about twenty miles south of Bison, the county seat, and near the Moreau River. Then Mary, an independent spirit who believed that women should do their own thing a generation before the emergence of the women's liberation movement, filed on 277 acres close to the land she and the Shoffs had purchased together. She filed under the Enlarged Homestead Act of 1909, which was extended to South Dakota in 1915. Her land was along Rabbit Creek, a small stream that flowed into the Moreau River. She was among the thousands of pioneers who moved into the Western Dakotas and Eastern Montana between 1900 and 1920. This was chancy country, where rainfall usually ranged from twelve to sixteen inches a year, but it did not intimidate the McCardle girls. Perhaps it should have!

In July 1917 Mary McCardle married Clyde Fite who had migrated to South Dakota from Ohio in 1914 as a magazine salesman. They settled down on Mary's homestead until Clyde was called for military service in January 1918. After he returned from France a year later, they resumed a small farming and livestock operation on Rabbit Creek. Mary received title to her land on 27 January 1922.

Meanwhile, things were turning sour for Frank McCardle on his Jerauld

County farm. The prosperous times of World War I suddenly ended, and by 1921 farmers were suffering from a severe economic slump. Commodity and land prices fell with a sickening thud, placing farmers who were in debt in a particularly unfortunate position. In the previous decade McCardle had gone heavily into debt purchasing, mainly on credit, some 600 acres of land. As prices fell in late 1920 and 1921, his debts became a crushing burden. In South Dakota, however, hard-up farmers had a possible way out. In 1917, under the governorship of Peter Norbeck, the South Dakota legislature had passed a rural credit law which permitted the state to make thirty-year real estate loans to farmers at relatively low interest rates. With his back against a wall of debt, McCardle applied for and received a loan of $5,000 in March 1921. He applied this amount against his other indebtedness.

Paying off some old loans with new borrowings did nothing to relieve the economic pressure on McCardle. As commodity prices continued to fall, his expenses remained high. Like hundreds of thousands of farmers all over the United States, he found himself in a severe cost-price squeeze. For example, as cattle prices dropped from $14.95 to $7.31 a hundred pounds between 1919 and 1921, McCardle's taxes on land and personal property remained at wartime highs. In some cases tax rates in the early 1920s were actually higher than in 1918 or 1919. In 1921 McCardle had 11 horses and mules, over 100 head of cattle, 69 sheep, and other personal property that was assessed at nearly $4,000, the fourth highest in the township. By community standards McCardle did not appear to be bad off. But he was. During the early 1920s he continued a general family farm operation, but he simply could not produce enough income to service his debts, pay taxes, meet operating costs, and make a living. What he made he spent for operational costs and living expenses, leaving debts to multiply and his interest obligations unpaid.

Financially pressed from every side, McCardle decided to convey his children's land inheritance to them at once. They would get deeds to their land, and he would be rid of his debts. The fact was, McCardle was land poor in those hard times after World War I. On 6 October 1923 he legally transferred a half section of grass land to his daughter and son-in-law, Mary and Clyde Fite. He deeded his home quarter to his daughter, Hazel, and 128 acres to his son, Mike. Then he deeded his last 160 acres to his wife. When the papers were all signed, McCardle did not have an acre in his own name. Incidentally, he had not done his children any favors. All of the land was transferred "subject to encumbrances," the legal jargon for assuming mortgage debt and unpaid interest. Unless conditions got better, the land would not produce enough to service the debt in the depressed 1920s.

Nevertheless, the Fites decided to make a determined effort to save the land McCardle had given them. In 1924 they left their homestead west of the Missouri River in Perkins County and returned east to live with the McCardles on the old home place. By this time Frank and Mary McCardle were sixty-two years old and needed help with farm and household work. This joint farm family made enough for a modest living, but debts continued to accumulate. Both Mary and Clyde Fite took off-farm jobs teaching nearby in rural schools in hopes of earning enough cash to make principal and interest payments on their land. Their efforts, however, proved futile.

The financial roof began falling in on the McCardle family in 1927. After giving notice of foreclosure on August 10, McCardle's home place, where he and the Fites lived, was sold at public auction on the court house steps in Wessington Springs. The only bidder was the State of South Dakota which held a mortgage on the land. McCardle had not made a single principal or interest payment on his $5,000 loan, negotiated in 1921 with the Rural Credit Department. By then the principal, interest, delinquent taxes, and miscellaneous expenses amounted to $7,994.14. In effect, McCardle had sold his land to the state in 1921 and lived on it for six years without making payments of any kind. Thousands of South Dakota farmers did the same thing in the 1920s. The same day the sheriff sold the land owned by McCardle's son. Again, the state was the only bidder. The Fites managed to hold onto their land in Jerauld County until April 1929 when it, too, went under the auctioneer's hammer. By 1929 all of the 768 acres of McCardle family land had been foreclosed on except one quarter. Somehow, the family held that last 160 acres until 1936. Meanwhile, beginning in 1927, unpaid taxes were building up on Mary McCardle Fite's 277-acre homestead. In 1934 the Perkins County Treasurer billed her for $533.77 in delinquent taxes. In the depth of the Great Depression, the figure might just as well have been $5,000 or $5 million as far as her ability to pay was concerned. After years of trying to collect taxes, Perkins County officials finally resorted to legal action and gained title to the land in 1942.

By any economic criteria, Frank McCardle was an economic failure. A pioneer settler on the last frontier, he won some initial successes, but after farming for more than forty years he died a virtual pauper in 1948, twelve years after his wife's sudden death in 1936. He experienced only one fairly prosperous period, the era of World War I. Otherwise, it was a constant struggle with debt, and he experienced that final humiliation feared by every farmer—loss of his land.

How should historians assess the thousands of Frank McCardles who occupied the western frontier in the late nineteenth and early twentieth centuries? I submit that it is inaccurate and unfair to judge them and their contributions only by their land holdings or bank accounts—or, in other words, by their economic progress. Adverse economic and climatic conditions combined to ruin the dreams of tens of thousands of these hardy pioneers as they came to the end of their working lives in the 1920s and 1930s. The Rural Credit Department foreclosed on nearly 7,000 farms in South Dakota alone during those years, to say nothing of the banks, insurance companies and other lenders who foreclosed on thousands of additional farmers in that vast prairie-plains region from Canada to Texas.

Yet until he gave up farming in 1934 at age seventy-two, Frank McCardle and many other pioneer farmers on that last frontier had enjoyed a fairly decent standard of living for the times. He and his wife raised three children, all of whom eventually left the farm for better things. The McCardles paid taxes to support schools, roads, and other needed facilities, and they helped organize the political and social institutions of their community. They contributed to nation-building by helping to open up the vast cattle and wheat lands valuable to the country's welfare.

While the land occupied by these last American pioneers provided only a modest living for most settlers, it did support a transitional generation. That is, the children and grandchildren of those farmers represented by Frank McCardle gained sustenance from the farm long enough and in sufficient amounts so that the next generations could enter into the expanding manufacturing, commercial, and service economy of the nation. Farms, of course, had been fulfilling that function in American society for generations. But the McCardle generation was the last in which the farm supported a large number of people and then launched them into society with their rural values and outlooks intact. Jefferson may have exaggerated the values people supposedly derived from a close association with the land and farming, but agricultural fundamentalism was one of the dominant strains in American thought up through the early twentieth century.

. . . I would illustrate my point by mentioning two individuals well known to [historians of the American West]. The late Robert G. Athearn, a former president of the Western History Association, forsook land that had been homesteaded to pursue a brilliant career in teaching and writing about the region he knew so well. Wayne D. Rasmussen, too, left the homestead of his parents in Montana in the 1930s and trekked to the East Coast, where he worked for the United States Department of Agriculture for some fifty years, becoming the outstanding authority in the field of agricultural history. Not all of those who were temporarily supported by homesteads on the last frontier gained such distinction as Athearn and Rasmussen, but the time and place produced its quota of outstanding Americans. This was made possible by the hard work and sacrifices of the tens of thousands of unknown and unheralded pioneers typified by Frank McCardle. Those who have been calling on historians to spend more time studying the lives of common people are on the right track. The unknown and unrecognized legions contributed to nation-building and deserve our best scholarly efforts. I say hail to the ordinary men and women on that frontier such as Frank and Mary McCardle.

⅄ *F U R T H E R   R E A D I N G*

Annette Atkins, *Harvest of Grief: Grasshopper Plagues and Public Assistance in Minnesota, 1873–78* (1984)

Sidney Baldwin, *Poverty and Politics: The Rise and Decline of the Farm Security Administration* (1968)

Paul Bonnifield, *The Dust Bowl: Men, Dirt and Depression* (1979)

Allan G. Bogue, *From Prairie to Corn Belt: Farming on the Illinois and Iowa Prairies in the Nineteenth Century* (1963)

George A. Boyce, *When the Navajos Had Too Many Sheep: The 1940s* (1974)

Leonard A. Carlson, *Indians, Bureaucrats and Land: The Dawes Act and the Decline of Indian Farming* (1981)

Sucheng Chan, *This Bitter-Sweet Soil: The Chinese in California Agriculture, 1860–1910* (1986)

Edmund Danziger, *Indians and Bureaucrats: Administering the Reservation Policy during the Civil War* (1974)

David M. Emmons, *Garden in the Grasslands: Boomer Literature of the Central Great Plains* (1971)

Gilbert C. Fite, *American Farmers: The New Minority* (1981)

——, *The Farmers' Frontier, 1865–1900* (1966)

——, "The Pioneer Farmer: A View over Three Centuries," *Agricultural History,* 50 (1976), 275–89

James R. Gibson, *Farming the Frontier: The Agricultural Opening of the Oregon Country, 1786–1846* (1985)

Mary Wilma M. Hargreaves, *Dry Farming in the Northern Great Plains, 1900–1925* (1957)

——, "Homesteading and Homemaking on the Plains: A Review," *Agricultural History,* 47 (1973), 156–63

R. Douglas Hurt, *The Dust Bowl: An Agricultural and Social History* (1981)

——, *Indian Agriculture in America: Prehistory to the Present* (1987)

Terry G. Jordan, *German Seed in Texas Soil: Immigrant Farmers in Nineteenth-Century Texas* (1966)

Anita Kunkler, *Hardscrabble: A Narrative of the California Hill Country* (1975)

Donald Parman, *The Navajos and the New Deal* (1976)

Charles S. Peterson, *Take Up Your Mission: Mormon Colonizing Along the Little Colorado River, 1870–1900* (1973)

Sarah Ellen Roberts, *Alberta Homestead: Chronicle of a Pioneer Family* (1968)

Theodore Saloutos, *The American Farmer and the New Deal* (1982)

John T. Schlebecker, *Whereby We Thrive: A History of American Farming, 1607–1972* (1975)

Fred A. Shannon, *The Farmers' Last Frontier: Agriculture, 1860–1897* (1945)

Homer E. Socolofsky, "Success and Failure in Nebraska Homesteading," *Agricultural History,* 42 (1968), 103–7

Joanna L. Stratton, *Pioneer Women: Voices from the Kansas Frontier* (1981)

Robert A. Trennert, *Alternative to Extinction, Federal Indian Policy and the Beginnings of the Reservation System* (1975)

Richard White, *The Roots of Dependency: Subsistence, Environment, and Social Change Among the Choctaws, Pawnees, and Navajos* (1983)

Donald L. Winters, *Farmers Without Farms: Agricultural Tenancy in Nineteenth-Century Iowa* (1978)

Donald Worster, *Dust Bowl: The Southern Plains in the 1930s* (1979)

The Popular Imagination

Y

For most Americans and non-Americans alike, the dominant image of the West is one created by popular culture. The mass marketing of dime novels by Erastus Beadle and his competitors, the international success of Buffalo Bill Cody's Wild West Show and its imitators, and the production of numerous western films in both the silent and sound eras have all contributed to this imagery. One might assume that these popular perceptions have not changed from the early nineteenth to the late twentieth centuries. Yet they have changed, and substantially. The same Indians who were the great villains of captivity accounts have become heroic but abused figures in modern novels. Buffalo Bill has fallen in stature from a heroic scout of the plains to an elderly, buffoonish showman. The reasons these changes occur is a challenge for scholars. Change may be a function of some combination of mass memory, contemporary values, marketing campaigns, and media manipulations. However these changes proceed, the West of the popular imagination continues to have a major influence on countless artists, novelists, and historians depicting the region.

Y D O C U M E N T S

While residing in South Carolina, Pennsylvanian Owen Wister wrote a book about a Virginian who lived in Wyoming. He dedicated his 1902 best seller to Theodore Roosevelt, who, before he became president, had written several well-received articles on ranch life in the Dakotas. The first four documents focus on Wister and his highly influential novel *The Virginian*, which may well be the archetype for popular western fiction. In the first document, taken from an 1895 *Harpers' Weekly*, Roosevelt praises his friend's writing. He commends Wister's stories on nationalistic more than on artistic terms. In the second selection, Wister's introduction to the 1902 edition, the author explains why he considers *The Virginian* to be a historical novel. The third document, an excerpt from the novel itself, captures the spirit of the book as well as its most famous line. The final selection in the set, a review of a 1929 Hollywood production, demonstrates the novel's continuing appeal. This film helped launch Gary Cooper and the era of sound, much as the novel helped launch a genre of fiction.

George Armstrong Custer has changed dramatically over time as a figure in the popular imagination. After Custer's death, even Sitting Bull had words of praise for the fallen general, as an 1877 newspaper interview, reprinted here as the fifth document, reveals. The sixth selection, Ella Wheeler Wilcox's epic poem of 1896, goes well beyond the Hunkpapa chief's words. The seventh document, an excerpt from the beginning of Frederic F. Van De Water's 1934 biography, shows that the tide had turned against Custer. But a 1941 review of the film *They Died with Their Boots On*, the eighth selection, indicates that Hollywood had not yet caught up with the debunkers.

The final two documents show how playing western heroes in popular films elevated John Wayne to the status of a symbol for the nation as a whole. The congressional medal that honored Wayne's career and the adulation that appeared when he died are telling tributes to the power of popular imagery.

Theodore Roosevelt Praises Owen Wister's Stories, 1895

Mr. Owen Wister's stories . . . turned a new page in our literature, and, indeed, may almost be said to have turned a new page in that form of contemporary historical writing which consists in the vivid portrayal, once for all, of types that should be commemorated. Many men before him have seen and felt the wonder of that phase of Western life which is now closing, but Mr. Wister makes us see what he has seen and interprets for us what he has heard. His short sketches are so many cantos in the great epic of life on the border of the vanishing wilderness. He shows us heroic figures and a heroic life; not heroes and the heroic life as they are conceived by the cloistered intellect, but rough and strong and native, the good and evil alike challenging the eye. To read his writings is like walking on a windy upland in fall, when the hard weather braces body and mind. There is a certain school of American writers that loves to deal, not with the great problems of American existence and with the infinite picturesqueness of our life as it has been and is being led here on our own continent, where we stumble and blunder, and still, on the whole, go forward, but with the life of those Americans who cannot swim in troubled waters, and go to live as idlers in Europe. What pale, anaemic figures they are, these creations of the émigré novelists, when put side by side with the men, the grim stalwart men, who stride through Mr. Wister's pages!

It is this note of manliness which is dominant through the writings of Mr. Wister.

Owen Wister's Introduction to *The Virginian: A Horseman of the Plains,* 1902

Certain of the newspapers, when this book was first announced, made a mistake most natural upon seeing the sub-title as it then stood, *A Tale of Sundry Adventures.* "This sounds like a historical novel," said one of them, meaning (I take it) a colonial romance. As it now stands, the title will scarce lead to such interpretation; yet none the less is this book historical—quite as much so as any colonial romance. Indeed, when you look at the root of the matter, it is a colonial romance. For Wyoming between 1874 and 1890 was a colony as wild as was Virginia one hundred years earlier. As wild, with a scantier population, and the same primitive joys and dangers. There were, to be sure, not so many Chippendale settees. . . .

Had you left New York or San Francisco at ten o'clock this morning, by noon the day after to-morrow you could step out at Cheyenne. There you would stand at the heart of the world that is the subject of my picture, yet you would look around you in vain for the reality. It is a vanished world. No journeys, save those which memory can take, will bring you to it now. The mountains are there, far and shining, and the sunlight, and the infinite earth, and the air that seems forever the true fountain of youth,— but where is the buffalo, and the wild antelope, and where the horseman with his pasturing thousands? So like its old self does the sage-brush seem when revisited, that you wait for the horseman to appear.

But he will never come again. He rides in his historic yesterday. You will no more see him gallop out of the unchanging silence than you will see Columbus on the unchanging sea come sailing from Palos with his caravels.

And yet the horseman is still so near our day that in some chapters of this book, which were published separate at the close of the nineteenth century, the present tense was used. It is true no longer. In those chapters it has been changed, and verbs like "is" and "have" now read "was" and "had." Time has flowed faster than my ink.

What is become of the horseman, the cowpuncher, the last romantic figure upon our soil? For he was romantic. Whatever he did, he did with his might. The bread that he earned was earned hard, the wages that he squandered were squandered hard,—half a year's pay sometimes gone in a night,—"blown in," as he expressed it, or "blowed in," to be perfectly accurate. Well, he will be here among us always, invisible, waiting his chance to live and play as he would like. His wild kind has been among us always, since the beginning: a young man with his temptations, a hero without wings.

The cow-puncher's ungoverned hours did not unman him. If he gave his word, he kept it; Wall Street would have found him behind the times. Nor did he talk lewdly to women; Newport would have thought him old-fashioned. He and his brief epoch make a complete picture, for in themselves they were as complete as the pioneers of the land or the explorers of the sea. A transition has followed the horseman of the plains; a shapeless state, a condition of men and manners as unlovely as is that moment in the year when winter is gone and spring not come, and the face of Nature is ugly. I shall not dwell upon it here. Those who have seen it know well what I mean. Such transition was inevitable. Let us give thanks that it is but a transition, and not a finality.

Sometimes readers inquire, Did I know the Virginian? As well, I hope, as a father should know his son. And sometimes it is asked, Was such and such a thing true? Now to this I have the best answer in the world. Once a cowpuncher listened patiently while I read him a manuscript. It concerned an event upon an Indian reservation. "Was that the Crow reservation?" he inquired at the finish. I told him that it was no real reservation and no real event; and his face expressed displeasure. "Why," he demanded, "do you waste your time writing what never happened, when you know so many things that did happen?"

And I could no more help telling him that this was the highest compliment ever paid me than I have been able to help telling you about it here!

"When You Call Me That, *Smile*"

. . . Through folding doors I passed from the bar proper with its bottles and elk head back to the hall with its various tables. I saw a man sliding cards from a case, and across the table from him another man laying counters down. Near by was a second dealer pulling cards from the bottom of a pack, and opposite him a solemn old rustic piling and changing coins upon the cards which lay already exposed.

But now I heard a voice that drew my eyes to the far corner of the room.

"Why didn't you stay in Arizona?"

Harmless looking words as I write them down here. Yet at the sound of them I noticed the eyes of the others directed to that corner. What answer was given to them I did not hear, nor did I see who spoke. Then came another remark.

"Well, Arizona's no place for amatures."

This time the two card dealers that I stood near began to give a part of their attention to the group that sat in the corner. There was in me a desire to leave this room. So far my hours at Medicine Bow had seemed to glide beneath a sunshine of merriment, of easy-going jocularity. This was suddenly gone, like the wind changing to north in the middle of a warm day. But I stayed, being ashamed to go.

Five or six players sat over in the corner at a round table where counters were piled. Their eyes were close upon their cards, and one seemed to be dealing a card at a time to each, with pauses and betting between. Steve was there and the Virginian; the others were new faces.

"No place for amatures," repeated the voice; and now I saw that it was the dealer's. There was in his countenance the same ugliness that his words conveyed.

"Who's that talkin'?" said one of the men near me, in a low voice.

"Trampas."

"What's he?

"Cow-puncher, bronco-buster, tin-horn, most anything."

"Who's he talkin' at?"

"Think it's the black-headed guy he's talking at."

"That ain't supposed to be safe, is it?"

"Guess we're all goin' to find out in a few minutes."

"Been trouble between 'em?"

"They've not met before. Trampas don't enjoy losin' to a stranger."

"Fello's from Arizona, yu' say?"

"No. Virginia. He's recently back from havin' a look at Arizona. Went down there last year for a change. Works for the Sunk Creek outfit." And then the dealer lowered his voice still further and said something in the other man's ear, causing him to grin. After which both of them looked at me.

There had been silence over in the corner; but now the man Trampas spoke again.

"*And* ten," said he, sliding out some chips from before him. Very strange it was to hear him, how he contrived to make those words a personal taunt. The Virginian was looking at his cards. He might have been deaf.

"*And* twenty," said the next player, easily.

The next threw his cards down.

It was now the Virginian's turn to bet, or leave the game, and he did not speak at once.

Therefore Trampas spoke. "Your bet, you son-of-a———."

The Virginian's pistol came out, and his hand lay on the table, holding it unaimed. And with a voice as gentle as ever, the voice that sounded almost like a caress, but drawling a very little more than usual, so that there was almost a space between each word, he issued his orders to the man Trampas:—

"When you call me that, *smile.*" And he looked at Trampas across the table.

Yes, the voice was gentle. But in my ears it seemed as if somewhere the bell of death was ringing; and silence, like a stroke, fell on the large room. All men present, as if by some magnetic current, had become aware of this crisis. In my ignorance, and the total stoppage of my thoughts, I stood stock-still, and noticed various people crouching, or shifting their positions.

"Sit quiet," said the dealer, scornfully to the man near me. "Can't you see he don't want to push trouble? He has handed Trampas the choice to back down or draw his steel."

Then, with equal suddenness and ease, the room came out of its strangeness. Voices and cards, the click of chips, the puff of tobacco, glasses lifted to drink,—this level of smooth relaxation hinted no more plainly of what lay beneath than does the surface tell the depth of the sea.

For Trampas had made his choice. And that choice was not to "draw his steel." If it was knowledge that he sought, he had found it, and no mistake! We heard no further reference to what he had been pleased to style "amatures." In no company would the black-headed man who had visited Arizona be rated a novice at the cool art of self-preservation.

One doubt remained: what kind of a man was Trampas? A public backdown is an unfinished thing,—for some natures at least. I looked at his face, and thought it sullen, but tricky rather than courageous.

Something had been added to my knowledge also. Once again I had heard applied to the Virginian that epithet which Steve so freely used. The same words, identical to the letter. But this time they had produced a pistol. "When you call me that, *smile!*" So I perceived a new example of the old truth, that the letter means nothing until the spirit gives it life.

The New York Times Reviews *The Virginian,* 1929

From the pages of Owen Wister's old Western classic, "The Virginian," Paramount-Famous-Lasky have produced a noteworthy talking film, in which the voices are nicely modulated and the acting pleasingly restrained. The story is cleverly developed by the director, Victor Fleming, who deserves great credit for the production and especially for the effective but at the same time gentle humor that pops up periodically. It is also a capitally timed picture, with characters going here and there with natural movements.

Gary Cooper impersonates the Virginian, the cowboy foreman of Medicine Bow Ranch, in Wyoming, and Walter Huston plays Trampas, the bad man who finds more than his match in the Virginian. Both are believable characters brought to life from the days of half a century ago. There is good suspense when the Virginian gets the drop on Trampas and in the latter stages of this film the glimpses of Trampas looking for the Virginian recall the doings of Wild Bill Hicock, Bret Harte's men and even Buffalo Bill's thrilling encounters. It is a picture with a fine conception of the necessary atmosphere and one in which Mr. Fleming has happily refused to introduce extraneous incidents.

"When you call me that, smile!" is filmed in a highly satisfactory fashion, for this famous line occurs a second after the Virginian has his pistol in Trampas's abdomen. That scoundrel is not without a sense of humor, however, and he avers that he will smile any time in such circumstances.

The romance between Molly Wood and the Virginian is appealing. Mr. Fleming and those concerned with the adaptation of this tale have shrewdly availed themselves of action and words that build up the characters as well as the plot.

The nearest approach to this excellent piece of work, in its own particular line, was James Cruze's old silent film, "The Pony Express." In this present offering it is evident that the calling upon players to deliver lines causes them to give firm, understanding interpretations of their respective rôles, far more so than they ordinarily would do in a silent film.

It may not be a yarn jammed with thrills, but it is one that always compels attention. The moment that Molly Wood, the school teacher, arrives in Medicine Bow, there is good humor in which the lass from the East clashes with the lads from the West.

There are some adroitly sketched scenes in Miss Wood's school and Mr. Fleming has reproduced in a merry fashion the incident where the

Movie Review of "The Virginian" by Mordaunt Hall, 1929: *New York Times,* December 23, 1929. Copyright © 1929 by The New York Times Company. Reprinted by permission.

unfortunate Steve and the Virginian mix up the babies at the christening party. This episode elicited uproarious mirth at the theatre yesterday afternoon.

The happy-go-lucky Steve comes to a bad end, for he dies with a noose around his neck for cattle rustling. And the Virginian superintends the hanging. Here, again, Mr. Fleming scores, for he leaves enough to the imagination and yet is able to give a clear idea of what cattle stealing meant in those wild days.

Aside from the intelligent acting of Mr. Huston and Mr. Cooper, Richard Arlen gives an agreeable portrayal of Steve. Mary Brian does her share to help the picture along, but she might have been more persuasive with less rouge on her lips.

The sounds, whether footfalls, horses' hoofs, rumbling wheels or voices, are really remarkably recorded and reproduced. A good deal of this film was made in the open and it would seem that stories of Western life, if pictured in a rational fashion, would be unusually successful, for they are aided immeasurably by the audibility of the screen.

Sitting Bull Praises General Custer, 1877

I went on to interrogate Sitting Bull:—

"This big fight, then, extended through three hours?"

"Through most of the going forward of the sun."

"Where was the Long Hair [Custer] the most of the time?"

"I have talked with my people; I cannot find one who saw the Long Hair until just before he died. He did not wear his long hair as he used to wear it. His hair was like yours," said Sitting Bull, playfully touching my forehead with his taper fingers. "It was short, but it was of the color of the grass when the frost comes."

"Did you hear from your people how he died? Did he die on horseback?"

"No. None of them died on horseback."

"All were dismounted?"

"Yes."

"And Custer, the Long Hair?"

"Well, I have understood that there were a great many brave men in that fight, and that from time to time, while it was going on, they were shot down like pigs. They could not help themselves. One by one the officers fell. I believe the Long Hair rode across once from this place down here (meaning the place where Tom Custer's and Smith's companies were killed) to this place up here (indicating the spot on the map where Custer fell), but I am not sure about this. Any way it was said that up there where the last fight took place, where the last stand was made, the Long Hair stood like a sheaf of corn with all the ears fallen around him."

"Not wounded?"

"No."

"How many stood by him?"

"A few."

"When did he fall?"

"He killed a man when he fell. He laughed."

"You mean he cried out."

"No, he laughed; he had fired his last shot."

"From a carbine?"

"No, a pistol."

"Did he stand up after he first fell?"

"He rose up on his hands and tried another shot, but his pistol would not go off."

"Was any one else standing up when he fell down?"

"One man was kneeling; that was all. But he died before the Long Hair. All this was far up on the bluffs, far away from the Sioux encampments. I did not see it. It is told to me. But it is true."

"The Long Hair was not scalped?"

"No. My people did not want his scalp."

"Why?"

"I have said; he was a great chief."

Custer, An Epic Poem by Ella Wheeler Wilcox, 1896

I.

ALL valor died not on the plains of Troy.
Awake, my Muse, awake! be thine the joy
To sing of deeds as dauntless and as brave
As e'er lent luster to a warrior's grave.
Sing of that noble soldier, nobler man,
Dear to the heart of each American.
Sound forth his praise from sea to listening sea—
Greece her Achilles claimed, immortal Custer, we.

.　.　.　.　.　.　.　.　.　.　.

XXX.

Ah, grand as rash was that last fatal raid
The little group of daring heroes made.
Two hundred and two score intrepid men
Rode out to war; not one came back again.
Like fiends incarnate from the depths of hell
Five thousand foemen rose with deafening yell,
And swept that vale as with a simoon's breath,
But like the gods of old, each martyr met his death.

XXXI.

Like gods they battled and like gods they died.
Hour following hour that little band defied
The hordes of red men swarming o'er the plain,
Till scarce a score stood upright 'mid the slain.
Then in the lull of battle, creeping near,
A scout breathed low in Custer's listening ear:

"Death lies before, dear life remains behind
Mount thy sure-footed steed, and hasten with the wind."

XXXII.

A second's silence. Custer dropped his head,
His lips slow moving as when prayers are said—
Two words he breathed—"God and Elizabeth,"
Then shook his long locks in the face of death,
And with a final gesture turned away
To join that fated few who stood at bay.
Ah! deeds like that the Christ in man reveal
Let Fame descend her throne at Custer's shrine to kneel.

XXXIII.

Too late to rescue, but in time to weep,
His tardy comrades came. As if asleep
He lay, so fair, that even hellish hate
Withheld its hand and dared not mutilate.
By fiends who knew not honor, honored still,
He smiled and slept on that far western hill.
Cast down thy lyre, oh Muse! thy song is done!
Let tears complete the tale of him who failed, yet won.

Frederic F. Van de Water's *Glory Hunter* (Excerpt), 1934

He followed Glory all his days. He was her life-long devotee. She gave him favor withheld from most men, and denied herself when his need of her was sorest.

When, desperately pursuing, he died on the heights above the Little Bighorn, Glory, the perverse, relented and gave eternal brilliance to the name of George Armstrong Custer, Lieutenant-Colonel, 7th United States Cavalry, Brevet Major-General, United States Army, the "Boy General with the Golden Locks," "the Murat of the American Army," the good sword, the hero, the martyr.

His memory has been clothed in glamour by the mystery of his death. He rode away at the head of five troops into the bare brown hills, and dust, smoking up beneath the hoofs of weary horses, hid him. Men found his stripped body at the apex of a corpse-littered angle of rout. No one will ever completely know his purpose or learn the instant and manner of his end.

Wherefore he is immortal, by his enigmatic death, by the no less vivid inconsistencies of his immoderate life. His body lies at the United States

Reprinted from *Glory-Hunter: A Life of General Custer*, 17–19, by Frederic F. Van de Water, by permission of University of Nebraska Press. Copyright 1934, 1962 by Frederic F. Van de Water.

Military Academy where his brief and furious career began. There is no such rest for those who follow the singular course that body took through life. Angry controversy beclouds his every step. It is as though the unbridled spirit of him still were clearly discernible to mortal eyes.

In the flesh, he was greatly loved and hated. So he remains, almost sixty years since he fell, twice pierced by bullets of the Sioux. Few still endure who saw him in the flesh, but over his memory, his deeds, his character and particularly his death, Custerphobe and Custerphile strive with the heat of the man's actual intimates. No winds of partisanship disturb the ashes of other warriors of his day. Merritt, Kilpatrick, Devin, MacKenzie, Crook, captains of Union horse and Indian fighters alike, have the peace that is obscurity's twilight. Men keep the fame of Custer burnished while that of equal or better soldiers grows dim.

While he lived, few saw him accurately. Contemporaries accorded him the unreliable tributes of infatuated praise or vindictive condemnation. He was a person whom it was impossible to regard with balance. His death did not placate, though it hushed, his enemies. The years that elapsed before their own ends never diminished the clear loyalty of his adherents.

Major and Brevet Brigadier-General Frederick W. Benteen, most valiant and able of his troop captains, hated him profoundly. General E. S. Godfrey, who served as lieutenant under Custer, devoted much of his life to his hero's defense. The last of his officers, Colonel Charles A. Varnum, still protects the memory of his old chieftain. Later men, who never saw that golden head gleam in the murk of battle, speak and write of him with odd personal heat.

Death submerges heroes, hiding actual dimensions and qualities from inquiring eyes. The flood covers men and all that remains visible are islands that were peaks of their careers. Many of these vestiges, as the years pass, slip lower or disappear. From the scattered and incongruous archipelago that still endures, one must try to surmise the outline and substance of vanished actuality. Few have left to the biographer more wholly divergent islets of fact than the Glory-Hunter. He seems in his brief time to have been many men.

He followed Glory to his doom. Thereafter, woman-like, she followed him. The paradox is consonant with the career of George Armstrong Custer. He himself was paradox; the word made flesh.

Few men have been more vehemently positive in character. None has thwarted generalization with more baffling contradictions.

He was a popular hero who was scorned by many in his own profession.

He was the idol of a few subordinates and distrusted by others.

He was a tenderly devoted son and husband and a brutal commander.

He was gentle with his dogs and horses, yet blind to suffering he inflicted on men.

He was a dangerously insubordinate officer; he had been a most slovenly cadet and subaltern, but he enforced discipline on his own troops implacably.

He has been praised as a knightly and gallant foe; he had been decried as butcher and lyncher.

He was renowned for his flaming valor in battle, yet his record is marred by one stain, that is the blood of Major Joel H. Elliot and nineteen men, killed by what was, at best, the incredible callousness of George Armstrong Custer.

He is best remembered as the foremost Indian fighter of his day but his only positive victory in battle against the red men was massacre rather than conflict, and his chief surviving fame as a soldier is based upon a defeat as complete as ever United States regulars sustained.

These and lesser inconsistencies defy plausible solution unless the biographer abandon any attempt to harmonize discordant facts and admit that the man was demented. Custer was not crazy, though some contemporaries thought him so. He was the life-long infatuate of renown. Through the strange contradictions of his character, that one trait runs constant. He loved fame with insatiable ardor. His pursuit of renown was medieval and adolescent. All his life, he rode after Glory.

The New York Times Reviews *They Died With Their Boots On,* 1941

The Warners have been generous to a fault in paying their respects to General George Armstrong Custer. Certainly the man who is more famed for his celebrated last stand against the Sioux and allied tribes at Little Big Horn than for any of his several other exploits receives his due as a courageous soldier, and then some, in "They Died With Their Boots On," which thundered into the Strand yesterday. Dismiss factual inaccuracies liberally sprinkled throughout the film's more than two-hour length and you have an adventure tale of frontier days which for sheer scope, if not dramatic impact, it would be hard to equal.

Wave upon wave of cavalry charges packed with breath-taking thrills have been handled in masterly fashion by Director Raoul Walsh, and they alone are worth the price of admission. Mr. Walsh, it is obvious, spared neither men, horses nor Errol Flynn's General Custer in kicking up the dust of battle. But the director was not so fortunate in handling the personal drama and as a consequence "They Died With Their Boots On" has little verve between campaigns.

With all the action of the Civil War sequences, it is not surprising that the intervening account of the General's domestic life and his battle against political intrigue, which lacks genuine dramatic sustenance, should become a little wearying. After all, two hours and seventeen minutes requires a powerful lot of sustained drama. Mr. Walsh would have had a more compact and compelling entertainment had he whittled a half hour or so out of the script. But he more than makes up for this with his action shots.

From what the records show, "They Died With Their Boots On" is

Movie Review of "They Died with Their Boots On" by Thomas M. Pryor, November 24, 1941. Copyright © 1941 by The New York Times Company. Reprinted by permission.

the screen's first full-fledged attempt at spanning Custer's remarkable career from his hazing as a West Point plebe, his almost story-bookish rise from second lieutenant of cavalry at the first Battle of Bull Run in 1861 to his appointment two years later as brigadier general of volunteers and commander of the Michigan brigade, which performed so brilliantly at Gettysburg.

However fanciful the film's account of his early Army career and the events in between his assignment as lieutenant colonel, Regular Army, of the Seventh Cavalry, may be, it nevertheless provides a broad view of a complex personality. In the massacre at the Little Big Horn in 1876 the film credits Custer with knowingly sacrificing his small forces to prevent the warring Indians from swooping down upon General Terry's unsuspecting regiment, a viewpoint in variance with certain historical accounts of the tragedy.

Errol Flynn, who approximates the general in physical characteristics, is excellent as the dashing, adventuresome cavalryman. Olivia de Haviland is altogether captivating as his adoring wife. Others in the long cast who acquit themselves with credit are John Litel as General Phil Sheridan, Sidney Greenstreet as General Winfield Scott and Stanley Ridges as the fictious Major Taipe who engineers Custer's court-martial. George P. Huntley Jr. gives a magnificent performance as Custer's fellow-officer and buddie.

John Wayne Receives a Congressional Gold Medal, 1979

The consumer-affairs subcommittee of the House Banking, Finance and Urban Affairs Committee had no trouble yesterday getting an audience and television coverage of hearings on whether Congress should authorize a special gold medal in honor of John Wayne. A key witness was Maureen O'Hara, often Mr. Wayne's co-star, who tearily told the subcommittee; "John Wayne is not just an actor, John Wayne is the United States of America."

Miss O'Hara received a consoling pat on the back from Elizabeth Taylor. She said to the subcommittee chairman, Representative Frank Annunzio, Democrat of Illinois: "Please let us show him our appreciation and love. He is a hero, and there are so few left." Later the subcommittee approved the measure, calling for the medal to read—at Miss O'Hara's suggestion—"John Wayne, American."

Mr. Wayne, who is gravely ill with cancer, will be 72 years old on Saturday. President Carter supports legislation, already approved by the Senate, authorizing him to issue a gold medal in Mr. Wayne's honor. Similar legislation has been enacted 83 times for the striking of Congressional gold medals, given to Americans as diverse as George Washington, Charles A.

"Notes on People," John Wayne Receives a Congressional Gold Medal, May 22, 1979. Copyright © 1979 by The New York Times Company. Reprinted by permission.

Lindbergh, Robert Frost, the Wright Brothers, Dr. Jonas Salk and Bob Hope.

The Duke: "More Than Just a Hero," 1979

John Wayne was an American folk hero by reason of countless films in which he lived bigger, shot straighter and loomed larger than any man in real life ever could.

His death in Los Angeles on Monday at the age of 72 deprived the world of the last active survivor and exponent of the classic American action film. In the more than 200 features in which he appeared in a career that spanned half a century, "Duke" Wayne projected an image of rugged, sometimes muleheaded and always formidable masculinity.

His name was synonymous with the Western and, beyond that, with Hollywood and with what many Americans would like to believe about themselves and their country. He became a figure whose magnitude and emotional conviction took on an enduring symbolic importance.

Mr. Wayne's films earned about $700 million. For 25 consecutive years, he was listed among the top 10 box office attractions of American films. His only Academy Award came late in his career for his role as the cantankerous Marshal Rooster Cogburn in "True Grit" in 1969. The critic as well as the public thought it was well deserved.

Perhaps no Hollywood actor had a more distinctive appearance—a slightly tilted stance and a loping stride, an emphatic, syncopated way of speaking which delighted many a mimic, professional and amateur, and an awesome physical presence. His physicality was expressed most engagingly, perhaps, in a peerless ability to kick in locked doors.

In an interview in 1976, Mr. Wayne described the typical hero he portrayed:

"The man I played," he said slowly, "could be rough, he could be immoral, he could be cruel, tough or tender, but" his hand hit the table smartly—"he was never petty or small. Everyone in the audience wants to identify with that kind of character. He may be bad, but if he's bad, he's BAD. He's not just a petty little whiner."

Mr. Wayne died of cancer at 8:35 P.M. (Eastern time) at the UCLA Medical Center in Los Angeles. His death was announced three hours later by Dr. Bernard R. Strohm, the hospital administrator. The actor's seven children were at his bedside at the end.

The character Mr. Wayne played on the screen and the gallantry and stubbornness with which he fought repeated illnesses in recent years were evoked in the messages of sympathy that came from around the world.

In a statement issued by the White House, President Carter said that "in an age of few heroes" Mr. Wayne was "the genuine article."

"The Duke: 'More Than Just a Hero' " by Gary Arnold and Kenneth Turan, June 13, 1979. Reprinted by permission of *The Washington Post*.

"But he was more than just a hero," the president said. "He was a symbol of many of the most basic qualities that made America great. The ruggedness, the tough independence, the sense of personal conviction and courage—on and off the screen—reflected the best of our national character. It was because of what John Wayne said about what we are and what we can be that his great and deep love of America was returned in full measure." . . .

Mr. Wayne starred in Hollywood action films beginning with a grandiose Western epic, "The Big Trail," and ending with "The Shootist" in 1976. Although he enjoyed success in many non-Western roles—at one time his identity as a movie soldier probably took precedence over his identity as a movie cowboy—Mr. Wayne's fame and appeal are likely to rest on such Westerns as John Ford's "Stagecoach," "She Wore a Yellow Ribbon," "Rio Grande," "The Searchers," and "The Man Who Shot Liberty Valance," Howard Hawks' "Red River" and "Rio Bravo," and Henry Hathaway's "North to Alaska" and "True Grit."

At once the most venerable and durable of Western stars, Mr. Wayne sustained this genre by the force and clarity of his personality years after other stars of his generation had abandoned it. Although some critics have felt that Mr. Wayne did little more than play himself in his movies, the image he projected was one he devised with considerable art. His walk and his manner of speaking, for example, were copied from his friend Yakima Canutt, the stunt man.

Film historian David Thomson wrote that "Wayne's sincere wrong-headedness may yet obliterate the fact he is a great screen actor. . . . It is a matter of some . . . importance that the student of film appreciate that Wayne is an actor of noble bearing. Good enough to survive innumerable bad films, he is a presence that makes meaning and appearance exactly congruent—one can ask for no more."

Υ *E S S A Y S*

Have westerners created their own popular view of their past? Clyde A. Milner II teaches western and American Indian history at Utah State University and is coeditor of the *Western Historical Quarterly*. In the first essay, which received the Palladin Writing Award from the Montana Historical Society, he examines memoirs and reminiscences, and demonstrates that Montana's pioneers created a shared memory that includes certain emblematic stories about the overland journey, Indians, outlaws, and vigilantes.

Paul A. Hutton, an expert in military and western history, teaches at the University of New Mexico, where he also edits the *New Mexico Historical Review*. His book *Phil Sheridan and His Army* won three major awards, including the Billington Prize of the Organization of American Historians. In the second selection, Hutton analyzes the changing popular image of General Custer as a western hero, and shows that over time, fame can be separated from heroism.

Michael T. Marsden and Jack Nachbar, both faculty in the popular-culture program at Bowling Green State University, believe that despite the popularity of Louis L'Amour's novels, the western novel is today in demise. In the third essay, they contend that a shift in national mood may resurrect broad interest in western stories. May we assume that the Virginian, George Armstrong Custer, and John Wayne have not breathed their last in the popular imagination and the shared memory of Americans?

The Shared Memory of Pioneers

CLYDE A. MILNER II

In the beginning there was no Montana, but Harriet Sanders was already there. By arriving in the gold camp of Bannack in 1863, well before the 1864 creation of Montana Territory, Harriet Sanders and thousands of others could lay claim to being Montana pioneers. But Sanders's claim had more substance than merely being present before the creation. She and her immediate family played prominent roles in the new society. Her husband, Wilbur Fisk Sanders, who gained early fame as the prosecutor who aided the vigilantes in their campaign against the "road agents" and other outlaws, later served as a territorial delegate to Congress and eventually became a U.S. Senator. Her older son, James, like his father practiced law and also served as secretary of the Society of Montana Pioneers. The younger son, Wilbur, became a mining engineer and for a term was librarian of the Montana Historical Society. The elder Wilbur Sanders served as president of that same organization from 1865 through 1890.

When Harriet Sanders wrote her memoir in 1897, she, her husband, and her two sons had not only lived through more than thirty years of Montana's history, but they also had helped promote and preserve that history. Nonetheless, despite her long-standing prominence and her recent election as the first president of the Montana Women's Suffrage Association, Harriet Sanders did not write a full-scale autobiography. Nor did she write a family history. Instead, she focused on only sixteen years of her life in what she called her "Reminiscences of My Trip across the Plains and My Early Life in Montana, 1863–1879." More than half of this memoir described the three earliest years, 1863 through 1865, when Harriet Sanders and her family traveled overland to the goldfields and settled in the mining camps of Bannack and Virginia City.

Many other pioneers who wrote memoirs also concentrated on the same story—the overland trip and the early days in the mining camps—and Sanders recognized that her readers may have heard pioneer accounts like her own. In the second paragraph of her memoir, she modestly wrote: "Our experiences across the plains were, I presume, similar in many respects to those of others. . . ." Later, when she described her family's arrival in the

Clyde A. Milner II, "The Shared Memory of Montana's Pioneers," *Montana the Magazine of Western History,* 37 (Winter 1987), 2–13. Reprinted by permission of the Montana Historical Society.

gold camps and she began to discuss "the reign of terror by the road-agents," she assumed that "You have all heard of those dark and terrible days when justice was meted out at the hands of the Vigilance Committee. . . ."

With these words as important signposts, Harriet Sanders's memoir indicates that at least by the 1890s a pattern of shared memory about the overland experience and the early days of the gold camps had emerged among many Montanans. This shared memory allowed many Montanans to consider themselves pioneers, but it also altered their personal memories.

In his scholarly effort to explain how people remember the past, David Lowenthal asserts, "we need other people's memories both to confirm our own and to give them endurance. . . . In the process of knitting our own discontinuous recollections into narratives, we revise personal components to fit the collectively remembered past, and gradually cease to distinguish between them." Memoirs of life in early Montana seem to follow this process. Some elements of these memoirs, regardless of their accuracy, take on great emblematic significance in confirming the narrator's status as a "pioneer" and thus seem to represent a collectively remembered past. The Indian threat during the overland journey was one such element; another was the activities of the vigilantes in the early mining camps. The first may well apply to other overland pioneers who settled elsewhere in the West; the second has clearer ties to the history of early Montana. Each is a potential altering of either factual recall or personal memory in order to participate in the collective memory of a pioneer history.

Diaries, letters, and memoirs often may discuss the same overland journey. For example, three women in addition to Harriet Sanders who traveled from Omaha to Bannack with the Sanders family wrote of their experiences. Sidney Edgerton, Wilbur Fisk Sanders's uncle, made this trip after President Abraham Lincoln had appointed him Chief Justice of the newly organized territory of Idaho. Sidney's wife, Mary, was part of the group, and she wrote a series of letters home to her sisters in Tallmadge, Ohio. The Edgertons' twenty-three-year-old niece, Lucia Darling, kept a diary during the trip, and their thirteen-year-old daughter, Martha, later included an account of the journey in her lengthy, unpublished autobiography.

Each of these women wrote only one account of the same trip. Harriet Sanders wrote two. During the overland journey in 1863, she kept a daily diary; thirty-four years later, she composed her memoir. These two documents show how one woman transformed her daily journal into an example of pioneer history. Internal evidence clearly demonstrates that Sanders used her original diary when she wrote the first part of her larger memoir. At one point, she asked that readers "Refer to my remarks in the Journal." Yet, despite having her diary at hand, Sanders created a memoir that differed in significant ways from her original account and from the accounts of her fellow overlanders.

Sanders made Indians appear in her memoir. In 1897, Sanders claimed that the party saw Indians "every day" or, on the next page, "daily" between Fort Kearny and Fort Laramie (between June 29 and July 22 in the diary). The account in the 1863 diary reports on only four days over this period, July 7–8 and July 20–21, when Indians are either met or sighted. In fact, the diary notes when Indians are *not* present. On July 9, for example, Sanders wrote: "Kept guard last night but were not troubled by the Indians." On July 14, making light of the monotony of the travel, she noted: "Nothing of interest has transpired thus far today. We have killed neither Indian nor buffalo."

Sanders also made an Indian disappear in her memoir. The diary contains a description of a nearly disastrous crossing of the Snake River on September 7. In this account, an Indian on his pony carried Harriet Sanders's maid, Almaretta (Amerette) Geer, safely to the far shore. The helpful Indian is absent in the memoir, despite an elaborate retelling of "the narrowest escape that we had thus far experienced." The memoir concludes one page after this Indianless episode with Harriet Sanders maintaining that their party during the entire journey ". . . had been continually in danger of attacts [*sic*] from the Indians." Both the letters that Mary Edgerton wrote during the trip and Lucia Darling's diary confirm that the Edgerton-Sanders emigrant party had no difficulties with the Indians.

By making the Indians a greater danger in her memoir, Harriet Sanders did what many other pioneers had done. In his massive study of the overlanders on the California and Oregon trails, John D. Unruh, Jr., notes: "Encounters with hostile Indians—often much embellished—are far more conspicuous in latter-day reminiscent accounts." As Unruh explains, letters home that summarized the trip "tended to give Indian affairs much more prominence" than did the same people's daily journals and diaries. It seems that some retrospective reference to the "Indian threat" became a way to certify a pioneer's overland journey. It was expected to be part of the story, but it served a greater purpose than merely telling an exciting tale.

These accounts of the Indian danger created a shared memory and, therefore, a shared identity for the pioneers. If Harriet Sanders had wanted to tell an exciting story, she could have stressed the sickness, storms, and stampedes that she recounted more frequently in her diary than in her memoir. But Harriet Sanders could make a grand statement about the destiny of the pioneers if she emphasized the Indians rather than other problems. Her memoir provided ample opportunity for such a grand, retrospective pronouncement. Early in her memoir, she paused in her description of travel along the Platte River to assert:

> This boundless country had belonged to the Indians and the buffalo from time immemorial. . . . The emigrants who passed through the country previous to 1868 did so at the peril of their lives. The Indians becoming jealous at the appearance of the whites, lay in ambush for the unsuspecting victims, and many a scalp-dance was danced and war-songs chanted over the forms of those who aspired to plant an empire in the unknown west. But in the end, however, the pioneers conquered the wilderness and transformed it into a land of peace and plenty.

As revealed in this statement, Harriet Sanders created a historical rationalization of the pioneer experience in her memoir. Sanders declared that by surviving the Indian danger of the overland journey, the pioneers eventually conquered the "wilderness" and transformed Indian lands into a new and "civilized" order. The pioneers ultimately became new natives in what they considered a new land. If the old natives had not been prominent enough on the original journey, they could be made more prominent in the memory of it. In this way, the shared identity of pioneer could be maintained *along* with the idea of cultural and even physical conquest. Such self-serving, ethnocentric bias permitted the pioneers, and those who followed them, to justify their own emigration and settlement.

Many scholars have looked closely at the diaries and letters of overlanders. Historian Glenda Riley has found that rumors and alarmism about Indians did create anxieties during the trip, especially for women. Yet, what they feared rarely became reality. In her examination of 150 primary accounts from all the major overland trails between 1830 and 1900, Riley discovered that in only 15 were major troubles with the Indians reported and in none were claims made about extensive loss of life. Historian Lillian Schlissel studied ninety-six overland diaries written by women. She found that only 7 per cent contained accounts of attacks by Indians and these reported the deaths of only two families, two men, and one woman. Unruh's analysis of the California/Oregon trail demonstrates that fewer than four hundred emigrants were killed by Indians from 1840 to 1860, when approximately two hundred and fifty thousand people took this overland route. Yet, rumors of raids and massacres spread beyond the overland trails, and newspapers occasionally published vivid accounts of what proved to be fictitious attacks.

The trails to Montana's gold camps during the 1860s saw roughly 10 per cent of the number of emigrants that traveled to California and Oregon between 1840 and 1860. Yet, this smaller migration may have been subject to greater Indian hostility, especially when crossing the bison ranges of the Teton Sioux and Northern Cheyenne. Certainly the record of warfare on the northern plains between the army and the native peoples was far greater during the 1860s than during the 1840s and 1850s. How direct and deadly such hostilities proved to be for emigrant trains to Montana needs careful analysis. The personal accounts from eight emigrant trains that traveled across the northern plains from Minnesota between 1862 and 1867, for example, reveal that only the 1864 expedition suffered a serious Indian attack.

Whatever the reality, the description of an Indian threat became a dramatic element in many Montanans' memoirs. Perhaps the most excessively dramatized report of an Indian attack appeared in David J. Bailey's lengthy 1906 reminiscence. Bailey, who grew up in Georgia, Alabama, and Kentucky, decided to travel west to the Montana goldfields in 1865 at age twenty-one after working as a clerk in Evansville, Indiana. His account of the overland journey, which began after he took a steamboat to Leavenworth, Kansas, contains descriptions of four Indian attacks. After the largest of these battles, he confessed:

> The story that one hundred men withstood the furious onslaught of three hundred wild, fiendish savages without serious injury seems almost incredible.

I remember now how they looked and acted when coming toward us. Some were on ponies and others on foot, naked, save breechclouts and cartridge belts, guns in hand, faces painted, hair tangled, with quill feathers inserted and finger in mouth, yelling like demons from the veritable hell below.

Whereas Harriet Sanders had her dairy to help shape the writing of her memoir, David Bailey appears to have had dime novels and popular adventure stories. His overland story recounted many courageous acts by his companions and included a highly stylized courtship between Thornton, a heroic young man, and Mildred, a sweet young woman. During one Indian attack, Mildred and Bailey's own valorous young bride risk their lives to bring Bailey and Thornton their guns. Bailey concluded, "These were instances of female bravery seldom equalled in modern times or paralleled in history."

Other memoirs did not readily mirror Bailey's overblown rhetoric, but they still referred to the Indian threat. In her brief 1908 reminiscence, "A Story of Pioneer Days," Elizabeth Busick O'Neil recalled the 1867 journey that she took at age four with her mother and sister. In mid July, they left the family farm in Des Moines, Iowa. When they were halfway to Virginia City, there appeared a "band of Indians, swinging their lariat ropes and yelling at the top of their voices. When they were opposite us they all stopped their horses and in one breath shouted, 'How!' " This fanciful, childlike description then goes on to recount that an Indian from the same band shot Mr. House, "the man driving the loose stock." With the arrowhead deeply embedded in his back and Mr. House in great pain, the point was finally extracted by a Mrs. Floecer (or Fleecer) using her teeth. "After this experience we were very much afraid of Indians and both men and women carried guns and ammunition."

References to an Indian threat became so common in the shared memory of the pioneers that people who experienced no Indian trouble felt obligated to comment on their good fortune. Michael Lewis Geary arrived in Virginia City in 1864, having traveled from Vienna, Missouri, up the Platte River, through South Pass to the Bear River, and then north across the Snake. In 1937, at age ninety-four, he recalled:

> Of course we saw wolves and coyotes, and along the Platte we saw Indians at several places but had no trouble with them at any times. Some other outfits on the same trail were attacked by Indians that summer but we were lucky and they let us alone. At Fort Laramie we saw the most Indians hanging around the Fort where the soldiers were, but after leaving the Platte we saw no more of them.

James Madison Page, in his reminiscence of an 1866 trip from Leavenworth, Kansas, to Virginia City via Salt Lake City, also commented on Indian attacks and his good fortune:

> We had some interesting Indian scares, but were not seriously troubled by them although we traveled alone most of the distance which was very unwise, as there were massacres and serious Indian trouble both in front and back of us through the Indian Country.

An overland traveler to Montana in the 1860s could have remembered a range of events and a variety of landscapes. The longer memoirs are often full of details on changing weather, impressive landforms, personal interactions, and humorous incidents. Hardships and difficulties are not ignored, although many memoirs take on a nostalgic tone because they were often written at least thirty years later and reflect a grand adventure that took place when the writers were young adults or even children. Nor are the facts always lacking. A large number of memoirs contain precise information on the routes followed by overland parties.

Such factual information and narrative details are forms of personal elaboration. When presented at length, these facts and details can enrich the account of the overland journey and prove that the narrator has a full story to tell. Some of these elaborations, like the accounts of harsh weather or confrontations with wild animals, may carry on the theme of "conquering the wilderness." In this way, they correlate to the Indian threat as an emblem of pioneer identity.

When the memoirs of Montana pioneers focus on the early years of the mining camps, narrative details and emblematic elements also abound. Pioneers regularly commented on the high price of goods and food. They remembered the difficulty of either finding or building some rude form of housing. They also recalled the excitement created by rumors of new gold strikes in the region and the rushes that followed. These pioneer memoirs also usually contain an account, often at length, of some of the robberies and murders committed by the road agents [bandits] and of some of the trials and hangings carried out by the vigilantes.

Ironically, a history of the vigilantes of Montana had been published well before the upsurge of pioneer memoirs began during the 1890s. Thomas J. Dimsdale, an educated Englishman, had come to Virginia City during the summer of 1863, in part to improve his health. During the winter of 1863–1864, when the vigilance committee carried out its successful six-week campaign against the road agents, Dimsdale taught school and also gave singing lessons. On August 26, 1865, the first of his series of articles appeared in the *Montana Post*. Collected and republished in 1866 as *The Vigilantes of Montana or Popular Justice in the Rocky Mountains*, Dimsdale's writings had the distinction of being the first book published in Montana.

In their memoirs, some Montanans mentioned Dimsdale and his book. Harriet Sanders wrote that she could not end her reminiscences of Virginia City "without making brief mention of Professor Dimsdale." In Conrad Kohrs's 1913 autobiography, the successful cattleman recounted his pursuit of some highwaymen who were later hanged and informed his readers that "The particulars of this execution may be found in Dimsdale's Vigilantes." In the 1920s, when Paul C. Phillips edited the extensive journals of pioneer prospector and latter-day cattleman Granville Stuart, he excluded Stuart's writings on the vigilantes. Phillips noted that Stuart had close associations with Dimsdale as well as with Nathaniel P. Langford, who wrote a second history of the vigilantes in 1890. Phillips concluded that although Stuart in "his last years" wished to retell the vigilante story, "he was influenced

. . . by the writings of his friends to such an extent that his own contribution added little to what had already been published."

These references to Dimsdale demonstrate that published accounts can influence shared memories, just as reminiscences of the overland trails may have been influenced by false reports of Indian massacres in the newspapers and fictionalized presentations of Indian attacks in popular novels. Dimsdale's book, because it appeared so quickly after the actual events, became part of people's memories of those events. But the interconnections are even more fascinating. In all likelihood, Dimsdale talked to Wilbur F. Sanders and Granville Stuart before he wrote his articles. He may even have talked to Conrad Kohrs and Harriet Sanders. No doubt they all read Dimsdale's book, if not his articles in the *Post*. Ultimately, when they wrote memoirs, they could think back both to the events of the day and to the accounts they or their friends had given to Dimsdale. Langford's later book may have replicated this form of double memory. In Wilbur Fisk Sanders's 1913 memoir of the trial of George Ives—an event that brought Sanders early fame and that also precipitated the formation of the vigilance committee— Sanders wrote:

> In fact, the written authorities of Langford and Dimsdale are hearsay, neither one of these gentlemen having been present but their information was gathered from actors in this stirring tragedy, and I consider them reliable.

Although both Dimsdale and Langford relied on the memories of observers from the vigilante days, the accuracy of these books still may be questioned. Each book is an uncritical apology for the vigilantes' actions. Later pioneer reminiscences retain this same attitude and the same possibility for error; and many of them, consciously or not, seem to modify, elaborate, or possibly misrepresent what is found in Dimsdale and Langford. Wilbur Sanders in his memoir, for example, wrote that George Ives tried to compose a letter to his mother and only completed "a half dozen lines" before being hanged. In 1903, Reginald Stanley, in a long reminiscent letter to Sanders's son, James, claimed that Ives's last words were " 'Tell my mother I died an innocent man.' " Neither Wilbur Sanders nor Dimsdale reported these last words, and Dimsdale included no last letter from Ives to his mother. Dimsdale did claim that Ives took off his boots; evidently, Ives had often declared that he would never die with his boots on. Sanders admitted that he had heard this story, but could not remember if it had happened. Stanley made no reference to Ives's boots.

Regardless of the variations on boots, letters, and last words, all three accounts agree that Ives was hanged. Unlike the overland memoirs where Indian attacks may or may not have occured, the memoirs of the mining camps did not include fabricated hangings. Enough occurred at the time. Also, whereas the Indians remained a constant but vague threat—specific tribes or particular warriors rarely being mentioned—the road agents are vividly, even positively, characterized. Reginald Stanley described George Ives as he stood ready for his execution as a "fine handsome young fellow" who was "a born leader of men. . . . he had the making of a hero in him had he taken the right course." Harriet Sanders had a similar opinion of Henry Plummer, the elected sheriff of Bannack who directed the operations of the road agents:

> He [Plummer] was slender, graceful, and mild of speech. He had pleasing manners and fine address, a fair complexion, sandy hair and blue eyes— the last person whom one would select as a daring highwayman and murderer.

Such comments underscore an important aspect of the vigilante story. The road agents were members of the pioneer community. Indians had different racial and cultural characteristics and were perceived as an external threat to the overlanders. Plummer, Ives, and the twenty-three other men hanged by the vigilantes, however, were not that different from their executioners and could have been mistaken on appearances alone as everyday residents of the mining camps.

Surviving the Indian threat had been an emblematic representation of the struggle to bring civilization to the wilderness. The eradication of the road agents continued this theme, but here the threat to civilization was the internal evil of the road agents and not the external wilderness and its native peoples. Ironically, in terms of murderous actions, the internal threat from the road agents had greater factual reality than the often imagined threat of Indian attack. Plummer and his cohorts may have murdered over one hundred people in less than two years.

Outlaws are often viewed as heroes in the folklore and popular literature of the American West. Stories and songs have glorified such figures as Jesse James and Butch Cassidy. These outlaw heroes are presented as good men forced to do wrong. They robbed institutions such as banks and railroads that the singers and storytellers viewed as more evil than the "bad men." As presented in the memoirs of Montana's pioneers, the story of the road agents is very different. These outlaws robbed and murdered the pioneers, so the fellow pioneers who hanged these murderers—the vigilantes—are presented as heroes.

At least one story, the hanging of Captain J. A. Slade, tempers the heroic image of the vigilantes. Slade is not characterized in positive terms. His early murderous career is often stressed, especially his notorious *mementos mori:* the severed ears of a man he killed in Colorado that he carried in his vest pocket. Apparently, Slade's hanging came about because of his bad reputation and his riotous, drunken conduct. Some members of the vigilance committee may have opposed his execution; but according to Dimsdale, a gathering of six hundred miners insisted that the hanging be carried out. In effect, the vigilantes executed Slade because of his *potential* to do evil in the mining camps. Even Reginald Stanley in his hagiographic reminiscence of the vigilantes wrote: "Slade was not a Road Agent."

Linked to memories of Slade's hanging is the story of his wife's daring ride in an attempt to save his life. Harriet Sanders recalled that Mrs. Slade "was a large, fine looking woman of commanding presence. Report says that she did not wait for a saddle but sprang upon her fleet horse, reaching

Virginia [City] in the shortest time possible only to find that her husband was not alive.'' Other accounts reported Mrs. Slade's great grieving over the death of her husband.

The ambivalent attitude evident in these recountings of Slade's hanging may reveal that some pioneers saw both the vigilantes and men like Slade as figures near the social boundary between deviant and acceptable behavior. Whatever the case, the dramatic story of the ride of Slade's wife lends itself easily to variations. In his 1903 memoir, Aaron T. Ford described Mrs. Slade on horseback, arriving too late, but instead of grieving over her husband's hanging, ''she said had she been there she would have killed him before they could hang him.'' Ford believed her capable of this act because she was the ''best shot'' in the area and could ''take a Revolver and shoot a chicken Head off every time.'' David Bailey wrote in his 1905 memoir: ''It was said that Slade's wife, a beautiful woman, a good horse-woman, and an expert shot, dashed into town on her charger during the trial and demanded her husband's release.'' Mrs. Slade's angry pleadings failed, and the hanging went on.

It is too easy to dismiss Ford and Bailey as oldtimers who got the basic story of Slade's hanging wrong. Instead, it is more informative to consider what they have in common with other versions. Each attributes remarkable characteristics to Mrs. Slade; each remembers her daring ride; and each has Slade hanged despite her efforts. In other words, each has the same core to his story as do Sanders and Dimsdale.

The search for the core of a story may not be a familiar task for a historian, but it is for a folklorist. Indeed, folklorists often deal with narrative materials that have many of the same characteristics as pioneer memoirs. Variations in content are expected with folk narratives. In addition, folktales are *not* necessarily false, fictionalized accounts. Factual information can be contained in a folk story just as it may be found in a pioneer memoir. Most importantly, the way that folklorists look at narratives reminds us to consider the larger *context* of the intended audience for whom pioneers wrote their memoirs.

Each memoir tried to tell a personal story. The pioneer's immediate family—grown children and grandchildren—probably made up the primary audience for that story, but there was also a broader audience of fellow pioneers and residents of the local community. Memoirs represented a self-conscious valedictory, a reminiscent summing up of a life. Typically, they were written during the author's later years. Some of the stories in a memoir may have been told numerous times before they were written down. Therefore, they may be the anecdotes and accounts that were most popular among family, friends, and the local community, the groups for whom the memoir was written. In the case of historical events in which others in the audience participated, the chances would increase that the memoir contained reminiscences that represented the knitting together of a collectively remembered past.

The sharing of collective memories also may have created important conceptual boundaries. Folklorist William A. Wilson believes, ''If the story is to live, [the storytellers] cannot, in the telling of it, depart too far from the value center of the audience whose approval they seek." Memoirs may contain such a value center shaped over time through a similar process of interaction with the audience for whom they are ultimately written. In the memoirs of Montana's pioneers, attitudes toward Indians and accounts of the vigilantes do not stray far from the same value center.

The idea of a value center refers to a shared historical perception that is based on what is emotionally believed whether it is factually accurate or not. A people's beliefs about its past are what Wilson calls "people's fact." These beliefs are also part of what historian Carl L. Becker considered "living history." In his essay, "Every Man His Own Historian," Becker maintained, "The history that does work in the world, the history that influences the course of history, is living history, that pattern of remembered events, whether true or false, that enlarges and enriches the collective specious present."

As living history, the memoirs of pioneer Montanans revealed not only what they believed about their past but also what they believed in their present. Stories about Indians on the overland trails and accounts of murders by road agents and hangings by vigilantes indicate attitudes about outsiders and violence prevalent during the 1890s and later, but supposedly remembered from the 1860s. It is worth pondering how such attitudes, which were expressed in a living history, also had become part of the institutions and daily life of post-1890 Montana. Indians remained outsiders to Montana society, often living as a separate people on reservations, and expressions of personal or even corporate violence could be observed in labor relations and political campaigns.

Yet, the value center and living history of Montana's pioneers were not unique. Other memoirs in other western locations readily present an Indian threat on the overland trails or describe the lawlessness of the mining camps. Many California pioneers may have memoirs directly comparable to those in Montana, including accounts of an active vigilance committee in San Francisco.

Beyond their western themes, Montanans' memoirs are indicative of a broadly American process of creating historical identity through an insistence on new beginnings. The American Revolution, the creation of a new nation, and the near cult of the Founding Fathers have been the greatest expressions of this process. In her memoir, Harriet Sanders compared the 1863 arrival of her overland party at Bannack to the 1620 landing of the Pilgrims at Plymouth. Her comparison implied that her group of pioneers had, for Montana, a similar historical significance, but she did not claim the Pilgrims as ancestors of her own "little band." Instead, she saw each group as an example of people who had survived a dangerous journey.

Other pioneers showed the same inclination. They might present a family genealogy or point to historical parallels, but they let Montana history begin with themselves and assumed the status of founders merely by being present at the beginning. But when did the beginning end? The Society of Montana Pioneers, established in 1884, tried to date formally the latest time that an individual could have arrived in the gold camps and still claim to be a "pioneer." The initial deadline was May 26, 1864, before the legal creation of Montana Territory. Eventually, by 1901, the deadline for membership had advanced to December 31, 1868. The search for an appropriate deadline demonstrated the artificiality of trying to define a "pioneer." Nonetheless, it underscored what was also revealed in the memoirs, that two qualifications determined a pioneer: early immigration and long-term residence.

The leaders of early Montana could not exclusively call themselves pioneers. Instead, the term included all survivors of the early days. Ethnocentrism and vigilantism excluded Indians and outlaws, but even deceased residents of the gold camps could be called pioneers in the memories of those who survived. This generous and broad definition incorporated nearly everyone who came to Montana by the 1860s. But when these pioneers arrived, they did not bring a shared identity. This quality had to be created over time and reinforced through shared memories.

The emigrants to the gold camps brought a range of personal histories and cultural heritages. Those who chose to stay would build another layer of identity that could be laminated onto a plurality of identities. This new layer took shape in shared memories, which at their core revealed a striving for social definition and social cohesion. These memories defined temporal as well as social boundaries. They marked the early events and emblematic incidents that formed Montana in its beginning. By presenting native peoples as a threat to their coming to Montana and by remembering outlaws as a threat to their first communities, the pioneers established who they did and did not consider to be "true" Montanans from the early days of the overland journey and the gold camps. Through their collective view of Montana's past, the pioneers created a powerful social identity that in its regional setting had a resonance similar to American nationalism. The pioneers may not have created a "new order for the ages" or "a more perfect Union," but they had in their own memories provided vital beginnings for a new state in what they perceived as a new land.

Custer's Changing Image

PAUL A. HUTTON

Heroes are not born, they are created. Their lives so catch the imagination of their generation, and often the generations that follow, that they are repeatedly discussed and written about. The lives of heroes are a testament to the values and aspirations of those who admire them. If their images change as time passes they may act as a barometer of the fluctuating attitudes of a society. Eventually, if certain attitudes change enough, one

Copyright by Western History Association. Reprinted by permission. The article first appeared as "From Little Bighorn to Little Big Man: The Changing Image of a Western Hero in a Popular Culture," by Paul Andrew Hutton. *Western Historical Quarterly*, 7 (January 1976), 19–44, with some abridgements.

hero myth may replace another. Such is the case with George Armstrong Custer. Once a symbolic leader of civilization's advance into the wilderness, within one hundred years he came to represent the supposed moral bankruptcy of Manifest Destiny.

The historical literature on Custer is voluminous and can be divided into strongly pro or con factions with few moderate voices. Nearly a century of scholarship has resolved little of the controversy surrounding the general or his last campaign, although the latest major scholarly works, Edgar I. Stewart's *Custer's Luck* (1955) and Jay Monaghan's biography, *Custer: The Life of General George Armstrong Custer* (1959), are sympathetic toward the controversial cavalryman. As is often the case, the work of diligent historians seems to have had only marginal effect upon the public mind. Most of the conventional information, or misinformation, about Custer comes from elements of popular culture rather than scholars. It is through novels, motion pictures, newspapers, paintings, television, and mass circulation magazines that one can best trace how the changing image of Custer has partially reflected American opinions and values.

Custer had all the qualities of greatness admired by Americans of the late nineteenth century. A son of the Middle Border, he had firm Anglo-Saxon roots, was born into a modest social position, and rose to be a flamboyant general of extraordinary courage and individualism. He was the perfect hero for a people whose ideal characters were Napoleon and Horatio Alger, Jr. They craved the solace of believing that the individual was all-important, that he could climb to success through his own abilities, and could master other men and his own environment.

Long before his death Custer noted what the people expected of a hero and attempted to conform to that image. As the son of an Ohio blacksmith the young Custer was faced with social and economic barriers to success. He overcame many of these obstacles by obtaining an appointment to West Point in 1857. After squeaking through the academy at the bottom of his class he was thrust into combat at Bull Run. Custer's dominating personality and aggressive spirit won him the admiration of Gen. George McClellan, whom he served as an aide, and then of Gen. Alfred Pleasonton, who promoted him in 1863 from captain to brigadier general. Custer made his debut at Gettysburg sporting a floppy, broad-brimmed hat, crimson scarf, and a black velvet jacket trimmed with gold braid onto which flowed his shoulder-length hair. He had studied the life of Napoleon's flamboyant cavalry leader Murat and understood the usefulness of dramatic flair to impress soldiers and civilians. The press was drawn to him and avidly reported the exploits of the Boy General—he was only twenty-three in 1863. They followed him from charge to charge until he helped cut off Lee's retreat and personally received the white flag at Appomattox. When the war ended he wore the stars of a major general and commanded a division of Philip Sheridan's cavalry.

The army was reorganized after the war, and Custer accepted a commission as lieutenant colonel of the new Seventh Cavalry. Although technically second in command, he actually ran the regiment since the colonels in charge were usually on detached duty. With his bride of two years, Elizabeth Bacon Custer, the new colonel set up headquarters at Fort Riley, Kansas, and began whipping his motley troops into shape. Custer, ever conscious of his image, now adopted the fringed buckskin suit of the frontiersman, but kept his favored wide-brimmed hat and crimson scarf.

In the spring of 1867 the Seventh Cavalry joined the expedition of Gen. W. S. Hancock against Indians of the southern plains who were harassing the crews building the transcontinental railroad. The expedition ended in failure and Custer was court-martialed for being absent without leave to visit his wife during the campaign. He was suspended from rank and pay for one year but was recalled by General Sheridan for a winter campaign in 1868. Along the Washita River in Oklahoma the Seventh Cavalry wiped out the Cheyenne village of Chief Black Kettle. Although some characterized the battle as a massacre, the reputation of Custer and his regiment as great Indian fighters was firmly established in the popular mind.

Throughout the next eight years Custer's name was kept before the public in press accounts of his expeditions into the Yellowstone region and the Black Hills, in his own articles that appeared in *Galaxy* magazine, and in his memoirs, *My Life on the Plains,* published in 1874.

In 1876 Custer became involved in political controversy when his testimony on government corruption before a congressional committee proved embarrassing to President Grant and Secretary of War Belknap. In retaliation Grant stripped Custer of the command of a proposed expedition against renegade Sioux. Only the intercession of Gens. Alfred Terry and Philip Sheridan saved Custer from the humiliation of having his regiment go into battle without him.

The plan of attack required that three columns converge on the region in southern Montana where the Sioux were expected to be. But Custer, often night marching his troops, reached the Indian encampment ahead of the other columns. Disregarding the advice of his scouts, he divided his regiment into three prongs, just as he had done so successfully at Washita, and attacked. But everything went wrong. The center column, under Maj. Marcus Reno, was routed after attacking the Indian village and was saved only by the timely arrival of the left column under Capt. Frederick Benteen. Although firing was heard in the distance and enemy pressure on their position slackened, Reno and Benteen made only one effort to join Custer, even though Benteen had earlier received written orders to do so. When their one effort failed they dug in and withstood two days of Indian siege until General Terry arrived with the main body of troops and the Indians triumphantly withdrew.

They found Custer and his two hundred men scattered along the hills above the Little Bighorn River. The Boy General lay with fifty of his troopers inside a twisted circle of horses just below the crest of the battlefield's highest hill. His once proud regiment was shattered, the victim of the army's ignorance of the size of the enemy force and of his own rash overconfidence.

The mystery and tragedy of Little Bighorn immediately captured the nation's imagination. The press, and especially the papers controlled by

Democrats, turned from singing the praises of the United States on its centennial to singing Custer's praises. With a presidential election coming in November, the battle quickly became a club for the opposition to beat Grant and his faltering party. The *Dallas Daily Herald* may have had problems with its spelling, but its sentiments came across plainly: "Grant exiled Custar and doubtless is glad that fear[less] soldier and unpurchaseable patriot is dead." In the debate over who was to blame for the disaster, the publicity given the battle by the press led to vicious denunciations of almost everyone involved in the campaign, and especially of Grant, Terry, and Reno. The groundwork was then laid for a historical debate unsettled to this day.

The wide press coverage of the battle also created many of the myths that surround the last stand and contributed greatly to Custer's heroic image. The *New York Herald* reported that the troopers had "died as grandly as Homer's demigods." In deference to the democratic tradition the paper noted that "as death's relentless sweep gathered in the entire command, all distinctions of name and rank were blended," but then added that "the family that 'died at the head of their column' will lead the throng when history recalls their deed." Some newspapers were not so generous. The Republican *Chicago Tribune* editorialized that Custer had needlessly brought on the disaster because he "preferred to make a reckless dash and take the consequences, in the hope of making a personal victory and adding to the glory of another charge, rather than wait for a sufficiently powerful force to make the fight successful and share the glory with others." President Grant was just as blunt, telling a reporter that he regarded the battle "as a sacrifice of troops, brought on by Custer himself, that was wholly unnecessary—wholly unnecessary." The official military reports of Terry and Reno echoed Grant.

A hack writer named Frederick Whittaker then appeared on the scene to champion the cause of the "dead lion." Such a champion would seem as necessary to the creation of a hero as the "great man" himself. Many historic characters from the past have had their architects of glory: George Washington had Parson Weems, Paul Revere was selected for immortality by Longfellow, Daniel Boone owes his legend to Timothy Flint and James Fenimore Cooper, Kit Carson was blessed by the writings of John C. Frémont, and Buffalo Bill Cody burst from the fanciful pens of Ned Buntline, Prentiss Ingraham, and John Burke. In that pantheon of mythmakers Whittaker ranks among the best. The dust had barely cleared on the battlefield before Whittaker began work on his biography of Custer. Using newspaper reports and Custer's own writings as his sources, he turned the book out with remarkable speed, publishing it in December 1876. The hero who emerged from the pages of Whittaker's *A Complete Life of Gen. George A. Custer* was a figure of epic proportions, no less than "one of the few really great men that America has produced," and "as a soldier there is no spot on his armor." As might be expected, he was compared favorably to the great Napoleon.

Whittaker's biography was more drama than history and every good drama naturally required villains. There were three in his book: Grant, Reno, and the Sioux warrior Rain-in-the-Face. The author, a Democrat, asserted that Grant wanted to humiliate Custer because of his testimony against Belknap. In Whittaker's eyes the president's revenge proved disastrous, for if Custer had commanded the expedition as originally planned it would have been a success. Furthermore, he stated that "Reno and Benteen would never have dreamed of disobeying their chief, had they not known he was out of favor at court."

This latter charge was widely accepted and repeated. Whittaker made Reno his special target and repeatedly urged his court-martial. Getting no response from the military he turned to Congress and in 1878 managed to get a petition introduced seeking a court of inquiry against Reno. Even though the petition was not voted on, Reno, hounded by Whittaker's accusations, asked President Hayes to appoint a court to investigate the charges against him. Although the military court of inquiry, which met in Chicago for four weeks in 1879, damned Reno with faint praise, Whittaker declared it a whitewash and continued his one-man crusade. Such a crusade, after all, was worth considerable free publicity which aided lagging book sales. The unfortunate Reno, court-martialed twice on other charges, was dismissed from the army in 1879 and died ten years later. To the time of his death he was still attempting to clear his name, but the growing legend was too much for him to fight.

Whittaker discovered his Indian villain, Rain-in-the-Face, in the lurid newspaper reports that followed the slaughter. The story, as reported in the press and repeated by Whittaker, was that Rain-in-the-Face held a grievance against Custer for an 1874 imprisonment and so avenged himself by killing Custer at Little Bighorn and then cutting out his heart. This occurred only after Custer, his pistol empty, fighting "like a tiger . . . killed or wounded three Indians with his saber."

Whittaker's spotless hero, a poor boy who rose through his own efforts to stand in greatness with Napoleon, was finally betrayed by evil politicians and jealous subordinates and died gallantly facing a savage foe. This interpretation, along with numerous factual errors in the book, was repeated over and over in the next fifty years. Popular histories such as D. M. Kelsey's *Our Pioneer Heroes and Their Daring Deeds* (1888), J. W. Buel's *Heroes of the Plains* (1881), John Beadle's *Western Wilds and the Men Who Redeem Them* (1881), and W. L. Holloway's *Wild Life on the Plains and Horrors of Indian Warfare* (1891) followed Whittaker closely and sometimes plagiarized his work.

As important to Custer's growing legend as the bitter work of Whittaker were the loving writings of Mrs. Custer, who devoted the rest of her long life to perpetuating a shining image of her dead husband. Her first book, *Boots and Saddles* (1885), was a great success, selling over twenty-two thousand copies. The reception of that work encouraged her to continue writing, publishing *Tenting on the Plains* in 1887 and *Following the Guidon* in 1890. Custer emerged from her books as a man who found it impossible to hate or hold a grudge, who was devoted to his family, loved children, and who was a great patron of the arts. Although a superb marksman and hunter, he had respect for all living creatures, and although a bold man of action, he was never impetuous, simply quick of mind. In short, he was a saintly hero who was entirely capable of accomplishing all the deeds attributed to him by Whittaker and the pulp writers.

The poets of the day tendered considerable assistance to Mrs. Custer in memorializing her husband. Within twenty-four hours of receiving the news of Custer's fall Walt Whitman had a poetical tribute in the mail, accompanied by his bill for ten dollars. On July 10 the *New York Tribune* published "A Death Song for Custer" (the title was later changed to "Far from Dakota's Canyons").

> Thou of the tawny flowing hair in battle,
> I erewhile saw with erect head, passing ever in
>   front, bearing a bright sword in thy hand,
> Now ending well in death the splendid fever of thy
>   deeds.

It mattered little that Custer's hair was closely cropped before the campaign and that no one carried a saber; these were the props of high drama and would be called into use again and again.

Not to be outdone, Henry Wadsworth Longfellow hurried into print his version of the tragedy, entitled "The Revenge of Rain-in-the-Face."

> "Revenge!" cried Rain-in-the-Face,
> "Revenge upon all the race
>   Of the white chief with yellow hair!"
> And the mountains dark and high
> From their crags reëchoed the cry
>   Of his anger and despair.

The poem proved to be quite popular and the soldier's repeated testimony that Custer's body was found unmutilated could not dispel the myth that Rain-in-the-Face had cut out the general's heart.

In 1887 the *Atlantic Monthly* published "On the Big Horn" by John Greenleaf Whittier in which the poet pleaded for the nation to forget Rain-in-the-Face's past deeds and allow him to enter General Armstrong's Industrial School at Hampton, Virginia.

> The years are but half a score,
> And the war-whoop sounds no more
>   With the blast of bugles, where
> Straight into a slaughter pen,
> With his doomed three hundred men,
>   Rode the chief with the yellow hair.
>
> O Hampton, down by the sea!
> What voice is beseeching thee

For the scholar's lowliest place?
Can this be the voice of him
Who fought on the Big Horn's rim?
Can this be Rain-in-the-Face?

Whittier's efforts were to no avail, and the old warrior was not afforded the blessing of a white education. He eventually met the same fate as many other Indians of note by being displayed as a curio for white audiences. At Coney Island in 1894 a pair of sensation-seeking reporters got him drunk and he "confessed" to his part in the fight. Rain-in-the-Face claimed it was Thomas Custer, the general's brother, he had mutilated. "The long sword's blood and brains splashed in my face . . .," he told them, "I leaped from my pony and cut out his heart and bit a piece out of it and spit it in his face."

The reporters had gotten just what they wanted and published it as documented fact. Rain-in-the-Face had not come to believe the legend but he had come to realize the futility of denying it. Just before his death in 1905 he told a fellow Sioux, Dr. Charles Eastman, that he had done none of the acts attributed to him. "Many lies have been told of me," he said. It was a fitting epitaph.

Unlike Rain-in-the-Face and Reno, William "Buffalo Bill" Cody actively sought identification with the Custer fight and greatly benefited by it. Cody, already immortalized in the dime novels of Ned Buntline and others, had been busy since 1872 inventing the Wild West on eastern stages. Upon receiving word of the Indian war, he closed his show and informed his audience that he was needed far more in the West than on the stage. That was debatable, but the army seemed to want him and he was soon scouting for the Fifth Cavalry. At War Bonnet Creek on July 17, 1876, Cody was given an opportunity to exhibit his prowess as a scout and abilities as a showman when challenged to a duel by the Cheyenne warrior Yellow Hand. Between a line of Indians on the one side and troopers and reporters on the other Cody rode out and promptly shot the Indian. It was quite a sight as the long-haired scout, dressed in a silver trimmed and red sashed suit of black velvet, lifted his fallen foe's topknot and triumphantly proclaimed it to be "the first scalp for Custer!" This accomplishment was worth nearly a column in the *New York Herald*.

Having done his duty, Cody quickly returned to the stage to reenact his duel in *The Red Right Hand; or, Buffalo Bill's First Scalp for Custer*, exhibiting Yellow Hand's scalp to the audiences. It was one of his most successful seasons.

The ever popular dime novel also hlped to identify Cody with Custer. In Prentiss Ingraham's *Buffalo Bill with General Custer* the scout was depicted as the battle's only survivor. Just as fantastic was *Buffalo Bill's Grip; or, Oath-bound to Custer*, in which Cody arrives on the field while the bodies are still warm. Captured by the white renegade who had led the

Sioux against Custer, the scout's life is saved by one of the scores of beautiful Indian girls who have populated our frontier regions since the days of Pocahontas. Upon his escape he engages in a knife duel with Yellow Hand and avenges Custer. Only the most unsophisticated of readers would have accepted the events of the dime novels as fact, but since they were based on historical fact such works aided in the creation of lasting myths.

The last stand itself became a standard attraction in many of the wild west shows. Adam Forepaugh staged "Custer's Last Rally" as part of his show's "Progress of Civilization" pageant. Buffalo Bill, who had exhibited Sitting Bull for a season as Custer's conqueror, used the last stand as his show's climax. Buck Taylor played the general whose tiny group of men were reduced to an ever tightening circle in the middle of the great arena. When the last trooper had fallen the spotlight moved to Buffalo Bill who slowly approached the scene of carnage, removed his hat, and sadly bowed his head. Projected on a screen at the end of the arena were the words, Too Late!

It was only natural that, when the popularity of the wild west shows declined after the first decade of this century, Cody would turn his attention to motion pictures. The early western film was a direct descendant of the wild west show, retaining many of its conventions and stereotypes. Cody's 1913 film effort to recreate the Indian wars was not successful either commercially or artistically, but others were also eager to apply themselves to the task. Custer's last stand became a popular subject on the silent screen. The portrayal of Custer, when character was allowed to intrude, was invariably heroic.

The first Custer film was most likely William Selig's 1909 one-reeler, *Custer's Last Stand*. Thomas Ince's 1912 version of *Custer's Last Fight* concentrated on the Rain-in-the-Face myth and starred Francis Ford as Custer. In that same year D. W. Griffith turned his talent to a loose interpretation of the battle entitled *The Massacre*. Two Custer films, *Campaigning with Custer* and *Camping with Custer,* were released in 1913. Thereafter no Custer movies were made until Marshall Neilan filmed *Bob Hampton of Placer* in 1921. As the fiftieth anniversary of Custer's death approached movie producers commemorated the occasion with a bumper crop of Custer films. J. G. Adophe's 1925 nine-reeler, *The Scarlet West* with Clara Bow and Johnnie Walker, was the first of a string of Custer films, which included *The Last Frontier, With General Custer at Little Big Horn,* and *The Flaming Frontier,* all released in 1926. The last named was billed as the epic of the group and featured Hoot Gibson as its hard riding hero and Anne Cornwall as his sweetheart. Their attempts to warn Custer of the trap awaiting him are foiled by the film's black-mustachioed villain. Dustin Farnum portrayed Custer, who was labeled in the film's advertising as "the bravest man that ever lived." Although commercially successful, *The Flaming Frontier* was the last silent film tribute to Custer.

An event occurred in 1890 that had more influence upon Custer's heroic image than all the dime novels, stage shows, and motion pictures combined.

This was the bankruptcy of John G. Furber's Saint Louis saloon, in which hung Cassily Adams's twelve-by-thirty-two-foot-painting, *Custer's Last Fight*. The Anheuser-Busch Brewing Company acquired the canvas as a creditor's asset and eventually gave to the Seventh Cavalry. Before making this donation the company employed F. Otto Becker of Milwaukee to copy the painting and reduce it to a manageable size for lithography. Becker, however, made numerous changes in Adams's painting so that the end result could easily be accepted as a different work. Adams's painting complied with Whittaker's fanciful account of Custer's death, and the buckskin clad, long-haired soldier was portrayed just as he dispatched the last of three bold warriors who had dared approach him. Rain-in-the-Face was painted aiming his pistol from a safe distance to kill Custer, as hundreds of other warriors advanced in parade ground ranks. Becker retained all the errors of Adams's painting by depicting Custer as long-haired, fighting with a sword, and the last man standing. But he added a greater sense of confusion and carnage by filling the Little Bighorn Valley behind Custer with hordes of Indians rushing in all directions. Custer was portrayed in much the same way as in the Adams version, although with sword upraised instead of in a lunging position. No less than five warriors are dead around the general while four others take aim to kill him. The foreground of the picture is filled with savages hacking and carving at dead or dying troopers. It is not difficult to discern the representatives of progress and civilization in the painting.

The lithograph was copyrighted in 1896 and over 150,000 copies were distributed by the brewing company as an advertising gimmick. Soon it became a standard prop of saloon furnishing and remained so for at least fifty years. Possibly only Gilbert Stuart's *Washington* has been reproduced more, and in that case only because of efforts to put a print in every schoolroom in the country. While the children labored under the dour visage of the nation's father, their elders consumed alcohol and contemplated the nuances of Becker's *Custer's Last Fight*. As Robert Taft aptly stated, the print "has been viewed by a greater number of the lower-browed members of society—and by fewer art critics—than any other picture in American history. Thus Anheuser-Busch was aided in becoming a corporate giant and Custer a heroic legend in a partnership that must rank as one of the great triumphs of American capitalism.

The Becker lithograph became so identified with the last stand that it was repeatedly invoked when someone wanted to instantly convey an image of the battle. Film producers paid particular attention to it. Thomas Ince posed a number of actors in a photographed copy of the Becker lithograph that was released as a still for his 1912 Custer film. As part of prerelease publicity for *They Died with Their Boots On,* Warner Brothers anounced that the last stand in the movie would be carefully based on the picture, a decision which probably contributed to the film's many historical errors. The advertising campaign for the 1951 film, *Little Big Horn,* was based entirely on a reproduction of Becker's print, below which were the words "fifty painted Sioux to every one of their gallant few." The "gallant few" referred to a squad of troopers trying to warn Custer since the general and his last stand were not depicted in the film.

The Adams-Becker version of the last stand was, of course, not the first, and far from the last, painting of the battle. Many early depictions were made to illustrate accounts of the slaughter in newspapers and magazines, and a number, most notably John Mulvaney's epic canvas, were painted for exhibition around the country. Mulvaney's twenty-by-eleven-foot canvas, which depicted a spotlessly attired Custer surrounded by a few kneeling men and encircled by a moving horde of war bonneted savages, was a great commercial success on tour and received laudatory reviews in the press. One such review by Walt Whitman in the August 15, 1881, edition of the *New York Tribune,* clearly shows the nationalistic and chauvinistic manner in which nineteenth-century Americans viewed Custer's stand: "Nothing in the books like it, nothing in Homer, nothing in Shakespeare; more grim and sublime than either, all native, all our own and all fact."

Whitman might well have been speaking of all the Custer paintings that would appear over the next fifty years, for they reflected the high drama and heroic romance of that struggle. In most of them Custer is the dominant figure; usually wielding a saber, his long locks blowing in the wind, standing alone while his comrades kneel at his feet to fire. The dramatic scene would attract artists of all nations and varying degrees of talent, and when a checklist was compiled in 1969 nearly a thousand depictions of the battle were counted. Over the years, even as Custer's public image changed radically, there was no slackening in the production of pictures, not only as paintings, but as book and magazine illustrations, advertisements for motion pictures, pageants, and television programs, comic book illustrations, political and humorous cartoons, posters, play money, bubblegum, greeting, and post cards, record album covers, and advertisements for products ranging from whiskey to children's cereal. Little wonder that Custer's last stand is an event known throughout the western world. . . .

By the time of the fiftieth anniversary of the battle in 1926, the heroic legend of Custer was firmly established. That year saw the release of numerous books, articles, and films based on the Custer story. An observance was held at the Little Bighorn on June twenty-fifth with a number of the surviving antagonists of the battle in attendance. As a large crowd applauded and bands played, an Indian and a white officer shook hands next to Custer's monument, signifying that old wounds had healed. However, a full page spread in the *New York Times* of June 20 testified to the fact that some wounds still festered. Praising Custer's skill and daring, the article blamed his defeat on the hatred of Reno and Benteen and credited the defeat with bringing about the reform of the Indian bureau that Custer had long sought. But the days for such an interpretation were numbered as a changing America began to look anew at its heroes and found many of them lacking.

Biographical writing of the late 1920s and 1930s was dominated by a style called debunking, which sought to correct past errors of interpretation by exposing the clay feet of idols. Blessed with a cynical wisdom evidently obtained in the disillusioning years after the first global war, the debunkers concentrated on the human frailties of previously revered individuals. Considering that even George Washington came under attack in 1926, it is a wonder that Custer escaped scrutiny until 1934 when Frederic Van De Water published *Glory Hunter.*

Van De Water's Custer had little resemblance to the hero of Whittaker or Brady. The new Custer was an immature seeker of fame, a brutal and strict commander, though himself a dangerously insubordinate officer, and one distrusted by most of his officers and men. He had no military talent, his Civil War victories were the result of providence and more cautious subordinates, and his lone victory over the Indians was a massacre. A callous, often sadistic egotist, he alone bore the blame for Little Bighorn, which resulted from a combination of his military ineptitude and headlong pursuit of fame.

The *New York Times,* which eight years before had unlimited praise for Custer, now hailed Van De Water's biography as the definitive book on the subject. As such, the review reflected a growing disenchantment with "an unjust and unhappy Federal [Indian] policy" in particular and military leaders in general. This is not to say that Van De Water's interpretation found universal acceptance. In a long and bitter letter published in *Today* magazine, Gen. Hugh S. Johnson accused the author of muckraking and of stooping to "scalp an heroic warrior found dead on the field of honor." Such complaints were to no avail, however, for the heroic image of Custer was fading before the widely accepted Van De Water version.

On the heels of the Van De Water biography came the first anti-Custer novel, Harry Sinclair Drago's *Montana Road.* In it, a glory-seeking Custer frustrates the efforts of Indian agent Stephen Glen to avoid war. Glen rides with Reno's detachment at Little Bighorn and it is Custer who fails to provide the expected support, not Reno. Drago echoes Van De Water by having the ambitious Custer disregard his scout's advice and foolishly lead his men into a trap.

The motion pictures of the period did not share the debunking spirit of the printed media. The filmmakers, faced with producing for a much wider and often less sophisticated audience than that of the historians and novelists, found it safer to concentrate on swashbuckling adventure than on psychological analysis. Two low budget serials were churned out in the 1930s dealing sympathetically with Custer—*The Last Frontier* (1932) and *Custer's Last Stand* (1936). In 1937 Cecil B. De Mille decided to "do justice to the courage of the Plainsmen of the West" in a film of epic proportions that displayed a remarkable disregard for history. *The Plainsman* told the story of Wild Bill Hickok as scout and peace officer and brought together in one film nearly every cliché associated with the western genre. John Miljan played Custer as a great Indian fighter—cool, courageous, and natty in tailored buckskins. At the last stand he calmly picked off circling redskins until a bullet hit home and, clutching at his heart, he slowly sank alongside the American flag. As for the Indians in the film, they were presented as nothing more than targets. Naturally the movie was an enormous commercial success.

Heroic Custers also appeared in two films that did not concern the Little Bighorn. Ronald Reagan portrayed a soft-spoken, level headed Custer in Warner Brothers' *The Santa Fe Trail* (1940). In it Custer aided Jeb Stuart in halting the misguided schemes of John Brown at Harpers Ferry. The following year Addison Richards as Custer helped Wild Bill Hickok and Calamity Jane clean up the Black Hills in *Badlands of Dakota*.

Hollywood's pro-Custer era was climaxed in 1941 by Raoul Walsh's *They Died with Their Boots On*. The film demonstrated little regard for historical fact in following Custer's career from West Point to Little Bighorn. Errol Flynn's Custer was a spotless knight, a devil-may-care adventurer who loved a fight for a fight's sake, but who, upon seeing the plight of the Indians resulting from government corruption, sacrifices all in an effort to block the plans of railroad tycoons and dishonest politicians. At Little Bighorn Custer knowingly sacrifices his regiment to halt the Indian advance on General Terry's force of infantry. Custer kidnaps the film's villain and on the eve of battle the terrified captive inquires of their destination. "To hell or to glory—it depends on one's point of view," replies Custer. As the villain dies the next day he confesses to Custer that he "was right—about glory." The general had known that all along, and with his troopers dead around him, his pistol empty, his long hair blown by the western breeze, he draws his saber and falls before a charge of mounted warriors.

Although *Life* magazine lamented that the film "glorifies a rash general" and the *New York Times* accused "writers in warbonnets" of scalping history, the movie was a great success. Walsh never intended for the film to reflect historical fact, but rather to reflect how history should have been. The myth had become more important than the reality, and it was the myth that the public wanted to be entertained by and believe in. Coming as it did on the eve of war, and following years of economic depression, the film's portrayal of villainous businessmen and gallant soldiers struck a responsive chord. As the nation reeled from the shock of Pearl Harbor, Wake, and Bataan, it could easily identify with Custer's last stand. Following the fall of Bataan a cartoon in the syndicated "Out Our Way" series illustrated this identification by depicting Custer and his huddled men awaiting the final charge over the verse:

My Country

You can take back
All you've gave me
And you'll never
Hear a yelp
For we've let too
Many heroes die
A-lookin' back
For help.

Ernest Haycox, on the other hand, continued the Van De Water tradition in his novel, *Bugles in the Afternoon* (1944). The story revolves around a disgraced officer attempting to redeem himself and portrays Custer as an irresponsible and often cruel commander who sacrifices his men to advance himself. The novel proved quite popular, being serialized in the *Saturday Evening Post* and then reprinted numerous times in cloth and paper editions.

The first anti-Custer film was John Ford's *Fort Apache* (1948), which changed the locale and names to interpret the Custer story. Henry Fonda played the Custer character, Col. Owen Thursday, as an arrogant, stiff-backed officer contemptuous of his native foe and anxious to regain his Civil War rank of general by some glorious deed. His martinet attitudes antagonize his men, especially his second-in-command, Captain York (John Wayne). His ambition finally leads him to attack a large force of Indians who wipe out his command. Ford, usually a defender of the military and western traditions, had Thursday portrayed as an aberration, representing neither the military nor the government, and thus absolved those groups from blame.

Part of Ford's intent was to convey an idea of the importance of heroes to society. York, now in command, is depicted in the film's last scene discussing an upcoming campaign with a group of reporters. One of them mentions with awe that it must have been an honor to know Thursday. "No man died more bravely," replies York, his voice full of irony, "nor won more honor for his regiment." Another newsman noted that Thursday had become "the hero of every schoolboy in the nation," but that the men who died with him were forgotten. York disagreed, stating that the men live on in the regiment, which was better because of the gallant example set by Thursday. York, who had hated Thursday, realized that society understands little of the true motivation of heroes but still needs to idealize them as figures to emulate. The character of York was obviously based on Captain Benteen, who had expressed the same sentiments, although more bluntly, in an 1879 letter. "Cadets for ages to come will bow in humility at the Custer shrine at West Point," he wrote, "and—if it makes better soldiers and men of them, why the necessity of knocking the paste eye out of their idol?" Ford, like Benteen years earlier, was sensitive to the needs that legends and heroes fill in a society.

The films of the 1950s continued the anti-Custer trend, but for different reasons. The success of Delmar Daves's 1950 film, *Broken Arrow,* which dealt sensitively with the plight of the Indians, proved that a motion picture with Indian heroes could be profitable. It was followed by a number of films which were generally more interested in exploiting a new trend than in righting past wrongs.

In *Sitting Bull* (1954), a film so historically inaccurate it would have made De Mille blush, Douglas Kennedy portrayed Custer as an ambitious, arrogant Indian hater who forces the peace-loving Sioux Chief, Sitting Bull (J. Carrol Naish), into war. The following year a biographical film entitled *Chief Crazy Horse* gave that chief credit for defeating Yellow Hair, although its budget was too small to allow filming of the battle. By 1958 Custer's image had fallen so low that even Walt Disney, as great an upholder of traditional heroes as the movie factories ever produced, turned on him. In *Tonka* (1958), the story of the horse Comanche, the only living creature found on the battlefield, Disney treated Custer as a vain racist. Even the gallant death scenes from *Fort Apache* and *Sitting Bull* were now gone, the Custer of this film being shot early in the battle as he crouched low behind a dead horse. Although perhaps cynically motivated, these films were representative of Hollywood's deepening concern with social problems. They were accepted by a society that had learned in World War II the horrors to which racist dogma could lead, and that was struggling, however timidly, with its own inherent racism.

Custer fared no better with the novelists of the 1950s. In Will Henry's novel, *No Survivors* (1950), Custer was again an incompetent glory hunter but was allowed to redeem himself in the end by realizing his folly (and even dictating a letter during the battle accepting responsibility for the defeat), and then dying gallantly. The same author, writing under the pen name of Clay Fisher, was not so generous in his *Yellow Hair* (1953). Dealing only with Custer's activities on the southern plains, Fisher climaxed his novel with the Washita attack which he characterized as a massacre of innocents.

In the same year Mari Sandoz dealt briefly with Custer in *Cheyenne Autumn,* her tale of the flight of a band of reservation Cheyenne toward their northern homeland. Not only was Washita a massacre, but Sandoz also claimed that the lecherous Custer had bedded the Indian maiden Monahsetah after the battle and that she bore him a son. The story quickly became a popular club with which to beat the Custer legend.

By the time Frank Gruber published *Bugles West* (1954) the glory hunter interpretation was becoming a standard stereotype. His novel had nothing to distinguish it from the others, although his portrait of Reno was sympathetic. As Custer turned from hero to villain it was only natural that Reno would be redeemed. Ken Shiflet's novel, *Convenient Coward* (1961), completed the transformation by having a constantly oppressed Reno as hero and a mentally unstable Custer as his tormentor.

A partisan biography of Reno published in 1966, *Faint the Trumpet Sounds,* told the same story. One of that book's authors, George Walton, along with a great-nephew of Reno and the American Legion, successfully petitioned the army to review the major's dismissal. In May 1967 the army concluded that Reno's dismissal had been "excessive and, therefore, unjust." Reno was restored to rank and given an honorable discharge. Soon after, Reno's body was removed from its unmarked Washington grave and reburied at Custer Battlefield amid much ceremony.

The 1960s gave no respite to the tarnishing of Custer's legend. If the 1950s had seen a budding racial conscience in America, it came to full bloom amid the tumult of the 1960s. The plight of oppressed minorities became the concern of many Americans, and there was no longer room in the pantheon of heroes for those who had engaged in repression. Young people especially began to wonder if the values and heroes of American society were worthwhile and relevant. To an ecology-minded generation the winning of the West became synonymous with environmental exploitation and destruction. The settlement of the frontier was no longer a glorious affair but a murderous conquest accomplished over the dead bodies of innocent Mexicans and Indians. To many, Indian life offered a valid counterculture, a more organic, rational, and natural existence than that of white society. The Vietnam conflict, with its array of political and military blunders, gave rise to a bitter disdain of the military in particular and arrogant leadership in general. By the late 1960s comparisons of the Vietnam War with the Indian wars were becoming commonplace, and Custer, though his image had changed, was still a symbol of those earlier conflicts.

Novelists continued to interpret Custer along the same lines. In William Wister Haines's award winning book, *The Winter War* (1961), the Little Bighorn slaughter is brought on by Custer's "vain stupidity" and flagrant violation of orders. Thomas Berger's *Little Big Man* (1964) portrayed a much more complex Custer than the usual stereotype that had dominated Custer fiction since Van De Water. The book's hero, a frontier Candide named Jack Crabb, starts out hating Custer and attempts to kill him, but finally, after Little Bighorn, gives the dead man a grudging respect. Vain, cruel, and with an irrationality bordering on insanity, Custer leads his men to their deaths in the hope of winning a victory that could lead him to the presidency. In the eyes of Crabb, Custer redeems himself by the strength of his character and the manner of his death. Crabb, who is beside Custer when the general dies, is "imbued with the glory and the tragedy of it all." Upon viewing Custer's body later he concedes the dead man's greatness: "Custer had had to die to win me over, but he succeeded at long last: I could not deny it was real noble for him to be his own monument."

Such sympathies, however limited, were becoming rare. Lewis B. Patten wrote a bitter denunciation of Custer in his novel, *The Red Sabbath* (1968). Once more Custer disobeys orders in his blind search for glory, once more he does not give Reno promised support, and once more he is a cruel and callous commander who sees his men as "tools of his ambition, to be used, dulled, sacrificed and thrown away."

Although television had dealt only sporadically with Custer, a series entitled "Legend of Custer" had a brief run in 1967. The program's producers attempted to exploit one current movement and in the process ran head on into another. Appealing to youth, the show's advertising referred to Custer as a young maverick and a long-haired rebel. The tribal Indian Land Rights Association was not impressed and announced that it would petition in the courts for an injunction against the series, claiming that "glamorizing Custer is like glamorizing Billy the Kid" because Custer "endorsed a policy of genocide and massacred village after village of Indians." *Newsweek* magazine, reporting on the furor, noted that Custer "had a reputation for cruelty" and a habit of wenching Indian maidens. *TV Guide* ran an article criticizing the sympathetic image of Custer presented in the show. All the protests were really not necessary since poor quality doomed the show and it went off the air in mid-season.

Four Custer motion pictures were released in this period, and they also conformed to the popular trend. Columbia's *The Great Sioux Massacre* (1965), focused on the efforts of Major Reno and Captain Benteen to dissuade the ambitious and ruthless Custer from bringing on an Indian war in his efforts to win national recognition. They fail when Custer attacks the Indians at Little Bighorn in the hope of winning a victory that could carry him into the White House. In the same year a thinly disguised portrait of an evil Custer was given by Andrew Duggan in Arnold Laven's *The Glory Guys*.

Robert Siodmak's *Custer of the West* (1968) presented the title character as a mass of complexities and contradictions. Custer (Robert Shaw) was a troubled soldier whose only wish was to do battle, yet who loathed the one-sided conflict on the western plains. Although sympathetic to the Indians' plight, he was willing to butcher them mercilessly on orders from Washington. Torn between his sense of humanity and his duty as a soldier, Custer finally decides to use his popularity to inform the nation of the terrible moral price it must pay to conquer the Indians, but his efforts destroy his military career. Frustrated and embittered, Custer knowingly goes to his doom at Little Bighorn. The film's potential to expose the hypocrisy of American Indian policy as seen through Custer's troubled eyes was lost in a jumbled script and poor editing. The film's mediocrity and the complexities of the main character doomed the film to commercial failure. Nor did this film escape litigation from those opposed to even a semipositive view of Custer. Charles Reno, a grandnephew of Major Reno, claimed that his ancestor was slandered in the film. The court backed the film, but that was about all the support it received.

In 1970 Arthur Penn's *Little Big Man* was released and soon proved an immense success, becoming the second biggest money-maker of the film season. Although the film retained much of the humor of Berger's novel, it had none of its realism or deep sense of irony. By patronizing the Indians the film idealized them beyond recognition, and Custer was played in one-dimensional comic book style as a devil in human form.

Penn makes no pretense of objectivity; he envisions Custer as not only vain and ambitious, but also insane. Custer was "so infatuated with his capacity to win, so racially assured that he belonged to a superior breed" that he led his men into a hopeless trap. Penn uses the film as a vehicle to attack the Vietnam War and the arrogant leadership that he felt led America deeper into an Asian quagmire rather than admit a mistake. Contemporary terms such as "higher moral right" and "legal action" appear. In depicting the Washita massacre Penn concentrates on the slaughter of innocent women and children. As a herd of Indian ponies are killed, Custer comments on his humanity in sparing the Indian women who surrendered since "they breed like rats." At Little Bighorn, with all the evidence pointing to a trap, he charges blindly on rather than "change a Custer decision." The last stand is depicted as a rout with no semblance of order, and Custer, entirely mad, wanders about the battlefield ranting until struck down by Cheyenne arrows. There was to be no glory or redemption for this Custer, only a senseless but well-deserved death. The general, however, is not presented as an aberration, for the soldiers under his command are depicted as being just as cruel and racist as their leader. It is a harsh, ideological portrait, as far removed from reality as the early dime novels, yet it seems to have been widely accepted as historical fact.

The increasing media exposure and growing political power of the Indian rights movement also popularized a negative view of Custer. As white Americans became aware of the gross injustices perpetuated on the Indians it became obvious to them that the man who symbolized the Indian fighter in history must himself have been evil since he carried out an immoral policy. Vine Deloria's plea for Indian equality, *Custer Died for Your Sins,* reinforced that view. Custer, Deloria wrote, "represented the Ugly American of the last century and he got what was coming to him."

After the enormous commercial success of Dee Brown's *Bury My Heart at Wounded Knee* (1971) there was an orgy of publication on Indians, much of it of dubious quality. One such work, *The Memoirs of Chief Red Fox,* announced on the cover of the paperback edition "He's 100 years old. And he can tell you the truth about Custer." It became a national bestseller before being exposed as a plagiarized fraud. Still, it seemed that people had an insatiable appetite for the "truth about Custer" and the terrible things he had done to the Indians. Just as Whittaker had needed Rain-in-the-Face and Reno as villains in his drama of Custer's fall, so now the writers turned on Yellow Hair, also finding it necessary to have a villain to offset their Indian heroes.

In a 1971 *Life* article entitled "The Custer Myth," Alvin Josephy quoted an Idaho Nez Percé who summed up the relationship of Custer to the new writings: "The white man's knowledge of Indians is based on stereotypes and false, prejudiced history. Custer is the best known hero of that myth to the whites. . . . Destroy the Custer myth, the biggest one of all, and you'll start getting an understanding of everything that happened and an end to the bias against the Indian people." Josephy then proceeded to aid in that task by labeling Custer a crazed glory hunter and calling his monument in Montana "a sore from America's past that has not healed." The most striking characteristic of the writers of the late 1960s and early 1970s was their commitment to demythologize Custer and finally expose the truth—as if no one had tried before. . . .

There appears to be a filtering-down process in popular culture whereby interpretation is passed from the more sophisticated medium to the least sophisticated. The comic book, that unsophisticated bulwark of one-dimensional characterization, retained the heroic Custer until the 1970s. Evidence on comics is hard to come by since systematic collections are rare, but those found seem to reflect a definite trend. Custer died with cool bravery facing a savage foe in an issue of *Westerner Comics* (1949), and in two 1950 comics, *Indian Fighter* and *Custer's Last Fight, Massacre at Little Big Horn.* Although a darker side was portrayed in Walt Disney's *Tonka* (1958), Custer was back in full glory the following year in Classics Illustrated's *Story of the Army.* In *Famous Indian Tribes* (1962) rashness was hinted at, but Custer was praised for his courage and skill. In the 1970s the shift of sympathy toward the Indian and the negative popular image of Custer emboldened comic book producers to join in the attack on the general's legend. It was a time of new maturity for comics as they began to deal with a number of social issues. The September 1971 issue of *Rawhide Kid* featured a story, "The Guns of General Custer," in which a racist, sadistic Custer disregards the hero's warning and rides to his doom. Only four years earlier in "Massacre at Medicine Bend," the Rawhide Kid had fought alongside Custer whom he considered the "finest battle commander" he had ever seen. The same portrait of a glory-seeking Custer was repeated in the April 1973 issue of *Star Spangled War*.

The Custer legend has thus been completely reversed. What is extraordinary is that over the entire period, long after the clay feet of the idol were exposed, Custer remains an extremely popular figure. The constant production of books and motion pictures on his life and last battle attest to this continuing public interest. Custer's youth, appearance, flamboyance, and adventurous life during a colorful era have all contributed to his popular appeal, but it was the high drama and intrigue about his death that earned him immortality. While few people know of Custer's Civil War exploits, most Americans recognize Custer's last stand. Battles in which one side has been annihilated have long fascinated mankind, and people of many nations point pridefully to such events in their homeland. The leader of the defeated band is often revered as a national hero while the battle becomes a point of cultural pride, an example of patriotism and sacrifice: Leonidas at Thermopylae, Roland at Roncesvalles, Crockett at the Alamo, or Gordon at Khartoum.

Although the last stand assured continuing fame for Custer, it was not enough to guarantee him a perpetual positive image. As the values of society change so does its vision of its history, and one Custer myth is replaced with another. The collective popular mind is unable or unwilling to deal with the complexities of character; its heroes are pure and its villains are evil with no shading in between. As the American view of militarism and Indians changed, so the view of Custer changed. As society's image of the frontier altered from that of a desert stubbornly resisting the progress of civilization to that of a garden of innocence offering refuge from the decadence of civilization, so the expectations for the western hero changed. The conquering military hero was replaced by the frontiersman or Indian who could live in harmony with nature. Thus, from a symbol of courage and sacrifice in the winning of the West, Custer's image was gradually altered into a symbol of the arrogance and brutality displayed in the white exploitation of the West. The only constant factor in this reversed legend is a remarkable disregard for historical fact.

The Modern Popular Western

MICHAEL T. MARSDEN AND JACK NACHBAR

Few story forms have gone through as many transformations as the Western story, from its origins in the nineteenth century to contemporary variations on classic themes. Over the last seven decades the American Western story has fulfilled more social and cultural functions for its audience than has any other American story form. Indeed, the Western can be seen as a record of America's national self-awareness.

By the mid-1970s, the popular Western in its several forms of print, radio, television and film had just begun to receive the intensity and depth of critical analysis it deserves. There is little doubt that popular Westerns up to that point had not dealt with the historical West as it was, but with the West as we wish it had been. Thus, the evolution of the idealistic Western to the more realistic contemporary one reveals much about the state of American society along the way. The persistence of the Western format, even in its evolved state, indicates American preoccupation with a time of optimism about the American Dream, thus placing the popular Western of both yesterday and today in the American romantic tradition.

Critics are quick to point out a basic flaw in the popular Western—that the authors have used the same basic plots and character types since the beginning days of the genre. What the critics fail to acknowledge is that it is this very repetition of the "formula" that is aesthetically satisfying to audiences. A Western fan, upon hearing or seeing a Western, is like a person meeting an old friend. He simply expects to share old news. John Cawelti has illustrated the viability of this formulaic approach to the study of popular story forms in *The Six-Gun Mystique* and *Adventure, Mystery, and Romance: Formula Stories as Art and Popular Culture*. Both books should be required reading for anyone who attempts critical analysis of the popular arts. . . .

Unlike the Western radio or television series whose popularity waxed and waned according to various media-specific developments, the popular Western novel has enjoyed a consistent and notable following from the nineteenth century to the present. With its foundation firmly in the dime novels, the Wild West shows, the pulps, and the popular Western formula, Western fiction has simply been more fully developed than its counterparts in the other mass media. From its earliest manifestations through the writings of Owen Wister, Zane Grey and Max Brand, the popular Western novel appealed to eastern sensibilities rather than western. Other Western writers, such as Ernest Haycox, Luke Short and Louis L'Amour, weaned the form away from its eastern mindset and planted it more firmly in western soil.

The Western of post–World War II years is marked by two major tendencies. First, because novels, like radio, had to compete against the ever more popular television, like radio they fought back with realistic, tough-minded content. However, despite changes in content, the tone has continued to be romantic and idealized. The contemporary Western novel thus strikes a precarious balance between the audience's need for realism

"The Modern Popular Western: Radio, Television, Film and Print," by Michael T. Marsden and Jack Nachbar from *A Literary History of the American West,* 1263–1280, with some abridgements. Reprinted Courtesy of Western Literature Association and Texas Christian University Press.

and romanticism; however gritty the plot becomes, the results remain hopeful and optimistic.

The second major distinguishing characteristic of the postwar Western is its emphasis on reality of setting. What Western writers and Western readers are interested in is a good story which not only entertains but also informs them about the American West. In his fine study *The Dime Novel Western,* Daryl Jones notes that the late nineteenth-century public grew less and less tolerant of the increasing sexual and violent content of many of the dime novels, whose sales fell off notably. The Western story, in fact, seems to have gone through several cycles of birth, sordid adulthood, and rebirth during its one hundred and fifty-plus years of existence. Jones quite accurately pinpoints the popular appeal of the "cleansed" Western story:

> That we are still reluctant today to abandon our vision of an ideal world, a moment's glance at a newsstand, a theater marquee, or a television program guide will instantly confirm. The medium has changed, but the popular Western lives on. To be sure, the message is neither so simple nor so reassuring as it once was. With the advance of the twentieth century have come cultural and world-wide dilemmas which have brought about significant alterations on the familiar formula. . . . Altered, inverted, even parodied, the popular Western formula nonetheless survives. And it will continue to survive as long as it extends to humanity some glimmer of hope that a golden age still lies ahead.

The modern popular Western, like its early predecessors, views the American West as a "golden age" which did not allow spiritual or physical weaknesses among the survivors. The heroes of the modern Western, however, can be philosophers on the range, men used to wrestling with ideas as well as cows, like those found in the novels of Ernest Haycox. Haycox, like a number of his contemporaries in the post-1930 period, added a historical dimension to some of his Westerns which, while heightening the realism, did not diminish the idealism. The author of twenty-four novels from the late '30s to early '50s, Haycox penned several classic Westerns, including *Trouble Shooter, The Border Trumpet, Alder Gulch, Bugles in the Afternoon,* and *The Earthbreakers.* Henry Wilson Allen in his "Will Henry" Westerns followed in the same tradition. In his *Maheo's Children,* the Sand Creek massacre plays a prominent role in the plot, and his *From Where the Sun Now Stands* depicts the annual trek of the Nez Perce Indians to follow the buffalo. Luke Short also wrestled with the realities of the West in his works of romance. In *Paper Sheriff,* which is considered one of his best Westerns, the focus is on the importance of "group needs over individualistic interests," a theme which marks a certain maturity of the Western formula. The emphasis on the historical West in each of their works allowed these writers to meet effectively the changing needs of the audience by providing them with hard information about the West, while at the same time engaging them in a romance. This compromise is not without its price, however. Paperback Westerns, which had been a staple of the publishing industry for more than three decades, have begun to decline in popularity. In 1975, for example, only sixty-five new paperback Westerns were published out of a total of 177 which were distributed; the other 112 were reissues.

The most dominant type of Western on the newsstands at present is the adult Western series, which does not exclude sex and violence. George G. Gilman's "Edge" series, Jake Logan's "Slocum" series, and Tabor Evans's "Longarm" series are only three of the many adult Western series now commanding an impressive part of the popular Western marketplace, leaving the casual peruser of the paperback racks with the impression that in the Western market the only competition adult Westerns have are reissues, or Louis L'Amour's novels. While adult Westerns do not seem to be consistent with the mainstream popular Western tradition, at least one critic, Gary Hoppenstand, has suggested that rather than a "bizarre outgrowth of the genre," adult Westerns might be an evolution of the approach of the Western romance towards sex and violence. He argues that the sex and violence of the adult Western series have been there all along—they have simply been more fully developed in this stage of the Western romance's evolution.

While other writers like Jack Schaefer, whose *Shane* helped to elevate the Western paperback to new levels of respectability, deserve serious analysis as well, perhaps the most representative author of the mainstream popular Western tradition is the best-selling and prolific Louis L'Amour, who has been ranked by *Saturday Review* as the third top-selling writer in the world. L'Amour clearly believes in a responsible and responsive West populated by the restrained and civilized. He has a considerable talent for perceiving the needs and interests of his audience and, after three decades of writing Western novels, has been able to establish his own genre against which the works of other popular Western writers are judged. L'Amour has developed a strong, personal relationship with many of his readers. He writes:

> As for myself, whatever else I may be I am a storyteller. I see myself as carrying on the story of my people just as the shanachies in Ireland and the Druids before them, and as Homer did in Greece. . . .
>
> Telling stories is my way of life. . . . My intention has always been to tell stories of the frontier, the sort of stories I heard when growing up.

L'Amour's fiction can be used as a touchstone for the modern popular literary Western because of its universal appeal and continuing success in the marketplace. In addition to providing his audience with enjoyable stories, he also provides them with a popular history of the settlement of America by focusing on family dynasties, vernacular architecture, the cultural history of the American Indian, women's roles on the American frontier, cowboy customs, and myriad other details of nineteenth-century American life.

From the 1950s *Hondo* to his most recent Sackett novel, Louis L'Amour's works remain convincing examples of the viability of the mainstream popular Western story, presenting the historical West in something like an oral tradition. But the successes of the adult Western series also serve as convincing examples of what many perceive to be the evolution of the Western story form into a distinctly different type of story. Still others perceive the two forms, the mainstream popular Western story and the adult Western series, as linked in an evolutionary process where the latter is developing elements already present in the former. Whatever the specific form or forms the popular Western story takes, it seems reasonable to suggest that it will continue to remain a strong force in the popular literary marketplace. One possible explanation for the longevity of the popular Western story in its many forms is that writers like Ernest Haycox, Luke Short, and Louis L'Amour are really telling versions of one, long epic tale unfolded over an extended period of time through the efforts of a number of skilled storytellers.

The death of John Wayne, the movies' greatest Western star, symbolically suggests a place to mark the demise of the modern popular Western. By that date, hoofbeats on the radio had been silent for a generation. Both the film and television media had become incapable of producing a Western hit. Even the long-lived Western novel showed signs of aging. However, though the popularity of the Western theme has declined, its struggle to maintain a place in American life has brought about a thematic maturity and dignity to the popular Western formula. Where early or "classic" Westerns had affirmed the European-American taking and taming of the West, modern Westerns often did not. Radio and television Westerns such as *Gunsmoke* sometimes suggested that pioneering could mean no more than a slow death on a barren prairie. Movies often explored the negative side of the settlement of the West, such as the pathology behind much outlaw violence and the racism at the heart of the Indian wars. Even Western novels, the form that most strongly retained the values of "classic" Westerns, moved in the direction of stronger characterization and a closer fidelity to historical accuracy.

During the 1980s the formula Western refuses to pass completely from the scene. Western novels stubbornly maintain their slots in paperback book racks. Just as significant, perhaps, is the persistence of images from popular Westerns in the media. Popular music stars such as Willie Nelson and Waylon Jennings still sell millions of records featuring songs about cowboys. During the early '80s, Western-style bars and cowboy clothes were a billion-dollar fad. On television, ads for chewing tobacco, gum, beer, after-shave lotion and numerous other products all ride into American homes on the shoulders of popular Western heroes. The continuing presence of these images suggests the remaining, latent attraction of the popular Western. When the national mood changes and is again receptive to frontier stories, it is not unlikely that a third significant period of popular Western storytelling will engage America's national imagination.

Y *F U R T H E R   R E A D I N G*

Robert G. Athearn, *The Mythic West in Twentiety-Century America* (1986)
Susan Armitage, "Women and Men in Western History: A Stereoptical Vision,"
     Western Historical Quarterly, 16 (1985), 381–95

Gretchen M. Bataille and Charles L. P. Silet, eds., *The Pretend Indians: Images of Native Americans in the Movies* (1980)

Ray Allen Billington, *Land of Savagery, Land of Promise: The European Image of the American Frontier* (1981)

Patricia Janis Broder, *The American West: The Modern Vision* (1984)

Jenni Calder, *There Must Be a Lone Ranger: The American West in Film and in Reality* (1975)

Richard Etulain, *The Popular Western: Essays toward a Definition* (1974)

Philip French, *Westerns: Aspects of a Movie Genre* (1974)

Edwin Fussell, *Frontier American Literature and the American West* (1965)

Dawn Glanz, *How the West Was Drawn: American Art and the Settling of the Frontier* (1982)

William H. Goetzmann and William N. Goetzmann, *The West of the Imagination* (1986)

Charles W. Harris and Buck Rainey, *The Cowboy: Six-Shooters, Songs, and Sex* (1976)

Annette Kolodny, *The Land Before Her: Fantasy and Experience of the American Frontiers, 1630–1860* (1984)

Patricia Nelson Limerick, *Desert Passages: Encounters with the American Deserts* (1985)

Leo Marx, *The Machine in the Garden: Technology and the Pastoral Ideal in America* (1964)

John R. Milton, *The Novel of the American West* (1980)

Rita Parks, *The Western Hero in Film and Television: Mass Media Mythology* (1982)

Earl Pomeroy, *In Search of the Golden West: The Tourist in Western America* (1957)

Joseph C. Porter, "The End of the Trail: The American West of Dashiell Hammett and Raymond Chandler," *Western Historical Quarterly*, 6 (1975), 411–24

John T. Reid, *Spanish American Images of the United States, 1790–1960* (1977)

Cecil Robinson, *Mexico and the Hispanic Southwest in American Literature* (1977)

William W. Savage, Jr., *The Cowboy Hero: His Image in American History and Culture* (1979)

Paul Seydor, *Peckinpah: The Western Films* (1980)

Richard Slotkin, *The Fatal Environment: The Myth of the Frontier in the Age of Industrialization* (1985)

Henry Nash Smith, *Virgin Land: The American West as Symbol and Myth* (1950)

C. L. Sonnichsen, *From Hopalong to Hud: Thoughts on Western Fiction* (1978)

Kent Ladd Steckmesser, *The Western Hero in History and Legend* (1965)

——, *Western Outlaws: The "Good Badman" in Fact, Film, and Folklore* (1983)

G. Edward White, *The Eastern Establishment and the Western Experience: The West of Frederick Remington, Theodore Roosevelt, and Owen Wister* (1969)

Will Wright, *Six-guns and Society: A Structural Study of the Western* (1975)

CHAPTER
12

Cultural Complexities

Y

The cultural pluralism of the West's population has grown more diverse in the one hundred and forty years since the California gold rush. In terms of immigration and population growth, California has become the most dramatic story since World War II. Today it has the largest state population in the country. Peoples from Southeast Asia, the islands of the Pacific, Central America, the Middle East, and seemingly every other region of the world have helped make California the state with the largest population in the nation. Yet the older Indian and Hispanic cultures that inhabited the Far West before 1848 have not been submerged under the waves of new arrivals. In fact, the cultural identity and political activity of Native Americans and Mexican-Americans have been revitalized during the last twenty-five years. Why new peoples appear in great numbers and why older peoples refuse to disappear are both aspects of the present-day cultural complexity of the American West.

Y D O C U M E N T S

The first selection consists of three tables drawn from the 1980 United States last census. The first table examines four urban counties in California, including Alameda for the Oakland area. The last two illuminate the diversity and mobility of people in the states west of the Mississippi River.

The next four documents reveal the political attitudes of Mexican-American activists. The second document, *El Plan de Delano,* is a manifesto released in 1966 during the height of the Delano grape strike and national boycott. It helped greatly to increase public awareness of the National Farmworkers' Association, led by César Chávez. The third document has a militant separatist tone. It was released in 1969 by the Chicano Liberation Youth Conference in Denver, Colorado, which had three thousand participants. This gathering was initiated by Corky Gonzalez through his organization, Crusade for Justice. The following selection provides another militant political statement about the rights of undocumented aliens. It was released in 1977 by the California Conference on Immigration and Public Policy. Finally, a western historian, Patricia Nelson Limerick of the University of Colorado, wrote a brief editorial, reproduced as the fifth document, for the national newspaper *USA Today* in 1985. In it she argues against the official stance of the government that immigration across the southwestern border from Mexico to the United States has gotten out of control; her position is that the border has never been controlled.

The last three documents consider American Indian activism. Compare the 1969 National Indian Youth Council *Statement of Policy* to the document from the Chicano Liberation Youth Conference of the same year. The National Indian Youth Council had existed since 1961. Members participated in several demonstrations, including the occupation of Alcatraz Island in 1964 and 1969. Ramona Bennett, who had been a Puyallup Tribal Council Member, and Gerald Wilkinson, a Cherokee-Catawba who served as executive director of the National Indian Youth Council, participated in the Red Power activism of the 1960s and 1970s. Their recollections, delivered at a national conference on Indian self-rule held in 1983 at Sun Valley, Idaho, are reprinted as the seventh document. At that same conference, Philip S. Deloria, a Standing Rock Sioux and the director of the American Indian Law Center in Albuquerque, New Mexico, presented some ideas about federal policy that he hoped President Ronald Reagan would consider; they appear here as the eighth selection. Bennett, Wilkinson, and Deloria demonstrate that American Indians are willing to take action to secure the survival of their societies.

Selected Statistics of Western Population, 1980: Three Tables

Table 1 Population, Race and Mobility: Four Urban Counties of California

STATE AND COUNTY	LAND AREA 1980 (SQ. MI.)	POPULATION, 1980				
		TOTAL PERSONS	PERCENTAGE CHANGE 1970–1980	PER SQUARE MILE	PERCENTAGE URBAN	MALES PER 100 FEMALES
California	156,299	23,667,902	18.5	151.4	91.3	97.2
Alameda	736	1,105,379	3.2	1,501.1	98.9	94.6
Los Angeles	4,070	7,477,503	6.2	1,837.2	98.9	95.3
San Diego	4,212	1,861,846	37.1	442.1	93.2	103.6
San Francisco	46	678,974	−5.1	14,636.2	100	99.1

RACE (PERCENTAGE)					MOVERS, 1975–1980 (PERCENT)		
White	Black	American Indian, Eskimo, and Aleut	Asian and Pacific Islander	Spanish Origin (Percent)	SAME COUNTY	DIFFERENT COUNTY, SAME STATE	DIFFERENT STATE OR ABROAD
76.99	7.68	0.98	5.55	19.19	30.2	12.1	13.2
67.83	18.43	0.75	8.04	11.73	29.6	11.5	11.2
68.68	12.61	0.73	6.11	27.62	34.9	3.7	13.4
81.93	5.61	0.88	5.11	14.75	31.2	9.6	21.8
59.23	12.69	0.53	21.98	12.40	25.1	8.7	18.4

Table 2 Western Population by Race

REGION, DIVISION AND STATE	MALES PER 100 FEMALES 1980	WHITE 1980 TOTAL (× 1,000)	BLACK 1980 TOTAL (× 1,000)	AMERICAN INDIAN, ESKIMO, AND ALEUT, 1980	ASIAN AND PACIFIC ISLANDER, 1980	PERCENTAGE OF TOTAL, 1980			
						WHITE	BLACK	INDIAN	ASIAN
United States	94.5	188,372	26,495	1,420,400	3,500,439	83.1	11.7	0.62	1.54
West North Central	95.0	16,044	789	142,486	87,006	93.4	4.6	0.82	0.50
Minnesota	96.1	3,936	53	35,016	26,536	96.6	1.3	0.85	0.65
Iowa	94.6	2,839	42	5,455	11,577	97.4	1.4	0.18	0.39
Missouri	92.7	4,346	514	12,321	23,096	88.4	10.5	0.25	0.46
North Dakota	101.3	626	3	20,158	1,979	95.8	0.4	3.08	0.30
South Dakota	97.3	640	2	44,968	1,738	92.6	0.3	6.50	0.25
Nebraska	95.3	1,490	48	9,195	7,002	94.9	3.1	0.58	0.44
Kansas	95.9	2,168	126	15,373	15,078	91.7	5.3	0.65	0.63
West South Central	95.8	18,599	3,527	231,027	168,107	78.3	14.9	0.97	0.70
Arkansas	93.5	1,890	374	9,428	6,740	82.7	16.3	0.41	0.29
Louisiana	94.2	2,912	1,238	12,065	23,779	69.2	29.4	0.28	0.56
Oklahoma	95.4	2,598	205	169,459	17,275	85.9	6.8	5.60	0.57
Texas	96.8	11,198	1,710	40,075	120,313	78.7	12.0	0.28	0.84
West	98.0	34,890	2,262	720,739	2,080,869	80.8	5.2	1.66	4.81
Mountain	98.7	9,961	269	364,381	98,433	87.6	2.4	3.20	0.86
Montana	99.6	740	2	37,270	2,503	94.1	0.2	4.73	0.31
Idaho	99.7	902	3	10,521	5,948	95.5	0.3	1.11	0.62
Wyoming	105.0	446	3	7,094	1,969	95.1	0.7	1.51	0.41
Colorado	98.5	2,571	102	18,068	29,916	89.0	3.5	0.62	1.03
New Mexico	97.2	978	24	106,119	6,825	75.0	1.8	8.13	0.52
Arizona	96.9	2,241	75	152,745	22,032	82.4	2.8	5.61	0.81
Utah	98.4	1,383	9	19,256	15,076	94.6	0.6	1.31	1.03
Nevada	102.4	700	51	13,308	14,164	87.5	6.4	1.66	1.77
Pacific	97.8	24,929	1,993	356,358	1,982,436	78.4	6.3	1.12	6.23
Washington	98.7	3,779	106	60,804	102,537	91.5	2.6	1.47	2.48
Oregon	97.0	2,491	37	27,314	34,775	94.6	1.4	1.03	1.32
California	97.2	18,031	1,819	201,369	1,253,818	76.2	7.7	0.85	5.29
Alaska	112.8	310	14	64,103	8,054	77.1	3.4	15.94	2.00
Hawaii	105.2	319	17	2,768	583,252	33.0	1.8	0.28	60.33

Table 3   Spanish Origin, Ancestry, Languages Spoken, and Place of Birth

| REGION, DIVISION, AND STATE | PERSONS OF SPANISH ORIGIN, 1980 TOTAL (× 1,000) | PERCENTAGE OF TOTAL 1980 | PERCENTAGE LEADING ANCESTRY GROUP 1980 | PERCENTAGE LEADING SINGLE ANCESTRY GROUP 1980 | PERCENTAGE SPEAKING OTHER THAN ENGLISH AT HOME 1980 | BORN OUTSIDE OF STATE OF RESIDENCE (PERCENTAGE) | PLACE OF BIRTH, 1980 | | | |
| | | | | | | | FOREIGN COUNTRY | | LEADING COUNTRY OF ORIGIN | |
							NUMBER (× 1,000)	PERCENTAGE OF TOTAL POPULATION	COUNTRY	PERCENTAGE OF FOREIGN BORN
United States	14,609	6.4	EN-26.3	EN-12.6	11.0	36.1	14,080	6.2	Mexico	15.6
West North Central	209	1.2	GN-46.4	GN-20.3	4.6	28.3	344	2.0	Germany	12.2
Minnesota	32	0.8	GN-47.5	GN-19.0	5.6	25.1	107	2.6	Canada	11.4
Iowa	26	0.9	GN-52.7	GN-23.7	3.4	22.4	48	1.6	Germany	13.7
Missouri	52	1.1	GN-39.8	GN-16.0	3.1	29.9	86	1.7	Germany	14.1
North Dakota	4	0.6	GN-50.3	GN-27.9	11.3	27.1	15	2.3	Canada	23.3
South Dakota	4	0.6	GN-51.8	GN-28.7	7.8	29.3	10	1.4	Germany	13.8
Nebraska	28	1.8	GN-51.5	GN-25.1	4.8	29.8	31	2.0	Germany	15.0
Kansas	63	2.7	GN-43.1	GN-18.5	4.7	37.0	48	2.0	Mexico	14.1
West South Central	3,160	13.3	EN-28.3	EN-15.6	15.5	30.8	1,020	4.3	Mexico	49.6
Arkansas	18	0.8	EN-38.0	EN-25.2	1.8	30.8	22	1.0	Germany	14.2
Louisiana	99	2.4	FR-28.5	A-A-27.4	10.0	21.9	86	2.0	Vietnam	10.7
Oklahoma	57	1.9	EN-35.4	EN-17.7	4.0	37.0	56	1.9	Germany	12.0
Texas	2,986	21.0	EN-27.0	MX-20.9	21.8	32.2	856	6.0	Mexico	58.2
West	6,254	14.5	EN-27.3	EN-10.5	17.9	54.7	4,565	10.6	Mexico	31.5
Mountain	1,443	12.7	EN-33.1	EN-14.4	14.6	55.9	485	4.3	Mexico	27.6
Montana	10	1.3	GN-37.4	GN-15.9	5.2	43.0	18	2.3	Canada	25.7
Idaho	37	3.9	EN-43.3	EN-21.4	5.6	50.9	23	2.5	Mexico	26.2
Wyoming	24	5.2	GN-34.9	GN-15.9	6.3	61.3	10	2.0	Mexico	16.3
Colorado	340	11.8	GN-34.3	GN-12.2	10.6	58.3	114	3.9	Mexico	14.8
New Mexico	477	36.6	S/H-25.1	S/H-22.2	37.8	48.2	52	4.0	Mexico	47.9
Arizona	441	16.2	EN-27.7	MX-14.4	20.1	67.0	163	6.0	Mexico	43.6
Utah	60	4.1	EN-60.9	EN-31.2	7.4	33.7	50	3.5	Germany	11.8
Nevada	54	6.7	EN-30.0	EN-11.6	9.7	78.6	54	6.7	Mexico	15.7
Pacific	4,811	15.1	EN-25.3	MX-11.4	19.1	54.2	4,080	12.8	Mexico	32.0
Washington	120	2.9	EN-32.1	EN-10.3	6.9	52.0	239	5.8	Canada	19.6
Oregon	66	2.5	EN-34.8	EN-12.3	5.4	55.7	108	4.1	Canada	17.6
California	4,544	19.2	EN-23.8	MX-14.7	22.6	54.7	3,580	15.1	Mexico	35.7
Alaska	10	2.4	GN-24.3	EN-10.9	12.5	68.0	16	4.0	Canada	14.6
Hawaii	71	7.4	JA-27.3	JA-23.9	25.8	42.2	137	14.2	Philippines	42.7

Note: A-A = Afro-American, S/H = Spanish/Hispanic, EN = English, GN = German, FR = French, JA = Japanese, MX = Mexican

The National Farmworkers' Association
El Plan de Delano, 1966

We, the undersigned, gathered in pilgrimage to the capital of the state in Sacramento, in penance for all the failings of farmworkers as free and sovereign men, do solemnly declare before the civilized world which judges our actions, and before the nation to which we belong, the propositions we have formulated to end the injustice that oppresses us.

We are conscious of the historical significance of our pilgrimage. It is clearly evident that our path travels through a valley well known to all Mexican farmworkers. We know all of these towns of Delano, Fresno, Madera, Modesto, Stockton, and Sacramento, because along this very same road, in this very same valley, the Mexican race has sacrificed itself for the last hundred years. Our sweat and our blood have fallen on this land to make other men rich. Our wages and working conditions have been determined from above, because irresponsible legislators who could have helped us have supported the rancher's argument that the plight of the farmworker was a "special case." They saw the obvious effects of an unjust system, starvation wages, contractors, day hauls, forced migration, sickness, and subhuman conditions.

The farmworker has been abandoned to his own fate—without representation, without power—subject to the mercy and caprice of the rancher.

We are suffering. We have suffered unnumbered ills and crimes in the name of the law of the land. Our men, women, and children have suffered not only the basic brutality of stoop labor, and the most obvious injustices of the system; they have also suffered the desperation of knowing that that system caters to the greed of callous men and not to our needs.

Now we will suffer for the purpose of ending the poverty, the misery, and the injustice, with the hope that our children will not be exploited as we have been. They have imposed hungers on us, and now we hunger for justice. We draw strength from the very despair in which we have been forced to live. WE SHALL ENDURE!

This pilgrimage is a witness to the suffering we have seen for generations. The penance we accept symbolizes the suffering we shall have in order to bring justice to these same towns, to this same valley. This is the beginning of a social movement in fact and not in pronouncements.

We seek our basic God-given rights as human beings. Because we have suffered—and are not afraid to suffer—in order to survive, we are ready to give up everything, even our lives, in our fight for social justice. We shall do it without violence because that is our destiny.

To the ranchers and to all those who oppose us we say, in the words of Benito Juárez, "Respect for another's rights is the meaning of peace."

We seek the support of all political groups, and the protection of the

From *The Chicanos: Life and Struggle of the Mexican Minority in the United States,* 107–110, by Gilberto Lopez y Rivas. Copyright © 1973 by permission of Monthly Review Foundation.

government, which is also our government. But we are tired of words, of betrayals, of indifference. To the politicians we say that the years are gone when the farmworker said nothing and did nothing to help himself. From this movement shall spring leaders who shall understand us, lead us, be faithful to us, and we shall elect them to represent us. We shall be heard!

We seek, and have, the support of the Church in what we do. At the head of the pilgrimage we carry the Virgin of Guadalupe because she is ours, all ours, Patroness of the Mexican people. We also carry the Sacred Cross and the Star of David because we are not sectarians, and because we ask the help and prayers of all religions. All men are brothers, sons of the same God; that is why we say to all men of good will, in the words of Pope Leo XIII, "Everyone's first duty is to protect the workers from the greed of speculators who use human beings as instruments to provide themselves with money. It is neither just nor human to oppress with excessive work to the point where their minds become enfeebled and their bodies worn out." God shall not abandon us!

We shall unite. We have learned the meaning of unity. We know why these United States are just that—united. The strength of the poor is also in union. We know that the poverty of the Mexican or Filipino worker in California is the same as that of all farmworkers across the country, the Negroes and poor whites, the Puerto Ricans, Japanese and Arabians; in short, all of the races that comprise the oppressed minorities of the United States. The majority of the people on our pilgrimage are of Mexican descent, but the triumph of our race depends on a national association of farmworkers. We must get together and bargain collectively. We must use the only strength that we have, the force of our numbers; the ranchers are few, we are many. United we shall stand!

We shall pursue the Revolution we have proposed. We are sons of the Mexican Revolution, a revolution of the poor seeking bread and justice. Our revolution shall not be an armed one, but we want the order which now exists to be undone, and that a new social order replace it.

We are poor, we are humble, and our only choice is to strike in those ranches where we are not treated with the respect we deserve as working men, where our rights as free and sovereign men are not recognized. We do not want the paternalism of the ranchers; we do not want the contractor; we do not want charity at the price of our dignity. We want to be equal with all the working men in the nation; we want a just wage, better working conditions, a decent future for our children. To those who oppose us, be they ranchers, police, politicians, or speculators, we say that we are going to continue fighting until we die, or we win. We shall overcome!

Across the San Joaquin Valley, across California, across the entire Southwest of the United States, wherever there are Mexican people, wherever there are farmworkers, our movement is spreading like flames across a dry plain. Our pilgrimage is the match that will light our cause for all farmworkers to see what is happening here, so that they may do as we have done.

The time has come for the liberation of the poor farmworker. History is on our side. May the strike go on! Viva la causa!

The Chicano Liberation Youth Conference's
El Plan Espiritual de Aztlán, 1969

In the spirit of a new people that is conscious not only of its proud historical heritage, but also of the brutal "Gringo" invasion of our territories: We, the Chicano inhabitants and civilizers of the northern land of Aztlan, from whence came our forefathers, reclaiming the land of their birth and consecrating the determination of our people of the sun, declare that the call of our blood is our power, our responsibility, and our inevitable destiny.

We are free and sovereign to determine those tasks which are justly called for by our house, our land, the sweat of our brows and by our hearts. Aztlan belongs to those who plant the seeds, water the fields, and gather the crops, and not to the foreign Europeans. We do not recognize capricious frontiers on the Bronze Continent.

Brotherhood unites us and love for our brothers makes us a people whose time has come and who struggle against the foreigner "Gabacho," who exploits our riches and destroys our culture. With our heart in our hands and our hands in the soil, We Declare the Independence of our Mestizo Nation. We are a Bronze People with a Bronze Culture. Before the world, before all of North America, before all our brothers in the Bronze Continent, We are a Nation, We are a Union of free pueblos, We are Aztlan. . . .

Aztlan, in the Nahuatl tongue of ancient Mexico, means "the lands to the north." Thus Aztlan refers to what is now known as the southwestern states of this country.

El Plan espiritual de Aztlan sets the theme that the Chicanos (La Raza de Bronze) must use their nationalism as the key or common denominator for mass mobilization and organization. Once we are committed to the idea and philosophy of El Plan de Aztlan, we can only conclude that social, economic, cultural, and political independence is the only road to total liberation from oppression, exploitation and racism. Our struggle then must be the control of our barrios, campos, pueblos, lands, our economy, our culture, and our political life. El Plan commits all levels of Chicano society— the barrio, the campo, the ranchero, the writer, the teacher, the worker, the professional—to la Causa.

I. Punto Primero: Nationalism

Nationalism as the key to organization transcends all religious, political, class, and economic factions or boundaries. Nationalism is the common denominator that all members of La Raza can agree upon.

II. Punto Segundo: Organization Goals

1. Unity in thought of our people concerning the barrios, the pueblo, the campo, the land, the poor, the middle class, the professional is committed to liberation of La Raza.

2. Economy: economic control of our lives and our communities can only come about by driving the exploiter out of our communities, our pueblos, and our lands and by controlling and developing our own talents, sweat, and resources. Cultural background and values which ignore materialism and embrace humanism will lend to the act of cooperative buying and distribution of resources and production to sustain an economic base for healthy growth and development. Lands rightfully ours will be fought for and defended. Land and realty ownership will be acquired by the community for the people's welfare. Economic ties of responsibility must be secured by nationalism and the Chicano defense units.

3. Education must be relevant to our people, i.e., history, culture, bilingual education, contributions. Community control of our schools, our teachers.

4. Institutions shall serve our people by providing the service necessary for a full life and their welfare on the basis of restitution, not handouts or beggar's crumbs. Restitution for past economic slavery, political exploitation, ethnic and cultural psychological destruction, and denial of civil and human rights. Institutions in our community which do not serve the people have no place in the community. The institutions belong to the people.

5. Self-defense of the community must rely on the combined strength of the people. The front line defense will come from the barrios, the campos, the pueblos, and the ranchitos. Their involvement as protectors of their people will be given respect and dignity. They in turn offer lives for their people. Those who place themselves on the front for their people do so out of love and carnalismo. Those institutions which are fattened by our brothers to provide employment and political pork barrels for the Gringo will do so only by acts of liberation and la Causa. For the very young there will no longer be acts of juvenile delinquency, but revolutionary acts.

6. Cultural values of our people strengthen our identity and the moral backbone of the movement. Our culture unites and educates the family of La Raza towards liberation with one heart and one mind. We must insure that our writers, poets, musicians, and artists produce literature and art that is appealing to our people and relates to our revolutionary culture. Our cultural values of life, family, and home will serve as a powerful weapon to defeat the gringo dollar value system and encourage the process of love and brotherhood.

7. Political liberation can only come through an independent action on our part, since the two party system is the same animal with two heads that feeds from the same trough. Where we are a majority we will control; where we are a minority we will represent a pressure group. Nationally, we will represent one party, La Familia de La Raza.

III. Punto Tercero: Action

1. Awareness and distribution of El Plan espiritual de Aztlan. Presented at every meeting, demonstration, confrontation, courthouse, institution,

administration, church, school, tree, building, car, and every place of human existence.

2. September 16th, on the birthdate of Mexican Independence, a national walkout by all Chicanos of all colleges and schools to be sustained until the complete revision of the educational system—its policy makers, its administration, its curriculum, and its personnel—to meet the needs of our community.

3. Self-defense against the occupying forces of the oppressors at every school, every available man, woman, and child.

4. Community nationalization and organization of all Chicanos re: El Plan espiritual de Aztlan.

5. Economic program to drive the exploiter out of our communities and a welding of our peoples combined resources to control their own production through cooperative effort.

6. Creation of an independent local, regional, and national political party.

IV. Punto Cuarto: Liberation

A nation autonomously free, culturally, socially, economically, and politically will make its own decisions on the usage of our lands, the taxation of our goods, the utilization of our bodies for war, the determination of justice (reward and punishment), and the profit of our sweat.

EL PLAN DE AZTLAN IS THE PLAN OF LIBERATION!

A Call for Amnesty for Undocumented Workers, 1977

President Carter's administration has shown that it is not concerned with a humane solution for the undocumented and the civil and democratic rights of the Mexican population here in the U.S. While waving the banner of human rights abroad and putting forth an apparent concern during pre-election campaigning, the Carter administration has done little to quiet the anti-immigrant hysteria at home. In fact, Secretary of Labor Ray Marshall said it was necessary to prevent the rise of a "new civil rights struggle of the 1980's by having an underclass of people come into this country, unable to protect themselves, easily exploited, dissatisfied with their status and yet fearful of being deported." He said that the sons and daughters of these immigrants would demand their civil rights as occurred in the civil rights movement of the '60s.

Appeasing liberals and conservatives, big business and agribusiness, the labor aristocracy is what is behind the Carter administration's immigration proposals.

The so-called amnesty Carter proposes is already a right under current immigration laws, while the requirements for eligibility would actually apply to only about 200,000 persons if not less. The lack of guarantees under this proposal poses possible mass deportations for those registering but found to be ineligible. Yet it is significant that this proposal recognizes that the undocumented do contribute to society but the Carter administration engineers a political ploy and makes a cruel hoax upon the lives of millions.

The non-deportable status is nothing more than a temporary five-year work permit similar to the temporary worker importation, a bracero, modern slave labor program. This status forbids workers any rights, denies them social services for which they pay, forbids them to bring their families and guarantees nothing beyond five years.

The bracero program put workers at the mercy of the employers and agribusiness and was their weapon against the organization of agricultural workers.

The employer-sanction measure would make immigration agents of unqualified and untrained employers, who could abuse this authority and discriminate against Latinos and others who speak another language or are non-white. It is another convenient union-busting and strike-breaking tool.

The above measures isolate one sector of the population, citizen and non-citizen alike, and impose requirements to the exercise of their rights to work and live in this country as well as to obtain social services. It makes the scapegoat out of a people because of their vulnerability through using racism and nativism. It is a situation that can only be compared to the internment of the Japanese in concentration camps, apartheid in South Africa and Nazism in Germany.

Civil and democratic liberties are further threatened by the proposed national I.D., the non-counterfeitable social security card, which must be presented to gain employment, and the increase in the border patrol. Without any concern for the killings and abuses committed by the Border Patrol, the Carter administration only seeks to increase their numbers.

The Carter administration's immigration plan abuses the preoccupations of working people, particularly the oppressed nationalities who are hardest hit by the economic crisis. While at one point saying that undocumented workers displace U.S. workers, the proposals call for bringing in more workers without mention of the runaway shop. While saying they depress wages, the administration brings in workers under minimum wages. While saying the government will insure the rights of Latinos in the U.S., the administration proposes measures which further curtail the rights of this segment of the population.

The solution to the problem of immigration must be just and humane. The Carter amnesty is no amnesty at all and clearly leads to further abuses and repression. Unconditional and General Amnesty is the only solution which can prevent this and which recognizes that undocumented workers are not criminals but have in fact contributed to this society.

The recognition of all civil, democratic and human rights for the undocumented is the only protection for working and poor people of the U.S. as for oppressed nationalities.

Patricia Nelson Limerick on the
Border Never Controlled, 1985

The immigration debate rests on an unexamined premise—the tired old cliche, "We've lost control of our borders."

In the U.S. Southwest, which was once Mexico's North, Latin America and Anglo-America ran into each other. The border has been "out of control" ever since the Spanish Empire tried to keep French and U.S. traders, the "illegal aliens" of their day—out of its vulnerable northern borderland.

After its independence in 1821, Mexico tried the risky experiment of allowing U.S. settlers into Texas, hoping they would assimilate and become Catholics and Mexican citizens. Instead, the result was the U.S.-Mexican War and the loss of half of Mexico's territory. By comparison, Mexican nationals in the USA today do not look like much of a threat.

Far from being a threat, Mexican immigrants have for nearly a century provided the crucial labor source for the development of western agriculture and transportation. To this day, all of us who purchase affordable fruits and vegetables benefit from the availability of low-paid Mexican labor.

Most of what's said in the congressional debate over immigration has been said over and over throughout the 20th century. There is one change: the conventions of public discussion no longer permit open admissions of racism. But the veneer of politeness leaves the question open: How much is hostility to Mexican immigration still based on racism, on the old fear of a "brown horde" sweeping north to threaten a "white man's country."

The USA shares a 2,000-mile border with a nation of the impoverished Third World. Much of that border runs through open, arid, unsettled country. Two centuries of history carry a clear lesson: If people on one side of that border want something on the other side, they will cross that arbitrary line.

Just as Anglos defied the border in the 19th century, as long as the Mexican economy remains troubled and unstable, Mexicans will continue to follow in the path set by history.

Mexicans do not cross an ocean to a distant and alien land; instead, they walk or ride to a contiguous country closely related to their homeland.

The evidence of kinship is everywhere. Out here, the earthquake in Mexico City was no remote and abstract tragedy. The West is full of people directly concerned for the welfare of relatives and friends in Mexico. If we in the USA are responding compassionately to the catastrophe of that earthquake, then the long-range catastrophe of Mexican poverty surely deserves equal compassion.

Both problems ask for the same change in our attitude: Stop thinking of these peoples as "aliens" and try considering them as neighbors in trouble.

The National Indian Youth Council's
Statement of Policy, 1969

Since earliest contacts with western man, the American Indian has been considered unproductive, unprogressive, and unco-operative. Because we have been classified as a culturally deprived people, we have been subjected to systematic study by foreign cultures, resulting in the imposition of institutions and programs to "improve our condition." Millions of dollars have been poured into projects by the government to help the American Indian; somehow, this money has bypassed the majority of tribal communities and ended up in the pockets of administrators and so-called Indian consultants.

Abandoning a program of militant extermination of the Indian, the government has tried to dictate, through the establishment of colonial structures, the direction of Indian life. Concepts of tribal integrity and cultural equanimity have been overlooked in favor of enculturating the Indian and assimilating him into the American mainstream as fast as possible. The failure of this policy can be evidenced by the existence of 400,000 Indians still living within a tribal system in reservations through the United States. Most of these people live in communities with economic levels well below the poverty criterion. . . . The unwillingness to submit to the government's system of cultural death by allowing oneself to exist under these living standards seems, to us, to be a fight as real as the Indian Wars of the previous century. The weapons employed by the dominant society have become subtler and more dangerous than guns—these, in the form of educational, religious, and social reform, have attacked the very centers of Indian life by attempting to replace native institutions with those of the white man, ignoring the fact that even these native institutions can progress and adapt themselves naturally to the evironment.

The major problem in Indian affairs is that the Indian has been neglected in determining the direction of progress and monies to Indian communities. It has always been white people or white-oriented institutions determining what Indian problems are and how to correct them. The Establishment viewpoint has neglected the fact that there are tribal people within these tribal situations who realize the problems and that these people need only the proper social and economic opportunities to establish and govern policies affecting themselves. Our viewpoint, based in a tribal perspective, realizes, literally, that the Indian problem is the white man, and, further, realizes that poverty, educational drop-out, unemployment, etc., reflect only symptoms of a social-contact situation that is directed at unilateral cultural extinction.

Realizing the rise of ethnic consciousness and the dangers of policies directed at that consciousness, the National Indian Youth Council was formed to provide methods of action to protect the tribal communities through the implementation and co-ordination of educational resources. The nature of this work has, basically, been directed into research, training, planning, and programming at community, tribal, and national levels. Believing firmly in the right to self-determination of all peoples, we attempt to reverse the hierarchical structure of existing agencies such that "the People" directly determine the policies of organizations and bureaucracies established to serve them: Therefore, we act as resource individuals to serve our people.

The American Indian has been communicating for the past two centuries; it is time that someone listened. The era of the young Indian as spokesman for his people has, we hope, ended. Realizing that we are of a marginal nature, we are not qualified to act as representatives for a tribal people in voicing, deciding and, judging issues relevant to these people. We are prepared to address our people, not as "potential leaders," but as resources. Leaders arise from the people; an Indian leader cannot be delegated by the BIA [Bureau of Indian Affairs] or manufactured out of the tribal community by American society through an education that largely ignores his native culture.

Ramona Bennett and Gerald Wilkinson Remember Activism and Red Power, 1983

Bennett:

About sixteen or seventeen years ago, I was involved with voluntary programs sponsored by the American Indian Women's Service League in Seattle. I met many Indian people who had moved to Seattle because of the BIA relocation program. They had all come to the city to secure improved educational opportunities and find good jobs.

But I discovered that these families had lots of problems. One time, I went to a powwow and met a pretty little girl. She wore a buckskin dress that was sewn with the sinew from a deer. That little girl had rickets and she could not dance. But the dress revealed that her family had at one time been proud and independent. I started to think about that. I wondered how a race of people had become so impoverished that they could not even feed their children.

A short time later, I attended a Puyallup tribal meeting to find out what was going on with my own tribe. I discovered that my tribe had been unofficially terminated by the failure of the federal government to maintain services. The Bureau of Indian Affairs had set up a land office and had alienated the land. Then, the BIA folded up its carpetbag and moved on down the road. The Puyallup tribe did not have a recognized reservation nor any fishing rights.

I had the opportunity to serve on the tribal council. We inherited a broken typewriter and a broken filing cabinet. There had not been an updated enrollment in forty years. Only about twenty out of a thousand people in the tribe received Indian health services. The tribe was in pretty bad shape.

From *Indian Self-Rule: First-Hand Accounts of Indian-White Relations from Roosevelt to Reagan* edited by Kenneth R. Philp. Copyright © 1986 by the Institute of the American West. Reprinted by Permission of Howe Brothers.

I worked with Hank Adams, who lived with a family at Frank's Landing. Adams was an idea person. He was a very creative, innovative, and slightly madcap individual. When we would go to tribal general meetings, we would encounter a negative attitude. Previously entrenched tribal representatives would say: "No, we tried that in the 1920s and the 1930s. That idea will not work." We started doing research to combat this state of lethargy. We found out that many Puyallup people had been murdered. Their death certificates stated that they had fallen asleep on railroad tracks. We also discovered that the reservation had been taken, literally, at gunpoint through a whole series of thefts. That was why the Puyallup people were scattered around Tacoma and elsewhere without much organization.

I had an opportunity through the Puyallup tribe to meet people who had occupied Alcatraz Island in San Francisco Bay. I read some of the press releases that came out of Alcatraz. One statement indicated that Alcatraz was perfect for Indian purposes. Like many reservations, it had no schools, roads, jobs, or economic opportunities. During that period of time we closely followed the events at Alcatraz, and all kinds of light bulbs started flashing.

We concluded that it was not an accident that Indian people were living in poverty. The federal government had planned the alienation of Indian land. For over ninety years it had been responsible for preventing Indian fishermen from supporting their families with dignity. Because of my increased awareness of social injustice, I attended a National Indian Youth Workshop that was being held in Washington D.C. At this time, President Richard Nixon's self-determination statement was released. We finally realized that we were going to have to defend Indian fishing rights. It was clear that the federal government would not use troops to save our fishermen from the game wardens hired by the state of Washington.

I went back home and joined an armed camp that was set up to protect our fishermen. We were defending the fishermen on our river under a treaty right. We encountered 550 enforcement agents from all of the state agencies. They threatened and physically attacked us. The federal government had an obligation to protect Indians. Instead, it called us radicals. We were only upholding our tribe's treaty right to be self-supporting. When we tried to protect ourselves, they attacked our group, which consisted of only 60 people.

Indians had come from Canada and all over the country. One young Canadian boy was there because white men had raped and murdered his mother. The people would sit around and tell stories about why they were there. Very few of the people had come for the purpose of opening the river so our tribe could safely fish again. They were simply angry because of something horrible that had happened in their lives.

I was part of the Trail of Broken Treaties caravan. I was in the Bureau of Indian Affairs building when the war drums came out. We literally faced death for many nights in that building. We expected federal forces to kill us because the government did not want to abolish the Bureau of Indian Affairs, institute a national Indian government, or address the other issues that we raised.

The most beautiful pictures were drawn in the BIA building. It was fantastic. For a week, Indian artists from all over the country decorated that building. Brave people were involved in this protest movement. They were prepared to sacrifice themselves so that the next generation of Indians could live a better life. I was blessed and fortunate to associate with those people.

This era of Red Power and activism was a very special time. The people that engaged in protest were misunderstood. Hopefully, the well-established and secure reservation Indians will never know what it felt like to be a Puyallup. We looked death in the eye and were threatened with termination. I feel that as long as there is one acre, one fish, or one Indian child remaining in our care, we are always going to be under attack. If we ever forget this, white people will have us for breakfast. They are out to get us. I do not think that is paranoia. To me, that is a conditioned reflex.

Wilkinson:

Indian activism and Red Power, as movements within the Indian community, have changed. Ten years ago, when there was an issue before Congress that affected the lives of Indian people, everybody would get involved. Indians in Washington would gather around the Xerox machine at the National Congress of American Indians before trooping in to see their congressmen. This kind of activity also happened on many different levels outside of Washington D.C.

Today, one of the basic problems is that Indian organizations have become highly specialized groups. We used to have people who were generally involved in education. Now, we have people involved with the education of handicapped Indians. When an omnibus bill is introduced in Congress that affects Indians, only those people interested in a specific aspect of it are there. Indian people are not to blame for this kind of specialization. The nature and the direction of the country has forced Indian groups to become more specialized.

One of the consequences of specialization is that almost no one thinks holistically about Indian problems anymore. Very few people relate what they are doing to a broader context or develop some kind of vision about where Indian people are going and what should be done. Another consequence of specialization is that the market place of ideas has dried up. We have made tremendous progress in many areas, but in terms of intellectual growth, our people have not advanced much over the last ten years.

It was quite a contrast when I recently attended a meeting of Indian organizations in Mexico. There were Indians from Mexico, Guatemala, Bolivia, and Peru. We sat around and talked about things of a philosophical nature. We discussed ideas such as the relationship of Indians to Christianity and the nation state. We also examined the relationship of peasant Indians in Mexico to tribal Indians in the United States. That level of discourse was much different than the kinds of discussions that Indian people have in the United States.

Contact with Indian people in other countries is absolutely essential if we want to intellectually reinvigorate the Indian community. In order to move again, as we did in the 1960s and 1970s, we must have an Indian intellectual revolution. It is essential that we think about who we are as a people and where we are going as a people.

I want to refer to a political study that we did in the Third Congressional District of New Mexico because it illustrates at least one point that is related to what I have said. On the Navajo Reservation, there is a community called Crown Point. During the tribal council election, we went up to Crown Point to pretest our survey and obtain political information about the people. We assumed that the people at Crown Point, for the most part, were concerned about being exploited by the big energy companies and about combating racism from the white ranchers in the area. We also assumed that they agreed with tribal leaders about the need to expand the medical clinic and refurbish the high school.

In our survey, we discovered that those things were not really on many people's minds. The most important issue at Crown Point was dogs. On the Navajo Reservation, ten thousand people a year are treated by the Public Health Service for dog bites. The people also were concerned about clean water and improved roads.

The point is that, even though you are intimately involved with Indian people, you can lose track of what they are thinking. The biggest task before Indian intellectuals is to relate to the common people. We are entering a new era. The development and implementation of ideas is absolutely essential, if we are going to have another Red Power revolution.

Philip S. Deloria's Suggestions
for Ronald Reagan, 1983

I would like to identify some issues that might be worthy of consideration by Ronald Reagan or any other president. From my brief experience in helping to found the World Council of Indigenous Peoples, I learned that a fundamental issue is the relationship between industrial societies and tribal peoples. All around the world, village and tribal people are seeking to hold on to their land and their identity, but they are being forced off the land and into cities because of the needs of industrial societies. The economic promises that are implicit in plans for world development simply do not have the arithmetic to back them up. There are not going to be enough jobs created in light industry to employ everybody in Rio de Janeiro, Mexico City, or other large cities that are absorbing tribal and village people. In many respects there is a time bomb that is ticking.

From *Indian Self-Rule: First-Hand Accounts of Indian-White Relations from Roosevelt to Reagan* edited by Kenneth R. Philp. Copyright © 1986 by the Institute of the American West. Reprinted by Permission of Howe Brothers.

That leads to some fundamental issues that have to be clarified for American society. In America, as I see it, the conflict has never really been between cultures. Those clashes have been only surface manifestations of a deeper problem. The real issue in this country has been over the control of land and natural resources and the relationship of Indians to the economy.

Historically, Indian policy has been largely bipartisan. For example, both termination and self-determination received bipartisan support. It is not going to be enough for both candidates in the next election, or the election after that, to make the same kind of campaign promises about self-determination and respect for treaties.

From recent Supreme Court opinions, it appears that the fundamental view of this society is that Indians do not belong in this economic system and their resources should be used and developed by somebody else. The Supreme Court has now invented the notion that federal agencies have a trust responsibility to their constituent groups that is comparable in the law to the federal trust responsibility for Indians. This is an astounding and drastic judicial viewpoint. It deserves a great public outcry.

The tools for the solution to many Indian problems already exist. The will and the spirit of Indian tribes must be harnessed to bring about political and economic advancement. And Indian communities have to realize that they are the only ones that can decide how to do this. The federal government also has the tools to coordinate the federal resources available to tribes, in order to achieve economic results. But the bipartisan will to do this has been lacking. Neither political party has had its feet held to the fire. They still think that Indians are willing to settle for platitudes.

The Carter administration, in my experience, was constantly in a state of public embarrassment. Whatever it did with respect to Indians simply added more embarrassment to an already humiliating four years. The Reagan administration seems to lack the capacity for embarrassment. This indifference to criticism greatly affects our strategies for changing the policies of this administration.

I agree that we should ask President Reagan to stop his war on poor people. But he did not stumble into that war and the poor people did not attack him. Officials in the Reagan administration made a calculated decision to follow this course of action, and they are not embarrassed about it. Until there is a strong public consensus in this country which says that the nation will no longer tolerate such a public policy, Indians will continue to pay the price of poverty for continuing to be Indians. Reorganizing the Bureau of Indian Affairs is not going to have the slightest effect on ending this war.

The basic issue that Indians face is are we going to use our own resources, or is somebody else going to use them? The answer, for the last two hundred years, has been very clear. Somebody else is going to use our resources. I do not see the slightest indication that there is any demand for this process to change except from Indians and a few of our friends.

We showed, in response to the termination policy, that we can lobby very effectively against something. Our record since that time of demonstrating that we could lobby effectively for something has been less dramatic. There is an apparent absence of a will in the American political community to find a solution to our problems. So we must define the answers ourselves and keep pushing until something begins to happen. But we still will need public support. I am not ready to say what Indians want in specific details. But, in general, it is clear that Indians do not want to be poor anymore. The economic and political issues involved in the control of our resources are paramount and are most often ignored in the federal policies. There are still vast resources in the government to help us, but they are not being mobilized and targeted by federal officials.

Since the early 1970s, tribes have begun to face the need to act as governments that regulate and tax. In the process, we have created a set of issues with respect to federal, state, and municipal governments that were beyond the wildest imagination of people twenty years ago. A whole new set of issues has to be confronted. It involves the development of institutions and the implementation of political philosophies in a very short time. That is an almost impossible task, but we are going to have to do it. In order to be successful, we must stave off attempts to interfere with and abolish our governments.

Nobody went in and abolished the city of Cleveland when it almost went bankrupt under the direction of a youthful mayor. But tribes are constantly faced with the reminder, that in the view of much of the society, we are transitional governments. This makes it very difficult for us, over the long haul, to implement plans. We can not make even one percent of the false starts and the mistakes that every other government in this country is entitled to, as a matter of right, because they have a permanent existence.

Most people are not aware of the enormous growth and power of the Office of Management and Budget in the federal government. It no longer just deals with management issues or adding up numbers and giving them to the president. The OMB is a major policy-making force in America. Every person that works for OMB, in theory, speaks for the president. The levels at which Indian policy questions are decided in the OMB are so low that no one who is appointed by the president even knows they take place, unless they are very major issues.

The OMB is an unaccountable bureaucracy that essentially has the freedom to impose its policy preferences on Indians. There is no due process or access to policy formulation on the part of Indians. This situation happens in every administration.

We must find a way to break through that bureaucratic barrier and establish the permanency of Indian societies and governments in this system. This must not be done at the price of our continued poverty. We have to discover how to work our way out of poverty and still be permanent. That involves a conceptual framework that simply has not been developed, and we have to do it very quickly.

Y *E S S A Y S*

Moses Rischin, a distinguished historian of immigration at San Francisco State University, examines the astoundingly diverse population of California in the first essay. Giving a historical overview of California's growth, Rischin notes the challenge that it creates in terms not only of cultural pluralism but also of what he calls "cultural democracy." In the second selection, William T. Hagan's presidential address to the Western History Association, this noted scholar of American Indian history from the State University of New York College, Fredonia, considers the revitalization of Indian tribalism since the 1950s. He believes that political activism, federal policies, and court decisions have influenced this rejuvenated sense of Indianness. John R. Chavez is a historian of Mexican-Americans and the American Southwest at Texas A&M University. In the third essay, he gives an overview of Mexican-American political activism in the 1960s and 1970s. His conclusions about Chicanos as a dispossessed people in the 1980s have a far bleaker tone than Hagan's conclusions about Indians. Both groups share similar demands for political recognition, economic opportunity, and cultural autonomy. Are these interests doomed, or will Indians and Chicanos be able not only to survive but also possibly to flourish in the future?

Minorities in California

MOSES RISCHIN

For Californians, the drama of migration has been an experience without parallel anywhere else in the United States, or in the world, in volume, velocity, scope, continuity, and variety. Here, however unevenly and selectively, have settled natives of every state and of most of the nations of the globe. Here the westward migration and overseas immigration have simultaneously converged at land's end. In the mid-1960s, the drama peaked with historic intensity as California attained primacy among the nation's states.

"The single most distinctive fact about the culture of California has been the perpetually high proportion of newly arrived residents among its inhabitants," reiterated Carey McWilliams, and few will contest this assertion by the veteran interpreter of the human maelstrom that has always been California. Indeed, in each generation, exodus has been reenacted in California almost as if millenarian scriptural expectations were to be accepted literally, not merely to be commemorated by lapsed Christians, errant Jews, and nakedly unconscionable sun worshippers. A sea of strangers, sojourners, newcomers, and footloose wanderers has borne witness to the perpetual spectacle of migration that informs every aspect of the state's history and institutions, or the dearth thereof, the absence of genuine party organizations, the novel political and religious sects, the yeomanless agriculture, the powerful maritime unions, and the absence of a state-supported historical society.

Moses Rischin, "Immigration, Migration, and Minorities in California: A Reassessment," © 1972 by the Pacific Coast Branch, American Historical Association. Reprinted from *Pacific Historical Review*, Vol. 41 (February 1972), 71–90, by permission.

California's ungilded ghost towns of the Mother Lode and its sun-gilded phantom new cities testify, if at times eerily, to the insistent myth of Argonaut days proclaimed by land developers and chambers of commerce, reminiscent, but now justifiably so, of the paradisiacal promises of steamship agents of the great trans-Atlantic migration that featured date palms and olive trees, if not citrus groves, covering the Great Plains.

Yet in our time the mass electronic media, the automobile and the jet-plane successors to the covered wagon, the sailing ship, and the railroad have dangerously obscured the sense of radical upheaval and psychological displacement that migration has exacerbated, the extreme rootlessness that has unhinged the lives of so many Californians. Although the most perceptive historian of the contemporary West, Earl Pomeroy, a grandson of California pioneers, has been especially sensitive to the normative problems that the stress of extreme change have entailed, California-centered historians have been until recently too intoxicated by a sunny euphoria to freshly reexamine the state's social and psychological ills. Even Carey McWilliams, for well over a decade the New York based editor of the *Nation* but once the state's most imaginative and distinguished publicist and immigration and minority expert, has failed to sustain his earlier grasp of the social realities of California. A recent book that he has edited lacks authority and curiously omits a discussion of minorities, although it does include a few essays that are at least suggestive of the unprecedented strains of the past two decades.

But perhaps the recent emergence of a new population equilibrium will stir historians to a more sober confrontation. For the first time in California's history, a state which has consistently derived its major population growth from migration seems destined to make its major future population gains by natural increase. Since 1966, with the exception of 1967, the state's annual natural increase has regularly exceeded its annual increment by migration. Since it is anticipated that this pattern will persist, self-knowledge for the mounting numbers of native Californians becomes more relevant and critical than ever.

In the last half century a distant province has become the center of a new American civilization of the semitropics. High technology has transformed Edward A. Ross's "last asylum of the native-born" not simply into a year-round all-American Mediterranean sanctuary against icy winters, industrial strife, and cultural cleavage but into an avant-garde showcase of a brave new world. The old frontier of rural hardship has given way to a new frontier of urban comfort with no collective anticipation of its challenges and hazards. Frederick Jackson Turner's frontiersmen have been ill-prepared for the Riviera and ill at ease in Zion. The lurking fear that here ontogeny may not recapitulate phylogeny runs deep.

Changes of such vast proportions have yet to find their paradigm. Early in the century a young writer's efforts to extrapolate from the pioneer experience of the Middle West by identifying "A Californian Example of the Welding of Southern and New England Stocks of People," in "Our Town" (Fresno, California), seems as idyllic as Thornton Wilder's poetic drama of Groves Corners and as delightfully remote:

We used to have a "plaza" in our town, where the hoboes rested in the shade at noon, and where at night twice a week we went to hear the band concerts. Now we have a "courthouse park." It is the same thirteen acres of grass and trees and flowers, with the same courthouse in the centre. But we call it by a different name. The transition from "plaza" to "courthouse park" in our vocabulary marks the path of our evolution from a frontier town in California with many traces of Mexican influence in our "lingo" to a civilized modern little city dominated intellectually by New England schoolma'ams.

The diversity of human ingredients, influences, contrasts, and dilemmas activated by the migrations that have contributed to California's original and rapid social transformation can merely be suggested here. Such categories and pairings as trans-California Americans and native sons, Europeans and trans-migrants, Occidentals and Orientals, Catholics and Protestants, Mormons, Jews, and Gentiles, the "old" immigration and the "new," the unaffiliated and the indifferent, the Anglo and the Chicano, the black and the white seem gross and inadequate in the face of the discontinuities of so many group experiences alongside the continuities of others. The rough-edged asymmetrical temporal and spatial relations of groups totally unaware of one another's existence, linked only by the accident of migration, have nowhere in the United States been more transparent than they have been in California.

Clearly the Gold Rush years set the terms for California's unique and varied peopling and the patterns to be followed, as McWilliams has argued so forcefully. But their implications became fully apparent only with the march of the twentieth century into California when the state became a pacemaker rather than an illustration of national trends. "After 1900, population growth achieved proportions unprecedented in any American state." The great westward migration to California began after the historical westward migration had ended. Between 1900 and 1970, the growth of California's population by nearly 19,000,000 has been virtually equal to the total national increment by immigration for the whole nineteenth century. The 67 percent increase in population between 1920 and 1930, not exceeded in any other decade, only reflected a persistent and unbroken trend since 1850, unabated even during the Great Depression, in which the migration gain in each successive decade has exceeded the natural increase, a condition without parallel for any other state. As a result, with its population almost doubling every twenty years for a dozen decades, California has never had a respite to consolidate its institutions or to firm up its identity, to assert the authority of tradition or reputation in the face of a cruel individualism, as Josiah Royce so well knew.

The individual, who by public action or utterance, rises above the general level in California, is subject to a kind of attack which strong men frequently enjoy, but which the stranger finds on occasion particularly merciless. That absence of concern for a man's antecedents . . . contributes to this very mercilessness. . . .

The quasi-mechanical and agglutinative growth of the past generation continued to keep California off balance. An increase of over 5,000,000 between 1950 and 1960, an increment nearly equal to the total population of the state in 1930, and another increase of 4,250,000 by 1970 have resulted in a growth in the past twenty years that has almost matched the state's total population in 1950. The resultant leviathan exceeding all consciously regulated norms virtually eludes comprehension or comparison.

With less than two percent of the nation's population in 1900, the twelfth state in the nation became, in 1964, the premier state. With nearly ten percent of the American population, California surpassed New York, the nation's most populous state for over a century and a half. New York, which had moved ahead of Virginia shortly after 1810, did not attain its maximum relative population growth until 1830. Following the opening of the Erie Canal, it accounted for almost fifteen percent of the American people, even though by 1860 for every migrant that New York gained three New Yorkers were lost to other states. New York's preponderance was not to be sustained but its preeminence was uncontested until California's phenomenal surge; in the last century, New York consistently counted slightly less than ten percent of the national total.

The generous projection that California may number every seventh American among its residents by the end of the twentieth century would still bring it barely abreast of New York in its imperial take-off decades between 1820 and 1850, when the joint thrust of New England and European immigration tethered to a transportation revolution created the Empire State. California, however, would come nowhere close to Virginia's dominance in 1790, when the Old Dominion accounted for 19 percent of the nation's population, two fifths slave (and two-fifths of all American slaves), as a consequence of the massive importations of the previous century.

Yet New York and certainly Virginia offer no migration and population patterns to fit California's unique development. Free and transcontinental, the California migrations have defied the strictures and prognostications of migration theorists and offer no ready parallels. One historian in speculating about the significance of the push and pull factors has concluded that the pull factors were more important than the push factors, especially when half a continent had to be crossed, and that individual psychological factors outweighed economic and environmental motives. Professor Dorothy Johansen has persuasively juxtaposed California and Oregon, so different in scale, tone, magnitude, and psychology, to document the critical influence of the pull factors. Whether the leading state from which the migrants came was New York (from 1860 to 1900), Illinois (from 1910 to 1940), or Texas (since 1950) seems less critical, therefore, than the selective forces that attracted them to California rather than to Oregon.

To what extent migrants fully understood the implications of their decision to take the California trail rather than the Oregon trail is debatable; but that the California migrants quite appreciated the significance of the urban trail on which they embarked seems dubious at best. By contrast with the agricultural frontiers of the historic westward migrations, California's heavy migrations came in an era of unprecedented urbanization. Significantly, in 1890 when the frontier officially was declared closed, 41 percent of Californians lived in cities of 10,000 or more and the state ranked behind only Massachusetts, Rhode Island, New York, New Jersey, Maryland, and Connecticut, the embryonic American megalopolis of our own day, as a center of urban life. By 1960, California ranked second behind New Jersey, and tied with Rhode Island, the nation's smallest state, as the most urbanized state in America. Californians, living in the nation's leading agricultural state, made the shift to a potential megalopolitan future with an abruptness and deceptiveness made even sharper by the simultaneous double stress of both regional and ecological dislocation. If Americans "entered a great period of city building . . . protestingly, metaphorically walking backward," Californians did so on the hop, skip, and gallop.

Just as the westward migration and the urban trail acquired a special character in California, so the coming of its immigrant peoples reflected California's unique relationship to the United States and to the world. This became especially apparent again in the 1960s when California became for the first time the nation's foremost Mecca for immigrants, surpassing New York as it has in population. In 1940, New York still accounted for two and one-half times as many aliens as did California. By 1960, California had passed New York, and by 1969 it accounted for 22 percent of all registered aliens as compared to New York's 17 percent, a fall from 25.6 percent in 1940. In these years, California edged New York, as well, in the number of immigrants choosing to settle in the state annually, accounting also for 22 percent of the national total. This westward tilt, derived primarily not from the east but from the southwest, reflected a decisive shift of Mexican immigration from Texas to California in the early 1960's which transformed the state's leading ethnic minority into the largest ethnic or racial minority in any state in the country. Between 1950 and 1960, when New York registered a decline in the proportion of its foreign white stock from 20.2 to 19 percent, California's foreign white stock rose from 8.8 to 11.3 percent, the only state in the nation to reflect such a gain. California thus reversed a trend of many decades that had seen it become progressively less foreign than it had been in the opening decades of its statehood. In the 1870s foreign immigrants had outnumbered migrants from other states; in the 1920s American migrants outnumbered immigrants nearly four to one; and by 1940 immigration had virtually ceased to be a factor in the state's population growth. Yet between 1950 and 1960, of the eight American cities with the largest numbers of foreign white stock, only Los Angeles and San Francisco registered increases. Indeed, in 1960, some 30 percent of the population of the San Francisco–Oakland metropolitan region was of foreign stock deriving from eighty-four different countries.

Yet California's renewed cosmopolitanism has been famously flawed by the accident of geography and an extreme frontier racist mentality. To Chester Rowell, the epic view from the Berkeley hills proved spectral and Spenglerian rather than inspiring. Looking to the Golden Gate, that representative Californian saw the sunset of westward expansion rather than a vision of merging hemispheres.

The American Pacific Coast is the window through which one world looks out upon another. And on what we have eyes to see through that window, rests the future of the human race. . . . Here is visibly the final portal of the white man's world; the entrance doorway to the storied East. It is the goal of all the ages. Out of the East and the past our eldest fathers came, driven by an ever-westward urge. Celt and Teuton, Roman, Hellene and Slav, they flowed in successive waves across Europe, and their descendants braved the Atlantic, conquered the wilderness, crossed mountains and plains, and finally at the Golden Gate reached the end of the journey which is the story of our race. Beyond is again East, and another world which, except as visitors, we can never penetrate. The Gate marks the end in time of the oldest fact in history, and the boundary in space between two worlds. . . . Whatever the truth or the right of the matter may be, there is no doubt [that] the European peoples around the Pacific unanimously think of . . . their borders as a racial frontier, which they are determined to maintain inviolate.

Significantly, Angel Island, designated as an immigration inspection center in 1892, unlike Ellis Island opened at the same time and Castle Garden earlier, has never come to occupy even a latter-day niche in the pantheon of liberty. No Museum of Immigration has been projected for Angel Island or is likely to be. Until recently, the lamp has burned dimly, if at all, at the Golden Gate. No new colossus with an invitation on its base to "the tempest-tossed" has graced Yerba Buena. Asia and Europe, the Pacific and the Atlantic, have aroused polar emotions even among cosmopolites. Those who reversed the familiar immigration pattern, those "Westerners from the East," crossing the Pacific rather than the Atlantic, have too often seemed to come surreptitiously by night even if they in fact came openly by day. Until recently, organizations with the noblest intentions side-stepped the Pacific dilemma. David Lubin's Commission of Immigration and Housing, created in 1913, was directed to the plight of Atlantic immigrants and counted on the Panama Canal to link California to the immigrant European countries. With the outbreak of World War I, the sealing off of the anticipated mass European migration just as the first ocean steamer passed through the canal's locks drastically curtailed the commission's program that, in any case, had never been intended for Pacific immigrants.

Yet Pacific immigrants fulfilled a significant role in California. From the very beginning their presence conferred instant status on all European immigrants that was not to be their lot elsewhere except in the South, where slavery was endemic. This was especially the case between 1860 and 1880, when the Chinese constituted one-fourth of all the state's immigrants, competing until 1890 with the Irish for first place among the state's foreign-born. In 1914, the prominent California spokesman, Chester Rowell, informed Sydney Gulick, American Protestant missionary to Japan and deviser and promoter of the immigration quota system as an expedient to salvage Japanese pride, of the rank order of nativism. "The ordinary Californian's view of the Japanese is compounded, first, of his notion that all foreigners are inferior, second, of his notion that all persons of any color except white are in the same class with 'niggers'. . . ." For European immigrants, the common bond of origin was to persist as a key advantage in law and public opinion into our own time.

For Atlantic immigrants, notably Catholics, who were to experience slights, rebuffs, and even violence elsewhere in the United States, California proved remarkably benign. Indeed, European immigrants seemed less threatening in California, for like native-born migrants they comprised a broader and more diffuse spectrum than was the pattern in other states. Although the Irish and the Germans were the leading European immigrant groups in California as elsewhere through the most of the nineteenth century, their numbers were proportionately fewer and their impact less clearly felt. The trans-European, no less than the even more decisively trans-American pattern of the native-born migrants, lent an atomistic tone to the California immigration. In addition, the initial Catholic traditions of the state, augmented by the early, heavily Catholic immigration that antedated the Protestant migrations of the late nineteenth century, reversed the traditional American social etiquette of precedence and subtly affected ethnic and religious relations. A considerable Italian immigration impressed itself early upon the state and flowered better there than anywhere else in the United States. An impressive French migration, modestly represented elsewhere, patronized a profusion of French periodicals exceeded only in Louisiana. The Irish, especially, have been prone to describe the California, particularly the San Francisco, experience in panegyrics, as have the Jews. Later, less familiar European strains attracted to California also have prospered, despite initial strains, in the isolated rural areas. Wilson D. Wallis, a young sociologist commissioned in 1919 to do a series of articles on the foreign-born of Fresno County by Chester Rowell, editor of the *Fresno Morning Republican,* approvingly registered the accomplishments and prospects of the Armenians, the Portuguese from the Azores, and the Russo-Germans, the most numerous group in the county from 1890 to 1940. These peoples, he explained, were "an atoll amid a sea of various influences which surround, but do not permeate. . . ."

Without doubt the relatively advantageous lot of all European immigrants in California was attributable, in part at least, to the low esteem in which all non-whites were held. If "the evils of intoxication and of mixed races" that obsessed Governor Peter H. Burnett in the 1850s could not be avoided, it was not for lack of effort. Indeed, one contemporary scholar is convinced that the relations between whites and Indians proved the critical determinant of all subsequent racial attitudes.

> An animosity which reached almost the level of mass psychosis . . . still persists in attenuated form to the present day, and in the meantime it has colored the relations between the white man and not only the red man but almost all other ethnic stocks very slightly represented in California until recently as well.

Ironically, the Negro, the classic American outsider, proved less vulnerable in California in the twentieth century, since other colored groups—Mexicans and Orientals—more historically identified with the region and its prejudices absorbed the larger impact of white hostility. As late as 1940, only 40 percent of California's non-whites were Negroes, comprising but 1.8 percent of the state's total population. In the inter-war years, the California sojourns of Ralph Bunche and Jackie Robinson proved fortunate for the development of their sense of self-esteem, doubtless fortifying them for the statesmen roles that they subsequently were to assume.

Despite its vaunted racism, and perhaps because of it, California more than any other state in America early stirred visions of a color-blind new world where racial amalgamation would prove inevitable. In the 1920s, Robert E. Park detected a special challenge in the complex racial situation of the last West. The research director of the Survey of Race Relations on the Pacific Coast saw this "racial frontier" not in the negative terms of Chester Rowell but as the harbinger of a new "cosmic process" that would eventually lead to the breakdown of racial barriers, rather than to their preservation.

> The race relations cycle which takes the form, to state it abstractly, of contacts, competition, accommodation and eventual assimilation, is apparently progressive and irreversible. Customs regulations, immigration restrictions and racial barriers may slacken the tempo of the movement; may perhaps halt it altogether for a time; but cannot change its direction; cannot[,] at any rate, reverse it.

This "cosmic process," slated to take place first on the Pacific Coast, in the wake of the Hawaiian example, proved slow in coming. Instead of apocalyptic sociology, for a generation, Emory S. Bogardus, a Park student, found ample opportunity in California to gauge the wide range of racial antipathies with refined gradations by the use of his social distance scale.

The end of World War II, however, saw a radical reversal of earlier extreme racist practices that had culminated in the forced removal of Japanese Americans to detention camps. In 1948, the California Supreme Court invalidated the state's anti-miscegenation statute, applying originally to Negroes and mulattoes, and amended in 1905 to include Mongolians and in 1933 members of the Malay race, viz. Filipinos. In the first year after the law's invalidation, of 21,000 marriages in Los Angeles County, 100 were interracial; Filipino males, the most womanless of immigrants, were the most numerous participants. Yet, if interracial marriages with European-Americans were few, the estimated 25,000 Japanese war brides in the United States by 1960 testified to a social transformation that Robert Park had anticipated and that now seemed irreversible.

Most impressive was the entry of Asians into public life. In 1956, for the first time in the nation's history, an Asian-American, Dalip Singh Saund, was elected to Congress from California. . . . Three years later, Hawaii, in so many ways a satellite of California, was admitted to statehood and quickly sent the first Chinese American and first Japanese American to the United States Senate. More recently, San Francisco State College president and semanticist, S. I. Hayakawa, has played a conspicuous role in higher education nationally, and in San Jose a Japanese American who spent two years in World War II relocation centers became the first Asian American to be elected chief executive officer of a major mainland American city.

Perhaps the most conspicuous consequence of the migrations of the past few decades has been the qualitative transformation of California by a cultural and scientific elite. Writing to William James in the year that saw the publication of Henry George's *Progress and Poverty,* Josiah Royce in his first semester at Berkeley after his return to California despaired of another kind of poverty:

> My first impressions have passed away now, and I have quite a settled opinion of the place and opportunities about me. . . . There is no philosophy in California—from Siskiyou to Ft. Yuma, from the Golden Gate to the summit of the Sierras. . . . I trumped up a theory of logical concepts last term and preached it to the seniors. . . . It was somewhat monstrous, and, in this wilderness with nobody to talk with about it, I have not the least idea whether it is true or not. . . .

The geographical isolation and provincialism that troubled Royce at Berkeley in 1879 was broken in the 1920s. Then the onset of the intellectual migration that crested in the 1950s and early 1960s moved California into the front rank of American cultural innovation, transforming a state that had been a region into a world center. None other than Fredrick Jackson Turner, writing in 1927 to Max Farrand, first director of the Huntington Library, heralded the grand prospects for the productive higher life of the mind. "You will have a career as the organizer and leader of a new center of scholars in this wonderful land that has already produced such notable results in science and will in art, as well as the humanities in general." Robert A. Millikan, who had a few years earlier been awarded a Nobel prize, was transforming the new California Institute of Technology into a center of modern physics and international science in association with Linus Pauling and Robert Oppenheimer and many others, while Ernest O. Lawrence, also destined to be a Nobel Laureate, was at work laying the foundations for Berkeley's great scientific work. After some years of quiet growth, World War II set the stage in California for a revolution in higher education and Pacific-consciousness that brought with it a westward migration of intellectual and scientific talent, American and foreign-born, comparable perhaps only to the migration to America during the Hitler years of leading European scholars and intellectuals. Drawing heavily upon the fertile crescent that extends from the banks of the Potomac to the banks of the Charles and from the rim of the Great Lakes, California moved suddenly from a colonial outpost of academic gentility and respectability to a center of unprecedented and dazzling innovation. Clark Kerr's unparalleled entre-preneurship in filling California's educational and cultural void stamped the model of the multiversity, so reflective of the state's great new institutional needs, upon American higher education. Projected as model new cities, the university's new campuses were to be islands of urbanity and culture to stir the creative and intellectual juices of the state's adults as well as its youngsters. Robert Hutchins' Center for the Study of Democratic Institutions, Ralph Tyler's Center for Advanced Study in the Behavioral Sciences, the Rand Corporation, and others brought with them a vitality and a cosmopolitanism that promised to bring Californians abreast of their sudden new responsibilities.

Inevitably such vast migrations have made planning difficult. In certain respects, California's habitual reliance upon migrants to fill its many gaps has encouraged a colonial mentality that has inhibited the growth and development of quality institutions at the grass roots. Without such centers to sustain an atmosphere of art, science, and culture, the gaps between aspiration, opportunity, and performance in many vital areas may well leave talented native sons frustrated, culturally impoverished, and at loose ends. This vacuum has been especially noted in medicine. For many reasons, California very early in its history had a high physician-population ratio; in 1940 it was the highest in the nation and California still ranks behind only New York and Massachusetts in this respect. Yet only one of five or six of its physicians has been trained in California, which has had little incentive to develop extensive and expensive medical centers. As a result, the number of students from California seeking a medical education has narrowed to fit the opportunities available. It has been estimated that in relation to population, California has only from one half to one quarter the number of potential medical students of the northeastern states. By contrast, the number of engineering students has increased in California, while declining elsewhere. Between 1946 and 1965, defense spending, so critical a feature in the California economy, accounting for one half of its net immigration, has clearly provided the major incentive for immediately practical, remunerative, and subsidized vocations to the dangerous neglect of the state's long-term needs.

The strains of migration also have elicited a personal price. Personal, familial, ethnic, and religious ties have been fractured, often with little concern for the consequences. California's first millionaire, first newspaper publisher, and major entrepreneur was written off as an apostate by the Mormon Church, fell victim to drink and domestic troubles, and died in poverty and obscurity in the arms of his third wife, a Mexican boarding-house keeper. This is by no means an apocryphal story but the telescoped biography, of course, of Sam Brannan. California at the end of the American rainbow, half a continent and more away from the points of origin of so many migrants, has provided few cushions for failure, no easy return or ready retreat.

> California . . . resembles Eden: it is assumed that those who absent themselves from its blessings have been banished, exiled by some perversity of heart. Did not the Donner-Reed party, after all, eat its own dead to reach Sacramento?

Wayward emotions, mental imbalance, and sheer accident have constantly propelled migrants to California on the flimsiest pretext. Horatio Alger's villains all appear to have fled west, though whether they reached California is not at all certain. More calculatedly, the officials of the Leavenworth and Atlanta federal prisons reputedly sent their most intractable inmates to Alcatraz. Most recently, the closeness of the Vietnam War has generated a new social casualty, as California with 23 percent of the convictions for draft evasion has come to lead the nation in this category.

In the absence of authoritative studies of the relationship between mental disease and migration for Californians, it does not seem unreasonable to assume that studies of New York should cast light on the California situation, to which it seems most analogous. The atypicalness of these two states doubtless has made them especially alluring to the footloose as well as to the unusually gifted and ambitious, while their urban and ethnic mix has been particularly baffling to migrants from rural areas. In New York, and probably in California, the incidence of mental disease has been highest for interstate migrants, somewhat lower for the foreign-born, and lowest of all for non-migrants. The incidence of alcoholism presumably has also been considerably higher for migrants than for non-migrants. In California, where the divorce rate and the suicide rate have been twice the national average and clearly related one to the other, loneliness has exacted a heavy toll. Suicide has been more frequent among the single than the married, even more frequent among the widowed, and most frequent of all among the divorced.

The rootlessness, sensed or unsensed, of so many Californians has readily led to what Erik Erikson has called "locomotive self-intoxication." Particularly apposite for Californians is the joke about the man, who, to the puzzlement of his friends, boasted that he paid $5,000 for his tiny new electric automobile. "The car itself only cost a thousand dollars," he explained to them, "but the extension cord cost four thousand." For many, the extension cord has been frazzled to the near breaking-point. Agonized and uneasy in California, Hamlin Garland, the passionate writer and lecturer on the Middle Border pioneers, was possessed by "a feeling of guilt, a sense of disloyalty to my ancestors," and proved unable to forgive himself for deserting the Middle West for New York, for Europe, and, finally, for building a "Monterey Colonial casa." Most pathetic were the dust bowl victims, who on the eve of their exodus mourned the death of their identities.

> The women sat among the doomed things, turning them over and looking past them and back. This book. My father had it. He liked a book. *Pilgrim's Progress*. Used to read it. Got his name in it. . . . Think you could get this china dog in? Aunt Sadie brought it from the St. Louis Fair. . . . Wrote right on it. No, I guess not. Here's a letter my brother wrote the day before he died. Here's an old-time hat. . . . No, there isn't room.
> How can we live without our lives? How will we know it's us without our past? No. Leave it. Burn it.

Most recently, native Californians of pioneer antecedents have added their plaints to those of other exiles. "It is hard to find California now, unsettling to wonder how much of it was merely imagined or improvised. . . ."

In the last few years the slackening of migration has suggested that the historic California migration patterns of a dozen decades, and especially of the past two, may have at last induced "the dynamics of repulsion." It has even been argued that migration to California will not level off but will drop precipitously in the face of insurmountable problems and, indeed, that some Californians will find another West, perhaps in Australia. It may very well be that a marked decline in the momentum of migration will drive Californians to confront their "easiest failing," which Josiah Royce described nearly a century ago as their "general sense of social irresponsibility." A new "reverence for the relations of life," to cite Royce's phrase, may impel Californians, both old and young, to examine and to reflect upon their many histories, upon the meaning of community and the many human challenges that Robert Park optimistically projected for "the racial frontier." Perhaps a reverse migration by native Californians to an older America and to foreign lands will induce a growth in consciousness of the fragility of history, the dangers of amnesia, and an appreciation of the promise that is California, both as extension and as a break with the pasts of its many peoples. Perhaps like Lincoln Steffens, a representative native Californian who had not experienced the drama of migration until young manhood, they will return not to retire but rather to bring balance to a remarkable state of whose rare potential and setting they have not been aware or appreciative.

> The overland approach is still an element in the overwhelming effect of a first impression of California. To me as a child, the State was the world as I knew it, and I pictured other States and countries as pretty much "like this." I never felt the warm, colorful force of the beauty of California until I had gone away and come back over my father's route: dull plains; hot, dry desert; the night of icy mountains; the dawning foothills breaking into the full day of sunshine in the valley; and last, the sunset through the Golden Gate. And I came to it by railroad, comfortably, swiftly. My father, who plodded and fought or worried the whole long hard way at oxen pace, always paused when he recalled how they turned over the summit and waded down joyously, into the amazing golden sea of sunshine—he would pause, see it again as he saw it then, and say "I saw that this was the place to live."

Permeated by a trans-American ground change, a displacement perhaps analogous to the immigrant sea change, Californians have been fashioned into new men, the ultimate in new Americans both statistically and mythically. They may also be approaching a new stability. In 1967 California's population was identified as .03 percent Indian, 2 percent Oriental, 7.2 percent Negro, and 11.1 percent of Spanish surname. Non-whites totaled 10.1 percent; whites, 89.9 percent. Except for minor fluctuations such as a slight rise in the Indian and Oriental populations, it seems likely that the ethnic and racial makeup of the state will change little for some time. The new immigration law, divested of national origins quotas, is not likely to markedly affect the future composition or balance of ethnic groups in California if the immigration figures of the revised law's first year of operation are to be judged as typical. California, however, will continue to attract a high proportion of certain ethnic groups, especially Orientals, led by Chinese and Filipinos, who in

1969 for the first time comprised over twenty percent of the total immigration to the United States. This was in contrast with New York, which attracted the predominant number of immigrants from southern Europe and the Caribbean. "In 1969," noted the Commissioner of Immigration and Naturalization, "most immigrants from Mexico and Canada, and from the Far East, chose to reside in California: one of every two Mexicans did so; 13 percent of the Canadians; 39 percent of the Filipinos; 36 percent of the Chinese; 18 percent of the Koreans; and 16 percent of the Indians. Twenty percent of all new Portuguese immigrants planned to reside in California, in keeping with the well-established Portuguese population of that state.

The drama of migration to California has not ended but is entering a new and more mature phase as an experiment in human relations. Descendants of colonial Americans, both black and white, no less than the latest comers from a Montana reservation or Hong Kong, have experienced in California a journey of flesh and spirit, "a step into the world" that has transformed many of them into the first Americans in their families. Hopefully this vital state peopled by so many new Americans will be able to draw upon the rich diversity of its heritages to implement a cultural democracy not fully imagined until recently anywhere and with no more promising setting than California.

Tribalism Rejuvenated

WILLIAM T. HAGAN

Within the last year the spokesman for a native group has deplored the possibility of a gradual termination of United States aid to his people. He charged that as a result of previous government policies, his people's traditional fishing and hunting economy had been destroyed and they had been reduced to dependency. The spokesman implied that this was a poor way to prepare native peoples for local autonomy.

The spokesman in this instance was not a Menominee or Klamath Indian, or a Sioux. He was a Micronesian from the Truk Islands in the western Pacific—islands we seized from the Japanese in World War II. However, the fears he expressed were startlingly similar to those being expressed after World War II by American Indians as they felt themselves threatened by a new government policy.

In the late 1940s and early 1950s United States Indian policy had changed course. What came to be called "termination" had come into vogue. It proposed the tapering off of government programs for the Indians, the transfer of some programs to the states, and planning for the dismantlement of the Bureau of Indian Affairs. Several thousand native Americans had their ties with the federal government severed, the most publicized cases being those of the Menominee and Klamath tribes.

Copyright by Western History Association. Reprinted by permission. The article first appeared as "Tribalism Rejuvenated: The Native American since the Era of Termination," *Western Historical Quarterly*, 12 (January 1981), 5–16.

To supporters of termination it seemed simply a return to the antitribal, assimilationist policies that had prevailed for a hundred years before the Indian New Deal of the 1930s. To the terminationists, the reforms of the 1930s designed to strengthen the tribe as a political, economic, and cultural unit had been at best an aberration, at worst a bad mistake.

During its first half-century the United States had pursued a contradictory policy on tribalism. On the one hand, through the negotiation of treaties and the manipulation of annuity payments to encourage selected chiefs and tribal councils, it had helped develop and sustain a political unity that in most cases had not existed before. When the European invaders reached these shores, the political unit for Indians living in the eastern part of the American continent had been the village. What would later be designated by the United States as a tribe or nation, and treated as a political entity, was most likely at time of contact to have been several autonomous villages whose common culture provided the only real bond among them. The Indian nations, kingdoms, and confederacies which appear in such profusion in the literature of the seventeenth century were largely the result of a common phenomenon—the tendency of Europeans to apply to other cultures the political vocabulary with which they were familiar.

Farther west this nomenclature had even less relevance. The unit for the nomadic tribe of the plains was the band, membership in which could shift dramatically over a period of a few years with the fortunes of war and hunting and the vagaries of the personal relationships of its members. If for no other reason than to have tribal leadership with which binding agreements could be made and maintained, it was in the interest of the United States to encourage centralization of authority and the development of credible tribal governments where they had not previously existed.

From the 1840s down to the end of the nineteenth century, even as the Indians were being concentrated on reservations and being stripped of all but a fraction of their land, administratively it still was in the interest of the United States to develop a more coherent tribal leadership. Anyone who has studied the history of a tribe's relations with the United States in this period has seen this happening. Moreover, for Indians who previously had lived in scattered autonomous villages, or as the members of the smaller and less permanent plains bands, reservation existence produced a tribal identity that was more intense and more real than they had experienced before. It usually was a devastating experience for the individual, but the reservation life made tribes of what had been loose aggregations of bands or villages.

The United States, although it might find the new situation administratively convenient, had no intention of perpetuating tribalism. Assimilation of the Indian into American society was the long-range objective, not perpetuation of separate tribal identities. Reservations were simply to be way stations for the Indian on his road to assimilation. What one commissioner of Indian Affairs referred to as "this empty pride of separate nationalism" was not to be permitted to stand in the way of assimilation and integration.

The result was a contradiction between a day-by-day policy requiring the development of tribal political institutions to ease administration and long-range policies calling for their abolition. Meanwhile, Indian agents would experiment with tribal councils, business committees, and other political bodies to enable them to control reservation populations. What the agents hoped to do was to identify Indian leaders who could command respect in their tribes and yet be thoroughly amenable to direction by the agent. Such an ideal combination was seldom found, but the search went on. In the meantime, the confines of the reservation afforded a commonality of experience that was a boon to tribalism.

The tribe as a political institution was supposed to be dealt a mortal blow by the attack on communal ownership delivered by the land in severalty policy. It did result in the breakup of most Indian reservations, as individual Indians were allotted farms and the surplus land was opened to settlement by whites. By the early 1900s fewer than thirty-five reservations remained intact, and over half of these tribes were the atypical pueblos along the upper Rio Grande. Nevertheless, those tribes whose reservations had lost their territorial integrity did not automatically lose their ties with the federal government. Perhaps as a bureaucratic survival ploy, perhaps, as a secretary of the interior argued, because the Indian struggling to exist on his new farm needed guidance at this critical stage, the Bureau of Indian Affairs did not wither away. Indeed, it grew. In 1900 it had less than 6,000 employees and a budget of less than $9 million. Today the bureau has 16,000 employees and a budget of about $1 billion.

A principal argument for maintenance of an agency, or superintendency as it was labeled early in this century, was the provision in severalty agreements that Indian allotments should be held in trust by the federal government for twenty-five years. In 1906 it became possible for this trust period to be extended indefinitely at the discretion of the secretary of the interior. Thus the United States continued to pursue a contradictory policy, on the one hand pledged to eliminating tribalism and integrating the tribesmen, and on the other hand continuing to deal on a day-by-day basis with Indians as members of tribes. Even tribes that no longer held reservations in common, and that was most of them, continued to maintain nominal governments.

Thus, when John Collier became Indian commissioner in the New Deal era and sought to revive the tribe as a political, economic, and social unit, he had more to work with than reformers of the 1870s and 1880s had presumed would survive. Today, students of the Collier era may differ among themselves about the value of the New Deal reforms, but they agree that they did breathe new life into tribalism.

When this heightened tribal consciousness and loyalty was threatened by termination in the post–World War II period, it was Native Americans themselves who took the lead in opposing it. Paradoxically, it was the extent to which they had been assimilated that gave them the skills to resist effectively. They now knew how to generate support in the media, how and whom to approach in the halls of Congress. Their agitation set the stage for the repudiation of termination. Both national political parties denounced it in their 1960 platforms. A task force on Indian policy established in the Kennedy administration recommended that termination give way to self-determination. Presidents Lyndon B. Johnson and Richard M. Nixon stated their unequivocal support for the maintenance of Indian identity, and politically this meant the tribe.

Tribalism also gained strength from the Red Power movements of the sixties and seventies. Although most of it was urban oriented, Indian activism placed increasing emphasis upon tribal identity, on reservation roots. Leaders of the several militant groups sought to demonstrate their reservation connections, to establish their credentials as what would come to be called, sometimes in jest, "grassroots Indians."

But the resurgence of tribalism required more than sentiment and emotion, slogans and demonstrations. In the final analysis, tribalism could amount to little unless the federal government cooperated, and cooperate it did. In 1973 Congress, which had set the ball rolling on termination a generation earlier, began to reverse the process by restoring the Menominee tribe to federal recognition. Other tribes that had been terminated also had their special ties to the government restored, and more have requested reinstatement.

Besides the nearly 300 tribes or other Indian groupings which have federal recognition, there are about 130, principally in the East, that do not enjoy this status. Most of these are currently seeking recognition. Indeed, one enterprising university-based anthropologist has proposed establishing a research center, financed of course by federal grants, to help authenticate tribal claims to federal recognition.

As an example of one tribe that has been successful in regaining federal recognition we have the Coushatta of Louisiana. A small tribe of about 250 people, in earlier periods it had received some federal services in the area of health and education, but these were terminated in 1953. In recent years when the tribe sought reinstatement, the Coushatta discovered failure to meet one of the criteria laid down by the government for recognition—holding land in common. This deficiency, however, was corrected by an association which purchased fifteen acres for the tribe.

The great attraction to tribes like the Coushatta in federal recognition, aside from certain psychological benefits resulting from acceptance of their Indian identity, clearly is the cornucopia of federal programs for which they become eligible. Today over $2 billion is expended in federal programs for the less than a million Indians, about half of whom live on or near reservations. One tabulation of grant programs available to Indians lists seventy-two. Unfortunately, many different departments and agencies are involved, and there is no coordination of the many programs. This inevitably leads to duplication and to what one tribal chairman called "haphazard spending." It does, nevertheless, represent a great increase in funding for Indian programs since 1960, when virtually all were administered by the Bureau of Indian Affairs, which had a budget of less than $120 million. In contrast, today's BIA budget is about $1 billion, and that probably represents less than half of what is going into Indian programs in 1980.

The change began in the Kennedy administration when Commissioner of Indian Affairs Philleo Nash emphasized the need for Indians to become eligible for more programs. Nash helped qualify them for redevelopment aid, and he interested federal housing agencies in Indian reservations.

When President Johnson succeeded Kennedy and launched his war on poverty, the reservations really came into their own. With unemployment rates as shockingly high as 80 percent, infant mortality and suicide rates higher than the national average, and Indian longevity significantly less than that of non-Indian citizens, reservations were an obvious place for antipoverty programs to be instituted. At least in part as a result of Indian lobbying, when the Office of Economic Opportunity was established, Indian needs became the responsibility of a special section—"Indian desk" in bureaucratic jargon—of that new federal agency. When the OEO spawned programs like Job Corps, Neighborhood Youth Corps, and Head Start, tribesmen got their share of the dollars. As Congress created still other programs, the Indians were taken care of in the eligibility sections of the laws which included the phrase "and/or Indian tribes."

The result has been a veritable revolution in tribal funding. Tribes which before 1960 might have had budgets of $50,000 have today multi-million-dollar budgets. As an example of this, we have the Seneca nation of Indians in western New York. The Seneca nation has over 5,000 members, only about half of whom live on the nation's two reservations. Currently, annual funding from federal sources for the Senecas is estimated to be about $6 million.

This funding in recent years had done a number of things for the Senecas. Not the last of these is making their reservations more attractive places to live, thus reinforcing tribalism. In 1980 Senecas need not go to Buffalo or Rochester to find jobs and decent housing. Indeed, some have left cities to return to the reservation and tribal life. Federal funds have built community buildings on the two Seneca reservations, also a bowling alley, a sports center, and a campground, all to be operated by the nation. Nearly a hundred units of housing have been funded, and federal grants have provided bilingual education programs and a large CETA [Comprehensive Employment Training Act] operation. Among the many other grants were ones enabling the Senecas to hire secretaries and bookkeepers, health aides, and recreation directors. The Seneca nation, with a reservation population of less than 3,000 people, has about 300 employees, most of them paid from grant money.

What is happening to the Senecas is happening to other tribes as well. One estimate is that in 1979 the seven tribes in South Dakota received grants totaling about $185 million. It is little wonder that grantsmanship has become a major preoccupation of tribal leaders. A former tribal chairman, and the current president of the National Congress of American Indians, Ed Driving Hawk, has said that "tribal governments have become more administrators of federal programs than tribal governments." Like many research-oriented universities and municipalities from New York City to Manhattan, Kansas, tribes have become dependent upon these grants. As another Indian phrased it, "The government is the Indian's new buffalo."

Federal funding has not only greatly increased in volume and variety, an effort is being made to involve the tribes in the administration of the programs. In 1974 Congress passed the Indian Self Determination and Education Assistance Act, which offered tribes significant opportunities to regain control of their community affairs. Under the new law tribes could contract to take over federal programs, with the Bureau of Indian Affairs providing technical assistance. This was the legislative fulfillment of President Nixon's 1970 charge: "We must assure the Indian that he can assume control of his own life without being separated involuntarily from the tribal group . . . [or] being cut off from Federal concern and Federal support."

It is not intended, of course, that federal funding become a permanent crutch for reservation economies and tribal budgets. But the question is: where can the tribal government find other support? They usually do not have the tax base available to local governments. Much effort and federal funding have gone into trying to attract industry to reservations to remedy this situation and also to provide employment for reservation residents. But the results have not been impressive. Most of the plants have been marginal operations which had a brief life. Reservation environments generally are not attractive to industry, which needs good transportation, proximity to markets and raw materials, and a well-trained and experienced pool of workers.

Tourism has been offered as another solution to reservation economic problems. Several tribes have opened ski lodges, motels, and campgrounds, usually with the assistance of federal grants, but again without outstanding success.

Very few tribes are in the enviable position of holding large reserves of gas and oil, uranium, and other minerals. Although probably no more than ten tribes can expect to derive substantial income from natural resources, twenty-five belong to CERT—the Council of Energy Resource Tribes— which is sometimes described as a native American OPEC, one incidentally launched with federal funding.

For all but a very few tribes, continued dependence on the federal government seems to be the price for a tribal existence, if living standards for the tribesmen are to approach those of mainstream Americans. Nevertheless, there has been considerable talk in the last twenty years of tribal sovereignty. Just what tribal sovereignty is is something Indians do not agree upon. A handful, like the Mohawks who recently have located on 6,000 acres provided by the state of New York, claim sovereignty in the pure sense—untrammeled autonomy, with no ties to New York, much less to the United States.

For most tribes, however, what they seek is control over their own populations and reservation land bases. They want the framework of federal, state, and local governments expanded to include tribal governments. One unlikely recent proposal is to give tribes representation in Congress, the senators and representatives to be selected by an intertribal caucus.

The question of tribal sovereignty is hardly a new issue. A century and a half ago John Marshall's Supreme Court declared tribes to be domestic, dependent nations immune from state control. Neither Georgia nor the federal government chose to honor that decision, and today there are many ambiguities in state-tribal and federal-tribal relations.

Recent controversies between states and tribes usually have stemmed from efforts of tribal governments to assert themselves, particularly against Public Law 280. This 1953 enactment transferred to some state governments jurisdiction over reservations in those states. This was a part of the termination era legislation and has been denounced by Indians and their friends as "a noose choking Indian Tribes and the Indian way of life out of existence." However, the influx of dollars from federal programs has given tribes new muscle, and a reawakening of tribal pride and Indian nationalism has given them the will to resist.

All kinds of legal questions have arisen as a result of these confrontations, for example:

1. Do tribes have the right to tax non-Indians, as well as their own people?
2. Can states levy severance taxes on minerals mined on reservations?
3. Must reservation store owners collect state sales taxes?
4. Can tribes ignore state liquor-licensing regulations and enact their own?
5. Can tribes ignore state game conservation laws and enact and enforce their own?
6. Particularly in the Southwest, where water is an increasingly scarce commodity, what rights do Indians have to the water in streams crossing their reservations? If booming communities like Phoenix are downstream, this can be a question of considerable import in the arid Southwest.

There are dozens of other questions that have been raised, and slowly a body of law is being arrived at by the courts. However, lawyers have a faculty for demonstrating that their client's case is unique and requires a new interpretation of the law. With 389 treaties, 5,000 statutes, 2,000 federal court decisions, and 500 attorney general's opinions to choose from, a good lawyer can usually find what he needs.

By and large, court decisions in recent years have clearly affirmed the right of tribal governments to tax and control their own populations. In one important case, *Oliphant,* however, the Supreme Court in 1978 has held that a tribe cannot have criminal jurisdiction over non-Indians.

Greatly complicating the question of jurisdiction is the fact that most reservations no longer exist as territorial entities. What might have been a three-million-acre reservation in 1880, and still appearing on many maps a century later as a solid block of Indian land, may actually have been broken up by allotment in severalty, the result being "checkerboarding" with Indian and white holdings intermingled. Most of that three million acres may now be in non-Indian hands. In fact, non-Indians may outnumber the Indians within what had been the boundaries of the old reservation. And of the Indian-owned land, not all of that may be held in trust by the federal government.

Despite these changed circumstances, there can still be a tribal government with a police force attempting to exercise jurisdiction over all of what would have been the original three-million-acre tract. But over whom do they have authority? If you run afoul of the law in any village or city in the United States, there is no question of the authority of the local police to arrest you and hold you for trial. In contrast, an Indian policeman must determine if the crime took place on Indian or non-Indian land and make certain that the suspect is a local Indian over whom he has jurisdiction. As one tribal chairman put it: "Policemen need tract books, surveyors, and a battery of lawyers to determine the probable extent of their jurisdiction." Other have suggested that genealogical charts would be helpful.

While those problems are being confronted principally in the West, some of the most dramatic developments involving the revival of tribalism are going on in the East. They are the outgrowth of suits tribes have filed against states, claiming that the states obtained land from them in treaties not supervised by the federal government as required by a 1790 law.

In the most publicized case, the Penobscots and Passamaquoddies have reached a tentative settlement with the state of Maine which could bring the Indians a $27-million trust fund, plus 300,000 acres—if Congress will appropriate the $81.5 million required. Not only is the federal taxpayer to finance the settlement, the Indian position in the suit has been supported by attorneys of the Justice Department.

The settlement does require the Penobscots and Passamaquoddies to relinquish all other land claims—too high a price for those who put the greatest value on sovereignty. They would have preferred that the tribes hold out for a treaty guaranteeing exclusive jurisdiction, even if the financial settlement had been less satisfactory.

A precedent for this type of settlement was set in a case last year which had the Narragansett Indians suing Rhode Island. The Indians won and got 1,800 acres, purchased by $3.5 million provided by the federal government. The land is not of particularly good quality, but it will provide the Narragansetts with a basis for going after federal recognition and grants for development. They are already talking about schools, housing for the elderly, a vocational training center, and a community building.

Incidentally, these cases are not related to those brought by tribes before the Indian Claims Commission. Some 475 cases out of over 600 settled before the commission ceased to operate in 1978, and those remaining on the docket were turned over to the Court of Claims. Over $800 million in judgments against the United States have been awarded.

The financial benefits of tribal membership, stemming from these judgments, have been a factor, though one difficult to measure, in determining individual attitudes toward maintenance of tribal ties. A major motivation for Congress establishing the Indian Claims Commission in 1946 had been to expedite disposal of claims Native Americans had against the government, as a prelude to termination. Over twenty years later the Indian Claims Commission went out of business after disposing of most of the claims. However, the financial settlements have given a new value to tribal affiliation and Indians are more firmly entrenched than ever as wards of the government, despite all the talk about sovereignty.

Some native Americans are troubled by the contradiction inherent in tribes insisting on remaining wards of the federal government, and continuing to be recipients of federal funding, while talking sovereignty. Alfonso Ortiz, a San Juan Pueblo and a prominent anthropologist, has observed, with pardonable exaggeration, that "dependence upon Washington is the greatest threat that Indians face today, certainly greater than pestilence and flood or famine. . . ." Indian traditionalists are particularly concerned, noting that reservation populations that thirty years ago were poor but relatively self-supporting are today becoming welfare states at the mercy of congressional committees determining appropriation levels. Sometimes the argument for traditional values comes from unlikely sources, for example, an Indian who is a university and law school graduate, with service in a state legislature and currently special counsel for a Senate committee—presumably living the good life in Washington, D.C. He advocates reservations being kept "as primitive as possible," denounces all economic development as "a colonial approach to exploiting Indians," and suggests Indians would save money and be healthier without automobiles.

Tribalism enters the 1980s alive and flourishing, despite the efforts of the terminationists of the post–World War II era. The impetus for tribalism in the last twenty years would seem to have come from three sources: (1) the heightened pride in tribal identity, the Indianness, which was both a cause and a result of the Red Power movement, (2) the switch in government policy from termination to self-determination, and (3) the substantial financial benefits accruing to tribal membership from the judgments awarded by the Indian Claims Commission and from the greatly increased level of federal funding since the early 1960s.

Of these factors contributing to the rejuvenation of tribalism, two of them obviously depend on the vagaries of government policy. Given the present trends in government, it is unlikely that the current levels of funding enjoyed by the tribes will be maintained, much less increased. However, it is difficult to envision a return to the terminationist and assimilationist policies of the 1950s. The larger tribes, with a clearly definable territorial base and assured sources of income, should have a degree of autonomy comparable to that enjoyed by local governments throughout the United States. But such autonomy will be impractical for the average tribe of two or three thousand members, with no real land base, and heavily dependent upon federal grants.

As usual, the great variety of tribal conditions makes generalizing about Native Americans a risky pastime. However, tribalism has survived two centuries of the United States, and there seems to be no reason to assume it cannot survive another two. Of one thing I am confident. If I were to return to western New York in the year 2180, I would expect to find a people calling themselves Senecas and easily distinguishable from the surrounding population. Tribalism is an enduring institution.

Aztlán Rediscovered

JOHN R. CHÁVEZ

During the middle and late 1960s, the political situation in the United States developed into a crisis that permitted a resurgence of the image of the lost land. The myths of the Spanish Southwest and the American Southwest, which the Mexicans of the region had accepted for much of the twentieth century, were suddenly set aside. During that period when so many myths were being reexamined by U.S. society in general, many Mexican-Americans found it possible to challenge the images of themselves and their region that had been imposed by the Anglo majority. The shattering effect that the civil rights and the antiwar movements had on the Anglo self-image led many Mexican-Americans to believe that their attempts to be like Anglos were against their own interests. They began to feel that perhaps they had more in common with blacks and even the Vietnamese than with the dominant Anglo-Americans. Reviewing their own socioeconomic position after two decades of "Americanization," Mexican-Americans found themselves lower even than blacks in income, housing, and education. Though they were not as discriminated against or segregated as blacks, Mexican-Americans realized that they had in no way become the equals of Anglos. In searching for the causes, the view that all "immigrant" groups initially experienced such problems seemed to explain less and less, for by 1960, 81 percent of Mexicans in the Southwest were United States–born. Furthermore, the condition of longtime residents in New Mexico and Texas was no better and often worse than that of other Mexican-Americans.

The nationalist movements of such peoples as the Vietnamese and the Cubans inspired a significant number of Mexican-Americans to reexamine their own condition through history and conclude that they too had been the victims of U.S. imperialism. As a result, the nineteenth- and early twentieth-century image of the Southwest as lost and of themselves as dispossessed reemerged from the collective unconscious of the region's Mexicans. As we have seen, that image had persisted, largely because of the intense Mexican nationalism that radiated from across the border, but in the 1960s it was reasserted and reshaped under the influence of contemporary ideas. Increasingly after World War II the former colonies of the world gained political independence and established nonwhite rule. Nonwhites sought to reestablish pride in their own racial backgrounds to combat the feelings of inferiority that colonialism had imposed. In the United States this phenomenon manifested itself in calls for black pride and black power, and also in cries for Chicano pride and Chicano power. The use of the term "Chicano," derived from *mexicano* and formerly used disparagingly in referring to lower-class Mexican-Americans, signified a renewed pride in the Indian and mestizo poor who had built so much of the Southwest

"Aztlan Rediscovered," from *The Lost Land: The Chicano Image of the Southwest*, 129–155, with some abridgements, by John R. Chávez, © 1984 by University of New Mexico Press. Reprinted by permission.

during the Spanish and Anglo colonizations. While investigating the past of their indigenous ancestors in the Southwest, activist Chicanos rediscovered the myth of Aztlán and adapted it to their own time.

After gaining independence from Spain and again after the revolution of 1910, Mexicans had turned to their ancient past for inspiration. It is no surprise that Chicano activists did the same thing during the radical 1960s, especially given the example of contemporary nationalist movements. In the ancient myth of Aztlán, activists found a tie between their homeland and Mexican culture that antedated the Republic of Mexico, the Spanish exploration of the borderlands, and even Tenochtitlán (Mexico City) itself. As we have seen, ancient Aztec legends, recorded in the chronicles of the sixteenth and seventeenth centuries, recounted that before founding Tenochtitlán the Aztecs had journeyed from a wondrous place to the north called "Aztlán." Since this place of origin, according to some of the chroniclers, was located in what is now the Southwest, Chicano activists reapplied the term to the region, reclaiming the land on the basis of their Indian ancestry. And although the preponderance of evidence indicates that the Aztlán of the Aztecs was actually within present Mexico, the activists' use of the term had merit. While the Aztlán whence the Aztecs departed for Tenochtitlán was probably in the present Mexican state of Nayarit, anthropological studies suggest that the distant ancestors of the Aztecs centuries prior to settling in Nayarit had inhabited and migrated through the Southwest. Thus, on the basis of Indian prehistory, Chicanos had a claim to the region, a claim stronger than any based only on the relatively brief history of Spanish settlement in the borderlands.

Since Aztlán had been the Aztec equivalent of Eden and Utopia, activists converted that ancient idealized landscape into an ideal of a modern homeland where they hoped to help fulfill their people's political, economic, and cultural destiny. Therefore, though "Aztlán" came to refer in a concrete sense to the Southwest, it also applied to any place north of Mexico where Chicanos hoped to fulfill their collective aspirations. These aspirations in the 1960s, it turned out, were more or less the same hopes Southwest Mexicans had had since the Treaty of Guadalupe Hidalgo. Chicanos sought bilingual/bicultural education, just representation in the government, justice in the courts, fair treatment from the police and the military, a decent standard of living, and ultimately that which controlled the possibilities of all their other aspirations—their share of the means of production, for this, intellectuals at least now believed, was what the Anglo conquest had fundamentally denied Southwest Mexicans. The northern homeland had been lost militarily and politically in the 1840s; the economic loss had come in subsequent decades with the usurpation of individually and communally owned lands that produced the wealth of the region. During Mexican rule the wealth of the land had been largely agricultural, but later the land of the Southwest had also given forth gold, silver, copper, coal, oil, uranium, and innumerable other products that enriched the Anglos but left Mexicans impoverished. In this respect, Chicanos increasingly saw a parallel between themselves and the native peoples of other colonized lands: all had been conquered, all had been reduced to menial labor, and all had been used to extract the natural bounty of their own land for the benefit of the conquerors.

The Chicanos' historic loss of the economic power inherent in the land of the Southwest underlay the manifestations of militant nationalism that erupted in the late 1960s: the farmworker strikes in California, the land grant struggle in New Mexico, the revolt of the electorate in Crystal City, Texas, the school walkouts in Denver and Los Angeles, and the other major events of what came to be called the Chicano movement. Though these events exploded with suddenness, they were preceded by calmer yet significant developments in the previous decade that prepared a sizable number of Mexican-Americans for the move away from Americanization. As we have seen, the 1950s and early 1960s had been the nadir in the history of Mexican nationalism in the Southwest. But even though Mexican-American organizations had generally been weakened by the assimilation of potential members into the Anglo world, several new groups had managed to establish themselves during that time. The most important of these were the Mexican-American Political Association (MAPA) founded in California in 1959 and the Political Association of Spanish-Speaking Organizations (PASO or PASSO) founded in Arizona in 1960 and most influential in Texas. These two differed from the League of United Latin American Citizens, the G. I. Forum, and other earlier groups because the new organizations believed in activating the political power of Mexican-Americans for the overall good of Mexican-Americans. Earlier groups, more assimilationist in perspective, preferred a defensive posture, protecting the rights of Mexican-Americans in the name of all U.S. citizens. While the difference may seem subtle, the new emphasis on self-interest rather than universality prepared the way for the rebirth of Chicano nationalism. . . .

On 16 September (Mexican Independence Day) 1965, César Chávez's predominantly Mexican-American National Farm Workers Association (NFWA) voted to join a grape strike initiated in Delano, California, by the Filipino Agricultural Workers Organizing Committee (AWOC). Because of their greater numbers, Mexican-Americans soon dominated the strike and later controlled the United Farm Workers' Organizing Committee (UFWOC), which came into being as a result of the merger of the two original unions. This strike was to lead to the first successful agricultural revolt by one of the poorest groups of Chicanos in the Southwest. Interestingly, this revolt was led by a man who believed in nonviolence, democracy, and religion; who had little faith in government programs; and who distrusted the very Chicano nationalism he inspired.

Chávez, whose grandfather was a "pioneer" in Arizona in the 1880s, was born near Yuma in 1927. "Our family farm was started three years before Arizona became a state," Chávez once remarked. "Yet, sometimes I get crank letters . . . telling me to 'go back' to Mexico!" As a result of the depression the family's land was lost in 1939 because of unpaid taxes, and the Chávezes migrated to California where they became farm workers. After years of such work and a period in the navy, César Chávez joined the Community Service Organization which, though overwhelmingly Mexican-

American in membership, stressed the acquisition and exercise of the rights of citizenship by the poor of all ethnic groups. This early influence later helped Chávez gain widespread support for the farm workers, even though it prevented him from becoming a true spokesman for Chicano nationalism. After ten years in the CSO, Chávez in 1962 decided to organize farm workers on his own when the CSO decided the task was beyond its range of activities.

Shortly after the NFWA voted to strike, Chávez appealed to religious and civil rights groups for volunteers. By doing so, he converted a labor dispute into a social movement, and expanded his Mexican-American and Filipino base of support by including all others who wished to help. At the same time he nonetheless acknowledged that race was an issue in the strike. Chávez encouraged nationalism among the farm workers because he knew it could be a cohesive force against the Anglo growers who were accustomed to treating racial minorities as inferiors. Indeed, the Virgin of Guadalupe, the patroness of Mexico, became one of the chief nationalistic symbols used in the movement's demonstrations. Luis Valdez, playwright and propagandist for the farm workers, described her significance:

> The Virgin of Guadalupe was the first hint to farm workers that the pilgrimage [to Sacramento in the spring of 1966] implied social revolution. During the Mexican Revolution, the peasant armies of Emiliano Zapata carried her standard, not only because they sought her divine protection, but because she symbolized the Mexico of the poor and humble. It was a simple Mexican Indian, Juan Diego, who first saw her in a vision at Guadalupe. Beautifully dark and Indian in feature, she was the New World version of the Mother of Christ. Even though some of her worshippers in Mexico still identify her with Tonatzin, an Aztec goddess, she is a Catholic saint of Indian creation—a Mexican. The people's response was immediate and reverent. They joined the march by the thousands, falling in line behind her standard.

Thus, through the Virgin, Chávez and the Chicano workers linked their struggle to their aboriginal Mexican past.

Although the Mexican symbols used by the movement were generally associated with Mexico proper, Chávez was also aware of the Chicano farm workers' indigenous background in the Southwest. He had a personal interest in the history of the California missions and in their treatment of the Indians, the first farm workers. Chávez believed that though the missionaries had indeed used coercion on the Indians, they had saved them from far worse treatment at the hands of the secular authorities and the settlers. They had done this by making the missions sanctuaries where the Indians could work the land communally and by forcing the settlers to treat the Indians as human beings. As a result, Chávez once commented, "The Spanish began to marry the Indians . . . they couldn't destroy them, so instead of wiping out a race, they made a new one." The relative autonomy of the missions, politically and economically, together with the Franciscans' belief in the equality of all human souls, permitted the Indians a certain amount of security and even on occasion complete acceptance through intermarriage with the settlers. Like their Indian predecessors, twentieth-century farm workers, in Chávez's eyes, could only gain their rightful place in society if they believed in their own racial equality with other men and established themselves as an independent political and economic force capable of challenging the new owners of the land.

Chávez fully realized what the historic loss of the land had meant to the Indians and to their Mexican successors. The "Plan of Delano," a Mexican-style proclamation stating the discontent of the farm workers and the aims of Chávez and his movement, reminded society of the oppression Southwest Mexicans had endured: "The Mexican race has sacrificed itself for the last hundred years. Our sweat and our blood have fallen on this land to make other men rich." Chávez knew that the power of the Anglo growers rested on their ownership of the land, and he also realized that Chicanos and the other poor would ultimately achieve full equality only when they had recovered that land: "While . . . our adversaries . . . are the rich and the powerful and possess the land, we are not afraid. . . . We know that our cause is just, that history is a story of social revolution, and that the poor shall inherit the land." Though Chávez stated this belief publicly, he knew land reform was a distant ideal, and he was much too practical to make it a goal for his union. Despite this, the growers claimed that such statements, together with the symbols of Mexican nationalism, revealed Chávez to be communistic and un-American. One rancher remarked,

> Mr. Cesar Chavez is talking about taking over this state—I don't like that. Too much "*Viva Zapata*" and down with the Caucasians, *la raza* [the Latin American race], and all that. Mister Cesar Chavez is talking about *revolución*. Remember, California once belonged to Mexico, and he's saying, "Look, you dumb Mexicans, you lost it, now let's get it back!"

Despite such distortions and in spite of his actual encouragement of nationalism, Chávez feared the divisive effects it could have within the movement. Since the growers were quick to exploit such divisiveness, he would not allow intolerance to split the ranks of his Chicano, Filipino, and liberal Anglo supporters. He was especially concerned that Chicanos not let their incipient nationalism get out of hand: "We oppose some of this La Raza business. . . . We know what it does. When La Raza means or implies racism, we don't support it. But if it means our struggle, our dignity, or our cultural roots, then we're for it." Because of this guarded attitude, however, Chávez could never become a fully committed advocate of Chicano nationalism. His struggle after all was economic, rather than cultural; his concerns were those of the poor as a whole, rather than more specifically Chicano issues, such as bilingual education. On the other hand, Chávez showed Chicanos that their cultural problems could not be solved by politics alone, since these problems were economic at their source:

> Effective political power is never going to come, particularly to minority groups, unless they have economic power. . . . I'm not advocating . . . brown capitalism. . . . What I'm suggesting is a cooperative movement.

Such power lay in numbers and could best be harnessed if minority groups joined together with liberal Anglos in a broad interracial consumer movement.

During the grape strike, Chávez demonstrated how a cooperative movement could generate economic power, enough power to force the capitulation of the growers in 1970. His major weapon was a grape boycott extending beyond the Chicanos' Southwest, throughout the United States, and even into Europe. Since he had made the strike a moral and civil rights movement, many outsiders were willing to cooperate in the boycott. Within the UFWOC itself, as we have seen, Chávez made the workers understand that the struggle was for human equality, not merely for better wages and working conditions. As a result, in practical terms, the UFWOC itself became more a cooperative than a trade union: "It . . . developed for its members a death benefit plan; a coöperative grocery, drug store, and gas station; a credit union; a medical clinic; a social protest theatre group . . .; and a newspaper. . . ." Such cooperative policies together with the nonviolent, mass protest methods of the civil rights movement (methods Mexican-Americans had earlier disdained to use) effectively countered such traditional grower tactics as the employment of strikebreakers from Mexico. After the grape growers agreed to sign contracts with the UFWOC in 1970, the farm-worker movement in the succeeding decades became an ongoing force as the union entered the lettuce fields, fought for the renewal of old contracts, and expanded to other parts of the nation.

"Across the San Joaquin Valley," proclaimed the "Plan of Delano" in 1966, "across California, across the entire Southwest of the United States, wherever there are Mexican people, wherever there are farm workers, our movement is spreading like flames across a dry plain." Within a short time the farm-worker front of the Chicano movement had indeed spread to Arizona and Texas, but, more important, other fronts of the movement had opened independently throughout the Southwest in other sectors of Chicano life. One of these fronts was the renewal of the land grant struggle in northern New Mexico. As we saw earlier, after the Treaty of Guadalupe Hidalgo, Mexicans in the Southwest were gradually deprived of their lands by an Anglo-American legal and economic system that constantly challenged land grants made under previous governments. In his investigation of problems resulting from the land grant issue during the 1960s, Peter Nabokov wrote that in northern New Mexico:

> These ancestral holdings had originally been awarded to single people or to communities of at least ten village families. A man had his private home and a narrow rectangular plot which usually gave him access to river water. But the community's grazing and wood-gathering acreage, called *ejido*, was understood to be held commonly, and forever, a perpetual trust. A large percentage of the New Mexico *ejido* lands had been put in the public domain by the surveyors general of the period 1854–1880 because they recognized only claims made on behalf of individuals, not communities.

During the twentieth century much of this "public domain" was turned over to the Forest Service, which in turn was given the authority to lease the lands to private individuals and companies for the use and development of natural resources. Unfortunately for the long-settled small farmers of northern New Mexico, large out-of-state corporations, engaged in mining, logging, and tourism, received preferential treatment in their dealings with the Forest Service. The impoverished small farmers, on the other hand, were gradually denied their grazing rights by an agency that was unconcerned with and even hostile to their needs; in her study of the problem, Patricia Bell Blawis observed that "while logging firms contracted with the Forest Service for immense areas on their ancestral land, the grantees were forbidden to cut stovewood without a permit." Thus, according to Blawis, in the twentieth century the imperialism of the nineteenth continued surreptitiously: "The Forest Service is evidence of the colonial policy of the Federal government. . . . Through this Service, resources of the West are exploited by Washington, D.C. and its friends." As we have seen, the native Mexicans had in the past reacted violently to this colonialism: between the 1880s and the late 1920s, for instance, at least two groups of nightriders, Las Gorras Blancas and La Mano Negra, had burned buildings, torn down fences, and committed other such terrorist acts to protest the seizure of their lands. During the late 1960s such violence flared again.

In 1963 the militant Alianza Federal de Mercedes (the Federal Land Grant Alliance—always popularly known as the Alianza, even though the official name changed several times) was incorporated under the direction of a dynamic leader named Reies López Tijerina. Tijerina, whose great-grandfather had been robbed of his land and killed by Anglos, was born in Texas in 1926; he lived and moved throughout the Southwest and beyond as a farm worker and later as a poor itinerant preacher. During these wanderings, he came to believe that the problems of his people had resulted from their loss of the land, for as he later stressed, "the ties of our culture with the land are indivisible." As a consequence, he became interested in the land grant issue, spent a year studying the question in Mexico, and in 1960 settled in New Mexico where he felt there was the best hope of recovering the grants. After organizing many of the heirs into the Alianza, Tijerina unsuccessfully petitioned the U.S. government to investigate the land titles for violations of that portion of the Treaty of Guadalupe Hidalgo that guaranteed the property rights of Mexicans in the Southwest. He had also requested the Mexican government to look into the matter, but Mexico, having gradually become economically dependent on as well as ideologically aligned with the United States since the 1930s, had not and would not support any radical claims made by dissident Chicanos. Rebuffed in his efforts to get consideration through regular legal and political channels, Tijerina turned to civil disobedience.

In October of 1966 Tijerina and other *aliancistas* occupied the Echo Amphitheater, a section of the Carson National Forest that had once been part of the land grant of San Joaquín del Río de Chama. Since the original Spanish and Mexican grants had permitted the villagers a good deal of autonomy, the *aliancistas* declared themselves the Republic of San Joaquín and elected as mayor a direct descendant of the original grantee. When several forest rangers attempted to interfere, they were detained by the "republic," tried for trespassing, and released on suspended sentences. By allowing this, Tijerina hoped to challenge the jurisdiction of the Forest Service over the land, thus forcing the land grant issue into the courts, possibly as far as the Supreme Court. Also, the declaration of autonomy would make public the Chicanos' need for self-determination, their need to escape a whole range of problems caused by their incorporation into U.S. society. Not least of these was the war in Vietnam, which even the traditionally patriotic *nuevomexicanos* were beginning to oppose: "The people," as Tijerina had once remarked, "generally feel that our sons are being sent to Vietnam illegally, because many of these land grants are free city states and are independent." The "liberation" of the Echo Amphitheater had been a dangerous act, but as the increasingly radical Tijerina declared during the occupation: "Fidel Castro has what he has because of his guts. . . . Castro put the gringos off his island and we can do the same." Unfortunately for the Alianza, Tijerina would later serve two years in prison for assault on the rangers at the Echo Amphitheater; furthermore, the courts would refuse to admit discussion of the land grant issue.

During May of 1967, according to Nabokov, "private northern landowners . . . began suffering from the traditional symptoms of unrest—selective cattle rustling, irrigation ditch and fence wreckage, shot-up water tanks, and arson." Although there was no evidence the Alianza had committed these acts, the authorities actually feared that guerrilla warfare might break out in northern New Mexico. When Tijerina revealed that his group planned to have a conference on June 3 at Coyote, a small town near the San Joaquín grant, the authorities anticipated another occupation and prevented the meeting by declaring it an unlawful assembly, blocking the roads to the town, and arresting any *aliancistas* who resisted. This proved to be a mistake, for it brought on the very violence the authorities had feared. Feeling that their right to free assembly had been violated, the *aliancistas* decided to make a citizen's arrest of the district attorney responsible for the police action. On June 5, in the most daring move of the contemporary Chicano movement, Tijerina and about twenty other armed *aliancistas* attacked the courthouse at the county seat at Tierra Amarilla. In the ensuing shoot-out two deputies were wounded, the courthouse was occupied, and the Coyote prisoners were freed. Finding that the district attorney was not present, the *aliancistas* then fled the town with two hostages.

The reaction of the authorities brought the cause of the Alianza to the attention of the entire nation. Imagining "a new Cuba to the north," the state government in Santa Fe sent out four hundred National Guardsmen to join two hundred state troopers in an expedition into northern New Mexico that included the use of helicopters and two tanks. After a few days Tijerina was captured and charged with various crimes connected with the raid, though he was subsequently released on bail. Once in the national spotlight, Tijerina elaborated on the issues and goals of the land grant struggle, issues that were important to Chicanos throughout the Southwest; "Not only the land has been stolen from the good and humble people," he commented, "but also their culture. . . ." And he remarked, "A major point of contention is that we are being deprived of our language. . . ." Tijerina also argued that in addition to property rights, the cultural rights of his people were guaranteed by the Treaty of Guadalupe Hidalgo. Once the guarantees of this treaty were honored and discrimination was ended, Indo-Hispanos, as Tijerina often called his people, would take their rightful place as intermediaries in the pluralistic Southwest:

> We have been forced by destiny to adopt two languages; we will be the future ambassadors and envoys to Latin America. At home, I believe that the Southwest is breeding a special kind of people that will bridge the color-gap between black and white. . . . [Moreover] We are the people the Indians call their "lost brothers."

While the many charges against him were being handled in the courts, Tijerina continued his activities with the Alianza and also participated in the interracial, antipoverty Poor People's March on Washington in 1968. In 1969, however, the Alianza was deprived of Tijerina's leadership when he was imprisoned for the Echo Amphitheater incident. Suffering from poor health, he was paroled in July 1971, but on condition that he no longer hold office in the Alianza. Deprived of his full leadership and lacking the organized economic power of an institution such as the United Farm Workers, the Alianza lost much of its drive, and not until 1979 was it able to convince the government to give even nominal reconsideration to the land grant issue. Nonetheless, Tijerina and the Alianza did rejuvenate the ethnic pride of a good number of *nuevomexicanos*. Though many Hispanos considered Tijerina an outsider, many others joined his organization, and in doing so reaffirmed their ties to Mexico through reference to the Treaty of Guadalupe Hidalgo, and to their Indian ancestors through acceptance of the facts of *mestizaje* (Indo-Hispano intermarriage). In New Mexico no longer could "Spanish-Americans" easily deny their background. No longer could Spanish-American politicians, who had generally held a representative number of positions in government, ignore their economically depressed constituents without opposition from Chicano militants around the state—for increasingly among *nuevomexicanos* the image of the Spanish Southwest was giving way to the image of Aztlán.

The person most responsible for the adoption of the term "Aztlán" by the rapidly spreading Chicano movement was Rodolfo "Corky" Gonzales, leader of the Chicano community in Denver, Colorado. In modern times the term was first applied to the Chicano homeland in 1962 by Jack D. Forbes, a Native American professor who argued that Mexicans were more truly an Indian than a mestizo people; his mimeographed manuscript, "The Mexican Heritage of Aztlán (the Southwest) to 1821," was distributed among Mexican-Americans in the Southwest during the early 1960s. The term gained popularity, but was not universally accepted by the Chicano movement until, in the spring of 1969, the first Chicano national conference, in Denver, drafted "El plan espiritual de Aztlán," a document that declared the spiritual independence of the Chicano Southwest from the United States.

Paradoxically this sentiment was expressed in a city never legally within the confines of Mexico; however, like arguments for Puerto Rican independence presented in New York, this declaration from Denver signified the desire of a minority group for independence from the colonialism that had subjugated its native land and that continued to affect the individuals of the minority no matter where they resided within the United States.

Born in Denver in 1928, Corky Gonzales was primarily a product of the urban barrios, even though he spent part of his youth working in the fields of southern Colorado. He managed to escape poverty by becoming a successful boxer. As a result of the popularity gained from this career, he became an influential figure in the barrios and was selected to head various antipoverty programs in the early 1960s. By 1965, however, he had become disenchanted with the antipoverty bureaucracy. He concluded earlier than other Chicanos that the War on Poverty was designed to pacify rather than truly help the poor. Had he read it, he would have agreed with a later comment made by a Chicano editor when government and foundation money poured into northern New Mexico in the aftermath of Tierra Amarilla:

> They're trying to create *Vendido* power (sellout power) . . . trying to bring Vietnam to New Mexico and trying to create "leaders" the system can use as tools. But it hasn't worked with the Vietnamese and it's not going to work with Raza here in the United States.

Disgusted with the strings attached to funds from the government and foundations, Gonzales organized the Crusade for Justice, a community self-help group. Through their own fund-raising efforts, the members established a barrio service center, providing such assistance as child care, legal aid, housing and employment counseling, health care, and other services especially needed in poor urban areas. The Crusade was, moreover, outspoken in its concern for Chicano civil and cultural rights.

More than Chávez and even more than Tijerina, Gonzales felt that nationalism was the force that would get Chicanos to help one another, and that the success of his Crusade exemplified the possibilities of self-determination. Although his participation in the Poor People's March of 1968 revealed his belief in the necessity of interracial cooperation, at heart he felt that Chicanos would have to help themselves and would do so if they became aware of their proud history as a people. Of Chicanos in his state, he once said, "Colorado belongs to our people, was named by our people, discovered by our people and worked by our people. . . . We preach self-respect . . . to reclaim what is ours." Regarding the region as a whole, he commented, "Nationalism exists in the Southwest, but until now it hasn't been formed into an image people can see. Until now it has been a dream. It has been my job to create a reality out of the dream. . . ." The Crusade was part of that reality and so was the Chicano Youth Liberation Conference, called by Gonzales to bring together Chicanos from throughout the nation, but especially from the cities, where 80 percent of all Chicanos lived. In Gonzales urban youth found a leader, unlike Chávez or Tijerina, who had successfully attempted concrete solutions to city problems. Consequently, 1,500 Chicanos from many different organizations attended the conference of this urban nationalist.

As if in exhibit of the problems of urban Chicanos, the week before the conference riots broke out in the Denver barrios, resulting from events that began with a racist remark made by a teacher at a local high school. A student and community protest led to confrontation with police; according to Gonzales, "What took place . . . was a battle between the West Side 'liberation forces' and the 'occupying army.' The West Side won [police suffered some injuries and damage to equipment]." Although Gonzales opposed violence and tried to stop the rioting, he clearly felt the trouble was justified and was proud that Chicanos were capable of defending themselves against the government he believed had made internal colonies of the city's barrios. After the riots, the conference convened in an atmosphere permeated with nationalism and proclaimed the following in "El plan espiritual de Aztlán:"

> Conscious . . . of the brutal "Gringo" invasion of our territories, we, the Chicano inhabitants and civilizers of the northern land of Aztlán, from whence came our forefathers, reclaiming the land of their birth. . . . We [who] do not recognize capricious frontiers on the bronze continent. . . . we declare the independence of our mestizo nation.

In that proclamation the Chicano delegates fully revived their people's traditional image of the Southwest and clarified it for their own time: the Southwest was the Chicano homeland, a land paradoxically settled by an indigenous people who were subsequently conquered. Furthermore, these people were now seen as native, not merely because their Spanish ancestors had settled the land hundreds of years before, but because their Indian ancestors had resided on the land thousands of years earlier, tying it permanently to Indian and mestizo Mexico.

With this image of the Southwest, the Chicano delegates established a context for a variety of demands that would gain impetus in the near future. Before long in the name of Aztlán and its people, activists would demand restitution from the United States for its conquest of the region and for its economic, political, and cultural oppression of the Southwest Mexican population. From the institutions of the United States, Chicanos would reject token representation and poverty programs with strings attached; from state and national institutions they would expect unrestricted compensation; over local institutions they would demand control. With such control, Chicanos hoped to establish bilingual/bicultural education, promote their own arts and customs, tax themselves, hire their own police, select their own juries, sit on their own draft boards, and especially found cooperatives to prevent further economic exploitation. Thus, the separatism at the conference, while expressing itself in the ideal of complete political independence from the United States, more importantly would promote the pragmatic goal of local autonomy. Gonzales' Crusade offered a practical example of how such autonomy might be gained. Another practical means, discussed at the conference, was the creation of a third party independent of Democrats and Republicans, especially in local elections. Many of these ideas found a national forum in the Chicano Youth Liberation Conference. This was Gonzales' major achievement. While his Crusade for Justice continued its work in Denver, as an organization it never spread far beyond that city. However, the delegates to the conference returned to their homes throughout the Southwest inspired by the urban nationalism that the Crusade exemplified. . . .

In urban areas, students from high school through graduate school had been the major force behind the Chicano movement at least since 1968. In the spring of that year Chicanos in five East Los Angeles high schools walked out of classes to protest conditions in the schools that resulted in extremely high drop-out rates. This led, over the next few years, to a series of walk-outs in one city after another, as Chicano students and instructors throughout the Southwest demanded new schools, more sensitive teachers, and bilingual/bicultural education. Although Chicano student groups had been organized before 1968, the activism of that year put those groups into the forefront of the urban movement. In the colleges and universities of the Southwest, these groups successfully demanded Chicano studies and affirmative action programs, programs that would help produce the first group of Chicano college graduates committed to the cultural survival of their people. Even before they had graduated, these students became involved in off-campus groups to organize the poor and uneducated in the barrios and rural towns. . . .

As time passed, campus groups that in 1967 had given themselves names such as the United Mexican American Students and the Mexican American Student Confederation became more militant. After many walk-outs and after Corky Gonzales's Chicano Youth Liberation Conference in 1969, most campus groups changed their names to El Movimiento Estudiantil Chicano de Aztlán (MECHA—The Chicano Student Movement of Aztlán), revealing their increasingly radical nationalism. At the Second Annual Chicano Youth Conference in the spring of 1970, representatives of student and other youth groups, reflecting their disenchantment with the United States, declared their opposition to the war in Vietnam. Many Chicanos were no longer proud of the fact that they, as a people, were once again dying in a U.S. war in disproportionately high numbers; moreover, they opposed dying in a war fought against a people they believed were victims of the same colonialism they themselves were experiencing. To demonstrate their opposition, a national Chicano antiwar rally was planned for August 1970 to be held in East Los Angeles, the barrio with the largest concentration of Mexican-Americans in the nation. Unfortunately, the rally became a riot when the police attempted to break up the demonstration and only succeeded in provoking the participants into the worst mass violence in East LA since 1943. For months thereafter violent protests erupted periodically, and the number of police on the streets of East LA visibly increased. Rarely had the colonial status of Chicanos seemed so evident.

After 1970 the open confrontations of the previous five years became less frequent as the Chicano movement entered a period of consolidation. Having had many of its hopes and grievances dramatized, the Chicano community was gradually able to take advantage of the advances the movement had attained, especially in education and self-awareness. With a renewed pride in their culture, Chicano intellectuals set out to express a world view that had long been suppressed. That their image of the Southwest as Aztlán was an important part of that world view was clear from the titles of many of the publications that appeared as Chicano culture experienced a renewal in literature, art, and social thought. A scholarly quarterly entitled *Aztlán: Chicano Journal of the Social Sciences and the Arts* was first issued in 1970 by Aztlán Publications at the University of California, Los Angeles. A bibliography by Ernie Barrios published in 1971 bore the title *Bibliografía de* Aztlán. In 1973 Luis Valdez and Stan Steiner edited a work called *Aztlán: An Anthology of Mexican American Literature*. Two novels, *Peregrinos de Aztlán* (1974) by Miguel Méndez M. and *Heart of Aztlan* (1976) by Rudolfo A. Anaya, also carried the ancient name of the Southwest. As if to secure that name for posterity, *Aztlan: The Southwest and Its People*, a history for juveniles by Luis F. Hernández, was published in 1975. Many other works with less obvious titles also reflected the rediscovered Chicano image of the Southwest. Among the most important was . . . *Occupied America* (1972) by Rodolfo Acuña. In this history of Chicanos, Acuña interpreted the tradition of the lost northern homeland according to the modern theory of colonialism, a theory that made the image of Aztlán more meaningful to contemporary Chicanos.

Needless to say, not all Mexican-Americans accepted the image of Aztlán. Among the masses the images of the Spanish Southwest and the American Southwest continued to predominate during the 1970s, and into the 1980s, largely because these were still promoted by the educational system and the mass media. Through bicultural and Chicano studies programs, Chicano intellectuals worked to change this situation. However, a small group of Mexican-Americans conversant with the affairs of their ethnic group refused to abandon borrowed images of the Southwest, usually because their lives had been formed within those images or because those views continued to help them accommodate themselves to the standards of Anglo society. Congressman Henry B. González of San Antonio, Texas, for example, had built his political career around the integrationist civil rights movement of the 1950s and early 1960s; as a result the nationalism of the Chicano movement struck him as nothing less than reverse racism. Since González accepted the integrationist melting pot ideal, he also perceived his region as the American Southwest, to which his parents, like European arrivals on the East Coast, had come to join the "nation of immigrants." Thus, in an address to Congress in 1969, he remarked:

> As it happens my parents were born in Mexico and came to this country seeking safety. . . . It follows that I, and many other residents of my part of Texas and other Southwestern States—happen to be what is commonly referred to as a Mexican-American.

Since his background only "happened" to be Mexican, González could see little importance in notions such as Aztlán and vigorously opposed Chicano militancy. . . .

Even though borrowed images of the Chicanos' place in the Southwest persisted, by the late 1970s some of the new group of educated Chicanos were in positions where they could reveal the image of Aztlán to the general public. For example, Tony Castro, a graduate of Baylor University, spent several years writing for various major newspapers around the country and was then hired in the late 1970s as a regular columnist for the conservative *Los Angeles Herald Examiner*. Devoting most of his columns and later his special reports to Chicano issues, Castro repeatedly exposed the generally conservative readership of that newspaper to the Chicano image of the Southwest:

> The Chicano has been here since the founding of California and the Southwest. His pre-Columbian ancestors wandered here from the north, migrating farther south and establishing the great civilizations of the Maya, the Toltecs, the Aztecs. . . . [Yet] Mexican-Americans . . . have been the conquered people, strangers in their own land. . . .

Young professionals like Castro who were willing to argue for their people's rightful place in the Southwest and the United States were the most successful product of the 1960s movement. As we have seen, educational improvement had been a major goal of the movement; consequently during the 1970s education was the area where Chicanos made their greatest strides. With Chicano college enrollment having tripled by 1978 (despite a leveling off of progress by that time), more teachers, social workers, writers, social scientists, and others influenced by the nationalism of the 1960s were echoing that nationalism, albeit with caution, from new positions throughout the Southwest.

Despite the emergence of this educated, nationalistic leadership, the progress of Chicanos as a whole was uneven in the 1970s and stagnant in the early 1980s. They continued to fit the description of a colonized people. In California, for example, where Chicanos were most heavily concentrated and where opportunities were often considered best, "Hispanics" over the age of twenty-five had completed high school at only 56 percent of the rate at which Anglos had gained the same level of schooling. And financially, the median Hispanic family income was only $16,140 or 71 percent of the equivalent white family income (1980 U.S. Census figures). While these figures did indicate some improvement over the 1960s, the gains were threatened by a backlash that persisted into the 1980s. Many of the educational and consequently the income gains of Chicanos had come as a result of affirmative action programs, compensatory programs that gave minorities preferential treatment in schooling and employment. These programs were attacked in the courts as reverse discrimination in case after case by Anglos who, though they failed to destroy the programs, managed to impede their effectiveness. Also, programs in Chicano studies and bilingual/bicultural education, while surviving, constantly met opposition from those who regarded them as contrary to the tradition of the nation of immigrants who learned English and forgot the old country. Given the fact that their educational and income gains were so recent, it is no surprise that Chicanos had accumulated little personal wealth and had made little progress toward recovering the means of production in their southwestern homeland.

This continuing lack of economic power in the 1970s and 1980s caused Chicano gains in the political arena to be inconclusive at best. While U.S. presidents generally appointed an increasing number of Chicanos to positions in their administrations, these appointees usually found themselves beholden to their benefactors and isolated in government with little real power to help their people. Even those Chicanos elected to political office could rarely represent fully the interests of their people, since as politicians they generally owed their elections to the Anglo-controlled coalitions that funded their campaigns. In many cases, of course, the politicians themselves continued to be ideologically traditional. For example, in 1974 Arizona and New Mexico elected as governors conservative Raúl Castro and moderate Jerry Apodaca, the first southwestern governors of Mexican descent since Octaviano Larrazolo fifty years earlier. If traditional electoral politics had been the best way to the improvement of Chicano life, the election of two Mexican-American governors should have brought significant social change for Chicanos in those states, but this did not happen because the ideological frame of mind and the political structures within which the governors worked were developed to protect the status quo. As we have seen, even the radical La Raza Unida party often found the traditional structures impregnable. Without such a radical organizational base, individual Chicano politicians, regardless of any personal nationalism, found themselves coopted by a system that defended the Anglo owners of the means of production. Many newly educated Chicano leaders in other fields found themselves bound by the same strictures. Since their salaries were bestowed on them by the system they often opposed, nationalistic Chicanos could not easily put their more radical beliefs into practice. Thus, though new leaders were more conscious of the forces in control, they were not yet in a position to topple neocolonialism in the Southwest.

This situation, however, failed to prevent Chicano nationalists from voicing their disapproval of the neocolonial practices of the United States. In Latin American affairs, for example, many Chicanos had long since become disillusioned with North American motives; President Johnson's armed intervention in the Dominican Republic in 1965 had shown the United States to be as imperialistic as ever. In 1973 North American cooperation in the overthrow of a democratically elected Marxist government in Chile convinced more Chicanos that the United States was more concerned with its economic interests than it was with democracy or social change in Latin America. In the early 1980s U.S. opposition to the new government of Nicaragua and to the leftist guerrillas of El Salvador caused renewed fears among Chicanos of possible U.S. military intervention in Central America. As we have noted, Mexicans in the United States had always seen their fate as closely tied to that of other Latin Americans, and as a consequence a significant group now believed continuing neocolonialism in Latin America to mean continuing neocolonialism in the Southwest. Quite naturally, Chicanos were most concerned with relations between the United States and Mexico, relations which intellectuals now interpreted as between metropolis and "neocolony."

José Angel Gutiérrez in 1971 remarked concerning Chicanos and Mexico, "the Rio Grande never has separated us and never will." During the 1970s and 1980s the growing dependence of Mexico on the United States would verify Gutiérrez's statement. Although the Mexican Revolution had been fought in part to free the country from foreign, specifically North American, economic domination, by 1978 the United States was once again the major investor in and chief trading partner of Mexico. Similar to the situation during the Díaz dictatorship, the Mexican government was stable, but the economy was erratic—at times superficially prosperous, but ultimately deeply troubled. Unfortunately most of the wealth was once again accruing to foreign investors and to the few Mexicans belonging to the middle and upper classes. The masses, burdened by one of the highest birth rates in the world, continued their struggle with poverty and, as in the past, looked to the north for employment. The most important pattern in Chicano history during the 1970s and 1980s was the renewed migration of Mexicans into the Southwest. Composed almost entirely of undocumented workers, commonly called illegal aliens, this movement was the largest yet from Mexico. Though estimates of their number, based on apprehensions of the undocumented by the Immigration and Naturalization Service (INS), varied tremendously, the actual figure was undoubtedly in the millions.

The arrival of so many undocumented workers presented problems for Chicanos; nevertheless, it could be argued that the migration was beneficial. As in previous migratory waves, the new arrivals competed with U.S. Mexicans for low-paying jobs and low-cost housing; they seemingly depressed wages and helped cause unemployment; they occasionally served as strikebreakers, and sometimes competed with Chicanos for aid from the government. Since the undocumented generally settled in the southwestern barrios, Chicanos not only bore the brunt of competition from the newcomers, but were also exposed to renewed Anglo-American xenophobia. With the appearance of so many un-Americanized newcomers, the Anglo notion that all people in the barrios were foreigners once again seemed plausible. As a result, harassment of Chicanos by INS agents increased, and some employers became more cautious about hiring anyone who looked Mexican since that person might be an undocumented worker. During the 1970s and 1980s, the illegal alien question, of all issues concerning Chicanos, was by far the most commonly discussed in the Anglo communications media. Though the undocumented were usually discussed in terms of a social problem, for example as an alleged tax burden on the citizenry, these terms usually hid a very real Anglo fear that the Southwest was being culturally and racially reconquered by Mexicans—a fear not entirely unfounded.

"There is a distinct possibility," wrote one openly racist Anglo, "if the legal and illegal seepage of Mexican genes across the Rio Grande and the high Mexican-American birthrate continue at present levels, that Mexican-Americans will regain their lost territories of Alta California and Texas . . .—not by violence or minority politics but simply by exercising squatters' rights." In October of 1977, this fear of Mexican invasion was so aroused by the media that the Ku Klux Klan announced it would conduct its own armed surveillance of the boundary to assist the undermanned Border Patrol in arresting illegal aliens. With the tacit approval of certain officials in the INS and of the San Diego (California) police, some Klan patrols were planned, but this activity ceased after strenuous protests from Chicano and other minority groups. Their nationalism having been revived during the 1960s, most U.S. Mexicans no longer disassociated themselves from their fellows across the border; they were no longer willing to stand by, as they had in the 1930s and 1950s, and watch Mexicans mistreated simply for lacking proper documents. Even though undocumented workers competed directly with Mexican-Americans, most Chicanos now felt their common national heritage outweighed their practical differences. Indeed, this feeling was strong enough that Chicano activists threatened to form their own armed patrols to counter the Klan's.

That Chicanos had to some extent readopted their Mexican imagination was evident from the similarity of their image of the Southwest to the image of the region perceived by the undocumented. "Undocumented workers," reported Grace Halsell, author of *The Illegals,* "do not feel they commit a crime in traveling north from Mexico. They call it going to *el norte.* As far as the Southwest is concerned, 'we are the legals, the Anglos the illegals,' one Mexican said." In spite of the artificial international boundary, many Chicanos now realized more than ever that both they and Mexicans belonged in the Southwest, and that the fate of Chicanos in that region would always be influenced by people from Mexico. Because of this, as long as Mexico existed in a neocolonial relationship with the United States, the Chicano barrios and hamlets in the Southwest would continue to be internal colonies of the United States. Deprived of a living by a Mexican economy profiting North American investors and a domestic elite, undocumented workers would continue to pour into the Southwest to provide capitalists with cheap labor and consumers with lower prices. Since the undocumented would continue to compete with Chicanos at the bottom of the economic ladder, Chicanos would continue to have a difficult time climbing out of poverty, especially given the cooptation, discrimination, and other forms of subjugation traditionally used in the Southwest to keep the Spanish-speaking colonized.

In the past Mexican-Americans had at times supported efforts to seal the border against their competitors from Mexico, but after the 1960s many concluded that, besides being practically impossible, sealing the border would not eliminate domestic forms of subjugation and would only deprive the Mexican poor of desperately needed income. Many Chicanos concluded it was immoral to deny employment to the undocumented, especially when many were friends and relatives. For this reason, in fact, some Chicanos by 1979 were quietly hoping for a completely open border. Journalist Richard Reeves noted:

> I'm convinced that the real Chicano position on undocumented workers is total amnesty . . . , and a totally open border. . . . No one will say that . . .—but many people said things like this . . . : "We know where the undocumented workers are—they're sleeping on the couches in our living rooms. . . . They're family and they're just trying to feed their families back home."

Moreover, the undocumented and other recently arrived Mexicans provided Chicanos with the best hope that their culture would survive in the Southwest. Because of the newcomers, Chicanos were forced to maintain their language and culture or suffer a breakdown in barrio communication.

In fact it was the new influx of people from Mexico, together with the emergence of an educated nationalistic leadership, that made Chicano activists in the late 1970s guardedly optimistic about the future, despite the obstacles set up by the dominant society. Of course, they had no illusions that they were about to establish a politically independent Aztlán, nor did they then wish to do so. Several years earlier, this idea had been considered and rejected for obvious reasons. "Would a separate state be viable?" journalist Armando Rendón had asked in 1971. "My guess is that the United States Government would act very quickly to suppress Chicano efforts toward this end." While such a utopian course of action would never be permitted, by the late 1970s Chicano activists were optimistic that more practical social plans would have to be taken seriously by Anglo society, for that society could not continue to ignore the fastest growing minority group in the nation. Given the perpetually high Chicano and Mexican birth rates, Chicano voting strength was growing by the year; if the newly nationalistic leadership ever organized that power, Anglo supremacy throughout the Southwest would be challenged as it had been in Crystal City [Texas]. Faced with such a possibility, Anglos would have to make concessions because, as columnist Tony Castro commented, "The Mexican-American in the Southwest today is like a Palestinian in the Middle East. An accommodation has to be made."

The analogy with the Palestinians had some merit because, being a dispossessed group, Chicanos continued to have the potential for violent rebellion. That potential became a reality on May 7, 1978, when Houston Chicanos rioted in response to news that city policemen responsible for the death of a young Chicano the previous year had received light sentences for their crime. The Houston riot served as a warning that if Chicano optimism about the 1980s were to become disillusionment that decade could see more violence than had the late 1960s. The analogy with the Palestinians was appropriate in at least one other way—in the mid-1970s the fate of Chicanos began to be influenced by oil. At that time a major oil discovery was made in southern Mexico, and though there was a good deal of controversy concerning its exact size, speculation that the discovery might equal the reserves of Saudi Arabia caused everyone involved to reconsider the relations between the United States and Mexico, and consequently the relations between Anglo-Americans and persons of Mexican descent.

In the late 1970s some North American businessmen began to consider the advantages of a common market including the United States and Mexico, a common market that, according to Carey McWilliams, would "permit the free movement across their borders not only of all commodities— particularly oil and gas—but also of people." In their need for petroleum, some North Americans were beginning to consider the idea that the boundary between the Southwest and Mexico might indeed be artificial. In return for increased supplies of energy, North Americans were beginning to think about legalizing the seemingly inevitable migration of Mexicans into the Southwest. Such a concession to the Chicano image of the region, while not eliminating the neocolonial status of the Mexican and Chicano masses, would certainly improve their condition by providing economic opportunities for the former, and numerical and cultural strength to the latter. The thought of this is what made Chicano activists optimistic about the future of Aztlán. While such concessions would not end neocolonialism in the Southwest, they would permit Chicanos to entrench themselves until revolutionary changes in the general society of the United States could allow true self-determination.

However, the guarded optimism of the late 1970s decreased as the 1980s proceeded. In the United States the backlash of the former decade increased with the introduction of conservative federal policies on such matters as the enforcement of civil rights laws; moreover, the economic position of minorities suffered during a period of recession and slowed government spending. Declining petroleum prices left Mexico unable to repay huge loans secured with its oil discoveries, and this development stifled idealistic hopes of a common market between the two nations and of swift progress toward equality between Anglos and Chicanos in the Southwest. Significant recovery of control in the region, the myth of Aztlán, seemed as far off as ever. As a result, for the foreseeable future, the Chicanos' image of the land as lost, and of themselves as dispossessed, would continue to have credibility.

Y *F U R T H E R   R E A D I N G*

Mario Barrera, *Race and Class in the Southwest: A Theory of Racial Inequality* (1979)

Larry W. Burt, *Tribalism in Crisis: Federal Indian Policy, 1953–1961* (1982)

Sandra L. Cadwalader and Vine Deloria, Jr., eds., *The Aggressions of Civilization: Federal Indian Policy Since the 1880s* (1984)

Albert Camarillo, *Chicanos in a Changing Society* (1979)

Lucie Cheng and Edna Bonacich, eds., *Labor Immigration under Capitalism: Asian Workers in the United States Before World War II* (1984)

Fay Cohen, *Treaties on Trial: The Continuing Controversy over Northwest Indian Fishing Rights* (1986)

Arthur F. Corwin, ed., *Immigrants—and Immigrants: Perspectives on Mexican Labor Migration to the United States* (1978)

Douglas Henry Daniels, *Pioneer Urbanites: A Social and Cultural History of Black San Francisco* (1980)

Roger Daniels, *The Politics of Prejudice: The Anti-Japanese Movement in California and the Struggle for Japanese Exclusion* (1962)

Vine Deloria, Jr., *Custer Died for Your Sins: An Indian Manifesto* (1969)

Sarah Deutsch, *No Separate Refuge: Culture, Class and Gender on an Anglo-Hispanic Frontier in the American Southwest, 1880–1940* (1987)

David H. Dinwoodie, "Indians, Hispanos, and Land Reform: A New Deal Struggle in New Mexico," *Western Historical Quarterly,* 17 (1986), 291–323

Donald Fixico, *Termination and Relocation: Federal Indian Policy, 1945–1960* (1986)

Richard Griswold del Castillo, *The Los Angeles Barrio, 1850–1890* (1979)

Abraham Hoffman, *Unwanted Mexican Americans in the Great Depression* (1974)

Masakazu Iwata, "The Japanese Immigrants in California Agriculture," *Agricultural History,* 36 (1962), 25–37

Alvin Josephy, Jr., ed., *Red Power: The American Indians' Fight For Freedom* (1971)

Leigh Dana Johnsen, "Equal Rights and the "Heathen 'Chinee' '": Black Activism in San Francisco, 1865–1875," *Western Historical Quarterly,* 11 (1980), 57–68

Frederick C. Luebke, "Ethnic Group Settlement on the Great Plains," *Western Historical Quarterly,* 8 (1977), 405–30

Elizabeth McLagan, *A Peculiar Paradise: A History of Blacks in Oregon, 1778–1940* (1980)

Carey McWilliams, *North From Mexico,* (1948)

Mauricio Mazon, *The Zoot-Suit Riots: The Psychology of Symbolic Annihilation* (1984)

John Modell, *The Economics and Politics of Racial Accommodation: The Japanese of Los Angeles* (1977)

David Montejano, *Anglo and Mexicans in the Making of Texas, 1836–1986* (1987)

Kenneth R. Philp, *Indian Self-Rule: First-Hand Accounts of Indian-White Relations from Roosevelt to Reagan* (1986)

——, "Stride Toward Freedom: The Relocation of Indians to Cities, 1952–1960," *Western Historical Quarterly,* 16 (1985), 175–90

Francis Paul Prucha, "American Indian Policy in the Twentieth Century," *Western Historical Quarterly,* 15 (1984), 5–18

Moses Rischin, "Beyond the Great Divide: Immigrants and the Last Frontier," *Journal of American History,* 55 (1968), 42–53

Stanley R. Ross, ed., *Views Across the Border: The United States and Mexico* (1978)

Vicki L. Ruiz, *Cannery Women, Cannery Lives: Mexican Women, Unionization, and the California Food Processing Industry* (1987)

Theodore Saloutos, "The Immigrant in Pacific Coast Agriculture," *Agricultural History,* 49 (1975), 182–201

Graham D. Taylor, *The New Deal and American Indian Tribalism: The Administration of the Indian Reorganization Act, 1934–45* (1980)

William Toll, *The Making of an Ethnic Middle Class: Portland Jewry over Four Generations* (1982)

Charles Wilkinson, *American Indians, Time, and the Law: Native Societies in a Modern Constitutional Democracy* (1986)

Charles Wollenberg, ed., *Ethnic Conflict in California History* (1970)

The Federal West

Y

The history of the trans-Mississippi West of the United States began with the federal government's acquisition of land from France in the Louisiana Purchase of 1803. The "feds" cannot today claim to own all the land, but some disgruntled westerners would disagree. Resentment over eastern intrusion into western affairs gave rise in the late 1970s to a political protest movement known as the Sagebrush Rebellion. Seeing the interests of the West pitted against the interests of authorities in Washington, or "easterners" in general, has been a regular theme in the nineteenth and twentieth centuries. Disputes over statehood, especially for Utah and New Mexico; the rise of the silver issue and western populism; and westerners' opposition to the Progressives' interest in the conservation of natural resources are but three examples of western confrontations with "eastern" policies and government programs.

Yet the federal government has also played a major role in the economic development of the West. The New Deal programs of the 1930s aided countless westerners during the depths of the Great Depression. Military budgets during and after World War II brought growth and prosperity. For many westerners, the presence of the federal government through its national parks, its military bases, and its water, forest, and land-management programs has created a love-hate relationship. In the West, as elsewhere, there are those who appreciate the federal money but detest the federal regulation.

Y *D O C U M E N T S*

The first selection consists of four tables reprinted from Gerald D. Nash's book *The American West Transformed.* The statistical evidence shows how the push for victory in World War II affected the economy and population of the West. In the second document, Roger Daniels, a historian at the University of Cincinnati, traces in quantitative terms the wartime impact of another federal program. In other studies, Daniels has dealt with the tragedy of relocation for Japanese-Americans and the injustice of interning these people behind barbed wire. Here he gives a broad picture of how many people suffered under this policy.

Another tragedy resulting from federal actions is the subject of the next two documents. The effects of nuclear fallout from above-ground test explosions in the 1950s appear now to have been responsible for high rates of cancer in southern Utah. In the third document, dating from 1979, a scientist at the University of Utah explains his findings on this matter. A Utah senator, Orrin Hatch, in the fourth selection considers the larger question of justice for the victims of fallout. Japanese-Americans waited forty-six years for Congress to apologize and to work out the final compensation for their losses during World War II. Residents of southern Utah may have to wait even longer.

The final three documents focus on the Sagebrush Rebellion. In the fifth document, a Nevada state senator explains the reasons for the "rebellion," and an official of the Council of State Governments reports on the status of public land policy in the West. The sixth selection is made up of two cartoons that appeared in the *Deseret News* of Salt Lake City as commentaries on the targets and supporters of the political protest. In the first cartoon, the president who is shown having his jogging shoes laced up is Jimmy Carter. The final document, a 1986 newspaper account by James Coates of the *Chicago Tribune,* reports on what has happened to the Sagebrush Rebellion after its heyday in the late 1970s and early 1980s. Coates believes that the highly urbanized West now has other concerns. Yet the history of western protest against federal policies indicates that other movements akin to the Sagebrush Rebellion are likely to appear in the future.

The Impact of World War II on Western Growth: Four Tables

Table 1   Major War Supply Contracts and War Facilities, 1940–1945 (in thousands of dollars)

| | MAJOR WAR SUPPLY CONTRACTS, JUNE 1940–SEPT. 1945 | | MAJOR WAR FACILITIES PROJECTS, JUNE 1940–JUNE 1945 | |
STATE	COMBAT EQUIPMENT	OTHER	INDUSTRIAL	MILITARY
Arizona	94,854	31,115	100,592	134,116
California	14,255,117	2,195,524	1,013,778	1,511,447
Colorado	244,634	116,920	170,350	174,479
Idaho	12,049	6,421	27,049	101,992
Montana	12,966	15,081	12,956	41,106
Nevada	1,521	32,402	151,542	88,050
New Mexico	11,133	9,356	13,325	101,506
North Dakota	1,582	5,938	120	1,572
Oregon	1,629,809	182,825	100,603	163,842
South Dakota	201	4,584	150	65,908
Texas	3,749,561	2,224,979	1,166,836	837,582
Utah	79,136	34,345	284,394	153,097
Washington	3,408,305	379,331	341,058	327,949
Wyoming	12,770	68,419	25,535	23,431

Source: U.S. Census, *County Data Book* (Washington, 1947), p. 7.

Table 2   Paid Civilian Employment in the Executive Branch of the Federal Government, 1938 and 1945, by State

STATE OR OTHER AREA	DECEMBER 1938	JUNE 1945
Continental U.S.	831,833	2,915,476
Washington, D.C., metro. area	119,874	257,808
48 states	711,959	2,657,668
Arizona	7,477	17,900
California	48,334	317,236
Colorado	8,692	28,839
Idaho	3,780	9,877
Montana	8,157	9,150
Nevada	1,819	6,753
New Mexico	7,201	16,206
North Dakota	3,820	6,047
Oregon	9,113	18,827
South Dakota	3,886	10,488
Texas	27,777	149,899
Utah	3,886	37,665
Washington	15,520	100,359
Wyoming	3,095	5,067

Source: U.S. Census, *Statistical Abstract,* 1951 (Washington, 1951), p. 196.

Table 3   Personal Income: Select Western States, 1940, 1948 (in millions of dollars)

STATE	TOTAL INCOME 1940	1948	PER CAPITA INCOME 1940	1948
Arizona	251	879	502	1,274
California	5,802	17,633	835	1,752
Colorado	615	1,810	544	1,433
Idaho	235	725	—	1,407
Montana	316	876	566	1,616
Nevada	101	283	890	1,814
New Mexico	198	655	373	1,084
North Dakota	218	813	340	1,401
Oklahoma	851	2,390	366	1,140
Oregon	671	2,278	648	1,621
South Dakota	231	916	360	1,497
Texas	2,762	9,142	430	1,199
Utah	266	810	482	1,241
Washington	1,140	3,608	655	1,600
Wyoming	151	429	606	1,595

Source: *Historical Statistics of the U.S.,* pp. 242–245.

Table 4 Population Growth of Western States, 1920–1950

DIVISION AND STATE	1920	1930	1940	1950	PERCENT INCREASE 1940 TO 1950
United States	105,710,620	122,775,016	131,669,275	150,697,361	14.5
Mountain	3,336,101	2,701,789	4,150,003	5,074,998	22.3
Montana	548,889	537,606	559,456	501,024	5.6
Idaho	431,866	455,032	524,873	588,637	12.1
Wyoming	194,402	225,565	290,742	290,529	15.9
Colorado	939,629	1,035,296	1,123,296	1,325,089	18.0
New Mexico	360,350	423,317	531,818	681,157	28.1
Arizona	334,162	435,573	499,261	749,587	50.1
Nevada	77,407	91,058	110,247	160,083	45.2
Utah	449,396	507,847	550,310	688,862	25.2
Pacific	5,566,871	8,164,423	9,733,262	14,486,527	48.8
Washington	1,356,621	1,563,396	1,726,191	2,378,963	37.0
Oregon	783,389	753,786	1,089,684	1,521,311	39.6
California	3,426,861	5,677,251	6,907,387	10,586,223	53.3

Source: U.S. Census, *Historical Statistics of the U.S.*, p. 31.

Roger Daniels's Quantitative Note on the Forced Migrations of Japanese Americans, 1942–1946

It is often assumed that all Japanese Americans suffered a common fate during World War II: imprisonment in a War Relocation Authority concentration camp. This was not the case; the purpose of this note is to indicate the variety of Japanese American experiences during the war and to establish a uniform terminology.

According to the Census of 1940, there were 126,947 persons of Japanese ancestry living in the United States, another 157,905 in the Territory of Hawaii, and 263 in the Territory of Alaska, for a total of 285,115 persons. More than two-thirds of these were native-born American citizens. Because, except for a few World War I veterans, no Japanese person could be naturalized, there were close to 100,000 aliens of Japanese birth who became, after Pearl Harbor, enemy aliens.

Some of these enemy aliens were the first forced migrants of the war. Starting on December 7, some 3,000 adult aliens, almost all of them male, were arrested by the FBI and interned in such places as Missoula, Montana, or Lordsburg, New Mexico. This was a well-established governmental policy, recognized in international law, and represented no innovative action. The men were interned under military guard but were in the custody of the Immigration and Naturalization Service (INS), part of the Department of Justice. Eventually, each man interned received a hearing, and some were freed as a result of those hearings. The vast majority of adult male enemy aliens were not interned, nor were any women and children. Several hundred of the internees were repatriated during the war on the exchange ship *Gripsholm,* a Swedish passenger liner.

In December and January 1941–42, most, but not all, of the more than 3,000 Japanese American citizens who had been inducted into the armed forces since the institution of the draft in October 1940, were discharged because of their ancestry, and they, and all other Japanese Americans were placed in a special category, IV-C, normally reserved for enemy aliens, and making them ineligible for military service.

After the promulgation of Executive Order 9066 by President Franklin D. Roosevelt on February 19, 1942, the U.S. Army took control of all persons of Japanese ancestry—aliens and citizens, men, women, and children—who lived in California, in the western parts of Oregon and Washington, and in part of Arizona, and forced them to leave their homes for the duration of hostilities. According to the 1940 census, 111,938 persons lived in what became the forbidden zone. In the more than two years between the census and the forced removal, that population gained from natural increases and was also affected by voluntary migration. According to the army's statistics,

"The Forced Migrations of West Coast Japanese Americans, 1942–1946," by Roger Daniels in *Japanese Americans: From Relocation to Redress,* 72–74, edited by Roger Daniels, Sandra C. Taylor and Harry H. L. Kitano, 1986. Permission granted by University of Utah Press.

117,116 persons were "eligible" for *incarceration* between March and October 1942. But it took charge of only 110,723. They were *incarcerated,* first in assembly centers under the jurisdiction of the army, and then in relocation centers under the jurisdiction of the War Relocation Authority.

This process has been given many names. Franklin Roosevelt was willing to call the places of confinement *concentration camps.* The War Relocation Authority abhorred that term and preferred to talk about the process as "relocation," although it sometimes referred to its prisoners as "evacuated" or "impounded people." The problem with the word "relocation," apart from its euphemistic nature, is that it also has been used to describe the process by which some Japanese Americans "voluntarily" moved out of the forbidden zone, and to the process by which, during and just after the war, thousands of Japanese Americans moved out of the camps to new homes and businesses in the interior of the United States. To further the semantic confusion, it has become common in recent years to speak of the "internment" of Japanese Americans as describing all the procedures affecting aliens and citizens, a practice that has been given official sanction by Congress, which created the Commission on the Wartime Relocation and Internment of Civilians (CWRIC) in 1980.

Most of the few thousand Japanese Americans resident on the West Coast who were neither interned nor incarcerated were allowed to migrate voluntarily outside of the forbidden zone. Japanese Americans who already lived in such places as Salt Lake City, Chicago, or New York were, if they were not interned, left in nervous liberty. The army's data indicate that nearly 5,000 voluntarily migrated east between March and October 1942. Clearly, others had already done so between December 7 and the beginning of March, but there are no good data on the numbers involved.

To complicate matters further, some Japanese Americans not subject to incarceration because of their residence returned to the forbidden zone to join their families, as did some discharged servicemen. In addition, some 1,000 persons were in various institutions, medical and penal, and not otherwise incarcerated; however, some patients were concentrated into a few institutions, such as Hillcrest Sanitorium outside of Los Angeles.

According to the War Relocation Authority, it had, at one time or another, 120,313 individuals in custody. It received 111,236 from the army, 1,118 from Hawaii, 1,735 who were transferred from INS internment camps, 219 "voluntary residents" (mostly individuals who joined families already in camp), and 24 from various institutions. In addition, 5,981 U.S. citizens were born to incarcerated mothers.

The overwhelming majority of Hawaiian Japanese Americans were left at liberty; all but a few thousand of the mainland Japanese Americans were interned or incarcerated, as was every such person who had lived in Alaska. . . .

At the very outset, even before the relocation centers had been filled, several hundred persons received "work release furloughs" to assist in harvesting crops, such as sugar beets in the western states outside of the forbidden zone. Others were allowed to volunteer for service with military intelligence units of the U.S. Army. In the fall of 1942, hundreds of students were allowed to leave to attend colleges and universities outside of the forbidden zone. And, particularly after the beginning of 1943, a process of controlled resettlement in the interior states was encouraged.

Thousands were moved from camp to camp: while some transfers were to reunite families and others at the convenience of the government, the major reason for intercamp migration was caused by a desire to *segregate* those considered disloyal in one camp—Tule Lake, California. Loyalty was largely determined by inmate answers to a questionnaire administered to all adults in WRA custody early in 1943. The two crucial questions asked were:

27. Are you willing to serve in the armed forces of the United States on combat duty, wherever ordered?
28. Will you swear unqualified allegiance to the United States of America from any or all attack by foreign or domestic forces, and forswear any form of allegiance or obedience to the Japanese emperor, to any other foreign government, power or organization?

Those who answered "No" to one or both questions—some 6,700 of the 75,000 respondents—were considered disloyal and most of them were segregated in the camp at Tule Lake. This segregation involved moving some 13,000 inmates, for about 6,200 "loyal" persons were moved from Tule Lake to other camps and some 6,800 persons were moved to Tule Lake.

Input-Output Data for WRA Centers, 1942–1946

FROM	TO
90,491 assembly centers	54,127 return to West Coast
17,491 direct evacuation	52,798 relocated to interior
5,918 born in camp	4,724 Japan
1,735 INS internment camps	3,121 INS internment camps
1,579 seasonal workers (furloughed from assembly centers to work crops, then to camp)	2,355 armed forces
1,275 penal and medical institutions	1,862 died
1,118 Hawaii	1,322 to institutions
219 voluntary residents (mostly non-Japanese spouses)	4 unauthorized departures
120,313 Total population ever under WRA control	120,313

By the end of the war almost half of the incarcerated people were out of camp, having received what the WRA came to call "leave clearance" to work, to go to college, or to enter the armed forces. By March 20, 1946, the last camp was empty. The accompanying table shows the movement of people in and out of the camps.

Joseph L. Lyon on Leukemia
and Atom Bomb Tests in Southern Utah, 1979

A University of Utah researcher has released findings of a link between leukemia deaths and nuclear fallout in Utah that will open the door to new studies on the hazards of radiation exposure.

Dr. Joseph L. Lyon, assistant professor of family and community medicine and co-director of the Utah Cancer Registry, reported his findings in the New England Journal of Medicine.

Leukemia death rates for children under age 15 born in southern Utah during the intensive period of above-ground nuclear testing in Nevada (1951–58) were about two and a half times that of children born in the same region before and after, Lyon reported. The leukemia death rates for northern Utah children born during that period were about 1.3 times greater.

The study is the first to report an association between fallout and an increased number of childhood leukemia deaths in Utah and comes at a time of growing controversy over what constitutes a safe level of radiation exposure. Two other studies of workers exposed to low levels of radiation in Portsmouth, N.H., and Hanford, Wash., have drawn fire because of the research methods used.

The Department of Health, Education and Welfare is planning an award of a one-year contract to the U for follow-up work to confirm Lyon's findings. The U will also test the feasibility of reconstructing radiation doses received by each community in Utah.

"The average risk of leukemia death for all children born in Utah during that eight-year period increased 40 percent," Lyon says. "Our studies show an excess of 18 and 19 childhood leukemia deaths above what would normally have been expected in southern Utah. Northern Utah, with less exposure but a larger population, experienced 30 to 32 excess deaths.

"We can't say from this study that fallout causes cancer. Studies of this nature don't establish cause and effect. We particularly can't establish a cause-effect relation in any specific death," he notes.

"But I think we can say without question there is an association between fallout exposure and the increased incidence of childhood leukemia deaths in Utah," Lyon says.

The researcher also stresses that the risk to children no longer exists,

"Leukemia and Atom Bomb Tests in Southern Utah, 1979" in *University of Utah Review*, 12 (February 1979). Permission granted by University of Utah Press.

and there is currently no detectable "cancer epidemic" among adults or children in southern Utah.

There were 97 documented above-ground atomic bomb tests in Nevada from 1951 to 1958, when a moratorium took effect. Another 10 tests were set off in 1962. The United States and Russia then signed a test ban treaty in 1963, moving all testing underground.

"We defined 1951 to 1958 as the period of heavy exposure," Lyon says. "We obtained Atomic Energy Commission or Public Health Service maps from 26 of the tests showing fallout bands over Utah. The other tests purportedly did not result in fallout reaching Utah. Because of recent disclosures about government attitudes and actions during that period, we consider this official exposure data conservative at best.

"Although 26 blasts represent only one-fourth of the known tests, in terms of kilotonnage they represent half. It was the most massive blasts that sent fallout over Utah," Lyon notes.

Orrin Hatch Considers the Fallout Victims, 1979

Some time after hearing the blast I noticed the cloud drifting eastward a few miles south of where I was gathering cattle to take back to the ranch . . . Before getting to the ranch, I began to feel rather nauseated . . .

Awhile later, brown spots began to appear on each side of my face, ears and neck with a burning sensation . . . When I consulted the doctors, they said, "Oh, it's just a little sunburn" . . . These spots have continued to affect me for over 20 years.

—Roger Mathews, Washington County, 1955

No sunburn could cause the suffering borne by Mr. Mathews and several hundred other Utahns. Only a nuclear detonation with a minimum of health protection can inflict such an injury.

Mathews and others reported massive deaths in cattle herds throughout Washington County and the surrounding area. "In 1957 or 58, I met some of the crews monitoring the fall-out and invited them to come to our ranch to investigate.

"They never showed up."

But cattle, sheep and other livestock were not the only fatal victims of the fall-out. Read the testimony of Elmer Pickett, who lived to tell his story this past April 17 during a special town meeting I sponsored in St. George:

In my own family we have had nine cancer victims . . . all since the fall-out. I cannot find anywhere in our family records as far as we can go evidence of any cancer-related deaths . . . We have been a very healthy family."

To me, the fall-out is the only thing that has happened in this area of a nature that could cause such disaster . . . We cannot recall a single leukemia case in a great many years, and possibly a half-dozen cancer cases (during the same period)."

The Courage of Faith

Were it not for Elmer Pickett's personal strength and faith, he might not have come forward to tell his story. But what of the Elmer Picketts all over Southern Utah whose stories have not yet been told, whose lives and the lives of their loved ones have been similarly ravaged? I believe we should spare no effort to find them. Listen to them. And then help them.

The repercussion of what the federal government did or failed to do during the years of and since the tests affect all of us. But there is no one person or agency to blame. Like the radiation itself, such negligence has been cumulative.

The lack of safety and health measures taken by test officials was atrocious for several reasons. We now know that the Atomic Energy Commission was primarily concerned about keeping the tests on schedule. Perhaps more importantly, our knowledge of radiation's effects was at that time severely limited. The maximum acceptable dose of radiation then was *four times* the maximum accepted today. So ignorance may well have been the real killer in Southern Utah.

What We Can Do

What are we to do now? The only acceptable action, in my view, is some form of financial retribution. Money is a poor compensation for the agony of familial loss and personal suffering caused by the tests. Fortunately, it is not the only thing we can do. As a member of the Health Subcommittee of the Senate's Judiciary Committee, I am introducing legislation with the following provisions:

- Compensation for fall-out victims, with no-fault compensation for those with certain doses of radiation in the area at the time of the tests. Others would be handled on a case-by-case basis.
- Establishment of a research center, probably at the University of Utah, to study the continuing effects of the fall-out.
- Transfer of most of the Nuclear Regulatory Commission's research authority to the Department of Health, Education and Welfare.

Some may see this as an expensive approach. I believe the bill is the most practical and, more important, the most humane alternative available to our government. Especially when we witness the steadfast faith and patriotism of Utahns like Elmer Pickett, who, even after the terrible hardships he has suffered, can still examine this issue with not a trace of bitterness:

> The time has long since gone when public officials hid behind the skirts of the government. I've never lost faith in the government. But we've got people in the government who I am not proud of. And they have to be corrected.

It was necessary to test the bombs, but was it necesary to put the bombs above the safety of the citizens?

I say it was not and I am sparing no effort to assure that responsible compensation is made and that the same mistakes are never, ever again repeated. Our people have suffered too much.

Two Reports from Nevada on the Sagebrush Rebellion, 1979

State Senator Richard E. Blakemore, Nevada:

The "sagebrush rebellion" is a catchy but somewhat misleading term used to describe the western states' demands for a greater role in determining the future of the west.

Unlike the dictionary definition, in this rebellion there is no armed or unlawful resistance to government. Neither is western land desolate or worthless as the term "sagebrush" connotes.

Moreover, if much of the land in the west ever was considered of little worth, the need for energy has changed that.

Statistics show that much of the west is controlled by the federal government. The federal government controls about one third of the 2.1 billion acres of land in this country or 700 million acres. Over 90 percent of all federal land is from the Rockies west. The federal government controls 96 percent of Alaska, 87 percent of Nevada, 66 percent of Utah, 64 percent of Idaho, and 45 percent of California. The lowest percentage of western federal lands is in Washington at 29 percent. On the average, the federal government controls 52.6 percent of the land in the 12 western states, excluding Hawaii.

By contrast, the federal government controls only 4.3 percent of the land in the other 38 states. Many counties in the west are 99 percent federal land.

What does this large federal presence mean to westerners and why are westerners protesting?

For many years, the public domain was open to ranching, mining, and outdoor recreation. But a number of federal acts, passed to protect and conserve the environment, have closed great parts of the public domain to traditional uses. Westerners see these restrictions in the use of public lands as a portent of things to come—that eventually most of today's public lands will be locked up in wilderness or other restrictive uses. Matters are made worse for agricultural interests by urban growth, which gobbles up the little private land open to development.

Two Reports from Nevada on the Sagebrush Rebellion, 1979, in *State Government News*, 22, No. 10 (November 1979) 3–5. Reprinted by permission of The Council of State Governments, Publisher.

Meanwhile, the west today is at the confluence of two major movements—that for protection of the environment and that for production of energy.

To a great extent, the success of the attempt for U.S. energy independence depends upon resources of the west. In addition, the west is looked to for increased agricultural production and for its reserves of minerals necessary to modern industry.

The environmental movement prompted the passage of federal legislation aimed at protecting the environment and maintaining great portions of the country in a natural state. Among the major environmental acts of the past 15 years are the Wilderness Act, the National Environmental Protection Act, the Federal Land Policy Management Act (BLM Organic Act), the Wild and Scenic Rivers Act, and the National Forest Management Act.

The genesis of the sagebrush rebellion can be found in the conflict between the desires to protect and preserve the environment and the demands for food, minerals, and energy from the west.

The rebellious spirit in the west today can be traced to several federal policies and actions in recent years.

Constraints on the uses of public lands and obstacles to disposal of public lands into nonfederal ownership have increased over the past 15 years.

Most federal land is managed by two agencies—the U.S. Forest Service and the Bureau of Land Management (BLM). The BLM never even processed most proposals for land exchanges to eliminate checkerboard patterns of private-public ownership. Privately owned land can be exchanged for public lands, but appraisals must be made so the values are equivalent. Exchanges make it possible to consolidate ownership of contiguous land tracts. However, the BLM has not given staff priority to exchanges.

Of the 275,000 acres of public land in Nevada for which exchanges have been proposed since 1968, only 3,000 acres have been exchanged. In those 10 years, there have been denials on less than 20,000 acres, meaning that the BLM has not rendered decisions on 92 percent of the land requested for exchange.

This illustrates the general opposition of land management agencies to land disposal or any changes in ownership patterns. These attitudes were sanctioned by Congress in 1976 with passage of the Federal Land Policy Management Act, commonly called the BLM Organic Act. (Until then it was U.S. policy to dispose of public lands, although there was very little disposition in the preceding 30 years. The Organic Act made retention of public lands the policy, unless land use planning under the act showed disposal was in the national interest.)

At the same time, the Forest Service was engaged in a wilderness review, known as RARE II. The Organic Act also required the BLM to begin wilderness review on the land it administers.

Another blow to the west was President Carter's hit list of western water projects, which was issued without consultation with governors of the affected states.

Also in the water area, a recent opinion by the U.S. Department of the Interior could open the way to federal intervention in state administration of water laws. The opinion, not yet tested in court, concludes that the Department of the Interior should comply with state water law, but that compliance would not prevent the federal government from taking whatever water rights it needs.

These federal policies and activities make the west apprehensive about what's next. Nonwesterners may appreicate this frustration with federal land policies more if they consider the growth in federal regulation throughout the country in the past 15 years.

Overregulation is bad anywhere. Imagine how much worse it is for states in which the federal government is also the landlord over most of the land in the state. Excessive regulation and heavy-handed bureaucracy are magnified where land is federally controlled.

While the particular issues on which the sagebrush rebellion are based are more common to the west, the principles behind the movement are national in scope. It is a question of the extent to which the destiny of the country is controlled by federal agencies and bureaucrats. States, local governments, and the people should make more of these determinations and the federal government less.

Because of the federal omnipresence in the west, westerners have reached the crisis first. But reversing the trend towards centralization that threatens the economy, our lands, and our freedoms is of concern to all Americans.

Westerners have started drawing lines and pushing back. We ask non-westerners to join with us for the benefit of all.

Susan S. Munroe, Council of State Governments, Washington Office:

Approximately 300 state and county officials making up the Western Coalition on Public Lands met in Reno, Nevada, September 5–7, to hammer out policy proposals that would remedy what members believe to be growing federal encroachment into states' purview over land and water use.

The Nevada legislature's introduction of a measure to secure transfer to the state of a portion of federally owned lands has been dubbed a "sagebrush rebellion." The move, which could end up in the U.S. Supreme Court, appears only to be a first salvo.

The state and county officials proposed other possible remedies to federal intervention, including:

- Expeditious disposal of unmanageable and isolated tracts of federal lands;
- Full payments to counties under the payments in lieu of taxes program to compensate for the tax immunity of federal lands;
- Support for wilderness decisions based on the multiple-use concept of public lands;
- Support for Alaska lands legislation that would guarantee the conveyance of statehood entitlement lands to that state;
- Support for a comprehensive energy impact assistance program;

- Support for the goals of the National Forest and Rangeland Resources Planning Act; and
- Support for comprehensive state and local land use planning.

The recommendations were subsequently approved, with some modifications, by the Western Conference of the Council of State Governments and the Western Interstate Region of the National Association of Counties (NACo).

Soon after the Western Coalition meeting, the U.S. Senate passed a measure to speed energy development that will further diminish western states' land and water rights. By a vote of 68–25, the upper house moved to establish a powerful, four-member Energy Mobilization Board.

Opponents believe the legislation will mandate far-reaching energy efforts that will trample federalism and ignore environmental consequences.

If the bill passes undiluted by the U.S. House (where action is expected shortly) and is signed into law, once again western attempts to control land use will have been thwarted, this time in favor of federal governmental interest in expediting massive energy development.

Passage of the Energy Mobilization Board bill would add substantial fuel to the already flaming sagebrush rebellion. By giving the energy board such broad powers, particularly a grandfather clause that allows waiver of any laws enacted after beginning construction of a priority project and authority to make decisions for state, local, and federal agencies which miss deadlines, Congress and the president will almost assure a barrage of lawsuits that will result in a slowdown of project developments for perhaps years to come.

Lawsuits are but one weapon in the sagebrush rebellion's arsenal to protect and regain land from federal control.

For example, western interests are pushing S. 1680, introduced August 3 by U.S. Senator Orrin Hatch (R–Utah), and companion legislation in the U.S. House, H.R. 5426, introduced by U.S. Representative James Santini (D–Nevada), that will provide for conveyance of federally owned, unreserved lands to the states by Congress.

The measures provide for states to set up their own land commissions and protect existing leases and revenues prior to transfer by application to a federal land transfer board.

The Western Conference of the Council of State Governments and the National Association of Counties' Western Interstate Region support the bills, which are still in committee.

Two Cartoons, 1979–1980

Reprinted by permission of NEA, Inc.

Camp followers.

Reprinted by permission of NEA, Inc.

*"By the way, Mr. President, Agents Lewis and Clark of the BLM have
returned from their fact-finding mission to Utah."*

James Coates Asks,
Is the Sagebrush Rebellion Dead? 1986

Lean and lanky as the Marlboro man, David Flitner sat behind James Watt's old desk at the Mountain States Legal Foundation here and told how the "Sagebrush Rebellion" had been shackled by conservationists' victories and modern urban problems.

The Sagebrush Rebellion, which captured the spotlight during Ronald Reagan's 1980 presidential campaign, was a package of legislative proposals that would have allowed the federal government to sell large amounts of the land in the American West and speed up development of natural resources.

"I happen to be one who cheers and supports the Sagebrush Rebellion," Reagan said in a campaign speech in Salt Lake City. "Count me in as a rebel."

As interior secretary, the newly elected president chose Watt, the first director of the foundation, which had been set up in 1977 by conservative Colorado braumeister Joseph Coors and others as a mirror of such liberal groups as the Sierra Club.

With the help of the administration and a Republican-dominated Senate, pro-development forces won some big battles—increased offshore oil exploration, mining on national forest lands and a freeze on federal grazing fees.

But though the rebels continue to "fight the good fight" on many fronts, the rebellion has become a holding action, Flitner said.

"Things were going well at first but the bureaucracy is so entrenched. It's almost immaterial in the end which administration gets in. So, yes, things have slowed down for us," he said.

A coalition of ranchers, sheepherders, miners and other leaders of the wide open West had formed the Sagebrush Rebellion with the goal of taking control of about 500 million acres of mostly arid land west of Omaha that is owned by the federal Bureau of Land Management.

"We were getting our fannies kicked all over the place," recalled Flitner, a wealthy Wyoming rancher who succeeded Watt as director of the foundation in 1981.

"People were getting so frustrated that the most intimate policies about our lives—how our grazing was done, how our forests were managed, how our water was used—were being made by bureaucrats in far-away big cities."

The Reagan administration came riding to the rescue with proposed sales of massive Western coal tracts and of offshore oil and gas leases. Cuts were attempted in the creation of new wilderness areas and there even were plans to allow mining within the boundaries of the country's sacrosanct national parks.

The coal sales created a furor in Washington.

James Coates, *Chicago Tribune*, March 16, 1986. © Copyrighted 1986, Chicago Tribune Company, all rights reserved, used with permission.

Meanwhile, plans to develop mineral rights in national parks were stalled by a raft of lawsuits filed by such groups as the Sierra Club, Wilderness Society and Friends of the Earth. The drive to halt wilderness areas also fizzled.

A major bid to expand timber cutting in the national forests was stymied when environmentalist lawsuits forced the U.S. Forest Service to cut back on plans to build access roads for the loggers. The Wilderness Society showed that the roads would cost more than the timber companies paid the government for taking its trees.

And the rebels' key proposal to sell off public land—the Western Lands Distribution and Regional Equalization Act—also ran into a mass of environmentalist lawsuits and finally was shelved by administration leaders beset by Gramm-Rudman deficit-cutting issues.

Today, as the sagebrush rebels look for support among their fellow Westerners, they find a highly urbanized society in which roughly 75 percent of the population live in towns and big cities; it is a society that has moved on to other concerns.

Υ *E S S A Y S*

Gerald D. Nash of the University of New Mexico is one of the leading historians of the twentieth-century West. His essay considers the economic growth that World War II brought to the region. As Nash explains, the war effort helped begin the transformation of the West from an underdeveloped area to a pacesetter in technological fields and the service economy. The late Robert G. Athearn taught western history at the University of Colorado for many years. In 1983 he was the first recipient of the Western History Association prize for lifetime achievement. His final book, published posthumously, is the source of the essay reprinted here as the second selection. With his characteristic wit and energy, Athearn examines the state of the twentieth-century West as a colonial region dominated by the federal government and eastern interests. In the final essay, Alfred Runte, an authority on national park history and management who lives in Seattle, Washington, presents a recent case study of Alaska and its national parks. He explains how the wilderness movement, political interests, and congressional maneuverings produced the Alaska Lands Act of 1980. Runte's essay indicates that confrontations over who controls the West are likely to continue.

World War II and Economic Transformation

GERALD D. NASH

Between Pearl Harbor and V-J Day the economy of many portions of the West underwent a profound transformation. The colonial economy of the region, heavily dependent on raw materials production before 1941, now

Gerald D. Nash, The New West: War and Economic Transformation,'' from *The American West Transformed: The Impact of the Second World War,* excerpts from pages 17–22, 29, and 35–36. Reprinted by permission of Indiana University Press.

became increasingly diversified and self-sufficient. Changes that would have taken more than a generation in peacetime were accelerated by war mobilization in a four-year period. Mobilization speeded up the activities of the extractive industries such as mining, accelerated industrial development, and ushered in what Daniel Bell has described as the post-industrial era. As a region rich in natural resources the West profited from the nationwide demand for its raw materials as it had not for more than a decade during the depression. At the same time military demands stimulated the establishment and expansion of manufacturing and industrial assembly plants. Somewhat unexpectedly, the war crisis greatly spurred new aerospace and electronics industries in the West and, in their wake, a host of profitable new service industries so characteristic of the post-industrial society. In short, as no other single event in the history of the West, the war stimulated economic growth. The erstwhile colony emerged from the war as an economic pace-setter for the nation.

How was this transformation accomplished? A major influence was the dynamism of the federal government, which invested at least $40 billion in the West during wartime. More than ever, the West became a federal province. Federal monies poured in through the establishment of new factories and award of vast contracts for war materiel. At the same time the large-scale expansion of military installations—air and naval bases, supply depots and training camps—provided an extraordinary stimulus to the regional economy. It would be inaccurate to say that the federal government was solely responsible for the spurt in the area's economic growth. But the federal presence provided the spark that set a pattern of other economic activities into motion. The influx of federal monies created hundreds of thousands of new jobs; these openings attracted men and women from all over the nation (not unlike the Gold Rush of 1849) and set off a population boom, increased population, particularly in towns and cities, proved a boon to service industries of all kinds, and created demands for new social and cultural services.

Of course, the ingredients for the realization of this vast economic potential had long been present. As Walter P. Webb bemoaned in 1937, eastern industrial interests had been consciously seeking to inhibit western economic growth. Webb pointed to the discriminatory freight rate system then sanctioned by the Interstate Commerce Commission as one important reason for western subservience to the East. The concentration of investment capital in eastern financial centers was undoubtedly another contributory factor. As one admirer of Webb, John Crowe Ransom, himself a distinguished spokesman, said:

> We all know about the inequalities of the economic structure. . . . Within the Northern states you have your masters of capital on the one hand, and against them your farmers and employees. . . . But . . . [in] the West you have almost your whole population in this latter status. . . . The North owns and operates the national economy; the South and West work under its direction. . . . The West bears a colonial relation to the North because the North actually colonized the West.

Webb's arguments had a ring of truth, of course, although they over-simplified a somewhat more complex situation. As a relatively young and underdeveloped section, the West reflected many of the characteristics of third-world underdeveloped nations in the twentieth century. Before the Second World War its population in many areas was still too sparse to sustain local manufactures; its internal transportation arteries were not as well developed as those in eastern states; it lacked well-developed financial institutions that could provide the capital necessary for further growth; and in a national and international economy wracked by depression, as in the 1930s, westerners could hardly expect to find markets for their goods.

But in 1941 the potential seemed limitless. The West still had open spaces to harbor a vast new population; changing transportation patterns, particularly the growth of the motor truck industry and the emergence of expanding air traffic, lessened the importance of rail transport and freed the region from the shackles of the basing point system; remoteness became a positive virtue with the development of new scientific and technological processes which required vast open spaces for testing and development; and the balmy climates of many portions of the West became a positive attraction with the growth of more affluent life styles. The development of air conditioning and climatic control further enhanced the economic potential of the desert areas which in previous years had been considered by many easterners to be uninhabitable.

In a sense, then, the boom triggered by World War II was not entirely unexpected. Wartime mobilization stimulated an expansion in which the West cast off some of the constraints which had hampered its growth in the preceding decade and at the same time acquired vast sums of new capital investments which made expansion possible. How this process took form contitutes a fascinating chapter in the annals of western history.

The exigencies of war prompted a massive influx of federal monies into the West. Certainly such an investment was not a totally new departure for the federal government. To bolster the first American settlements in the trans-Mississippi West during the early nineteenth century Congress had poured large sums into the region—through military installations, trans-portation development, and river and harbor appropriations. During the 1930s New Deal programs accelerated the flow of public expenditures into the West. But beginning in 1941 the scale of federal investment reached unprecedented levels. Congress authorized the expenditure of approximately $70 billion in the West from 1941 to 1945, with almost half of that sum earmarked for California. In fact, that state secured one-tenth of all federal monies expended during World War II.

This federal largesse flowed westward through various channels. Some was expended by existing agencies such as the U.S. Army Corps of Engineers and the Bureau of Reclamation; in addition, Congress created new agencies to purvey capital to the West. One major source was the Reconstruction Finance Corporation which established various subsidiaries to carry out plant expansion in the West. The challenge of creating "instant industries" in the region was met by the Defense Plant Corporation (DPC), the Rubber

Reserve Corporation, and the Metals Reserve Corporation, to name three of the subsidiaries which were especially significant in the West. The experience of new manufactures had usually been accomplished by private enterprise—at times perhaps with federal aid. Even in the First World War, 90 percent of new war-induced investments ($6 billion) came from private sources. But in the Second World War the situation was very different. The Defense Plant Corporation supplied the capital for 96 percent of new rubber plants, 58 percent of new aluminum plants, 90 percent of new magnesium plants, and 71 percent of the aircraft factories. With the exception of synthetic rubber, almost all of these enterprises were west of the Mississippi River. Of the fifteen largest aircraft plants built in World War II fourteen were financed by the Defense Plant Corporation. If before 1941 the federal government had been a junior partner with private business in financing new enterprises in the West, during World War II it became a dominant influence in western industrial expansion.

Established by Congress on August 22, 1940, to expedite the lagging mobilization program, the DPC came to be the largest investor in the history of the region. During the next five years it built 344 plants in the West at a cost of $1,853,634,000. These included a wide range of manufacturing facilities. Outstanding were the vast new steel mills established in Provo, Utah, and Fontana, California, the only such complete steel fabricating facilities west of the Mississippi River. The DPC also erected the largest magnesium plant in the world near Boulder Dam, just outside the sleepy little railroad town of Las Vegas. And it constructed a whole new complex of aluminum fabricating plants in the Pacific Northwest. As noted, virtually all of the aircraft manufacturing plants on the Pacific Coast were built with DPC funds.

Although most of the DPC's projects were designed to increase production, the Corporation also engaged in research and development. Such was the case with the plan hatched by Howard Hughes and Henry J. Kaiser for the "Spruce Goose," a giant cargo plane. With their vivid imaginations, Hughes and Kaiser in 1942 envisaged an eight-engine, 200-ton aircraft capable of carrying an entire company of soldiers with all of their equipment. At a time when German submarines were seriously impeding the flow of American supplies to England such a proposal seemed attractive to the administration and the President himself gave a green light for the program. The DPC spent $18 million for a proposal to build three of these planes, one prototype and two for use in testing. As metals were scarce in 1942, the DPC directed that they be made of wood.

Hughes undertook construction of one of the planes in his California plant, indulging his ever-increasing penchant for secrecy. No outsiders were permitted to watch progress in the building of this, the world's largest aircraft, not even Henry Kaiser, it was rumored. But even after the DPC had expended more than $13 million, the prototype was still far from completion. Thus, in 1943 Donald Nelson, chairman of the War Production Board, decided to cancel the contract. Hughes hurried to Washington to plead his case. His persuasiveness led President Roosevelt to order Donald

Nelson to reinstate the contract. Although the DPC agreed to pay the remaining $5 million of the loan to Hughes, it also required him to pay additional needed costs out of his own pocket. At that point Kaiser dropped out of the project while Hughes invested at least $10 million more, according to the estimate of Jesse Jones, chairman of the Reconstruction Finance Corporation. Not until November 2, 1947, with Hughes himself at the controls of the prototype, did the Spruce Goose lift off for a two-minute flight near his plant in California. As public confidence in the venture waned, that of Hughes increased. His faith in the project remained unshaken, but he placed the plane in storage in a huge hangar in Long Beach, California, where it languished until 1980 when the Hughes estate sold it to promoters who made it a public tourist attraction in Long Beach.

The West was also affected by the activities of the Metals Reserve Corporation. Another major subsidiary of the Reconstruction Finance Corporation, it became the federal government's principal agent for the purchase of more than $2,750,000,000 of metals in the western states, not to speak of another $1 billion of purchases overseas. As the major metals procurement agent for the armed services it scoured the West for copper, tin, tungsten, zinc, chrome, bauxite, and more exotic metals. It also constructed the world's largest tin smelter in Texas City, Texas, despite efforts by executives of Phelps-Dodge and American Metals Company to retain the facility in the East, near their operations in Baltimore. Through the subsidies it paid to western miners the Metals Reserve Corporation greatly stimulated metals production in California, Idaho, Nevada, Colorado, and Utah, and in most other western states. Even metals that had been imported into the United States before 1940, such as chrome, were produced domestically during wartime as miners—spurred by the Corporation's subsidies—combed unexplored reserves throughout the region. In Montana, for example, they discovered rare chrome deposits in the Custer National Forest. These finds supplemented limited quantities imported from South Africa and Rhodesia. And the western aluminum industry could not have flourished during wartime had it not been for the Metals Reserve extensive program to exploit Arkansas deposits.

Synthetic rubber was another of the new industries fostered by the federal government in the West. Twenty-three new synthetic rubber plants built by the Rubber Reserve Corporation were erected either on the Pacific Coast or in the Texas Gulf region. Almost overnight, the Rubber Reserve Corporation created an important new industry for the West. . . .

Businessmen and state officials in western states that were primarily agricultural saw the war mobilization program as an unusual opportunity to secure long-desired manufacturing facilities. In North Dakota, for example, the Governor and other state officials were eager in the fall of 1941 to secure federal contracts. They encouraged a group of local businessmen to form the North Dakota War Resources Committee to develop specific proposals. Another group of businessmen organized the Greater North Dakota Association, which hired a paid lobbyist to solicit federal funds in the nation's capital. In 1942, this individual, Frederick Frederickson, introduced the state's political leaders and members of the Association's War Resources Committee (of which he was chairman) to key federal officials. They made the rounds of the War Production Board, the Reconstruction Finance Corporation, and the War Department, but unfortunately met with no success. A somewhat similar experience befell a group of businessmen and political leaders from Wyoming.

On the other hand, when a western state had a powerful politician as a spokesman, it fared better. Nevada was a case in point. With Senator Key Pittman's death in 1940 the state lost an influential voice in the United States Senate. But within a short time Senator Pat McCarran took up his mantle. A shrewd political manipulator, he was instrumental in 1941 in securing more than $200 million from the Reconstruction Finance Corporation for the construction of the world's largest basic magnesium plant at Henderson, near Las Vegas. The site—between Las Vegas and Boulder City—was not far from the recently completed Boulder Dam, which promised to provide an ample supply of cheap power. Nearby Nye County also contained extensive magnesium deposits. McCarran intervened at the highest level and secured President Roosevelt's direct, personal support. "I am glad to be able to advise you," Roosevelt wrote him in 1941, "that a project for producing 23,000,000 pounds of magnesium annually has already been approved by the Materiel Division, U.S. Army Air Corps. . . . The new plants will be located at Gables, Mead, and Las Vegas, all in the state of Nevada." With evident pride McCarran reported his accomplishment to Joe Cook, editor of the *Nevada State Journal*, noting that he had first written to the Chief Executive on this matter on June 14 after holding several conferences in Washington, D.C., with "appropriate authorities." As McCarran wrote, he had done "all to securing for Nevada a share in this defense program," for he was sure that the plant was a "promise of increased industrial development activity for our state."

By September 1941 the RFC had rushed the completion of the plant, which operated until November 1944, at times with more than 15,000 employees. When federal stockpiles of magnesium grew large toward the end of the war, the Defense Plant Corporation closed the facility. During the period of operation, however, Basic Magnesium not only created the new boom town of Henderson, but invigorated the economy of the entire southern portion of the state.

Although disappointed about much hoped-for federal funds to speed industrialization, those western states that failed to receive substantial war orders nevertheless still prospered from the wartime boom, which spurred mining and agriculture and new military installations. Almost as a consolation prize western states were the beneficiaries of government largesse in the form of new military installations. Remoteness and isolation now came to be virtues that provided a magnet for vast new facilities in every western state. A recapitulation of their history would entail many volumes. It is true, of course, that since 1850 the West had received a substantial portion of its income from army posts and supply depots. But the scope of this expansion in World War II was unprecedented, and more than ever made the West increasingly dependent on federal largesse.

The defense installations of Utah provide a striking example of the growing pervasiveness of the federal presence in the West. In Utah, by 1942 the federal government established ten major military bases. Three were training facilities, one a research and testing installation, while the others were huge supply depots and repair and maintenance bases. They included the Ogden Arsenal, Hill Air Force Base, Ogden Defense Depot, Deseret Chemical Depot, Tooele Army Depot, Naval Supply Depot at Clearfield, Camp W. G. Williams and Fort Douglas, Wendover Air Force Base, Kearns Air Force Base and Dugway Proving Ground. In addition to more than 60,000 military personnel stationed in Utah in wartime, the bases employed another 60,000 persons.

In fact, a sizable portion of federal investment throughout the West during wartime came through the establishment of new military installations. Training camps, air bases, testing facilities and storage depots came to dot the West, making the region—in contrast to World War I—a major site for the nation's expanding military-industrial complex. Its open spaces, remoteness, and mild climates made the West particularly desirable for such installations, given the state of technology at the time. Moreover, in 1941 the United States was also engaged in a Pacific war and the proximity of the West to that area made it more important than ever as a major arsenal.

Although the federal government provided about 90 percent of the new investment capital that flowed into the West during wartime mobilization, it also did much to stimulate private banking in the West. Capital funds of banks west of the Mississippi River increased by about 20 percent between 1940 and 1945. The Bank of America was certainly not a typical western financial institution, but its wartime growth did mirror the expansion of other banks throughout the West. During World War II it supplied increasing amounts of capital to local industries and significantly freed many western businessmen from their reliance on eastern financiers. Between 1941 and 1945, for the first time in its history, the bank entered upon large-scale investment programs in cooperation with eastern syndicates. To stimulate corporate expansion on the Pacific Coast, it floated large debt issues for corporations like Bendix, Chrysler, RCA, and Westinghouse. It also supplied most of the private funds needed for the expansion of private shipyards on the Pacific Coast, in collaboration with the major banks in the Pacific Northwest. Although the influence of the western banks in Washington was still less than that of Wall Street lobbyists, war mobilization significantly increased their importance and their influence. The Smaller War Plants Corporation and the Federal Reserve Board's Regulation V were among the concrete manifestations of that influence. At the same time the war-induced boom on the Pacific Coast greatly boosted the bank's business. Although in 1942 the Comptroller of the Currency was loath to issue the Bank of America more permits to open new branches, he really had no choice. The extraordinary demand for new banking facilities in new housing developments, army camps ad naval installations, and war-related factories forced his hand. Thus, the war accelerated the trend toward branch banking, particularly for the Bank of America. But its experience was closely watched—and soon widely imitated—in many other western states.

The large influx of federal investment funds—supplemented by expansion of private financial institutions—sparked an enormous economic boom throughout the West. It spawned new factories and new service industries, stimulated many spheres of Western mining, and created a vast network of military installations and new science centers. That boom, of course, did not affect all parts of the West in an even-handed fashion. It was most pronounced on the Pacific Coast, quite noticeable in the Southwest, muted in the Rocky Mountain area, and perhaps least significant on the Great Plains. On the other hand, wartime-induced demands for agricultural goods brought a revival of prosperity to the Plains and ended more than a decade of hardship inaugurated by the Great Depression.

Industry on the Pacific Coast experienced the most striking wartime boom. California alone secured 12 percent of all war orders in the United States with heavy concentration in shipbuilding, aircraft manufactures, food processing, and clothing and light manufactures. In 1939, California was in a good position to attract war orders. Its large metropolitan areas contained a vast array of small machine shops, auto assembly and food processing plants, and clothing manufacturers who could convert to wartime production on short notice. And shipyards and aircraft manufacturers who had developed during the First World War had managed to survive the hazards of the Great Depression. Blessed with a mild climate and strategically located near the Pacific theater of war, California appeared particularly appealing to the Washington chiefs of staff who favored some decentralization of the nation's industrial capacity in the interests of national security.

The influx of more than $70 billion in federal funds into California between 1941 and 1945 set a chain of events into motion that ultimately created the nation's largest urban military-industrial complex in the state. In that complex the aircraft industry was preeminent, stretching from San Diego northward to Long Beach, Santa Monica, Burbank, Inglewood, and other communities in the Los Angeles area. During the peak of production in 1943 the aircraft plants of southern California employed 243,000 workers drawn from all parts of the nation. Their function was not unlike that of the mines in the Gold Rush of 1849. By June of 1945 aircraft plants in Los Angeles had secured $7,093,837 in federal orders while those in San Diego received $2,136,119. The names of once obscure airplane manufacturers now came to be household words in America. Who in World War II had not heard of Douglas Aviation's Flying Fortresses (B-17s) or Liberator Bombers, or of Lockheed's famed P-38 fighter? Not only aviation enthusiasts but the general public now followed the latest production records of Hughes Aircraft or Northrop, Consolidated-Vultee or North American Aviation as popular magazines and newspapers filled their pages with the exploits of the nation's newest corporate heroes in the West.

Much of California's boom town atmosphere during wartime was due to its vast shipbuilding activities. As southern California became the hub of the West's aircraft industry, so the northern part of the state became a significant shipbuilding center. By 1943, the shipyards in the San Francisco area and those in Los Angeles employed 280,000 workers. Three-fourths of the $4.7 billion which the federal government spent for shipbuilding on the Pacific Coast was awarded to yards in the Bay region, and Richmond, Vallejo, Sausalito, Alameda, and South San Francisco became boom towns over night, complete with trailer camps, ramshackle streets, and bawdy entertainment houses.

Of the Big Three manufacturing industries that sprang up in the West during World War II steel was another newcomer. President Roosevelt himself decided early in the rearmament program, in the spring of 1941, that steel manufacturing in the West needed to be greatly expanded. Consequently, in 1942 the Reconstruction Finance Corporation provided subsidies and loans for the construction of a vast new steel manufacturing complex in Fontana, California. The proximity of Fontana to the major shipyards of the Pacific Coast was a major factor in the decision to build this, the only major steel manufacturing facility west of the Mississippi River with the exception of the Geneva Steel Works in Provo, Utah.

The Big Three industries in California generated a vast network of subcontractors, resulting in the extraordinary expansion of thousands of small businesses. Airplane parts, electrical equipment, plastics, machinery, and pumps of infinite variety were made and processed. The value of California's manufactures jumped from $2,798,000 in 1939 to $10,141,000 just five years later. And the number of production workers in California employed in manufacturing grew as dramatically, from 271,290 in 1939 to 530,283 eight years later.

In many ways the "can do" spirit of western industry was personified by the West's (and the nation's) outstanding industrialist, Henry J. Kaiser. He was born in Canajoharie in upstate New York of a poor family. Forced to leave school at the age of eleven, he went to work for a local photographer as an errand boy. Before he was out of his teens, he had bought out his boss and operated the photography business, spending summers in Lake Placid and winters in Florida to tap the tourist trade. When he fell in love with one of his photographic subjects, Bessie Hannah Fosburgh, and asked for her hand, her father insisted that he ply a more "regular" trade. So in 1907 Kaiser went to Spokane, Washington, where he secured a job with J. B. Hill and Co., a paving contractor who was then building Spokane's expanding street network. Within six years Kaiser founded his own paving firm specializing in highway construction as increasing use of automobiles created a boom in that field by the 1920s. In 1921, his first large project was building the road between Redding and Red Bluff, in California. With wife and children in the back of his car he was always on the move during these years, supervising his various construction projects while building a modest home in Oakland and earning a reputation for efficiency. Kaiser's was one of the Six Companies that built Boulder Dam, completed in 1935, and also built the piers for the Oakland–San Francisco Bay Bridge. From these vast ventures he moved to even greater challenges with the building of Bonneville and Grand Coulee Dams just on the eve of World War II. Meanwhile, in 1939 he had also entered into the cement manufacturing business with the establishment of the Permanente Company.

Kaiser came to shipbuilding somewhat accidentally. While he was having two old cement carrier ships repaired in the Todd Shipyards in Seattle, he talked with the president, John Reilly, in January 1941. He decided on a partnership—Todd–California Shipbuilding Company—to garner lucrative government contracts. They separated just two months later, but by then Kaiser was well on his way. Using the good offices of his friend and sometime financier, A. P. Giannini of the Bank of America, he made initial contacts with the White House. Within a year Kaiser had secured contracts for fully one-third of all the merchant ships then under construction.

Once engaged in large-scale shipbuilding, Kaiser became concerned about securing a steady supply of prefabricated steel for his yards, and so became involved with the expansion of the western steel industry at Fontana. Eastern industrialists still had a virtual monopoly on the manufacture of finished steel products and did not look favorably on losing control of their western markets. But President Roosevelt himself felt strongly that the decentralization of industry—particularly the steel industry—was highly desirable. Such decentralization was needed not only for greater national security but also in the event of possible enemy air attacks. Dispersion would also limit the monopolistic practices of industries such as steel which had just recently been laid bare by the investigations of the Temporary National Economic Committee and the Anti-Trust Division of the Department of Justice under Thurman Arnold. Thus, Kaiser's plans found receptive ears in the Roosevelt administration. In 1942, Jesse Jones, chairman of the Reconstruction Finance Corporation, authorized a $150-million loan to Kaiser to enable him to build a brand-new steel manufacturing facility at Fontana, California, largely at government expense.

The restless vision of this remarkable entrepreneur also led him to assume leadership in the development of a new aluminum industry in the West. Kaiser keenly perceived that light metals would have burgeoning markets in the immediate future, not only for the building of aircraft, ships, and autos, but for thousands of other civilian uses. Thus, he applied to the Reconstruction Finance Corporation for federal loans to build and operate five new aluminum plants in the Pacific Northwest. Since the power to be used by these factories was to be supplied by Bonneville and Grand Coulee Dams which he had just completed, Kaiser was in a particularly favorable position to win approval for his plans, once again financed largely by federal funds.

Kaiser's career paced the West Coast's economic growth. He was representative of the region's outlook and its desire to utilize its undeveloped capacity and its still untried potential. The war forever demolished the myth that the frontier had closed and ended the West's capacity for growth and expansion. The war stimulated the West's traditional optimism which had been blunted—if not virtually extinguished—during the Great Depression. The war unlocked a sense of purpose and determination that westerners quickly translated into striking accomplishments in industrial expansion. With a growing population, a highly skilled labor force, vast areas of un-populated lands, abundant natural resources, and an increasing array of scientific and technological skills the West was in an excellent position to embark on another surge of economic growth. The ingredients that had been missing in the 1930s—namely a supply of new investment capital and also a sense of optimism—were now provided.

If the pace of war-induced industrialization was slightly less hectic in the Pacific Northwest than in California, the transformation there was no less complete. Between 1941 and 1945 manufactures increased 265 percent in the region. Seattle alone secured war contracts totaling $5.6 billion. A significant portion of this total flowed to the Boeing Company in Seattle which hired 40,000 new workers. Although headquartered in Seattle, Boeing's activities reached into many parts of the region in view of extensive sub-contracting and the establishment of branch plants in Renton, Bellingham, Aberdeen, Chehallis, and Everett, Washington. Seattle and Portland hummed also with extensive shipbuilding activities as the vast new Kaiser shipyards in Portland and the Puget Sound area helped to pace large-scale construction of Liberty ships and baby aircraft carriers. The shipyards of the Pacific Northwest were also involved in large-scale repair activities. Much of the Navy's fleet salvaged from the disaster at Pearl Harbor, for example, was refitted in the Portland shipyards. In addition, many smaller plants were engaged in significant war production, such as the Pacific Car and Foundry Company which converted to producing Sherman tanks.

The Pacific Northwest also benefited from wartime demands for aluminum. The recent completion of the Bonneville Dam in 1942—and the availability of cheap power from that source—was a key factor that led the Roosevelt administration, particularly Donald Nelson and Jesse Jones, to locate nine major new aluminum plants on the Pacific Coast, built primarily with funds advanced by the Defense Plant Corporation, and operated by the Aluminum Corporation of America (Alcoa), Reynolds Aluminum, and Henry Kaiser. Federal intervention in the industry effectively broke the monopoly which Alcoa had cherished until 1941. Moreover, it brought a major new industry to the Pacific Northwest and established mutually advantageous relationships with the booming aircraft industry.

In the Rocky Mountain area the war also stimulated industrial devel-opment, if on a smaller scale than on the Pacific Coast. Denver, Colorado, secured a significant share of wartime contracts. The Rocky Mountain Arsenal there, operated by Remington-Rand, employed more than 20,000 people at the peak of wartime production, fabricating munitions and poisonous gases. Denver became something of a shipbuilding center as well, specializing in the fabrication of submarine chasers. The yard produced more than sixty such vessels, which were shipped to the Mare Island Naval Yard in the San Francisco Bay Area by railroad. It was an eerie sight indeed to see ships moving over mountains. Once they arrived at Mare Island, workers there undertook assembly and gave them a second launching.

War industries moved into selected areas of the Southwest, most notably Arizona, where the Goodyear Company opened a vast new plant in Phoenix that attracted a number of smaller companies. Tucson profited from war orders also, primarily with the growth of small establishments that worked as subcontractors for the large corporations on the Pacific Coast. . . .

The war thus had a profound influence in transforming the western economy. Mobilization wrought major changes in the economic life of the region and brought long-sought-for diversification. In addition to the basic resource industries, the massive influx of new capital provided by the federal government now resulted in the establishment of major new manufacturing facilities—mainly in aircraft, shipbuilding, aluminum, and steel—with related industries. But the West did more than gain a new manufacturing base in World War II. Its economic growth was further stimulated by the founding of new technologically oriented industries characteristic of a post-industrial society, namely aerospace and electronics. These had as yet barely developed in the older and more stratified economy of the industrial Northeast. In a sense, the underdeveloped economy of the West in 1941 proved to be an advantage, because it offered unlimited opportunities for experimentation with new industries such as nuclear energy, aerospace, and electronics. Along with extensive military installations, these industries did much to promote the service trades which were already becoming increasingly significant in the national economy. In 1941 the Western economy had been backward, characterized by a raw-materials, nonindustrial base. By 1945 the region had not only developed the bases for a manufacturing complex; it had moved into the next stage of economic development with the growth of a technological and service economy. In four short years, the erstwhile backward section had become a pace-setter for the nation.

Colonialism: The Enduring Dilemma

ROBERT G. ATHEARN

As late as 1897 William E. Smythe, who was well known for his studies on reclamation, viewed the trans-Missouri West as a great place to plant colonies. He remarked that it was common to think of colonialism as a thing of the dead past but that all growing nations tended to employ it as a means of economic expansion, the United States being no exception. The difference, he explained, was that this country had no need to go beyond its borders to find homesites for its growing population because the colonial movement "of today and of the future" would be directed toward the arid

Robert G. Athearn, "Colonialism: The Enduring Dilemma," in *The Mythic West in Twentieth-Century America,* 108–130. Copyright © 1986, reprinted by permission of the University Press of Kansas.

regions of the West. As the new century approached, there remained in American thinking the picture of a "desert" West that waited only to be "reclaimed"—that is, watered and colonized. Smythe was writing in a day of hope, of prospects for the further "developing" of American real estate out there some place. A little over three decades later, in the depths of an unprecedented depression, such optimism no longer existed. Presumably the hinterland had been drained of anything worthwhile, and now taxpayers were being billed for a dead horse. . . .

For their part, westerners also were taking a fresh, hard look at their place in the economic scheme of things. It took some time, but they gradually came to see themselves as poor relatives, not legitimate offspring who had hereditary rights to the family fortune. Around the turn of the century they had been called "the children of the nation—and favored children," a status they had accepted with some reservations in the years that preceded American participation in World War I. It was in this phase that westerners had begun to display signs of an emerging resentment toward the spiritual domination of the East, and they even exhibited a certain political restlessness. But then came the troublous twenties, when agriculture, stock raising, and mining declined sharply. It was then that the pangs of a regional inferiority complex began to become obvious.

In this period of nationwide disillusionment and self-doubt, the West began to think of itself not only as a neglected colonial but also, more precisely, as a weaker element in an organization in which stronger factions were taking advantage of those who were less able to protect themselves. As the haze of optimism was burned away, westerners, their jaws clenched and their brows furrowed, were analyzing their situation and defining their grievances much more clearly than in the past. And they were feeling trapped. The conviction was growing that what was once thought of as development was, indeed, nothing more than exploitation by outsiders. The main burden of colonialism was, in their eyes, the economic tether by which they now were being constrained. It enforced a thralldom that went straight to the pocket nerve, overshadowing all other forms of subordination. In the eyes of easterners it threatened to create, for the first time in the nation's history, an American peasantry.

The traditional target of those who complained about outside control was, of course, the railroad industry. Discriminatory rates long had been a western grievance, one that dated back to the 1870s, climaxed about twenty years later, and remained a dormant dissatisfaction during the ensuing years. As was true in an earlier day, the outrage generated by the levying of inequitable freight rates ebbed and flowed with the price of grain and the general level of prosperity in the West. Not unexpectedly, the downturn in western economic conditions during the 1920s generated a search for a villain. An old and sure-fire one was waiting in the wings: rail rate schedules.

In 1926 an Idaho senator introduced a bill that was designed to better balance the differential between long-haul and short-haul rates. All mountain-state senators except those from Colorado voted for it. It goes without saying that the bill failed; even the Pacific Coast states voted against it. It was ironic that Colorado should have been among the negative votes, for its mineral and agricultural industries were no better off than were those of its sister states. Perhaps Colorado had not felt the bite sufficiently by 1926, but three years later there was evidence that times were changing. By then, Frederick Bonfils, publisher of the *Denver Post*, had come forth as a champion of those who wanted to control rail rates. He conceded that in an earlier day, when the West was thinly populated and railroads were fighting for their lives, they had to charge more, but now there was no justification for such conduct. He recommended the formation of a Rocky Mountain League of States, the combined power of which would force roads to moderate their charges. Bonfils argued that the region ought to be free from outside financial control, and in his demands for collective action he used such terms as *justice* and *square deal*.

In Colorado it was not only the little people, the small users, who had grievances against the financial giants who wielded power from afar. The sting of the lash had been felt by local corporations, the most recent of which had seen New York bankers and rival railroads stop David Moffat's efforts to build a line from Denver to Salt Lake City in the years before World War I. Before that, the Denver and Rio Grande Western Railroad had faced a similar situation, one that dogged it all during its early years; and one of the road's major goals while coming out of bankruptcy after World War II was to maintain control of its own financial destiny. That it succeeded was heralded by its directors as a landmark of progress for the line.

Although railroads were the traditional "enemy" and a favorite topic when westerners talked about financial peonage, the influence of the "foreign" money masters and large corporations had extended far beyond that by the twenties. "Even if you start a grocery store in a small town," said a western lawyer in 1927, "some chain may come along and beat you to it." He admitted that one could own a farm or practice a profession in the West, but any other avenue reached a dead end in the backyard of big business. And where were the big businesses? In the East, he said. As historian Walter Webb wrote of those years, the small-town merchants of the West were locked into a form of bondage that necessitated the payment of tribute to northeastern financial centers.

Lamentations of this nature failed to move a great many residents in other parts of the country. Those who lived in the depression-ridden East already had expressed concern about supporting poor relatives out West, and now, at a time when belt tightening at home was called for, they were to have even greater complaints when New Dealers began to hand out money with a lavish hand to these sufferers of the sagebrush. Once again, said those from older sections of America, the country cousins were getting a larger proportionate slice of the federal pie.

Westerners did not object to generous helpings at the family table. Not yet. For the moment they were perfectly happy to see the New Deal bail them out. When criticized as deadbeats, they pointed out that they could hardly support themselves entirely, because much of their land was owned by the government and therefore was beyond their power to tax. Here was a refrain to be heard for generations to come. By the 1930s the government had given away or sold about all the land it ever would. A lot of the West was left under federal control, and it remains so today. In 1980 the federal government owned about 1 percent of New York and Ohio, 6 percent of North Carolina, and 9 percent of Michigan. Across the hundredth meridian, however, the numbers changed dramatically. Uncle Sam owned about 35 percent of Colorado and New Mexico, 50 percent of Wyoming, 65 percent of Utah and Idaho, and nearly 90 percent of Nevada. Particularly during the hard depression years, it seemed only fair that the Great White Father should pay his rent on the far side of the river.

Besides that, the western "colonists" during the 1930s still felt at ease accepting support from the national capital, though many of their children and grandchildren would feel differently. During the depression, westerners lived in the last of the "contiguous forty-eight" to be settled. They had waited as territories outside the union of equal states much longer than had their predecessors east of the Mississippi, and they were accustomed to thinking of Washington, D.C., not their own capital cities, as the controlling force. Federal agencies had been among them from the start and had parceled out the allotted money. Not infrequently these dispensers had constituted some of the better oases in the financial desert.

Thus, when the New Dealers arrived and renewed the greening of the West, the locals took their customary places in line—sometimes twice— and took all they could get. Then, as was the custom, when times got better, they attacked their benefactors and accused them of trying to prostitute the innocents with temptations from the big city.

Such behavior recalled earlier times, when westerners had damned the army for its bungling, for not killing off the red natives fast enough; but at the same time they eagerly had sought the establishment of posts to which they could sell horses and hay, beef, and booze. Now, in the thirties, government offices, often manned by outside political appointees, were doling out the largess. Local politicians, who did not have that kind of money, could not compete for votes on even terms, so they began to complain about remote control and to moan over the enslavement of a once-free people.

A foretaste of the militancy that was to emerge among western States' rights advocates made national news in 1943 with the outbreak of the comic-opera "Jackson Hole War" in Wyoming. That spring, when Franklin Roosevelt's executive order set aside 221,610 acres of land adjacent to Grand Teton National Park to establish Jackson Hole National Monument, local Paul Reveres saddled up and spread the cry that an invasion of outlanders was taking place. Those who felt that they had been set upon were further irritated by the realization that the withdrawn tract included 32,117 acres that had been acquired gradually by the Rockefellers, with the intention of giving it to the federal government for preservation purposes. As these westerners saw it, a second enemy, one representing financial royalty, had thrown in with the tyrants from Foggy Bottom to drive honest yeomen of the Rockies from the king's forest. Wyoming newspapers and politicians rallied around the folks of Teton County, who complained that they had been robbed of valuable taxable property, not to mention the loss of grazing, hunting, and fishing possibilities. The aggrieved struck back by calling for a moratorium on the buying of war bonds; Teton County quickly sank to the bottom of the state's list.

True westerners could do better than that. Talk was cheap, and passive resistance had no part in the pioneer tradition. Onto the scene now rode forty horsemen, armed to the teeth and accompanied by old-time movie actor Wallace Beery, who hit the saddle for some real-life drama. Well, almost hit the saddle; an ugly rumor had it that he was obliged to use a ladder to board his steed. Billed as a "rancher," Beery's sole claims to the title were a lease that he had on a half-acre of Forest Service land and his lone bovine, an old milk cow, which recently had expired.

The campaign fizzled as the light brigade drove a few startled cows across the newly forbidden land in a pallid show of defiance. The park superintendent, who had no taste for cattle wars, made no effort to deter the vigilantes in their quest for justice. Such acquiescence brought roars of protest from feisty Harold L. Ickes, secretary of the interior, who called the horsemen "ghost-hunting cowboys" running around in "mail-order regalia" and engaged in mock heroics.

Nay, cried the head of the Wyoming Stockgrowers Association, no such thing. This was a mounted Boston Tea Party, carried out by patriots who were determined to preserve their God-given rights. "We will never rest until we are in fact, as well as in name, sovereign states," he informed his critics. Following along in the historical jet stream, Governor Lester Hunt struck a Lincolnesque pose and announced that his domain was "half free and half slave." Implications of revolution or a miniature civil war wafted eastward from Wyoming.

Washington listened. In December 1944, Congress passed a bill that abolished the Jackson Hole National Monument, and Roosevelt promptly gave it a pocket veto. But the complaints continued, and in 1950 another bill was passed that abolished the monument. As a trade-off, most of the contested land was added to Grand Teton National Park; the act had been performed, but under another cover.

By the end of World War II the western states were openly denouncing the degree to which federal control had fastened itself upon their part of the land. Early in 1945, governors and other western representatives, meeting at Reno, Nevada, spoke out against this encroachment by the central government and formally demanded the return of their "rights and functions lost to the federal government during the war." It was a public admission that the West simply had moved from one form of colonialism to another.

The war extended federal colonialism even in a negative way. During those years the region lost population to enlistments and to war industries outside the area. The vacuum thus created tended to drive out people who were not affected directly by either of these forces but whose businesses suffered; tourism serves as one example. There were, of course, isolated exceptions to the outflow. Cities such as Denver, Salt Lake City, and Las Vegas grew, but the fact remained that by V-J Day in 1945, the region's head count was smaller than it had been in 1940.

Lack of growth—which has traditionally been regarded as an American disgrace—generated cries of dismay and a sharpened antagonism from those who felt oppressed. Now it became popular to turn on the federal government and to accuse it of trying to stifle the West by smothering private enterprise. The Missouri Valley Authority, for example, was loudly opposed by a group of westerners who listened to power-company lobbyists and came away convinced that their hereditary rights were being eroded.

These were merely signs that once more the natives were getting restless. Colorado poet Thomas Hornsby Ferril, a sensitive and perceptive man, watched the western emotional seismograph at the end of the war and noted some rumblings in the Rockies. In those early peacetime days he predicted: "The westerner is going to become more rampant, more articulate. He bristles and foams at hearing Thurman Arnold say that the western states are being treated as 'colonies of the mother country—the industrial East.' " The folks in Laramie, Arnold's home town, probably bristled and foamed a little more when, in 1937, he commented that anyone who had any sense would not settle in Wyoming, where he thought both money and intellectual contacts were in short supply. He was not mimicking [Bernard] De Voto, the expatriate who had heaped scorn upon Ogden, Utah; rather, he was trying to show that colonialism stunted development. "Economic disadvantage creates a backward country," he wrote. Like De Voto, however, Arnold felt that the West's lack of development was not simply a natural occurrence; it had been imposed. These critics were willing to compare the region to the American colonies before the Revolution in the mother country's denial of industry. Charges such as these brought nods of agreement from westerners and added to their already-well-developed sense of inferiority. As always, they welcomed a scapegoat when they were unable to pinpoint their own difficulties.

If all the charges of colonialism were true, then the West appeared to be held in thralldom by, not one, but two masters: Wall Street and Washington. In a series of articles, from his perch in the "Easy Chair" at *Harper's,* De Voto thundered his charges against the eastern establishment for half a decade after the war. Much of his writing simply reiterated or expanded upon his "Plundered Province" article of August 1934. Rail-rate inequities, usurious interest charges, absentee ownership, tariff protection for eastern manufacturers, the control of capital by easterners, the stifling of western industries by driving them to the wall with eastern monopolistic branches, and economic favoritism to the East in general—all were favorite launching pads for De Voto's multiple literary rockets. None of them was new, but there was a readership for these recycled ideas, and De Voto packaged them very attractively.

The surfacing of this postwar populism was not entirely surprising, if one considers the restlessness of the West during the preceding two decades, but it was not cast quite in the classic pattern. No William Jennings Bryan came forth; there was no "Sockless Jerry" Simpson, no Mary Elizabeth Lease, and no "Bloody Bridles" Waite to whip angry voters into a froth before sending them wild-eyed to the ballot boxes. There were writers, commentators, and university professors who held that the West still was a "company domain," and their warnings about the dire consequences of such a condition were gladly printed by eastern publishers, whose interest in the colonies was one of long standing.

This time, however, there was something hollow about the West's protest. Looking back, it was World War II that shifted and redefined the terms of the debate over colonialism, just as the global conflict changed so much else in the region. The war returned prosperity to the country at large and triggered a boom in the West that in many ways continues today. Though the East's complaints about the worthless hinterland continued in some quarters, businessmen began to look beyond the Missouri with a new interest after 1945. The view of the West as a wasteland and as an economic rathole no longer held the stage alone. In the West, business-oriented community leaders were working hard to wipe the dust off and to pound the dents from the old image of the country as a land of opportunity and sure profits. Under these circumstances, there was a need for a different villain. Western complaints about outside control still were heard, but now the oppressor was, not Eastern businessmen, but the national government, which had helped prop up the West during the depths of the depression.

So as Colorado economist Morris Garnsey noted, there was little outcry from the old Populist country about absentee ownership; instead, there was loud complaint about the government as landlord and as an enemy of States' rights. He was convinced that the traditional control that big business had exercised over the West's political apparatus had resulted in an ingrained notion that the federal government was out to stifle economic exploration and development. Garnsey strongly opposed the absentee ownership by the business world, but he also admitted that the federal government was the biggest absentee owner of all, a landlord in whose grasp most of the West lay. He added, however, that Washington had created more economic activity than it had suppressed and so was less harmful. Future western development, therefore, depended directly on the area's transportation, communications, and other major areas of economic activity.

In effect this is what the business-courting community leaders of the postwar West were complaining about. They wanted development at any cost, and they regarded the central government as the principal barrier to that expansion. They did not, to be sure, want Washington to release its western lands to them. Little of it would be profitable in private hands. Instead, they wanted to be able to use it with the fewest possible restraints. In the terms of the day, the debate raged over whether growth was to be "natural"—that is, unregulated and presumably "free"—or a controlled hothouse growth, supervised by planners from afar. The outriders and trumpeters of these latter-day business pioneers were the cattlemen, who still held a strong and somewhat disproportionate influence in various western legislatures and who were fond of making loud noises about the diminution of their legendary rights to grazing on the public domain. They were ready to ride once more, at the customary drop of a hat.

Meanwhile the argument grew hotter over just how tightly the West was being held in the coils of its ancient colonial subservience. Depending upon whom one read, the answer varied from no to yes, from somewhat to maybe. The freight-rates tether remained a popular part of the argument, with journalists and professors alike joining in the cry against these transportation companies, but in the decade and a half after the end of the war, there were those who contended that despite remoteness and discriminatory long-haul rates, the West had established a measure of economic independence.

Leonard J. Arrington, Utah's widely respected economic historian, supported this view in his study of the regional economy for the years 1940–60. He concluded that the West was moving in the general direction of economic maturity because of its declining reliance upon the exportation of its resources to sustain itself.

From the vantage point of 1940 the great "break through," which later was said to have resulted from the war and its immediate aftermath, did not appear to hold much promise. Scholars of that day still regarded the West as a "vast, new colonial empire," one that was potentially rich but was still poor because of its lack of development. The region continued to be viewed as a raw-material resource annex, one that was "destined to remain for many years to come a vast, unused storehouse of wealth, awaiting the needs of a future America."

However, said Arrington, the ensuing two decades belied that prediction. In citing four important changes in the Mountain West during those years, he summarized the observations of a great many people who had watched the unfolding panorama. Figures for tourism had soared, making climate and scenic attractions a major industry. There was far less dependence upon agriculture and mining than before. For the first time in history the Mountain West could boast of manufacturing on a significant scale, the steel complexes of Utah and Colorado being important examples. And lastly, the area was a beneficiary of enormous outlays for defense spending, a market that the West was now sharing with other portions of the country. While his tests applied especially to the mountain portion of the region and were true only in varying degrees to the plains country, there is enough application to the entire West that is being considered here to use the broader generalization when talking about colonialism.

As western financial leaders watched the peacetime economy emerge from the war years, they saw changes around them. They noticed that western bank assets, which had totaled a little over $7 billion in 1940, had tripled by 1948, giving rise to the feeling that local projects increasingly were able to rely upon "inside money" for assistance. Elroy Nelson, vice-president of Salt Lake City's First Security Corporation, expressed a hope that was shared by his colleagues when he said, "We're growing up industrially." The war, he thought, had accounted for a recent speed-up in that evolution. It was an episode that had "telescoped decades of development into a few years," and he thought it suggested the end of a century of colonialism.

Efforts to bring industry, and hence independence, to the West during these postwar years provided a new scenario, but even that was not without its problems. For about a quarter of a century after 1945, state and local community leaders made a concerted effort to attract new business to the western states. Each year, little groups of commercial missionaries were sent eastward to sing the praises of a new frontier and to woo capital. They offered climate, a cheap and docile labor force that could boast of little or no organization, favorable building sites, tax breaks, and other inducements. However, these solicitations in the big city were not indiscriminate. The scouting parties were on the lookout for small, clean "Swiss type" industries that would not pollute physical or civic atmospheres out there where the skies are not cloudy all day. It was hoped that through this selectivity the residents, both old and new, would have fewer complaints about the resultant growth; but as it turned out, these expectations were not realized.

As always, the eastern corporate establishment responded to the call, especially when the natives indicated a renewed urge to fondle a few trade beads. "Clean" industries began to plant outposts along the mountain front and throughout the Rockies. When *Esquire-Coronet*'s subscription department, Minneapolis-Honeywell Regulator, Hewlett-Packard, Beech Aircraft, Eastman Kodak, and IBM came to such a state as Colorado, they added to the tax base and hired the "right" kind of employees. Governmental installations, such as the Air Force Academy at Colorado Springs, the Central Radio Propagation Laboratory of the National Bureau of Standards (on donated land), the Atomic Energy Commission's cryogenics engineering laboratory, and the National Center for Atmospheric Research, all at Boulder, brought large payrolls and some highly trained personnel to the area. When Ball Brothers Research Corporation, a descendant of a well-known Indiana fruit-jar manufacturer, located at Boulder and began to process a number of federal contracts that were important to the space program, another nonpolluter had nestled against the Rockies.

The solicitation of these carefully selected industries offered yet another variation of the colonialism that had so annoyed westerners. As commercial implants, they were operated by remote control and were staffed, at least at the upper levels, by outsiders who at once sought to shape their new, if temporary, homes by demanding that these places retain their size, quaintness, and outlook. At the same time they lamented the fact that culturally the West was a desert. Those who followed the corporate flag westward were themselves colonists in a commercial sense. Frequently they thought of their jobs merely as assignments to one of their employer's outposts, and upon retirement, they would settle somewhere in a land of their particular dreams. They did not always hit it off well with the "old" colonists who, in the case of Colorado, responded by displaying bumper stickers that read "Native," a kind of family crest meant to put strangers in their places. The "strangers" posted "Who Cares?" bumper stickers on their cars. . . .

In the agonizing over its status, there were arguments that the West also remained a colonial region in a cultural sense. In 1973, *Newsweek* carried a complaint from a westerner to the effect not only that his area was shackled in an intellectual sense but also that the condition was getting worse. Once, he said, the West had had a score of vigorous regional magazines, but they no longer existed. Nor, he said, did a single national news program or political commentary originate in the West. Programming decisions, as well as media investment policies, had their sources in New York. "So gradually," he wrote, "I have grown to accept that I live in an intellectual, artistic and political suburb, a colony of the East."

There were other signs that in this sense the West remained a virgin land. Historian Gerald Nash suggested that the underdeveloped nature of the prewar West had left it open and available as a testing ground of all sorts, a place for experiments in education, science, architecture, cultural departures, and life styles. It also was a place where the original atomic bomb had been tested.

Use of a barren land as a testing laboratory speaks more of colonialism than it does of an emerging society. Even in residential land use, where suburban enclaves were developed in an irregular pattern within the conventional rectangular patterns, the effort was made to transplant an eastern trend rather than to originate. Despite arguments that the West was used as a hothouse for sprouting seeds of change, the results of which experiments sometimes were accepted elsewhere, the West that we are considering here remained mainstream and conservative in its outlook.

The political side of that conservatism emphasized increasingly the cry that it was not the business masters who posed the greatest threat from outside; rather, the bureaucratic overlords from the nation's capital were manipulating the sovereign's western satrapies. Part of this attitude derived from frontier days, when men were supposed to have moved west to get more breathing room and to find freedom from restraint. Settlers who came out, took up free land, demanded protection against the Indians, and complained when the rural-free-delivery carrier couldn't make it through the mud always reserved the right to be "agin the guvmint." It helped to preserve the fiction of their independence.

The hard liners among the conservatives were the cattlemen. The end of the open range had meant a considerable loss of political power; nevertheless, the one-time "Kings" were not without influence in the legislatures. In 1916, at a time when these lords of the open range were near the end of their heyday, a Nevada sociologist by the name of Romanzo Adams looked at the situation in his state and concluded that their fall from grace was more apparent than real. The 1910 census, he wrote, revealed that 82 percent of Nevada's so-called farmland was controlled by cattlemen. There were 344 "farms" that ranged in size from 1,000 to 175,000 acres, and although the amount of Nevada that was devoted to even this form of agriculture was relatively small, only 1 percent of it was "improved." For Nevada the Homestead Act had been a signal failure; the state's stockmen simply had moved from one kind of control to another. Adams suggested that the grazers should rent government land, subject to rules that would protect the grazing, and should pay nominal fees, only a portion of the full rental value of the range land. He anticipated the Taylor Grazing Act of 1934.

The Taylor Act was only part of the New Deal's efforts to alleviate the stockmen's difficulties and to provide a sensible, equitable plan for grazing. During the depression, problems on the range made many a rancher wonder if the days of raising cattle were about over; severely depressed prices and drought had withered their future, just as it had that of the farmers. But the federal government came to the aid of these rugged individualists with substantial financial injections, and for many of them, it saved the day. Lorena Hickok wrote to Harry Hopkins from Cheyenne, in the fall of 1934, saying: "By and large, the cattlemen appear to be deeply appreciative of what the Government is doing to help them out. 'Many of us are desperate,' one of them told me. 'I think we'd just pack up and move out and leave our stock to starve if the Government hadn't stepped in. This gave us new hope, to try again.' "

But in the West, gratitude is a particularly fragile, evanescent quality, and memories of favors done by the government are spectacularly brief. War followed depression, and there was demand for agricultural products, especially beef. Within a very few years those agents who rode tall in the saddle or in the Ford pickup, who doffed their Stetsons to womenfolk, and who paid homage to no man had moved back into the nineteenth century, and cussing the feds again became a favorite indoor sport. The postwar years spawned a new generation of home-grown entrepreneurs, young business types who took up the cry that Washington controlled the purse strings; and here the cattlemen found new allies. Various interests that were desirous of utilizing the West's federal domain now joined in a propaganda campaign that would force this foreign power, which was located on the banks of the Potomac, to "give back" land to states that had never owned it in the first place.

It was entirely appropriate to western history that the cattlemen provided the outriders for the modern army of liberators. Theirs was the image of white hats riding to the rescue, of sacrifice and selfless contribution to the forces of right—the far Right in this case—and of justice in the land of the free. Actually they were motivated by no such high ideals; all they wanted was their own key to the range lands' executive washroom. They were not descendants of Owen Wister's hero; rather, they were men whose political views recalled the attitudes of their forefathers, who had once ruled the cow country; they were modern beef producers who had seen too many John Wayne movies.

What especially moved these latter-day beef barons to reach for their figurative shooting irons was the trumpeting of a fresh group of colonials, modern "nesters" who had fled the crowded regions of both coasts for the free air of the open and unsullied West. Many of these recent arrivals were attracted by the evangelism of a crusading element known to their detractors as "Ecofreaks," folks who appeared to be ready to fight against so much as the turning of a stone in a wilderness that they implied they had discovered and now claimed as their very own. Ironically the nature lovers tended to accept the garb of the cowmen and saw nothing inconsistent in wearing oversized Stetsons and in hobbling around in uncomfortable cowboy boots while admiring their recently claimed wilderness domain. The difference between the two groups lay in what was contained under the hats.

The average westerner fell between these two highly vocal groups as a faceless figure who appeared to have no opinion on the vital question of the day. This may have been due to the taciturnity attributed to his kind or because he was busy making a living and, as always, was chary of political noises in the background. He was not an alarmist, and therefore he came on as a mute and, even worse, an indifferent mute. Westerners, who long had complained about exploitation and tearing up the countryside, themselves were opposed to the destruction of the past, but they experienced some annoyance at the extremes to which some of the preservationists wanted to go.

What really generated the commotion over the use of western lands was the increased amount of economic activity in the postwar West, a transition that perhaps suggested the noisy birth pangs of the very independence that the area presumably was seeking. By the 1960s that growth was enough to excite westerners with its promise, while at the same time it alarmed a nationwide group of environmentalists, who began to push for wilderness areas. Lyndon B. Johnson's signature on the Wilderness Act of 3 September 1964 signified the extent of that group's strength, and it brought new cries from some westerners that the Old West was about to be turned into a preserve for bird watchers.

Earlier that year, Congressman Wayne Aspinall (D, Colo.) had identified the enemy when he had said, "If we let the East lock up these lands [for wilderness] it will destroy the economy of the West." He argued, as did many of his constituents, that lands could be conserved while they were being utilized for limited and carefully controlled timbering, mining, grazing, and reclamation.

The threat of bureaucratic aggrandizement remained popular as one of the tools of the political trade. Fifteen years after Aspinall's warnings, presidential aspirant John Connally brought cheers from a group of Colorado Republicans when he declared: "I want to free the West of the bondage of bureaucracy in Washington." When he became president, he said, he would bring these colonials into the Union. Connally allowed as how he'd like to join the Sagebrush Rebels. Later, Ronald Reagan expressed the same wish. Both men understood western Republican audiences.

During the tumultuous decade of the 1960s, when Americans were feeling a political irritation and a social nervousness, the complexities and contradictions in western attitudes toward the outside only deepened. For most of the region these were good years that promised to become even better. In such times, a leading news magazine noted, colonials were becoming leery of taking money from Washington on the ground that it merely would lead to tightened control over resources they wanted developed. The swelling conservation movement tended to stiffen the resolve of those who were trying to reduce the role of government regulation.

Even so, it was hard to break old habits. It was obvious that the new prosperity was due in part to the money that the federal government was shoveling across the hundredth meridian. During the '60s, New Mexico received more than $450 million from expenditures by the Atomic Energy Commission. Coloradans benefited from the payrolls of some thirty-seven thousand military personnel, not to mention some fourteen thousand civilian federal employees, and the spin-off from an additional $444 million in prime contracts. Neighboring Utah did only slightly less well at the national fiscal trough, while in Montana, government payrolls exceeded all others. In the "Treasure State" some forty-three thousand people worked for the state and local governments, and eleven thousand worked for the federal government, a figure that had doubled in twenty years. In 1969, Washington poured $644 million into Montana and got back $343 million in taxes. By 1981, Wyoming, Montana, and New Mexico were among the top five, per capita, in the amount of federal aid to state and local governments.

During these years this golden flow caused local politicians some problems. A good example of the dilemma facing those who stumped for reelection was the case of Republican Wallace Bennett of Utah in 1962. His published advertisements spoke out for better, not bigger, government and argued that federal aid should be sought only when state and local government could not afford to do the job. At the same time, Bennett reminded his constituents that he had worked hard for water projects, for aid to the Small Business Administration, and for research money to aid the local coal industry. In appreciation of this endorsement of independence, but one that included carefully drawn exceptions, the voters returned that solon to office. As one critic pointed out, the region argued that it could not live with the federal government, yet it gave every indication that it could not live without it. Its businessmen always endorsed cuts in federal spending while assuring the congressional delegation that their particular neighborhood had nothing it could sacrifice to the budgetary ax.

There were other evidences of the western political crunch. In 1963, when Senator Gale McGee (D, Wyo.) obtained for Park County, Wyoming, designation as an area of "persistent unemployment," in order to qualify it for emergency federal assistance, he was criticized by local residents. Yet his action was in response to a petition from the townsmen at Cody, the county seat, not a few of whom earlier had signed a "declaration of independence" from the federal government. Obviously these people had divided loyalties. Their city was the home of the state's first John Birch Society; and the Cody Club, a Chamber-of-Commerce-oriented organization, had originated the above-mentioned declaration. The fact that H. L. Hunt, one of the old-time economic gentry whom westerners had become used to saluting, had a summer place in the neighborhood added to the conservative ambience.

If westerners experienced a certain amount of bewilderment over the question of who were their masters, if indeed they had any masters, one of the explanations was to be found in the postwar changes being experienced by their part of America. At the beginning of that era one still heard numerous references to the sagebrush colonials, a sentiment that was most frequently evinced by liberals, both eastern and western, but as the years passed, there was more frequent talk of economic independence, one proof of which was said to be the region's increasing access to local capital. By the time the anticipated "Soaring Sixties" had come into view, the West was sharing a national expectation of prosperity, along with which came the cautious hope that the end of its own financial bondage was near. By then a national news weekly could say, "Today the West offers an industrial entity all its own," an entity that was said to be moving toward a long-cherished autonomy.

In many ways this was little more than a pat on the back from big brother. It cannot be denied that there was growth and development in the land of the Old West, but it was spotty and uneven. Colorado, with its historic economic connection with the East, worked hard to induce outside money and industry, while at the same time encouraging local enterprise, and the businesses that sprouted along this section of the Rocky Mountain front indicated a degree of success. Across the mountains, in Utah, there was similar development. These bits of evidence were encouraging to those who were promoting independence, and much was made of them in the press.

But others had second thoughts. In 1978 a writer for *American Heritage* looked again at De Voto's "plundered province" and concluded that while the Pacific Coast increasingly had found and developed its own resources, there was evidence to show that a replay was taking place in the part of the West that was traditionally accustomed to pillage. This time it included the strip mining of coal.

The picture was familiar. The energy-rich mountain region again was the scene of a boom, but it was one that appeared to pose more problems than it solved, and once more, the investment money had come largely from outside. Instead of being grateful for fresh income, the residents complained about overcrowded towns, a shortage of schools, an inability to cope with the imported crime wave, and, generally, of being brushed aside in the rush for riches by those who came to "git and git out."

As one visiting writer saw it, these industry-seeking communities had for so long been the poor stepchildren of the nation that when good fortune smiled, they "do not know how to react when the glass slipper finally fits." In other words, as De Voto once had suggested, it was again being inferred that the West did not really want to be liberated from the bondage that it so long had resented; rather, it wanted to "buy into it, cumulative preference stock if possible." There is, however, a difference between lying back supinely as the glass slipper is fitted and of owning part of the coach, the horses, and the coach-owners' kingdom. For a long time, westerners viewed the glass-slipper ceremony as one that suggested seduction, as opposed to a promise of wedlock and community property.

Thus, the notion of buying in was somewhat chimerical. A desire, a dream, but not a real prospect. At best the mineral-rich areas stood a chance to sell some of the subsurface holdings to outsiders. The mountain portions promised to remain largely as "diggin's" for the new prospectors, while out on the plains the modern coal miners were merely looking on the other side of the sod for a crop. As a well-known agricultural historian has remarked, the plains country would continue to be primarily a producer, surface or subsurface, and "its colonial status in relation to the rest of the nation will not change substantially." If anything, that status promised to become more pronounced because of a continuing decline in population among the agrarians. A diminished representation in Congress would reduce the already dwindling political influence of this group.

The prospect of a continued colonial role has not deeply concerned some elements of the western business community. The more aggressive commercial types have regarded the area, not as a cap-doffing dependent, but as one that had something to sell, as it always had something to sell; and from such transactions, westerners were supposed to make a living in the manner of their forebears. These latter-day traders, who still affected boots and broad-brimmed hats, like to sit down with the monied folks from other parts and to join in economic games of chance—games called development—as opposed to acts of exploitation. They understood *independence* to be a word with positive connotations, but when dealing with land or resources, they held the short-run view that it mattered not if the money was local or imported. The long-run implications of financial control were not always a burning issue with those more interested in today than tomorrow and not at all interested in yesterday.

Therefore, those who regarded the central government's ownership and control of vast western regions as being a barrier to future development, not to mention a blot on the much-cherished notion of private enterprise, continued the arguments of yesteryear that the land was to be used, not hoarded. An opposing view held that a great body of westerners owed their living, not to mention their spiritual and physical well-being, to the fact that their government not only stood between them and the "developers" but also contributed to the West in a very positive way. They argued that even the cattlemen, who had spearheaded the "Sagebrush Rebellion," consistently had been helped, not hurt, by the officialdom that they appeared to hate so much. In addition to the vast amounts of land that stockmen earlier had controlled through an extremely liberal land policy, there were numerous instances of direct assistance from Washington. Mentioned were such things as help rendered in fighting foot-and-mouth disease, favorable legislation that offered protection against unfair packing practices, the subsidization of meat prices on occasion, and finally, numerous instances of direct, low-interest government loans.

As De Voto had suggested, the pervasiveness of the New Deal all across that thinly populated and yet undeveloped West later may have led to cries of a new servitude, but in truth, this penetration of the West rescued much of that region from the further ravages of economic colonialism by reversing the wasteful exploitation of resources with a program of rehabilitation, repair, and rebuilding. It offered alternative sources of credit, inexpensive electricity, which had never before been available to rural residents, badly needed water from expanded reclamation developments, and an impressive reforestation program by the Civilian Conservation Corps. It not only made life better for thousands of individual westerners, but in a field such as power development the government also helped to establish a base for the expansion of small industries, thereby initiating the first steps in the direction of economic independence.

And so it went. To some degree the relationship between the East and the West had always been one of parent and child, but the disastrous depression and the boom years that followed put new strains on the feelings between mom and her restless youngster. The West had stood for opportunities of various sorts—the chance to move and maneuver and wring fortunes from the land. But always westerners have required support from the outside, money from home to protect them and to get their various schemes off the ground. Behind this was the troublesome question of just how much profit and control the East could expect in return. The Great Depression threatened to destroy the mystique of a land of limitless possibilities. As eastern pundits advised cutting off the hinterland as a hopeless investment, westerners raged that all along, Wall Street had been milking them of their just rewards. Then, when businessmen of both regions again began to court one another after the war, the programs and controls of the government seemed to threaten both the image of opportunity and another sacred element of the mystique—independence.

The dilemma between support and control, investment and exploitation, has grown naturally from the economic realities of the West and the imagery of its myth. Consequently the debate over colonialism is probably with us for good. Often it has given the world a chance to see both sides at their worst. Eastern critics have sounded like a mother who has worked her children ragged on the family farm, then clutched a hankie to her bosom and sobbed how the brats have bled her dry. Westerners have taken advantage of eastern investment and, above all, government aid; but in the manner of ungrateful children, they have tried to bite the hand that fed them. True to their history, they have ignored the benefits and lashed out at their benefactors. As adolescents in the national family, they wanted the freedom to roam, but they still have turned up at mealtime and have always been around when the allowances were handed out. To them, Big Daddy in Washington remained the tight-fisted tyrant who unaccountably expected some kind of responsibility from the offspring.

National Parks in Alaska

ALFRED RUNTE

Born of romanticism and cultural nationalism, the first great national parks of the United States were clearly the result of nineteenth-century perceptions of the American landscape. Outside of the continental United States, only Alaska offered preservationists of the twentieth century one final opportunity to have national parks in keeping with the principles of biological management.

In preservationists' own words, Alaska was "our last chance to do it right," to design national parks around entire watersheds, animal migration routes, and similar ecological rather than political boundaries. "This will require the largest possible blocks of land to be set aside as national-interest lands," wrote Peggy Wayburn, arguing the case for expansive parks on behalf of the Sierra Club: "This alone can prevent the loss of perhaps the greatest remaining wildlife, wilderness, and scenic resources on earth."

Even the largest national parks in the lower forty-eight states, among them Yellowstone, Yosemite, and the Everglades, were but pieces of far larger biological wholes. Alaska in contrast, offered the best of both the monumental and the biological in nature. Scenically, its mountains, glaciers, and volcanic areas were unsurpassed on the North American continent. In other words, preservationists need not speak against their own traditions in their quest for Alaskan parks. More importantly, however, Alaska's vastness and near complete ownership by the federal government made the realization of the biological ends in national park management no less attainable. At least, preservationists had good reason to be optimistic at the outset of their campaign for parklands in the forty-ninth state.

In Alaska, as elsewhere in the United States, organized opposition to the expansion of the national park system came from a wide variety of resource interests. For industrialists, Alaska's importance lay beyond its role as the last great refuge for plants and animals. Instead, the nation's last major repository for timber, minerals, oil, natural gas, fresh water, and hydroelectric power seemed to be at stake. "I think we are all acutely aware," noted John H. LaGrange, representing the Kennecott Copper Corporation, "that our Nation and, indeed the world, is passing from an era of surplus to an era of shortage in many mineral and energy commodities." New national parks in Alaska, it followed, again should be restricted to monumental topography, areas rich in scenery but poor from the standpoint of natural resources. "National park and critical habitat withdrawals should not contain more than 15 million acres," LaGrange argued. Otherwise national parks would conflict with the nation's pressing need to find more oil and, in the meantime, to exploit its vast deposits of coal and other minerals. Alaska had all of those resources in abundance. Unfortunately, between 40 and 80 percent of the richest copper deposits alone were located in areas where preservationists wanted to establish national parks.

For preservationists, the opposition of resource interests to the establishment of national parks—as typified by LaGrange's remarks—was nothing new. As preservationists soon discovered, the problem in Alaska was the tendency of the resource issue to overlap the question of Native American rights. Unlike the continental United States, where Indians had been forced

Reprinted from *National Parks: The American Experience,* second edition, revised 236–258, with some abridgements, by Alfred Runte, by permission of University of Nebraska Press. Copyright 1979, 1987 by the University of Nebraska Press.

onto reservations outside the national parks long before the parks themselves had been created, Alaska was still largely inhabited by groups of native peoples. In Alaska, the creation of national parks could not be divorced from the issue of civil rights. Drawing the boundaries of each new park demanded simultaneous respect for native traditions, cultures, and means of subsistence—customs deeply intertwined with national park lands. "If we are to err," argued Elvis J. Stahr, president of the National Audubon Society, "let us not err on the side of destroying a truly unique culture."

Indeed, it was almost as if the national park idea had come back full circle to 1832 and George Catlin's plea for "a *nation's Park,* containing man and beast, in all the wild and freshness of their nature's beauty!" On the plains of South Dakota, the artist had called for precisely the kind of sensitivity that planning for the Alaskan parks demanded if the right of Native Americans to reside on their ancestral hunting grounds was also to be protected. Of course, his perspective was as much a product of the period's romanticism as it was evidence of embryonic concern in the United States for the rights of native peoples. For Catlin, preserving the Indians of the plains added charm to the landscape at the same time it advanced the morality of American culture. Alaska was the final opportunity not only to establish national parks with biological boundaries but to create parks that did not—as Catlin himself would have opposed—drive out or exclude native cultures in the process.

With the establishment of Yellowstone National Park in 1872, Catlin's revolutionary point of view was rejected in favor of the strict protection of monumental scenery. By preservation was meant to protect landscapes, not to preserve the historical relationships between landscapes *and* people. Not until the 1960s was the policy of protecting natural features in the national parks exclusive of natural processes widely criticized. Biologists at last fully acknowledged the role of Native Americans in changing park landscapes through the use of fire. The Alaska lands issue also drew attention to the fact that native peoples throughout North America had long exerted great influence on the biological composition of the continent.

Native Americans, it followed, were themselves "part of nature," a key link in the chain of natural processes so many biologists hoped to reintroduce to national park environments. At least in Alaska, preservationists conceded, the chain had not been broken. "Indeed," argued Anthony Wayne Smith, president of the National Parks and Conservation Association, "the practice of subsistence hunting, as understood by the Native cultures, can well be looked upon as part of *a natural ecosystem* which has sustained itself in Alaska for something like 10,000 years and which has proved itself compatible with the stability and diversity of both wildlife and human population" [italics added]. The historical opposition of the National Parks and Conservation Association to hunting, Smith said, elaborating on his point, dealt "only with sports hunting, and if the distinction is kept quite clear along the lines of the pending legislation, no violence can be done to established traditions of national park management."

The naïveté of preservationists like Smith was their assumption that native cultures, like park environments, could be maintained at a fixed approximation of their appearance at some earlier and more ideal period of history. Catlin's romanticism might not be dead but neither were the forces that made changes in the native cultures inevitable. Perhaps the best that could be done in Alaska was to honor the civil rights of the natives and hope that change would not overwhelm their traditions at the expense of the parks. "No conservation group of which I am aware," remarked Louis S. Clapper, a representative of the National Wildlife Federation, "would deny a Native the right to take whatever fish and wildlife he needs for his own family's welfare." That said, so-called subsistence hunting was often "a much abused practice," a "subterfuge" for "the recreational practices" of "employed and 'modernized' natives." Clapper's outspoken comments were compromised by the National Wildlife Federation's own defense of sport hunting among its members. Yet even the most ardent defenders of subsistence hunting could not dismiss the impact of modern technology on native cultures. Ideally, Alaskan natives would resist the temptations and pressures of modern life. It was just as likely, however, that the national parks would be eroded from within as well as from without by what was in fact a vain attempt to uphold the past against the relentless forces of the present.

The resource at stake was wilderness—remote, pristine, and teeming with animals. Before World War II, the natives of Alaska had hardly made a dent in either its wildness or its wildlife. But that was before modern firearms and the introduction of airplanes in effect shrank the boundaries of the Alaskan wilderness. Still, as late as the 1970s, preservationists saw legitimate reason to compare Alaska to Yellowstone a hundred years earlier. Much as Yellowstone had been America's frontier in the nineteenth century, so Alaska was its frontier in the twentieth. The difference was nonetheless striking—Americans must make do with Alaska for centuries to come, at least with respect to wilderness on earth. "What we save now is all we will ever save," declared another popular slogan of the period. Especially in the forty-ninth state, no statement seemed to be a more appropriate— or compelling—call to action.

The wilderness movement, as distinct from campaigns to establish new national parks per se, won its most important victory on September 3, 1964, when President Lyndon B. Johnson signed the Wildrness Act into law. For eight years wilderness enthusiasts had sought its passage, citing the need to protect not only the remote unspoiled corners of the national parks but the best of the nation's roadless areas remaining in the national forests and elsewhere on the public domain. Nine million acres of land within the national forests were immediately designated as wilderness; meanwhile, the National Park Service was authorized to study and recommend to Congress which portions of the national parks should also be protected in a wild and undeveloped state.

For a variety of reasons, the study and establishment of wilderness areas in the national parks, especially the largest preserves, moved slowly.

Preservationists themselves were far more concerned about the fate of wilderness areas controlled by the U.S. Forest Service and Bureau of Land Management. In contrast to the Park Service, those were the agencies historically renowned for their determination to open the public domain to multiple use, including logging, grazing, and mining. Granted, the National Park Service itself was often accused of overdeveloping the most popular points of interest within the national parks. Still, the agency had neither the authority—nor the incentive—to open its backcountry areas to resource exploitation.

Of greater concern to the Park Service was the threat wilderness posed to the agency's bureaucratic autonomy. The management of wilderness areas came under the directives of the Wilderness Act of 1964, not the Park Service's own Organic Act of August 25, 1916. Prohibitions in wilderness areas against the use of any motorized means of access or equipment, not to mention roads, clearly restricted the Park Service's discretion in managing its backcountry zones. Formal wilderness designations would also forfeit the potential for using at least some of those areas to accommodate overflows of visitors in the future. That restriction, too, concerned many concessionaires, themselves an influential body in determining national park policy. Like tradition-minded Park Service employees, concessionaires were highly skeptical of anything that might undermine their own options for further expansion of visitor services.

Not until October 23, 1970, six years after the passage of the Wilderness Act, did Congress designate portions of Petrified Forest National Park, Arizona, and Craters of the Moon National Monument, Idaho, as wilderness. In October 1972, parts of Lassen Volcanic National Park and Lava Beds National Monument, both in California, also received wilderness status. Four more years elapsed before Congress approved the first truly major additions to the wilderness system in national parks. On September 22 and October 1, 1976, the House and Senate, respectively, approved legislation creating wilderness areas in portions of thirteen existing parks and monuments—Badlands National Monument, Bandelier National Monument, Black Canyon of the Gunnison National Monument, Chiricahua National Monument, Great Sand Dunes National Monument, Haleakala National Park, Isle Royale National Park, Joshua Tree National Monument, Mesa Verde National Park, Pinnacles National Monument, Point Reyes National Seashore, Saguaro National Monument, and Shenandoah National Park. President Gerald R. Ford approved the legislation on October 20, 1976.

The Omnibus Park Bill of 1978, also known as the National Park and Recreation Act, further designated 1,854,424 acres of wilderness in eight additional units of the national park system—Buffalo National River, Carlsbad Caverns National Park, Everglades National Park, Guadalupe Mountains National Park, Gulf Islands National Seashore, Hawaii Volcanoes National Park, Organ Pipe Cactus National Monument, and Theodore Roosevelt National Park. In addition, the bill declared another 119,581 acres in the eight preserves as "potential" wilderness, bringing the grand total to nearly two million acres. Supporters of the legislation in Congress, eager to draw attention to their achievement, were quick to point out that this figure exceeded "the total acreage of all lands previously designated as wilderness in the National Park System."

Most of the largest and most popular national parks, however, among them Yellowstone, Yosemite, Glacier, and the Grand Canyon, still lacked approval for their wilderness proposals. Designating wilderness in those parks remained controversial. Although the Park Service endorsed the wilderness idea in public, many high level officials privately expressed their doubts about the wilderness movement. The larger the roadless areas within the national parks, the less opportunity remained for the Park Service to expand its traditional visitor services and overnight accommodations. The Park Service would be left with no alternative but to restrict the number of visitors in the already developed portions of its parks. For an agency that measured its success by how many people it served, such restrictions seemed politically unwise. And even in those parks where management seemed strongly in favor of formal wilderness designations, concessionaires usually were quietly suspicious of, if not overtly hostile to, the concept.

With each frustration of their attempts to establish large wilderness areas in the national parks of the continental United States, preservationists looked upon Alaska as a battleground of even greater importance. If national parks were in fact to be managed as sanctuaries, not merely as scenic wonders divorced of biological considerations, wilderness appeared to be the crucial prerequisite. Wildlife biologists warned repeatedly that the remote roadless corners of America were the only remaining refuges of any real consequence for many species of plants and animals. The management of habitat could accomplish only so much. The alternative to greater and greater reliance on the manipulation of plant and animal populations was providing both with enough territory to survive on their own in the first place.

For a land so rich in natural resources and wilderness, the history of Alaska as an American possession began on a distinct note of irony. Ratification of the treaty in 1867 authorizing purchase of Alaska from the Russians passed the Senate over the objections of opponents who denounced the territory as nothing but a worthless region of snow, rocks, and icebergs. Among most Americans that image of the frozen north held well into the twentieth century. Occasionally, authors, artists, and travelers broke down that perception, yet it was not until World War II, following completion of the Alaska Military Highway through Canada, that Americans finally began to appreciate the true richness and diversity of what was to become the forty-ninth state.

Statehood, which came in 1959, still did not end the bitterness among many Alaskans over their decades of treatment as second-class citizens by the federal government. For a territory of roughly 365 million acres, Alaskans believed federal officials had been far too conservative in allowing the exploitation of its natural resources. In either case, residents were eager to get on with development, not only logging, fishing, and trapping—pursuits comprised in the state's traditional economy—but also opening oil and gas fields and mineral deposits. The legislation granting statehood allowed Alaska to select approximately 104 million acres of federal lands in the state; similarly, the federal government relinquished title to tens of millions of acres of submerged lands along the continental shelf. Only one major obstacle stood between Alaska and the process of completing its selection of federal lands—few politicians had stopped to consider the claims of Native Americans to many of those same properties. Finally, in 1966, as Aleuts, Eskimos, and Indian tribes prepared to take their grievances to court, Secretary of the Interior Stewart Udall froze all land selections pending congressional consideration of the argument that Native Americans as well as the state of Alaska were entitled to share in the allocation of the public domain.

The ensuing stalemate was not resolved until October of 1971 and passage of the Native Claims Settlement Act. The legislation awarded forty million acres of land and one billion dollars in additional compensation to the Alaskan groups. During the five years Congress considered this apparent departure from federal Indian policy, preservationists themselves were no less aware of the unique opportunity the bill presented to voice their own concerns about the future of public lands in the forty-ninth state. Although most preservationists sympathized with the demands of the natives for a secure land base, native selections, in addition to the selections already guaranteed to Alaska, conceivably might undercut the protection of the best wilderness areas even before they had been identified and established. Alaska, to reemphasize, represented the final opportunity to establish national parks, wilderness areas, and wildlife refuges of irrefutable ecological significance and integrity. Without simultaneously addressing the need to preserve the Alaskan wilderness, preservationists argued, all hope of coordinating the development of the state with its protection would be lost.

With the environmental movement, like the civil rights movement, at the peak of its influence, Congress was in little mood to ignore the concerns of preservationists any more than the grievances of Native Americans. Accordingly, Section 17(d)(2) of the Alaska Native Claims Settlement Act further recognized the desirability of designating up to eighty million acres of the public domain in Alaska as national parks, national forests, wildlife refuges, and wild and scenic rivers. The act gave the secretary of the interior nine months to withdraw lands deemed suitable for consideration as additions to each of the four categories; similarly, the secretary was given until December 19, 1973, to make his final recommendations to Congress concerning which of the lands initially withdrawn from entry should in fact be protected in perpetuity by the federal government.

Yet another opportunity for preservation was provided by Section 17 (d)(1) of the Alaska Native Claims Settlement Act. Under its provisions, the secretary of the interior was allowed ninety days after the enactment of the legislation to select additional "public interest" lands for withdrawal from entry. Apparently the provision did not affect state and native selections around native villages but took precedence over all other state and native selections elsewhere on the public domain. In the confusion over interpretation of the (d)(1) provision, however, the state of Alaska, in January 1972, proclaimed the selection of its entire remaining allotment of seventy-seven million acres under the Statehood Act of 1958.

Such complexity and confusion only foreshadowed the coming battle over Alaskan lands, a struggle that would last for nearly a decade. By September of 1972, Secretary of the Interior Rogers C. B. Morton had withdrawn seventy-nine million acres of the public domain under subsection (d)(2) of the Native Claims Settlement Act, in addition to forty-seven million acres under subsection (d)(1). The state of Alaska immediately protested that the withdrawals conflicted with many of its own selections and, as a result, filed suit in federal court to have Secretary Morton's duplicate choices that were in dispute revoked. In an out-of-court settlement, Alaska won concessions affecting some fourteen million acres of the (d)(1) and (d)(2) withdrawals; for its own part of the compromise, the state agreed to relinquish its claims to thirty-five million of the seventy-seven million acres it had selected in January.

In the end, Secretary Morton's own final recommendations for lands to be protected in Alaskan parks, wilderness areas, and wildlife refuges pleased no one. The state of Alaska again filed suit; meanwhile, preservationists also protested against his proposal to include over eighteen million acres of the (d)(2) lands in national forests rather than in wilderness areas. The objective of the act, preservationists argued, was the protection of those lands rather than the development of their resources, even on a sustained-yield basis. Adding urgency to preservationists' concerns was the deadline established by Congress for the resolution of the entire debate by December 18, 1978. That gave preservationists but seven years to make their case, and already two of those years had slipped by without an acceptable compromise between development and preservation of the state even in sight.

Despite their frustration, preservation groups still used the interval preceding congressional consideration of the Alaska lands issue very wisely. The lull offered them an opportunity for further study and redefinition of their park proposals, for educating their memberships, and, most importantly, for unifying on behalf of a concerted political effort on Capitol Hill. The so-called Alaska Coalition, representing the National Audubon Society, Wilderness Society, Sierra Club, National Parks and Conservation Association, and Defenders of Wildlife, officially organized in 1971 during the debate about native claims in the state. Cooperation among the groups was still relatively informal until January 1977, when Congress itself took up the Alaska lands controversy. Under the circumstances, the five member organizations of the Alaska Coalition agreed to pool both staff and financial resources as they prepared to contest what they collectively considered "the most important conservation issue of the century."

The battle was finally joined on January 4, 1977, when Representative Morris Udall of Arizona introduced his bill, H.R. 39, to the Ninety-fifth Congress. By early April, H.R. 39 was accompanied by a host of similar bills; numerous cosponsors had also attached their names to Udall's original legislation. To sift through the complex array of proposals and to assess public opinion, the House Committee on Interior and Insular Affairs, with Udall as chairman, approved the creation of a special Subcommittee on General Oversight and Alaska Lands. On April 21 and 22, Representative John F. Seiberling of Ohio, chairman of the subcommittee and a cosponsor of H.R. 39, convened the first public hearings on the Alaska lands issue in Washington, D.C.

Five months and sixteen volumes of testimony later, the Subcommittee on General Oversight and Alaska Lands concluded its work. In addition to holding hearings in Washington, D.C., the committee took testimony in Chicago, Atlanta, Denver, and Seattle. Afterward the committee moved to Alaska, where it heard the residents of sixteen separate towns and cities, including Sitka, Juneau, Ketchikan, Anchorage, and Fairbanks. Never before in national park history had any issue sparked so much public interest and discussion. Even the more noted controversies of the recent past, such as the campaign to preserve the redwood groves of the California coast, had not come close to arousing such a nationwide insistence that the general public, as well as renowned figures in the preservation movement and their principal adversaries, should be heard by a major congressional panel.

By itself, however, the sheer number of people who participated in the controversy still had little effect on the arguments used to sway the opposing sides. To be sure, although many people took the opportunity to speak their minds before Congress, their positions were both traditional and pre-dictable. The hearings, in other words, contained no real surprises. Simply, those with a personal stake in the economy of Alaska pushed for smaller parks and greater development of the state's natural resources. Likewise, those who looked to Alaska as the last American wilderness wanted des-perately to protect its mountains, forests, rivers, and wildlife in parks that were not only spacious but clearly of ecological as well as scenic significance.

It followed that support for the Alaskan parks was greatest outside the state. Indeed, much as people living on the Alaskan frontier universally opposed the parks, so citizens in the lower forty-eight states overwhelmingly endorsed H.R. 39. Not surprisingly, supporters and opponents of the legislation lined up similarly in the halls of Congress. Senators Ted Stevens and Mike Gravel of Alaska, in addition to the state's lone member of the House, Don Young, strongly opposed H.R. 39 in its original form. . . .

The entirety of 1977 passed without any action on H.R. 39, with the exception of the public hearings conducted by the House Subcommittee on General Oversight and Alaska Lands. As preservationists feared, the delay only worked to the advantage of their opponents, especially Rep-resentative Don Young, who succeeded in adding no fewer than eighty-five amendments to the original bill once the subcommittee convened early in 1978 to draft the final version. Not until April 7, 1978, was the Interior Committee prepared to report to Congress as a whole; by then only eight months remained until December 18, 1978, the deadline established for the resolution of the Alaska lands issue under the Native Claims Settlement Act. If the controversy had not been resolved by that date, technically all of the lands withdrawn from entry pending congressional review would once again revert to the unreserved public domain and be subject to both state and native selections.

Under the circumstances, preservationists were indeed fortunate to have the support of the new administration. Granted, President Jimmy Carter and his secretary of the interior, Cecil Andrus, proposed a ceiling of only 92 million acres of parks and wilderness as opposed to the 115 million acres of land sought by the Alaska Coalition and specified in the original version of H.R. 39. Still, with Senators Mike Gravel and Ted Stevens threatening delay of the legislation in the Senate, and in light of their call for the protection of a mere 25 million acres of territory, the endorsement of the White House was crucial. On May 17, 1978, the House of Representatives began debate on H.R. 39 and two days later approved the bill by a vote of 277 to 31. Preservationists were jubilant, not only because the House proposed to protect more than 120 million acres as national parks, wildlife refuges, and wild and scenic rivers, but because passage of the bill had been won by such a stunning, lopsided margin.

The celebration, however, proved to be premature. In the Senate, Mike Gravel successfully thwarted serious consideration of the Alaska lands bill throughout the summer and into the fall. Although his delaying tactics grew unpopular, even with Senator Stevens, they nonetheless had the desired effect of preventing final action on H.R. 39 in 1978.

The December 18 deadline, in other words, would not be met. Once again preservationists were extremely fortunate to have the support of the Carter administration. Even as the Ninety-fifth Congress disbanded, President Carter and Secretary of the Interior Andrus had considered their options. As early as October 11, Andrus had informed the public in a signed editorial: "If Congress is unable to act, President Carter and I will." On November 16 Andrus made good his promise by withdrawing 110 million acres of public lands in Alaska from entry under the authority of the Fish and Wildlife Act of 1956 and the Federal Land Management Act of 1976. Each allowed the secretary of the interior broad discretion in the protection of wildlife and wilderness areas on the public domain. Finally, on December 1, further invoking the articles of the Antiquities Act of 1906, President Carter gave added protection to 56 million of the 110 million acres withdrawn by Andrus as national monuments. Andrus's withdrawals were to stand for only three years; Carter's designation of the national monuments would be permanent if Congress itself refused to decide the Alaska lands issue.

Carter's objective was in fact to force Congress to make the final decision. In that respect, his action was like President Franklin D. Roosevelt's veto in 1943 of the bill to abolish Jackson Hole National Monument in Wyoming. Like Roosevelt, Carter believed the protection of Alaska transcended local prejudices and special interests; at least, the decision was too important to allow a few legislators manipulating the political process to forestall the ultimate test of the nation's true will. Nevertheless, 1979 was another year of postponement; indeed, the political season began as another period of frustration and despair for preservation interests, with new amendments threatening the integrity of the original legislation passed by the House of Representatives in 1978. In the second House vote, taken on May 16, 1979, preservationists withstood the new opposition by a tally of 268 to 157, only to lose ground once again in the Senate. Its final version of the bill not only considerably weakened the management safeguards approved by the House but granted protection to twenty-six million fewer acres of Alaska lands in the process.

Ironically, the fate of Alaska was sealed in 1980 not only by compromise but by the intimidation of preservation interests. On August 19, the Senate finally passed a considerably less protective Alaska lands bill. Dismayed but defiant, preservationists would have worked to postpone the legislation yet another year, but for the election on November 4 of Ronald Reagan as the next president of the United States. Unlike Carter's, Reagan's attitude toward environmental legislation was openly hostile. Fearing that he might kill the Alaska lands legislation entirely, preservationists both within and outside the Congress saw no choice but to make their peace with the Senate version of H.R. 39. "Political realities dictate that we act promptly on the Senate-passed bill," Representative Morris Udall said, issuing a personal warning. "We must accept the fact that Reagan is here for four years." On November 12, the House agreed to recognize the wisdom of the Senate, and on December 2, 1980, President Jimmy Carter signed the compromise legislation into law. Granted, the bill was a disappointment for preservationists, although it did, in Udall's words, "accomplish 85–90 percent of the things the House wanted." The penalty of further delay under the Reagan administration might well have been the sacrifice of legislation of any kind.

Considering what they might have lost, preservationists understandably celebrated what they had won in Alaska as a milestone of American conservation. "Never has so much been done on conservation for future generations with one stroke of the pen," wrote Charles Clusen, chairman of the Alaska Coalition. The acreages protected were indeed impressive, a total of more than 100 million acres or 28 percent of the state, including 43.6 million acres of new national parks, 53.8 million acres of new wildlife refuges, and 1.2 million acres for the national wild and scenic rivers system. Of those lands, 56.7 million acres were to receive further protection as wilderness, subject only to accessibility by foot, horseback, raft, or canoe. "Not since the days of Theodore Roosevelt's large public land withdrawals," Clusen concluded, "have we seen such boldness, dynamism, and leadership for the protection of our land heritage. The Alaska 'victory' also shows that the American people believe in a conservation ethic and support environmental protection more than at any previous time in history."

Only after more careful reflection were most preservationists willing to concede that their battle for Alaska may in fact have just begun on December 2, 1980. In park after park, critical wildlife habitat had either been fragmented to accommodate resource extraction or excluded entirely. As a concession to copper mining interests, for example, approximately one million acres in Gates of the Arctic National Park were denied wilderness protection. Similarly, state selections threatened grizzly bear habitat, salmon streams, and caribou breeding grounds bordering Mount McKinley National Park. The Alaska Lands Act renamed the park Denali and expanded it by a whopping 3.7 million acres. The point again was that size by itself was no guarantee that wildlife, especially migrating populations such as caribou, could be sustained without further extending protection to their lowland breeding grounds.

Other preservationists sensed a troublesome precedent in the use of the term "preserve" to describe large expanses of wilderness that historically would have been labeled "national parks" or "national monuments." The management principles of national parks and monuments were clearly defined by precedent, but what was a "national preserve"? One unsettling answer could be gleaned from the legislative histories of the Big Thicket National Preserve in Texas and the Big Cypress National Freshwater Preserve in Florida. In each instance, Congress had granted wide discretion to the secretary of the interior to allow mining, oil drilling, grazing, hunting, trapping, and other extractive uses both within and adjacent to the parks. On the roughly twenty million acres of land designated as "preserves" in Alaska, much the same discretion prevailed. The management of a preserve, in other words, could easily be determined by administrative fiat rather than established by public consensus.

Ideally, preserves would act as buffers for more sensitive park areas. In fact, however, often the preserves themselves were in greater need of protection. The mountainous, inaccessible landscapes forming the core of the new parks and monuments rarely had the same potential for economic development. In keeping with the size and ruggedness of Alaska, its parks could be far larger than those in the lower forty-eight states. In the final analysis, however, national park history had repeated itself. The only unchallenged mandate in Alaska was the endorsement of monumentalism. Beyond its mountainous terrain, especially along the seacoasts of Alaska and in the forests of its southeastern panhandle, entrenched commercial interests, both native and non-native, successfully resisted most long-range efforts to effect preservation over economic use.

In defense of their right to make such a choice, Alaskans argued that pioneer Americans in the past had also enjoyed the freedom to exploit the land as each saw fit. Now that the rest of the country had been developed, residents of the lower forty-eight states had no right to dictate to Alaskans that they and they alone must sacrifice economic opportunity for wilderness preservation. Besides, Alaskans loved the frontier way of life and themselves wished to preserve the land base supporting it.

In rebuttal, preservationists asked again whether or not Alaskans could in fact resist unwanted or undesirable forms of change indefinitely. "Big, outside corporations are looking all over the world for resources," noted Representative John F. Seiberling, for example. He warned Alaskans to support H.R. 39: "And with the kind of machinery and airplanes and the kind of money that people have in the outside, they are going to come in here and each one is going to take a cut of the salami and when he gets through, there will not be much left for the people of Alaska unless we set aside certain areas." Persistent opposition to H.R. 39 on the question of personal freedom led to the allowance of subsistence hunting and the establishment of national preserves to accommodate it. Gradually, however, even preservationists who supported the practice came to recognize the potential for its abuse, especially since the snowmobile, airplane, and high-powered rifle had replaced the dogsled, spear, and hunting knife as tools of the chase.

Alaska, it seemed, eventually would change much as the rest of America had changed. Writing on behalf of the Alaska Coalition, an anonymous preservationist was among those who conceded the point, "For a land which is expected to give so much material wealth to the nation, we only ask in return that the nation seek to protect certain lands and wildlife so that this priceless natural heritage will survive for future generations." Margaret Murie, the noted author and longtime Alaskan adventurer, was even more eloquent, "My prayer is that Alaska will not lose the heart-nourishing friendliness of her youth, . . . that her great wild places will remain great, and wild, and free, where wolf and caribou, wolverine and grizzly bear, and all the Arctic blossoms may live in the delicate balance which supported them long before impetuous man appeared in the north. This is the great gift Alaska can give to the harrassed world." On a scale unique in American history, the passage of the Alaska Lands Act of 1980 realized this fondest of preservationists' dreams. But could the dream be sustained? Indeed, even in the vastness of Alaska, one fundamental accomplishment still eluded the movement—effecting its dreams in perpetuity, in physical reality as well as in transitory laws.

Y *F U R T H E R   R E A D I N G*

John Baden and Richard L. Stroup, eds., *Bureaucracy vs. Environment: The Environmental Costs of Bureaucratic Government* (1981)

Howard Ball, *Justice Downwind: America's Atomic Testing Program in the 1950s* (1986)

C. W. Buchholtz, *Rocky Mountain National Park: A History* (1983)

Alston Chase, *Playing God in Yellowstone: The Destruction of America's First National Park* (1986)

Robert E. Ficken, "Gifford Pinchot Men: Pacific Northwest Lumbermen and the Conservation Movement, 1902–1910," *Western Historical Quarterly*, 13 (1982), 165–78

Phillip O. Foss, *Politics and Grass: The Administration of Grazing on the Public Domain* (1960)

Samuel P. Hays, *Conservation and the Gospel of Efficiency: The Progressive Conservation Movement, 1890–1920* (1959)

Norris Hundley, *Water and the West: The Colorado River Compact and the Politics of Water in the American West* (1975)

William Kahrl, *Water and Power: The Conflict over Los Angeles' Water Supply* (1982)

Daniel McCool, *Command of the Waters: Iron Triangles, Federal Water Development, and Indian Water* (1987)

Richard Lowitt, *The New Deal and the West* (1984)

Roderick Nash, "The American Invention of National Parks," *American Quarterly,* 22 (1970), 726–35

Claus-M. Naske, "Governor Ernest Gruening, the Federal Government and the Economic Development of Territorial Alaska," *Pacific Historian,* 28 (1984), 5–16

Donald J. Pisani, "Conflict over Conservation: The Reclamation Service and the Tahoe Contract," *Western Historical Quarterly,* 10 (1979), 167–90

——, "State vs. Nation: Federal Reclamation and Water Rights in the Progressive Era," *Pacific Historical Review,* 51 (1982), 265–82

Elmo R. Richardson, *Dams, Parks, and Politics: Resource Development and Preservation in the Truman-Eisenhower Era* (1973)

Robert Righter, *Crucible for Conservation: The Creation of Grand Teton National Park* (1982)

William G. Robbins, *Lumberjacks and Legislators: Political Economy of the U.S. Lumber Industry, 1890–1941* (1982)

Joseph L. Sax, *Mountains Without Handrails: Reflections on National Parks* (1980)

Karen L. Smith, *The Magnificent Experiment: Building the Salt River Reclamation Project, 1890–1917* (1986)

Harold K. Steen, *The U. S. Forest Service: A History* (1977)

Ferenc Morton Szasz, *The Day the Sun Rose Twice: The Story of the Trinity Site Nuclear Explosion, July 16, 1945* (1984)

William K. Wyant, *Westward in Eden: The Public Lands and the Conservation Movement* (1982)

C H A P T E R

14

The Changing West

Υ

In the contemporary West, certain historical trends are evident. Population growth and economic expansion have affected the quality of the environment. They have also influenced where many people live. Cities are now a home off the range for most westerners. In addition, the West's economy, outside that of California, may have moved beyond its postwar boom into an era of decline. Where the West may be headed in terms of its environment, its economy, and its quality of life are questions that westerners cannot ignore.

Υ D O C U M E N T S

The growth of greater Los Angeles over the last half-century is a major story in urban history. Now the second largest city in the nation, Los Angeles is projected to surpass New York City after the turn of the next century. The first three documents present a snapshot analysis of Los Angeles at different times. A. Edward Newton's 1932 report for the *Atlantic Monthly* depicted a sprawling city where automobiles were already a necessity and where the abundant use of electrical power created an artificial beauty in the night. In the second document, which appeared in *Harper's Magazine* in 1949, Carey McWilliams, one of the best writers on California and its history, observes that the astounding postwar growth of greater Los Angeles was producing instant suburban communities, much as the gold rush of 1849 had produced instant mining camps. Finally, David Brodsly, a Los Angeles native, wrote an impressive book-length essay on the city's freeways in 1981. The excerpt reprinted here as the third selection captures his thoughts about these monumental testimonies to urban life.

In eastern Montana in the early 1970s, plans for massive energy development loomed large. With the imposition of drastic price hikes or embargos by many overseas oil producers, the possibility arose that America would need to become self-sufficient in energy resources. A public forum held in 1973 explained why eastern Montana's coal resources were especially attractive and presented a range of opinions about environmental and economic issues that Montanans needed to consider. The viewpoints of some of the participants are reprinted as the fourth document.

In less than fifteen years, the economic picture has changed dramatically. The final document, a 1987 report by Michael Zielenziger of the Knight Ridder newspapers considers whether the West's economy is now in so deep a decline that an era of expansion and opportunity has ended.

A. Edward Newton Spends a Few Days in Los Angeles, 1932

A few days later I was in Los Angeles. What is one to say to this amazing city? The late Henry E. Huntington said to me some years ago, when I asked him why he placed his wonderful library and picture gallery in San Gabriel, a suburb of Los Angeles: 'Because I am a foresighted man. I believe that Los Angeles is destined to become the most important city in this country, if not in the world. It can extend in every direction, as far as you like; its front door opens on the Pacific, the ocean of the future. The Atlantic is the ocean of the past. Europe can supply her own wants; we shall supply the wants of Asia. There is nothing that cannot be made and few things that will not grow in Southern California. It has the finest climate in the world: extremes of heat and cold are unknown. These are the reasons for its growth.' I thought of this remark when I was dining with some friends. My hostess, a charming lady, much younger than I, told me she had been born in Los Angeles. 'I remember,' she said, 'when we had a population of ten thousand.'

'And what is it now?' I inquired.

'One million, six hundred thousand,' was the reply.

A city that has grown as fast as this is like a boy who has suddenly grown to six feet—the city has, in a way, outgrown its strength. It needs filling out; there are many spots filled with sordid and miserable shacks, but they are no worse than similar spots were in New York,—not, indeed, as bad,—on Fifth Avenue, where the magnificent shops and palaces now are. I remember when, fifty years ago, the district above Fifty-ninth Street was a rocky waste, with here and there a disreputable shanty, where nanny goats, tethered by a rope, were expected to thrive, or at least survive, upon a diet of ashes and tin cans. Let those of us who criticize Los Angeles remember this.

Of filling stations there are more than enough. The Sherman Anti-Trust Law has outlived its usefulness—if it ever had any. The greatest economic waste in this country of colossal waste is the oil business. A man who makes two ears of corn grow where only one grew before does more essential service to his country than the whole race of politicians put together, says Dean Swift. Very true, but what shall be said of the politician who makes ten service stations grow where one would serve? These horribly garish, smelly, and noisy establishments occupy and temporarily ruin strategic corners everywhere. But can anyone say that these crimes are peculiar to Los Angeles? In this respect, as in many others, we are setting a bad example to the world, which is quick to follow.

If rapid growth is desirable,—and I am sure it is not,—it should be blamed upon the automobile. Not elsewhere in the world is its use so common: in California it is quite impossible to get along without one. You get an invitation for luncheon, which you accept, and you find you are going seventeen miles out in the country. In some trepidation you tell your hostess you have an engagement for tea. 'Where?' she inquires. You tell her and she says, 'Oh, very well, I'll send you in my car,' and you find you have a thirty-mile drive ahead of you. You dash back to your hotel, get into a dinner jacket, and again are whisked out into the country and again into a city, the magnificence of which amazes you. Of the hospitality of California I had heard much, but, as the Queen of Sheba said of the glory of Solomon, 'the half was not told me.'

We were in Los Angeles so short a time, and out of it so many times, that I lost all count of where I went, but I shall never forget the magnificence of the scene when one night, coming home from a party, our course took us over a very high hill. Beneath us lay Los Angeles, surrounded by its satellites, each glowing with the blaze of what seemed to be millions of electric lights. I was reminded of a night up the Nile, some years ago, when, after spending an hour in the gloom of the Temple of Abu Simbel, I came out into the night to see the dark blue dome of heaven lit with millions of stars. Now, as then, the stars were above us, but beneath us were Los Angeles and her surrounding cities with their gorgeous display of lights sparkling in the clear, dry atmosphere. *Sic itur ad astra*, 'Thus to the stars,' might well have been the motto of Thomas A. Edison. One thinks of the New York Edison, the Boston Edison, the Chicago Edison, the California Edison, and bows—or should—in reverence at the thought of the great inventor. What a testament of beauty to leave the world! 'Let there be light,' and there *was* light—and power, too, and heat.

Carey McWilliams on the Postwar Growth of California and Greater Los Angeles, 1949

During the war and the ensuing years, Californians were vaguely aware of a phenomenal increase in population. But the full shock of recognition did not come until August 1947, when the Bureau of the Census released a report on population shifts for the period from April 1, 1940 to July 1, 1947. Then came amazing news. California had gained *three million new residents in seven years*—had absorbed, in less than a decade, about as many people as live in the whole state of Virginia, or the whole state of Iowa, or as lived in California itself at the time of the first world war. Thus the state had reached a total population of ten million—more people than there are in all of New England. California had passed Illinois and Ohio in population and had edged close to Pennsylvania, the second most populous state in the Union. . . .

Just what does it mean, in human terms, to dump 3,000,000 people into a state—even a state as large as California—in the brief period of seven years? Although the absorptive capacity of the state is still very great, the latest rush of people to California has produced an impact not unlike that

Reprinted by permission of Harold Ober Associates Incorporated. Copyright 1949 by Harper & Bros.

of the gold rush a hundred years ago. (Actually thirty times as many people have come to California in the past eight years as came during the gold-rush decade.) The effect of this latest migration has been all the greater by reason of the fact that the war migrants surged into a limited number of already crowded cities, mainly San Francisco, Oakland, San Diego, and Los Angeles. Since most of the migrants came to Los Angeles, it is to this city that one must turn for illustrations of the new type of community that has come into being. Westchester, "the fastest growing community in the United States," is perhaps the most interesting of these.

In 1940, Westchester was merely a name on the map for a large, vacant area near the Los Angeles Municipal Airport, green in the rainy season, brown in the summer, of gently rolling slopes and level plains planted to lima beans. In 1941, there were only seventeen widely scattered homes in the entire area; today 30,000 people live in Westchester. Everything about Westchester is new and shiny: its streets, its homes, its growing shopping center, its schools. Only within the past year has it begun to emerge from its camplike, squatter phase. In 1948, precisely 5,492 homes, most of which sold for about $7,000, were built in Westchester, and eight thousand additional homes are planned or under construction at the present time. Here, on the plains, a good-sized city has come into being in the past eight years, trim and neat and painfully, incredibly new. Although its development was almost wholly unplanned, by some miracle Westchester has the appearance of a fairly well-planned community.

The settlers of Westchester were war workers who wanted homes near the aircraft factories. This seemed to be an ideal place to build them. At the onset, no one thought of Westchester as a community, much less as a city; it was just a wartime improvisation, a "camp," and many of the settlers were not sure that they intended to stay in California. But it was not long before people began to say that they "lived in Westchester." And at some point it began to occur to people that a new community had been born. This consciousness of community identity is indeed a strange thing. Six homes, a dozen homes, two dozen, do not make a community; even a hundred homes will not always do so. Community consciousness is not necessarily a function of size: it is more closely related, perhaps, to such factors as time and place. In the case of Westchester, everyone arrived at about the same time, under approximately the same circumstances, and built or bought much the same kind of home; and the area was just sufficiently removed from other community-centered areas to set it apart, to give it an impetus toward self-recognition and a sense of identity. Whatever the cause, this collection of homes, bungalows, and cottages began to emerge as a community within a year after the first war migrants began to move in.

The population of Westchester is as young as the community is new. The adult population, for example, is highly concentrated in the thirty to thirty-four age bracket. About 75 per cent of the men are veterans of World War II. There are practically no old people. Most of the residents are in the middle of the middle class; the extremes of wealth and poverty are largely absent. For the most part, the men work in the skilled trades, the professions, civil service, and in manufacturing plants; few of the women work outside the home. Nine out of ten families own or are purchasing their homes. The school population, of course, is as young as the adult population: only 49 per cent of the children have yet reached the age of school enrollment, a circumstance which has created a great interest in kindergartens and nursery schools. Westchester is remarkably homogeneous, a fact which probably accounts for the rapid growth in community-consciousness. It is made up of people very similar in age, background, income, and interests; a community with an unusual interest in schools, playgrounds, and recreational centers because of the unusually large number of children. "Our children," as one Westchester housewife has said, "have not yet reached the age of delinquency, and we do not intend to have any delinquency in Westchester."

This statement throws a clear light on at least one aspect of the widespread postwar social ferment in California. The amount of lethargy in community attitudes probably increases in direct ratio to the age of the community. To change a pattern—to change anything, in fact—seems to be more difficult than to establish a new pattern, and this is particularly true with Americans, a notoriously impatient and restive people. Thus, by a paradox, the lack of planning created in Westchester the challenge to plan; the newness of the community, the youth of its population, and its homogeneity provided the dynamics which made planning possible. It has been said that newcomers in California are reluctant to develop an interest in community affairs, but in Westchester the interest is unusually great.

This ferment of newness is shown in other matters. Not enough churches have yet been built to take care of the religious needs of the community. By necessity, therefore, the existing churches have had to share their facilities; the Jewish congregation uses the Baptist Church, and most of the churches exchange pastors. Inter-faith activities of all kinds have been stimulated, and the existing churches have come to occupy a new relationship to the community. In the absence of facilities, churches have become the equivalent of a town hall or city council. No one factor, of course, explains the absence of a warring sectarianism in Westchester; it has come about as a result of a peculiar combination of social circumstances.

Here, then, is an eight-year-old city of 30,000 inhabitants with no local fire or police stations and without emergency hospital facilities; with no direct telephone line to Los Angeles—though it is an integral part of the city—so that the residents must pay a toll charge on all calls; with a "city library" about as big as a box car; with a collection of hastily thrown together bungalows for its elementary schools; without even—at last report— a barber shop. Never formally planned, the streets of Westchester are a jumble of unrelated numberings and sharp, criss-crossing turns; only the oldest inhabitants can find their way about with ease. Yet despite these omissions, inconveniences, and limitations, Westchester is going ahead, raising money to build a town hall, seeking by a variety of devices to improve community services. This is the 1949 California equivalent of the Poker Flats and Hangtowns of 1849—and how different it is! . . .

With all these inhibitions of the planning function, how then does it happen that the influx of 3,000,000 people did not produce a state of sheer chaos? There are many answers to this question. For one thing, California has space to burn. The city of Los Angeles has a larger land area than any other city in America: 44 miles by 25 miles, enough land to support a population of between eight and ten million people. The county of Los Angeles, with 4,038 square miles, is about the size of the state of Connecticut. If Los Angeles had been a compact, centralized city, the migration of the past eight years would have had a devastating impact; as things are, the newcomers simply fill up the vacant spaces.

The spread-out character of Los Angeles, plus the volume and velocity of migration, has resulted in a natural, and from many points of view a highly desirable, dispersion of population. Industries are widely scattered in Los Angeles. For the most part the wartime growth has taken place round the edges of the community, rather than at the center. By an accident, therefore, Los Angeles has become the first modern, widely decentralized industrial city in America. For, with the growth taking place in the peripheral areas, the city has found it more convenient to decentralize services and facilities than to attempt a new integration from the center. As fast as new areas have developed, the chain stores, the department stores, and the drive-in markets have chased after the people, setting up new shopping districts and establishing new neighborhood centers. With more automobiles per capita than any other city in America, and with the worst rapid-transit system, Los Angeles was almost ideally prepared for a decentralization which it did not plan but from which it will profit in the future. . . .

But the *newness* of sections of Los Angeles has created opportunities of which planners have dreamed for many years. San Fernando Valley, not so many years ago a "rural section of Los Angeles County," today has a population of 350,000 and, by the end of the century, may well have 1,000,000 residents. In other parts of the world, planners look hopefully forward to the coming of the "satellite" city, the decentralized community of from 35,000 to 50,000, with its own services, residences, and industries. But Los Angeles is already made up of a series of "satellite" cities, all unplanned.

Another clue to the success with which California has assimilated, after a fashion, 3,000,000 new residents in seven years, is to be found in the character of the migrants. They represent a selection rather than a cross section of the American population. They are young people, active, in their best working years; 45 per cent, for example, are between fifteen and thirty-four years of age. On the whole, they are much younger than the resident population, the median age of which in 1940 was four years older than the average for the nation. Often referred to by the California press as "undesirable," the war migrants show a higher proportion of college graduates than is to be found in California, and a higher proportion of high-school graduates than is to be found in the states from which they have come. Three-fourths of them come from points west of the Mississippi River. Although many of them are "unskilled," there is a high percentage of skilled workers included in the total of recent migrants to the state.

For the most part, then, the migration of the past eight years has been made up of people who have quickly and easily adjusted themselves to the conditions of their new life in California. The same characteristics of the total migrant group can be found, for example, in the large wartime influx of Negroes to California. Today Los Angeles County has the third largest concentration of Negroes outside the Southern states, with perhaps 350,000 Negroes now residing in the county.

There are, however, certain sections of the migrant population that present a special problem, particularly the "senior citizens." In 1940 there were 10,000,000 people in the United States over sixty-five years of age, of whom 750,000 lived in California; and of this group 325,000 lived in Los Angeles County. In the same year, 6.8 per cent of the nation's population was over sixty-five, but the percentage in Los Angeles was 8.5. It may now be close to 10 per cent. One-fourth of Los Angeles County's "senior citizens," those over sixty-five, are receiving some form of public assistance.

This, then, is California in 1949, a century after the gold rush: still growing rapidly, still the pace-setter, falling all over itself, stumbling pell-mell to greatness without knowing the way, bursting at its every seam. Today it has 10,000,000 residents; tomorrow it may have 20,000,000. California is not another American state: it is a revolution within the states. It is tipping the scales of the nation's interest and wealth and population to the West, toward the Pacific.

David Brodsly on Los Angeles Freeways as Monumental Structures, 1981

The freeway is literally a concrete testament to who we are, and it continues to structure the way we live. Both the dominant role the freeways play in transportation and their sheer permanence have made them the backbone of southern California. They rank with the mountains and the rivers in influencing the organization of a changing city, and uncontestably they are the single most important feature of the man-made landscape. Driving the freeway is absolutely central to the experience of living in Los Angeles, and any anthropologist studying our city would head for the nearest onramp, for nowhere else would he or she observe such large-scale public activity. Time spent on the freeway is for many of us a significant chunk of our lives. The way we think about place, both the city at large and our home turf, is intimately tied to cars and freeways. Perhaps the most basic feature of freeways, and the one most overlooked by the preoccupied commuter, is that they are impressive structures, the most awesome works of design in the daily lives of most of us. They can even be beautiful.

Although tourists and schoolchildren look to Olvera Street for a visible sign of Los Angeles' illusive history, the freeway stands as a living monument

David Brodsly, "L.A. Freeway: An Appreciative Essay," 2–5, 1981, University of California Press. © 1981 The Regents of the University of California.

to our past. It is a final product of succeeding generations of transportation systems which have been superimposed on the southern California landscape: the early Indian and Mexican colonial trails, the steam railroads, the electric railways, and the automotive highways. Through a hundred-year-long process of transportation development an urban metropolis was etched out of the desert, an act of creation which is revealed by a historical view from the road.

The original Spanish settlement, founded in 1781 as El Pueblo de la Reina de los Angeles, was a village located about fifteen miles due east of the Pacific Ocean and another fifteen south of the San Gabriel Mountains on a coastal plain now called the Los Angeles Basin. The basin is ringed by the high, often snowcapped mountains of the coastal range, its flatness interrupted by a few smaller ranges including the Santa Monica Mountains and La Puente Hills.

The early and continuing pattern of transportation in the basin comprises five lines of movement radiating from the Los Angeles pueblo (present downtown Los Angeles) toward other early Spanish settlements: a line running northwest toward San Fernando, another west toward Santa Monica, a third south toward San Pedro, a fourth southeast toward Santa Ana, and a fifth east toward San Bernardino. This pattern is implicit in the physical geography of the region, dictated in large measure by points of access to the outside world through mountain passes and natural harbors. The introduction of railroads set these routes as the primary matrices for all subsequent development, and their courses remain more or less faithfully articulated by the freeways. A quick genealogy shows that the route northwest along the Los Angeles River into the San Fernando Valley became a Southern Pacific line and later the Golden State freeway; the route west to Santa Monica became the Los Angeles and Independence Railroad and later the Santa Monica freeway; the route south to San Pedro became the Los Angeles and San Pedro Railroad and later the Harbor freeway; and the route southeast to Santa Ana became another Southern Pacific line and later the Santa Ana freeway. Three railroads headed east through the San Gabriel Valley, as do three freeways today. The Pasadena freeway and the Foothill freeway east of Pasadena descend from the Santa Fe, the Pomona freeway descends from the Union Pacific, and the San Bernardino freeway is partial heir of the Southern Pacific. Both the Foothill and the San Bernardino freeways now have railroad tracks built within sections of their center dividers.

The legacy of Los Angeles' once extensive electric railways, though not so obvious, can also be found in the freeway system. The freeways were designed to serve the same territory covered by the trolleys. They could not have done otherwise, as it was through the electric streetcars, especially the interurbans, that a metropolitan Los Angeles first suggested itself. The most striking testament vanished when the Pacific Electric disappeared. We no longer have the red cars sharing the rights-of-way of the Hollywood freeway over Cahuenga Pass or the early segments of the San Bernardino to remind us of this continuity. Some railway lines actually met their fate as a direct result of freeway construction. Several Pacific Electric rights-of-way were usurped by their land-hungry stepchildren, the freeways striking the final blow to a system long suffering from public neglect.

The relationship of the freeways to their highway predecessors is the most obvious and the easiest to understand. The freeways were built to relieve the most popular surface highways of through traffic. The names associated with the freeways in the early master plans of the 1930s and 1940s make this intended superimposition particularly clear: Sepulveda Parkway, Colorado Parkway, Ramona Parkway, Atlantic Parkway, Olympic Parkway, Crenshaw Parkway, and so on. The parallel was even more pronounced in the plan for a freeway and expressway system adopted by the state legislature in 1959, which was to replace practically every major state highway with a freeway. What was actually built, however, more closely resembles the earlier rail patterns than a comprehensive highway grid. The radial routes usually received higher priority and were constructed first, and several major bypass routes were subsequently deleted owing to funding shortages and routing controversies.

The Los Angeles freeway is a silent monument not only to the history of the region's spatial organization, but to the history of its values as well. Rather than representing a radical departure from tradition, the freeway was the logical next step in making the Los Angeles dream a reality. Los Angeles' appeal lay in its being the first major city that was not quite a city, that is, not a crowded industrial metropolis. It was a garden city of backyards and quiet streets, a sprawling small town magnified a thousandfold and set among palms and orange trees and under a sunny sky. When the city began drowning in the sheer popularity of this vision, the freeway was offered as a lifeline. The L.A. freeway makes manifest in concrete the city's determination to keep its dream alive.

The L.A. freeway embodies a tension long present in American culture: the pastoral versus the technological. It is a drama that historian Leo Marx called, in an excellent book of the same title, the "Machine in the Garden." American arts and letters have, since Jefferson expounded his agrarian ideals, been struggling with acceptance of the urban industrial age. Only a few have suggested reconciliation through acceptance, replacing the bucolic imagery with some technological counterpart. Henry Adams, in his autobiography, made an uneasy truce with the technological age through the image of the dynamo. He saw the electric generator as a modern equivalent of the medieval Virgin, as a new goddess of power and fecundity. As the Virgin had inspired the building of Chartres, so the force of the dynamo would infuse the works of technological man. The American poet Hart Crane, in his most famous collection, *The Bridge*, supplied the missing element in Adams's equation. For Crane, the Brooklyn Bridge was like a cathedral of the machine age. In steel, concrete, and cable he could see, as Adams had at Chartres, the evocation of an entire epoch.

Both Adams's essay, "The Virgin and the Dynamo," and Crane's American epic function better as literature than as modern secular theology. The electric generator is simply too far removed from our experience to have any symbolic force, and the Brooklyn Bridge seems today more a monument to our past. As I survey the world I live in for a better metaphor to evoke the contours of the machine-age soul, I find none more appropriate than the freeway. For here the abstract image of the dynamo becomes an active metaphor in the automobile. It is the machine most fully integrated into our lives, the dynamo with a face; it has become an extension of our bodies, both as appendage and as an expression of personality, a technological icon. And the freeway is the automotive basilica.

Joan Didion . . . calls the freeway experience "the only secular communion Los Angeles has." The more I think about the parallel, the more I realize how correct she is. Every time we merge with traffic we join our community in a wordless creed: belief in individual freedom, in a technological liberation from place and circumstance, in a democracy of personal mobility. When we are stuck in rush-hour traffic the freeway's greatest frustration is that it belies its promise.

The L.A. freeway is the cathedral of its time and place. It is a monumental structure designed to serve the needs of our daily lives, at the same time representing what we stand for in this world. It is surely the structure the archeologists of some future age will study in seeking to understand who we were.

A Public Forum on Coal and Energy Development in Montana, 1973

Richard L. Reese, Helena, Montana:

The Fort Union Formation, underlying parts of Montana, North Dakota, South Dakota, Wyoming and Saskatchewan, is perhaps the largest coal basin in the world. The coal bearing section of this formation contains estimated reserves of one point three trillion tons. Hundreds of billions of tons of this coal underlie a large area of eastern Montana; some thirty billion tons are estimated to be "strippable", i.e., it lies in thick seams close to the surface.

Recently, interest in the rich coal reserves of eastern Montana has intensified dramatically. Increasing national demands for electricity coupled with chronic metropolitan air pollution problems which demand relatively clean, low sulfur, low ash coal of the type found in Montana, have touched on an unprecedented Montana coal rush.

The stakes are high, and America's largest coal, oil and energy combines are among the participants. The payoff may ultimately be measured not in millions of dollars or even in billions of dollars, but rather in hundreds of billions of dollars. A single acre of Montana coal land underlain by a fifty-foot seam, for example, will produce over eighty-eight thousand tons of coal. Even at the current price of one dollar and eighty cents to two dollars per ton at the mine (it sells for four times this in Chicago), the operation would gross one hundred seventy-six thousand dollars an acre.

But the highest stakes may lie not in coal production itself, but rather in potentially vast energy conversion facilities including mine mouth electrical generation plants, coal gasification and liquefaction plants, petrochemical complexes, and uranium enrichment plants. A single coal-fired uranium enrichment plant now planned by Reynolds Metals for the coal fields of Wyoming, for example, will cost a staggering two point two billion dollars and will increase the taxable valuation of the entire state of Wyoming by two and one half times. Clearly, western coal is big business.

During the early weeks of 1973, a group of Helena, Montana citizens organized a public forum to deal with some of the issues regarding coal and energy development in eastern Montana. Partially funded by a grant from the Montana Committee for the Humanities, the forum was held in Helena on February third and fourth, 1973.

Representatives of industry, government, agriculture, environmental groups, and the general public were invited to participate on panels dealing with energy and public policy, air quality, water resources, strip mining and reclamation, and the socio-cultural impact of coal and energy development. . . .

[I]t is important to remember that the forum was held in February, 1973, about one-third of the way through the First Session of the Forty-Third Montana State Legislature. Almost from the time the Legislature convened in January, 1973, it was clear that coal was going to be the dominant issue of the session. . . .

By the time the First Session of the Forty-Third Legislative Assembly ended on March 24, 1973, several highly significant bills had been passed. Senate Bill ninety-four, the Montana Strip Mining and Reclamation Act of 1973, was signed by Governor Judge on March 16. It may indeed be "the strongest strip mining reclamation law in the history of this country", as the Governor had called for in his State of the State Message. On the same day the Governor signed into law House Bill one hundred twenty-seven, the Montana Utility Siting Act of 1973. This act, which grants the state a remarkably comprehensive degree of authority over the construction of energy related facilities, may, over the long run, prove to be the most significant piece of legislation to emerge from the Forty-Third Legislative Assembly.

In addition to the above, the Legislature passed and the Governor signed a bill which quadrupled state coal production taxes on the two highest grades of coal and tripled the tax on the lower grades; a water use act which requires the issuance of a permit for water appropriation and which will provide the state with much needed information on industrial as well as agricultural water use; and the Strip-Mined Coal Conservation Act, the intent of which is to prevent the waste of coal and insure that once strip-mined land is disturbed and reclaimed, it will not be disturbed again.

These new laws, while not sufficient in themselves, could have a far reaching and profoundly beneficial effect in protecting Montana from the ravages of strip mining and uncontrolled energy production. Whether in fact, they will afford our state the protection they intend will depend upon the manner in which they are administered and the vigor with which they are enforced. The months and years immediately ahead will tell the tale.

Robert J. Labrie, Assistant Chief Engineer, Montana Power Company:

We are here today to discuss the increased industrialization that we can see coming in eastern Montana. This area of eastern Montana has been losing population since 1920. We can all now see the possibility of considerable population influx into the area due to the development of a coal mining industry. This industry is going to grow due to the much publicized energy shortage. The electric power industry can't keep up with the demand for electric power with nuclear plants only. They must use coal to fill the gap until the fast breeder reactor comes into commercial operation. In addition, sources of fossil fuels in this country are dwindling. Coal is going to have to be gasified to provide natural gas for cities and liquified to provide gasoline. The big controversy around our state right now is just how fast will this industrialization come upon us, and what will be its effect.

Let me speculate a bit on these questions from the point of view of someone in the electric power industry. First of all, the demands for electric growth in Montana must be met through the use of coal-fired generating plants until about the year 2040. By that time, the breeder reactor will have become a reality and nuclear power will have taken over. The first demonstration plant breeder reactor should be in service in about 1985. Breeder reactors will probably be available and more or less "de-bugged" by about 1995. So some time around the year 2000, I predict that the last coal-fired power plants will be built in Montana. The then existing plants will continue to operate, however, for another thirty or forty years. . . .

What effect will all this have on the air pollution potential in eastern Montana? First of all, . . . we are constructing two three-hundred-and-fifty MW generating plants at Colstrip, Montana at the present time. These plants will be equipped with scrubbers that will remove ninety-nine and one half per cent of the particulates or fly ash. Estern Montana coal is low in sulfur content, but these scrubbers will also remove much of the sulfur dioxide that is generated. A scrubber of this type is also most effective in removing the little fluorides that might exist in either the particulate or gaseous form. . . .

As we look to the 1980's and 1990's, I think that we can see continued improvement in technology. For instance, there is much research being done on fluidized bed furnaces which will absorb sulfur dioxide right in the furnace. Low btu coal gasification for electric power production, where the sulfur will come out with the ash in the bottom of the system, is being proposed. We certainly will have improved scrubber technology and fuel cells. Some geyser power sites will probably be developed. Big storage batteries for peaking will be developed. In the 1990's, I think I can see magnetohydrodynamics and high temperature topping turbines coming into play to improve the efficiency of electric power generation. And some time in the 1990's, fast breeder reactors will become commercially available to increase our available nuclear fuel by thirty-fold. Sometime after the year 2000, fusion power probably and some form of solar power will be developed. They should make available energy sources almost infinite.

With these things in the future, provided that we work hard toward them, there is every reason to believe that there will not be a long-term energy shortage and that we will be able to keep ahead of and diminish our air pollution problems.

Harry Mitchell, Dairy Farmer and Former Montana State Senator:

Should full development of the twenty-one proposed power sites in Montana occur, some sixty-nine thousand megawatts of electric energy would be produced annually. Most of these plants would range in size from one thousand to five thousand megawatts.

One of the serious problems associated with these plants is their airborne emissions. Mr. Labrie talked about this earlier. Even with the best pollution control technology, large volumes of pollutants will still be given off. The emission of particulates, sulfur oxides, and nitrogen oxides can be expected. Now sulfur oxides in the air, according to what President Nixon said back in 1971 in his message to the House, "are among the most damaging air pollutants. High levels of sulfur oxides have been linked to increased instances of diseases such as bronchitis and lung cancer. In terms of damage to human health, vegetation and property, sulfur oxide emissions cost society billions of dollars annually." I have stacks of information to back this up. . . . Electric power plants generated over half of the estimated thirty-two million tons of sulfur oxides released into the atmosphere in 1970. This is the biggest single source for sulfur oxides, not the smelting industry. The report of the North Central Power Study states that the coal from the Gillett-Colstrip area may preclude the need for sulfur oxide removal because of its low sulfur content. This was written in 1971. The management of the Four Corners plant near Farmington, New Mexico also claimed "that since the plant burns low sulfur coal, it creates no sulfur pollution problem." This plant, when operating at full capacity, can generate about thirteen hundred megawatts; small by comparison with those projected for Montana. Testimony given before the Senate Interior Committee in 1971 indicated that since the fully operating Four Corners plant burns about twenty-five thousand tons of coal each day, it spews into the atmosphere over one hundred thousand tons of sulfur dioxide, (equivalent to about one hundred and fifty thousand tons of sulfuric acid) every year *in spite of* the low sulfur content of the coal and relatively low concentration of sulfur oxides in the flue gasses. When such quantities of pollutants are involved, it is quite apparent that quality air cannot be maintained by imposition of regulations based on concentration of flue gas or upon maximum emission allowed per unit of power produced or fuel consumed. It is the *total amount* of pollutants released to the atmosphere that determines the degree of environmental degradation.

In 1969, when the astronauts were circling the globe getting ready for their Apollo trip, the only man-made activity that they could positively identify was the smoke plume from the Four Corners plant in New Mexico. That plant was producing about thirteen hundred megawatts. The North Central Power Study has programmed a maximum capacity (and this is programmed, it doesn't mean it will ever come about) of about sixty-nine thousand megawatts. Reduce that by half, or take only ten per cent of that, and we still have a tremendous pollution source destined for eastern Montana. I suggest to you that here in Montana we have a microcosm of the problem that's facing the world in terms of energy consumption. Somewhere this consumption has got to level off. Nothing can grow forever. And if we can't recognize this and do something about it in Montana, then I doubt if it's going to be able to be done anywhere.

Rick Applegate, Research Associate, Montana Environmental Quality Council:

[O]ne is uncertain precisely how to get a handle on the impending coal development, and specifically how to assess its effects on water resources and water quality in the state.

There are, however, ominous prospects. First, massive and continuous, not seasonal, consumption of water from the Yellowstone River would seriously affect agricultural, fisheries, tourist, recreational and esthetic uses of water. Second, the central role water plays in various coal development technologies suggests that it may be *the* crucial variable in thermal electric generation, MHD [millions of gallons per day] conversion to electricity, gasification, liquifaction, or slurry pipeline transportation. Third, there will be increased water demands resulting from uncertain increases in population in southeast Montana. Fourth, the unknown plans of energy development companies for development of alternative technologies yields very different water demands, whether we're talking about thermal electric generation as opposed to gasification, or wet as opposed to dry cooling. Fifth, the possibility of coal companies buying up irrigated lands to acquire water rights, and many more.

Again quoting from the Coal Task Force, "Until more is known as to likely timing and magnitude of these demands, the resulting effects on physical, natural and human systems can only be speculated upon." Needless to say, these doubts and prospects leave one unsettled in the face of potentially enormous disruption of the aquatic ecosystem of eastern Montana. . . .

House Bill four hundred ninety two . . . provides a healthy delay of further energy development while specified state agencies carry out a co-ordinated, comprehensive study of coal related issues. The studies would be reported to the 1976 session of the Legislature. By that time, the Legislature should also have before it a Department of Interior study of Northern Great Plains resources and an energy policy study from the Environmental Quality Council. The State Department of Health and Environmental Sciences would report on potential surface and ground water pollution and diminution, including recommendations to prevent significant degradation of water quality.

The Bureau of Mines would study effects on aquifers and recharge areas; these are especially critical for operations near Decker. The Departments of Natural Resources and Fish and Game would study surface and underground hydrology with recommendations to prevent depletion of water resources to the detriment of agricultural and recreational uses. This would give the Department of Natural Resources additional time to rectify shortcomings in the state water plan and the Water Resources Act and to require federal, local and private planners to cooperate further with the state. . . .

[T]he only approach is one of caution, supplemented by detailed steady-handed study of all relevant problems. Should we fail to spend the time which a moratorium will provide to determine the numerous unresolved questions of coal development, we will be guilty of what economists sometimes refer to as sub-optimization. In this case, there will be a panic-stricken rush to determine the best way to do something, which perhaps ought not to be done at all.

Fred Wetzstoen, Rancher, Sula, Montana
Chairman, Natural Resources Committee, Montana Farm Bureau:

I am convinced, in my own mind, that available knowledge, experience and dedication to responsibility are sufficient to insure that coal-burning systems will not be constructed that will be harmful to [the] Montana environment, and that improvements that show up will be incorporated as construction progresses.

What was luxury day before yesterday, was convenience yesterday, and is necessity today. We have built our lives around electric energy. Our existence as farmers and ranchers and our ability to produce necessary food and fibre is today dependent to a very great extent on electrical energy. We have built our lives around electrical and other mechanized devices, partly because of convenience but mostly because of necessity.

We are rapidly depleting, throughout the world, non-renewable natural resources that can and will be substituted for by renewable resources that will be produced on our lands. Great amounts of electrical energy will be needed to convert these resources to products usable by man and it is our responsibility to devise means of creating this electrical energy.

Just a few years ago, power companies and other utilities were several years behind the desires of the public because of an economic theory which said that in order to stay in business and on the job there had to be a guarantee of dividends for share holders. Recently, a bolder, more imaginative and courageous personnel has taken over and proven, I think, that the way to success is to be equal to or ahead of public demand. "Ecoenvirocrats" along with recreationists, sportsmen, and similar classifications have turned our energy developers away from hydro-electric systems, and coal presently is the other known sensible, safe and sane place to go.

I have no patience with those who expound that we can do without some or cut back on our use of electricity. I see no reason why we should. Our increasing needs and desires should be met insofar as it is possible to do so, and the rapidly increasing needs and desires of our society should be programmed for with imagination, courage and creativity. I believe our energy producers are soon coming back to our streams with low-level energy producing plants and if our impact researchers are behind in their work they had better "get to it" because there has been and are plenty of "on the ground labs" to work from and with. It is unfortunate that government is greatly in the picture and always several years behind the times.

Not because of age, but because it just isn't so long ago, I can remember the old scrub board which I had to learn to manipulate, then the old push lever washer, the Maytag with the gas engine, the thirty-two volt electric motor and then the REA [Rural Electrification Administration project] up the canyon. My son-in-law and I cleared eight miles of right-of-way through a heavily timbered canyon in less than thirty days to get that high line to my ranch. We have built our lives around electric energy and when brown-outs appeared during our two cold spells this winter it crystalized my resolve to do all I could towards an ever-increasing supply of electrical energy within the bounds of good judgment in relation to those other so important resources, air and water.

And finally, I cannot be convinced that any utility is going to spend millions to construct an energy-producing plant that is going to be closed down by environmental considerations before it can get into production. I believe that knowledge and sincerity is sufficient, and that a moratorium in the coal fields could be likened to a moratorium on a six-months pregnant mother because someone has determined that doctors do not know all there is to know about childbirth.

Michael Zielenziger on the West's Economy, 1987

After a decade of dazzling growth, the economy of the American West has collapsed, consigning a region that has embodied the nation's grandest ambitions to a future of adversity and decline.

From Oklahoma's oil fields to the mines of North Idaho and Montana and the wheat fields of Washington, the West's basic commodities are languishing. After years of speculation, many of its biggest cities are overbuilt, its small towns depressed. States such as Colorado and Oregon, which once worried about managing growth, now labor to revive it. Blue-collar workers take pay cuts, or lose their jobs altogether. And as unemployment rises and tax revenues shrink, banks fail and bankruptcies soar, leaders wonder when and how the West can regain its old economic vitality.

"This region is suffering from shock," said Mike Fitzgerald, head of the Washington state economic development board. "The trends of 10 years ago have so completely reversed; it's just astonishing. These states are

Michael Zielenziger, *The Spokesman-Review/Spokane Chronicle*, April 12, 1987. Reprinted with permission, Knight-Ridder Newspapers.

losing economic capacity at a rate that nobody can deal with. There's a sense of devastation out there. If we can't undo current trends, we'll be in a declining spiral which may take a full generation to reverse.''

Said Raymond Plank, chairman and chief executive officer of the Denver-based Apache Corp.: "There's a flood washing over this region, and a lot of people are drowning."

Economists say the West has fallen victim to fundamental changes in the world economy: the emergence of a global marketplace for resources and labor; the precipitous spread of technology and capital to Asia and the Third World; the crash of commodity prices. Lacking in diversity, dependent on foreign trade and natural resources, the West's economy is unraveling.

And although the region has always been prey to cycles of boom and bust, a growing body of economic experts, business leaders and scholars see an age of economic despair.

"Forces in global economics have really shaken the whole structure of the resource-based economy," said Paul Cunningham, executive director of the Western Governors' Association in Denver.

"In the West, various regions are teetering precariously, tied to one or two declining industries," said Harold T. Gross, a professor of business at Southern Methodist University. "The West is an underdeveloped economic region. As a result, what we will see is an erosion of incomes, of job opportunities and of standards of living."

Already, some areas of the West have begun to resemble what some economists say the entire region could become: a neo-colonial economy that exports raw materials, bulk commodities and waste products to foreign competitors while importing high-tech and processed goods.

"The sad reality is that much of what we're sending to Japan and Asia is waste paper, scrap metal and animal feed," said Tom Tabasz, chief economist for the First Interstate Bank of Washington, describing exports from the Port of Seattle. "Today, our list of exports lined up next to that of Paraguay or Argentina wouldn't be that much different."

If—as many economists forecast—basic Western commodities like copper and soybeans, timber, oil and cattle are never again central to economic growth, the solutions to the West's economic plight may be few, painful and piecemeal.

"We're staring at a future of depopulation and economic depression," said Robert Lee, chairman of the college of forest resources at the University of Washington.

Added Doug Henton of SRI International in Menlo Park: "The West can no longer take its future for granted."

Everywhere you look, the news is bad.

In the 1980s, for the first time, personal incomes in the West are growing more slowly than the national average. From 1982 to 1985, personal income grew 7 percent a year across the nation; in the 14 non–Sun Belt Western states, it grew 4.7 percent, according to the U.S. Commerce Department.

In 1980, residents of Washington state had incomes 8 percent above the national average; by 1985, they were right at the average. Idaho, where personal income was 87 percent of the national average in 1980, had fallen to 80 percent; Wyoming went from 16 percent above to 5 percent below.

The price at which the West can sell its goods has eroded at a fearsome rate. Oil, which sold for more than $35 a barrel only two years ago, now sells for $18 or less. Soybeans, which brought $7.57 a bushel in 1980, brought $5.10 in 1985. Copper, which peaked at $1.01 a pound in 1980, was 68 cents a pound four years later. Farmland in Nebraska, worth $635 an acre in 1980, was worth $444 in 1985.

From 1981 to 1985, the economies of the 14 states grew an average of 1.1 percent a year, while the gross national product rose by 2.3 percent annually.

In 1986, unemployment exceeded the 7 percent national average in all the non–Sun Belt states except the Dakotas, Nebraska, Kansas and Utah.

The average unemployment rate in the 14 states was 7.5 percent, but demographers say that statistic would have been far worse had it not been for record farm subsidies.

Mass migrations always have fueled the West's prosperity. But in 1985, the 14 Western states grew more slowly than the rest of the nation. Oregon and Wyoming showed net declines in population, and in many other states the waves of immigration that created economic vitality during the 1970s suddenly began to slow. Last year, for the first time in two decades, more people left Colorado than moved in.

"The 1970s were the first decade in which the non-California segment of the West accounted for more than half of the West's growth," said Calvin Beale, chief demographer for the U.S. Agriculture Department's Economic Research Service. Beale first forecast the "back to the country" movement of that era, an economic and sociological phenomenon that seemed to bode well for the rural West.

"In this decade, however," Beale said, "it doesn't look as though that dispersed growth pattern will continue to be true, a clear indication that a slump has taken place."

What these statistics mean, said Kenneth L. Deavers, director of the rural economics division of the U.S. Department of Agriculture, is that the West is undergoing a "fundamental structural adjustment," a downturn that will "permanently affect agriculture, mining, energy and manufacturing"— in short, every traditional Western industry.

Seventy years ago, historian Frederick Jackson Turner argued that "the true point of view in the history of this nation is not the Atlantic Coast, but it is the Great West. The perennial rebirth, the fluidity of American life, the expansion westward with its new opportunities, its continual touch with the simplicity of rural society, furnish the forces dominating American character."

As in Turner's era, the West again may prove to be a model for America's development—but a model of economic vulnerability in a changed world.

Some of the realignments through which the West is passing mirror the "deindustrialization" that has swept through America's Rust Belt, shutting steel mills, tire plants and other basic industries.

"The East went through a difficult period of dislocation in the early 1970s," Gross said. "It had a depth of economic structures and the diversity to rebound. The Western states—they don't have that depth. They'll come back, but unless they do something drastic, it might take 30 or 40 years."

Herman Bluestone, an economic development researcher at the Agriculture Department, said the West's generally high levels of education may be its greatest asset.

But Don Dillman, director of the Social and Economic Sciences Research Center at Washington State University, said much of the West is not equipped to take advantage of emerging technologies.

"A lot of the rural areas don't even have the telephone infrastructure to move into high tech," he said.

Other analysts note that many American firms are moving toward the Japanese model of "just in time" manufacturing, in which more components are made to order. That means that suppliers will need to be closer to main assembly plants, a difficult proposition in the wide-open West.

"To be that new, flexible, customized manufacturer, you've got to be moved closer to your market," said Daniel Garnick, associate director of regional economics for the Commerce Department's bureau of economic analysis.

Despite such built-in disadvantages, states such as Colorado and Washington are pressing forward with a variety of innovative projects, including initiatives to:

• Develop small, localized production firms that manufacture items now imported from outside the region.

• Encourage farmers to replace undifferentiated commodities such as wheat and soybeans with specialized products such as asparagus, grapes and miniature vegetables.

• Teach producers how to successfully repackage their goods and sell them in overseas markets where requirements and specifications are different.

• Create recreational and tourist centers to attract out-of-town money and spur local business.

• Establish retirement communities in rural areas where extractive industries once held sway.

• Develop the ports of the Pacific, especially Portland and Seattle, as centers for increased trade with the fast-growing nations of Asia's Pacific Rim.

But even if those ventures succeed, they are likely to leave many workers behind, wishing for their old jobs and high wages.

"As we move toward 'specialty niche' markets and high-tech automation, it's that broad middle that will disappear," said Fitzgerald. "The middle-sized companies, the middle managers, the middlemen . . . maybe even the middle class."

"Whatever train the West was riding, it certainly has stopped," said David Harrison, a senior public policy researcher at the University of

Washington. "We're undergoing a fundamental change, and that train just ain't gonna be out there anymore."

Y E S S A Y S

Richard White of the University of Utah has written extensively about the West; another of his essays appears in Chapter 9. His essay here, the first selection, is in his field of special interest, environmental history. Using the Pacific Northwest as his case study, White shows in the first essay how the human population has shaped the environment over time. He considers what the cost of these changes may turn out to be. In the second selection, Bradford Luckingham, an urban historian at Arizona State University, affirms the historical significance of urban growth in the American West, especially the Southwest. Urban pioneers helped develop this region, and the existence of urban centers explains the attractiveness of the Sun Belt for contemporary Americans. Michael Malone, a well-established scholar and the dean of graduate studies at Montana State University, is an authority on the history of western metal mining. In the final essay, he discusses whether this major segment of the region's economy has collapsed. If economic trends and world markets were to spell doom for western mining, Malone wonders what will happen in other economic sectors.

The Altered Landscape of the Pacific Northwest

RICHARD WHITE

Any region of the United States, no matter how one defines regional criteria and boundaries, is a physical place with its own geography and climate, its own flora and fauna. Once this rather obvious statement was the heart of regionalism. During the early 20th century, geographical determinists argued that environment translated readily into culture, social structure, personality, and politics. In their crudest formulations, determinists argued, for instance, that rugged land regularly produced rugged individualists.

Even in the current intellectual climate, where the only things still being recycled are simplistic social theories, this kind of geographical determinism has so far failed to make a comeback. Still, reports of its demise may be premature. Geographical determinism, after all, seems no more unlikely than the currently fashionable assertions that laissez-faire economics and appeals to greed will create universal prosperity and social justice, and that militarism will prevent war. Nevertheless, geographical determinism remains momentarily dead, although its unfortunate legacy has been to turn attention away from regional studies of the relationship between the environment and the human societies which inhabit the land.

Richard White, "The Altered Landscape: Social Change and the Land in the Pacific Northwest," in *Regionalism and the Pacific Northwest*, 109–124, ed. William G. Robbins et al., 1983, Oregon State University Press.

In a real sense, the determinists had gotten it all backwards. As George Perkins Marsh noticed more than a century ago, the land shaped societies decidedly less often than societies shaped the land. The implication of Marsh's insight is that a region is less likely to get men to match its mountains, than mountains to match its men (and women). This neat reversal is, however, too simple. Nature is not infinitely malleable. In the end the relationship between landscape and society, between environment and culture, is reciprocal. Human beings create landscapes, and these landscapes in turn have consequences for the society which created them.

The Northwest is, at least superficially, an apt place to examine the reciprocal influences of land and society. To Easterners, Northwesterners seem particularly tender in their concern for the land. This is an opinion maintained despite years of Hanford's nuclear wastes leaking into the Columbia River and eventually Dixie Lee Ray [governor of Washington, 1977–1980] leaking into the political system. It is an apt region, too, because, by defining the Pacific Northwest narrowly as everything between the Cascades and the Pacific and between British Columbia and California, it is possible to create a crudely homogeneous environmental region to study. Here vast changes have taken place in the land; a society has arisen, which claims (for vague and ill-defined reasons) to be regionally distinctive; and a vocal concern for the land has become a legitimate political issue.

In the Pacific Northwest, as in any region of the United States, there are diverse feelings and opinions about the land. Personal feelings and opinions, however, are not really at issue here; my concern is with how they develop, what power they exert, and with what results. These are basically historical questions even though they are often defined in excessively presentist and functional terms.

History matters a great deal in understanding the regional relationship to environment, but history cannot be confused with myth. What the American West spawns (for the good, I think) are the great myths of American culture which revolve around the clash of civilization and savagery and nature. These are, however, cultural divisions and must be understood as such; they are not useful historical divisions of the past. Untamed nature plays only a minor role in the history of the Northwest (or any part of the West). The high country of the Cascades and Olympics was (and still is) wilderness, but calling the land American settlers found "wilderness" only obscures the relationship between people and the land.

The first American settlers who penetrated into western Oregon and Washington entered a relatively stable and productive environment. For centuries Indian peoples had been burning forests and prairies, encouraging some species and discouraging others; more recently, they had adopted exotic plants and animals such as the potato and the horse. The species composition of both the forests and prairies were to a significant degree the result of Indian practices. The Northwest that American settlers found was an Indian-managed Northwest. This point is an important one. Any environment inhabited by human beings is, to varying degrees, a human-dominated ecosystem. The question is not domination per se, nor civilization versus wilderness, but rather how an environment is dominated and with what results. In the 1840s the environment west of the Cascades remained not only stable and productive, but also botanically distinctive. Indians manipulated native species, and few exotics were introduced; the managed ecosystem maintained itself without costly imports or serious deterioration.

White settlement destroyed the Indian Northwest. Indeed most whites failed to recognize that it even existed. Farmers simply mistook Indian handiwork for virgin nature. They sought out the prairies and openings to farm in preference to the massive fir forests, without realizing that Indian burning often created and maintained these prairies and shaped the species composition of both prairie and forest. Treating those Indians who survived the ravages of smallpox and influenza, murder and war, and displacement to reservations as so many primitive pyromaniacs, settlers banished the fires and in so doing began to change the forest composition and the balance between prairie and forest in ways they did not suspect. Settlers might think that they were putting the mark of human use on the land as they displaced the Indians and plowed and fenced and planted, but they were only reordering the land and imposing a different vision, one developed far from the place they settled.

Early settlers in the Pacific Northwest almost automatically sought familiar landscapes. They were newcomers in what remains a region of newcomers, and the familiar was not the native. Settlers, therefore, sought not so much to create as to recreate. A frontier in this sense was not the cutting edge of change, but rather the most conservative region of the country. As historians are increasingly emphasizing, settlement was not a process of individualists breaking ties and heading west, but instead the relocation of existing kinship groups and community groups. The connections between settlers in the Willamette Valley or the Puget Sound region created a web of kin and old neighbors. Settlers husbanded the familiar, and the new land became merely a foundation upon which to reestablish existing ways.

Settlers brought with them to the new land an idea of an ordered landscape—a cultural model, rather than a specific ecology. What was meaningful for the frontier farmer was the traditional sense of landscape reflected in the census categorization of land as either improved or unimproved. Improved land was essentially that from which native plants and animals had been eradicated; unimproved land was where they remained. In the traditional mixed farming of the Midwest and Border South (from which most migrants came), these categories implied different perceptions and uses of the land. Farmers invested great labor in improved land, fenced it, and limited its production to familiar useful species. They controlled it by means that went back centuries to other continents.

Unimproved land was not untouched, but it was largely unexamined. Early diary accounts of western Washington, for example, often praised the land's beauty, but few diarists either knew, noticed, or named specific plants. Someone like James Swan, who took a detailed interest and delight in the peoples, plants, and animals of the native Northwest, was unique and eccentric. Most settlers contented themselves with hunting the land's game, destroying its predators, and releasing their cattle and hogs to fatten on (and destroy) camas and other native plants of the region. However, unimproved land, no matter how altered, still retained marks of older systems and different orders.

Of course, not all improved land was the same. In western Oregon different farming systems emerged within a decade of settlement, but nonetheless, the agricultural landscape still lacked the variety and distinctiveness of the unimproved land it replaced. A prairie wheat field in Oregon differed little from a prairie wheat field in Illinois, while a native prairie in Oregon differed a great deal ecologically from a native prairie in Illinois.

Anglo-American influence on the Pacific Northwest, then, began simply as a result of attempts to impose old ways on a new place. As long as settlers remained subsistence farmers, domestic considerations shaped production decisions. These considerations seem to have been clearly utilitarian: farmers managed the land to feed and clothe their families. But arguments of simple utility are deceptive and deserve closer examination. To say something is useful explains little. It is not that people want only the useful, but rather that people define as useful and necessary whatever it is that they want. For instance, people have to eat, but why do they eat what they do? Northwestern Indians relied on salmon for animal protein; the whites largely preferred pork. Both pigs and salmon are useful sources of protein and, on the Northwestern frontier, salmon were arguably more useful since they were rarely known to get into the fields and destroy growing crops. Yet frontier whites preferred the pig, even though in some areas hogs became ecological frankensteins that ate up both Indian and white food sources.

Utility clearly lies in the eye of the beholder (or rather the beholder's culture), and the Northwest settler's eye had a narrow range of vision indeed. Faced with the majestic forests of the region, T. J. Cram, a member of one of the government's expeditions of the 1850s, could only dismiss the trees as "timber of inferior quality for everything but spars, yards, and piles." Cram's crabbed view of the forest is a fair sample of unreflective utilitarianism, which even on its own terms is limited and shortsighted. Its arguments are necessarily geared to a present and culturally limited utility. To the immigrant, the usefulness of something new may not be immediately apparent, or its possible uses may be considered culturally unacceptable. The useful always exists within constricted cultural and temporal boundaries.

The logic of unreflective utility quickly established itself in the Northwest. The native landscape was neither sacred nor sentimental; it was merely an opportunity. And opportunity quickly became the opportunity to make not just a living but a profit. This change was part of the larger transition to commercial farming in the United States. Its consequences appeared in the attitudes of northwestern farmers and through them in the landscape. As Walter Crockett, an early settler in Washington Territory, phrased it, his main object in settlement was:

> to get the land subdued and wilde nature out of it. When that is accomplished we can increase our crops to a very large amount and the high prices of

everything that is raised here will make the cultivation of the soil a very profitable business.(sic)

Crockett's ambitions and those of the settlers in the Willamette Valley for large profits in the commercial market were doomed to frustration for much of the 19th century. Farmers producing staple crops increasingly operated in a world market over which they could exert little influence. A farmer could accurately plan what his family would need, but he could not predict what the price of wheat would be or what specialty crop would sell. In relatively isolated, commercially marginal areas like the Pacific Northwest, what was profitable could change yearly. Some farms became a kaleidoscope of different crops and animals, while other farmers engaged in steady staple crop production could not compete and actually abandoned land. In both cases care of the land suffered, exotic weeds invaded the fields, and fertility declined. In the Willamette Valley there was actually an absolute decline in improved land between 1880 and 1900.

By the end of the 19th century, agricultural settlement had significantly contributed to a less distinctive northwestern landscape, one that was increasingly shaped by markets hundreds or even thousands of miles away. By introducing exotic species into the region and by trying to make it over in the image of other places, settlers had sparked an ecological invasion one botanist characterized as the most cataclysmic event in the natural history of the area since the Ice Age. In 1919 an examination of a seemingly native prairie landscape in the Willamette Valley revealed that one-half the species of grasses present were not indigenous.

In time, such introductions combined with surviving native species might have formed a new stable landscape. But the domination of the agricultural economy by large and impersonal markets insured that the only criterion of success in farming would be profit, and profit came only to those who quickly adjusted their fields to market demands. Thus commercial farming usually insured ecological instability. As the 20th century wore on, weeds and insects were only held at bay by increasingly costly applications of energy and poison to the land. There was little unique or regionally distinctive about successful farming in the Pacific Northwest.

The impact of the market reached well beyond the farmer's fields into the forests which surrounded them. Initially, the 19th century market demanded only fir, and available technology limited logging to areas only a mile or two from tidewater. The resulting logging for piles, masts, and spars produced operations of prodigious wastefulness, but surprisingly little ecological damage resulted. Loggers left cedar and hemlock standing as well as those Douglas fir either too large or too diseased to be cut. These trees provided the seeds necessary for the rapid repropagation of the forest. In Island County, Washington an untrained eye could mistake land cut 30 years before for a virgin forest. That the forest could maintain itself was, however, an accident. Loggers did not plan for sustained yield. It simply was not yet profitable to engage in the sort of lumbering that would destroy the forest. Again, the real forces at work were market forces. Concern with the land or the communities upon it was subordinate to making money. Advocates of the free market claimed then, as now, that private profits eventually translate into healthy communities and stable environments. The history of the Pacific Northwest belies this.

With the depletion of the forests of Michigan, Minnesota, and Wisconsin, accompanied by improvements in logging technology, changes in transportation and markets, and an influx of logging capital, the real assault on northwestern forests accelerated after the turn of the century. The donkey engine (a steampowered winch that could drag logs to a central place for shipment) and logging railroads allowed the logging of areas far removed from tidewater. The markets gradually expanded to include cedar and hemlock. Loggers took out immense amounts of timber cheaply and efficiently, but they left huge amounts of waste. Stumps, tops, branches, and trees shattered in the felling amounted to an average of 24,000 cubic feet of waste per acre. When this slash ignited, it burned at temperatures as high as 1,814 degrees and consumed not only the slash but 89 percent of the duff layer on the forest floor.

The seedlings that sprang up from fallen seeds in the wake of logging were often destroyed in these fires, which left unpromising conditions for any new trees that might follow them. By destroying the humus, fire lessened the moisture retention of the soil which was essential for the germination and survival of Douglas fir seedlings. It changed the nutrient balance of the soil and altered its ph. The sudden abundance of potassium, nitrogen, and calcium released from debris by burning encouraged those seedlings that survived to develop shallow root structures and large crowns and thus made them vulnerable to even short droughts. The black ash and charred debris also exacerbated drought by increasing heat retention in the soil on hot summer days by 25 degrees or more. Even to get a second crop of seedlings on the land following fires was difficult, since loggers no longer left an abundance of cull trees, and the logging of small tracts which could be reseeded by neighboring forests gave way to operations that covered huge areas.

Lumbermen cared little about all this. They realized the utility of protecting standing forests, but they ignored the fires that devastated cutover lands. Lumbermen claimed taxes prevented them from reforesting the lands they cut, but the evidence indicates such claims were specious. The real problem was that market prices did not justify restocking the forest. The logging companies cut and ran, and as a 1927 Forest Service report concluded, "whatever reproduction takes place, does so, for the most part, in spite of present methods, not as a result of them." Foresters estimated that 40 percent of privately held land in the Douglas fir region was not reforesting at all and that reforestation on most of the remainder was inadequate. In a good part of the reforestation that did take place, the returning trees were not Douglas fir, but rather alder.

By the early 20th century the new lumber industry, unlike farming, promised to provide a unique Northwestern landscape. It consisted of miles of huge shattered stumps surrounded by debris which, when accidentally ignited, burst into fires that burned for much of the summer. These devastated forests produced little but fire and bracken and filled the bays and rivers with eroded soil and logging debris, wiping out the spawning beds of the salmon. The ruin of the forest brought a generation of Northwesterners abruptly to the realization that ecology and society were connected; it became apparent that it is impossible to maintain human institutions, build roads, support schools, and meet public needs on a wasteland.

It is, however, naive to believe that the mere recognition of a problem insures its solution. The response to the logged-off lands took shape within the same cultural boundaries that produced the problem. The result was a back-to-the-land movement which was a complex brew of commercialism, class interest, and sincerely held agrarian beliefs.

The movement to settle the logged-off lands of the Pacific Northwest, like similar back-to-the-land movements in Michigan, Minnesota, Wisconsin, and the arid West, justified itself largely in regional terms. The northwestern back-to-the-land movement originated in the cities. City people promoted it, and ultimately the movement served urban interests. The West, and the Pacific Northwest in particular, have always been largely urban regions, but Westerners often manage to reconcile an urban reality with antiurban rhetoric. Proponents of the settlement of logged-off lands proceeded from the assumption that the cities were overpopulated while the rural districts were correspondingly underpopulated. From this fundamental imbalance flowed the myriad of social problems—unemployment, poverty, disease, moral decline—which they feared could destroy the Northwest and eventually the nation. This rhetoric was antiurban, but it paradoxically served urban interests. Blaming urban ills on too many poor people in the city not only avoided any serious analysis of the economic and social system, it proposed a simple solution to a pressing environmental problem. Urban poverty could be eliminated by shipping the poor to the logged-off lands, which they would then redeem with their labor. Ideally, the socially expendable poor of the cities would cultivate the surrounding land and alleviate the need to import millions of dollars worth of dairy products, pork, poultry, and veg-etables from outside the Northwest. Not only would these new settlers retain needed capital in the area, they would also consume the products of urban industries and thus stimulate urban prosperity.

This vision was partly a response to the wasteland left behind by the loggers, but it was also a rejection of the forest itself. It represented an inability to come to terms with the realities of the ecology of the Northwest. Boosters of the movement denounced the Forest Service for its fledgling attempts to replant the forest on federal lands. When one enthusiast con-demned the Forest Service for "trying to grow trees on land that should grow men," he was only underlining the logic of the whole movement.

Having denounced the city to serve the city's ends and having rejected the forest, the boosters of settlement offered all the venerable agrarian homilies. They argued that the attraction of people to the soil was instinctive, that urban life was unnatural, and that moral and civic virtue sprang directly from agriculture. They put these evocative and emotional appeals, however, firmly within a commercial context. Organizations from local chambers of commerce to the state government of Washington assured settlers that farming logged-off lands would surely make them comfortable and might very well make them rich.

To read the propaganda of these years is to witness the creation of a cultural landscape, but one which had only the most tenuous relation to the environmental realities of the land. The primitive soil science of the era before 1930 was of little help in guiding settlement. All soil seemed capable of producing something marketable, if only by supporting cows and chickens. When boosters claimed that the "land which grew the sturdy evergreen will grow anything else," few challenged them. As late as 1931, the state director of agriculture for Washington advised prospective settlers to choose land with plenty of big stumps because such land was certain to be fertile. In the promotional literature, the region's biggest drawbacks became assets. The logging debris which made land clearing so tedious and expensive became "fuel for all time . . . at the doors of the home." The heavy rains which leached the limited fertility of thin soils were "just enough to make everything grow to perfection."

How many people were convinced by this propaganda is impossible to determine, but people did settle these lands. Western Washington alone gained 17,000 farms between 1900 and 1920, and 15,000 of them were under 50 acres, the farm size typical of the cutover region. By 1940 there were 36,370 such farms in western Washington. The ethnicity and social origins of these settlers shifted over time. Predominantly Scandinavian between 1900 and 1920, by the 1930s the flood of settlement was made up of drought-stricken migrants from the northern plains and urban workers who often sought little more than a small plot to grow food while they searched for work.

Settled on infertile lands and provided with little capital, these farmers were anachronisms in the commercial economy. Rural virtue didn't feed their families. Even boosters, while arguing that federal aid for settlement could fix matters, conceded that "isolation from markets, lack of roads, lack of neighbors, and lack of school facilities" often made farming logged-off lands a "life of dreary existence . . . without any practical rewards." State and federal surveys only verified such subjective impressions. The movement weakened in the 1920s, but quickened again in the 1930s as the cities disgorged their desperate poor, and environmental and economic disaster on the plains pushed people west. The cutover lands were hardly a haven. A survey in 1939 found that one-third of the farmers had been on relief sometime in the past two years, and among those who had settled in the 1930s, the figure was over 50 percent.

The damage the movement inflicted was not confined to the settlers. Their hilly infertile farms suffered with them. Depending on farming techniques and terrain, they eventually turned their fields into dense patches of bracken, watched them erode down hillsides, or abandoned them to the alder which thrived on the degraded land and replaced the original forests of Douglas fir. Even those rare areas (such as the floodplains of the Willamette) where logged-off farms eventually became productive benefited the original settlers little. This was a post–World War II development that demanded both flood control and a capital investment the original settlers could not muster.

The collapse of the back-to-the-land movement at the end of the Great Depression, while a blessing to both land and people, did nothing to check the commercial forces shaping the Northwest. Concern with the regional landscape now resided largely within the organized conservation movement, which had probably always been more powerful than the back-to-the-land movements. Conservation, like the market, provided a national context in which regional groups operated.

Conservation represented a reaction to the environmental disasters and waste brought by unrestrained entrepreneurial capitalism. The movement itself, however, was neither anticapitalist nor antidevelopment. As Samuel Hays has persuasively demonstrated, conservationists of the late 19th and early 20th centuries shared with corporate executives a strong belief in efficiency and planning as opposed to unrestrained competition. Their major goal was efficient production, with an emphasis on the renewal of resources whenever possible. In practice, conservation bureaucrats and corporate bureaucrats have always worked well together.

National conservationists such as Gifford Pinchot worked through the federal bureaucracy, but from necessity they had to deal not only with national groups (such as large corporations) but also with various regional groups (such as local conservationists interested in specific issues, municipalities, and local economic interests). All of these people put claims upon the public lands; in practice conservation in the Northwest was the result of shifting, complicated alliances between various interest groups and federal (and later state) bureaucrats. For example, irrigators, cattlemen, and members of the Oregon Alpine Club supported early forest reserves in the Cascades; sheep owners and miners opposed them. Federal management did not completely remove market influences from the land; it did, however, narrow the range in which these influences operated.

On federal and state lands the landscape evolved within the framework of national development policy, instead of within the older arena of unrestrained use. At any given time this planned use pleased some groups and antagonized others, depending largely on whom the planning benefited. Quite often demands for states' rights or regional rights in such issues represented no more than the protests of those special interests who had lost out in the bureaucratic planning process, while pious support for conservation measures came from those groups who benefited from the same process. Economic interests remained decisive in shaping the public lands, but now an advantage went to those groups who could at least claim that the resources they used were renewable and that their activities were compatible with other uses. In practice, this meant that "guild organizations of lumbermen and stockmen" came to shape federal policy in much of the Northwest.

This description of early conservation policy in the Northwest seemingly neglects an important segment of the movement—the preservationists like

John Muir, who sought to preserve land for scenery and recreation. Most of these people, however, also fit into the larger framework of planned land use for economic development. For a surprisingly long time, preservationists in Oregon concerned themselves largely with maintaining strips of scenic virgin timber along the highways for the tourists they zealously tried to attract. Scenery was but another engine for development. By such early 20th century standards, a recent governor of California who advocated sparing only enough redwoods to flank the highways might rank as a preservationist.

By the mid-20th century, planned development with an emphasis on renewable resources and a devotion to preserving scenery were all ensconced in northwestern land use. These basic tenets of conservation, however, were not always synonymous with a healthy environment. Nor were the conservationists who promoted them primarily concerned with the regional ecology. Conservation, too, reflected the needs of powerful economic groups within society. In the woods, conservation and economic rationalization produced managed forests, which grew ecologically simpler and simpler. At the extreme they have become genetically selected, chemically fertilized, aerially sprayed tree farms.

Like any radically simplified form of monoculture, these forests can become costly to maintain, and the poisoning of their predators and competitors can quickly shade over into the poisoning of human residents. The recent controversy over dioxins is a single example of this. The benefits of this policy largely accrue to the large timber companies. These forests are efficient, but efficiency is measured largely in terms of corporate profits and government revenues. The recent controversy over log exports shows that not everyone feels such measures reflect the larger economic wellbeing of the region, let alone the environmental health of the forest.

Similarly, local attempts to preserve scenery and wild resources often approached the land as a sort of environmental supermarket, in which one could choose to preserve certain natural populations while destroying others. As hunting and fishing became important to local and regional economies, both sportsmen and those who served their needs recognized that the wild populations they depended on were dangerously near elimination. The result was a flood of concern and regulation: hunting seasons enforced by local and state officials, laws to preserve shellfish beds, laws to ban fish traps and fish wheels, and the stocking of streams and lakes with hatchery-bred fish. Eventually such concerns encompassed attempts to preserve water quality, to protect the spawning beds of salmon, and to perpetuate endangered species. Most of this originally occurred, however, because a dollar value could be put on certain wild game populations.

Sportsmen became an economic interest group who secured members of a state bureaucracy (the fish and game agents) to serve their interests. The victories of sportsmen were victories over competing economic groups such as the canning companies who ran fish traps, the mill companies who polluted the rivers, or the Indian fishermen who competed for the catch. In many instances sportsmen's victories benefited the environment; in others, such as the Indian fishing controversy, conservation was a cynical mask. In virtually all cases, however, the aims of sportsmen remained quite selective. They could at once protect game animals and sponsor "predator days" to eliminate those species who competed with them for game. Until recently, the measures they sought had little sense of ecological balance and often rendered the regional ecology, if anything, less stable. Fish hatcheries, game farms, elaborate regulations, and a new bureaucracy are necessary to maintain the desired wild populations. These animals have often become mere commodities, valued not according to their place in the regional ecology, but rather according to their marketability. Like many state and local parks, they are maintained to attract visitors and further economic development.

Over the last decade many of the historical trends described here have been challenged and sometimes blunted. Ecology and ecosystem have entered common speech; environmentalists in the Northwest and elsewhere have searched for a language and a convincing rationale for creating a stable and ecologically distinctive environment. The results have been mixed. Wilderness areas have been preserved, the tendency to equate economic growth with wasteful consumption and environmental damage has been challenged, and the tendency of capitalism to reduce everything on the planet to a commodity has been questioned. Yet it would be premature to argue that the forces that have shaped the American landscape since settlement are no longer pertinent to its future.

In fact, environmentalism is currently receiving a vigorous counter-challenge. It can be forcefully attacked, in part, because it has too often been content with mystical or semireligious rationales for its efforts or else has taken the stance of a continuing protest against recurrent environmental catastrophes. The land ethic Aldo Leopold spoke of—a coherent vision of the human place in the ecosystem—has yet to be forcefully articulated. The real and vital connections between human societies and the natural world need to be stressed and understood. It is a dimension of human history too often oversimplified or neglected. The Northwest will certainly remain a center of environmental conflict, and it is a conflict to which the historical issues sketched here are pertinent.

Nearly a century and a half of American settlement has produced a regional landscape which has grown increasingly less distinctive and progressively less stable. That Northwesterners have not allowed natural systems to function without interference is neither surprising nor objectionable; all human societies shape their environment. What is more noteworthy is that alterations of the Northwest landscape have often proceeded with reckless disregard for the environmental limits of the area, as if ecosystems operated on a profit motive. Northwesterners have frequently acted as if the natural world exists largely as something to buy and sell and as if the regional ecology were infinitely malleable. The history of the region already shows that environmental destruction has social costs, but as long as these costs are borne by the powerless, this is an easy lesson to ignore.

The results of environmental destabilization and regional homogeneity may not be immediately catastrophic, but the costs are there, and they are incremental. The northwestern landscape, still a recent one, already grows increasingly costly to maintain and increasingly vulnerable to disruption. The costs of maintaining it are largely public; the profits of destroying it remain private. In an era which appears bent on repudiating public cost, this does not bode well for the land. Nor does it bode well for a distinctive regionalism in a section of the country which has repeatedly resorted to its mountains, woods, rivers, and oceans as symbols and sources of its distinctiveness. Northwesterners may still claim to be unique, but they will do so amid a landscape that reflects commercial homogeneity and ecological precariousness—a place where regional concerns and influence over the land have been thoroughly subordinated to national capitalist development. The mountains may then stand like skeletons, dead remains of an older and far more distinctive place.

An Urban View of the Southwest

BRADFORD LUCKINGHAM

In the past four decades scholars have created an important body of knowledge in the field of western American urban history. Articles and books have called attention to the urban dimension of the western experience, and urban dwellers have been given as much credit for developing the American West as other pioneers and promoters.

From the beginning, western cities served as "spearheads of the American frontier." Urban developers worked to reproduce familiar city patterns in the new country, and by 1830 Pittsburgh, Cincinnati, Louisville, and St. Louis represented the paramount influence in the Ohio Valley. A similar process occurred in the Great Lakes area. The builders of Cleveland, Detroit, Chicago, and Milwaukee, like earlier urban pioneers and promoters, were a conspicuous part of the westward movement. By 1870 the lake cities exhibited the same dominant influence over their region that older urban centers exerted over their respective hinterlands, and this rapid city growth in the West was viewed as fundamental to the development of the expanding nation.

In Texas, too, patterns of urbanization were established during the middle years of the nineteenth century. During the period from 1836 to 1865, Houston, Galveston, Austin, and San Antonio came of age as major centers of cultural, social, economic, and political influence in the state. Texans looked to the cities not only for culture but for vital services. As one urban historian has put it, "They read urban newspapers, sought out urban society, borrowed money, traded raw materials and purchased goods from urban merchants."

Even the Rocky Mountain mining camps and the Kansas cattle towns

Copyright by Western History Association. Reprinted by permission. The article first appeared as "The American Southwest: An Urban View" by Bradford Luckingham. *Western Historical Quarterly*, 15 (July 1984), 261–280.

served as agents of urban civilization, despite the myth of the "Wild West" popularized in the media. The rough and violent times were by comparison a relatively short interval in the lifespan of a typical mining camp or cattle town. Illustrating the urban impulse on the frontier, the maturing communities, led by businessmen and editors, quickly established urban institutions and sought to attain the coveted "prize of city status."

The quest for urban status was also evident in the frontier regions of the Far West. As Earl Pomeroy has observed, "From the time of the first American settlements, the Pacific slope was significantly urban. Even those Far Westerners who did not live in cities looked to them to an unusual degree; even in states and areas where population was sparse, society was remarkably urbanized." San Francisco, Los Angeles, Salt Lake City, Portland, Seattle, and other leading cities of the region played a crucial role in the development of the Far West, as had their counterparts in the East and Midwest. Indeed, this area did not evolve from rural beginnings to city endings but saw its cities develop at the same time as did its ranches, farms, and mines.

According to observers, a significant urban consciousness or urban pride existed in the West by 1890, and by that year, in virtually every aspect of life, as John W. Reps has noted, urban residents and institutions "dominated western culture and civilization." The lure of the city in the region continued into the twentieth century, and as it evolved, the West, led by its urban centers, became more prominent in the life of the nation. During the Great Depression and World War II, the federal government became increasingly involved in the growth of the Far West, and that relationship, along with new as well as traditional technological and social factors, gave impetus to the unprecedented economic boom and population explosion of the 1950s. During that decade and beyond, as Gerald D. Nash has detailed, the metropolitan Far West, notably in California, led the way in establishing the region as "a pacesetter for the nation."

That the cities led the way in making the Far West "a pacesetter for the nation" in the post–World War II years emphasized the persistent role of urban centers in the westward movement. Some 25 million people moved across the Mississippi River from 1945 to 1965, and the vast majority of them settled in the urban West. By 1965 more than two-thirds of the inhabitants of the American West were urban dwellers. In 1967 Wallace Stegner, new editor of *The American West*, urged contributors to be more aware of the urban dimension. As he put it, "The American West, whatever its frontier past, is in the twentieth century increasingly urban. The western American is, by the millions, a city dweller, even if he wears boots and a Stetson and grows whiskers for Frontier Days. Seven out of eight readers of this magazine are city dwellers." Moreover, according to Carl Abbott, the "level of urbanization" in the American West surpassed that of the rest of the country by 1880. During the next sixty years, the region maintained a slight edge, but following World War II it rapidly extended its lead. By 1980, 83 percent of the population of the American West lived in urban areas compared to 73 percent for the country as a whole. "To a greater

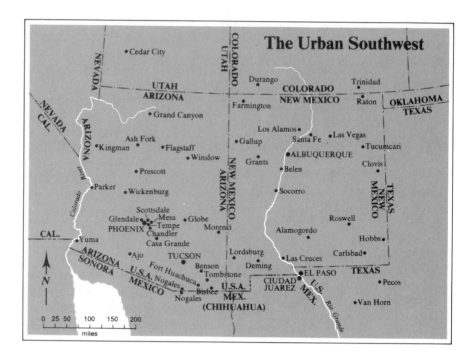

The Urban Southwest

extent than many of us realize," Abbott has declared, "the history of the West is the history of its cities."

A pattern of urban dominance may also be seen in the history of the Southwest—a region defined as including Arizona, New Mexico, and the western promontory of Texas. El Paso, Albuquerque, Tucson, and Phoenix have been the most important urban centers in the Southwest since the nineteenth century, and they are among the fastest growing cities in the nation today. In fact, since the beginnings of Spanish settlement in the seventeenth century, what Walter Prescott Webb called an "oasis civilization" existed in the Southwest. While the English established towns on the East Coast and in the interior, Spanish pioneers were creating Santa Fe (1610), Paso del Norte (1659), Albuquerque (1706), and Tucson (1776) on the northern frontiers of New Spain. These oasis towns served not only as centers of life in the region but also as outposts of civilization and spearheads of desert development. Urban growth accompanied or preceded the opening of the surrounding country, and the towns acted as links between vast, unpopulated areas and the outside world.

In 1821 Mexico won its independence from Spain, and more Anglos (white people of non-Hispanic descent) began to enter the towns to do business. In 1846 war broke out between the United States and Mexico, and following that conflict Anglos increasingly found their way to the oases—now the urban centers of the American Southwest. They joined with local Hispanics in the further development of El Paso, Albuquerque, and Tucson;

in 1867 Anglo pioneers created Phoenix. By 1880 promoters of all four of these river communities were involved in the coming of the railroads, which were the key to their emergence as the four principal cities of the Southwest.

The importance of the coming of the railroads to the Southwest cannot be overestimated. As on other frontiers, railroads encouraged urbanization. Leaders in the four towns, aware of the close relationship between transportation innovations and urban growth, promoted the presence of railroads. They knew that the "natural wealth" of the area could never attain "proper development" until a railroad system evolved. Railroad routes, an Albuquerque editor declared in 1872, would place developers "in communication with the outside world and offer inducements to population and capital."

Albuquerque leaders boosted their town and "cooperated" with company officials in order to attract the main line of the Atchison, Topeka and Santa Fe Railroad, and when it bypassed the towns of Santa Fe and Bernalillo and went to Albuquerque, the future of that town as "the metropolis of New Mexico" was assured. When the town celebrated the arrival of the railroad on April 22, 1880, William C. Hazeldine said it all when he declared it to be "the day of all days in Albuquerque, a day long expected and anxiously looked forward to by the friends of progress and advancement."

Hazeldine's declaration reflected the sentiment of leaders of all four of the communities regarding the significance of proper railroad connections. "We have sprung into a city," asserted Judge Allan Blacker when the Southern Pacific first arrived in El Paso on May 26, 1881. The railroads "will bring within our grasp great probabilities and grand possibilities." By late 1880 not one, but four, railroads were constructing tracks toward the Texas border town from four different directions, and this development promised to make it the future railroad hub of the Southwest.

When the railroads arrived in the four towns in the 1880s, they all gained considerably in population. Railroad contact with the outside world, including transcontinental routes operated by the Southern Pacific and the Atchison, Topeka and Santa Fe railroads, provided links to the national economy and helped the towns to expand as trade and distribution centers for productive hinterlands. Their emergence as vital hubs facilitated the economic exploitation of the Southwest, and they played a large role in civilizing the region. They became the centers of business districts, military posts, and universities. Stores and factories, schools and churches, banks and hotels, hospitals and courthouses, theaters and saloons, all served the people of the four cities and their surrounding areas.

As in other western towns, the four desert centers experienced the "business of sin" during their "Wild West" days, but by the turn of the century all four cities had creditably survived their youth and had achieved recognition as the centers of civility in the region. All four served as county seats, and Phoenix was the capital of Arizona Territory. Santa Fe had managed to retain the capital of New Mexico Territory, but in every other respect it lost out to Albuquerque, which by 1900 exceeded Santa Fe in population. Promoters worked diligently to develop the cities into desirable places for those looking for amenities as well as opportunities. The amenities included the climate, and the sun culture was boosted endlessly. Each of the towns became havens for health seekers as well as prime locations for tourist resorts; they became famous for their hospitals as well as their hotels.

The towns, in fact, stand as excellent examples of the impact of amenities on regional urban growth. Following the arrival of the railroad in the Southwest, doctors around the country started sending patients to the four oases for the winter. "The climate of El Paso is the finest in the Union," declared local boosters, "and the dry refined air of the region is a luxury to breathe." At the same time, Albuquerque promoters called their town "an ideal spot for the health seeker." In Tucson and Phoenix, observers noted the benefits of "perpetual sunshine." Many of those who came to the desert centers for their health did recover sufficiently to lead productive lives, and some made outstanding contributions to the development of the region. Affluent, healthy tourists also were given every encouragement to visit the cities, and they were provided with the services of several large, modern hotels equipped to meet their needs. For example, the Santa Rita Hotel in Tucson, the Hotel Adams in Phoenix, the Alvarado Hotel in Albuquerque, and the Hotel Paso del Norte in El Paso all enjoyed reputations as centers of luxury in the Southwest.

Opportunities in the Southwest included mining, farming, and ranching, but many people came to the region to share in the progress of growing communities. As a newcomer to El Paso in the 1880s declared, "I wanted to be in the coming metropolis; I was anxious to grow up with the frontier town." Many of these success seekers became effective leaders and boosters of the desert hubs. As members of the local business and civic elite who were willing to combine private interests with community interests, they often directed, with growth and development in mind, the economic, political, and cultural lives of their respective cities.

Among the outstanding leaders of the Phoenix elite, for example, was Dwight Heard. A successful businessman in Chicago, Heard moved to Phoenix in 1897 hoping the climate would help him recover his health. Heard and his wife Maie were both impressed with the Arizona capital, and he along with some of his friends in Chicago began investing in the economic growth of the city and the Salt River Valley, while Maie became involved in raising the cultural tone of the city. Heard opened his home, the finest in Phoenix, to potential investors from the East and Midwest and did everything he could to encourage their interest in the Phoenix area. His investment company, specializing in real estate, became a leading force in the development of the city and the valley. His newspaper, the *Arizona Republican*, exerted a strong influence on politics and other aspects of life in Phoenix and the rest of the state. Heard was an active civic promoter and an ardent booster; he and his wife were instrumental in securing many benefits for the city, including the Heard Museum. When Dwight Heard died in 1929, he was eulogized as "Arizona's greatest citizen."

While visionary leaders in the Southwest worked hard to make their cities transportation hubs, trade and distribution centers, health meccas, tourist attractions, gateways to Mexico, and the site of government agencies, military installations, and industrial firms, they also promoted the resource development of the hinterlands. They helped establish transportation and communication networks throughout the region that brought the countryside and the population centers into closer contact. The cities served as bases for the occupation of the territory, and as both the rural and urban sectors grew, they made demands on each other. By providing local markets and national and international transportation outlets, the desert communities stimulated farming, mining, and livestock-raising pursuits in the region. The cities as points of attachment operated as economic conduits between the Southwest and the outside world, as collectors of exports from the surrounding area, and as distributors of imports from around and beyond the nation. Urban promoters often acted as middlemen and mediators between the Southwest communities and the world beyond. Cotton, copper, cattle, and other regional interests were encouraged to look to the four hubs of the Southwest for vital services and facilities. A rural-urban interdependence developed, and cooperation was usually valued more than conflict. For the most part, mutual interest in growth and prosperity helped the cities and their surrounding areas to maintain a satisfactory association.

Local leaders often led the way in the struggle to gain advantages useful to regional as well as urban development. For example, following a severe drought in the late 1890s, Phoenix leaders and central Arizona farming interests decided that a water storage system was the answer to the area's problem. Joining together, they formed the Salt River Valley Water Users' Association, and that organization, taking advantage of the National Reclamation Act of 1902, supported the federal government in the construction of nearby Roosevelt Dam, completed in 1911. This and similar endeavors brought vital stability to the water supply, allowed irrigation control, assured agricultural growth in the valley, and as it prospered, so did Phoenix. The area became the leading agricultural producer in the Southwest. Urban promoters were behind other water conservation projects in the region as well; El Paso promoters, for instance, were instrumental in securing federal government support for the construction of Elephant Butte Dam on the Rio Grande River in 1916.

The success of the reclamation projects illustrated the importance of water to the development of the urban Southwest. Since the beginning, the oases towns had depended on adjacent river flows and deep underground wells for local sustenance, but the rivers were unreliable, and underground sources were limited. The "water management" systems created by Roosevelt and Elephant Butte Dams benefited the Phoenix and El Paso areas the most. Albuquerque suffered from floods caused by the erratic behavior of the uncontrolled Rio Grande River north of Elephant Butte Dam, and Tucson reaped the consequences of possessing the most limited water supply of the four major cities in the region.

The reclamation projects also demonstrated the vital contribution of the federal government to the growth of the urban Southwest. In each case, federal money and federal expertise proved indispensable in seeing the projects through to completion, and once in place they delivered a considerable advantage to the oases involved. But it took more than the cooperation of Washington to realize the successful urbanization of the desert. As on other frontiers, the progress of the towns often depended on the quality of the people who lived in and promoted them. In Phoenix and El Paso, local leaders spent considerable time both at home and in Washington lobbying in behalf of their goals. Urban developers realized "you cannot dream your town into a city; you must build and boost it into one." This attitude could make the difference between urban success and failure. To neglect to boost growth and development for the city and the surrounding area was to risk decline and defeat in the urban sweepstakes.

While Albuquerque and Tucson lagged behind El Paso and Phoenix as centers of business and agricultural life, they competed as climate and cultural centers. Health seekers and tourists continued to flock to the sunshine cities, while physical facilities and social amenities multiplied. New modes of transportation, including the automobile and the airplane, made it easier to travel to the desert centers, "where winter never comes." Some boosters were especially proud of local educational institutions. Because of the University of Arizona, for example, the *Arizona Star* called Tucson the "Athens of Arizona." The four oases, in addition to providing economic functions, served as transmitters of civilization, and urban promoters benefited the region by instituting social and cultural services in their respective cities. They encouraged and supported schools, colleges, churches, libraries, museums, theaters, and other agents of civilization. Exhibiting an urban consciousness, they helped to refine the Southwest by making the cities the social and cultural enrichment centers of the region.

The urban centers also influenced the social structure of the region. As the oases developed, they became increasingly attractive to Anglo elements, and as they assumed power in the regional centers of the Southwest, they utilized Mexicans as an underclass to help them realize their goals, including economic growth. Having achieved a dominant position in each community, the Anglos acquired more wealth, influence, and prestige, and from these positions of strength, dictated the terms of the ethnic arrangement, which invariably found the majority of the Mexicans and Mexican Americans living on the "wrong side of the tracks." For the majority of Hispanics as well as the less numerous blacks and Indians, upward mobility proved elusive and poverty remained a problem.

By the 1920s, developers had promoted into adoption a host of characteristics common to cities elsewhere, from street and park development to health, fire, and police protection. In this respect, the cities of the Southwest were not unique; they were more imitative than innovative, and they reflected the national culture. As on other urban frontiers, the maturing cities of the desert region were in many ways similar to those throughout the rest of the nation.

In some instances, however, urban leaders in the Southwest had secured advantages especially useful to desert development, such as water storage projects, and at times regional urbanites set the pace for their counterparts elsewhere in the country. For example, they were quick to accept the motor vehicle as a primary mode of transportation. In each of the centers the use of the auto and the bus sent streetcar systems into a decline from which they never recovered. Reliance on the automobile, the bus, and the truck contributed to residential and business dispersal, and as a result, the concept of decentralization gained impetus in the 1920s.

The motor age transformed the urban Southwest as much as the railroads had in the nineteenth century. Suburbs were seen as extensions of the urban cores, and despite their costs in extended services, the "wide open spaces" seemed to offer an escape from the problems of high-density city life. The automobile era enabled the desert cities and suburbs to expand in a low-density pattern of settlement, and this variety of spatial growth afforded a high degree of freedom and a pleasant atmosphere in which to live. The automobile was among the amenities that provided the "good life" promoted by boosters of the four oases.

Also in the 1920s each of the historic transportation crossroads embraced the airplane and its potential, and thus they became regional aviation centers by the end of the decade. In 1930, as in 1900, the four cities continued to serve as the principal junction points in the transportation structure of the Southwest, acting as vital links connecting the cities, not only with each other but also with national and international rail, highway, and air service networks. With the increasing importance of these cities as transportation hubs over the years, they became more dominant over their surrounding areas and more attractive to potential residents and business investors.

By 1930 these four cities, led by El Paso—called by some observers the "Chicago of the Southwest" because of its superior railroad and industrial facilities, including the largest copper smelter in the world—were well established as the leading urban centers in the region. Phoenix retained its position as the second largest city in the Southwest, enabling its leaders to laud it as "truly the capital of Arizona, the hub of new developments. As Phoenix goes, so goes Arizona." Tucson, the "second city of Arizona" since being surpassed by Phoenix in the 1920 census, edged out for third place in the regional urban hierarchy Albuquerque, which was "the metropolis of New Mexico" since it had surpassed Santa Fe in population in the 1900 census. The four cities had spearheaded the growth of civilization in the region, and they had exerted an important influence on the development of west Texas, Arizona, and New Mexico. (See Table 1.)

Each of the four cities suffered less from the Great Depression than many of their counterparts elsewhere, and except for El Paso, a border city that witnessed a large exodus of Mexicans, they all increased their populations in the 1930s. As in the past, people from not only outside the region but from within it migrated to the cities of the Southwest in search of a future. The urban centers seemed to offer more help to individuals, if not always in jobs, at least in services. New Deal programs especially provided welcome relief and gave impetus to recovery. During the decade

Table 1 Population Growth by Decades

CITY	1880	1890	1900	1910	1920	1930
El Paso	736	10,338	15,906	32,279	77,560	102,421
Phoenix	1,708	3,152	5,544	11,134	29,053	48,118
Tucson	7,007	5,150	7,531	13,193	20,292	32,506
Albuquerque	2,315	3,785	6,238	11,020	15,157	26,570

Source: U.S. Census of Population, 1880–1930.

a strong relationship developed between the federal government and the urban Southwest as the people of the cities turned to Washington for aid and received it.

After 1940 all four cities continued to benefit greatly from close relations with the nation's capital as the federal government poured large sums of money into the communities, helping to make them major military and high-technology centers. During World War II each of them became the home of important military bases and defense plants. Local organizations such as chambers of commerce worked closely with regional representatives in Washington to secure these valuable assets. Inducements, including building sites, materialized, as every form of cooperation was extended. Fine flying weather and the government's program to locate military bases and defense plants inland to protect them from possible air attacks also helped. As in the past, federal funds and projects stimulated the local economy, and a significant amount of growth and development in the region was due to government or public investment; in short, the crucial role played by "Uncle Sam" in creating the boom in the urban Southwest during and after World War II can hardly be overestimated.

During the cold war, military installations in the urban Southwest continued to serve as part of the national defense effort, and former war plants looked not only to the military but to civilian markets as well. A multiplier effect took hold, and as more industries moved to the urban centers of the region, they attracted others. Predominant were light and clean industries, especially electronics firms, and they flourished in the low-humidity climate so necessary to their success. Electronics plants used little water, and they produced high-value, low-weight products that could be easily shipped overland. The relatively isolated location of the cities was no problem in electronics production because, as one observer declared, "A truckload is worth a million dollars." The region's modern transportation network included everything from trucking lines and major highways to transcontinental railroads and international airlines.

It was important to tourist businesses in the "clean cities" of the Southwest that pollution-free industries settle in the region. City developers encouraged smokeless plants in order to preserve "the sunshine and pure atmosphere" of the oases. In Phoenix, for example, the sun shone 85 percent of the time, a statistic that pleased manufacturers. Business could meet production schedules without being interrupted by adverse weather.

Amenities, including the climate, continued to influence migration to the desert centers. The mass production of air conditioners in the 1950s and the consequent "age of refrigeration" not only attracted manufacturers and brought an extended tourist season to the cities but also made them more comfortable for those permanent residents unable to leave for the coast or the mountains during the hot summer months. Executives and workers also appreciated the nearby mountains and man-made lakes and the active, but casual, year-round life-style that emphasized informal outdoor leisure living. A Douglas Aircraft official in Tucson in the early 1950s revealed that "we came here for the flying conditions and the airport facilities but we've been pleasantly surprised by other advantages. The labor supply, for instance. We can recruit engineers, electronics people, machinists— anything we need. Workers like it here and don't want to move away." Suitable conditions for both work and play seemed to meet in the urban Southwest, and the opportunities and the amenities appealed to many technical and professional people and their families.

During the 1950s the air-conditioned regional hubs offered unprecedented opportunities and amenities, and led by Phoenix, the largest city in the Southwest by 1960, they were making strides toward metropolis status. In Phoenix, manufacturing had become the city's principal source of income by 1955. Between 1948 and 1960 nearly three hundred manufacturing enterprises opened their doors as manufacturing employment in the metropolitan area tripled. The annual income from manufacturing rose from under $5 million in 1940 to over $435 million in 1963. As a result, Phoenix achieved economic diversification, and the Valley of the Sun emerged as the metropolitan center of commerce and industry in the Southwest.

A major reason the Arizona capital moved ahead of the Texas city in the 1950s was the attitude and ambition of its leaders. Southwest urban promoters frequently noted the aggressive tactics of Phoenicians. As one El Pasoan declared, in the Arizona capital "industrial scouts are met at the plane, entertained, offered free land, tax deals, and an electorate willing to approve millions in business-backed bond issues." By comparison, he lamented, "El Paso does nothing," and as a result it "has lost its spot as the number-one city in the Southwest." And, he concluded, "Unless we start hustling after new industry, we're going to wind up in serious trouble."

Phoenix moved to the top of the urban hierarchy in the Southwest in the 1950s and remained there during the next two decades, with manufacturing holding its lead as the most dynamic growth sector. By the end of 1977, the Arizona capital had 74.4 percent of the total manufacturing employment in the state, and the annual income from manufacturing in the Phoenix area had increased to $2.5 billion, up from $4.8 million in 1940. Electronics and aerospace plants dominated the industrial landscape in the Valley of the Sun, and in 1980 the area ranked third in the nation behind metropolitan San Francisco and metropolitan Boston as a high-technology center. Other cities in the Southwest could not keep up with the promoters of the Arizona metropolis. As a bank president in El Paso put it in December 1978, "I hate to express it publicly, but it's true our leadership has been sort of mediocre. We didn't have the influx of well-educated people in the industrial and commercial world. Phoenix did. Some of these kinds of people are coming here now." At the same time, another El Paso businessman remarked that "we haven't always done a selling job of what we've got. Phoenix has done a better job."

In the 1970s the Texas city broadened its outlook. Early in the decade, the newly formed El Paso Development Corporation announced that "the western tip of Texas has always depended upon copper, cotton, cattle, and climate and more recently on the clothing industry as the basis of livelihood for the people living here." The city's "phenomenal growth during the past three decades has been reflected by a similar growth in the five C's as well as a steady expansion at Ft. Bliss." However, for the city to reach its true potential, it "must seek and acquire new industry." By the late 1970s, with the support of public officials and private interests on both sides of the border, major electronics firms such as RCA, General Electric, Sylvania, and Westinghouse had located in El Paso and Juarez. At the same time, Tucson and Albuquerque also attracted industry, including high-technology firms the caliber of IBM, Gates-Learjet, National Semiconductor, and Digital Equipment.

As the population rose, the urban centers not only continued to serve more tourists as well as their increasing resident populations but also remained the trading and distribution hubs for vast regions of towns, farms, ranches, and mines. They functioned as the service stations of the Southwest. Employment increases within the services and trade sectors accounted for a sizable percentage of the total increase in employment registered in the thirty years before 1980. In fact, by that year the services sector provided the most jobs in each of the metropolitan areas, and the importance of that sector to the regional economy was clear.

The growth of government programs and institutions, ranging from military bases to state universities, provided more jobs and also contributed to the population explosion and economic boom. Fort Bliss in El Paso became known as the air defense center of the world, and Kirtland Air Force Base in Albuquerque served as one of the major national defense installations in the Southwest. Others were Davis-Monthan Air Force Base in Tucson and Luke Air Force Base in Phoenix. Phoenix remained the capital of Arizona, and each of the cities continued to function as centers of government employment and government activity at all levels. Public institutions of higher learning in each of the urban areas served not only as economic generators but also as cultural and intellectual leaders in the Southwest. They offered excellent undergraduate and graduate programs and provided increasing instruction in business and engineering to satisfy the demands of the new high-technology society they and the cities of the region wished to represent. Arizona State University in Tempe (part of the Phoenix metropolitan complex) recorded 39,431 students in 1980, up from 11,128 in 1960. Record-breaking enrollments also occurred at the University of Arizona at Tucson, the University of New Mexico in Albuquerque, and the University of Texas at El Paso.

The growth of the universities reflected the magnitude of the great migration to the Southwest since World War II. The economy of the regional hubs, based largely on government spending, remained strong. Opportunities and amenities continued to increase in the Southwest urban centers, while cities elsewhere became increasingly less inviting. To continue to attract high-technology companies to the region, urban leaders promoted support for local institutions of higher learning. As each of the metropolitan hubs joined the competition to become another "Silicon Valley" of the West, pressure mounted to give massive amounts of dollars to local universities, especially their business and engineering schools. For example, an Arizona State University official recently noted that "a $38 million Engineering Excellence Program, designed to establish ASU as a major research center nationally, is on target." Prompted by a "burgeoning growth of high-tech industries," the "goal is to propel ASU into the ranks of the foremost engineering programs in the United States." The "school will be working closely with industry to turn the Valley of the Sun into a 'silicon oasis.'" The high-tech-oriented urban universities of the Southwest, with their new research facilities, boosters declared, were needed not only to encourage more private and public investment in the urban areas but also to help make the region a vital part of the new computer world. Quality institutions were necessary to educate the population to meet the scientific and social demands of business and society in the new Southwest.

Agriculture, despite urban encroachment, also continued to be important to the welfare of the metropolitan Southwest, but it is declining because of the heavy demands it makes on water supplies. For example, in Arizona in 1980, agriculture was using 89 percent of the water consumed, as opposed to 7 percent being used by the cities and 4 percent being utilized by industry. In 1979 in the Tucson area, farmers were using 75 percent of the water, although they accounted for only 2 percent of the work force. The city of Tucson, being totally dependent on groundwater, had already purchased and retired from cultivation some 11,000 acres of irrigated agricultural land in order to meet increasing urban needs. The fate of farming, therefore, in the Tucson area may well be doomed to extinction if metropolitan area growth continues to prevail.

Experts have declared that water shortages will not stem from the population influx because more of the water supply can be diverted from agricultural to nonagricultural users. Moreover, the conservation of water has become a planning priority on both the state and municipal levels. For example, the 1980 Groundwater Management Act in Arizona, which regulates the use of water by irrigators and requires better water management in the urban centers, will force groundwater conservation in the metropolitan areas, and that action could very well serve as a model for the region. Voluntary water conservation programs also have been encouraged in the cities, with Tucson leading the way. Higher water-use rate structures and public education programs implemented in the cities in recent years have resulted in voluntary reductions in water consumption. The goal is to cut waste by making water conservation a way of life in the desert cities. In addition, local leaders have continued to work with representatives and officials in Washington to secure support for water projects in the Southwest that will supply more of that precious commodity to the urban centers; for example, the completion of the federally funded Central Arizona Project by the late 1980s, which will bring Colorado River water to Phoenix and Tucson, is being vigorously promoted by a variety of metropolitan interests. As in the past, boosters aware that serious water problems could lead to limited growth have called for action.

Urban leadership has exerted a strong influence over the entire region. In practically every field of endeavor, urban leaders have stood out. An *Arizona Republic* survey in December 1981 declared that the twenty most powerful people in the state of Arizona were Anglos from Phoenix. Anglos were in control of each of the oases as well as the region. The *Albuquerque Journal* in February 1980 noted in a local power study that out of fifty-five "wielders of clout" in the city, only five were Hispanic. In December 1978 the *El Paso Times* reported that not a single Hispanic was among the twenty-five most influential men in the economic life of the city. At the same time, more members of minority groups, many of them business and professional people, moved into the middle class. The positive effect of such dynamic forces as the G.I. Bill, the civil rights movement, and the growth of the economy made it possible for individual Hispanics to benefit from new educational and employment opportunities, but progress for Hispanics as a group (the largest minority group in the urban Southwest) proved to be slow. In El Paso, for example, as Oscar J. Martinez put it in 1980, Hispanics "as a community have traveled only a short distance in their quest to achieve parity with the Anglo population. Economically and socially, a gulf still separates the two groups."

Meanwhile, newcomers of all ages from within and without the region continued to flock to the air-conditioned capitals of the Southwest where opportunities and amenities seemed to blend so well. Most of the newcomers were young, the median age of the population being below the national average. In Tucson in 1980, the average age was 28.2; in Albuquerque it was 24.7. For many newcomers, it was a chance to work America's newest boom frontier. As one observer put it regarding Phoenix, "The mood is here; the word is out; this is the place. The city is going somewhere, and it is attracting more than an average share of people who want to go somewhere with it." As a result of this dynamic appeal, the four oases experienced phenomenal growth, and Phoenix set the pace. By 1980 it ranked as the ninth largest city in the nation, up from twentieth in 1970. (See Table 2.)

The four major metropolitan areas of the Southwest were dominated by the central cities. In 1980, 78 percent of the population of El Paso County lived in El Paso, while 73 percent of the people of Bernalillo County lived in Albuquerque. In Arizona, 52 percent of Maricopa County's population resided in Phoenix, while 65 percent of the population in Pima County made

Table 2   Population Growth by Decades

CITY	1940	1950	1960	1970	1980
Phoenix	65,414	106,818	439,170	584,303	789,704
El Paso	96,810	130,485	276,687	322,261	425,259
Tucson	35,752	45,454	212,892	262,933	330,537
Albuquerque	35,449	95,815	201,189	244,501	331,767

Source: U.S. Census of Population, 1940–1980.

Tucson their home. Only in Maricopa County did sizable incorporated centers develop outside the central city. As Phoenix experienced more growth following World War II, nearby settlements, including Tempe, Scottsdale, and Mesa to the east and Glendale to the west, became larger satellites of Phoenix. Although they were small communities in 1940, they thrived along with Phoenix during the next forty years, and as a result, there emerged one vast, auto-connected metropolitan complex, with the capital city in the middle. (See Table 3.)

As time passed, the metropolitan hubs of the Southwest came to dominate the region more than ever. In 1980 Phoenix was the fastest growing among the top thirty metropolitan areas in the nation, and by that year the four urban complexes accounted for 67 percent of the regional population. An oasis civilization had prevailed in the Southwest; it was part of that larger "oasis civilization" in the American West, first noted by Walter Prescott Webb in 1957 and later developed by Gerald D. Nash in 1973, that has dominated much of the history of the trans-Mississippi country since the nineteenth century. The Southwest seemed less urban than other parts of the nation because of the vast stretches of land that remained unoccupied by people between the four oases, but it was an urban region, too, with urban dwellers comprising almost two-thirds of its inhabitants. The popularity of the cities was clear; in Arizona, for instance, nearly 80 percent of the entire state's population lived in metropolitan Phoenix and Tucson by 1980. The region contained four of the leading metropolitan centers in the burgeoning Sun Belt—a "new" American section that lay south of the 37th parallel

Table 3   Population of Phoenix and Neighboring Communities

CITY	1940	1950	1960	1970	1980
Phoenix	65,414	106,818	439,170	584,303	789,704
Mesa	7,224	16,670	33,772	63,049	152,453
Tempe	2,906	7,684	24,897	63,550	106,742
Glendale	4,855	8,179	15,696	36,228	97,172
Scottsdale	1,000	2,032	10,026	67,823	88,412
Chandler	1,239	3,799	9,531	13,763	29,673

Source: U.S. Census of Population, 1940–1980.

**Table 4   Population of the Four Southwest Standard
Metropolitan Statistical Areas**

CITY	1940	1950	1960	1970	1980
Phoenix	186,193	331,770	663,510	971,225	1,509,052
(Maricopa County)					
Tucson	72,838	141,216	265,660	351,667	531,443
(Pima County)					
El Paso	131,067	194,968	314,070	359,291	479,899
(El Paso County)					
Albuquerque	69,391	145,673	276,400	333,266	454,499
(Bernalillo County with parts of Sandoval County added in 1960, 1970, 1980)					

Source: U.S. Census of Population, 1940–1980.

and extended across the country from North Carolina to southern California. Since World War II, the ongoing decline of the old Snow Belt urban centers in the Northeast and Midwest had caused a shift in demographic and economic power toward the rising urban centers of the Sun Belt in the South, Southwest, and in southern California.

Currently, the four hubs are part of the "new" urban America, and it is part of the "big change" in the nation. In 1980 the census for the first time in American history indicated that the West and the South had more people than the North and the East. Among the fastest-growing states were those located in the Sun Belt Southwest. The census of 1980 also uncovered a massive shift in economic activity that had encouraged the population change. The Sun Belt Southwest gained new jobs as well as new people, while the Snow Belt lost both jobs and people. The shift appears to be irreversible, and experts have predicted that the four regional metropolitan complexes will be among the top ten employment centers in the country during the remainder of the century. The lure of the cities cannot be denied. Opportunities and amenities, despite the problems of growth, will continue to draw people to them as long as the new restructuring of America persists. The Phoenix metropolitan area, for example, contained a population of 1.5 million in 1980; demographers expect it to exceed 2.3 million by 1990. (See Table 4.)

From the beginning, the urban dimension has been a major factor in the history of the American Southwest. Without an appreciation of its crucial role in the growth and development of the region, the story is incomplete. The four metropolitan areas represent the centers of life in a land of wide open spaces. Although these areas are the focal points of an oasis civilization, in the past many historians either dismissed their role in the region entirely or accorded it an insignificant place. Until recently, there were no biographies of any of the cities, nor were there any comparative studies; but the urban Southwest can no longer be ignored or slighted. The urban pioneers of the Southwest deserve as much credit for developing the region as the trappers, miners, farmers, ranchers, and cowboys most often dwelled upon by historians. Living in the modern Southwest—an urban region—and searching for a "usable past," some scholars have found more meaning in an urban Southwest with an urban past; to them the urban dimension of the past deserves at least as much attention as other vital elements. From their perspective, it is clearly time to redress the imbalance in southwestern historiography. As it has for other regions, an urban view should provide a fuller understanding of the history of the American Southwest.

The Collapse of Western Metal Mining

MICHAEL MALONE

With what seems an incredible abruptness, the last five years have witnessed the utter devastation of the West's oldest industry, metal mining. True, this notoriously unstable and cyclical industry has fallen before, as in the 1890s or the 1930s, but this time there seems no possibility that metal mining can recover to anything like its former status in the region. When one considers how important mining has been to the evolution of the western economy, and to the region's social and political order, it seems appropriate to point out what has happened and attempt to place it in historical perspective.

First, the dimensions of the crisis: they are incredible. During the 1970s, energy conglomerates began buying many of the old western metal mining firms—ARCO acquired Anaconda, Sohio purchased Kennecott, Pennzoil bought the Duval Corporation, and so forth. They seemed like good investments, and the supercorporations promised to give them badly needed transfusions of capital. But alas, for reasons to which we shall return, the investments proved to be bad; and in the 1980s came the great unloading. The coming of the energy conglomerates proved to be one of the worst things to have ever happened to western mining.

Not long after ARCO acquired Anaconda in 1977, it began closing down that exploitative old firm's antique facilities in western Montana; and in 1983 came the final closures, ending a century of corporate dominance over this most "colonial" of western states. Meanwhile, in the neighboring "panhandle" of north Idaho, Gulf Resources and Chemical Company shut down its venerable old Bunker Hill silver-lead acquisition in the Coeur d'Alene district which for many years had been America's greatest silver producer. At historic Leadville, Colorado, Amax closed its large molybdenum mine in 1981, and most of its 3,000 workers lost their jobs.

In March 1985 came the not unexpected news that Kennecott Copper, which Sohio had recently purchased, would close its Utah Copper Division, shutting down the landmark Bingham Canyon open pit and its reduction works and cashiering the remaining 2,200 jobs. Sohio had lost nearly $483 million on its ill-starred Kennecott acquisition between 1981 and 1984.

Michael Malone, "The Collapse of Western Metal Mining: An Historical Epitaph," © 1986 by the Pacific Coast Branch, American Historical Association. Reprinted from *Pacific Historical Review*, Vol. 55 (August 1986), 455–464, by permission.

Pennzoil, in the meantime, announced that its Duval mining property was for sale. Those well established independent metal mining firms who had avoided the clutches of the conglomerates did little better. ASARCO, formerly American Smelting & Refining, shut down its giant Tacoma copper smelter in early 1985, cut back production at others, and slashed the salaries of its employees. Phelps Dodge, which is highly vulnerable as the most copper-reliant of the western mining companies, closed its Ajo, Arizona, smelter in 1985, amidst a wave of bitter strikes. Grimly, industry analysts predicted that one more recession would spell the end of this long-time colossus of the Southwest. With little seeming exaggeration, *Business Week* heralded "The Death of Mining" at the end of 1984, and in April 1985, the *Washington Post* proclaimed that "The Sun Is Setting in the West on the U.S. Copper Industry."

Business Week editors and other industry analysts have commented insightfully upon the causes of mining's decline, but any effort to view this issue in its full social and political—as well as economic—context requires that we place it also in historic perspective. The California gold rushes of 1849–1852 opened the Far West; then, during the period 1858–1876, the gold frontier rebounded into the interior, laying the foundations of the states of Nevada, Colorado, Idaho, Montana, South Dakota, and Arizona. Following the depression of the mid-1870s, industrial silver and gold mining boomed the Rocky Mountain and Great Basin regions. Clusters of colorful silver and gold towns, like Leadville and Cripple Creek, emerged in the high Colorado Rockies and in neighboring Utah. The great Homestake gold mine rose to become the national leader in South Dakota, and the colossal Bunker Hill and Sullivan mines led in making the Idaho Coeur d'Alene the much-abused queen of U.S. silver districts. In remote Montana, first a group of silver towns and then the great Butte copper district rose up to dominate the economy and political order. Similarly, copper came in the 1880s to dominate the economics and politics of Arizona with the rise of "camps" like Bisbee, Globe, Jerome, and Morenci.

Clearly, the period of roughly 1893–1907 marks the watershed era of western mining, the transition from frontier to modern conditions. By the early twentieth century, the best high-grade deposits of precious metals were either exhausted or being worked out. With the Grover Cleveland administration's precipitous demonetization of silver, that vital western industry collapsed in the calamitous Panic of 1893. Henceforth, with some exceptions like the Homestake and the Coeur d'Alene, precious metals would mean less and less to the western economy, with surges of mining activity when prices rose but more commonly languishing as they sagged. In the meantime, with the rise of the electrical and telephone industries, copper was becoming the dominant western metal.

The center of American copper mining moved dramatically westward in the midst of a mid-1880s price war, when the long dominant northern Michigan mines, led by Calumet & Hecla, lost out to the upstart Butte mines led by Anaconda. Montana prevailed in world production of the red metal for two decades and then fell into a tertiary role behind first Arizona and then also Utah. When Daniel Jackling and his associates at Bingham Canyon, Utah, proved the feasibility of mining low-grade, porphyry copper ores in mass quantities with steamshovels and rails, open-pit mining began, especially in Utah, Arizona, and Nevada, to supplant the older deep vein mines. Revolutionary new technologies, led by electrification, the flotation method of concentration, and electrolytic refining, also enhanced the productivity of the industry. Thus, copper became king in western mining, while the production of precious metals came increasingly to be a by-product industry dependent on the matte issuing from copper smelters.

In other ways, too, the industry began to take its modern form as the new century unfolded. Important new companies appeared: American Smelting & Refining, formed in 1899 as a silver-lead smelting trust and then led into new fields under the tutelage of the powerful Guggenheim family; Newmount Mining, formed in 1921 by the shrewd William Boyce Thompson; Kennecott, in which the Guggenheims also had a large hand, gained control of Bingham Canyon between 1915 and 1936. Labor relations became angry and sometimes violent as management frequently exploited workers, and as workers formed militant unions—first the Western Federation of Miners in 1893 and then its successor, the Mine, Mill and Smelter Workers Union. In states like Arizona and Montana, where mining was the dominant industry, the mining companies anchored the right side of the political order, while mining unionists, allying with other laborites and small farmers, held forth on the left. Sometimes the mining interests practiced outright repression, as in Idaho and Colorado in the 1890s, and at Butte and Bisbee during World War I.

With the passing years, the mining industry went through cycles of boom and bust: up during two world wars, down during the interwar period, and then into a slow decline after 1945. By the 1950s, high-grade tunnel mines were disappearing and low-grade open pits had most of the action. As a result, the angry old "Mine, Mill" union, racked by charges of Communist leanings, saw its membership dwindle and finally lost its copper clientele to the United Steelworkers in 1967. The newer unions which worked the open pits, mainly Teamsters and Operating Engineers, leaned much less to the left. As a partial result of the attrition of these mining unions, along with similar losses of their allies on small farms and in rail unions, the political order in the mining states shifted to the right—most obviously in rapidly industrializing and urbanizing Arizona, where the Barry Goldwater Republicans took over in the 1950s, but also in the other mining states as well.

The mining companies changed too. They did some diversifying, for instance into the new rival metal of aluminum and into the purchase of "down-stream" brass fabricating companies. Of greatest significance, they joined in the big post-1920 overseas expansion of U.S. industry. "Third world" copper mines were now becoming a major factor, especially those in the Chilean Andes, in the Congo (today's Zaire), and in Mexico. Both Anaconda and Kennecott moved heavily into Chile and came to rely upon it for large shares of their production and profits. Gradually, the western mining firms shed their old ways and adapted to the new order. Phelps Dodge found itself to be only one of a number of big outfits in booming Arizona, increasingly overshadowed by "high-tech" newcomers like Motorola. Kennecott had a similar experience in Utah, where the Mormon presence had denied it the kind of statewide hegemony that its sister firms had exercised elsewhere. The Nevada miners could no longer hope to compete with the fast-rising gambling industry for influence. Even in slow growing Montana, old Anaconda inched hesitantly toward modernity by selling its tightly controlled newspaper chain and closing its twenty-four-hours-per-day "watering holes" for legislators. The mining companies looked less and less like the behemoths of days gone by, more and more like other western corporations, fretting about tough new environmental laws, advertising to court public opinion, and lobbying hard in Washington and in state capitals.

As usually happens, the forces of change built slowly, but then erupted with startling suddenness. The dawn of the 1970s forecast the beginning of the end. Tough new federal and state environmental quality laws presented the miners with hard choices of whether to invest in expensive renovations of the antique smelters which they had failed to recapitalize or simply to close them down. At the same time, their dominant metal, copper, continued to lose its markets to aluminum, plastics, and, of major importance, its communications markets to fiber-optic wire. Precious metals derived from their smelter matte helped considerably when prices were high, as during the late 1970s, but little when they were low. Increasingly, companies like ASARCO have to reckon closely before opening a small new mine—whether the combined precious and base metals, in a period of declining prices, can render adequate profits against high labor, capital, and environmental regulation costs. Clearly, future metal mines in the West will employ hundreds, not thousands, and will merely supplement, not buttress, the regional economic structure.

Two factors, especially, sealed the fate of western metal mining: federal tax and antitrust policies, and foreign competition. Regarding the first, as Robert Reich notes in his insightful *The Next American Frontier*, most nations limit the ability of corporations to invest outside their areas of specialty and penalize them if they buy and then close other companies, throwing workers into unemployment. The trend in the United States has been, rather, to encourage the growth of conglomerates with a limp antitrust policy, and to encourage such buy-outs and shutdowns by allowing tax write-offs to compensate for them. Viewed from the national interest, this is incongruous; viewed from the perspective of abetting corporate profits, it makes sense.

Foreign competition is, by far, the main force which has devastated western metal mining. The copper mines of South America and Africa not only have larger quantities of higher grade ore than do those in the United States, they also employ labor forces that work for far less than do those in the U.S., and they are willing to mine at capacity even at low world prices in order to keep their expanding populations fed and pay their burdensome foreign debts. Chile is the Saudi Arabia of world copper; its nationalizations of American copper companies fifteen years ago under the socialist Allende regime did much to prompt the declines of Anaconda and Kennecott. In Chile, the Codelco miners, who are well paid by national standards, make only a tenth of what their counterparts earn in the U.S. American industrial leaders argue angrily that American dollars, through grants to the World Bank and the International Monetary Fund, enable Chile to flood the world market in what appears a calculated effort to destroy their American competitors.

No matter how well founded such complaints, the fact remains that there is no effective way to protect this ailing industry from world markets. Any effort to restrict copper imports with higher tariffs or tightened import quotas will only drive up the price and limit international sales of every U.S. product that uses the red metal. As in the steel industry, the decline is thus inexorable—but even worse because fewer than 25,000 jobs are left in this dying industry (there were 108,000 in 1981), and the western states lack the political clout of the midwestern and southern steel states. So, with prices hovering at sixty cents per pound, copper is down, and down to stay. It is unlikely to recover appreciably, since foreign rivals have large reserves, and since derelict mines are usually allowed to flood and are thus effectively lost for good. The lesser western metals are nearly as bad off as former king copper. Lead markets have been gutted by the upsurge in nonleaded gasoline, and aluminum markets (until this year) by the rising costs of energy for production. Gold and silver prices remain soft and unstable.

Thus a key factor in the economic, social, and political development of the West is fading from the scene. To the economist, or any other informed observer, the demise of metal mining is simply one aspect of America's loss of its basic "smokestack" industries to the more competitive "developing" world. In a flight of fancy, John Naisbitt tells us in his popular *Megatrends* that all this is inevitable and not bothersome anyhow, since America's future lies in clean "high-tech" industries; but common sense raises doubts about whether any major nation can long afford to import nearly all of its most important and basic raw materials.

To the student of the western region, mining's collapse raises other, more pointed issues. Viewed in the context of the crisis in other extractive industries of the West—for instance, agriculture and lumber (the latter is forsaking the forests of the Northwest for the perennial forests of the South)—the fall of mining is part of a greater whole. We are witnessing the close of the "colonial" period of western development, the frontier and post-frontier eras which saw the rise and fall of extractive industries and the often heedless exploitation of the region's natural resources. Tough new environmental laws similarly reflect the end of this epoch. To the optimists, all this is as it should be. The "developing" world is, after all, developing. The West is part of the world, and its proper role should be to develop high-tech and other clean industries which do not endanger its fragile environment. The cautious skeptic will not be so certain. As current events are demonstrating, high-tech industries may not be so stable and enduring after all. Any Utahn or Arizonan knows that the blue-collar workers and their families bear the brunt of the smokestack closures. And then there is the sobering possibility that the low-grade reserves of metals, which some mineowners are wastefully allowing to be lost under tons of flooding water, may be needed in a future national crisis.

The collapse of this great old industry represents more than simple inevitability and more than nostalgia for colorful frontier times. It also represents the ever increasing integration of the western economy into the global economy—just as does the shipping of unplaned logs to Japan while western sawmills lie idle or the unhampered acquisition of western farmlands by foreigners. The squandering of potentially valuable mineral reserves reminds us of the wastefulness of America's frontier past. The failure of national economic policy to do even what little was possible to buffer the mining industry from concerted efforts by foreign interests to destroy it, or to force conglomerate corporations to behave in the national interest, calls to mind the lack of intelligent national planning which has been so characteristic of the West's history. Thus one major phase of the West's frenzied and exploitative growth now comes to a close. Whether a better or a more troubled world lies ahead is impossible to say, but surely nothing more graphically symbolizes the region's transition from its exploitative, "third world" economic past than the passing of metal mining as a major force in its economic life.

Υ *F U R T H E R   R E A D I N G*

Richard M. Bernard and Bradley R. Rice, eds., *Sunbelt Cities: Politics and Growth since World War II* (1984)

Christopher Davies, "Life at the Edge: Urban and Industrial Evolution of Texas, Frontier Wilderness—Frontier Space, 1836–1986," *Southwestern Historical Quarterly*, 89 (1986), 443–554

Robert Gottlieb and Peter Wiley, *Empires in the Sun: The Rise of the New American West* (1982)

Richard V. Francaviglia, *The Mormon Landscape: Existence, Creation, and Perception of a Unique Image in the American West* (1978)

Lawrence H. Larsen, *The Urban West at the End of the Frontier* (1978)

Roger W. Lotchin, "The City and the Sword: San Francisco and the Rise of the Metropolitan-Military Complex, 1920–1942," *Journal of American History*, 75 (1979), 996–1020

———, "The Darwinian City: The Politics of Urbanization in San Francisco Between the World Wars," *Pacific Historical Review*, 68 (1979), 357–381

Gerald D. Nash, *The American West in the Twentieth Century* (1973)

———, "Stages in California's Economic Growth: An Interpretation," *California Historical Society Quarterly*, 51 (1972), 315–330

Roderick Nash, *Wilderness and the American Mind* (3rd ed., 1982)

Donald J. Pisani, *From the Family Farm to Agribusiness: The Irrigation Crusade in California and the West* (1984)

Marc Reisner, *Cadillac Desert: The American West and Its Disappearing Water* (1986)

John W. Reps, *Cities of the American West: A History of Frontier Urban Planning* (1979)

Susan R. Schrepfer, *The Fight to Save the Redwoods* (1983)

Duane A. Smith, *Mining America: The Industry and the Environment* (1987)

Douglas Strong, *Tahoe: An Environmental History* (1984)

Richard White, *Land Use, Environment, and Social Change: The Shaping of Island County, Washington* (1980)

Donald Worster, *Rivers of Empire: Water, Aridity, and the Growth of the American West* (1985)

CHAPTER 15

New Meanings of the West

Y

The year 1993 will mark the centennial of Frederick Jackson Turner's famous essay on the frontier. In the century after this anniversary, what will become important in explaining the significance of both the frontier and the West in American history? In search of answers, scholars will continue to examine new evidence, formulate fresh concepts, and revise old ideas. In the process, they will need to analyze the significance of the twentieth-century West as broadly as Turner attempted to analyze the colonial and nineteenth-century frontiers. The ultimate conclusions will have to withstand critical examination by others. Are there ways today of presenting the history of the West that in 2093 may still provide the focus for scholarly debates?

Y E S S A Y S

Frank J. Popper teaches in the urban studies program at Rutgers University. In the first essay, he takes stock of the large amount of "open" land left in the West and concludes that Turner's frontier has not closed. The potential uses for the West's relatively untouched territory are, he believes, significant for many future needs of the United States. William Cronon teaches environmental and western history at Yale University. A former Rhodes Scholar, he has received a MacArthur Grant to support any area of research that he wishes to pursue. In the second essay, he enlarges on Turner's ideas, bringing out new connections and concepts for consideration. While recognizing the significance of Turner, but not of his frontier, Cronon shows how the study of the West must create a new unity and direction. For those undertaking this task, he stresses the importance of many diverse and even opposing concepts, such as scarcity and abundance. Cronon challenges us to create our new understanding of the West not by ignoring older theories but by building upon their most useful elements. .

The Strange Case of the Contemporary American Frontier

FRANK J. POPPER

The West has always been the Great American Place. The mythic heart of the West has always been the frontier, whose finest nineteenth-century historian was Frederick Jackson Turner of the University of Wisconsin. His thesis was simple: the American people were the product of continual, centuries-long westering into the forests, plains, mountains, and deserts. But as the West became settled in the late nineteenth century, the previously abundant open frontier lands were increasingly rare and unavailable. Most of the Oklahoma land rushes, for instance, ended by the early 1890s. When such fertile, cheap, accessible lands disappeared, Turner wondered, what would the American people become? He had no real answer.

His twentieth-century successor as premier historian of the West, Walter Prescott Webb of the University of Texas, agreed that the American frontier was gone. In 1952 he wrote the *The Great Frontier:* "The end of an age is always touched with sadness for those who lived it and those who love it. . . . The people are going to miss the frontier more than words can express. For four centuries they heard its call, listened to its promises, and bet their lives and fortunes on its outcome. It calls no more, and regardless of how they bend their ears for its faint whisper they cannot hear the suggestion of a promise."

I would respectfully argue that the two most authoritative historians of the Western frontier that America ever produced were wrong: the frontier survives to this day as a distinct geographic region—a large remote land area beyond the farthest settlement—across huge stretches of the United States. It is likely to survive for many generations to come. It clearly influences modern-day American policies and attitudes concerning land use, natural resources, and the environment. The frontier never died and shows no signs of dying. I will examine the curious career of the concept of the frontier and demonstrate how we have misunderstood the winning of the West.

"Up to and including 1880 the country had a frontier of settlement, but at present the unsettled area has been so broken into by isolated bodies of settlement that there can hardly be said to be a frontier line." These undynamic words are the most famous the Census Bureau ever wrote, for Frederick Jackson Turner used them as the opening lines of his 1893 essay "The Significance of the Frontier in American History." He argued that the frontier, particularly the effort to acquire its land, had made the American people optimistic, energetic, pragmatic, expansionist, inquisitive, inventive, individualistic, anti-intellectual, egalitarian, materialistic, restless, insular, cruel (to the Indians, for instance), and inclined to restrain government and

Frank J. Popper, "The Strange Case of the Contemporary American Frontier," *The Yale Review* 76 (Autumn 1976), 101–121. Reprinted by permission.

to waste natural resources. The frontier had in fact given Americans all the national personality traits the rest of the world attributed to them (and still does).

Much of Turner's work focused on the nineteenth-century Midwestern frontier, such as the Wisconsin of his boyhood in the 1860s. He described a sequential settlement process, a predictable progression which began when whites entered the rich Ohio and Upper Mississippi valleys originally occupied only by Indians. The economic succession was increasingly intense: first came fur traders, next cattle raisers, then perhaps miners, then small subsistence farmers, and finally larger farmers who produced cash crops. All the settlers were drawn by abundant, fertile land that was inexpensive or free. As they displaced the Indians and cleared, cultivated, improved, and filled the land, the settlers were initially humbled by the frontier; then they conquered it. They acquired their distinctively American qualities from it; then they closed it. Turner contended that with suitable regional variations this sequence had recurred 'hroughout the white settlement of America, from the Massachusetts Bay Colony to the Far West.

Turner had no true objection to the closing of the frontier. He regarded it as the characteristic process of American history, a shift to a higher level of social development—progress of the kind dear to the nineteenth century. But as the frontier disappeared, he was concerned about what might replace it to shape the character of the American people. He worried about the ways in which Americans might respond to the loss of their accustomed frontier, about how a frontierless America might deteriorate. For almost a century, the frontier thesis has been one of American history's most influential ideas.

Turner and the Census had a specific demographic concept of the frontier. "An arbitrary line," Henry Gannett, a Census Bureau geographer, wrote in 1882, "must be drawn beyond which the country must be considered as unsettled, although it may not be absolutely without inhabitants." By convention the line usually bounded the zone with less than two people per square mile—a population density equivalent to Manhattan having no more than forty-five residents. From 1790 to 1880, the frontier line moved steadily westward, from the Appalachians through the Midwest to the Great Plains. Nineteenth-century researchers followed its progress closely. In 1876 Francis Walker, director of the 1870 and 1880 censuses, calculated that it was moving west and slightly north at a rate of seventy to seventy-five feet a day.

But the 1890 census was the first that could not show a national frontier line. The march of Western settlement, especially growth along the Pacific Slope, meant that the frontier had vanished west of the Sierra-Cascades and was no longer contiguous east of them. The frontier line, said the census, "can not, therefore, any longer have a place in the census reports." Turner interpreted the disappearance of the frontier line as "marking the closing of a great historic moment. Up to our own day American history has been in a large degree the history of the colonization of the West. . . . Now, four centuries from the discovery of America, at the end of a hundred years of life under the Constitution, the frontier has gone, and with its going has closed the first period of American history." Thus Turner, with the help of the census, declared the frontier dead.

Nearly a century later, however, the declaration looks odd and premature. The idea of a national frontier line as the boundary of a single national frontier zone now seems a vast statistical abstraction, a locally meaningless national average. Suppose we apply the nineteenth-century density standard another way, disaggregating it at the county level, and bring it up to date. The 1980 census shows 143 counties, all in Western states, with fewer than two people per square mile (see map 1). All but one of the counties lie west of the 98th meridian, the boundary Walter Prescott Webb used to define the arid West that averages less than twenty inches of rain a year; the 98th meridian, roughly where the great tallgrass prairies of the Midwest and South meet the shortgrass Great Plains of the West, is also the approximate location of the census's last national frontier line in 1880. All but the Alaskan frontier counties lie east of the Sierra-Cascades. In the 1980 census, the counties have a small total population of 572,000, representing one American in 396. But because they are large, the frontier counties have a total area of 949,500 square miles, over a quarter of that of the United States. For a place that is supposed to have disappeared generations ago, there is a lot of frontier left.

The frontier counties fall mostly in four areas: rural Alaska, the Owyhee-Bitterroot valleys of the Northwest, the Great Basin in Nevada and Utah, and the Great Plains from Montana to Texas. Alaska, whose license plates proclaim it "The Last Frontier," is 96 percent frontier. Nevada is 80 percent frontier, Idaho 44, Montana and Utah 41, New Mexico and Oregon 27, South Dakota 21, Colorado 17, and Wyoming 15. Even California, with four of the nation's sixteen largest cities, has two frontier counties, Alpine and Inyo, constituting seven percent of the state. The frontier counties of the "Lower 48"—the contiguous United States—contain thirteen percent of its total land area.

Many of the frontier counties consist principally of federal lands—the holdings, for instance, of the Bureau of Land Management (44 percent of the land in states from the Rockies westward), the Forest Service (16 percent of such land), the Fish and Wildlife Service (8 percent), and the National Park Service (6 percent). But a noticeable number of frontier counties lack large amounts of federal land. Sixteen percent of Texas is in frontier counties, but only two percent of the state is in federal holdings. Twenty-four percent of Nebraska is frontier, but only one percent is federal. Conversely, forty-four percent of Arizona and twenty-nine percent of Washington are federal, but neither state has any frontier counties. Thus many frontier counties are mainly in private or state holdings.

The nineteenth-century investigators sometimes drew a less stringent frontier line that delimited areas with less than six people per square mile (the equivalent of Manhattan having no more than 135 residents) rather than those with less than two. If one includes counties with this higher density, the surviving American frontier becomes truly impressive (see map 2).

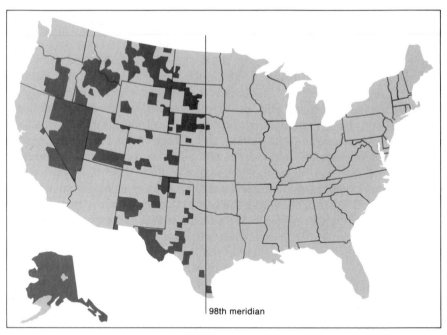

Map 1.   The American Frontier, 1980: counties with less than two people per square mile. (Adapted from maps produced by the Cartography Laboratory of the Geography Department, Rutgers University.)

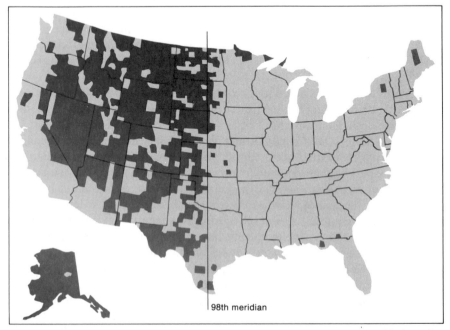

Map 2.   The American Frontier and its Borderlands, 1980: counties with less than six people per square mile.

East of the Great Plains, nine counties join the list, mostly in large national and state parks and forests: four of them lie on Minnesota's Canadian border, and there is one each in Florida, Georgia, Maine, Michigan, and New York. The Great Plains states themselves have four frontier counties totally east of the 98th meridian, seven straddling it, and 127 totally west of it. Starting with the Great Plains and going west, every state but Hawaii adds at least two counties, for an overall Western total of 251 new ones in eighteen Western states. States that previously had no frontier counties acquire substantial amounts: Arizona adds 4 counties covering 42 percent of the state, Kansas 28 covering 29 percent, and Washington 6 covering 16 percent.

The total population of the 394 Western frontier counties with less than six people per square mile is 2.239 million, around one percent of the American population. Their area is 1.614 million square miles, or forty-five percent of the United States. They cover thirty percent of the Lower 48 states. They are almost entirely contiguous, and come close to forming a nineteenth-century-style unified zone. On this map the national frontier line has still not crossed the Great Plains, just as it had not in 1880. Many of the contemporary West's large cities—for instance, Albuquerque, Anchorage, Boise, Denver, and Salt Lake City—amount to urban islands in a frontier sea.

The frontier, it turns out, never disappeared at all. Just beyond the West's peopled areas, it survives on a huge scale. It is a coherent place that seems in no serious danger of diminishing in coming generations. We have misunderstood the settlement of nearly half of America: we have thought of it as past history when much of it is still history to come.

There is a great deal of other evidence of the frontier's survival, in the frontier counties and elsewhere, that does not depend on nineteenth-century density standards. According to the Bureau of Land Management, 379 million acres of federal public land—all in the West, amounting to more than seventeen percent of the country—have never even been surveyed, and over fifty million more acres were surveyed inadequately over a century ago. Large chunks of Western territory have yet to be fully explored—for example, the northern Snake River Plain in Idaho, the Wah Wah Mountains in western Utah, Monument Valley in northern Arizona, the Wrangell Mountains in southern Alaska, the Brooks Range in northern Alaska, and the Owyhee River Canyons near the intersection of Idaho, Nevada, and Oregon. The Alaskan mountain ranges contain hundreds of peaks over ten thousand feet high that have never been named, much less climbed.

Homesteading—the most widespread and symbolic act of trying to people the frontier—continues to a surprising extent more than half a century after the Taylor Grazing Act of 1934 supposedly abolished it. Because Alaska's previous territorial status exempted it from the act, homesteading on federal land in the state lasted into the 1960s, and in 1982 the Bureau of Land Management revived it experimentally in central Alaska's Kuskokwim Mountains. On several occasions since 1934 the federal government relaxed its prohibition on homesteading to promote settlement near specific federal projects such as dams; for instance, in the late 1940s homesteaders occupied nearly two hundred thousand acres of irrigated farms in the Gila River project near Yuma, Arizona. Because of long legal delays stemming from clouded titles, multiple claimants, probated wills, and disputed Indian treaties, the federal government is still transferring Western homestead sites to latter-day settlers whose ancestors first filed applications before 1934. Some Western states, notably Alaska, still have widespread homesteading on state-owned land.

Then there is illegal homesteading that, whether temporary or permanent, amounts to frontier-style squatting on the vast Western public lands. At least four thousand Alaskans, almost one percent of the state's population, are squatting on the seventy-eight million acres of state land, many more are squatting on the larger federal holdings, and some are putting up "no trespassing" signs. In 1983 Alaska's governor, Bill Sheffield, was revealed to hold an interest in an illegal duck-hunting camp in a state waterfowl refuge; he publicly renounced his holding, but his opponent in the 1982 election and three state judges, including the chief justice of the Alaska Supreme Court, have not given up theirs. In Southern California's Mojave Desert, a former boomtown of the silver strikes of the 1920s, Red Mountain, is now a remote settlement of 130 retirees who until recently lived year-round as squatters on federal land. "The entire town is in trespass," a Bureau of Land Management official told the *Washington Post* in 1983. Late in 1984, after a twenty-seven-year squabble, the federal government gave most of the squatters title to their land.

The frontier is not what it was in the 1870s. It is smaller, less contiguous and isolated, more law-abiding and regulated, less rugged, dangerous, and impassable. It has less free land and no longer provides a safety valve for people who are unwanted or unneeded in cities or settled rural areas. The frontier's products account for a smaller proportion of the nation's natural resource economy, which in turn accounts for a smaller proportion of its overall economy. The frontier looks different: the cowboy culture that reached its height during the late nineteenth century has given way to high-tech agribusiness, big mining and timber companies, and large water projects. The highway has replaced the wagon trail, the trailer the sod house, the pickup truck the horse (mostly), the country-and-western station the campfire ballad, the bus and the mail plane the stagecoach, the snowmobile the dogsled. Except for Alaska, the frontier has not for generations been the dream of those who seek a fortune or a new life.

Yet the frontier lives on, protected from large-scale settlement by its climate (Alaska, central Nevada), its terrain (southern Utah, central Idaho, eastern Oregon), its distance from metropolitan areas (central Montana, the western Dakotas, most of Alaska and Wyoming), its lack of water, its frequent lack of exploitable resources, and most federal land policies. Thus much frontier land is almost unlivable, economically unattractive, and abundantly surrounded by more such land.

It seems remarkable that the nation does not acknowledge the unwon West as a huge empty region in our midst, but there are good reasons why we do not know what to make of it. The frontier is off the beaten track. Our governing classes, as well as many of the rest of us, have no reason to notice it except as a place to fly over. Barring occasional episodes such as the Sagebrush Rebellion (the recent unsuccessful attempt by James Watt to sell or give away large quantities of Western federal land to corporations and state governments), the public lands that form the core of the frontier are rarely a high-priority national issue. Their uses no longer determine the future of the American economy, and their disposal to settlers no longer controls the course of Western expansion. The high growth rate of many Western cities and towns masks the fact that they amount to burgeoning outposts scattered across the far larger frontier. (This clustering of growing urban populations has led to the ironic finding of recent censuses that the West is now America's most urban region.)

Most important, the nation accepted Turner's argument that the frontier was passing, that America was about to become what he called a "closed-room society"—more like what Europe was than what America had been. We therefore have difficulty grasping that the land future of the American West is not yet entirely decided; we assume that the settlement of the West is over. More precisely, we assume that most of the lands which have not been settled already are so useless or (in the less common case of preservation areas such as the national parks and wildernesses) so beautiful that they never will be settled. Thomas Jefferson had a more flexible, expansive view of what the uses of the West might turn out to be: he went ahead with the controversial Louisiana Purchase in 1803 largely because he believed Americans would need a hundred generations to settle the West and discover its uses, but then would be sustained by it for a thousand. Seven generations later, he may have been more prescient than we realize.

Because we ignore the survival of the frontier, we repeatedly misunderstand the West. We allowed the Great Plains portion of the West to become dependent on water-intensive farming methods and irrigation practices that cannot be sustained in arid frontier settings, and now are surprised when—just as in the 1890s and 1930s—nature and the economy turn hostile, Dust Bowls loom, and the Plains promise again to become one of the great failure sectors of American agriculture. We regard figures like James Watt and events like the Sagebrush Rebellion as aberrations when they are really the predictable products of the frontier, having appeared countless times before in the settlement of the West.

Similarly, environmentalists often seek to protect scarce, fragile Western areas that turn out to be neither scarce nor fragile, and developers often seek to exploit different scarce, fragile areas that indeed should be protected. Neither group trusts the other, so each exaggerates its own claims. The results are overuse in some resource situations and underuse in others. Because we do not realize that we still have a vast frontier, we are unlikely to arrive at a balanced or stable policy for it.

Yet the surviving frontier plainly affects Western land use and attitudes toward natural resources, pushing them in directions most Easterners (and people on the West Coast) find hard to grasp or admire. The surviving

frontier—particularly its wide-open spaces, endemic poverty, populist conservatism, tradition of geographic mobility, and myth of social mobility—
makes much of the rural West receptive to large extractive boom-and-bust
developments: big energy projects, copper and coal strip-mining and other
mineral enterprises, nuclear waste repositories, and the MX missile system.
Such environmentally risky projects, placed elsewhere, would cause far
more dismay than they do on the frontier.

The surviving frontier makes much of the rural West hostile to the
large federal holdings that seem to hinder the region's economic development.
So it makes the rural West sympathetic to once-a-generation divestiture
movements such as the Sagebrush Rebellion. And it makes the West hospitable
to the more frequent efforts—such as the Reagan-Watt initiatives and other
measures sought by large natural-resource corporations with headquarters
far from the frontier—to accelerate leasing for oil, coal, natural gas, other
minerals, timber, and grazing on federal land. It inclines the West to support
comparably motivated initiatives to slow down the acquisition of federal
parkland, wildlife refuges, and wilderness, and to give less weight to long-
term environmental considerations and more to short-term economic ones.

The surviving frontier also helps explain the West's special resistance
to federal and even state regulation of private land. It goes a long way
toward explaining why many Western rural localities have never adopted
zoning and probably never will. It clarifies why many Western urban areas
that were until recently frontier have adopted zoning reluctantly and in the
weakest form they could manage, and why Houston and other substantial
Texas cities (for instance, Baytown, Pasadena, and Wichita Falls) have
never adopted it at all. The surviving frontier is one of the main reasons
why Western states and localities are in the forefront of the national search
for alternatives to our present land use and environmental regulations.

Turner was not totally in error in 1893 to declare the frontier gone; the
lands that were both available and arable were disappearing fast in the late
nineteenth century. But the practical implications of his declaration have
frequently been misunderstood since. A frontier is often an area that can
be cultivated only marginally using the agricultural technologies of the time.
Since the 1890s our technologies, especially our means of handling water,
have not improved enough to make farming or ranching on the Great Plains,
or in northern Alaska or southern Utah, more than intermittently profitable.
The true architect of the West has never been governmental or even human—
it has been the desert, with its immense expansions and contractions and
its pitiless resistance to cultivation. Alaska too, except for the coastal strip
south of the Alaska Range, gets less than twenty inches of rain a year; it
is a cold desert, as Arizona is a hot one. The few available arable Western
lands may not have disappeared precisely by 1890, as a strict reading of
Turner and the census would imply, but almost all vanished sometime
between the completion of the first transcontinental railroad in 1869 and
the abolition of homesteading in 1934. After more than two hundred years
of frequently obsessive pioneering, the surviving frontier is what remains.

A prodigious amount is left. Consider Alaska, the sixth of America that bulks so large in Western development plans. The state, even after years of extremely fast population growth (thirty percent between 1980 and 1985, the highest rate for any state), still has an overall density of less than one person per square mile, easily qualifying all of the state, even including Anchorage and Fairbanks, as a frontier by the nineteenth-century standard. Alaska has half of the nation's coal reserves, almost half its supply of fresh water, its most fertile fishing grounds, huge stores of natural gas, and—because the summer's long northern light expands the growing season—a surprisingly bountiful agricultural potential. Alaska's Matanuska Valley has long produced, among other farm commodities, cabbages weighing seventy pounds and fields of wheat and barley eight feet high, all grown commercially, in marketable amounts, and without pesticides.

Alaska could produce as much oil in the next ten years as the rest of the country has since the first well in Titusville, Pennsylvania, in 1859. Alaska contains hundreds of uncharted, untrod mountains and valleys. It has dozens of bush villages that lack electricity, running water, telephones, and paving. The state capital, Juneau, along with scores of other towns, can only be reached by sea or air (or on foot); these are places for which road access from the outside is a project of the twenty-first century, if then. The state has a grand total of fifteen thousand miles of roads, mostly in the Anchorage and Fairbanks areas—fewer than Vermont, which has less than a sixtieth of Alaska's area (but a larger population). In the 1980s there is an American North almost as large, uninhabited, virginal, rich, and environmentally vulnerable as the American West was in the 1870s. In addition, much of the American West has not essentially changed since the 1870s.

It is difficult to predict the fate of the frontier. Coming decades will probably see continued development: more growth of Western cities, vast new mineral strikes, the unexpected (but inevitable) discovery of new kinds of minerals and extractive technologies that would make more frontier land economically attractive, renewed Sagebrush Rebellions, endless extractive boom-and-bust cycles, and perhaps some strengthening of water technologies that would allow agriculture on more of the frontier. These occurrences for the most part represent straight-line continuations of existing trends. They would not come close to filling the empty enormity of the frontier. Thus the happiest, most likely vision is that centuries from now the frontier will be roughly what it is today: the great, mythic, joyous West of big skies and cattle drives, lonesome roads and oasis towns, energy boomers and water shortages, of cactus and steppe and tundra—of purple mountain majesties that lack the fruited plain.

Yet the frontier could someday prove the solution to a national land emergency. The frontier may be thought of as a largely federal reserve, a gigantic bank account put aside to meet America's future land needs. During the energy crisis of 1973—1981, Alaska, of which ninety-six percent was then in federal hands, served this function to some extent, but the performance could become more obvious if the peril were worse. For example, there may come a time generations hence when the nation will rediscover the frontier and again want to settle or use it—after a major earthquake, a nuclear accident, a hazardous waste crisis, or some unforeseen economic, military, biological, or climatic defeat. If the emergency never comes, well enough—there was no active alternative use for much of the land anyway. But if it does come, the frontier will actively reenter American history.

The problem, as ever, is water. The desert, the scorched heart of the American West, is now expanding rapidly, largely because of urban and agricultural development. El Paso is bracketed east and west by two new areas of humanly caused desertification that the Council on Environmental Quality classified in 1980 as "very severe." A larger area with the same designation appears in the Rio Puerco Basin near Albuquerque and Santa Fe. The desertification of a wide Southwestern strip extending from central Texas and Oklahoma to central California, a tenth of the United States, was designated as "severe." The Ogallala Aquifer under the arid Great Plains portions of Colorado, Kansas, Nebraska, New Mexico, Oklahoma, and Texas—a nonrenewable groundwater source that nourishes more than eleven million acres of agriculture—is being inexorably depleted, notably by center-pivot irrigation. As in Dust Bowl days, farmland has been abandoned for lack of water in the Pecos Valley in New Mexico and between Amarillo and Lubbock in Texas. Throughout the West, the long-term meteorological outlook is for intensified drought.

The water constraints are probably worst in Arizona, which combines high growth rates, water-intensive agriculture, and an aridity unusual even for the West. Because the state's two-billion-dollar-a-year citrus, alfalfa, and cotton crops use nine-tenths of its well water, Arizona is buying up farmland to remove it from production and discouraging additional farming; the state has also made digging a new well a felony. In 1980 Arizona passed a water management act, the nation's most demanding, that requires all new urban developments to have an assured water supply for at least a century. In 1984 the state's Water Resources Department proposed that Arizona no longer allow the construction of all-grass golf courses or highway medians, large swimming pools, and decorative ponds, lakes, or fountains. (Such artificial bodies of water have been a prestige item in developments like Lake Havasu City, whose builders bought London Bridge, reassembled it block by block on the sandy site, and had to have it overarch something wet.) The department's plan is intended as the first of five that will impose progressively stricter limitations on water use over the next forty years.

The water deficit increasingly oppresses the entire West and has even begun to affect relations with Canada. The northern portion of the Canadian West contains even more fresh water than Alaska, and there have been repeated suggestions, American and Canadian, that it be exported south. Other schemes involving Canada have emerged. The North American Water and Power Alliance, proposed by the late California engineer Ralph Parsons, would reverse the present northern course of two large Alaska rivers, the Yukon and the Tanana, and send them south to the American West, with a courtesy diversion to the arid southern portions of Alberta, Manitoba, and Saskatchewan. An even more grandiose scheme, the Grand Canal project advocated by the Canadian engineer Thomas Kierans, would divert the flow from the Eastern rivers that now empty into James Bay, the large southern inlet of Canada's Hudson Bay. A dike one hundred miles long would separate the two bays, turn James Bay into a freshwater lake, and feed its flow into a canal that would carry the water southwest to the Great Lakes for release to the American and Canadian Wests (and Midwests).

Today such projects are visionary, at or beyond the edge of technological and intellectual respectability. They are extraordinarily expensive; they will cost at least three hundred billion dollars apiece, according to Frank Quinn, director of water planning for the Canadian counterpart of the Environmental Protection Agency. They are likely to have unintended ecological effects that would be devastating and irreversible. They could easily become white elephants before completion, in the manner of many contemporary nuclear power plants. Yet someday they may be possible, or may have to be made so; the Canadian government is now underwriting a long-term feasibility study of the Grand Canal project. "The desert," wrote Walter Prescott Webb in 1957, "is the guest that came to dinner never to go away. It is the great designer of the American West." If continued Western growth is to be practical in decades to come, we will need technical breakthroughs and new institutional arrangements for collecting, transporting, exchanging, conserving, and desalinating water, and perhaps for seeding clouds. An administration that truly wanted to settle the West, to build the Pacific side of America, would need to look no further for enterprises to support.

The administrations of future generations may also want to reconsider our practices of disposing of and retaining public land. The Sagebrush Rebellion is a dead issue today, but the frontier will probably see more land transfers over the next few decades, and the rebellion will have helped make them possible by reviving the sleepy field of public land policy. A number of plausible alternatives have already surfaced in its wake. Dean Rhoads, the Nevada state legislator and rancher who is often considered the father of the Sagebrush Rebellion, now supports allowing cattle and sheep raisers to buy surface rights to public land, keeping the mineral rights in federal hands, and letting the states take over day-to-day management and regulation. The 1982 report of the President's Commission on Housing advocates "townsteading" on public land. Others have suggested the creation of public/private development corporations, long-term leasing to private interests for terms as long as a hundred years, or, most sensibly, a series of experimental programs on relatively small tracts to test different approaches. The Bureau of Land Management's grazing system originated with such an experiment in the Mizpah–Pumpkin Creek area of southeast Montana in the late 1920s.

We are almost certainly moving into a new phase of America's expansion into its gigantic physical setting. From the Articles of Confederation to the Taylor Act, federal policy essentially was to acquire public land and then dispose of as much of it as possible. The Sagebrush Rebellion marks the transition back to what will probably be a lengthy period of disposal. For fifty years disposal has been interrupted; new land demands, new extraction and construction technologies, have now established themselves, and more will appear. The environmental movement—its laws and its protective technologies—is deservedly here to stay. Many public lands—all the national parks, monuments, and wildernesses, some national forests, and other quality recreation areas—are politically and physically sacred places that cannot and should not be touched. But disposal of lands less distinctive than the national treasures could take place gradually so as not to invite fraud, disrupt local land markets, or overburden states and localities. A key problem will be weaning Western resource-based industries and governments from their present dependence on federal subsidies such as cheap leases on public land, generous payments in lieu of property taxes, and federal assumption of what would otherwise be state and local public services.

A more important problem will be finding better ways to promote slow, small-scale disposal—incremental, tract-by-tract, year-by-year disposal that goes unpublicized but has significant local and cumulative regional consequences. The federal government has continually made small-scale disposals, even in periods when it opted against large-scale ones. Since 1926, under the Recreation and Public Purposes Act, the Interior Department has conducted an effective program to transfer land to local and state governments. The 1976 Federal Land Policy and Management Act, the successor to the Taylor Act as the prime federal statute governing the public lands, permits small-scale transfers and prescribes procedures for them. Modest increases in such disposals for the most part would transfer Bureau of Land Management holdings, especially those near cities and towns. Such disposals, when combined with the remnant homesteading described earlier, the ongoing federal-state land exchanges (for instance, Project BOLD in Utah), and the accelerating Alaska land transfers to the state, would offer a direct and practical way to reduce the federal holdings beneficially. The comparable but smaller state holdings are already being reduced; between 1972 and 1981, the Western states sold 193,000 acres of public land, while the Bureau of Land Management sold only 68,000.

Elsewhere on the frontier, the nation may in future generations decide that it wants to expand the federal holdings rather than reduce them. A probable area is the Great Plains (eastern Montana, Wyoming, Colorado, and New Mexico, and western North Dakota, South Dakota, Nebraska, Kansas, Oklahoma, and Texas), the area between the Rockies and the 98th meridian that accounts for nearly a fifth of the land area of the Lower 48 states and that Webb in 1957 called "the burnt right flank of the American desert." Agriculture—whether it involves cotton, cattle, corn, sheep, wheat, or hogs—is dying throughout much of the Plains both for economic reasons and for lack of water. The difficulties of Plains farming have historically been far worse than those of the neighbor region to the east, the Midwest's Corn Belt; even now, despite the genuine and well-publicized problems Corn Belt farmers face, they at least have water.

No replacement crops, federal subsidies, or foreseeable irrigation techniques are likely to save Plains farming. The Plains could undergo a large-scale 1930s-style depression, complete with dust bowls and rapid population losses. Much of the Plains is already becoming a place of old people and emptying towns. There will certainly be an uncomfortable number of farm bankruptcies and an unacceptable amount of soil erosion. All these conditions will be distinctly more severe than in the Corn Belt.

The federal government reacted to the agricultural crisis of the 1930s, one that in fact produced less soil erosion than is occurring today, by buying out five million acres of farm holdings, an area the size of New Hampshire. It made them into the national grasslands that are today administered by the Forest Service—locally unusable, nationally unneeded cropland that was turned back into the open prairie the settlers found in the nineteenth century. During the 1930s the Forest Service sought to return seventeen million more Plains acres to national grasslands, and Secretary of the Interior Harold Ickes urged that the federal government acquire still other substantial areas—including the entire Oklahoma Panhandle, which is larger than three Delawares.

As the Ogallala Aquifer runs dry, as other Plains agriculture succumbs, and as outmigration from the Plains increases, the nation may conclude that this part of America—a strip two hundred to seven hundred miles wide across the country's midsection—should never have been farmed or settled in the first place. It might not have been were it on the western edge of America rather than in its center. If Plains agriculture did not exist, the winning argument will go, it would not have to be invented. Nor would the federal government have to heavily and inefficiently subsidize its operation, especially its irrigation. The federal agencies will then offer incentives deliberately aimed at taking land out of cultivation and at speeding the depopulation of the Plains. In effect the federal government will work to enlarge the frontier.

The frontier has not been an issue in American society since the time of Turner. As David Potter suggested in *People of Plenty* (1954), Turner's frontier thesis, especially his notion of the closing of the frontier, was a brilliant metaphor for a form of historic American economic abundance that even in Turner's time was clearly being supplanted by other abundances Turner did not mention—those produced by such new industries and technologies as the automobile and television. It is these forms of abundance, Potter contends, that continue to shape American character and development, much as free land once did. But the result is that we have almost forgotten that we still have a land frontier.

Because we think that the West has been totally won, we ignore the immense surviving frontier—the lands that whites never learned to live on, but that centuries from now may have uses we cannot imagine. The frontier's unfilled vastness is still out there in our own time. It is even now a gift of history, an enduring part of our endowment, one of the reasons we remain a lucky country. We need to develop a coherent national idea of what to do with the frontier or at least to acknowledge that something can be done with it.

So progressive public policy has a great deal to contribute to the American frontier over coming generations. It can promote better and more efficient use of water; improving the West's spotty system of reservoirs would be a good place to start. It can find better means of soil conservation. Federal, state, and local governments can determine which public lands should be disposed of and which (presumably the larger part) retained. Conversely, if the federal government chooses to expand its frontier holdings—for instance, by restoring big chunks of the Great Plains to their original prairie condition—it can identify acquisition zones and devise fair buy-out contracts. In all these tasks responsive governments should work to alleviate the frontier's most persistent human problem, its poverty.

Across almost half the United States, the land awaits, as it has for generations and will for many more. The frontier has not disappeared; what Turner called the first period of American history has not ended. The most American of presidents, Thomas Jefferson, may have been more prophetic than Turner, closer to today's truth, in his assumption that uncountable generations of Americans would need to occupy the frontier before they remotely began to exhaust it, and in his vision that American history would just be getting under way generations after his own time. Gertrude Stein, of all people, may have said it best: "In the United States there is more space where nobody is than where anybody is. That is what makes America what it is." The frontier has not defined us as a people for nearly a century, but it remains a part of American life and a factor in the American future. We are no longer a frontier nation, but we are still a nation with a frontier.

Revisiting Turner's Vanishing Frontier

WILLIAM CRONON

What is there left to say about Frederick Jackson Turner? After all the articles and books and dissertations, what could possibly justify yet another excursion onto the "blood-drenched field" of the frontier thesis? That thesis is by now so familiar that even to summarize it is to engage in ritual. Its central claim is contained in a sentence which many of us have nearly memorized: "The existence of an area of free land, its continuous recession, and the advance of American settlement westward, explain American development." How did "free land"—"the frontier"—"explain American development"? According to Turner, the West was a place where easterners and Europeans experienced a return to a time before civilization when the energies of the race were young. Once the descent to the primitive was complete, frontier communities underwent an evolution which recapitulated the development of civilization itself, tracing the path from hunter to trader to farmer to town. In that process of descent and reevolution—as the frontier successively emerged and vanished—a special American character

Copyright by Western History Association. Reprinted by permission. The article first appeared as "Revisiting the Vanishing Frontier: The Legacy of Frederick Jackson Turner," by William Cronon. *Western Historical Quarterly* 18, (April 1987), 157–176.

was forged, marked by fierce individualism, pragmatism, and egalitarianism. Thus, fundamentally transformed as a people, Americans built their commitment to democracy, escaped the perils of class conflict, and overran a continent. Now, in the 1890s, the frontier was gone, and a new foundation for American life must somehow be discovered. So ran Turner's argument.

No less familiar than the Turner thesis itself, of course, are the complaints against it made by Turner's critics. In the half century since Turner's death, his reputation has been subjected to a devastating series of attacks which have left little of his argument intact. Some critiques have been epistemological. Turner's vocabulary was more that of a poet than a logician, and so his word "frontier" could mean almost anything: a line, a moving zone, a static region, a kind of society, a process of character formation, an abundance of land. His fuzzy language conferred on Turner's argument the illusion of great analytical power only because his central terms— frontier, democracy, individualism, national character—were so broad and so ill-defined.

Other critiques have been more empirical. Historians of non-Anglo-American regions—the Spanish Southwest, say, or French Canada—have argued that "democracy" simply was not a relevant category in their areas; for them, Turner consistently misunderstood the cultural complexity of frontier regions. Even in areas of Anglo-American settlement, critics argued, westerners looked to the East for whatever models of democracy they possessed, and were themselves models less of individualism than of dull conformity. Among the eastern institutions dominating western life have been the Federal government, the corporation, and the city, none of which were given adequate attention by Turner. Although those who went to the frontier in the United States sometimes found their opportunities for upward mobility enhanced, mobility rates in the West were not vastly different from those one might expect to find in the urban centers of the East. Far from being the crucible of "Americanization" which Turner made of it, the frontier was a region where racial and ethnic minorities remained significantly isolated from other communities: Blacks, Chicanos, Chinese, and Indians all had historical experiences that meshed neither with Turner's thesis nor with the dominant culture of Turner's day, and so he failed to study them. The same was true of women. Worst of all, because Turner's frontier necessarily ended in 1890, it left historians few clues about what to do with the West in the twentieth century: in an odd sense, Turnerian western history almost literally ended at the very moment that Turner created the field. Within three decades of his death, Turner's defenders were a distinct minority, and the master was now studied more for his rhetoric and ideology than for his contributions to historical knowledge. Those who speculated about the future of western history went so far as to wonder whether it would survive as a field at all.

What, then, justifies yet another essay about Frederick Jackson Turner and his frontier? Simply this: we have not yet figured out a way to escape him. His work remains the foundation not only for the history of the West, but also for much of the rest of American history as well. Textbooks still follow the basic outline which he and his students established in their lecture courses. For all the criticism his successors have directed against his work, no new synthetic paradigm for western history has yet emerged to replace Turner's. We continue to use the word "frontier" as if it meant something.

The remarkable persistence of the Turner thesis in the face of so much criticism might be attributable to any of a number of causes. It may simply signal the inertia which prevents universities from abandoning disciplines, courses, and professorships even after their original *raison d'être* has disappeared. It may be that we continue to use Turner's vocabulary only because it is so comfortably broad that it never gets in the way of our research and never forces us to adopt a more rigorous approach. Or it may be that Turner's thesis, in fact, retains more explanatory power than the critics have been willing to acknowledge in it; certainly it expresses some of the deepest myths and longings many Americans still feel about their national experience. Whatever may be the case, the continuing presence of the Turnerian paradigm in American history is itself a fascinating enigma. Why is it that the "vanishing frontier" refuses to vanish?

One way of beginning an answer to that question is to reflect on the influence Turner exercised during his own lifetime. Many of his contributions were of the sort that tend to be forgotten rather quickly: his work as library-builder and bibliographer, his role in shaping the AHA, his teaching in one of the most famous graduate seminars of his day. Of these, the last was probably the most important, shaping as it did a generation of scholars that included such names as Carl Becker, Merle Curti, Herbert Eugene Bolton, Frederick Merk, Marcus Lee Hansen, Samuel Flagg Bemis, and others.

There can be little doubt about Turner's electrifying effect in seminar. Years before James Harvey Robinson promulgated the doctrines of the "New History," Turner was telling his students that they must bring to the past their most urgent concerns of the present. *"Each age,"* said Turner in 1891, *"writes the history of the past anew with reference to the conditions uppermost in its own time."* Pursuing that idea, he argued for a history that would study not just politics and elites, but the social history of ordinary people: "The focal point of modern interest," he wrote, "is the fourth estate, the great mass of the people." A history that would do those people justice would have to study many fields—literature, politics, religion, economics, culture. It would have to focus on places and regions which past historians had ignored, places which, as luck would have it, were also home to many of Turner's students. It would have to turn to untapped documentary sources and apply new statistical techniques to their interpretation. It would have to set American history in the context of world history, and it would do so not by simple narrative but by studying *problems*. If these things were done, then the histories of ordinary people in places like Wisconsin or Kansas or California might come to have the significance they deserved. "History has a unity and a continuity," wrote Turner; "the present needs the past to explain it; and local history must be read as a part of world history."

There is a great deal in these lessons from Turner's seminar that our more recent generation embraces as its own. Change the vocabulary to match the modern jargon, and we find Turner championing social history, quantification, *l'histoire problèmatique*, interdisciplinary studies, local case histories, "history from the bottom up," and the search for a relevant past. But for the students in Turner's seminar, several additional things added to the excitement inherent in these ideas. One was the sense of being present at the creation of a new academic profession that was exploring the history of a continent's interior as it had never been studied before. Turner's role as a remarkably accessible and egalitarian mentor, his enthusiasm for exploring new documents and methods, his great flexibility in allowing students to choose their own research topics, only added to their sense that they were genuine colleagues working to build the profession. "The engaging theory," remembered Carl Becker, "was that we were all scholars together, surveying broadly the field of American history, each man having his particular subject . . . subjects large and unconfined, opening a career to talent."

Although Turner's students would do their best to defend their master against the criticisms that flooded in after his death in 1932, ultimately his reputation would stand or fall, not on his teaching, but on his writing. And here we encounter a central part of the enigma, for Turner was one of the great nonpublishing scholars of his generation, a man who seemed almost congenitally incapable of finishing a book. Turner's major scholarly writings fall into two rather meager groups: there are the two books, only one of which was finished during his lifetime, and there are the essays, which were eventually collected into two volumes.

The books and the essays are quite different. In this, they bear a striking resemblance to the work Turner required of his graduate students in seminar. Merle Curti reports that the seminar ordinarily centered upon an arbitrarily chosen period of a decade or two, and that "each student took, for the given period, some field in which he was interested, such as agriculture, transportation, immigration, internal improvements, banking, finance, tariff, land policy, literature, labor, or religion." The narrow period allowed students the diversity of topics that was the hallmark of Turner's interdisciplinary method, and still guaranteed that research remained tightly focused. To force students to keep track of both the forest and the trees, Turner required each to write two essays. One, known as the "problem paper," was meant to be a limited monograph on a well-defined research question; the other, known as the "correlation paper," gave the student an opportunity "to correlate his problem and to some extent his field with those his colleagues were studying." By the end of the year, in other words, each student had tried to synthesize the research of the entire seminar and relate it to the topic he or she was studying.

Turner's own writing echoed his seminar assignments. His two books consisted of a string of "problem papers," each chapter covering narrow research topics ranging from agriculture to transportation to the history of presidential administrations—the very subjects his students had examined in seminar. His essays, on the other hand, were usually "correlation papers," bold attempts to "explain" the history of American settlement in its widest sweep. Turner's fame rests on the very few of those essays which are still read, while most of his other writings are largely ignored. Struggle as he might to create a work that would equal the fame of his great 1893 essay on "The Significance of the Frontier in American History," he never managed to do so. Indeed, he never even succeeded in expressing the vision of that essay in a book that elaborated the original argument into a systematic presentation of western history as a whole. That task was left to his students.

Turner's failure to write such a book may, in part, be attributable to the anxieties which affect all writers to a greater or lesser degree, but his difficulty may also have been intrinsic to both his topic and his method. For Turner, "problem papers" and "correlation papers" somehow never quite came together. They always remained separate assignments, with different analytical frameworks and different rhetorical styles that persistently prevented them from merging. Although Turner, during his lifetime, was justly famed for having put American history on a new analytical basis that enabled it to escape older narrative historical writing, his books failed to discover a rhetoric to match his analytical vision. Both begin with long, static descriptions of the different regions on which Turner based his vision of American sectionalism, but these descriptions are overburdened with detail, weak in theory, and lacking in the dynamic energy of Turner's essays; in *The United States, 1830–1850,* for instance, they run to over 375 pages. Moreover, once the regional descriptions are done, both books become straightforward narratives of American national history organized by presidential administrations. Despite Turner's protest that "much that had passed as history is the merest frippery," his own books were not so very different from the traditional histories he criticized.

Turner is most boldly analytical in the essays. But there are problems here too. For one, the rhetorical style of the major essays is as much that of an orator as that of a scholar. Turner's first major successes as a writer came during high school and college oratorical competitions, and his essays never shed the flourishes he had learned in that context. Indeed, in his search for a history that would speak to the concerns of the present, he frequently adopted a pose that looked as much to the future as it did to the past. Turner the historian was not at all averse to playing prophet. Listen to his undergraduate oration on "The Poet of the Future":

> He will find beauty in the useful and the common. . . . In his ear humanity will whisper deep, inspiring words, and bid him give them voice. He will unite the logic of the present and the dream of the past, and his words will ring in the ears of generations yet unborn, telling them the grandeur of today which boils and surges with awakening life. He will reflect all the past and prophesy the future.

The youthful enthusiasm of this passage may be that of a college student captivated by his discovery of Emerson, but one nevertheless recognizes both the voice and the career it prophesies. Turner himself would seek to be that "Poet of the Future."

The most direct expression of Turner's prophetic impulse came in the essays whose titles began, "The Significance of. . . ." There were no fewer than seven of these, including three of his most important: "The Significance of the Frontier in American History," "The Significance of the Section in American History," and the remarkable early essay which laid the foundation for everything else, "The Significance of History." Turner's affection for essays devoted to "significance" revealed the essentially *interpretive* thrust of his historical projects. Like the prophets, he was drawn to exegesis and hermeneutics, to creating a web of verbal elaboration around a core set of ideas that never finally changed; like the prophets, he sought not to prove or disprove his vision, but to apply its sweep to all of American history. For all his commitment to problem-oriented history, his central concepts rarely expressed themselves as testable theories. Few could be falsified. The emphasis on "significance" was a black box which avoided the necessity of more rigorous analysis and theory.

It is only when one realizes the essentially hermeneutic nature of Turner's work that one understands why his legacy has been at once so powerful and so problematic. Prophets take the events of history and reorder them to give them new meaning, pointing them toward a future moment when history itself will finally come to an end. In that teleological act of interpretation, the past comes to have sequence, significance, direction; it becomes, in other words, *a story*. Turner's frontier thesis had all of these properties. Absorbing the Darwinian metaphors of evolution and organism that Herbert Baxter Adams had taught him to use at Johns Hopkins, Turner proposed a model of social change that placed the American West at center stage in world history. Although his goal was to explain the origins of American democracy, the tools he used to do so were at least as important as the democracy he was trying to explain. As we all know, the frontier thesis describes American history in terms of sequenced "stages" of social evolution, and it peoples those stages with a series of frontier "types." Turner by no means invented those "stages"—Americans had identified them as symbols of republican progress since the time of Jefferson—but he, more than anyone else, was responsible for canonizing them. To quote the key passage in the 1893 essay is again to engage in ritual:

> The United States lies like a huge page in the history of society. Line by line as we read this continental page from West to East we find the record of social evolution. It begins with the Indian and the hunter; it goes on to tell of the disintegration of savagery by the entrance of the trader, the pathfinder of civilization; we read the annals of the pastoral stage in ranch life; the exploitation of the soil by the raising of unrotated crops of corn and wheat in sparsely settled farming communities; the intensive culture of the denser farm settlement; and finally the manufacturing organization with city and factory system.

On this generous scaffolding, almost all American history could be erected as a case study in the progress of human civilization.

Here, then, is one of Turner's central ironies: the man who could not, and did not want to, write narrative history nevertheless codified the central narrative structure which has helped organize American history ever since. It was Turner who showed that the history of any given American place could be written in terms of a progressive sequence of different economic and social activities. It was Turner who showed that those activities could be embodied in representative figures who might serve as "types" for the community around them, so that Andrew Jackson became "the champion of the cause of the upland democracy," and Henry Clay "represented the new industrial forces along the Ohio." For lesser figures, the result was to raise ordinary people to heroic stature, so that their stories became "significant" simply by standing for the larger whole. And even if one accepted neither Turner's metaphors of social evolution nor his heroic typologies, there was still the underlying sequence of the frontier itself. Turner showed that one could write the history of the United States according to the order in which different regions of the country had been occupied by Anglo-American settlers. One could thus organize American history along geographical lines that were also temporal: the frontier thesis, in effect, set American space in motion and gave it a plot.

Whatever the merits of Turner's hypotheses about democracy and the national character, his stages and types had great rhetorical attractions. Seen through their lens, previously disparate phenomena and events suddenly seemed to become connected. This, surely, was one of the reasons that Turner's seminar generated such excitement in his students. All those wildly eclectic research topics were related to each other not just chronologically, not just by region, not just by their emphasis on the role of social and economic forces in politics, but by their place in the grand sequence of civilized ascent. The frontier, whether understood as geographic expansion or social evolution, was the "unity and continuity" which held everything together; without it, the "correlation papers" would dissolve into an over-abundance of fragmentary detail much as Turner's own books did. However much the frontier thesis has been criticized, western historians have been unable to replace the rhetorical sequence that Turner synthesized for them: when the chapters of the standard textbook of western history move from Indians to ranchers to farmers, they do so because no other arrangement seems properly ordered. We continue to follow the Turnerian plot.

There is, of course, a dark underside to all of this, and there, Turner himself came to grief. The Turnerian frontier had supposedly ended in 1890. With the passing of the frontier, the original forces which had created American democracy and the national character would begin to dissipate, and who could predict what might happen as a result? How would the immigrants be Americanized? How would the nation escape the class conflicts which had scarred the societies of the Old World? What could restrain the rise of corporate power and the decline of rural virtue? What would serve as an outlet for the nation's expansionist tendencies? Questions such as these gave Turner his prophetic opportunity, but they also masked the contradition that lay at the very heart of his frontier thesis.

For the whole point of the frontier had been to vanish. Like Timothy Flint's Daniel Boone or James Fenimore Cooper's Leatherstocking, its "purpose" in Turner's scheme was to prepare the way for the civilization that would ultimately replace it. Civilization had always been the teleological goal which had lent its force to Turner's historical sequence, and so there was no escaping the doom it must finally spell for the frontier thesis. If each new generation of historians must discover a past that spoke to the needs of the present, then western history, as Turner had framed it, would become more and more irrelevant. Turner himself saw this almost from the start, and it caused him increasing anxiety as he grew older. By 1910, in his presidential address to the American Historical Association, he was implicitly arguing for the replacement of his own frontier thesis by noting that "a comprehension of the United States of today . . . demands that we should rework our history from the new points of view afforded by the present." A year later, he acknowledged, in a letter to Carl Becker, that the historical processes he had studied were reaching "the point when the frontier becomes subordinated in influence to general social forces. . . ."

His own proposal was that historians should substitute for the frontier "another fundamental factor in American history—namely, the Section." With the disappearance of free land, as natural resources proved "no longer boundless," Americans would increasingly discover "sectional differences arising from unlike geographic regions." The United States would come to look more and more like Europe, with the peoples of different sections struggling among themselves for control of a nation that would seem more and more to be a kind of empire. Turner's hope was that this new prophecy would serve as a general application of the same geographical and social principles that had so successfully underpinned the frontier thesis. Sections could thus be used to "explain" American history in much the same way that the frontier once had.

It didn't work. Unlike the frontier, the sectional hypothesis had no overarching structure, no *narrative* that could be used to link monographic themes into an organic unity. What motion it had still came from the frontier. When Turner wrote of "the influence of the frontier and the West upon American sections," he was clearly seeing the frontier as the *primal* section whose energy had shaped all others. "The West," he wrote, "was a migrating region, a stage of society rather than a place." The frontier had been about movement; the section was about stasis. Whereas sections were bounded, motionless, and particular to their moment in time, the frontier was the moving embodiment of time, and so conferred on places it touched a universality the section could never attain.

Turner's generalizing inclination was to personify sections in much the same way he had personified frontier types, with the result that homogenizing regional "characters" came to dominate his sectional analysis. Although the sectional theme was rich in implications, suggesting the importance of conflicts between east and west, between city and hinterland, between old elites and new, it lacked both analytical precision and narrative force. Without a more sophisticated theoretical apparatus, the section remained inert. As Turner struggled to finish *The United States, 1830–1850,* the book that was to act as a showcase for the new hypothesis, he must have realized that he was fighting a losing battle. It was published only after his death, and showed little of the "unity and continuity" which the youthful Turner had held up as his historical ideal. The scholarship of the book was extraordinary, but as a fulfillment of its author's dreams, it could only be labeled a failure.

There are thus two quite different components of the Turnerian legacy. On the one hand, there is the West of the frontier, which at the height of Turner's fame seemed to be the key to explaining much of American history generally. On the other, there is the West as section, a locus for academic study in its own right, but one with no special claim to exceptional status. For western historians, there is no escaping the tension between these two poles of Turner's thought. The frontier had been the central reason for studying western history in the first place: it had given the field its "significance," and it had created the narrative trajectory which turned the peopling of the continent into an epic on the grand scale. Without the frontier, western history, like Turner's sectional thesis, lost its forward momentum. It became the history of a region that was not really a region, a section whose boundaries were never quite fixed until the 1890 census announcement left them stranded somewhere beyond the Mississippi River.

The years since World War II have seen proposals from a number of historians for new ways of researching and thinking about western history. One group of such proposals has sought to build on the inadequacies of the Turner school by focusing on those aspects of the West which remained invisible to the earlier generation. The result has been to reveal the masculine biases of Turner's frontier by exploring the lives of western women, to rediscover the racial and ethnic communities which somehow never quite melted into Turner's "line of most rapid and effective Americanization," and to provide a vastly richer and more accurate picture of the Indian peoples who were all but absent from Turner's vision. Such critics have been able to remain more or less agnostic on the question of whether the "frontier" is a useful category, since their research retains its importance whatever the merits of the original thesis.

A second group of proposals has accepted the criticisms of Turner's frontier by more or less inverting his original claims. These proposals have sought to show the derivative, conservative nature of western communities by exploring the complex transfer of institutions which enabled settlers in new communities to reproduce the worlds they had known back home. Here too are the works that emphasize the importance of the Federal government in shaping western life, along with those which have pointed to the urban character of much western settlement. Curiously, although such research explicitly rejects Turner's claims about the frontier sources of American character and democracy, it still relies on westward movement— the frontier—as its central analytical category.

A third and final group of proposals argues that the concept of "frontier" is powerful enough to deserve salvaging by redefinition. Here especially we can include the work of those who have sought to develop generalized models of frontier development by comparing the American experience with that of other areas of the world. Some have attempted to do this by using the Turner thesis directly; more often, broader definitions of the frontier have been offered to replace Turner's. In general, these broader proposals have veered toward defining the frontier as a region in which peoples of different cultures struggle with each other for control of resources and political power. Turner's central focus on frontier interaction with the landscape is thereby reduced—such redefined frontiers become essentially contact zones where culture, rather than environment, plays the pivotal defining role—but many of the other Turnerian arguments remain.

What is striking about all of these proposals is the extent to which they continue to rely on Turner for their direction and sense of synthesis. Whether we fill in his gaps, or turn him on his head, or redefine his vocabulary, western historians still look to Turner for their basic sequence. He still allows us to narrate our story from east to west, and to organize it around the continuous, albeit complicated, transition of economies and communities from one form of activity to another. However much we understand his *analytical* shortcomings, we still turn to him for our *rhetorical* structure.

If American historians are finally to come to terms with Turner, they must recognize the true nature of his legacy. The greatest attraction of the frontier thesis has been its simplicity and its sense of movement, its ability to shape and set in motion so many of the mere *facts* that American historians need to narrate. It supplies at least a rhetorical connection between those facts, and that connection in turn supplies the larger sense of order and unity that keep a reader turning the pages to find out "what happened." These are no small virtues, as recent debates about the rediscovery of historical narrative have suggested. The key question, then, is whether we can escape the analytical weaknesses of Turner's "vanishing frontier" and still retain his narrative strengths.

A full-scale resynthesis of western history is beyond the scope of this essay, but I do want to suggest that Turner's legacy may in fact have wider implications for such a synthesis than one might at first think. For myself, the most useful elements of Turner's frontier are its focus on the history of how human beings have interacted with the American landscape; its ability to relate local and regional history to the wider history of the nation; its interdisciplinary focus; and, not least, its commitment to putting ordinary people at the center of the story. None of Turner's weaknesses—the dubious arguments about democracy, the rather mystical search for "national character," the distorting collection of frontier "types," the teleological problems of a vanishing frontier whose closing marks a false end to history—are intrinsic to what I, at least, find most suggestive in Turner's work.

It is no accident that much of what we today call "environmental history" has been written in this country under the guise of *western* history. No other academic field, historical geography excluded, has proven to be a better home for those interested in studying human uses of the earth. This is Turner's doing. His initial frontier essay emphasized environment, but defined "free land" too narrowly in terms of unoccupied agricultural territory. Later in his life, he broadened this definition to include "the unpossessed resources of the nation.'' In so doing, he came close to anticipating the central thesis of David Potter's *People of Plenty,* a remarkable book that suggests at least one major linkage between Turner's work and a more general environmental history. For Potter, Turner's frontier was but a special case of the general abundance of natural resources that had made America exceptional from the start. "By failing to recognize that the frontier was only one form in which America offered abundance," Potter wrote, Turner "cut himself off from an insight into the fact that other forms of abundance had superseded the frontier even before the supply of free land had been exhausted. . . ." Potter's book has flaws that are akin to Turner's—he too chose to rest his argument on the fuzzy category of "national character"—but his central insight is surely a major key to the Turnerian riddle.

If the frontier represented only one kind of plenty, then it ought to be possible to rewrite western history—which in one rather Turnerian sense is actually the environmental history of North America—in terms of a transition not from free to occupied land, but from abundance to scarcity. Even that formulation is too sweepingly simple, since it attracts us to the same teleology that seduced Turner: we must be careful to avoid embracing frontiers that somehow "close." Turner's awkward transition from frontier to section has tended to keep western history fixated on the early stages of Euro-American settlement. But if we abandon the notion that regional history "closes," we can trace his environmental dialectic as far backward or forward in time as we like.

Neither abundance nor scarcity has ever been absolute. Instead, their definitions shift always according to natural and artificial constraints on systems of human activity, and according to people's *beliefs* about whether they are experiencing economic and environmental stasis, progress, or decline. Different forms of technology or social organization can produce entirely different levels of resource use, even when they exist on the same landscape; conversely, diminishing quantities of an essential resource, or newly discovered supplies of it, can produce drastic shifts in social organization and technology. People's notions of abundance and scarcity—of wealth and poverty—change accordingly, and so too does their political life. Communities that define abundance in one way all too easily come into conflict with those that define it otherwise. Much of regional history can be organized around these fundamental relationships. Western history, under this framework, can become what it has always been, the story of human beings working with changing tools to transform the resources of the land, struggling over how that land should be owned and understood, and defining their notions of political and cultural community, all within a context of shifting environmental and economic constraints.

Such an approach is quite Turnerian in its implications. Indeed, to study regional environmental history is to free what is best in Turner from the frontier thesis which made Turner's history seem to end in 1890. The vanishing frontier no longer needs to vanish. The dialectic between relative abundance and relative scarcity, as Potter showed, is something that can organize western history—and American history generally—without an arbitrary break at any particular moment. Such a theme applies as readily to the twentieth century as to the nineteenth. Better still, that dialectic retains the forward momentum Turner gave western history with his frontier: there is still a story here, albeit one with no definite beginning or end. The interplay between abundance, scarcity, innovation, politics, culture, and ideas may lack the high drama of the closing frontier, but it nevertheless retains the sense of *movement* that was Turner's most important contribution to American regional history. Equally important, scarcity and abundance can only be understood in terms of regionally specific environments, and so Turner's pivotal emphasis on "the importance of *space* in history," which allowed him to connect local history to national and world history, remains.

Ironically enough, Turner's sectional thesis may be more useful than his frontier thesis in pursuing this sense of interregional connection. The central weakness of the famous 1893 essay was its tendency to portray the frontier as *isolate,* a place whose importance derived from the very fact that it was so removed from the rest of civilization. In reality, even the most remote frontier was always connected to economic activities and demographic changes in the rest of the world, especially in the rising urban centers whose growth was central to frontier expansion itself. As several historians have suggested, cities did not wait for the final stage of Turner's frontier to make their appearance, but instead arrived with the first Euro-American pioneers. Indeed, Turner's frontier can easily be seen as the expanding edge of a metropolitan economy, along the lines that Harold Innis used in his synthesis of Canadian history. What is true of the nineteenth-century frontier is even more true of the twentieth-century West, whose urban centers lie at the core of the regional economy. If Turner's western history can be restated in terms of *connection* rather than *isolation*—so that the interactions among different regional economies, cultures, and environments come to be its central concerns—then we may find the *dynamic* sectional thesis that his original formulation lacked.

Cast in these terms, the questions Turner has left us remain very much alive. The challenge for western and environmental historians alike is to discover a subtler periodization for their fields to replace Turner's crude "frontier stages." Any such periodization must create a finer-grained sense of movement that will reflect interconnections between regional diversity and the shifting dialectic of scarcity and abundance. Western historians must abandon all illusions that "the vanishing frontier" is anything but a minor—and usually misleading—theme in the longer history of regional change and interaction. More comprehensive is the question of why "core" and "peripheral" American regions have experienced such different developments: if the "frontier experience" has at one time or another typified such diverse places as New England, the Old South, Appalachia, the Great Lakes, the Great Basin, the Pacific Slope, and the sub-Arctic North, why have the histories of these regions been so different? The answer will lie not in some homogeneous "frontier process," but in the diverse environments and cultures that have typified those regions.

And yet diversity is only half the story. The regions of the continent have developed within a larger system of political and economic relationships which have been affected by such things as changing international resource bases, the rise of the corporation, and the growth of the modern state, all within the framework of an expanding capitalist economy. To fulfill Turner's injunction that "local history . . . be viewed in the light of world history," these larger connections must be discovered in the dreams, joys, and tragedies of ordinary people—and in the ways those people have shaped and been shaped by the landscapes around them. Since the inhabitants of a given area are themselves diverse, an essential aspect of this last question must be the system of social relations that has shaped regional life. Here western historians—like other historians—must continue their turn away from the white northern European males who have fascinated them for so long, and explore how peoples of different racial, class, and cultural backgrounds have struggled with one another for control both of their regional resource base and their institutions of political power. Likewise, the divergent perceptions and experiences of men and women have significantly influenced how regional environments have come to be defined, and that in turn will affect the way we write their histories.

Underlying all of these things, giving them a kind of neo-Turnerian unity, will be the question of how American uses of, and attitudes toward, regional landscapes have shifted with the dialectical interaction of scarcity and abundance. The virtue of that dialectic is that it gives sequence to our story without necessarily entrapping us—as it entrapped Turner—in the snares of civilized ascent. It can lend *direction* to regional history without implying the existence of some larger, extrahistorical *progress*. Among the deepest struggles in American western history have been those among peoples who have defined abundance—and the "good life"—in conflicting ways. Such struggles must fit into this story without oversimplifying the values embraced by opposing sides, for ultimately "abundance" was as culturally contested a terrain as "community." In the West, to occupy the natural landscape meant, simultaneously, to occupy a human community; those two acts of belonging are among the most fundamental that a historian of the region can trace. And here we may as well return to Turner's most important questions as well: what *is* the relation between abundance and American notions of liberal democracy? To what extent *has* the peculiar nature of American class consciousness and republican government been shaped by the shifting resource base of our economic and social life? How *do* nature and humanity transform each other?

None of these are dead or answered questions, and all are part of Turner's continuing legacy. Turner's notion of the "frontier" may be so muddled as to be useless, but if Turner's "free land" is a special case of Potter's American abundance, then the general direction of Turner's approach remains sound. In his commitment to ignoring the walls between disciplines, in his faith that history must in large measure be the story of ordinary people, in his emphasis on the importance of regional environments to our understanding the course of American history—in all these ways, he remains one of the pathfinders whose well-blazed trail we continue to follow. And whether or not we ultimately abandon the frontier thesis, we are unlikely ever to escape its narrative implications. In fashioning a rhetorical framework for telling the history of the first continental republic, Frederick Jackson Turner, almost in spite of himself, gave American history its central and most persistent story. However much we may modify the details and outline of that story, we are unlikely ever to break entirely free of it.

Y *F U R T H E R   R E A D I N G*

H. C. Allen, *Bush and Backwoods: A Comparison of the Frontier in Australia and the United States* (1959)

Richard A. Bartlett, *The New Country: A Social History of the American Frontier, 1776–1890* (1974)

Robert F. Berkhofer, Jr., "Space, Time, Culture and the New Frontier," *Agricultural History*, 38 (1964), 21–30

Don Harrison Doyle, *The Social Order of a Frontier Community: Jacksonville, Illinois, 1825–70* (1978)

——, "Social Theory and New Communities in Nineteenth-Century America," *Western Historical Quarterly*, 8 (1977), 151–165

Gene M. Gressley, "Whither Western American History?" *Pacific Historical Review*, 53 (1984), 493–501

Richard Harrison, ed., *Crossing Frontiers* (1978)

Louis Hartz, *The Founding of New Societies* (1964)

Richard Jensen, "On Modernizing Frederick Jackson Turner: The Historiography of Regionalism," *Western Historical Quarterly*, 11 (1980), 307–322

Howard Lamar, "Persistent Frontier: The West in the Twentieth Century," *Western Historical Quarterly*, 4 (1973), 5–25

—— and Leonard Thompson, eds., *The Frontier in History: North America and Southern Africa Compared* (1981)

Patricia Nelson Limerick, *The Legacy of Conquest: The Unbroken Past of the American West* (1987)

Ralph Mann, "Frontier Opportunity and the New Social History," *Pacific Historical Review*, 53 (1984), 463–491

Michael P. Malone, ed., *Historians and the American West* (1983)

Roger L. Nichols, ed., *American Frontier and Western Issues* (1986)

Rodman W. Paul and Michael P. Malone, "Tradition and Challenge in Western Historiography, *Western Historical Quarterly*, 16 (1985), 27–53

Earl Pomeroy, "Toward a Reorientation of Western History: Continuity and Environment," *Mississippi Valley Historical Review*, 41 (1955), 579–600

——, "What Remains of the West?" *Utah Historical Quarterly*, 35 (1967), 37–55

David M. Potter, *People of Plenty: Economic Abundance and the American Character* (1954)

Paul F. Sharp, "Three Frontiers: Some Comparative Studies of Canadian, American, and Australian Settlement," *Pacific Historical Review*, 24 (1955), 369–377

Jerome O. Steffen, *Comparative Frontiers: A Proposal for Studying the American West* (1980)

—— ed., *The American West: New Perspectives, New Dimensions* (1979)

Mary Young, "The West and American Culture Identity: Old Themes and New Variations," *Western Historical Quarterly*, 1 (1970), 137–160